The Epistle of Forgiveness

Letter from the General Editor

The Library of Arabic Literature series offers Arabic editions and English translations of significant works of Arabic literature, with an emphasis on the seventh to nineteenth centuries. The Library of Arabic Literature thus includes texts from the pre-Islamic era to the cusp of the modern period, and encompasses a wide range of genres, including poetry, poetics, fiction, religion, philosophy, law, science, history, and historiography.

Books in the series are edited and translated by internationally recognized scholars and are published in parallel-text format with Arabic and English on facing pages, and are also made available as English-only paperbacks.

The Library encourages scholars to produce authoritative, though not necessarily critical, Arabic editions, accompanied by modern, lucid English translations. Its ultimate goal is to introduce the rich, largely untapped Arabic literary heritage to both a general audience of readers as well as to scholars and students.

The Library of Arabic Literature is supported by a grant from the New York University Abu Dhabi Institute and is published by NYU Press.

Philip F. Kennedy
General Editor, Library of Arabic Literature

About this Paperback

This paperback edition differs in a few respects from its dual-language hardcover predecessor. Because of the compact trim size the pagination has changed, but paragraph numbering has been retained to facilitate cross-referencing with the hardcover. Material that referred to the Arabic edition has been updated to reflect the English-only format, and other material has been corrected and updated where appropriate. For information about the Arabic edition on which this English translation is based and about how the LAL Arabic text was established, readers are referred to the hardcover.

The Epistle of Forgiveness

OR

A Pardon to Enter the Garden

BY

Abū l-ʿAlāʾ al-Maʿarrī

PRECEDED BY

Ibn al-Qāriḥ's Epistle

TRANSLATED BY

Geert Jan van Gelder and Gregor Schoeler

FOREWORD BY

Matthew Reynolds

VOLUME EDITOR

James E. Montgomery

NEW YORK UNIVERSITY PRESS
New York and London

NEW YORK UNIVERSITY PRESS
New York and London

Library of Congress Cataloging-in-Publication Data
Abū l-ʿAlāʾ al-Maʿarrī, 973–1057, author.
The epistle of forgiveness, or, A pardon to enter the garden / by Abū l-ʿAlāʾ al-Maʿarrī; preceded by Ibn al-Qāriḥ's Epistle ; translated by Geert Jan Van Gelder and Gregor Schoeler ; foreword by Matthew Reynolds.
pages cm
Includes bibliographical references, glossary, and indexes.
ISBN 978-1-4798-3494-5 (pb : alk. paper) — ISBN 978-1-4798-4810-2 (ebook) — ISBN 978-1-4798-6551-2 (ebook)
I. Gelder, G. J. H. van, translator. II. Schoeler, Gregor, translator. III. Abū l-ʿAlāʾ al-Maʿarrī, 973–1057. Risālat al-ghufrān. IV. Abū l-ʿAlāʾ al-Maʿarrī, 973–1057. Risālat al-ghufrān. English. V. Ibn al-Qāriḥ, ʿAlī ibn Manṣūr, b. 962. Risālat Ibn al-Qāriḥ. VI. Ibn al-Qāriḥ, ʿAlī ibn Manṣūr, b. 962. Risālat Ibn al-Qāriḥ. English. VII. Title.
VIII. Title: Pardon to enter the garden
PJ7750.A25R513 2016
892.7/134—dc23 2015045309

New York University Press books are printed on acid-free paper, and their binding materials are chosen for strength and durability.

Series design and composition by Nicole Hayward
Typeset in Adobe Text

Manufactured in the United States of America

10 9 8 7 6 5 4 3 2 1

To our spouses, Sheila and Christa, asking their Forgiveness for spending so many hours in al-Maʿarrī's company instead of theirs; and to Josef van Ess, who, like no other, knows about Islamic heretics, on the occasion of his eightieth birthday (. . . وبُلِّغْتَها!).

Contents

Foreword

MATTHEW REYNOLDS

The main character in this book is dead but seems intensely alive. He is a literary man and people call him "the Sheikh." He is also anxious, impetuous, curious, ineffectual, and amazingly, amusingly pedantic. When he is resurrected he can't bear the thought of waiting the standard fifty thousand years for entry to Paradise so he sets about pulling strings. He composes flattering verses for Paradise's Porter Angel, Riḍwān. In fact, he tries out every one of the metrical patterns that can accommodate the name "Riḍwān." It's no use: Riḍwān doesn't even know what a poem is.

Undaunted, the Sheikh tries the same trick on a couple of other spiritual eminences but again to no avail. Things look black when he realizes he has lost his certificate of repentance. But they improve when he encounters Muḥammad's daughter Fāṭimah: she intercedes on the Sheikh's behalf. Even so, he feels too wobbly to cross the Bridging Path to Paradise, so he asks for a piggyback from one of Fāṭimah's serving girls, reciting verse (as usual) in support of the idea. She has never heard of a piggyback (or the poet he is quoting) but all the same she picks him up and crosses "like a bolt of lightning."

A love of poetry ripples through this funny, cartoonish episode, and it animates the rest of the book as well. Perhaps "love" is too weak a word. When the Sheikh gets into Paradise the people he wants to meet are poets; and what he wants to do with them is seek illumination on fine points of interpretation and editing (as well as joining in a carnival of quotation and recitation). At one point, all the "learned transmitters of poetry" are brought together to be corrected on a detail of grammar. To the expert in classical Arabic, these passages must be a scholarly goldmine. To the general reader who knows nothing of Arabic (i.e., a reader like myself) they open a door onto a landscape of shimmering textuality, where alternative meanings proliferate and bloom. As the Sheikh asks one poet, "what did you mean by 'first-born'? The commentators have different opinions. Some say it is an egg; others say it is a pearl; or a meadow; or a flower; or a papyrus plant."

The Sheikh's literary obsessions are made to seem both admirable and absurd—a combination which the book's origins can help us to understand. *The Epistle of Forgiveness* was written by the brilliant, 11th-century poet and scholar Abū l-ʿAlāʾ al-Maʿarrī in response to a letter from another, older literary man, ʿAlī ibn Manṣūr Ibn al-Qāriḥ. The context is explained in detail in Geert Jan van Gelder and Gregor Schoeler's rich introduction to this book so I will just give a quick sketch here. Ibn al-Qāriḥ's letter is fussy and ingratiating. He wants to exculpate himself for having attacked a friend of Abū l-ʿAlāʾ's who had fallen out of favor with the Caliph. But he does so by attacking him even more, in cumbersomely elaborate prose (e.g.: "I was afraid of the madness of his madness, for his madness was in fact mad. A madman was sounder in mind than he!"). Evidently Abū l-ʿAlāʾ was not very impressed by this approach. In response, he imagines Ibn al-Qāriḥ dying and being resurrected as "the Sheikh," making a fool of himself in Paradise, and perhaps learning a little bit more tact and wisdom in the end.

So "the Sheikh" is a parodic figure of a literary man, created by another literary man. This is why the *Epistle* can be so cutting and so warm at the same time. Abū l-ʿAlāʾ makes fun of Ibn al-Qāriḥ but he also recognises that he and Ibn al-Qāriḥ share many of the same interests and impulses. The poetry the Sheikh recites is poetry that he himself knows—Abū l-ʿAlāʾ was blind and had a prodigious memory. The pedantic questions the Sheikh asks are questions that interest Abū l-ʿAlāʾ too. The *Epistle* becomes a vehicle for questioning, not only the behavior of Ibn al-Qāriḥ, but also the value of the literary life in general.

One poet was released from Hell to Paradise because of an especially impressive verse he had written: "it kept being recited while I was gradually freed of my fetters and chains." On the other hand, many of the poets in Paradise can't be bothered with the Sheikh's enquiries and can't even remember the poems that they themselves have written: they have more important things to occupy them now. Even so, it's hard not to feel that Abū l-ʿAlāʾ would have shared the Sheikh's enjoyment of the poetry recited by paradisal young women: "if it was matched with all the delights of the people of the Fleeting World since God created Adam until the time He folded up his descendants on earth, it would exceed them just as the billows of the deep sea exceed a toddler's tear, or as a lofty mountain exceeds a speck of dust that one flicks off one's saddle blanket."

Abū l-ʿAlāʾ's general idea of Paradise derives from Muslim beliefs and the culture of his time. The feasting and drinking, the happy animals, the beautiful, artificially-created young women: none of these are his invention. What is distinctive about the *Epistle* (I feel) is a canny, irreverent mood which comes through in the translation and which any reader can notice and enjoy. Since my own imagination is made from European materials, I relate this quality to works that are familiar to me. It reminds me of Chaucer's dream visions or the Pope's *The Rape of the Lock*, and I feel it forms a startling contrast to Dante's *Divine Comedy*, even though it too is a vision of the afterlife.

But really Abū l-ʿAlāʾ's *Epistle* has a searching brilliance all its own. Take the imagining of animals. At one point, the Sheikh goes hunting and excitedly launches his javelin at "a flat-nosed, long-tailed oryx bull." But then, when there is "a mere nail's length between it and the spear point, the bull says 'Stop.'" It turns out that the oryx has earned its place in Paradise by saving some humans in "the fleeting world." It is not available to be killed.

The Sheikh suggests that such worthy creatures should avoid getting mixed up with the run-of-the-mill animals that have been laid on in Paradise for the humans to exploit. But it turns out that they too are kept safe from harm. A blessed lion is rewarded by devouring "God knows how many animals"—but mysteriously his prey is never hurt and doesn't mind: "they enjoy it just as much as I do." People feast on a goose that is as big as a Bactrian camel. One has it roasted, another has it as a kebab, another spiced with sumac, another with milk and vinegar. But each time it returns to its winged and happy living state. The narrator comments: "the process continued for some time." I'm not completely sure of his tone here; but since Abū l-ʿAlāʾ was a vegan and hated animal suffering it seems likely there is some irony. "Here is a solution to the cruelty of my fellow humans"—he might partly think—"animals can be eaten without being harmed!" At the same time, he must surely have felt some revulsion at all this excited carnivorous gobbling.

Gender identities seem to be viewed with the same raised eyebrow. Delicious young women emerge from quinces, pomegranates and apples; geese turn into "full-breasted girls"; women who were ugly but virtuous in the fleeting world are reborn as beautiful. Though sparkily written, this is all standard-issue stereotyping (nobody ever expects the men to be attractive). But other elements of the *Epistle* are more surprising. There are women with superpowers, like the girl who gives the Sheikh a piggy-back. There is a note of absurdity in the men's desires, as when the Sheikh feels that a girl who has been created to please him "is rather skinny" and finds that she is immediately reconstructed so that her "behind rivals the hills of ʿĀlij, the dunes of al-Dahnāʾ, and the sands of Yabrīn and the Banū Saʿd." There is a snake who has the power to become "the most beautiful of the girls in Paradise," and who can quote poetry and discuss textual variants with the best of the men of letters: she desires the Sheikh but he gets scared and scuttles away. It feels relevant to these countercurrents that Abū l-ʿAlāʾ himself never married and apparently abstained from sexual intercourse. The heterosexual pleasures of Paradise move him to mockery as well as to celebration.

The English poet John Keats enjoyed very long poems because they give the reader a "Region to wander in where they may pick and choose, and in which the images are so numerous that many are forgotten and found new in a second Reading: which may be food for a Week's stroll in the Summer." This leisured, exploratory style of reading would suit the volume you are holding. On your first outing I would recommend you skip the first two items—the "Epistle of Ibn al-Qāriḥ" and the "Preamble"—reserving them for a later stroll, after you have tasted the delights of "Paradise." These delights are themselves variable and can be sampled at different speeds: not every reader will want to dwell at length on every detail of the philological explanations. Abū l-ʿAlāʾ's style is extremely elaborate and includes much rhyming prose (hence the alternative title offered by the translators: *A Pardon to Enter the Garden*). Not all of this is recreated in the translation but some of it is, and it offers unusual pleasures to readers who approach it with an open mind.

The second part of the *Epistle* abandons the imagining of Paradise and engages in more sober reflections. It has generally been omitted in previous translations: in fact, the current volume is the only complete translation of the *Epistle* into any language. The second part is certainly less fun than the first one; but it is valuable because it shows us Abū l-ʿAlāʾ speaking in a more direct voice. His ethical stringency is all the more compelling because of the scintillating vision that preceded it. Take for instance this reflection, where his love of animals re-appears in altered guise: "God is my witness that I am glad when someone finds fault with me, because he speaks the truth about his misgivings about me, and that I am worried by false praise, which leaves me like a hunted animal so thirsty it is unable to feed."

"Paradise" had been full of inventive compliments, not all of which (perhaps) were meant entirely seriously. But it is no false praise to re-apply one of them to the brilliant, acerbic and yet generous work that is *The Epistle of Forgiveness*: "if it were stagnant water it would never turn stale or stink."

Matthew Reynolds
Professor of English and Comparative Criticism
Oxford University

Abbreviations used in the Introduction and Translation

EI2	*Encyclopaedia of Islam*, New [= Second] Edition
Gh	*Risālat al-Ghufrān / The Epistle of Forgiveness*
IQ	*Risālat Ibn al-Qāriḥ / The Epistle of Ibn al-Qāriḥ*
L	(in prosody) long syllable
O	(in prosody) overlong syllable
Q	Qur'an
S	(in prosody) short syllable

Acknowledgments

We are grateful for the encouragement and help we received from the LAL editors, in particular Philip Kennedy, Shawkat Toorawa, and James Montgomery. Our labors were alleviated by the great efficiency and expertise of the LAL managing editor, Chip Rossetti; of the digital production manager Stuart Brown; of Carolyn Brunelle, who extracted a Glossary from our endnotes; and from the copy editor, Kelly Zaug. Of all these it was James Montgomery who contributed most, with his countless stylistic and linguistic improvements and his editorial accuracy. If, on very rare occasions, we disagreed with him and stuck to our own ideas, we hope for his forgiveness—which is, after all, the leitmotiv of the present work.

Introduction

The lengthy, mocking reply by a cantankerous maverick, obsessed with lexicography and grammar, to a rambling, groveling, and self-righteous letter by an obscure grammarian and mediocre stylist: this does not sound, prima facie, like a masterwork to be included in a series of Arabic classics. It is even doubtful whether it firmly belongs to the canonical works of Arabic literature. The maverick author, Abū l-ʿAlāʾ al-Maʿarrī, was certainly famous, or infamous, as we shall see, but in the entry on him in the biographical dictionary by Ibn Khallikān (d. 681/1282),[1] who calls him the author of "many famous compositions and widely known epistles," the present work is not even mentioned; in the very long entry on him in a somewhat earlier, similar work by Yāqūt (d. 626/1229) it is merely listed in a long list of works, without commentary.[2] It is true that the same Yāqūt has an entry on the rather obscure author of the original letter, the grammarian Ibn al-Qāriḥ, whom he describes as "the one who wrote a well-known letter to Abū l-ʿAlāʾ, known as 'the Epistle of Ibn al-Qāriḥ',"[3] which suggests that Abū l-ʿAlāʾ's reply was famous. However, the work is not often mentioned or discussed in pre-modern times, unlike Abū l-ʿAlāʾ's poetry.

As happens occasionally in the history of Arabic literature, the *Risālat al-Ghufrān* (*The Epistle of Forgiveness*), owes its present fame mostly to the rediscovery in modern times, by a western Arabist. Reynold A. Nicholson, in a letter to the *Journal of the Royal Asiatic Society*,[4] describes a collection of manuscripts gathered by his grandfather, to which, as he writes, "I would call special attention, because it is, as I believe, a genuine work, hitherto unknown and undescribed, of the famous blind poet and man of letters, Abū 'l 'Alā al-Ma'arrī." Over the following few years, between 1900 and 1902, he published a partial edition with a summary and at times paraphrasing translation of the contents in a series of articles in the same journal.[5] The *Epistle*'s subsequent rise to fame is mainly due to the fact that it seemed to prefigure Dante's *Commedia Divina* and that misguided attempts were made to prove the influence of the Arabic work on the Italian. This thesis has now been abandoned and one can appreciate *Risālat al-Ghufrān* in its own right.

Abū l-'Alā' al-Ma'arrī

The earliest appearance of al-Ma'arrī in Arabic literature is found in a work by a contemporary, one of the greatest anthologists of Arabic literature, al-Tha'ālibī (d. 429/1038). In the supplement to his *Yatīmat al-dahr*, he quotes a certain poet, Abū l-Ḥasan al-Dulafī al-Maṣṣīṣī, who told him:

> In Ma'arrat al-Nu'mān I came across a true marvel. I saw a blind man, a witty poet, who played chess and backgammon, and who was at home in every genre of seriousness and jesting. He was called Abū l-'Alā'. I heard him say, "I praise God for being blind, just as others praise Him for being able to see. He did me a favor and did me a good turn by sparing me the sight of boring and hateful people."[6]

Our author is usually called Abū l-'Alā' al-Ma'arrī,[7] the first part (literally "Father of Loftiness") not being a teknonym[8] in this case—for he never had children—but an added honorific name or nickname, and the second part derived from his place of birth, Ma'arrat al-Nu'mān, or al-Ma'arrah for short, a town in northern Syria, between Aleppo and Homs. The medieval biographical dictionaries, usually arranged alphabetically, list him under his given name, Aḥmad, and supply not only the name of his father, 'Abd Allāh, and grandfather, Sulaymān, but also some twenty to thirty further generations, tracing him back to the legendary realm of pre-Islamic Arab genealogy; he belonged to the famous tribal confederation called Tanūkh, entitling him to the epithet al-Tanūkhī. He was born toward sunset on Friday, 27 Rabīʿ Awwal, 363 (26 December AD 973) in a respectable family of religious scholars and judges. At the age of four he lost his eyesight due to smallpox. He made up for this disability by having a truly prodigious memory, about which several anecdotes are related; apparently he had the aural equivalent of a photographic memory and he stood out in a milieu that was already accustomed to memorization on a large scale. His blindness meant that he wrote his numerous works by dictating them; his pupil al-Tibrīzī mentioned that al-Maʿarrī at one stage had four well-qualified secretaries and a servant girl (*jāriyah*), who wrote down his dictations.[9] As a boy he studied with several teachers, including his own father, in his hometown and Aleppo; his main interest was poetry and he became an ardent admirer of the great poet al-Mutanabbī (d. 354/965), on whose poetry he was to write a commentary, entitled *Muʿjiz Aḥmad* (*Aḥmad's Miracle*), exploiting not only the fact that he shared his given name with the poet but also, rather daringly, alluding to the Qur'an, which was the prophetic "miracle" (*muʿjizah*) of the Prophet Muḥammad, who is sometimes called Aḥmad.

It seems that his own poetic efforts date from an early age, when he was eleven or twelve. Normally the poetry of a poet is collected in a single *dīwān*, in which poems are arranged alphabetically on rhyme letter, or chronologically, or thematically. Most of al-Maʿarrī's poetry however, as far as it is preserved (for many of his works are lost), is contained in two very distinct major collections; yet more poems are found in some minor works. His early poetry, in a *dīwān* called *Saqṭ* (or *Siqṭ*) *al-zand* (*The Spark of the Fire Stick*[10]), shows the influence of al-Mutanabbī. The second collection contains his later poetry and it is very different. Instead of more or less conventional odes, it offers nearly sixteen hundred mostly short pieces. Thematically and stylistically the collection is unusually coherent:

it is a sustained invective on mankind in general, a glorification of wisdom and reason, and it expresses skepticism to a degree that made the poet very suspect in pious circles. Dogmatically, however, it cannot be called coherent, for doubts about the Resurrection and afterlife or the value of prophethood alternate with professions of orthodox belief. The title, *Luzūm mā lā yalzam*,[11] literally "the necessity of what is not necessary," could also be translated as "the self-imposed constraints," one of these being a form of rich rhyme, involving two rhyme consonants instead of one and using all the letters of the alphabet as rhyme consonant. Another constant trait is the sustained use of figures such as paronomasia. The poems are riddled with allusions and studded with rare words and recondite expressions.[12] In order to refute allegations of unbelief detected in this collection he wrote a work called *Zajr al-nābiḥ* (*Chiding Away the Barking Dog*), parts of which are extant.[13]

Al-Maʿarrī's gloomy outlook on the world probably has something to do with his unsuccessful attempt to settle in Baghdad in 399/1008. He returned to al-Maʿarrah after some eighteen months, partly, it seems, because he was unable to secure suitable patronage and because he fell out with a leading personality in the cultural and literary life of the metropolis, al-Sharīf al-Murtaḍā. They quarreled about the merits of al-Mutanabbī; when al-Murtaḍā made a disparaging remark about the poet, al-Maʿarrī retorted with a cleverly allusive and insinuating quotation, after which he was unceremoniously dragged by his feet from the literary gathering. Henceforth, for the rest of his long life, with only one brief exception, he remained in his birthplace, describing himself as *rahīn* (or *rahn*) *al-maḥbisayn*, "hostage to two prisons," meaning his blindness and his seclusion; in an epigram he mentions a third prison, his soul being confined to his body.[14] Although contemporaries mention that he was wealthy and greatly esteemed in his town, he lived like an ascetic. He was obviously fond of various forms of self-imposed constraints. He abstained from marriage and sexual intercourse; the inscription on his grave says "This is my father's crime against me, | a crime that I did not commit to anyone."[15] His diet was extremely frugal, consisting chiefly of lentils, with figs for sweet;[16] and, very unusually for a Muslim, he was not only a vegetarian, but a vegan who abstained from meat, fish, dairy products, eggs, and honey, because he did not want to kill or hurt animals or deprive them of their food. This was an attitude he had to defend when he was attacked by the famous Ismāʿīlī ideologue and "chief propagandist" (*dāʿī l-duʿāh*), Abū Naṣr al-Mu'ayyad fī l-Dīn al-Shīrāzī, a kind of Grand Mufti of the Fāṭimids in Cairo (whose influence extended to Syria). This attack branded him as a heretic who tried to pose as someone "more merciful than the Merciful," i.e., God, who, after all, allowed the consumption of meat. The interesting exchange of letters between the theologian and Abū l-ʿAlā' has been preserved.[17] It is not clear from where he derived his ideas; his critics speculated that he might have adopted the vegan lifestyle from the Indian Brahmans.[18]

In spite of his ascetic attitude, Abū l-ʿAlā' was no true recluse, someone who cuts himself off from society. On the contrary, people flocked to him and scholars and viziers visited him, paying their respect and hoping to learn from him. Among his pupils were famous philologists such as the poet and critic Ibn Sinān al-Khafājī (d. 466/1074) and Abū Zakariyyā Yaḥyā ibn ʿAlī al-Tibrīzī (d. 502/1109). The latter reported that when Abū l-ʿAlā' died, after a short illness at the age of eighty-four in the month Rabīʿ al-Awwal of 449 (May, AD 1057), eighty-four poets recited elegies at his grave;[19] whether or not this is true, several such elegies have been preserved. Abū l-ʿAlā' also took a lively interest in the intricate politics of his own time and place (involving several dynasties and realms, such as the Ḥamdānids, Būyids, Mirdāsids, Fāṭimids, and the infidel Byzantines); an interest that is apparent from references in his poetry and from some of his letters and prose works. Probably the most interesting work in this respect is his *Risālat al-Ṣāhil wa-l-shāḥij* (*The Epistle of the Neigher and the Brayer*), a lengthy work in which the main characters are animals, notably a horse and a mule. Speaking animals had been familiar to the Arabs since the famous collection of animal fables, *Kalīlah wa-Dimnah*, was translated from the Pahlavi into Arabic by Ibn al-Muqaffaʿ (d. ca. 139/756),[20] but Abū l-ʿAlā'"s book, composed around the year 144/1021, does not contain fables; it is a commentary on contemporary politics involving the Mirdāsid and Fāṭimid dynasties and the Byzantines. It also discusses matters such as taxation. At the same time, like other works of his, it is full of digressions on highly technical matters in the fields of grammar, lexicography, poetics, prosody, and rhyme.

Abū l-ʿAlāʾ ranks as one of the great poets in Arabic literary history. Unlike most poets of the first rank he also excelled as a prose writer. In addition to the present work and the *Epistle of the Neigher and the Brayer*, mention should be made of a controversial work of his: *al-Fuṣūl wa-l-ghāyāt* (*Paragraphs and Periods*). It is composed in an exceptionally difficult idiom (the author regularly interrupts his text with a commentary and explanation of obscure words and expressions), but once one has grasped the sense the work is, at first sight, not shocking: it is a series of homiletic, sermon-like texts, containing praise of God, which call for piety, asceticism, and submission to Fate. The controversy that arose about the book is on account of its style and its form, together with the suspicion that the author's intention was to outdo the Qurʾan. It is composed in an intricate form of rhymed prose, with rhymes interwoven on two text levels: short range within the various sections or paragraphs (*fuṣūl*), and long range, because the last words ("ends", *ghāyāt*) of successive sections also rhyme in an alphabetic series. It uses many idioms that have a Qurʾanic flavor. Altogether, it is not surprising that some thought that its author intended to surpass the Qurʾan, an attitude clearly blasphemous to orthodox Muslims, who believe that the style of the Qurʾan, God's literal words, is inimitable and unsurpassable. When someone rhetorically asked how *al-Fuṣūl wa-l-ghāyāt* could possibly be compared to the Surahs and *āyāt* ("verses") of the Qurʾan, Abū l-ʿAlāʾ reputedly replied, "Wait until it has been polished by tongues for four hundred years; then see how it is,"[21] an answer that would not endear him to the pious.

Although he has been called "the poet among philosophers and the philosopher among poets," it does not do him justice to consider him a philosopher. It is probably wrong to see a consistent world view in his works. He is a humanist who generally hates humanity and loves animals, a Muslim who expresses many unorthodox thoughts (such as his frequently expressed doubts about a bodily resurrection), a rationalist, a skeptic, and a stoic, a precursor of Arthur Schopenhauer. But above all he is a witty and erudite man of letters, a satirist and moralist, with an incredible command of the Arabic language.

Among his other works that have been preserved is a treatise on morphology (*Risālat al-Malāʾikah*); a "prosimetrical" work, *Mulqā l-sabīl*, in which each section consists of a very short ethical paragraph in prose followed by a versification; a collection of letters in ornate style; and commentaries on the collected poetry by famous Abbasid poets: Abū Tammām, al-Buḥturī, and al-Mutanabbī. Many other works listed in the ancient sources are no longer extant.

Al-Maʿarrī lived at the end of what has been called "the Golden Age" of Arabic literature.[22] Whether or not this qualification and this periodization are justified, he firmly belongs to the "classic" Arabic authors. But his reputation has always been mixed throughout the pre-modern period. "People have different opinions about Abū l-ʿAlāʾ," says Yāqūt, "Some say that he was a heretic (*zindīq*) . . . , others say that he was a pious ascetic who subsisted on little and who imposed on himself a harsh regimen, being content with little and turning away from worldly matters."[23] Against the many admirers there are as many detractors. One of the latter, a certain Abū Ghālib ibn Nabhān, apparently had a dream shortly after al-Maʿarrī's death:

> Last night I had a dream in which I saw a blind man with two vipers on his shoulders, dangling down to his thighs. Each of them raised its mouth toward his face, biting off the flesh and devouring it. The man was yelling and crying for help. Shocked and frightened as I was by seeing the

> man in this state, I asked who he was. "This is al-Maʿarrī, the heretic (*mulḥid*)," was the reply.[24]

With this fancy about the afterlife of a presumed heretic we turn to the present work, al-Maʿarrī's imaginations about life in heaven and hell, much of which is devoted to heresy. It also has several passages about snakes.

Risālat Ibn al-Qāriḥ and Risālat al-Ghufrān

Around the year 424/1033 Abū l-ʿAlāʾ received a long and somewhat rambling letter from a grammarian and Hadith scholar from Aleppo, called ʿAlī ibn Manṣūr ibn al-Qāriḥ, also known as Dawkhalah.[25] The elderly writer, already in his seventies, obviously tries to ingratiate himself with the famous inhabitant of al-Maʿarrah. He complains at length of his infirmities and indigence, apologizes for his foibles, and attempts to impress the addressee in the customary ornate style, employing rhymed prose (*sajʿ*) with much display of erudition and orthodoxy, in the course of which he digresses with a discussion of a number of notorious heretics.[26] One of the aims of the letter to Abū l-ʿAlāʾ, whom he praises volubly, is to exculpate himself of allegations, which he knows Abū l-ʿAlāʾ has heard about him: he had been accused of ingratitude toward a family that had patronized him, a family some of whose members had close links with al-Maʿarrī. Abū l-Ḥasan al-Maghribī (d. 400/1009–10) was a man of letters who became state secretary, serving under the Ḥamdānids in Aleppo and later under the Fāṭimids in Cairo. He made Ibn al-Qāriḥ the tutor of his children, in particular Abū l-Qāsim (d. 418/1027), who later became vizier. When the family fell into disgrace and several were executed at the orders of the notorious Fāṭimid caliph al-Ḥākim, Abū l-Qāsim was the only prominent member of his kin who escaped. Ibn al-Qāriḥ not only disassociated himself from his former patron but even composed invective poems lampooning him.[27] One might expect that in his letter to Abū l-ʿAlāʾ, Ibn al-Qāriḥ would apologize for his vicious attacks on al-Maʿarrī's friend. Instead, he goes to some length in trying to justify his views, by describing Abū l-Qāsim as a madman, and a very unpleasant one at that.

It is easy to imagine Abū l-ʿAlāʾ being not a little irritated by this rather incoherent and self-righteous appeal and the attacks on a friend. Apparently he took some time before replying, and when he did it was in the form of this strange book known as *Risālat al-Ghufrān, The Epistle of Forgiveness.* Formally it is a *risālah*, a letter, but it is longer than many a book, and like many Arabic "epistles" addressed to one person it is obviously meant to be read by many. Abū l-ʿAlāʾ does not openly refute or rebuke his correspondent; he remains as polite and respectful as Ibn al-Qāriḥ. Both epistles are brimful with pious wishes and blessings, parenthetically added whenever the other is addressed or mentioned (in the polite epistolary style of the time, the third person is used instead of direct address, to refer to the recipient). Abū l-ʿAlāʾ's work opens with sections expressing his affection for Ibn al-Qāriḥ and praise of his letter, and the second part of *al-Ghufrān* opens with a discussion of hypocrisy, of which Ibn al-Qāriḥ is said to be wholly free. The reader will not be fooled, however: it is clear that all this is ironical. The very difficult Preamble (usually omitted by translators)[28] ostensibly expresses al-Maʿarrī's affection for Ibn al-Qāriḥ, but it is an exercise in double entendre, where words, said to refer to the writer's "heart," are closely linked to words for "black" and "snake." It is an odd way to open a friendly letter, and Bint al-Shāṭiʾ has suggested that al-Maʿarrī, with these snakes and the blackness, obliquely refers to what he really thinks of Ibn al-Qāriḥ's hypocrisy and malice.[29] There is a problem with this interpretation, because al-Maʿarrī is speaking of his own heart in this preamble, not that of Ibn al-Qāriḥ;[30] but in any case the ambiguous and punning diction seems to suggest that the fulsome praise is not to be taken at face value: al-Maʿarrī's epistle is steeped in sardonic irony, even though it is not always clear when he is being ironic.

When Abū l-ʿAlāʾ extols the qualities of Ibn al-Qāriḥ's letter, his irony takes a different direction. He imagines that this letter will help the writer to secure God's favor and forgiveness. Taking the theme of forgiveness as his starting point and as a leitmotiv for his text, he then embarks on a lengthy and extraordinary flight of fancy, which takes all of the first part (*Gh* §§1–20) of his *Epistle*. He imagines that on the Day of Resurrection, at the end of the world, Ibn al-Qāriḥ is revived like all mortal beings. He is admitted to Paradise, but not without difficulty. He has to cope, even at the Last Day, with what one could call the hardships of bureaucracy: one cannot be admitted without a document stating one's true repentance of sins. Unfortunately, the Sheikh (as Ibn al-Qāriḥ is often called) has lost this crucial document amidst the hustle and bustle and he must find someone to testify for him. When at last he has taken this hurdle and someone has duly attested that Ibn al-Qāriḥ showed true repentance in the nick of time, he still needs the intercession of the Prophet and the help of the latter's daughter and son. Having arrived in Paradise, after crossing the narrow Bridging Path in a rather undignified manner, riding piggyback on a helpful girl, he decides to go on an excursion. He meets with poets and grammarians—he is, after all, himself a grammarian with a great knowledge of poetry—and asks them how they have been able to attain eternal bliss. Some poets died before the coming of Islam; others composed verses of a dubious, irreligious nature, and one may wonder why they have been forgiven. The conversations are often about points of morphology, syntax, lexicography, and matters of versification, such as irregularities of meter and rhyme; in general, the Sheikh's interest is keener than that of the poets themselves, many of whom have forgotten, on account of the terrors of the Last Day, what they produced in the "Fleeting World."

The blessings and pleasures of Paradise are also described: the quality of the wine, at last permitted, and hangover-free; the food (a banquet is depicted), and the heavenly singing of beautiful damsels. Ibn al-Qāriḥ meets some ravishing girls who tell him that they were ugly but pious on earth and have been rewarded. Not all paradisial females had a worldly pre-existence: other black-eyed beauties emerge from fruits that can be plucked from a tree; Ibn al-Qāriḥ acquires his personal houri in this manner. Before settling with her he leaves for another excursion. He visits the part of Heaven reserved for the jinn or demons (for some of them are believing Muslims). There he meets the extraordinary demon called Abū Hadrash, who boasts in long poems of his devious exploits, but who has been forgiven because of his repentance. Then the Sheikh heads for the spot where there is (as the Qur'an states) a kind of peephole, through which one can look into Hell and gloat. Our Sheikh converses with poets who have been consigned to Hell for various reasons; he pesters them with queries about their poetry, but mostly meets with a less than enthusiastic response. He also talks to the Devil, who in turn asks him some perplexing questions about Paradise. On his way back the Sheikh visits yet another region: the relatively dusky and lowly Paradise of the *rajaz* poets, *rajaz* being an old and rather simple meter that is deemed inferior. Finally he rests, seated on a couch, carried by damsels and immortal youths, surrounded by fruit trees, the fruits of which move toward his mouth of their own accord.

This concludes the first part of the *Epistle of Forgiveness.* The author admits that he has been rather prolix and says, "Now we shall turn to a reply to the letter." This he does in the second part (*Gh* §§21–45), which is a point-by-point discussion of Ibn al-Qāriḥ's epistle. The bulk of this part is devoted to the various heretics and schismatics mentioned by Ibn al-Qāriḥ, after which al-Maʿarrī turns to the Sheikh's "repentance" and other matters. He concludes by apologizing for the delay in replying. The first part can be read on its own; indeed, most existing translations do not even contain the second part.

Yet the two parts hang together. Al-Maʿarrī's irony is present on a deeper level. There are strong indications[31] that the true purpose of his *Epistle* is to enjoin Ibn al-Qāriḥ to repent of his insolent and ungrateful behavior toward a former patron, of his self-confessed self-indulging in the past, of his hypocrisy in his own *Epistle*, of his sometimes tactless and self-righteous condemnation of poets and heretics, and of being generally obsessed with himself. The fictional Ibn al-Qāriḥ, in *al-Ghufrān*, only acquires forgiveness and reaches Paradise with much difficulty; it turns out that he only truly repented of his sins at the last moment: it may still happen in reality, implies al-Maʿarrī, if God wills. He also implies, therefore, that in his view Ibn al-Qāriḥ's own letter does not amount to true repentance. He mocks Ibn al-Qāriḥ's obsession with himself and his own profession (grammar and poetry) by imagining him in Paradise as being interested only in poets and philologists; even when he meets others, such as Adam, Abū Hadrash the jinn, or the devil, the conversation is mostly about poetry. The first part is therefore an elaborate and extremely lengthy introduction to the proper reply to the original letter. In the second part several points reappear, such as the importance of true repentance. The fictional Ibn al-Qāriḥ had seen the poet Bashshār in Hell, but al-Maʿarrī says in the second part that he will not categorically say that Bashshār's destination will be Hell; God is merciful and kind.

One of al-Maʿarrī's prominent methods in responding to Ibn al-Qāriḥ's letter is to treat the points made by Ibn al-Qāriḥ with profound and pervading irony, for it is rather obvious that, just as in the first part, the writer is mocking his correspondent. This begins right at the start: when al-Maʿarrī declares the Sheikh to be free of hypocrisy we can be certain that he means exactly the opposite of what he is saying. Much of the rest of the point-by-point reply should be read in the same light. When he objects to the Sheikh's praise by playing down his own learning, one suspects that he was not unaware of his superior erudition. The clearest instance of mockery is the passage in which he ponders the Sheikh's potential prowess on the marriage market, if he were to seek a mature spouse in the prime of life. It is impossible to decide to what extent, if at all, the lengthy section on heresy and heretics is to be read as irony. Abū l-ʿAlāʾ is a master of dissembling.

Another conspicuous method of al-Maʿarrī in commenting is to take up a theme or even a word and toy with it, in a manner that evokes the well-known description of the sermons of Bishop Lancelot Andrewes (1555–1626); a "Scotish Lord," asked by King James I how he liked them, replied that[32]

> he was learned, but he played with his Text, as a Jack-an-apes does, who takes up a thing and tosses and playes with it, and then he takes up another, and playes a little with it. Here's a pretty thing, and there's a pretty thing!

A good example, albeit a rather extreme one, is Ibn al-Qāriḥ's little story about the eighty-three dinars that were stolen from him by his niece.[33] Abū l-ʿAlāʾ begins with congratulating the Sheikh on retrieving his money; then he embarks on a mock eulogy on these dinars in prose, quoting many verses and some anecdotes about dinars, and mentioning a few people called Dīnār, comparing the Sheikh's dinars favorably with all of these. Next he takes up their number, quoting verses and stories involving the number eighty, followed by general thoughts on gold, and finally about sisters, women, and kinship. Thus an incident that in Ibn al-Qāriḥ's Arabic is told in some forty words is blown up by our author to a passage of approximately 2,200 words. In all this he displays his usual stupendous erudition. No doubt the author's ostensible purpose is to honor the Sheikh, but the reader cannot escape the feeling that the real point is to flaunt his vast knowledge and often rather ponderous wit. Moreover, the hyperbolic descriptions and comparisons involving the Sheikh's coins can be read as a form of ironic mockery of the triviality of the incident. Another example of his playing with words is the passage in which he takes up the titles of the heretic Ibn al-Rāwandī's books. His *al-Dāmigh* (*The Brain-Basher*) will only bash the brains of its author, his *al-Tāj* (*The Crown*) is not even fit to be a sandal, and so on.

Potentially the most interesting part of al-Maʿarrī's reply is his reaction to the lengthy passage in Ibn al-Qāriḥ's letter about heretics in Islam, particularly in the light of the many accusations leveled at al-Maʿarrī himself on account of his numerous aberrant or even heretical statements. Alas, he does not discuss theology or doctrine. One could hardly expect him to defend any of the alleged heretics listed by Ibn al-Qāriḥ, but he does not even discuss or attack their views apart from condemning them in general and strong terms. The long section on heretics contains much that is interesting, but one searches in vain for the author's ideas that could be connected with the often startling utterances that can be found the poems of his *Luzūmiyyāt* collection. Most of his "refutation" of Ibn al-Rāwandī consists of a long and somewhat excruciating series of puns on the titles of Ibn al-Rāwandī's books, as mentioned above, in a passage full of prose rhyme, without any comments on what these books actually contain.[34] It seems that Ibn al-Qāriḥ, with his insistence on the subject of heresy, wanted to provoke al-Maʿarrī. But the latter does not take the bait and carefully makes it clear from which heretical views he distances himself and presents himself as "orthodox."

We know nothing about Ibn al-Qāriḥ's reaction upon receiving the reply to his letter, so one can only speculate on the mixed feelings he may have had. No doubt he was honored by the extraordinary length of the epistle and the effort al-Maʿarrī bestowed on its composition. But unless he was wholly obtuse he cannot have been blind to the irony that pervades it.

While *Risālat al-Ghufrān* did not receive as much attention from pre-modern authors as his *al-Fuṣūl wa-l-ghāyāt* or the poems of *Luzūm mā lā yalzam,* it met with some mixed criticism. A note by al-Dhahabī (d. 748/1348) encapsulates it all: "It contains Mazdakism (*mazdakah*) and irreverence (*istikhfāf*); there is much erudition (*adab*) in it."[35] Ibn al-Qāriḥ's imagined experiences in Heaven (with glimpses of Hell) as told by al-Maʿarrī form an interesting kind of fiction. Overt fiction was often frowned upon in pre-modern Arab literary culture; hence, for instance, the condemnation of fairytales and fantastic stories such as are found in *The Thousand and One Nights.* But al-Maʿarrī did not pretend that his fantasies about his correspondent actually happened: the events are set in the future and the Arabic present tense (which can refer to the future, for events that will or merely might happen) is used consistently, rather than the perfect tense normally employed in narrative texts. If he cannot be accused of writing fictions or lies, one might think that his apparently irreverent descriptions of Paradise border on the blasphemous. There can, in fact, be no doubt that he is mocking popular and pious beliefs about the hereafter; after all, he himself frequently questioned the reality of bodily resurrection, one of the central dogmas of orthodox Islam. Yet he does not introduce anything in his descriptions of Paradise and Hell that has not been, or could not be, imagined or written by pious Muslims. As is well known, Qur'anic descriptions of the Last Day and the Last Things (Heaven and Hell) are vivid and full of concrete images; popular pious literature greatly expanded and elaborated the Qur'anic images, turning Paradise into a Land of Cockayne, where birds fly around asking to be consumed, not unlike the peacock and the goose in the *Epistle of Forgiveness* that are instantly marinated or roasted as desired, and are then revived again. The Qur'an (56:20–21), after all, promises the believers "whatever fruit they choose and whatever fowl they desire."

Eschatological tourism is known from several literatures, notably through Dante's *Divine Comedy.* That the latter was inspired partly by al-Maʿarrī was a hypothesis put forward by several scholars, notably Miguel Asín Palacios, and eagerly embraced, naturally, by some Arab scholars such as Kāmil Kaylānī, whose abridged edition of *Risālat al-Ghufrān* also contains a summary of Dante in Arabic, and who provides the first part of *al-Ghufrān* with the subtitle *Kūmīdiyā ilāhiyyah masraḥuhā l-jannah wa-l-nār*, "A Divine Comedy, Staged in Paradise and Hell."[36] One Arab writer even argued that Dante, having stolen al-Maʿarrī's ideas, produced a greatly inferior work, in which he should have made al-Maʿarrī his guide rather than Virgil.[37] The hypothesis that Dante was influenced by al-Maʿarrī has now been largely abandoned; if there is an Islamic root to Dante's *Commedia*, it is more likely to have been inspired by popular ideas about the Prophet's celebrated short excursion, his ascension to heaven (*al-miʿrāj*) after his "nocturnal journey" to Jerusalem (*al-isrāʾ*); a European translation of the anonymous *Kitāb al-Miʿrāj* (of which Latin, French, and Castilian versions were popular) was probably known to Dante. It has also been suggested that Dante may have been inspired by a Hebrew version of a work by Avicenna, *Ḥayy ibn Yaqẓān*, describing an imaginative "cosmic" journey.[38]

Nicholson rightly remarks[39] that while the *Risālat al-Ghufrān* "faintly" resembles the Sixth Book of Virgil's *Aeneid*, where Aeneas visits the Underworld, the *Divine Comedy*, or the Zoroastrian, Middle Persian *Book of Ardā Vīrāf*, a more significant parallel can be found in Lucian (d. ca. AD 180), who like al-Maʿarrī was a Syrian, though Greek-educated. In his ironically entitled *True Histories* (or *True Fictions*) Lucian describes his fantastic journeys on earth and even to the moon. He visits a Blessed Isle, the delights of which are depicted in some detail; there he meets not only ancient worthies such as heroes of the Trojan War but also Homer, whom he questions about his poetry.[40] All this is written in a lively and very irreverent style, altogether akin to that of al-Maʿarrī, who shared Lucian's rationalism, skepticism, and pessimism. It must not be supposed, however, that al-Maʿarrī knew Lucian's work, for he was not translated into Arabic and al-Maʿarrī did not know Greek. But Lucian was popular with the Byzantines: his works were much copied, annotated, imitated, and taught in schools[41] and one could imagine that some of Lucian's themes reached al-Maʿarrī orally. One also notes that the motif of the tree woman, exploited in *The Epistle of Forgiveness*, admittedly known in Arabic popular lore,[42] is also found in Lucian's *True Histories.*[43]

It has been suggested[44] that *Risālat al-Ghufrān* was inspired by *Risālat al-Tawābiʿ wa-l-zawābiʿ* by the Andalusian Arab poet and prose-writer Ibn Shuhayd (d. 426/1035), who composed it only a few years before al-Maʿarrī wrote his work. In this short, incompletely preserved work, translated by James T. Monroe as *The Treatise of Familiar Spirits and Demons*,[45] the author takes as his starting point the ancient Arab idea that a poet is inspired by a demon or genius, an idea that survived in Islamic times even though many would not take it more seriously than European poets would literally believe in the existence of the Muses or a personal muse. Ibn Shuhayd describes his imagined conversations with the demons of some famous poets: the pre-Islamic Imru' al-Qays, Ṭarafah, and Qays ibn al-Khaṭīm, and the Abbasid poets Abū Nuwās and Abū Tammām; he boldly expands the idea by assigning similar demons to prose writers such as ʿAbd al-Ḥamīd ibn Yaḥyā, Badīʿ al-Zamān al-Hamadhānī, and al-Jāḥiẓ (who no doubt would have been surprised by the fancy), and by describing some animal genii: a mule and a goose. It is not impossible that al-Maʿarrī (who in fact composed a short epistle on the same topic)[46] was aware of this work, but one would underestimate his powers of invention if one assumed he was unable to compose his *Epistle* without such inspiration.

The *Epistle of Forgiveness* builds to some extent on his own *Risālat al-Malāʾikah* (*The Epistle of the Angels*), mentioned above as a work on morphology. In this work, composed probably a few years before the *Epistle of Forgiveness*, al-Maʿarrī imagines that he himself discusses oddities of the Arabic lexicon with angels in the afterlife. He surprises the angels with his analysis of the word for "angel" (*malak*, pl. *malāʾikah*),[47] and he discusses other words with them. He argues that those who end up in heaven enjoying the *ḥūr* (black-and-white-eyed damsels) and other delights such as the *sundus* and *istabraq* ("silk and brocade") should at least be aware of the morphology and etymology of these words.[48] The imagined conversations are at times very similar to those in *al-Ghufrān*, for instance when al-Maʿarrī quotes poets and grammarians to prove a point, whereupon an angel exclaims, "Who is this Ibn Abī Rabīʿah, what's this Abū ʿUbaydah, what's all this nonsense? If you have done any pious deeds you will be happy; if not, get out of here!"[49] There is clearly some self-mockery here.

Similarly, although al-Maʿarrī is clearly mocking Ibn al-Qāriḥ in *al-Ghufrān*, one suspects that many of the philological concerns of the latter were also his own. Ibn al-Qāriḥ's fictional persona often uses obscure and rare words, which he immediately explains in plainer language; it looks as if he is being mocked for his pedantry. However, al-Maʿarrī does the same when he writes in his own voice; he appears to flaunt his extraordinary knowledge of the Arabic lexicon. A passage in the second part hints at another, practical reason why he added his glosses: our blind author fears that his dictations, with their recondite diction, may be misunderstood or garbled by his scribes.[50] Likewise, one assumes that some of the criticism voiced by Ibn al-Qāriḥ on points of grammar and versification is shared by al-Maʿarrī. A similar preoccupation with philology is found in other works by him, such as *The Epistle of the Neigher and the Brayer*. It is clear that for al-Maʿarrī and, as he imagines, for Ibn al-Qāriḥ the expected delights of Paradise are not primarily sensual but intellectual. The various delights provided by pretty girls, music, food, and drink are generally described in a somewhat ironical vein and the comparisons of heavenly substances with earthly equivalents are couched in ludicrously hyperbolic expressions; but the pleasures of poetry and philological pedantry are taken, on the whole, rather more seriously, even though here, too, a modicum of mockery is not altogether absent.

It is not surprising that in almost all translations of *The Epistle of Forgiveness* such passages about grammar, lexicon, and prosody have been drastically curtailed or omitted altogether, for a combination of reasons: they will not greatly interest those who do not know Arabic, they will seem an annoying interruption of the narrative to those who read the text for the story, and not least because they are rather difficult to translate and in need of copious annotation. When Bint al-Shāṭi' published her adaptation of the first part of the *Epistle of Forgiveness* for the stage, as a play in three acts,[51] she naturally excised much of the philology, even though she lets the actors discuss some matters regarding grammatical case endings and poetic meters on the stage. It is not known if the play has ever been performed and one cannot but have some doubts about its viability.[52]

Al-Maʿarrī's rationalist critique of religion has influenced and inspired neoclassicist and modernist Arabic writers and poets, such as the Iraqi poets Jamīl Ṣidqī l-Zahāwī (1863–1936) and Maʿrūf al-Ruṣāfī (1875–1945). The former wrote a verse epic, *Thawrah fī l-jaḥīm* (*Revolution in Hell*, 1931) in which he offers an interesting and subversive interpretation of the *Epistle of Forgiveness*, involving many well-known figures from Western and Arab history and culture. Heaven is the place for the establishment, Hell for the maladjusted and the socially ambitious, who are punished for their courage. Finally, supported by the angels of Hell, they storm Heaven, claiming it as their rightful place since it is they who have advanced mankind.[53] *Ḥadīth ʿĪsā ibn Hishām* (*The Story of ʿĪsā ibn Hishām*), a well-known work of fiction first published serially between 1898 and 1902 by the Egyptian author Muḥammad al-Muwayliḥī (1858?–1930), is often linked with the *Maqāmāt* of Badīʿ al-Zamān al-Hamadhānī (d. 398/1008) but it has several things in common with *Risālat al-Ghufrān*: a protagonist who is resurrected from the dead before an imaginary journey, implicit and explicit criticism of contemporary beliefs and customs, and a style in which rhymed prose alternates with ordinary prose.

The varied fate of the text, with its incomplete, truncated translations and its transformation into a play, clearly shows how difficult it is to classify it, to those who love neat classifications. Although called a *risālah* and addressed to one person, it is not an ordinary letter, nor is it intended to be read only by the addressee. While containing a narrative complete with a lengthy flashback it is not a normal story, *qiṣṣah*, *ḥadīth*, *khabar*, or *ḥikāyah*. It incorporates much of what normally belongs to the genre of philological "dictations," *amālī*. It contains, in al-Dhahabī's words quoted above, "much *adab*," which here has all its meanings of erudition, literary quotations including much poetry, moral edification, and entertaining anecdotes. Searchers for the "organic unity" of this heterogeneous literary work will have an arduous task. One could argue that part of its originality and its attractiveness lies precisely in the impossibility of pigeonholing it; but not every reader, critic, or publisher will be charmed by this.

A Note on the Text

Language, Style, and Translation

The present translators originally harbored some doubts about translating the text in full. However, it is the admirable purpose of the Library of Arabic Literature to present complete texts. We consented and took on the task as a daunting but stimulating challenge. The present translation, for the first time in any language, is complete, for the sake of the integrity of the text and in order not to distort its actual character, which reflects the author's character, as far as we can know it. Abū l-ʿAlāʾ is not first-and-foremost a storyteller: he is a satirist, a moralist, and a philologist who, in his physical blindness and linguistic insight, lives in a universe of language to such an extent that one could even say that, in addition to the two or three "prisons" mentioned above, he also lived in the admittedly very spacious prison of the Arabic language. It was a prison in which he felt at home like no other. The reader should be warned that *The Epistle of Forgiveness* is not exactly an easy read; but the philological passages can be skipped by impatient readers.

Telling a story could be done in a simple, unadorned style. The stories in *al-Faraj baʿd al-Shiddah* (*Relief after Distress*) by al-Muḥassin al-Tanūkhī (d. 384/994), for instance, are written in a relatively plain Arabic, and so are innumerable anecdotes and stories in various collections and anthologies. However, the aim of epistolary prose, in al-Maʿarrī's time, was not always primarily to express one's meaning clearly: that would be paramount to an insult, as if the recipient could only understand plain speech. One ought to employ a flowery style, rich in metaphors, allusions, syntactical and semantic parallelism, recondite vocabulary, and above all *sajʿ* or rhymed prose, usually in the form of paired rhyme (*aabbccdd*...). Such an ornate style is found especially in preambles of letters and books, and in descriptive, "purple" passages, or on any occasion where the author wishes to display his erudition and stylistic prowess. Already in al-Maʿarrī's lifetime interesting experiments had been done to introduce *sajʿ* into narrative prose texts continuously rather than on specific occasions, Badīʿ al-Zamān al-Hamadhānī (d. 398/1008) being a pioneer in this field, as the "inventor" of the *maqāmah* genre.

Al-Maʿarrī, in the first part of his *Epistle*, does not use *sajʿ* throughout but only at certain points. Since it is such a characteristic and striking element of classical Arabic prose, it has been imitated in the translation, at the risk of sounding somewhat quaint.[54] The same has not been done, except very occasionally, in the translation of Ibn al-Qāriḥ's epistle; likewise, the frequency of *sajʿ* in the second part of *Risālat al-Ghufrān* will make it impossible to imitate it in English. The reader should be aware that many a strange expression could have been caused by an Arabic rhyme; as Nicholson says, perhaps too harshly, "Abū'l-ʿAlā seldom escapes from his artificial prose with its forced metaphors and tyrannous rhymes."[55] Often, especially in the second part, he is not content with ordinary rhyme but employs the "rich rhyme" that also marks the poems in his *Luzūmiyyāt*. Where al-Maʿarrī uses an obscure word, the translation also uses an unusual English word, if possible. Fidelity to the text therefore overrides readability at times. The translators have stayed as close as possible to the Arabic text and have never resorted, unlike predecessors such as Brackenbury, Meïssa, and Monteil, to summary, large-scale paraphrase, and blatant glossing over difficulties by simple omission (Brackenbury and Meïssa cannot be blamed for this, since they relied on Kaylānī's edition, which leaves out everything that is difficult or obscure). Some concessions to

English style and usage had to be made, of course. Thus we have not hesitated to make pronouns (the ubiquitous and often confusing "he," "him," and "his" of Arabic narrative) explicit in order to make it clear who or what is meant, wherever this seemed desirable. Very often, when al-Maʿarrī refers to Ibn al-Qāriḥ, we have rendered "he" as "the Sheikh." Al-Maʿarrī's language is difficult and not all problems have been solved. Arab editors and commentators can ignore them, or pretend they do not find them problematical rather than confess their ignorance (we suspect this is often the case); a translator cannot hide in the same manner. In the notes we have discussed some of our difficulties and doubts or professed our inability to understand the text.

Many such problems are found in the poetry quoted in the text. Both epistles contain much of it, most of it by other poets, although the poems recited by the demon Abū Hadrash in *Risālat al-Ghufrān* are obviously by al-Maʿarrī himself. Classical Arabic poetry always rhymes (normally with "monorhyme": *aaaaaa*...), but our translations, with very few exceptions, do not use rhyme, which would normally be incompatible with accuracy; instead of the Arabic quantitative meters (not unlike those of ancient Greek, Latin, or Sanskrit) a loose English meter (e.g., iambic) has generally been chosen. In view of the difficulties of many verses and the fact that they do not contribute to the bare narrative, it is not surprising that all earlier translators drastically cut the verse. Needless to say, in the present translation nothing has been cut.

In the first part we have attempted to render the author's prose rhyme in the English translation, wherever it occurred. In the second part there is much more of it in the Arabic and we decided that it was impossible to imitate it, except sporadically. Al-Maʿarrī consistently employs "rich rhyme," involving two consonants rather than the usual one, which enables him to display his vast knowledge of obscure words. Translating such words and expressions is difficult enough; providing rhymes in addition is beyond the realm of the humanly possible without unacceptable sacrifices of the meaning.

Led by his rhyming skill and obsession the author often makes strange connections, leaping from one concept to another, very remote idea. Readers of the English, not alerted by rhyme, will have to take this into account whenever the text looks somewhat strange. On some occasions a note explains that the rhyme lies behind the odd juxtaposition of ideas, for instance when al-Maʿarrī comes up with a "mewing cat" (*māghin*, §31.2.1) because, unsurprisingly, it is the only word he can think of that rhymes with "brain" (*dimāgh*).

In the first part, just as in the second part a lot of poetry is quoted, sometimes with brief comments on technical matters. However, lengthy passages on grammar or lexicography such as are found in the first part, the direct result of imagined discussions with poets and grammarians, are lacking in the second part.

The text is often difficult and in need of much annotation to make it understandable to the reader. On several occasions we have acknowledged our ignorance. Extreme care should be taken in using Monteil's French translation, which seems to read well, being based on frequent guesswork, some of it inspired but very often wide of the mark. It is riddled with astonishing howlers.

The two translators have collaborated closely. The English text of the translation, annotation, and introduction, was made by van Gelder, who was helped, in varying degrees, by predecessors such as Nicholson, Brackenbury, Meïssa, Dechico, and Monteil,[56] by Bint al-Shāṭiʾ's excellent annotation, by Schoeler's published, partial, German translation, and by his unpublished rough draft of the complete German translation of the first part. Van Gelder's drafts were thoroughly revised by Schoeler and difficulties were discussed in frequent and fruitful email exchanges. The final English version was polished by two native speakers, Sheila Ottway and especially James Montgomery, our project editor at LAL. Translations from the Qurʾan are by van Gelder; they are marked by angle brackets (French quotation marks) to distinguish them from other quotations, just as in Arabic they are customarily given in special decorative "bow brackets." English titles of the various chapters have been added.

After the completion of Volume One of the hardcover, the translators were made aware of a new translation into Italian of the first part, by Martino Diez, who kindly sent a copy. Unlike its predecessors, it is virtually complete and includes the various digressions on grammar, lexicon, and prosody; it is provided with informative notes. We could make only limited use of this excellent translation.

The Arabic Edition

Reynold A. Nicholson may have been the pioneer in studying *The Epistle of Forgiveness* and making scholars acquainted with it, but the towering figure in the field is without question the Egyptian scholar ʿĀʾishah ʿAbd al-Raḥmān (1913–98), who named herself Bint al-Shāṭiʾ ("Daughter of the Riverbank"[57]), and whose doctoral dissertation at the University of Cairo in 1950 became the basis for the first scholarly edition of the epistles by al-Maʿarrī and Ibn al-Qāriḥ. Her richly annotated edition, a monument of scholarship, appeared in 1954 (Cairo: Dār al-Maʿārif) and was republished several times with minor revisions. The ninth edition that appeared in Cairo in 1993 forms the basis for the present translation; we have also used some of her earlier editions, notably the third (Cairo, 1963) and fourth (Cairo, n.d.), because even though the later edition corrects some mistakes and inaccuracies, some new typographical errors have crept in occasionally. Furthermore, we have consulted other printed editions, all of them uncritical. Nicholson's articles contain only selected parts of the Arabic text. The oldest of these printed texts is that by Ibrāhīm al-Yāzijī (Cairo: al-Maṭbaʿah al-Hindiyyah, 1903); rather fully voweled, the edition is devoid of annotation and does not contain Ibn al-Qāriḥ's letter. Kāmil Kaylānī, in an undated volume published in Cairo (Dār al-Maʿārif) in 1943, entitled *Risālat al-Ghufrān li-l-shāʿir al-faylasūf Abī l-ʿAlāʾ al-Maʿarrī* (*The Epistle of Forgiveness by the poet-philosopher Abū l-ʿAlāʾ al-Maʿarrī*), offered a shortened version of the epistles of Ibn al-Qāriḥ and al-Maʿarrī, stripped of most of the difficult passages, together with much relevant and sometimes irrelevant annotation and a selection of other epistles by al-Maʿarrī. Later editions, all uncritical, are obviously (but only rarely explicitly) dependent on Bint al-Shāṭiʾ: the lightly annotated one of Mufīd Qumayḥah (Beirut: Dār Maktabat al-Hilāl, 1406/1986, no indexes) and the more fully (but often erroneously) annotated one by Muḥammad al-Iskandarānī and Inʿām Fawwāl (Beirut: Dār al-Kātib al-ʿArabī, 2011/1432, provided with indexes).

In her critical edition of the two epistles Bint al-Shāṭiʾ explains that for Ibn al-Qāriḥ's *Epistle* she relied on two manuscripts from the Taymūriyyah collection in the National Library (Dār al-Kutub) in Cairo and one printed edition, the one incorporated by Muḥammad Kurd ʿAlī in his collection *Rasāʾil al-bulaghāʾ*.[58] The older, undated manuscript was apparently the basis for both the later one (copied in 1327/1909) and the edition in *Rasāʾil al-bulaghāʾ*, and Bint al-Shāṭiʾ took it as the basis for her own edition. We have also benefited from the only other critical edition of Ibn al-Qāriḥ's epistle, part of the unpublished doctoral dissertation by Michel Dechico, which also contains a study and a translation.[59]

For her edition of *Risālat al-Ghufrān*, Bint al-Shāṭiʾ used seven manuscripts, as well as Nicholson's publication and earlier printed editions. The most important manuscript, preserved in Istanbul, seems to date from the seventh/thirteenth century; its copyist remarks that he collated the text with a manuscript corrected by Abū Zakariyyā l-Tibrīzī, mentioned above as a pupil and great admirer of al-Maʿarrī, and an important scholar himself. The other manuscripts used by Bint al-Shāṭiʾ are obviously of less importance, being later, sometimes incomplete, and offering a less reliable text.

Bint al-Shāṭiʾ provides two kinds of footnotes. One supplies textual commentary, including meticulous, detailed information about variant readings in the manuscripts and parallel texts, occasional emendations, and glosses that explain difficult words. At times she cites Nicholson's readings and interpretations, often with gratuitously scathing remarks when he was wrong. The other set of footnotes gives basic information on persons and places mentioned in the text. Even though her editorial practice has been criticized,[60] altogether her notes display stupendous learning and she is almost always right. In our own annotation we have relied much on her notes, but we have not slavishly followed her and it would have been impossible simply to translate her annotation.

The original guidelines of the Library of Arabic Literature recommend that annotation be kept to a minimum. We are grateful to the editors for approving the increased volume of annotations included in the present work. Because of the difficulty of the present text and the plethora of names and allusions it contains, a great deal more explanation was considered essential; there would have been yet more if we had done full justice to the text. Instead, we have limited the annotation to a minimum. A full list of the names of individuals, places, tribes and dynasties which occur in the text is given in the Glossary of Names and Terms.

Notes to the Introduction

1 Ibn Khallikān, *Wafayāt*, i, 113–16; the same in al-Ṣafadī, *al-Wāfī*, iv, 94–111.

2 Yāqūt, *Muʿjam al-udabāʾ*, iii, 107–217; see p. 161.

3 Yāqūt, *Muʿjam al-udabāʾ*, xv, 83.

4 Nicholson, "Persian Manuscripts."

5 Nicholson, "The Risālatu 'l-Ghufrān by Abū 'l-ʿAlāʾ al-Maʿarrī," *Journal of the Royal Asiatic Society* (1900): 637–720; (1902): 75–101, 337–62, 813–47.

6 Al-Thaʿālibī, *Tatimmat al-Yatīmah*, p. 16; also in Yāqūt, *Muʿjam al-udabāʾ*, iii, 129–30; Ibn al-ʿAdīm, *Bughyat al-ṭalab*, p. 897; al-Ṣafadī, *al-Wāfī bi-l-Wafayāt*, vii, 96. Ibn al-ʿAdīm, always keen to defend al-Maʿarrī, doubts that he ever played games or even jested. Al-Maʿarrī's jesting cannot be denied but it is admittedly always of a serious kind.

7 Following Arabic usage, in this introduction he will be called either al-Maʿarrī or Abū l-ʿAlāʾ, for the sake of variety.

8 The Arabic term is *kunyah* (incorrectly translated as "patronymic" in the *Encyclopaedia of Islam*, New [= Second] Edition, v, 395).

9 Ibn al-ʿAdīm, *Bughyat al-ṭalab*, pp. 896–97.

10 An allusion to making fire by means of the friction between two pieces of wood, one hard and one soft.

11 The collection is often called *al-Luzūmiyyāt*.

12 For a good selection, with English translations, see Nicholson, "The Meditations of Maʿarrī."

13 Abū l-ʿAlāʾ al-Maʿarrī, *Zajr al-nābiḥ: Muqtaṭafāt*.

14 Al-Maʿarrī, *Luzūm mā lā yalzam*, i, 188 (rhyme *-īthī*): "I see myself in my three prisons | (so do not ask me about my secret story) || Because of my loss of sight, being homebound | and my soul's residing in an evil body."

15 See, e.g., Ibn Khallikān, *Wafayāt*, i, 115.

16 Al-Qifṭī, *Inbāh al-ruwah*, i, 85.

17 Yāqūt, *Muʿjam al-udabāʾ*, iii, 176–213; see Margoliouth, "Abū 'l-ʿAlāʾ al-Maʿarrī's Correspondence on Vegetarianism."

18 e.g., Yāqūt, *Muʿjam al-udabāʾ*, iii, 125.

19 Yāqūt, *Muʿjam al-udabāʾ*, iii, 126; Ibn al-ʿAdīm, *Bughyat al-ṭalab*, p. 910 mentions "seventy poets from al-Maʿarrah."

20 On speaking animals, see Wagner, "Sprechende Tiere in der arabischen Prosa."

21 There are several versions of this anecdote, see, e.g., Ibn al-ʿAdīm, *Bughyat al-ṭalab*, pp. 879–80.

22 Gibb, *Arabic Literature: An Introduction*, whose "Silver Age" begins two years before al-Maʿarrī's death, with the Seljuqs entering Baghdad.

23 Yāqūt, *Muʿjam al-udabāʾ*, iii, 142; cf. e.g. Ibn al-ʿAdīm, *Bughyat al-ṭalab*, p. 865.

24 Ibn al-ʿAdīm, *Bughyat al-ṭalab*, p. 909, al-ʿAbbāsī, *Maʿāhid al-tanṣīṣ*, i, 52. The two snakes growing on the shoulders are reminiscent of al-Ḍaḥḥāk/Zahhāk/Zuhāk, the evil Arabian king of Iranian lore; see, e.g., E. Yarshater, "Zuhāk." Ibn al-ʿAdīm gives the dream an interpretation that is favorable to al-Maʿarrī: the snakes are the false accusations of heresy and unbelief; the dream describes the sheikh's life, not his afterlife.

25 *Dawkhalah* or *dawkhallah* means "date basket made of palm leaves."

26 On Ibn al-Qāriḥ see Yāqūt, *Muʿjam al-udabāʾ*, xv, 83–88; shortened in al-Ṣafadī, *Wāfī*, xxii, 233–35; al-Suyūṭī, *Bughyat al-wuʿāh*, ii, 207. It is said that he died after 421/1030 (al-Ṣafadī, xxii, 234; Yāqūt, implausibly, has "after 461/1068").

27 For a fragment of four verses, see Yāqūt, *Muʿjam al-udabāʾ*, xv, 84.

28 For a German translation and study, see Schoeler, "Abū l-Alāʾ al-Maʿarrīs Prolog zum *Sendschreiben über die Vergebung*." For an

English translation and study see Stetkevych, "The Snake in the Tree."

29 ʿĀʾishah ʿAbd al-Raḥmān "Bint al-Shāṭiʾ," *Qirāʾah jadīdah fī Risālat al-Ghufrān*, pp. 52–54; *eadem*, "Abū ʾl-ʿAlāʾ al-Maʿarrī," p. 337.

30 Schoeler, "Abū l-Alāʾ al-Maʿarrīs Prolog," p. 421.

31 Schoeler, "Die Vision, die auf einer Hypothese gründet: Zur Deutung von Abū ʾl-ʿAlāʾ al-Maʿarrīs *Risālat al-Ġufrān*."

32 *Aubrey's Brief Lives*, ed. by Oliver Lawson Dick, 169.

33 *IQ* §9.3.

34 For this, see van Ess, *Theologie und Gesellschaft*, 4:295–349, 6:433–90. On heretics in general, see this work and idem, *Der Eine und das Andere. Beobachtungen an islamischen häresiographischen Texten.*

35 Al-Dhahabī, *Tārīkh al-Islām: Ḥawādith wa-wafayāt 441–50, 451–60*, pp. 199–200; the Arabic words are *mazdakah*, *istikhfāf*, and *adab*. The term *mazdakah*, instead of the normal *mazdakiyyah*, is unusual but found elsewhere, e.g., al-Ṣafadī, *Wāfī*, xv, p. 426. Since Mazdak is not mentioned in *Risālat al-Ghufrān*, Nicholson suggests (*Journal of the Royal Asiatic Society*, 1900, p. 637) that *mazdakah* could be a corruption of the common word *zandaqah*, which has a related meaning. The former is derived from Mazdak, who was the leader of a pre-Islamic revolutionary religious movement in Sassanid Iran in the early sixth century AD, while *zandaqah* is derived from *zindīq*, "heretic," often implying Manichaeism.

36 He is followed by Brackenbury in his English translation, which is based on Kaylānī's edition.

37 Qusṭākī l-Ḥimṣī, in articles published in *Majallat Maʿhad al-Lughah al-ʿArabiyyah* (Damascus), 7 (1927) and 8 (1928); see Hassan Osman, "Dante in Arabic."

38 See Strohmaier, "Chaj ben Mekitz – die unbekannte Quelle der Divina Commedia."

39 "The Risālatu'l-Ghufrān," p. 76.

40 *True Histories*, in Lucian (trans. Keith Sidwell), *Chattering Courtesans*, pp. 308–46; see esp. pp. 330–39.

41 Introduction to Lucian, *Chattering Courtesans*, p. xx.

42 See e.g. Tibbets and Toorawa, section “The tree” in the entry “Wāḳwāḳ,” *EI2*, xi (2002), pp. 107–8.

43 Lucian, *Chattering Courtesans*, p. 312.

44 See e.g. J. M. Continente Ferrer, “Consideraciones en torno a las relaciones entre la *Risālat al-Tawābiʿ wa-l-Zawābiʿ* de ibn Šuhayd y la *Risālat al-Gufrān de al-Maʿarrī*,” in *Actas de las jornadas de cultura árabe e islámica*, 1978, (Madrid, 1981), pp. 124–34; ʿAbd al-Salām al-Harrās, “*Risālat al-Tawābiʿ wa-l-zawābiʿ* wa-ʿalāqatuhā li-*Risālat al-Ghufrān*,” *al-Manāhil*, 9:25 (1982): 211–20.

45 Ibn Shuhayd, *The Treatise of Familiar Spirits and Demons.*

46 *Risālat al-shayāṭīn*, published in Kāmil Kaylānī's edition of *Risālat al-Ghufrān*, pp. 475–506 (only the beginning of the epistle deals with the demons of poets).

47 Al-Maʿarrī, *Risālat al-Malāʾikah*, pp. 5–8.

48 Al-Maʿarrī, *Risālat al-Malāʾikah*, pp. 26–28, 36–38; for *sundus* and *istabraq* see Q Kahf 18:31 and Dukhān 44:53.

49 Al-Maʿarrī, *Risālat al-Malāʾikah*, p. 8.

50 *Risālat al-Ghufrān*, p. 382.

51 *Qirāʾah jadīdah fī Risālat al-Ghufrān* (*A New Reading of The Epistle of Forgiveness*), subtitled *Naṣṣ masraḥī min al-qarn al-khāmis al-hijrī* (“A Dramatic Text of the Fifth Century of the Hijra”), see pp. 65–186; cf. “Moreh”, *Live Theatre and Dramatic Literature in the Medieval Arabic World*, pp. 112–13.

52 There is no drama in the classical Arabic “high” literary tradition; the texts employed in popular slapstick acting were almost never written down.

53 See Wiebke Walther's review of Schoeler's translation of *Risālat al-Ghufrān* in *Zeitschrift der Deutschen Morgenländischen Gesellschaft*, 157 (2007): 225–28, her article “Camīl Ṣidqī az-Zahāwī,” her entry “az-Zahāwī, Ğamīl Sidqī” in *Kindlers Neues Literatur Lexikon*, Bd. 22 (Suppl.) 1998, p. 741, and the German translation by G. Widmer in *Welt des Islams*, 17 (1935): 1–79.

54 Recent examples of prose rhyme in English translations from the Arabic may be found in Paul M. Cobb's translation (2008) of

al-Iʿtibār, the memoirs of Usāmah ibn Munqidh (d. 584/1188), as *The Book of Contemplation*, and in Humphrey Davies' translation (2007) of a seventeenth-century work, *Yūsuf al-Shirbīnī's Brains Confounded by the Ode of Abū Shādūf Expounded.*

55 *Journal of the Royal Asiatic Society*, 1902, p. 75.

56 Monteil's "translation" is full of wild guesses that are often wrong and without any solid basis in the Arabic text, even though they seem to produce a plausible sense.

57 She grew up in Dimyāṭ (Damietta).

58 Fourth ed. Cairo, 1954 (first ed. Cairo, 1908); for the *Risālah* see pp. 254–79.

59 "La Risāla d'Ibn al-Qāriḥ: traduction et étude lexicographique," Thèse pour le Doctorat de 3e Cycle, Paris: Université de Paris III, Sorbonne Nouvelle, 1980.

60 See Hellmut Ritter's review in *Oriens*, 6 (1953): 189–91.

The Epistle of Ibn al-Qāriḥ

In the name of God, the Merciful, the Compassionate

1.1 We commence in His name, seeking success through His benediction. Praise be to God, the originator of blessings, Who is alone in being pre-eternal; Who is exalted above any likeness to His creatures and above the attributes of those who have been brought into being; Who bestows benefactions but is not responsible for malefactions; Who is just in His acts and truthful in His words; the Creator and Originator of creation, who makes it last and annihilates it as He wills. His blessings be on Muḥammad and his pious family and relations, with a blessing that may gratify him, bring him nearer and closer to Him, and give him favor and good graces with Him.

2.1 *Ibn al-Qāriḥ's hopes for a meeting with al-Maʿarrī*[1]

I am writing—may God lengthen the life of my lord the venerable Sheikh and prolong his time; may He give him lasting protection and happiness; may He make me his ransom and may He present me before him[2] in truth and in reality, having been moved by good intention and firm belief, not only by way of speech and writing, without disrespect or guile, without the affectation of affection or complaisance; not as somebody said when visiting a sick friend of his: "How are you? May God make me your ransom!," merely intending to show affection and wanting to flatter, thinking that he had done a good deed for which his friend would thank him were he to get up and recuperate, and reward him were he to regain his health and recover—I am writing in a state of well-being that would be complete with being in the Sheikh's presence, and in a state of prosperity that would be in perfect order by being honored by his noble person, his blessed mind, and his countenance.

God, the most Noble—His names be sanctified—knows that if I had yearned to meet him—may God always support him!—as a bereft mother camel yearns for her calf, or a bird with chicks for its nest, or a dove for its mate, or a gazelle for its fawn, it would have been one of those things changed by the course of nights and days, years and ages; rather, it is the yearning of the thirsty for water, the fearful for safety, the snake-bitten for recovery, the drowning for rescue, the perturbed for quiet of mind—nay the yearning of the Sheikh's precious soul for God's praise and glory; for I have seen how it is drawn toward these things as components are drawn toward their elements and basic principles toward their substances.[3] If God grants me a fullness of life that enables me to delight in seeing the Sheikh and to hold fast on to the rope of his affection, then I shall be like the nocturnal traveler who lays down his staff, praises[4] his nightly journey, and whose heart and mind are gladdened and delighted; he is like someone untouched by evil, not betrayed by an enemy, not worn away by setting out at night and returning in the morning. Perhaps God will grant me this, today or tomorrow—in Him is our trust.

2.2 I ask God, despite the need to come closer, the distance, and the remoteness, to let the Sheikh enjoy the excellence that has risen high upon his shoulders and which has conquered East and West. For if one traverses his raging sea of knowledge and considers the brilliance of his radiant full moon, one's pen is apt to falter in one's fingers and one's natural talent will fail to impress itself[5] on one's epistles, unless one hands to him the keys or asks him to bestow one of the keys of his knowledge, so that one could be affiliated to him, in his debt, as someone who has come down to his mountain path, one of his associates and his party; a spark of his fire, a sliver of his gold dinar, a drop of his ocean, a puddle of his flood—Alas, how remote!

A span is too short for a journey;[6]

Applying kohl to the eyes is not like having coal-black eyes;[7]

They were created generous, not feigning to be generous:
the generous is he who does not feign generosity;[8]

—especially since the characteristics of the soul cleave to it like colors to bodies: white cannot turn black, nor black white. Nor can a brave man be cowardly, or a coward brave. Abū Bakr al-ʿArzamī says:

The coward among men flees, abandoning his nearest and dearest,[9]
while the brave among men will defend those unrelated to him.
A munificent man's favor will be granted to his enemy,
while the favor of a miser will be denied to his relatives.
He who does not refrain from brutishness to those who love him
will refrain from brutishness toward those who assail him.

How could a fog compare with a downpour from the clouds? How could the crow swoop like the eagle? How to compare oneself to the Sheikh, whose name, when mentioned in the sessions of recollection, has become a call to prayer, a tongue to express the landmarks of gratitude?[10] He who rejects the evidence of the eyes, who treats both mankind and jinn haughtily, and who clings to calumny and falsehood obstinately is like someone who in his insolence vies with the hardness of the stone in his obdurateness, who seeks to rival the beauty of the moon with his ugliness, who raves and babbles, who «takes in hand and hamstrings it».[11] He is like someone afflicted with fever who is delirious and who looks jaundiced,[12] like someone who proclaims his own shortcomings among the dwellers of the desert and the towns. He is—and this is unquestionable—like the person the poet meant:[13] 2.3

Like one that butts a rock, one day, hoping to cleave it,
but does not harm it, and the ibex only hurts his horns.

It is transmitted that the messenger of God—God bless and preserve him and increase him in honor with Him—said, "God curse him who speaks with two tongues, God curse every liar, God curse every slanderer!"

2.4 I reached the periphery of Aleppo—may God protect and guard it—after having been smitten in its outskirts with catastrophe, calamity, and casualty; nay, I was stricken with the rarest misfortunes and a crushing disaster. When I entered the town, not yet having a fixed abode, I did not recognize it, for I could not find any acquaintance or neighbor; then I recited to it, weeping:

> When, after long avoidance, I pay a visit to a land,
> I miss a loved one, though the place is still the same.

Abū l-Qaṭirān al-Marrār ibn Saʿīd al-Faqʿasī was in love with his cousin in Najd who was called Waḥshiyyah. A man from Syria took her as his wife to his country. He was grieved and afflicted by her being far away and by being separated from her. In a poem he said:

> Since Waḥshiyyah has left Najd, no doctor
> can cure your eyes of what they weep for.
> He saw a glance from her and he could not hold back his tears:
> her clothes, with underneath a rising sand dune![14]
> The winds that blow from Syria were once[15] disliked,
> but now those same winds have turned sweet.

What I had gained is gone with the wind, as happened to Abū l-Qaṭirān with Waḥshiyyah.

And then... and then... and then...[16]

2.5 Then the Sheikh's name was mentioned—may God always support him!—without any cause or occasion requiring it; and someone said, "The Sheikh knows more about syntax than Sībawayh and more about lexicography and metrics than al-Khalīl."

I replied, as the assembly gave ear, "I have heard that he—may God always support him!—belittles what is great in him, and even minimizes what is little in him; thus his belittling becomes a form of aggrandizement and his deprecation becomes an augmentation. I have witnessed the same thing in some other scholars I have met personally—may God have mercy upon them all, and may He make the Sheikh the inheritor of their longest, most flourishing, and most prosperous lifetime!—but there is no need for this: the flowers have blossomed, the light is bright, and dawn is shining for those with sight!"

Abū l-Faraj al-Zahrajī, state secretary at the court of Naṣr al-Dawlah—may God always protect him!—wrote a letter to me, which he gave me, and another letter to the Sheikh—may God always support him!—which he entrusted to me, asking me to deliver it to the venerable Sheikh, as speech, rather than as a dispatch, and quickly convey it and not to delay it. But my traveling companion robbed me of one of my saddlebags, which had the letter in it, so I wrote this letter instead, complaining of my state of affairs and explaining my needs, to inform the Sheikh of all my foibles and failings and of my experiences, during my travels, with all the petty people who pretend to have knowledge and erudition. True erudition is that of the soul, not that of study; but they are devoid of both. They commit errors when they read or write[17] but when I point them out, they gang up against me and impute the errors to me! **2.6.1**

I met Abū l-Faraj al-Zahrajī in Āmid. He had a library that he showed me. I told him, "These books of yours are Jewish and devoid of the Shariah of the True Religion!" He showed his annoyance and disapproval of this remark. So I said to him, "You are talking to an experienced man; someone like me does not talk rubbish about things he does not know about. Verify and you will be certain!" He and his son began to read, and he said, "First-hand knowledge has belittled reported knowledge!" He wrote me a letter, eulogizing me, for such is his good nature and unblemished character.[18] **2.6.2** *Criticism of heresy and heretics*

2.7.1 Al-Mutanabbī[19] says:

> I blame the manikins of these our times.

using the diminutive ("manikin" of "man"), out of deprecation and not veneration, and by making them few and not many; thus spitting out his words like someone with a disease of the chest,[20] by which his hidden mind was expressed. This is possible in the figurative language of poetry, and one is not forbidden to say such things in verse or prose, but he said it inappropriately and addressed it to people who did not deserve it. A time in which he has had the good fortune to meet Sayf al-Dawlah does not deserve to have its people blamed. How could it, when he himself said,

> I go to his fief in his clothes
> on his steed from his house with his sword.

He should have considered that these people are under Sayf al-Dawlah's protection; they were affiliated to him and his protégés. And one should not complain to a reasonless, dumb object about persons possessing reason and speech: for "time" is no more than the movements of the celestial sphere—unless he is one of those who believe that these spheres possess reason and have knowledge and understanding, aware of the effect of their actions, with intentions and volitions, and who by their belief are induced to bring sacrifices and burnt offerings to them. In that case he would contradict his own words:

> Perish the religion of the worshippers of stars
> and those who claim that these have reason.

Or he would be as God the Exalted says in His noble Book:[21] «Wavering between this, not to these, not to those»; he all but answers to this description.

2.7.2 In a book on which they collaborated—the people of Baghdad and Cairo claim that nothing like it was ever written on the subject, on account of its slim size and its great learning—al-Quṭrabbulī[22] and Ibn Abī l-Azhar[23] tell how al-Mutanabbī was taken from prison in Baghdad, to the court of Abū l-Ḥasan ʿAlī ibn ʿĪsā, the vizier (God have mercy upon him).[24] The latter asked, "Are you Aḥmad, the would-be prophet (*al-mutanabbī*)?" Al-Mutanabbī replied, "I am Aḥmad the prophet (*al-nabī*)!"[25] He bared his stomach and showed him a wen.[26] "This," he said, "is the stamp of my prophethood and the sign of my mission." The vizier gave orders that his shoe be removed and his head be slapped with it fifty times. Then he sent him back to his prison.

Al-Mutanabbī also said, addressing Sayf al-Dawlah:

You are angry with him who has obtained your support,
so that annoyance and gifts[27] torment him.[28]

He lies, by God! He had been badgering him about these acts of generosity and rubbing him up about them, jealously wanting them to come only from him and through him. But this does not detract from the polish of his poetry or the splendor of its fine style.

But I am furious about those heretics[29] and apostates[30] who make fun of religion and wish to instill doubts and skepticism among the Muslims, those who take delight in detracting from the prophethood of the prophets, God's blessings be on them all, and who are so satisfied with their sophistication and invention: 3.1

The conceitedness of a singer and the sophistication of a heretic.[31]

Al-Mahdī had Bashshār killed for heresy. When the latter attracted notoriety for this and began to be afraid, he defended himself by saying,

Ibn Nihyā,[32] my head is heavy for me,
and carrying two heads would be a heavy load!
Let others call for worshipping two Lords:
One is enough to keep me busy!

3.2 Al-Mahdī also summoned Ṣāliḥ ibn ʿAbd al-Quddūs. He called for the execution mat and the executioner. Ṣāliḥ asked, "Why are you sentencing me to death?" The caliph replied, "Because you said:

Many a secret I have hidden, as if I
were dumb, or my tongue were tied.
If I had exposed my religion to the people
the rest of my meals would be taken in prison.

"Enemy of God, and enemy of yourself!

A fine reputation veils scandalous deeds;
but you'll find no veil that covers good deeds."[33]

Then Ṣāliḥ said, "I was a heretic but I have repented and renounced heresy!" But al-Mahdī said, "How can that be! You yourself said:

An old man will not abandon his habits
until he is buried in the earth of his grave.
Though he may mend his ways, he will return to his error,
just as a someone chronically ill will relapse."

The executioner struck before he knew what was happening, and his head rolled on the mat!

3.3 In his reign, in a town beyond Bukhārā in Transoxania, there lived a one-eyed man, a fuller, who made himself a gold mask and who was addressed as Lord Almighty.[34] He also erected a moon on a mountain several parasangs high for his followers.[35] Al-Mahdī dispatched an army to him, which laid siege to him in his fortified town. Then the heretic burned everything in it, gathered all the townspeople and gave them poisoned wine to drink; they all died. He too drank and joined them; and God hastened his spirit to Hell.

3.4 Al-Ṣanādīqī, in Yemen, had his troops in al-Mudaykhirah and Safhanah. He was addressed as Lord Almighty, also in writing. He had a "House of Abundance," to which he brought all the women of the town, and he would let the men come and sleep with the women[36] at night. A trustworthy souce said: "I entered that place, to have a look. I heard a woman say, 'My dear son!' and he said, 'Mummy, we want to perform what God's Friend has commanded us!'"

He would say, "If you do this, private possessions will cease, and child will no longer be distinct from child. Thus you will become like one soul." Al-Ḥasanī conducted a campaign against him, from Sanaa, and routed him; he then entrenched himself in a citadel in that region. Then al-Ḥasanī sent to him a physician with a poisoned lancet. He used it to let his blood and thus killed him.

Al-Walīd ibn Yazīd reigned for one year, two months, and a few days. He is the one who said: 3.5.1

When I die, mother of the little dwarf, marry
 and do not hope to meet after the separation!
For what you have been told about our meeting
 is but "tales of Ṭasm," which leave one's reason feeble.[37]

He once shot arrows at a copy of the Qur'an, piercing it, and saying,

When you come to your Lord, on Resurrection Day,
 then say: O Lord, I have been pierced by al-Walīd!

He sent a Zoroastrian builder to Mecca, to build him a chamber to drink in on top of the Kaaba; but he died before its completion. The pilgrims would cry,[38] "Here we are, O God, here we are! Here we are, O Thou who hast killed al-Walīd ibn Yazīd, here we are!"

Once he called for a vessel(?)[39] made of gold which contained a jewel of great value, in the shape of a man. He prostrated himself before it, kissed it, and said, "Prostrate yourself before it, you lout!" I said,[40] "Who is this?" "Mani," he replied, "He was once great but his cause has dwindled with the passing of time." "One is not permitted to prostrate oneself," I said, "before anything but God!" He replied, "Leave us!"

Once[41] he was drinking on a rooftop with a large crater made of crystal set before him, which contained several cupfuls. He said to his drinking companions, “In which sign of the zodiac is the moon tonight?” One of them said, “In the crater!” “True!” he replied, “You have said what I had in mind, too. By God, I shall drink a hebdomad!”[42] i.e., drinking for seven consecutive weeks.

Once he was in a place called al-Bakhrāʾ,[43] in the environs of Damascus; then he said,

A Hāshimite played at being a prophet,
without a revelation that came to him, nor a book.

He was killed in that place. I saw his head in that crater, with which he intended to “hebdomadize.”

3.5.2 Abū ʿĪsā, the son of al-Rashīd, is the one who said:

The month of fasting has come to me as a disaster; may that month cease to be!
And may I never fast for another month!
If the caliph were to aid me and give me power over that month
I would appeal for aid against that month as long as I live.

Instantly he was struck with a fit and he died before he lived to see another month, God be praised!

3.6.1 Al-Jannābī killed thousands of people in Mecca. He took twenty-six thousand camels easily,[44] he set fire to their equipment and baggage, and seized so many women, youths, and small children, that the area was crowded with them. He took away the “stone of the place of attachment,”[45] thinking that it was the “magnet of the hearts,” and he took the waterspout.[46] I[47] heard him say to a tall, bulky, black servant, who, dressed in his two mantles, was strutting on top of the Kaaba, “Rakhamah, wrench it off, be quick!”—meaning the waterspout of the Kaaba. Then I became aware that the Hadith scholars had made a mistake when they said, “A boy called Raḥmah will wrench it off,”[48] just as they misspelled ʿAlī’s words—God be pleased with him—when he said, "Basra will perish through the wind," but it perished with the Zanj,[49] for the Alid pretender of Basra killed twenty-four thousand people there at a place called al-ʿAqīq; they counted them by tallying with reeds. He set fire to its great mosque. He addressed the Zanj in a sermon: "You have been helped by your ugly physique; to follow it up, an ugly reputation you must seek! To every habitation bring doom; turn every room into a tomb!" Abū l-Ḥusayn al-Yazīdī al-Warzanīnī[50] said to me in Damascus, "He attached himself to my ancestor's family and claimed to be related to him."[51]

Abū ʿAbd Allāh ibn Muḥammad ibn Rizām al-Ṭāʾī al-Kūfī reports: "I was in Mecca at the time when the sword of al-Jannābī had wrought havoc among the pilgrims. I saw one of them who had killed a number of people, saying, 'You dogs! Has Muḥammad, the man from Mecca, not told you that «Whoever enters it will be safe»?[52] But what safety is there here then?' I replied, 'Arab warrior, if you guarantee that I will be safe from your sword, I shall explain this to you.' 'Very well,' he said. I continued, 'There are five answers. First, it means: whoever enters it will be safe from My torment at the Resurrection. Secondly: safe from the religious duty that I have imposed on him.[53] Thirdly: it is expressed as a statement but a command is intended, as in God's words:[54] «and divorced women will wait by themselves». Fourthly: The prescribed punishment shall not be applied when someone commits a crime in a non-sacred territory.[55] And fifthly: God has granted it to them with His words:[56] «We have made a secure sanctuary, though around them people are being snatched away».' The man answered, 'You are right! Will this beard of mine[57] be forgiven?' I said, 'Yes!' Then he let me go and off he went." 3.6.2

Al-Ḥusayn ibn Manṣūr al-Ḥallāj from Nīsābūr—some say from Marw—claimed to possess all knowledge. He was a reckless, insolent man who wanted to overturn dynasties. His followers claimed that he was divine; he preached the doctrine of divine indwelling. 3.7.1

To rulers he made an outward show of the teachings of Shi'ism, to the masses he made a show of the ways of the Sufis, and implicitly in all this he claimed that divinity dwelled in him. The vizier ʿAlī ibn ʿĪsā questioned him in a dispute and found him to be devoid of any knowledge. He said to him, "You would have derived more profit from learning about your ritual purity and your religious duties than writing treatises where you do not understand what you say in them. How often have you not written to the people: 'Blessed be He with the glittering light that still gleams after its glittering!'[58] You are so much in need of education!"

Abū ʿAlī al-Fārisī told me: "I saw al-Ḥallāj when he was standing in the circle of Abū Bakr al-Shiblī. [. . .][59] 'You, by God, will one day corrupt the fear of Him!'[60] Al-Ḥallāj shook his sleeve in his face and recited:

O secret secret, subtle to the point of being
exalted beyond description by any living being;
Outwardly, inwardly, you manifest yourself
in every thing to every thing.
O whole of All, you are not other than I,
so why excuse myself then to myself?"

He believed that someone with mystic knowledge stands in relation to God as rays are to the sun: from it they appear, to it they return,[61] and from it they derive their light.

3.7.2 Al-Ẓāhir[62] recited to me these verses of his own:

I think the Sufi kind is the worst kind;
so ask them (how contemptible is this "divine indwelling!"):
"Has God then told you, when you fell in love with Him,
'Eat like beasts and dance for Me'?"

One day al-Ḥallāj moved his hand, whereupon the odor of musk spread to the people. Another time he moved it and dirhams were scattered. One of those present, someone with understanding, said to him, "Show me unfamiliar dirhams, then I shall believe in you, and other people will join me: how about giving me a dirham struck with your name and that of your father!" Al-Ḥallāj replied, "How could I, since such a coin has not been made?" The man answered, "He who presents that which is not present can make that which has not been made!"

In his writings one finds: "I am he who drowned the people of Noah and who destroyed ʿĀd and Thamūd." When his fame spread and the ruler[63] had gained reliable intelligence about him, he signed the sentence of one thousand lashes and the amputation of his hands, after which he had him burned in the fire, at the end of the year 309 [922]. Al-Ḥallāj said to Ḥāmid ibn al-ʿAbbās, "I shall destroy you!" Ḥāmid replied, "Now there is proof that you claim what you have been charged with."

The case of Ibn Abī l-ʿAzāqir Abū Jaʿfar Muḥammad ibn ʿAlī al-Shalmaghānī,[64] whose family is from a village near Wāsiṭ called Shalmaghān, was similar to the case of al-Ḥallāj: people claimed that he was a god, that God had dwelt in Adam, then in Seth, then in each successive prophet, legatee,[65] and imam, until He dwelled in al-Ḥasan ibn ʿAlī al-ʿAskarī, and finally in himself. He had led a number of people astray, including Ibn Abī ʿAwn, the author of *The Book of Simile*, who was beheaded along with him. They allowed him free use of their women and their property; he ruled over them according to his whims. He dabbled in alchemy, and he wrote some books that are well known. 3.8

Aḥmad ibn Yaḥyā al-Rāwandī, from Marw al-Rūdh, had a good reputation and was doctrinally sound. Then he divested himself of all this, for various reasons, and because "his learning was greater than his intellect."[66] He was like the one described by the poet:[67] 3.9

And who is able to repel someone in his youthful folly?
Who can stand up to a decent man when he casts off restraint?

He wrote the following books: *The Book of the Crown*, in which he argues for the pre-eternity of the world; it was refuted by Abū l-Ḥusayn al-Khayyāṭ. Also, *The Emerald*, in which he argues the invalidity of prophetic mission, also refuted by al-Khayyāṭ. In *In Praise of Wisdom* he declares that God the Exalted had been foolish to impose His command on His creatures; it was also refuted by al-Khayyāṭ. In *The Brain-Basher*[68] he attacks the composition of the Qur'an. In *The Rod* he establishes that God's knowledge is temporally originated, and that He did not have knowledge until He created knowledge for Himself. It was refuted by al-Khayyāṭ.[69] *The Coral* deals with the differences of opinion among the Muslims.[70]

3.10.1 ʿAlī ibn al-ʿAbbās ibn Jurayj al-Rūmī: Abū ʿUthmān al-Nājim says, "I visited him when he was ill with the disease that would carry him off. Near his head he kept a bowl of ice-cooled water and an unsheathed dagger so long that, struck in one's chest, it would have come out at one's back. I asked him, 'What is this?' and he replied, 'With the water I moisten my throat, for people seldom die unless they are thirsty. If my pain gets so bad I'll cut my throat with the dagger.' He added, 'I'll tell you my story, from which you can infer the true cause of my demise. I wanted to move from al-Karkh to Basra Gate. I consulted our friend Abū l-Faḍl, "Father of Favor," whose name is derived from "bestowing favor." He said, "When you come to the bridge, turn right"—"right" (*yamīn*) is derived from *yumn*, "right good fortune"—"Then go to Naʿīmah (Bliss) Street"—whose name derived from "bliss"—"Then live in the house of Ibn al-Muʿāfā, 'Son of Healthy'"—which is derived from "well-being." But, to my misery and misfortune, I did not follow his advice but went on to consult our friend Jaʿfar—whose name is derived from *jūʿ*, "hunger," and *firār*, "fleeing."[71] He said, "When you come to the bridge, turn left"—"left" (*shimāl*) is derived from *shuʾm*, "ill omen"—"And live in the house of Ibn Qilābah"—and sure enough, my world has been overturned (*inqalabat*)! And the worst thing of all: the birds on that lotus tree, chirruping *sīq sīq*, and here I am—sick!'[72] Then he recited:[73]

Abū 'Uthmān, you are the leader of your people;
You're above blame through your generosity toward the tribe.
Enjoy the presence of your friend, for I don't think
you'll see him or he'll see you after today.

"He found it difficult to stop urinating, so I said to him, 'You find it difficult to stop urinating!' He recited: 3.10.2

Tomorrow there will be an end to urinating
and there will be wailing and howling!
Indeed, meeting with God
is terror upon terror.

"He died the following day."

I hope that these words were an act of atonement for his idea of committing suicide. God's messenger (on whom be blessing and well-being) said, "He who stabs himself with a knife will be resurrected on the Day of Resurrection with his knife in his hand, and he will stab himself with it forever and ever in Hell. He who throws himself from a height will be resurrected on the Day of Resurrection and be thrown on to his nostrils in Hell forever and ever. He who drinks poison will be resurrected on the Day of Resurrection with his poison in his hand, drinking it forever and ever in Hell."

Al-Ḥasan ibn Rajā', the state secretary,[74] said, "Abū Tammām came 3.11
to me in Khorasan. I had heard that he did not perform the ritual prayer, so I appointed someone to stay close to him for some days, and he did not see him perform the ritual prayer one single day. I reproved him, but he said, 'My lord, I have come all the way from Baghdad to visit your eminence, I have borne hardship and suffered a long journey, which I did not find burdensome. If I had known that ritual prayer would benefit me, and omitting it would harm me,

I would not have omitted it!' I intended to have him executed but I was afraid that this would be ascribed to the wrong motive."

3.12 It is mentioned in many historical works that al-Māzyār was brought into the presence of al-Muʿtaṣim one day after the latter had become enraged with al-Afshīn, when the judge Ibn Abī Du'ād had said to al-Muʿtaṣim, "An uncircumcised fellow, and he sleeps with an Arab woman! Also, he has corresponded with al-Māzyār and encouraged him to rebel!"

Al-Afshīn's secretary was summoned; when al-Muʿtaṣim threatened him he confessed to having written on behalf of al-Afshīn to al-Māzyār as follows: "In this world and at this time there is no scourge other than I, you, and Bābak. I was keen not to have Bābak's blood shed, but his fate was otherwise. Now there is no one left but you and me. One of the armies of the Abbasids is heading for you. If you defeat it I shall attack their king, in his 'fixed abode,'[75] and the 'white religion'[76] will prevail." Al-Māzyār had written a reply, which he had with him in a red basket. The caliph confronted al-Afshīn with al-Māzyār and the latter confessed to what had been reported of him. Someone said to al-Muʿtaṣim, "Al-Māzyār has lots of money!" But the caliph recited,

The lions, the lions of the thicket, are intent,
on an evil battle day, on the despoiled, not on the spoils.[77]

It is said[78] that two men killed three million and five hundred *dhabbāḥ*(?) in red clothes and with long daggers, and that they found their names in every individual encounter in every individual location; from each they took a token: his signet ring, his cloak, his kerchief, or his waistband. "The torrent reached the wadi and flooded the riverbed."[79]

3.13 I have met somebody who disputed with me, arguing that ʿAlī—God be pleased with him— . . . and likewise al-Ḥākim . . .[80]

In Basra there appeared someone who claimed that Ja'far[81] was the son of Muḥammad—on both of whom be peace—, that he had a close connection with him, and that his spirit was in him and connected with him.

If I were to treat this topic exhaustively it would be very lengthy. However,

> He who suffers from a chest infection must spit;
> What his chest contains must be ejected.

In fact, if I mentioned all I know, "I would eat the rest of my meals in my prison,"[82] or rather I would recite:[83]

> I carry a head I am tired of carrying:
> Is there no lad who'll carry its load for me?

And I would rest and finally recite:[84]

> My wounds cannot heal another's wounds:
> he has his and I have mine.

4.1 *On fate*

If I complain of the time we live in and its decrees and blame its vicissitudes and evil days, I complain to someone who never heeds a complaint, and I blame someone who makes none content. His habit is to favor the ignoble and to maltreat the noble; he is bent on raising the lowly and obscure, and on debasing the virtuous and high-minded. If he grants a gift, look forward to being soon asked to return it! If he lends a thing (*a'āra*) I think he has carried out a raid (*aghāra*). Between turning toward you with a cheerful face and turning away from you with a glum frown lies but the wink of an eye, the flying of a spark. His ears have never heard of fidelity to promises, his eyes have never been touched by tears of embarrassment. His appearance gives joy and delight, but his inner self causes evil and despair. He disappoints those who expect his favors, he thwarts the hopes of those asking for support. He does not listen to complaint and gloats at people's torment.

4.2 For this I once cast blame, but now I do the same,[85] having fallen into it like a drowning man clutching at straw, or a prisoner lamenting his freedom. I think ʿAlī ibn al-ʿAbbās ibn Jurayj ibn al-Rūmī said it well:

Ibn al-Qāriḥ's complaints of old age

Ah, the grayness of your hairs will not be snatched away:
will you forswear the foibles of old age?
And will you stop complaining of the times,
complaining to a listener whenever you want?
To live to be gray-haired is everyone's desire,
but having gained it, one desponds.[86]

4.3 In my youth, my closest friend and dearest fellow, the man I deemed nearest to me, and the person I held in highest esteem was anyone who would say to me, "May God postpone your term, may God extend your life and grant you the longest of lives!" But now, with my eighth decade, come dismay and despondence. But why should I feel anxiety and agony, cherish ambitions in perpetuity, when I have attained what I desired and what my family wished for me? Because pretty women shun me? But, by God, I shun them more than they shun me, and I know them and the illnesses they bring only too well, for I am not one to recite, in grief over them:

Black [nights] have left their mark on black [hairs],
gleamings of white, by which the eyes of the white[-skinned women] are turned off.[87]

Or some other poet's verse:

But when I saw the vulture overcome the crow,
and settle in two nests, my soul grew agitated.[88]

Nor shall I recite Abū ʿUbādah al-Buḥturī:[89]

Its days were white, because of white-skinned women,
so long as they saw that my black hair stayed black.
Whenever a drought came on they rose as showers of rain,
whenever a dust cloud rose in battle, they would rise as lions.

It's good to mention them and tell their stories,
of iron swords that, clashing, talked to iron swords.[90]
A place[91] where lofty deeds grow; as soon as the young child among them sheds his milk teeth, he becomes a leader.

And this is how Maʿarrat al-Nuʿmān may be described, while the Sheikh is there—may God always support him, and may it never be parted from him, never cease to bring him blessings and to be blessed in his presence! I have found that its inhabitants acknowledge his acts of kindness, to say nothing of Abū l-ʿAbbās Aḥmad ibn Khalaf al-Mumattaʿ[92]—may God give him lasting vigor!—for I found clear evidence of his beneficence toward the Sheikh, while the latter's tongue is voluble with his approbation and his laudation, having filled heaven with prayer and earth with praise.[93] 4.4

The men of Quraysh said to the Prophet—blessing and peace upon him—: "Your followers who are freedmen—such as Bilāl, ʿAmmār, or Ṣuhayb[94]—are they better than Quṣayy ibn Kilāb, ʿAbd Manāf, Hāshim, or ʿAbd Shams?"[95] He replied, "Yes, by God, though they be few they will be many; though they be lowly, they will be noble, to the point of becoming stars by which one is guided and that are followed. Then people will say, 'This was said by So-and-so, or mentioned by So-and-so.' So do not boast to me of your ancestors who died in pre-Islamic ignorance.[96] Truly, what the dung beetle rolls about with its nose is better than your ancestors who died then! So follow me and I shall give you worthy lineages! By Him who holds my soul in His hand, you shall divide among yourselves the treasures of Chosroes and Caesar!" 5.1

The Prophet at the beginning of his mission

Abū Ṭālib, his paternal uncle, said to him, "Spare me and yourself!"[97] So he thought—blessing and peace be upon him—that his uncle was deserting him and forsaking him, and he said, "Uncle, I swear by God that even if, on condition that I abandon this, they put the sun in my right hand and the moon in my left, I shall never give it up until either God makes it prevail or I die!" Then he burst into tears and sobbed. He stood up and as he turned away, his uncle called him, "Come here, my nephew!" He did so and then Abū Ṭālib said, "Go and say whatever you want, for, by God, I shall never forsake you and let you come to any harm!"

5.2 One day the Prophet—blessing and peace upon him—mentioned the trouble and hardship he had experienced at the hands of his fellow tribesmen: "For days I went with no food but the fruit of the *arāk* tree in the mountain clefts. My companion here (pointing at Abū Bakr) went for more than ten days." ʿUtbah ibn Ghazwān, speaking of the distress and hardship they had suffered in Mecca, said, "We stayed for some time with nothing to eat except leaves of the balsam tree, which we ate until our jaws were sore. One day I found a date and I divided it between myself and Saʿd; and now every single one of us is a governor of a province!" They used to say that when someone found a date and divided it between himself and his friend, the luckier of the two was the one who got the stone, for he could chew it day and night, so scarce was food. The messenger of God—God bless and preserve him—also said, "I used to shepherd the small herds of the Meccans for a trifling sum."[98]

His mission began when he stood at al-Ṣafā and called out, "O dawn! O dawn!" They came hurrying toward him and said, "What has happened to you? What has come over you?" He asked them, "How do you know me?" "As Muḥammad, the trusted one," they said. He continued, "Do you think that if I said to you that horsemen are coming against you in the wadi, or that an army is attacking you coming from the mountain road, you would believe me?" "Yes, by God!" they said, "We have never known you to utter a lie." He said, "Your conduct is not for the sake of God, nor is it from God, nor is God pleased with it. Say: there is no god but God, and testify that I am His messenger! And follow me, and then the Arabs will obey you and you will reign over the non-Arabs. God has said to me, 'Draw them out, as they have drawn you out, and I shall send an army five times its size.' He guaranteed to me that He would grant me victory by means of some fellow tribesmen of yours, and He said to me, 'Join with those who obey you in fighting against those who disobey you,' and He guaranteed to me that my power would overcome the power of Chosroes and Caesar."

Then—blessing and peace be upon him—he carried out the raid of Tabūk with thirty thousand men.[99] This was due to God, who makes everything from nothing, and who makes everything into nothing; He solidifies liquids and liquefies solids, He causes the sea to solidify and then He cleaves rocks. All this is as if someone said, "With this thin, insignificant piece of glass I shall scratch these hard, lofty mountains and they will be crushed and broken thereby; and this weak, tiny ant will rout many well-equipped armies." 5.3

This is how it really was with the Prophet—blessing and peace be upon him. ʿUrwah ibn Masʿūd al-Thaqafī said to Quraysh, being their emissary to the Prophet—God bless and preserve him—at al-Ḥudaybiyah: "I have visited the Negus, Chosroes, and Caesar; I have seen their troops and their followers. But I have never seen people more obedient, more dignified, and more awe-inspiring than Muḥammad's companions when it comes to their Muḥammad! They stand around him 'as if birds were perched upon their heads.'[100] At the mere gesture of a command from him they hasten to act. When he performs the ritual ablution they divide the water among themselves. When he expectorates they rub their faces, their beards, and their skins with his sputum!" They were even more obedient after his death than they were during his lifetime, to the point that one of his companions said, "Do not revile the companions of Muḥammad, for they became Muslims for fear of God, whereas other people became Muslims for fear of their swords."

Consider, therefore, how he began his mission, when he was weak and alone, claiming that all this would happen. Friend and foe saw him, while his situation could only be likened to someone saying, "This speck of dust will grow and become a mountain that will 5.4

cover all the earth!" Then he warned people about this, while as weak as the speck of dust. One day he—God bless and preserve him—wanted to enter the Kaaba, but ʿUthmān ibn Ṭalḥah al-ʿAbdarī stopped him. "Don't do that, ʿUthmān," he said, "soon you will see me holding the key in my hand, which I shall put where I please!" Then ʿUthmān said, "Quraysh will be humbled that day, and few in number." But the Prophet said, "On the contrary, they will be many and mighty!"

6.1 *Ibn al-Qāriḥ's weaknesses and self-reproach*

I ask protection and success from God, making them my helpers in subduing my passions; I complain to Him about my indulging in my desires; and I ask Him to make me understand the admonishing lessons of the world. For I have become blind to the wounds inflicted by its vicissitudes, by the burning desire for it that has perched on my thoughts. I find nobody who will give me justice against it, no one who can restrain my longing for it. Where are the storerooms of reason and the treasuries of understanding, O ye with insight? We have condoned the evils of this world, shutting our eyes because of fleeting, obnoxious[101] troubles, to which the hand of extinction already points, and for which evils lie in hiding. Kuthayyir said:

> It is as if I'm calling to a rock when she averts herself,
> hard rock, where mountain goats, if walking there, would lose their footing.

6.2 And I say, following Kuthayyir: O world, at every glance you fill my eyes with tears, at every thought you cause me grief! O you who make turbid any purity, O you who breach any pact of loyalty: he who turns toward you has never prospered for a single instant, and he who prefers to remain well-disposed toward you has never been happy. Far from it! O children of this world, outwardly you are called rich, but inwardly and truly it is those happy with little who are rich in the true sense of the word. So many splendid days have I known, with many new moons, the sky bright, the shade stretching over me, the hours providing me all I desired, smilingly offering me all I longed for. But once it had attached itself to me in all my affairs,[102] the world begrudged me all this; it strove to break up my intimacy with it and to shorten its extent. Its splendor was eclipsed to gloom and the desolation of separation blighted its bloom. It has scattered us, dispersed to the horizons, after we had been like limbs held together, like bending, pliant branches;

O my grief, the day my youthful zeal
  was gathered in a shroud and grave!
I've squandered what I needed
  for what I did not need.[103]

I quote a verse by Ibn al-Rūmī:[104]

Ah, the grayness of your hairs will not be snatched away:
  will you forswear the foibles of old age?

I am perturbed, I weep though weeping is neither useful nor beneficial, and I should rather weep for my weeping and recite:

My tongue speaks but I do not act;
  My heart desires but I do naught.
I am aware of the right path but do not let myself be guided;
  I know, but act in ignorance.[105]

Some people offered me a cup of wine. I refused and said, "Leave me 6.3
with boiled wine, according to the doctrine of Sheikh al-Awzāʿī!"[106] I told them that Ibrāhīm ibn al-Mahdī once offered wine to Muḥammad ibn Ḥāzim, who refused and recited:

Shall I, with my gray hair, be foolish like a child?
  Gray hair is at war with brutish ignorance.
Old age, gray hair, and ignorance:
  upon your life, they're hard to reconcile.
O caliph's son, O for the days
  when I was strong and fresh,

When my gray hairs were few
    and drinking from love's spring was sweet,
When I was cured by pretty girls
    by conversation and proximity!
But now, when those who chided me
    see in me all they yearned to see,
And people see me taking the right path:
    shall I once more be chided and be foolish like a child?
I swear that I shall never drink wine
    as long as pilgrims ride to go on hajj for God!

6.4.1 I turned to myself, addressing and reproaching my soul; the address is phrased as if to others but is in fact to it:[107]

"He has given you respite as if He has neglected you. Are you not ashamed of how long you have been unashamed!"[108] Be like a newborn child, turned by a gentle hand in its cot, surrounded by affection, on whom benefits are showered without asking, because of his infancy, and from whom harm is averted without his being on his guard, because of his infirmity. Have you not heard the messenger of God— blessing and peace upon him—when he said in his prayer, "O God, guard me as a newborn child is guarded, who neither knows what is wanted from him nor what he wants himself!" Is there no one who will hold on to the shirttails of his guide?[109] Is there no one who readies a mount and a saddle for the day of his departure? You people! Departure at daybreak! Departure at daybreak! He who does not arrive before the others at a watering place will suffer burning thirst. I have refused to give you what you desire only in order to spare you and to protect you jealously. The messenger of God said— blessing and peace upon him—, "When God loves someone He protects him against the world." You complain about me when I protect you; you dislike my guarding you when I guard you. Is there no one who will seek refuge in our courtyard so that he may be achieve glory? Is there no one who flees to us, rather than from us? O Thou who canst dispense with everything, have mercy on him who cannot dispense with Thee in any circumstance! God is all-sufficiient, but one cannot do without Him in anything. It is for this reason that when Gabriel said to the Friend:[110] "Do you need anything?" he replied "Not from you." God deserves to be asked, even though He has already given sufficiently, because one cannot dispense with Him in anything. Obey Him in order to obey Him and do not obey Him in order that He may obey you and you grow lazy and bored. To him who abandons looking after his own affairs and leaves them to Our providence We shall give ease. Exalted is He whose hand holds the winding coils of the human hearts and human ambitions, who controls the decisions of decrees and apportionments.

Have you forgotten to think of loved ones 6.4.2
who forget your sins when they remember you?[111]
You treated them unkindly, even though so often,
unlike you, they have been at your beck and call.
And you endured it calmly when they left:
what was then your excuse when you endured it thus?

You abandon Someone whom you have treated unkindly, whom you forgot to remember, whose limit you have transgressed, whose prohibition you have abandoned, whose commands you have ignored; then you turned to Him in repentance, relying on His grace toward you, and saying: "O Lord!" Then He will say to you, "Here I am! «And when My servants ask you about Me I am near».[112] If you have a fly on your face, accuse yourself; but if I sever your limbs, you must not accuse Me. You are the one who abandoned Me and turned away, after I had given you what you hoped for. «And when We bless man he recoils and turns aside»."[113] O you who stands with these accusations—how many! How many! Will He not say to you, "What has deceived you about Me?"[114] and you will say, "Your forbearance! Or else, if Thou wouldst send a tiny bug against me, it would gather me unto Thee if it were Thy wish thus to gather me."[115]

After drinking from the cup of understanding,
and smelling the sweet herbal fragrance of the pious,
Have you fallen in love and turned a passionate lover, more
conspicuous than a piebald horse?
O world of mine, please take my hand before I drown
In the deluge of the sea of love!
I'll be your slave; so be then like the master who,
pleased with his slave, will set him free![116]

6.5 There was a man in Baghdad with a large head and elephantine ears, called Fādhūh. His head was uncovered during all the four seasons; he had no scruples about doing disgraceful things. People would say to him, "Hey Fādhūh, shame! Turn to God in repentance!" But he would reply, "People, why do you come between me and my Lord? It is He who accepts repentance from His servants!"

One day he was going along a certain street that was broad at the bottom but so narrow further up that the opposing houses nearly met. A woman handed her neighbor woman a mortar, but it slipped from her hand and fell on Fādhūh's head, pounding it to a pulp as if it were a *harīsah*. It fell too fast for him to repent! We had a pious preacher who used to say us, "Beware of a death like Fādhūh's!"

Gabriel says in a tradition: "I feared that Pharaoh[117] would complete professing the creed and his repentance, so I took some of the mud (*ḥāl*) of the sea and struck his face with it."—*ḥāl* here means "mud;" the word has eight meanings, including "mud"—So how can someone act who believes that repenting of a sin is not valid if one persists in another sin? There is neither might nor power . . .[118]

7.1 *The Sheikh exculpates himself*

I have heard about my lord the Sheikh—may God always support him!—that he said when I was mentioned to him, "I know of him by hearsay. He is the one who lampooned Abū l-Qāsim ibn ʿAlī ibn al-Ḥusayn al-Maghribī." These words are alarming to me, for I fear that he thinks ill of my character, and that he imagines me as someone who replaces gratitude with ingratitude. By acquainting him with what he does not know I would enhance my standing with him, with the greatness of his worth, his religion, and his pious asceticism. And so I shall inform him so that he is aware of the long and the short of it, and the high and the low of it.[119]

I studied with Abū ʿAbd Allāh ibn Khālawayh—God have mercy on him—and I often went to see Abū l-Ḥasan al-Maghribī. When Ibn Khālawayh died I left for Baghdad and stayed with Abū ʿAlī al-Fārisī. I frequented the scholars of Baghdad, such as Abū Saʿīd al-Sīrāfī, ʿAlī ibn ʿĪsā al-Rummānī, Abū ʿAbd Allāh al-Marzubānī, and Abū Ḥafṣ al-Kattānī, the companion of Abū Bakr ibn Mujāhid. I wrote down the Traditions of the messenger of God—God bless and preserve him—and achieved the goals I had set myself, to my best efforts (one is exculpated by giving one's best effort). Then I traveled from there to Egypt, where I met Abū l-Ḥasan al-Maghribī. He compelled me to stick to him like his shadow; I became like an equal, through the abundance of his equity, his affection, and our mutual friendship. He told me, in confidence, "I am afraid that the ambition of Abū l-Qāsim will draw him, and us with him, toward a watering place from which there is no return. If you can memorize and keep an accurate tally of even the breaths he takes, then do so and keep me informed!" 7.2

One day Abū l-Qāsim said to me, "We do not like how we live in obscurity." "What obscurity?" I replied, "You receive six thousand dinars each year from our lord—may God make him reign forever!—and your father is one of the leading men of the state; he is revered and honored." He said, "I want battalions and processions and squadrons to defile at our gates! I don't like being treated like boys and women!" I repeated these words to his father, who said, "I am really afraid that Abū l-Qāsim will dye this (he grasped his beard) blood-red with this (he touched his head)!" Abū l-Qāsim got to know this, and this brought about an estrangement between us.

7.3 General Abū ʿAbd Allāh al-Ḥusayn ibn Jawhar sent for me and honored me by employing me in his service. I saw that, whenever he had a leading person executed, al-Ḥākim would send his head to him, with the words "Ḥusayn, this is my enemy and your enemy!" I said to myself,

> He who sees something will one day be seen himself:
> One should have no illusions about Fate.[120]

I knew that he would be treated in the same manner. I asked leave to go on pilgrimage, which he permitted. I left in the year ninety-seven.[121] I went on pilgrimage, staying away for five years, and when I returned to Egypt he had been executed. His sons came to me in secret and wanted me to return to their service; but I said to them, "The best thing we all can do is to run away. Your father has deposited goods in Baghdad worth five thousand dinars, so run and I shall run too." They did so, as did I. I heard that they were killed in Damascus when I was in Tripoli.[122]

7.4 Then I went to Antioch and left it again for Malatya, where Mistress Khawlah,[123] the daughter of Saʿd al-Dawlah resided. I stayed with her until I received a letter from Abū l-Qāsim. Then I traveled to Mayyāfāriqīn. He was "secretly drinking the milk while pretending to sip the froth."[124]

One day he said to me, "I do not want to see you ever again!" I asked, "Has something happened?" "No," he said, "I want to curse you!" I answered, "Then curse me in my absence!" "No," he said, "it gives me more satisfaction to do it in your face!" "Why?" I asked. He replied, "Because you act against me, as you know very well!" Since there had been such a bond of close intimacy between us, I told him that there were three reasons why I deserved respect: the fact that we came from the same place, that his father had educated me, and that I had educated his brothers. But he retorted, "These reasons are to be torn to shreds. Coming from the same place is merely sharing walls. Being educated by my father was a favor we did you, and your education of my brothers was done in return for robes of honor and dinars!"

I wanted to say to him, "You had a comfortable life when noble people toiled!" However, I was afraid of the madness of his madness, for his madness was in fact mad. A madman was sounder in mind than he! One could not be madder than he. It has been said:

Your madness is mad and you won't find
 a doctor who's able to cure the madness of madness.[125]

Even the jinn who possessed him were mad[126] and his devil danced!

In him is a mad madness; yet, when it occurs,
 It's more intelligent and sensible than he's himself!

He said to me one evening, "I want to combine seven attributes of a candle in one verse, but nothing that comes to my mind pleases me." I said, "I'll do it now!" He said, "You are the well-rubbed little tree-trunk[127] and its well-propped palm-bunch!" So I took the pen from its inkwell and wrote in his presence, 7.5

A candle resembles me, in my passionate love,
 in my terror at what I encounter and what I expect:
Thin, and burning, and dwindling, and lonely,
 with wakeful eye, being pale, and tearful.

Then he said, "You composed this earlier!" I replied, "You deprive me of my quick wit and credit me with knowing the future! You will remember," I continued, "what your father said to us, to al-Battī the poet, and to al-Muḥassin al-Dimashqī, when we sat in the pavilion:[128] 'Compose an epigram, each of you! I shall reward the best by having his poem inscribed on this pavilion.'" Then I said:

The sky has been reached by the height of a house
 raised on the loftiest place;
A building so high that its roofs
 make the Little Bear's stars[129] sink beneath them.

So be happy in it and may you from bad
turns of fortune forever be safe.

"He liked my quick response and wrote it on the pavilion, also giving me a robe of honor."

7.6.1 Abū l-Qāsim was easily bored. Someone easily bored is sometimes bored with his own boredom; he, however, was never bored of being bored! He was full of resentment, like someone whose liver never softens[130] and whose joints are never relaxed.

A high official once reproached me, saying, "You are the one who is resentful; not him!" I said to him, "You do not know him. By God, he is inflexible and one cannot hope for any favors from him.[131] He has a frame of mind that encourages him to be disrespectful and that makes respect for people's rights seem hateful to him. He is far from having a character that rejects rejection but is amiable and loves mutual affection. It is as if he, in his arrogance, rides the celestial sphere and has seated himself on the galaxy-striped sky. Yet I am not the type to seek out anyone who seeks disassociation from his companionship, or to draw toward anyone who inclines toward withdrawal from his friendship.[132] When I saw how thoughtlessly he acted without doing me justice in his excessive pride, I wiped away his name from the page of my heart and considered my affection for him as something swept away by the river's flow.

For if the bonds with you are frayed, others will make ties;
There are places I can turn to on earth, away from an abode of hate."[133]

7.6.2 I recited some verses to the man, justifying myself in them for breaking off my contact with him:

If any good thing came from him, whose badness comes so readily,
then we could say: the good comes with the bad!
And if he had no bad, as well as nothing good,
we could endure it, saying: "he's no fletcher and no trimmer!"[134]

But he is bad and there's no good in him;
and badness, when it lasts, can't be endured.

My hatred of him, whether alive or dead—God is my witness—is the inevitable result of the fact that he appropriated the gold and silver niches of the Kaaba and coined them into dinars and dirhams, which he called "Kaaba coins."[135] He made the Bedouins plunder al-Ramlah and he laid Baghdad in ruins. So much blood did he shed, and so many women did he ravish, widowing free women and orphaning little children!

8 *Praise of al-Maʿarrī*

I ask the venerable Sheikh to excuse me when I laud him, even though I fall short of doing him justice, because his excellence has spread among all people and he has become a bright light on the brow of the sun and the moon. This has been immortalized in wonderful reports and has been written night-black on day-white. In writing to his noble person in verse and in prose I am like someone who fuels a fire with a spark, who presents the moon with a gift of light, who pours a mouthful into the sea, or who lends speed to that of the celestial sphere; for no shortcoming settles in his valley and no inadvertence nears his assembly.

I have heard the Sheikhs's epistles being read, which contain expressions so exquisite that if I extolled them I would have disgraced them, and which if I described them I would not have done justice to them. I was enraptured by them—God is my witness—as if enraptured by music. By God, if they were produced by someone who had his library and his books around him, turning his eyes now to this, and then to that—for "the pen is the tongue of the hand and one of the two kinds of eloquence"—it would be an amazingly difficult feat. By God, I have seen scholars such as Ibn Khālawayh who, when books were studied under their supervision, especially large ones, would consult their exemplars, like those who collate copies of texts in order to guard themselves against slips, misspellings, or errors.

But what is a truly amazing and an extraordinary and rare thing, is the Sheikh's memory—may God always support him!—of people's names and prose texts, just as other intelligent and eminent people memorize poetry. It is easy to say but hard to do; he who hears of it aspires to it, but if he aims for it, he finds it impossible to achieve it in meaning and form.[136]

On memorizing and forgetting; Ibn al-Qāriḥ complains again

9.1 Abū ʿAlī al-Ṣiqillī[137] told me in Damascus: "I was sitting in Ibn Khālawayh's assembly when he received some queries from Sayf al-Dawlah concerning lexicography. He became agitated about this, went into his library and got out dictionaries, distributing them among his companions, so that they could consult them and he could find the answer. I left him and went to Abū l-Ṭayyib al-Lughawī, who was holding a session and who had received the very same queries. He was holding a reed pen with red ink, with which he was writing the answers, without making any changes, such was his skill in replying. 'I recited from memory *The Pure Language* and *The Correction of Speech*[138] with Abū ʿUmar,' said Abū l-Ṭayyib, 'and Abū ʿUmar told me, "I would take notes in lectures on lexicography from Thaʿlab, writing the notes on pieces of pottery; I would sit on the bank of the Tigris memorizing them and then throwing them away."'"

9.2 I have exhausted myself spending the first half of my life memorizing things, and the second half forgetting them. I studied in Baghdad and left it when my memory was still fresh. I went to Egypt, letting myself indulge in animal desires and sinful designs. I wanted, in my eagerness, deceived by my blameworthy nature, to taste the sweetness of a life of pleasure, just as I persevered in seeking knowledge and erudition. I forgot that knowledge is the food of a noble soul and the burnisher of subtle minds. I used to write fifty folios each day and study two hundred; but now I write but one single folio and my eyes smart in pain and when I study five folios my eyes grow weary.

Then I was compelled to survive long enough to witness times in which no one desires knowledge or erudition; rather they want silver and gold! Though I may have been Iyās, I have become Bāqil.[139] I put a book down on my right and then look for it on my left. In spite of my weakness I try to make a living with a back that does not back me up but is broken and wounded, with a spinal column no longer firm. If I sit down it is like having a boil; if I walk I am all boils! All I have left is a trifle, a scant remainder of what was once a huge amount. If I could find a reliable person I would give it to him in return for something with which I could ease my body with not having to move, and my heart by not being preoccupied. I have, in fact, found someone to give it to, but it remains for him to render me his service.

A man gave a slave girl to a friend, entrusting her to his keeping 9.3
while he went on a journey. After a few days the latter said to someone with whom he was on intimate terms and whom he trusted, "My friend, one can no longer trust people these days! A friend has entrusted a slave girl to me, thinking that she was a virgin. But I tried her myself and she wasn't a virgin!"[140]

Another curious[141] story is that my sister's daughter stole eighty-three dinars from me. When the ruler—may God prolong his life, extend his term, and perpetuate his loftiness and his elevation!—threatened her and she produced some of them to him, she said, "By God, if I had known that matters would end up thus I would have killed him!"—"Be amazed about my *harīsah* and my customer!"[142]

By God, were it not that I am too weak and feeble to travel I would 10.1
go and visit the Sheikh, to be honored by sitting with him and talking to him. As for a learned discussion with him, I despair of this on account of the forgetfulness that has come over me and the worries and sorrows that have enveloped my heart. To God, not about Him, I complain; it would not be proper if I complained about Someone who has mercy upon me to someone who has no mercy upon

me. One who complains about a Merciful One to someone who is unmerciful is not wise.

Abū Bakr al-Shiblī used to say, "Other than God there is no other, and there is no good but with God." He said one day, "O Generous One!" Then he stood still, thinking. He raised his head; then he said, "How impudent am I! I say to Thee, 'O Generous One!' whereas someone has said about one of Thy servants:

> And if in his hand he held nothing but his soul,
> he would give it up freely; let him who asks him fear God![143]

"And on someone else the following was said:

> You see him, when you come to him, exulting,
> as if you had just given what you ask from him."[144]

Then he said, "But of course, I'll say 'O Generous One, who surpasses every generous one, and through whose generosity every one who is generous can be generous!'"

10.2 Ibn al-Sammāk[145] entered into the presence of al-Rashīd, who said to him: "Preach to me!" The caliph held a beaker containing water in his hand. "Wait, O Commander of the believers!" said Ibn al-Sammāk, "What do you think: if God made a divine decree about you and said, 'I shall only let you drink in return for half your empire,' would you do it?" The caliph replied, "Yes, I would." "Drink," said Ibn al-Sammāk, "May God let you enjoy it!" When he had drunk, the preacher said, "What do you think: if the same divine decree was applied to you[146] and God said, 'I shall only let you pass the water of this beaker from your body if I rob you of your empire,' would you accept?" The caliph answered, "Yes, I would." "Then fear God," said Ibn al-Sammāk, "and reflect upon an empire that is worth only a piss."

11.1 How could I complain about Him who fed me and sustained me for more than seventy years? When my shirt was two cubits long(?)[147]

He appointed for me two loving and caring parents, who spared no effort to make it fine and soft and pleasant. When it was twelve cubits long He took care of it and of my sustenance. He never let me go starving or naked. «And He who gives me food and drink»;[148] the speaker addressed his Lord tactfully and said, «And when I am ill He cures me»,[149] attributing the illness to himself, because one shuns mishaps and illnesses, though everything that befalls a person and which he is unable to prevent, such as sleep and wakefulness, laughter and weeping, sorrow and joy, fecundity and drought, wealth and poverty—all this comes from Him, sanctified be His names. Do you not see that He neither threatens[150] nor punishes for doing these things? Whereas anything a human being is able to prevent is his own doing, for instance when one wants to write something, and thus it happens that one does not build anything; or when one wants to build something, and thus it happens that one does not write. But someone who suffers from tremors is unable to steady his hand whereas someone who does not is able to hold it steady.

When I was in Tinnīs there was someone who was reciting the 11.2
Qur'an with a plaintive voice:[151] «They fulfill their vows and fear», and he wept. A thought occurred to me and I said to myself, "I am the opposite of those people, God's blessings be upon them. I neither make nor fulfill vows and do not fear misery and suffering. If I were fearful I would not be anything but[152] feverish"—And then I was!

An unimpeachable and trustworthy acquaintance told me the following story on the authority of his father, an ascetic, who had said, "I was with Abū Bakr al-Shiblī in Baghdad, in East Side in Bāb al-Ṭāq, when we saw a seller of roasted meat who took a lamb from the oven, which was as tender as a fresh, ripe date. Next to him was a pastry cook who was making *fālūdhaj*. Abū Bakr stopped and looked at them, lost in thought. 'My master,' I said to him, 'let me get some of both, along with some thin cakes and bread! My house is nearby; will you honor me by relaxing at my place today?' But he said, 'Really, do you think I have an appetite for these things? I was merely thinking that all other living beings enter the fire only after they have died, whereas we enter it alive!'"

O Lord, forgive a gray-haired, fearful man,
who's like a madman, fearful of the Fire!
He has committed, in the past, blameworthy deeds,
during the days he had no sense and no religion.[153]

12 The epistle is finished, praise be to God, giver of graceful gifts, and His blessings be on Muḥammad and the elect of his family.

I had hardly finished a draft when I was stirred by a bout of melancholy.[154] I apologize for the rambling or any error in this letter; for someone who makes a mistake is forgiven if it is accompanied by apology, effort, and careful scrutiny.

But who will be given perfection, then, and be perfect?[155]

'Umar ibn al-Khaṭṭāb said, "God have mercy on any man who points out my defects to me!"

And I ask the Sheikh—may God give him lasting power!—to honor me by answering my letter, for in spite of its imperfections it has been appreciated, taken down from my dictation, and received from me through lectures; I have honored it with the Sheikh's name and adorned it by mentioning him. The letter that al-Zahrajī wrote to me was the main reason why I came to Aleppo. If its answer comes I shall make it go round Aleppo and elsewhere, God willing. In Him is our trust, and God bless and preserve our lord Muḥammad and his family.

The Epistle of Forgiveness

Preamble

In name of God, the Merciful, the Compassionate

O God, give ease and help

The Mighty One (*al-Jabr*), from whom comes the name of Gabriel—He is the Way to all good things—knows that there is a tree (*ḥamāṭah*)[156] within me, one that never was an *afāniyah* tree, and on which there lived no stinging snake,[157] one that produces fruit for the love of my lord the venerable Sheikh[158]—may God subdue his enemy, and always, evening and morning, lead him to superiority![159] If a lofty tree were to bear these fruits its branches would sink to earth and all this fruit, once well-protected, would be trampled underfoot. 1.1

Ḥamāṭah is a kind of tree, which is called *afāniyah* when tender and *ḥamāṭah* when dry. A poet says:

When Umm al-Wulayyid[160] does not obey me,
I bend my hand around a stick of *ḥamāṭ* wood for her
And I say to her, "Get the Banū Uqaysh![161]
For you haven't got a nice figure!"

A characteristic of the *ḥamāṭah* is that it is a familiar haunt of snakes. A poet says:

Destined for her was—one from a numerous brood—
a bold male snake that hid in the *ḥamāṭah* tree.

He knows that the tree (*ḥamāṭah*) found in me feels a burning (*ḥamāṭah*) of great yearning which, as it happens, is not to be removed (*imāṭah*).[162]

Ḥamāṭah also means "heartburn." A poet says: "Many a worry that fills one's inside . . . ."[163] At the beginning of the Preamble, *ḥamāṭah* means "core of the heart." A poet says:

She shot at the core (*ḥamāṭah*) of my heart, unswervingly,
with arrows from her glance, the shooter unknown.

And God knows that in my two ragged robes[164] there is a "male snake (*ḥiḍb*)"[165] charged with harming me; if it could speak it would mention my misery. It does not live in a rocky crack or nook; down on to narrow mountain passes it does not look. It appears neither in winter nor in summer time; it passes neither by mountain nor by incline. It harbors for my lord, the venerable Sheikh—may God make the cornerstones of scholarship firm by giving him long life!—such a love as a mother cannot harbor for her son, no matter whether she is considered venomous or not.[166] This "snake" is no kin of the one meant by the *rajaz* poet[167] who said,

I curled up like a *ḥiḍb*.

1.2 The Sheikh—may God perpetuate beautiful performance by keeping him well!— knows that a *ḥiḍb* is a kind of snake, and that it is also used for the "bottom of the heart." He knows that this "black thing,"[168] which is dearer to me than ʿAntarah was to Zabībah, more precious to me than al-Sulayk was to al-Sulakah, and more entitled to my affection than Khufāf al-Sulamī was entitled to the innermost feelings of Nadbah, is always concealed, its coverings never removed and it never moves far afield. If it could travel it would, so that the Sheikh and it could meet; no mishap befalling it could make it retreat.

When mentioned in speech, it can be feminine and also masculine.[169] It is not known if it is really masculine; using it as a feminine is not rejected.

To please it, incessantly I take pains, although one cannot avert what God ordains. I esteem it more than Lakhm esteemed al-Aswad ("Black")[170] ibn al-Mundhir, more than Kindah esteemed al-Aswad ibn Maʿdīkarib, and more than the Banū Nahshal ibn Dārim esteemed al-Aswad ibn Yaʿfur, who composed such ravishing poetry. At the same time it never ceases to be as fond of mentioning the Sheikh as Suḥaym, be he in town or desert, was fond of his ʿUmayrah, or as Suʿdā was loved by Nuṣayb, the client of Umayyah.

Just such a thing[171] was found with al-Aswad ibn Zamʿah, al-Aswad ibn ʿAbd Yaghūth, the two men called al-Aswad mentioned in al-Yashkurī's[172] verse: 1.3

He guided them with the two Aswads; [173] God's command
strikes home: with it the wretched are made wretched

and with Aswadān, viz. Nabhān ibn ʿAmr ibn al-Ghawth ibn Ṭayyiʾ, and with Abū l-Aswad, mentioned by Imruʾ al-Qays[174] in his verse:

And that is because of what I have heard,
something that I was told about Abū l-Aswad.

Abū l-Aswad al-Duʾalī never parted from it in his lifetime for one second, whether during easy relaxation or tiring occupation. With Suwayd ibn Abī Kāhil it enjoyed a close link whenever he went to wells to drink. With Ibn al-Ṣāmit, another Suwayd, it was always closely allied, be he rejoicing gladly or gloating badly. It helped Suwayd ibn Ṣumayʿ as an ally, in days of poverty and prosperity. He was the one who said:[175]

When they demand from me an oath, I'll swear for them
an oath that's like a torn and tattered robe with yellow stripes!
And if they make me swear upon my wife's divorce, I'll come to her
as happily as ever, and we shall not part.
And if they make me swear upon the freeing of my slave,
ʿUbayd, my slave, knows well he won't be freed!

1.4 It was familiar with Sawdah bint Zamʿah ibn Qays's bed, when to the Prophet (God bless and preserve him) she was wed. God's messenger knew its force, and in good grace did not resort to divorce.[176] It entered the grave with Sawādah ibn ʿAdī, which is not a strange oddity. It is found in any congregation where the "two black things" are found, viz. water and dates, or maybe they are darkness and dusty volcanic ground. It flees from the "two things white" when these are exposed to a dustcloud raised by a fight—the "two things white" from which it flees are either two swords, or a sword and a spearhead. Yet it will bear with them both when it finds them,[177] as the *rajaz* poet says,

The "two white things" have cooled my bones:
Water and millet bread, no added condiments.[178]

And it will delight in two other "white things," as in the following verse:[179]

But a whole year has passed for me
without a drink of anything except the two white things.

As for the two white things that are youthfulness and fat, these are the things that al-Rabāb rejoices at,[180] and what perhaps other people are delighted to see. But they despair of getting anything out of *me*! It is the same with "the three, or two, red things"[181] that gratify the black (i.e. pupil) of a beholder's eye, which is then followed by something hidden away[182], as long as it has not yet been struck with mental decay.

2 I have received your letter, which is a sea with words of wisdom brimming, rewarding any reading or skimming, because it enjoins one to accept God's laws and to condemn holding the branches instead of the trunk. I drowned in the billows of its abundant ideas and its originality, amazed by these well-arranged jewels of great quality. Such a letter helps to intercede, and nearer to God's favor it will lead. I found its opening praise of our Lord's magnificence

Al-Maʿarrī's description of Ibn al-Qāriḥ's letter

to be by a master of eloquence. It is in the power of God (great is His might) to turn its every letter into a body of light, not mixed with falsehood's blight, which will ask for forgiveness for its writer until Judgment Day at the world's end, and which will remind him like a loving friend. Perhaps God has already made for its written lines, which will deliver from the Fire, silver or golden ladders going higher and higher, on which the angels from stagnant earth to heaven are ascending, and the veils of darkness rending, according to the Qur'anic verse,[183] «To Him ascend good words and a righteous deed He raises». Such «good words» seem to be meant also by God's word:[184] «Have you not seen how God has coined a comparison: a good word is like a good tree, its trunk stands firm and its branches are in the sky.[185] It brings its fruit every season, by its Lord's leave». In these lines there is many a word, all of which by the most Holy Creator to be favorably heard.

Paradise (I)

3.1 *Description of Paradise* On account of this praise, if God wills, for the venerable Sheikh trees will have been planted and their delicious fruit to him granted. Each tree provides shade from the East to the West extending, not at all like the "Tree of Suspending."—As you know, this was a tree that was venerated in pre-Islamic times.[186] It is said that someone asked the Messenger of God: "Make for us a Tree of Suspending like they have!" A poet said,

> We have the Guardian who protects us from our enemies,
> and we refused to have a Tree of Suspension.

Ever-living youths in the shade of those trees stand or sit and rest; with forgiveness truly one's life is forever blessed. They say—God is powerful over every difficulty—"We along with the trees are God's gifts to ʿAlī ibn Manṣūr, hidden for him alone, until the day the Last Trumpet is blown." Rivers drawn from the Water of Life flow at the roots of every tree; the river Kawthar (Abundance) feeds them incessantly. Whosoever drinks from one of those, will never die or suffer fortune's blows. Rivers overflowing with milk that will not sour but last, no matter how much time has passed. Rivulets of choice, pure wine that was sealed when retained—mighty is He with power over all things ordained. This is the wine eternal, not the wine vile and infernal. Rather, it is as ʿAlqamah[187] said (though he lied and never for forgiveness applied):

It cures a headache, its heat will not harm;
it does not befuddle the brain.

3.2 One scoops from it with cups of gold and jugs formed from peridot: the onlooker sees something novel, undreamt of even by Abū l-Hindī,[188] the poet (God rest his soul) who did not know it. The vile, available wine of the world he did cherish, though it was sure to perish. The Sheikh will no doubt have memorized and transmitted his collected verse; he is the one who said,

Abū l-Hindī does not need a perfect skin of milk:
he is content with jugs to which there sticks no greasy muck;
Provided with a strainer made of silk,
their necks like those of waterfowl, when thunderstruck.

Thus it is recited, with the rhyme defect called *iqwāʾ* in the rhyme words *zubdī* and *raʿdū*. Others read it as *mina l-raʿdī*,

their necks like those of waterfowl, frightened by thunder,

but the former reading is that of the grammarians.[189] Abū l-Hindī is a poet of the Islamic period; his proper name is ʿAbd al-Muʾmin ibn ʿAbd al-Quddūs. Both these names are Islamic. The verse is only quoted as evidence by people who think the poet uses correct Arabic. If Abū l-Hindī is a poet who could write and knew the letters of the alphabet he made a bad mistake with this rhyme defect. If he intended the verses to end with an unvowelled consonant, then Saʿīd ibn Masʿadah is correct in saying that the poetic meter called *ṭawīl* has four variants.[190]

3.3 If Abū Zubayd had seen those jugs he would have known that he was as good as a lowly knave, a mere little slave, that the subject of his lyrical verse was worth very little, and that he was content with scanty victual. He would have laughed at his verse:

Jugs with spouts like the necks of waterfowl, clothed with a linen
cover.[191]

Far from the mark! These *abārīq*, carried by *abārīq*, are brilliant like *abārīq*![192]

The first *abārīq* refer to the well-known "jugs." The second is from the expression *jāriyah ibrīq*, "radiant maiden," when she "shines" (*tabruqu*) with her beauty, as in the verse:

A radiant (*ibrīq*), graceful girl; it is as if her saliva
is nectar harvested by bees, mixed with the merchant's reddish
wine.

The third is from the expression *sayf ibrīq*, "a shining sword," derived from *barīq* ("glitter"). Ibn Aḥmar said,

You girded yourself with a shining (*ibrīq*; viz. sword) and slung on
a quiver,
to wipe out a populous tribe with a herd of their camels.

And if ʿAlqamah looked at them, he would be bedazzled and afraid, thinking he had lost his wits.—But how could poor ʿAlqamah see them? He may well be in a Fire that scorches the soil, where the drinking water will always boil. What has become of ʿAlqamah ibn ʿAbadah and his clan? His jug is broken and lost. But did he not say,

Their jug resembled a gazelle upon a hill,
wrapped in a cloth, and with a linen veil,
Adorned with necklace of sweet-scented herb sprigs, white,
brought by its keeper out into the light.

One look at these jugs is better than all the wine, daughter of the vine, of the world that passes, better than the saliva-sipping kisses[193] of sweet lasses one finds in the deceptive world, in which all pride is downward hurled. And if seen by ʿAdī ibn Zayd, from hunting and wine he would have been preoccupied, and would acknowledge that his wine jugs and all his drinking companions and friends in al-Ḥīrah were but a trifling thing: less than a blade of grass on sandy soil is its worth, less than a pebble lying on the earth.

When I was in Baghdad I saw a bookseller looking for the poem by ʿAdī ibn Zayd that begins with: 3.4

The women reproached him when morning
dawned: "Hey, aren't you sober yet?"
But he called for a morning drink of wine;
a songstress came, holding in her hand a jug.

The bookseller declared that Ibn Ḥājib al-Nuʿmān had asked for this poem; they searched for it in the copies of ʿAdī's collected poetry but did not find it. Afterward I heard a man from Astarabad recite this poem from the collected poetry of ʿAdī; but it was not contained in the copy in the library.

Take al-Uqayshir al-Asadī, he placed his bet on a bad horse in the event! Wretched until Judgement Day he may still repent when his skin is rent. He said, 3.5

My wealth, inherited or earned, has been consumed
by clinking cups on mouths of jugs.

What has happened to him and his wine? All his desires, without exception, have come to nought in the world of deception. If he beheld these jugs, he would know for certain that it was an illusion which seduced him, and that it was no joyful thing that to joy induced him. Likewise Iyās ibn al-Aratt, however pleased he was with jugs "like geese on a river bank," his fate played him a nasty prank. It is as if he never said,

The jugs of wine between them look like geese
high on the river bank, with their crooked necks.

And God have mercy on al-ʿAjjāj, whose *rajaz* verse is a hodgepodge: where is the jug that he mentioned when he said,

He picked a quantity of grapes,
He stored it for two years; then he examined it:
A red and potent wine that makes you shudder.
And this he poured into the jug in little spurts,
Like torrent-water over mountain ledge.

3.6 How many vessels are there at those rivers, made of engraved peridot, and of ruby, jacinth, or sapphire, carved like gazelles, of various hue: red, yellow, and blue; their sparkle is such that they burn to the touch, as al-Ṣanawbarī said,

You would think it ablaze
  and refuse to come close to its blaze.

In these rivers are vessels shaped like waterfowl that swim, or others that do not need the flowing stream. Some are formed like cranes, others resemble songbirds, or are shaped like peacocks and ducks. Some are in the water, others on the riverbank. From their spouts flows wine, like a mirage so clear and fine. If al-Ḥakamī Abū Nuwās had sipped it from a glass, he would have deemed it a cordial he had desired from times primordial. All those poets, both the moderns and the ancients,[194] who have described wine would testify in its favor, above all other kinds of wine that belong to the Perishable World, such as the old wine from ʿĀnah, Adhriʿāt, Gaza, Bayt Raʾs, or Palestine; the wine imported from Bostra on camelback, with which one hopes to make a profit on the market; the wine stored by Ibn Bujrah in Wajj,[195] on which he relied at the time of the Hajj, before alcoholic drinks were prohibited and base desires, for fear of God, were limited—Abū Dhuʾayb said:

Even if she had as much wine as Ibn Bujrah
she would not wet my palate with a sip

—or the wine pressed in Ṣarkhad or in the region of Shibām for any wise king, or the famed red wine of Ṣarīfīn and Babel made for all who are noble; or any type of intoxicating drink that makes the heavy drinker drink his fill, such as barley beer and wheat beer, mead made of honey, Abyssinian millet wine, and wine sired by date palms, made for both the miser and the generous man asked for alms; wines made from the days of Adam and Seth until Resurrection Day, for ready consumption or after long delay: they would testify that this drop of Paradise is a queen, who should never mixed up with her subjects be seen.

Opposite this wine are rivers of purified honey that has not been 3.7
gathered by bees that in the morning hours swarm out to flowers and not hidden in waxen bowers. Rather, the Almighty said "Be!" and it was; by His generosity it was granted the possibility to be. Such honey! It is not spoiled by fire; if some overheated drinker made it his morning drink forever, he would never be afflicted with pleurisy and he would never don the cloak of fever. All this is according to God's word:[196] «The likeness of the Garden that has been promised to the God-fearing: in it are rivers of water that is not stale, and rivers of milk whose taste will not go sour, and rivers of wine, a delight to the drinkers, and rivers of purified honey; and in it they have some of all kinds of fruit». I wish I knew if al-Namir ibn Tawlab al-ʿUklī was permitted to taste this honey! Then he would know that compared with it the honey of the Perishable World would resemble bitter colocynth. When he described Umm Ḥiṣn and the life of luxury and security that she led, he mentioned white bread, with butter clarified, as well as honey purified. God have mercy with him now that he has died! For he converted to Islam and transmitted a single saying of the Prophet. To have transmitted it correctly is for us sufficient profit. Poor al-Namir said,

To my companions,[197] when they all were sleeping tight,
 there came a phantom of Umm Ḥiṣn in the night.[198]
She has what she desires: honey purified
 whenever she wants, white bread with butter clarified.

3.8.1 The Sheikh knows (may God always empower him!) the story of Khalaf al-Aḥmar with his companions in connection with these verses. He asked them what the poet would have said in the second verse if the first had not rhymed in "Umm Ḥiṣn" but in "Umm Ḥafṣ." They did not come up with an answer; so he said: "white bread with *lamṣ*," which means a kind of sweatmeat.[199] One could expand this story[200] and ask: if the first verse had ended in "Umm Jazʾ," rhyming on the *hamzah*[201], what would he have said in the second? It would have been possible to say "white bread with *kashʾ*," from the expression *kashaʾa l-laḥm*, "to roast meat until it is dry," or *kashaʾa l-shuwāʾ*, "to eat meat that has been roasted until dry." Or he could have said "white bread with *wazʾ*," from the expression *wazaʾa l-laḥm*, "to roast meat." Possible, too, is "white bread with *nasʾ*." The best interpretation of this is that it is derived from the expression *nasaʾa Allāhu fī ajalih*, "May God postpone his end," and here meaning "she will have bread with a long life." This is better than explaining *nasʾ* as "milk mixed with a lot of water." It has also been said that *nasʾ* means "wine." Two interpretations have been given of the verse by ʿUrwah ibn al-Ward:[202]

> They gave me *nasʾ* to drink; and then those enemies of God
> surrounded me with lies and falsehood.

It would also be possible to interpret "white bread with *nasʾ*" as "with milk" or "with wine," because white bread is eaten with these things; i.e., "she has white bread with wine." Someone recounted how he saw Basīl, the king of the Byzantines, dipping bread in wine and eating it.

And if one would say "white bread with *lazʾ*," from the expression *lazaʾa*, "to satiate," it would not be too far-fetched; the preposition "with" would then mean "while (being satiated)" here.[203]

The rhyme letter of the verse could not be *alif*, since this *alif* is always unvowelled; the preceding consonant is unvowelled here, which is not possible with this rhyme.[204]

3.8.2 But if the poet were to turn to the letter *b*, and said "of Umm Ḥarb," he could rhyme the next verse with "white bread with *ṣarb*," which means "sour milk"; or "with *irb*," i.e. with a joint of roast meat or sliced dried meat; or "with *kashb*," meaning "eating roast meat greedily."

If he says "of Umm Ṣamt," he can continue with "white bread with *kumt*," i.e. the plural of *kumayt* (reddish-brown) dates, one of the ways to characterize dates. The following verse by al-Aswad ibn Yaʿfur is recited:

> Whenever the food was brought near I was fond
> of all those reddish-brown firm unpeeled dates.

Another poet said,

> I do not mind, now that my drying store is full of red-brown
> dates, if stars do not cause rain to fall on earth.[205]

Possible, too, is "white bread with *ḥamt*," as one says "*ḥamt* dates," i.e. intensely sweet ones.

If the poet turns to the letter *th* and says "of Umm Shathth," he could continue with "white bread with *baththth*." *Baththth* are dates that have not been well packed together, and are found loose.

If he moved on to the letter *j*, saying "of Umm Lujj," it is possible 3.8.3
to rhyme it with "white bread with *dujj*." *Dujj* means "chicken"; al-ʿUmānī used it in his *rajaz* poetry.

If he moved on to the letter *ḥ*, saying "of Umm Shuḥḥ," he could have said "white bread with *muḥḥ*" or "with *buḥḥ*," or "with *ruḥḥ*," or "with *juḥḥ*," or "with *suḥḥ*." *Muḥḥ* is "the yolk of an egg," *buḥḥ* is the plural of *abaḥḥ*, as in the expression "an *abaḥḥ* bone covered with meat," meaning one with lots of fat. A poet said,

> Many a reproaching woman got up to blame me,
> holding in her hand a bone that drips with fat.

Buḥḥ could also mean "arrows," i.e., this woman's kinsmen play the *maysir* game,[206] as al-Sulamī said:

> They regaled their guests on meat gained at play with arrow shafts,
> brown ones, and thanks to them the tribe lives comfortably.

Ruḥḥ is the plural of *araḥḥ*, "with broad hoofs," which is one of the characteristics of wild oryx bulls, i.e.,these are hunted for that woman. Or the word is used for the cloven hoofs themselves, as the poet al-Aʿshā said:

And (he has) broad hoofs with hair behind the fetlocks, firmly planted,
with which he outstrips all in fighting, and with which he scouts about the land.

3.8.4 *Suḥḥ* means "small dry dates." *Juḥḥ* means "small watermelons," before they are ripe. And if he said "of Umm Dukhkh," he could rhyme it with "white bread with *mukhkh*," i.e., "marrow," or something like it.

If he said, "of Umm Saʿd," he could say "white bread with *thaʿd*," which means ripe dates that are wholly soft.[207]

If he said, "of Umm Waqdh," he could say "white bread with *shiqdh*," viz. partridge chicks.

If he said, "of Umm ʿAmr," the closest match is "white bread with *tamr*," i.e., dates.

If he said, "of Umm Kurz," the closest match is "white bread with *urz*," i.e., rice; there are six variants of this word: *aruzz*, of the pattern ʾaC_1uC_2C_3, *uruzz* (pattern C_1uC_2uC_3C_3), *uruz* (C_1uC_2uC_3), *urz* (C_1uC_2C_3), *ruzz* (C_1uC_2C_3), and *runz*, with an *n*— but this is a bad form.

If he said, "of Umm Ḍibs," he could say "white bread with *dibs*" (i.e., honey); the Bedouin Arabs call *ʿasal* ("honey") *dibs*. Thus they explain the verse of Abū Zubayd:

An opportunity, indeed: I thought that those they met
were more delicious to him than cool *dibis*.[208]

The poet has inserted the extra vowel (in *dibis*) out of metrical necessity, as a poetic license.

If he said, "of Umm Qarsh," he could say "white bread with *warsh*," which is a kind of cheese. It may be a "post-classical" word.[209] Warsh, who transmitted a Qur'anic reading on the authority of Nāfiʿ, was called after it; his proper name was ʿUthmān ibn Saʿd.[210]

The letter *ṣ* has already been dealt with. If he said, "of Umm Gharḍ," he could say "white bread with *farḍ*," which is another kind of date, as in the verses by the *rajaz* poet:[211] 3.8.5

When I eat milk with with *farḍ* dates
I grow in length and I grow in breadth.

Al-Mubarrad and Sībawayh[212] differ on the precise function of the accusative in "length" and "breadth."

And if he said, "of Umm Laqṭ," he could say "white bread with *aqṭ*," a variant found in the dialect of the tribal group of Rabīʿah for *aqiṭ*, which means "sour cheese."

If he said, "of Umm Ḥaẓẓ," then there are few edibles ending in *ẓ*, which is infrequent anyway, for it is a letter that is very rare. He could say, "white bread with *kaẓẓ*," i.e., "eating a surfeit", or some such contrived expressions that could be used.

If he said, "of Umm Ṭalʿ," he could say "white bread with *khalʿ*," 3.8.6
i.e., with boiled meat carried in leather containers called *qurūf*. The following verse is recited:

Eat the tender meat! My food, for sure, is meat well-seasoned (*khalʿ*),
contained in leather vessels (*qurūf*).

If he said, "of Umm Farʿ," he could say "white bread with *ḍarʿ*," i.e., "udder," for udders are cooked. Kings sometimes love to eat them.

If he said, "of Umm Mubghī,"[213] he could say "white bread with *ṣibgh*," which is a seasoning made of gravy, olive oil, or vinegar, in which one dips a morsel.

If he said, "of Umm Nakhf," he could say "white bread with *rakhf*," which is soft butter, a lump of which is called *rakhfah*. A poet says:

We have sheep that give fresh milk that pleases lodging guests,
and we've soft butter for a morning meal, and slaughtered meat.

If he said, "of Umm Farq," he could say "white bread with *ʿarq*," i.e., a bone with meat on it, either roasted or boiled in a cauldron.

If he said, "of Umm Sabk," it would be possible to say "white bread with *rabk*," or " . . . with *labk*," (i.e., "with a mixture"), from the expression *rabaka* or *labaka l-ṭaʿām*, "to mix food with something;" that is, with things that are moist, for instance mixing it with milk, clarified butter, or similar things. One cannot use the verbs for mixing barley with wheat, except by way of metaphor.

3.8.7 If he said, "Of Umm Nakhl," he could say "white bread with *rakhl*," meaning a female lamb. There are four dialect variants: *rakhil*, *rakhl*, *rikhl*, and *rikhil*.

If he said, "Of Umm Ṣirm," he could say "white bread with *ṭirm*," i.e., honey. Clarified butter is also sometimes called *ṭirm*.

The letter *n* has already been dealt with, in "Umm Ḥiṣn."

If he said, "of Umm Daww," he could say "white bread with *ḥaww*," i.e. "kid," according to the Arabic expression quoted by a lexicographer: "He does not know a *ḥaww* from a *laww*," meaning "a male kid from a she-kid."[214]

If he said, "of Umm Kurh," he could say "white bread with *wurh*," which is the plural of *awrah*, "fat," as in the expression "*kabsh awrah* (a fat ram)."

And if he said, "of Umm Shary," he could say "white bread with *ary*," i.e. "honey."

This is a chapter that could be expanded[215]—such things happen in discourse that grows from such a theme, like an apparition that visits in a dream.

3.9.1 If a mere two pounds of Paradise honey were mixed with all the bitter things God created in this Treacherous World, such as colocynth, aloes, *Soelanthus*, *jaʿdah*, wormwood, and *habīd*, then they would be deemed delicious and superb, along with every other bitter herb. Then hateful colocynth would again taste like sugar pressed from cane; unripe colocynth would seem to have been made in al-Ahwāz, being sugar's equal. A woman herding camels, finding a colocynth,[216] would present it as a gift to her mistress who is *muḥẓalah*, which means a woman who is very jealously guarded; this is derived from the expression *ḥaẓala nisā'ahū*, "to guard one's women with excessive jealousy." A *rajaz* poet says:

You will not see a husband with his wives
like he and they but he will guard them jealously (*ḥāẓil*).[217]

For the owners of the plantations of sugarcane on the coast, their livelihood would be lost, and from bitter myrrh, without any wizardry, i.e. trickery, one would make *fālūdh*, honey-sweet and smooth.

If al-Ḥārith ibn Kaladah had tasted this honey he would have known that his description stands in relation to what is described here as bitingly bitter oleander[218] stands in relation to sweet jelly, or as an abhorrent medicinal concoction to sugar wine. I have in my mind the verses by al-Ḥārith: 3.9.2

Honey, to a thirsty drinker, with cold water
  from a raincloud mixed,
Is not more delicious than your meeting us:
  so when will it be and when will it return?

Likewise, the honey that is mentioned by the poet of the tribe of Hudhayl is, compared with the honey of Paradise, like the bitter *qār* tree—this is a tree that grows in the sand; Bishr says:

They're hoping to make peace in Dhāt Kahf,[219]
  but what is in it for them: bitter aloe trees and *qār*.

The verse by the poet of Hudhayl[220] I meant is:

He swore to them by God a forceful oath: "You are
  more sweet to me than honey when we gather it!"

When God—blessed be His name—grants someone the right to approach these rivers he can land sweet fish, not to be found on any dish. If Aḥmad ibn al-Ḥusayn[221] had seen them he would have despised the present he was given, on which he said: 3.10

The least of the least of this gift is a fish
that plays in a pond of honey.

As for the rivers of wine, in them too fishes of all shapes are playing: sea fish, river fish, in water salty or fresh, those that live in springs that gush and feed where plants are lush—but these are fishes made of gold, silver, jewels, and all things precious, a sight like dazzling light. When a believer stretches out his hand to one of these fish, he drinks from its mouth a drink so sweet that if a mouthful of it dropped into the salty undrinkable sea, its lowest depths and the crests of its waves would turn as sweet as could be. The briny stench would be found to smell as lavender on soft ground, where at night the dew will abound; or like the odor of an old, mild[222] wine that moves in small jugs but overpowers the brain.

4.1 *A drinking scene*

I imagine our Sheikh (may God make beauty perpetual by letting him live forever!), having gained a high rank, deserving entrance through true repentance. He has chosen fellow carousers from among the literate and erudite in Paradise, such as the man of the tribe of Thumālah, the man of the tribe of Daws, Yūnus ibn Ḥabīb al-Ḍabbī, and Ibn Masʿadah al-Mujāshiʿī.[223] They are as it is said in the Glorious Book:[224] «We have taken away the rancor that was in their breasts, as brothers, sitting on couches facing one another. No fatigue will touch them there and they will not be expelled from there». Thus the breast of Aḥmad ibn Yaḥyā has been cleansed there of its hatred of Muḥammad ibn Yazīd.[225] Now they are devoted and loyal friends, like Jadhīmah's two drinking companions, Mālik and ʿAqīl, who were never apart during the siesta and at night.[226]

Abū Bishr ʿAmr ibn ʿUthmān Sībawayh is there too. His innermost heart has been washed clean of any grudge against ʿAlī ibn Ḥamzah al-Kisāʾī and his followers, for what they did to him during a gathering at the Barmakids.[227] Abū ʿUbaydah only harbors thoughts of pure devotion toward ʿAbd al-Malik ibn Qurayb, their friendship now without any doubt beyond diatribe. They are now like the two brothers Arbad and Labīd, or Nuwayrah's two sons in the past, or like ʿAmr's two sons Ṣakhr and Muʿāwiyah in their amity:[228] they have extinguished the embers of enmity. «And the angels go in to them from every gate, saying "Peace be upon you, because you were patient. How excellent, the Ultimate Abode!"»[229] ʿAlī ibn Manṣūr (may God support knowledge through our Sheikh's life!) is there with them, just as al-Bakrī says,[230]

I took from friends the fragrant basil sprigs
 and a strong-tasting wine, its strainer always moist.
They do not sober up from it (it lasts!) except to shout
 for "More!"—no matter if it is their first or second time.
A page with pearls adorned with glasses serves them,
 his hose tucked up, a nimble page.
A lute responds—you'd think the harp can hear it,
 whenever the singer in her negligée plays the refrain.

Abū ʿUbaydah mentions to them the battles of the ancient Arabs and the fights of hero knights, while excellent poetry is what al-Aṣmaʿī recites. They delight in playing, so they throw their cups into the rivers of wine; filled by the liquid that offers itself, of taste divine. These cups clink and tunes are heard, by which even the dead would be stirred.

The Sheikh (may God adorn Time by prolonging his life!) says, "Alas for the fall of al-Aʿshā Maymūn! How many a reliable mount has he urged on! I wish that Quraysh[231] had not obstructed him when he turned to the Prophet (God bless and preserve him). I am reminded of him this moment by the clinking cups, on account of his verses: 4.2

Cool wine: when poured, the eye would think
 its bubbles are wild carrot blossom, red;
Its odor is like fragrant musk. The cupbearer
 pours it when people say 'Be quick!'

It comes from wineskins of the merchants, then
in a black, ample pitcher from al-Ḥīrah,
A deep one; on that day not minding being scooped from
by a jug and by a cup.
And when the wine produces foam in them,
the bubbles disappear from it and fade;
But when they hit the two sides of the cup
they reappear and swim upon the wine.
The wine is handed out, in well-used glasses, and
what has been depleted is topped-up.[232]
When all has gone we lift our wineskin, when
its strings are loose, and wine pours out!

"If he had embraced Islam he might have been sitting together with us, reciting many a rare-metered ode, which he composed in the Sad Abode, and tell us his stories with Hawdhah ibn ʿAlī, ʿĀmir ibn al-Ṭufayl, Yazīd ibn Mus'hir, ʿAlqamah ibn ʿUlāthah, Salāmah ibn Dhī Fāʾish,[233] and others on whom he composed eulogies or lampoons, those he feared at the time or from whom he expected boons."

5.1 *The Sheikh's excursion*

Then it occurs to him (may God give him lasting power!) to think of something called "excursion" in the Perishable World. He mounts one of the noble camels in Paradise, created of rubies and pearls. It is a mild day, neither hot nor cold. He takes a flagon with wine with him, and sets out in Paradise at random, on a whim. He brings along some of the food of eternity taken from a hoard for a happy father or son stored. When he sees how his mount speeds between the hills of ambergris, through fragrant *ḍaymurān* trees and then lotus trees, he raises his voice and recites two verses by the Bakrite: [234]

I wish I knew if my camel will ever trot with us
toward al-ʿUdhayb and al-Ṣaybūn,
With behind my saddle a skin of wine, a loaf of bread,
with some sweet-smelling basil, and fillet of fish!

By "sweet-smelling basil" he means sprigs of any herbs.

5.2 *The conversation with al-Aʿshā Maymūn*

Then a voice[235] calls, "Do you know, servant of God who has been forgiven, who composed this poem?" The Sheikh replies, "Yes, we have been told by scholars whom we trust and who have relied on trusted predecessors who have transmitted it from generation upon generation, all the way back to Abū ʿAmr ibn al-ʿAlāʾ, who transmitted it on the authority of Bedouin elders, hunters of the lizard in rough terrain and truffle-gatherers in desert and plain, those who have not eaten curds and whey, nor put fruit into their pocket to take away[236]—that this poem is by Maymūn ibn Qays ibn Jandal, of the clan of Rabīʿah ibn Ḍubayʿah ibn Qays ibn Thaʿlabah ibn ʿUkābah ibn Ṣaʿb ibn ʿAlī ibn Bakr ibn Wāʾil."[237]

The voice answers, "I am that man! God showed me His mercy after I was already on the brink of Hell's damnation, and despaired of forgiveness and expiation."

The Sheikh turns to him, happy, smiling, and glad. He sees a young man with a skin fair and light, who lives a life of blissful cornucopia. He now has beautiful black eyes after his former nyctalopia. His once crooked spine is straight and fine. The Sheikh asks him, "Tell me how you escaped from Hell's fire and flame and how you were saved from horrible disgrace and shame!" Al-Aʿshā says:

"Hell's angels dragged me to the Fire, but then I saw a man standing on the Courtyards of Resurrection. His face shone like the moon; people were calling to him from every direction: 'Muḥammad, O Muḥammad, intercede for us, intercede for us![238] We have such-and-such a connection!' So I also shouted, still held by the hands of Hell's angels, 'Muḥammad, save me, for I deserve to be spared by you!' He ordered, "Alī, go to him quickly and find out why he should be spared!' Then ʿAlī ibn Abī Ṭālib (God's blessings be upon him) came to me, as I was forcibly dragged away to be cast into the lowest reaches of Hellfire. But he drove them away and asked, 'On what grounds should you be spared?' I said, 'I am the one who has said:[239]

You there who ask me where my camels have been going:
they're due to meet some persons down in Yathrib.
I swore an oath: I will not pity them if they get tired
or suffer from sore feet, until I reach Muḥammad.
As soon as you[240] will halt at Hāshim's grandson's door
you will have rest and you'll experience his bounty.
Really, have you[241] not heard the counsel of Muḥammad,
God's prophet, when he counselled, when he testified?
If you don't travel with provisions of God-fearing,
and then see, after your death, someone who has,
Then you'll regret that you are not like him
and did not prepare yourself just as he did.
Beware all carrion, don't touch it![242]
Don't stab a camel with an iron arrow, bleeding it![243]
And don't approach a woman: her hidden, private parts
are not allowed to you; so marry or abstain!
He is a prophet who can see what you can't see; his fame
has reached—upon my life!—the lowlands and the hills.'"

5.3 The Sheikh—may God perfect the adornment of gatherings with his presence!—knows the various interpretations of this last verse. I only mention them because it is possible that some young person who has not heard it before may read this nonsense. Al-Farrā' is the only one to report the verb *aghāra* in the sense of *ghāra*, i.e. "to penetrate into the lowlands." If this verse is really by al-Aʿshā then he merely meant by it the opposite of *anjada*, "to travel to the hills." Two views are transmitted on the authority of al-Aṣmaʿī:[244] one is that *aghāra* means "to run fast"; in his *Book of Related Words* he quotes this verse:

Give up your quest of her; console yourself
with a fleet camel that, when it's spurred on, runs fast.[245]

The other is that the poet in fact used a different word order and said "—upon my life!—it has penetrated deeply (*ghāra*) into the lowlands and the hills," with a metrical shortening.[246] Saʿīd ibn Masʿadah, however, reads *ghāra* for *aghāra*, leaving out the first syllable at the beginning of the second hemistich.[247]

Al-Aʿshā continues, "I said to ʿAlī, 'I already believed in God and the final Reckoning and I believed in the truth of the Resurrection when I still lived in the pre-Islamic times of Ignorance. Hence my verses:[248] 5.4

No bell-ringing monk at a church
he has built, and in which he has crossed himself,
Who has prayed to the King of the World,
now lying prostrate, now wailingly praying,
Is more pious than you at the Reckoning, when
the people, revived, resurrected, will shake off the dust.'

"Then ʿAlī went to the Prophet (God bless and preserve both of them) and said to him, 'Messenger of God! This is al-Aʿshā of the tribe of Qays, whose poem in your praise has been transmitted. He has testified that you are a prophet sent with a message to the world.' The Prophet replied, 'But why did he not come to me in the previous world?' ʿAlī answered, 'He did come, but he was prevented by Quraysh and his love of wine.' Then the Prophet interceded for me and I was allowed to enter Paradise on condition that I should not drink any wine there. I was happy with that, for I have ample compensation with all the honey and the Water of Life. But whoever does not renounce drinking wine in the False World will not be given to drink it in the hereafter."

The Sheikh gazes out upon the meadows of Paradise. He sees two lofty castles and says to himself, "I'll go to these castles and ask to whom they belong." When he is close to them he sees on one of them an inscription that reads: "This castle belongs to Zuhayr ibn Abī Sulmā al-Muzanī" and one on the other that says: "This castle belongs to ʿAbīd ibn al-Abraṣ al-Asadī." He is amazed and says, "Both died in the time of Ignorance, but the mercy of our Lord 5.5.1

embraces everything.[249] I will seek to meet these two men and ask them how it is they were forgiven."

5.5.2 *The conversation with Zuhayr*

He begins with Zuhayr and finds him to be a young man like a flower freshly collected, who has been given a castle of pearls erected. It is as if he has never donned the cloak of decrepitude, nor ever sighed from lassitude. It is as if he never said, in his poem rhyming on *-mī*:[250]

I'm weary of life's burdens. Mind you, he who lives
for eighty years—alas!—gets weary!

or as if he never said, in another poem:

Have you not seen that I have lived for ninety years,
followed by ten I've lived, plus eight?[251]

The Sheikh exclaims, "Rather, rather! You are Kaʿb and Bujayr's father!" Zuhayr says, "Yes, I am." Then the Sheikh (may God keep him strong forever!) asks him, "How is it that you have been forgiven? For you lived in the interval without revelation,[252] when people were like cattle left to their own devices, practising only their vices!" Zuhayr replied, "I shunned falsehood as long as I was living, and I found a Lord who was forgiving. I believed in God Almighty. Once I dreamed and saw a rope that came down from heaven. The people on earth who held fast on to it of were saved.[253] Then I knew that it was a command from God, so I admonished my two sons and said to them, when I was on my deathbed: 'If someone stands up and calls upon you all to serve God, obey him then!' If I had lived to see Muḥammad I would have been the first believer! When Ignorance was still reigning and foolishness still firmly established, I said in my poem rhyming in *-mī*:

Hide not from God what is in your souls, as if
to conceal it! Whatever one hides, God knows!
It's postponed, it is kept in a book and stored
for the Day of Reckoning; or it is quickly avenged."

"But," says the Sheikh, "Did you not also say:

Oft I went out in the morn, at the head of troop of nobles,
 intoxicated, finding whatever we wanted to find.
They trailed behind them their mantles, after the strength
 of the wine in the cups and the singing had crept into them.

"Are you allowed to drink wine, like all others who have eternal life? Or are you forbidden to drink it just as al-Aʿshā of the tribe of Qays?" "That Bakrite," said Zuhayr, "lived in the time of Muḥammad, so he had to conform to the explicit command, because Muḥammad's message included the prohibition of alcoholic drinks and forbidding all ugly things. I died when wine was like any other thing and was drunk by the followers of former prophets. So the command did not concern me."

The Sheikh invites him for a drink and finds him to be a charming drinking companion. He asks him for stories about people from the past. The servant has a pitcher of emerald which contains some wine that has been kept under seal. It is mixed with ginger and water from Paradise's well-spring Salsabīl.[254] The Sheikh says (may God increase the number of his breaths!), "How can this pitcher be compared with the one that al-Sarawī mentions! He said:[255] 5.5.3

We have a pitcher, full,
 a black one, followed by its mug;
Whenever the pitcher yields us less, when it falls dry,
 the clay is broken from another pitcher's seal."

6.1

The conversation with ʿAbīd ibn al-Abraṣ

Then he turns to ʿAbīd. He, too, has been granted a life of eternity to lead.[256] "Greetings, friend of the tribe of Asad!" says the Sheikh. ʿAbīd replies, "Greetings to you too! Perhaps you want to ask me why I have been forgiven?" (Anyone who lives in the Garden has a clever mind; stupid people you will never find!) "Indeed I do," answers the Sheikh. "It is rather odd. Did you find a compelling reason for being forgiven and not being excluded from the mercy of

God?" "I'll tell you," says ʿAbīd, "I had already entered Hell's abyss. But when I was alive on earth I had said,

> He who asks of people will be denied;
> but he who asks of God will not be disappointed.[257]

"This verse traveled to the ends of the earth; it kept being recited, while I was gradually relieved of my pains and freed of my fetters and chains. It was repeated until God's mercy enveloped me through the blessing of this verse. «Our Lord is truly forgiving and merciful»."[258]

When the Sheikh (may God steady his steps!) hears what these two men have to say, he hopes that many different poets have obtained salvation.

6.2.1 *The conversation with ʿAdī ibn Zayd*

He asks ʿAbīd, "Do you know about ʿAdī ibn Zayd al-ʿIbādī?" "Yes," he replies, "He lives nearby, over there!" The Sheikh stops at his place and asks, "How did you cross the Bridging Path[259] and reach salvation, rescued after your life of immoderation?"[260] ʿAdī replies, "I adhered to the religion of Christ. Those who follow the prophets before Muḥammad's mission will come to no harm; but retribution shall come to those who prostrated themselves before idols and who are counted among the ignorant heathens." The Sheikh asks him, "Abū Sawādah, please recite for me your poem rhyming on the letter *ṣ*,[261] for it is one of the extraordinary poems of the Arabs!" Then ʿAdī begins to recite:

6.2.2.1 Inform ʿAbd Hind, my friend:[262] may you stay close
to the black, fertile land of al-Khuṣūṣ,
Facing al-Fūrah, or this side of it,
not distant from Ghumayr al-Luṣūṣ,
Where truffles will be gathered for you in the spring,
in the soft earth, so succulent, between the stems of the *qaṣīṣ*;
Where horses hunt for you and birds as well:
you will not be deprived of some distraction, hunting!

You'll eat what you desire, and drink
wine from al-Ḥuṣṣ, red, colored like gemstones.
May you be far from me, ʿAbd, when times 6.2.2.2
are bad, and kept away when times are difficult!
Do not forget to think of me during the pleasure of
a cup of wine, or when you hunt a fat and bulky she-ass!
You are a man who keeps his pledge, reliable,
refusing to be led by lying, cunning folk.
O ʿAbd, do you remember me a little while,
when riding in procession or when scouting on a hunt,
One day, together with the riders when they hastened,
while we, among them, raised our young she-camel's speed?
A slow man may attain his lucky share,
whereas good things sometimes escape the effort of the keen.
But in your breast you always harbored doubt,
thinking of me, how I might perish or escape.
My soul, spare me! Beware, do not revile the honor of
good people. Wise restraint will not abandon you.
I wish I knew—and I say it loud— 6.2.2.3
when shall I see again the drinkers round a wine vat's base
In a house that's built of broken earthy jugs: cool is its shade;
"gazelles"[263] are there, and palm leaf bins for dates,
And more "gazelles," their sleeves hemmed with brocade,
dragging their steps, the wary walk of one whose sole is hurt.[264]
Musk wafts from their sleeve cuffs, and ambergris,
and *ghalwā* perfume, and sweet storax from Qafūṣ.
A wind-chilled cup of vintage wine is poured for us,
dark, mixed with water of a pool.[265]
Much better that, than guardsmen at the door,
a pair of fetters, and a painful chain around the neck;[266]
Or being raised on top[267] of a male "ostrich,"
ulcered, restive, with a saddle[268]
(It will not fetch a high price at a sale,[269] nor will it
carry a second rider; it is not fed with choicest palm-tree leaves);
Or vultures gathered round the dead,
that eat the flesh, still fresh, between the shoulders and the ribs.

The Sheikh says, "Well done, by God, well done! That's what I think: if you were stagnant water you would never turn stale or stink! There 6.3

is an erudite man of the Islamic period who has composed a poem in this meter;[270] he is known as Abū Bakr Ibn Durayd. He said:

The fortunate are happy; wretched is the greedy one.
No creature can escape his fate.

"In this poem he says,

Where are on earth the kings of Ḥimyar,
the noblest men to whom a she-camel was ever urged?
Jayfar the Spender: destroyed by Time,
forever eager to demolish lofty things.

"But you, Abū Sawādah, are better since you were the first. However, I wish you had not said in your poem 'I wish I knew—and I (*wa-na*, or *wāna*, instead of *wa-ʾana*) say it loud,' because you are doing one of two things. Either you omit the glottal stop of *ʾana*, which is ugly, even though they recite the following verse:

If I don't fight, then dress me (*fa-lbisūnī*, instead of *fa-ʾalbisūnī*)
with a woman's veil
and put four rings on both my hands!

"And you went further than merely dropping the glottal stop, by shortening the vowel after the letter *n*, for if you elide the glottal stop at the beginning of the word, it consists of only one remaining letter, which makes it defective.[271] Or you realize the glottal stop, making it intermediate, but then you dare turn it into a pure long vowel![272] This is enough to violate normal practice. It is the same in the following verse:

They say: 'Gently! This old man has no dependents.'
But look at me, I had dependents, but I'm (*wāna*) childless now.

"If you had said, 'I wish I knew—I say it loud,' without 'and,' it would have been better in my opinion, and more normal." ʿAdī ibn Zayd replies, "I merely said what I have heard the people in my time say. All sorts of new things happened in Islam that we don't know of!"

The Sheikh says, "I see you do not understand my purpose. But I was about to ask you about a line of yours that is quoted as linguistic evidence by Sībawayh. It is when you say:

A farewell in the evening or a morning one?
You—see where you are going!

"Sībawayh claims that 'you' could be taken as a nominative, on account of an implied verb, which is explained by the following word, 'see!' But I think this explanation is far-fetched and not, I think, what you intended."[273] 'Adī exclaims, "O spare me all that nonsense! Actually, I was a great hunter in the Perishable World.

"You may have heard this poem of mine: 6.4.1

Oft I went out in the morning, riding a noble steed, adorned
with a face drained of blood[274] and a cheek like a whetstone,
With the length of his neck raised high,
easily led with the rein in the hand, strong and large, with locks of hair,
Smooth and slim like the shaft of an arrow that has no faults in it
to be seen, and no blemishing cracks:
He who trimmed it has shaped it, the touch of his hands
and the adze's planing have straightened its crookedness.
Whenever a dangerous spot in a fight is feared, it is charged to be there,
and when it is left without being led it is still guarded well,
As if brought up at home; its saddle blanket is torn
by obediently eating its wheat and drinking its milk.
We looked after it until, in the winter, it was in a happy mood,
stubbornly pacing and prancing.
Whenever a wild ass would roam,
or an ostrich, that fled at its first appearance,
A horse at the start of its run that amazed us would take us
so fast that we don't have to hide and seek cover in bushes.[275]

It combines a fast running, let loose like a downpour,
like a rainfall amassed, with a rapid pace(?)[276]
A brisk, fast horse that overtakes the young calves;
while biting its bridle it reaches the herd, not weakened.[277]
He who holds it will praise it,
an excitable, noble horse, like a lion, its halter stretched.
And when we have caught four beasts
a beggar for food will be guided by smoke from our fire.

6.4.2 "Or this poem, rhyming in *-āqī*:

A meadow, well rained-upon, that has blazed
into blossom, like the color of tufts of wool in sacks,
After an autumn season with rain from Aquarius, which
descended in buckets; the 'bucket handles' did not remain
hidden.[278]
The only blemishes there:[279] the places of ostriches' eggs, in which
some chicks sprouted down, between the cracked shells,
And the energy of the wild bulls around the cows
with their calves, defending themselves with their horns.
You can see them, like mighty men in a meeting,
or when they recline, at ease.
In that meadow I would ramble, with under my hands
a horse that often rides out, which excels in a race,
A tractable horse, a strong, large one, quick
in running, robust in his legs, and firm in his bones,
One not ridden during the midday heat,
not bridled for idle strolls or frivolous, trivial things,
But led only to any desirable aim, whenever it occurs,
or to war, when it tucks up its skirt.
It catches a milk-rich oryx cow in front
of the riders, a match for a far-roaming bull,
And an ostrich, big, with bare extra toes,[280] a young one,
its brain being close to its tearducts.

"Now, would you like us to mount two horses of Paradise and to drive them toward herds of wild cows, strings of ostriches, flocks of gazelles, and droves of onagers? For hunting is a pleasure for which I surely have raised your appetite!" But the Sheikh says, "I am a man of pen and peace, not a horse-riding type! I am not a man for ostentation and all that hype. I have come to visit you at your place to congratulate you on having been saved from Hell, you who, through the Merciful One's pardon, are now blessed and well! I do not want to take the risk of mounting a noble steed that is brisk, who has fed on pastures paradisiacal and has turned wild and demoniacal! I am like the one who said,[281] 6.5

They never rode horses until they were old;
now they sit heavily, clumsily on their steeds' flanks.

"I might suffer the same that befell Jalam, the friend of al-Mutajarridah,[282] when he was made to ride al-Yaḥmūm: doing what one is not wont to do leads to one's doom. You have heard what happened to the son of Zuhayr, who broke his neck when he fell from the courser Dhū l-Mayr. He rode out on a high road, but it did not avail him that his brother Kaʿb lamented him in an ode. Likewise your own son, ʿAlqamah, who came to grief in the Fleeting World when, hunting he went for a ride, and became like his grandfather Zayd.[283] You said of him:

Good morning to you, ʿAlqamah, the son of ʿAdī!
Have you stayed at home today and not departed?[284]

"I am bewildered, all you Arabs, about what reliable informants have transmitted about all these metrical variations, used by subsequent generations; and about your poem that rhymes in *-r*:[285]

Now it is time to sober up or else you'll be remiss;
ages have passed since those old times you spent
With girls with sparkling rings, with bracelets that
appeared upon their flashing wrists,

White-skinned, in silken clothes, and at their necks,
below the earlobes, pearls.

"The swiftly running horse may throw me on to the emerald rocks, breaking my arm or leg! I would be the laughingstock to the people of the Garden."

6.6 ʿAdī smiles. "Come now! Don't you know that of accidents in Paradise one need have no fear, and that mishaps never happen to those that dwell here!" So they mount two fleet coursers from among the horses of Paradise. If either were compared with all the empires of the Fleeting World, from the first to the last, it would outweigh them and be more valuable. When our Sheikh sees a herd that grazes on the leas of Paradise (and "leas" means "meadows") he aims his javelin (which is a short spear) toward a flat-nosed, long-tailed oryx bull, who there did graze for long nights and days. When there is but a mere nail's length between it and the spear point, the bull says, "Stop! God have mercy upon you! I am not one of the wild beasts created by God, praised be He, those that never existed in the Transitory World. But I lived in the abode of delusion; while I was searching pasture grounds in some wasteland or other, a caravan of believers came past. Their provisions had run out, so they killed me. They survived their journey because of me, and therefore God (exalted be His word) gave me compensation by making me dwell in Eternity." Thus our lord, the venerable Sheikh, spares him.

He then at a wild ass aims his spear, from which he has nothing to fear. However, when the tip of the spear is no more than a fingertip away from it, the ass says, "Stop, servant of God! For God has blessed me and saved me from harm. That was because once a hunter hunted me with a scythe; it was my skin that he was keen to make his prize. He sold it in a certain town, where somebody cut the skin down, to make a bucket for a waterwheel, which many an ailing person with its water did heal. With it, pious people performed their ablutions. So the blessings of all these encompassed me and I entered the Garden, where I subsist without any reckoning."

The Sheikh says, "You ought to distinguish yourself, for those of you that have lived in the Perishable World ought not to mix with the beasts of the Garden." The wild ass replies, "You have given us good advice, like a kind friend. We shall do as you tell us."

Our lord, the venerable Sheikh and his companion, ʿAdī, proceed. 7.1

The conversation with Abū Dhuʾayb al-Hudhalī

They see a man who is milking a camel in a pail of gold. "Who is this man?" they ask, and he answers, "Abū Dhuʾayb, of the tribe of Hudhayl." They say, "Long life and joy! May you never be unhappy in your life and never die!—But are you milking, with all these rivers of milk around? That does not seem sound!" "That is all right," he replies, "It occurred to me, just as it occurred to you to go hunting. I was thinking of the verses I composed on the olden times:

> Words from you—if only you knew—are honey
> of bees in milk of suckling camels,
> Mothers of calves firstborn and newly born,
> and mixed with water found in mountain streams.

"Then this she-camel that has given birth to her first young was for me by the Omnipotent God decreed, Whose blessings are guaranteed. So I got up and milked as usual. And now I want to mix it with the honey of bees that in the Garden followed their king bee."[286]

As soon as his pail is filled with milk, by the Creator (exalted is His glory) a beehive made of precious stones is formed, of which the pasturing bees over flowers have swarmed. Abū Dhuʾayb gathers the honey and mixes it with the milk. "Will you not drink?" he asks them. They drink from his pail a few mouthfuls so nice—had it been distributed among the inhabitants of Hell, they would have been as if in Paradise. ʿAdī says, "«Praise be to God Who has guided us to this! We would not have been guided to it if God had not guided us.

The messengers of our Lord came with the Truth. It is proclaimed to them: This is the Garden that you have been given as inheritance for what you used to do.»"[287]

7.2 The Sheikh (may God make his abilities last!) says to ʿAdī: "There are two things in your poetry that I wish you had not said! One is your verse

In the summer it rends the covering on its back;
it humiliates the horses in the racecourse; brisk, and well-proportioned.[288]

"The other is your verse:

Would that you had dispelled my worries for a while!
For then, in spite of what one could imagine, both of us would have been happy."[289]

ʿAdī replies in his ʿIbādī dialect,[290] "Got help you! You have been blesst with somesing zat ought to distract you from poetry. You ought to behafe as it is sait: «Eat and drink with relish, for what you used to do.»"[291] He said "*magbūr*," i.e., *majbūr*, turning the *j* into a *g*, which is a bad dialect pronunciation, used by the people in Yemen.[292] It is said in some tradition that al-Ḥārith ibn Hāniʾ ibn Abī Shamir ibn Jabalah al-Kindī, in the midst of the fray at the battle of Sābāṭ, exclaimed "Ḥugr, hey, Ḥugr!", meaning Ḥujr ibn ʿAdī al-Adbar, who turned to him and rescued him. ʿAdī also said *yagibu*, i.e., *yajibu*.

The Sheikh says (may God increase the number of his breaths!), "I have asked my Lord the Almighty not to deprive me in the Garden of the pleasure I have in my literary erudition, from which I derived such pleasure in my ephemeral life; and He has answered my prayer. «Praise be to Him in heaven and on earth, in the evening and at noontide»."[293]

7.3 *The conversation with the two Nābighahs, al-Dhubyānī and al-Ja'dī*

Continuing his excursion the Sheikh meets two young men who are talking together. They stand each at a palace with a pearly door free of any damage or flaw. He greets them and says, "Who are you? May God have mercy upon you!—but He has done so already!" They answer, "We are the two Nābighahs, al-Nābighah of the tribe of Ja'dah and al-Nābighah of the tribe of Dhubyān."[294] The Sheikh says (may God steady his steps!), "Al-Nābighah of Ja'dah has deserved his present state by his adherence to the true religion. But what's with thee, Abū Umāmah?" (He means: "What about you?"). Al-Dhubyānī replies, "I used to profess belief in God and I have been on pilgrimage to the Kaaba before the coming of Islam. Surely you have heard my verses:

No, by the life of Him whom I visited in pilgrimages,
by the blood that was shed on the sacrificial stones,
And by Him who protects the shelter-seeking birds, where the stones
of the Kaaba are stroked by Mecca's riders between al-Ghayl and al-Sanad![295]

"I also said:

I swear, not leaving any doubt within your mind
(Can any pious man obedient to God commit a sin?),
By camels drinking in the morning at Laṣāf and Thabrah
coming to Ilāl, while struggling keeping up the pace.

"I have not lived long enough to meet the Prophet (God bless and preserve him) so I cannot be accused of having acted against his commands. God, whose names be sanctified, mighty and glorious King, forgives great sins for the sake of a little thing."

7.4.1 The Sheikh (may his speech always be lofty!) says, "Abū Sawādah, Abū Umāmah, and Abū Laylā,[296] let us have a drink together! Our worthy 'Ibādī poet has said,

My heart, divert yourself with pleasure:
I long for music and for listening,
And for imperial Persian wine:[297] when tasted by
an old man he will sing and swing his body!

"He also said,

Music, appreciated even by old men,
and conversation sweet like honey gathered from the hive.

"But we want Abū Baṣīr, how do we get him here?"[298] He has not finished speaking, when who does appear but Abū Baṣīr! He is the fifth of the company. They praise and sanctify God, thanking Him for bringing them all together. The Sheikh (may God spread beauty through his longevity!) recites this Qur'anic verse: «He is able to gather them whenever He wishes».[299]

7.4.2 While they are eating from the good things of the Garden and drinking its wine, which God has stored for His God-fearing servants, he says (may God subdue the noses of those that snub him!), "Abū Umāmah, you have a sound judgement and you are intelligent, so how could you find it proper to say to al-Nuʿmān ibn al-Mundhir:[300]

The great man stated that her mouth is cool
and sweet; whenever you taste it, you say: more!
The great man stated (I've not tasted it myself):
a parched man will recover through the coolness of her gums.

"And then you went on to say things such that everyone, high and low, condemned you!"[301]

Al-Nābighah, sensibly and intelligently, replies: "Those who found fault with me have wronged me. If they were fair they would understand that I had been extremely careful. Al-Nuʿmān was besotted with that woman and he told me to describe her in my verse. I turned it over in my mind and said to myself: If I depict her in terms that are general, they could be applied not merely to her but to several. However, I was afraid to mention her name in verse, because the king would not agree, for kings do not like their women to be mentioned. So I thought I would put her description into his mouth and say 'The great man stated,' for if I had omitted to mention him the listener would think that my description was based on personal observation. The verses that follow still belong to the description by the 'great man.' Therefore, if one considers the sense one will find it to be not incorrect. But how do people recite my verse,

When I look I see a shining moon[302]

"and what follows?"

The Sheikh (may God humble his haters!) says, "We recite it as 'when you look,' 'when you touch,' 'when you stab,' and 'when you withdraw,' all in the second person singular." "That is a possibility," admits al-Nābighah, "but it is better to put it in the first person singular, as direct speech in quotation, because when I say 'the great man stated' it means 'the great man said.' That is safer; for then the king himself is the speaker. But when you read it in the second person it is improper: if you attribute the words to me it would be an affront to him, and if you attribute them to al-Nuʿmān it would be shameful and lacking in respect."

"Bravo, star of the tribe of Murrah!" says the Sheikh (May God lend assistance to virtue through prolonging his term!), "but the learned transmitters of your verse have corrupted it. I wish they were all here, Abū ʿAmr al-Māzinī, Abū ʿAmr al-Shaybānī, Abū ʿUbaydah, ʿAbd al-Malik,[303] and the other transmitters of poetry, that I could ask them in your presence how they read the lines, and you could know I neither falsely accuse you nor put a slur on you."

No sooner has he impressed these words on Abū Umāmah's 7.4.3
audile organs than all the transmitters of poetry are made to appear at God Almighty's call, without any trouble or effort to them at all. They greet politely and gracefully. The Sheikh (may God raise the

prestige of his words!) asks them, "Who are these paradisial persons?" "We are the transmitters," they reply, "those whose presence you have just now requested!" "There is no god but God," exclaims the Sheikh, "He who forms and records everything, praise be to God who resurrects and inherits,[304] blessed be God who is almighty and does not betray! How do you read, O deceased gentlemen—God rest your souls—the verses by al-Nābighah in his poem rhyming on *d*: 'when you (or I) look,' 'when you (or I) touch,' 'when you (or I) stab,' and 'when you (or I) withdraw:' do you read them as second or first person singular?" "As second person singular," they answer. The Sheikh continues, "Here is our master poet, Abū Umāmah, and he prefers the first person singular. He informs me that it is direct speech put into the mouth of al-Nuʿmān." The transmitters say, "That is as it is said in the Holy Book: «The matter rests with you, so consider what you will command.»"[305]

7.5 The Sheikh says (may God grant him success in whatever he says!), "Enough said about this, Abū Umāmah. But recite for us your poem that begins:

Alight, you two,[306] on the rain-soaked desolate meadow,
where once, in springtime, al-Mutajarridah stayed!
Anointed with musk she is, with hennaed hands and feet,
while pearls and rubies are hanging around her neck.
Her teeth—but I never tasted them—seem
like honey of bees mixed with chilled wine:
May al-Nuʿmān be happy with her! She's a blessing
to him, renewed from day to day!"

"I don't remember ever to have walked that path," replies Abū Umāmah.[307] Then our master, the Sheikh (may God adorn his days by making him live forever!) says, "Amazing! Who is it then who has knowingly attributed them to you?" "It was not done knowingly," says al-Nābighah, "but it was a mistake, a false assumption. Perhaps the verses are by a man of the tribe of Thaʿlabah ibn Saʿd."[308]

Then the other al-Nābighah, of the tribe of Ja'dah, joins in and says, "Once, in the days before the coming of Islam, a young man accompanied me; we were going to al-Ḥīrah. He recited this poem, as his own composition. He told me that he belonged to the tribe of Tha'labah ibn 'Ukābah.[309] But when he arrived, King al-Nu'mān was ill and he was not granted access to him." Al-Nābighah al-Dhubyānī remarks, "In all probability that is what happened."

The Sheikh (may God write down for him the recompense of the god-fearing!) says to al-Nābighah of the Banū Ja'dah, "Abū Laylā, recite to us your poem on the rhyme letter *sh*,[310] in which you say: 7.6.1

I often went out in the morning with drinking companions
proud, before the grass's verdancy was seen.
A wineskin with us, to a trencher of palm fronds, laid
with dishes both fresh and dried.
We dismounted on a wide and deserted plain,
that was touched by dew, by rain and by drizzle.
With us was a singing girl, chanting to us,
her ample behind not in need of a woollen bustle.
And then we suddenly saw a herd of fleeing oryxes,
and a string of ostriches, black like Ethiopians.
We brought with us a servant who helped us,
riding a fast and loudly neighing horse.
We said to him, 'Go, catch the quarry with it! Then you
will win, through us, your loved one and live happily!'
He brought us a sprightly oryx bull
and a male ostrich with a dam of a fawn.
We roasted the tender, tasty meat,
«a reward unfailing»,[311] and returned at dusk."

But al-Nābighah of the Banū Ja'dah replies, "I have never composed any poetry on this rhyme letter! And there are words in this poem that I have never heard myself: 'verdancy,' 'trencher,' 'dam of fawns,' indeed!"

Our master, the erudite, learning-loving Sheikh says, "Abū Laylā, You were familiar with the diction of the eloquent for so long! But you have been too busy drinking wine—a wine not found in Babel nor in Adhri'āt[312]—and you have been diverted by the meat of birds that feed on the meadows of Paradise, and now you have forgotten all you knew. However, you cannot be blamed if you have forgotten it: «The people of the Garden are busy today, rejoicing, they and their spouses on couches, reclining. There they have fruit and all for which they are calling.»

"As for the word *rabash* ('verdancy'), it is derived from the expression *arḍ rabshā'* ('verdant land'), when vegetation is visible on it; it seems to be an inversion of *barshā'* ('verdant'). A *summahah* ('trencher, or mat of palm fronds') is like a *sufrah* ('traveler's provision bag') made of palm leaves. Finally, *khushash* ('fawn'), as mentioned by Abū 'Amr al-Shaybānī in his lexicon, means 'young of a gazelle.'

7.6.2 "And how do you recite your verse:

It would not be proper for us to bring them back
in sound condition, nor reprehensible to have them slaughtered.[313]

"Do you read *mustankaran* ('reprehensible') in the accusative, or *mustankarin*, with a genitive?"

Al-Ja'dī replies, "In the accusative." "But what will you do," continues the Sheikh, "if someone recites it in the genitive?" "I would chide and reprimand him for speaking of things he does not understand!" The Sheikh says to himself (may God lengthen the extent of his life!), "«We belong to God and to Him we return!» [314] Sībawayh must have been mistaken about this verse, I think, because Abū Laylā al-Ja'dī lived both before and after the coming of Islam. Hence, as a young lad he was fed and bred on a diet of pure diction and eloquence."

7.7 The Sheikh turns to al-A'shā of Qays and says to him, "Abū Baṣīr, recite to us your poem:

Is there a dwelling place, now uninhabited,
of Qatlah midst the sand dunes?
It is as if this plump and white-skinned woman
never walked there with her tribe!
Languid she was; a look at her would make
a monk prostrate himself in awe.
A reddish wine from ʿĀnah,
carried in a wineskin,
(its vine was tended by a ruddy man,
who watered it each morning),
Stored in its cask for many years,
but now brought out and 'killed'
With water from a rain cloud bright,
cooled by the northern wind:
Such wine is to a thirsty man not more delicious
than you are—if only you could be available!"

Al-Aʿshā of Qays says, "This does not come from me! You seem to have developed a taste for spurious poems today!"

8.1 *The geese of Paradise*

A gaggle of heavenly geese goes by. Immediately they descend on that meadow and stand as if awaiting a command. Since the birds in the Garden are able to speak, the Sheikh asks them, "What do you want?" They reply, "We have been inspired to alight in this meadow in order to sing to those that are drinking there." "With God Almighty's blessing!" says the Sheikh. They shake off their plumage and turn into full-breasted girls, who strut in the garden, an embroidery of flowers. They carry lutes and instruments for musical entertainment. The Sheikh is amazed, and with reason; but it is in fact not so wonderful, coming as it does from the omnipotence of God the Glorious, whose Word is mighty, whose blessings flow abundantly on the world, whose mercy encompasses every thing, and whose vengeance falls on the unbeliever.

8.2 The Sheikh says to one of them, to test them, "Sing for us, in the 'first heavy' rhythmical mode, the verse by Abū Umāmah, that man who is sitting over there:

> Will someone come from Mayyah's clan, in the evening or morning,
> in a hurry, with provisions or without any food?"[315]

The girl does this. With her music she enraptures; the listener, in whose limbs it creeps, it captures. An idol, carved from stone, or a tambourine sawn by a carpenter, if, by any chance, they heard that song would dance. If they stood on high they would fall, and if they broke their necks they would not mind at all. The Sheikh (may God send all kinds of lovely things into his heart!) is faced with marvellous scenes that cannot be resisted by any means. "Come on," he says, "let's now have it in the 'light first heavy' mode!" The girl starts to sing, with a melody such that if heard by al-Gharīḍ he would have to concede that by comparison his own singing was feeble indeed. When the girl, to general admiration, has exceeded expectation, he says, "And now let the 'second heavy' mode follow suit, between the second and third strings of your lute!" She proceeds in a manner such that if ʿAbd Allāh ibn Jaʿfar had heard it, he would have to declare that the songs of Budayḥ could only compare to a camel's blare. When the Sheikh realizes this he exclaims, "God be praised! Whenever His omnipotence is made clear, unsurpassable marvels appear. And now turn to the 'light second heavy'! For you are doing a truly excellent thing; you banish slumber when you sing!" When she does what he has told her to do, she produces things that are fearfully good,[316] and says to the people, "Are you not in a cheerful mood?" Then he suggests that she should use the *ramal* mode and its "light" variety, and its brother the *hazaj* with its fast modality. All these eight modes to the ears she does impart, a master in her art.

When the Sheikh knows how well she can execute, and is aware of her skill with the lute, he proceeds to state that there is no god but God, that God is great, and that his Lord be praised, for he is truly amazed. "Mind you," he says to her, "weren't you a goose just now, that was flying? Then God turned you into a rightly guided being, no longer straying! So how did you acquire this skill? You seem to be an intimate friend of the soul's thrill. Even if you had grown up between Maʿbad and Ibn Surayj, with such exciting songs you would not have been able to oblige! How could you shed the goose's stupidity and excite your listeners with such rapidity?" She answers, "What have you seen then of your Creator's omnipotence? You are on the beach of a sea so wide that one cannot reach the other side. Praised be He «who revives the bones when they are decayed»!"[317]

8.3.1 *The first conversation with Labīd*

While they are talking like this, a young man passes by. In his hand he holds a ruby crook, which through a divine decree he took. He greets them and they ask, "Who are you?" "I am Labīd ibn Rabīʿah ibn Kilāb," he replies. "Noble man! Noble man!" they say, "Why did you not merely say 'Labīd'? For more there is no need: your first name has sufficient fame. How did you obtain the forgiveness of your Lord?" Labīd says, "I live here, God be praised, a life of which every description would fail. I have servants, female and male. Youth that does not fade, a life that does not jade!" The Sheikh says, "Blessed be the Holy King, whose certainty cannot be guessed by any intuiting! It is as if you never said in the Perishable World:

> Tired I am of life and of its length,
> of people asking, 'How's Labīd?'

"Or as if you never uttered these words:

> Whenever I may die—I do not care.
> Enough, this life of mine now, enough!
> A life so long we're tired of it;
> A lengthy life is apt to be found tiresome.

"Please recite to us your poem rhyming in *m*, the *Muʿallaqah*!" But Labīd replies, "Out of the question! I gave up poetry in the Treacherous World[318] and I shall not return to it in the Hereafter, now that I have been given something in return that is better and more righteous."

8.3.2 "Tell me then," says the Sheikh, "about your verse:

Abandoning places when I don't like them
or when some soul is bound to its death

"when you say 'some soul,' do you mean 'any soul'?" "No," answers Labīd, "I meant my own soul. It is just as when you say to a man, 'If your money is gone someone will give you money,' meaning in fact you yourself even though the literal meaning is 'any person,' or 'any group that is part of mankind.'"

The Sheikh says (may his opponent always be silenced), "Tell me about your words 'or when . . . is bound (*aw yartabiṭ*)': do you mean 'when I don't like them or when . . . is not bound,' where the verb is dependent on *lam* ('not'), or do you intend 'abandoning places when I don't like them,' so that *aw yartabiṭ* ('unless . . . is bound') is to be connected with 'abandoning places?'" Labīd replies, "I intended the former."[319]

Then the Sheikh (may God enlarge his share of reward!) asks, "What do you mean with your words:

A morning drink of clear wine, and a lute-playing girl who plays upon
a stringed instrument, adjusted by her thumb (*ta'tāluhū ibhāmuhā*)

"For people have read this verse in two ways. Some read it as *ta'tāluhū* ('adjusting it'), deriving the form from the verb *āla*, 'to lead, conduct (something).'[320] Others read it as *ta'tā lahū* ('to which [the thumb] comes'), from the verb *atā* 'to come.'"[321] Labīd answers, "Both readings are possible." The Sheikh says (may God spite those who envy him!), "Abū 'Alī al-Fārisī[322] used to claim that the form *ta'tā* is like saying *istaḥā, yastaḥī* ('to be ashamed'),[323] in the opinion of al-Khalīl and Sībawayh, because they think that *istaḥaytu* ('I was ashamed') is formed on the analogy of *istaḥāya*,[324] just as *istaqamtu*

('I was upright') is based on *istaqāma* ('he was upright'). This is a curious view; he believes that *ta'tā* is derived from the verb *awā* ('to seek refuge'), as if it were from form VIII of it: the verb would them be *i'tāya,* in which the *W* is made weak, as it is when we say: *iʿtāna* ('to help one another'), from the word *ʿawn* ('help'),[325] or *iqtāla* ('to choose') from the word *qawl* ('word, speech'). Then one says *i'taytu* ('I sought refuge'), in which the long vowel is shortened, just as *iqtāla* becomes *iqtaltu* ('I chose'), and then, in the future tense,[326] it is pronounced with elision, just as one says *yastaḥī.*"[327]

Labīd answered, "Someone who objects to a phenomenon that does not concern him! The matter is easier than this fussy pedant thinks."

Labīd turns to al-Aʿshā and says, "God be praised, Abū Baṣīr! Having confessed to you-know-what, have you been forgiven and are you now in the Garden of Eden?" Our master the Sheikh speaks on behalf of al-Aʿshā, "You seem to refer, Abū ʿAqīl, to al-Aʿshā's verses: 8.4

I'm drinking in the countryside—so that they say:
He has been staying in the country for some time!—
A wine from Ṣarīfūn that is delicious,
poured out 'twixt cup and jug.
And I amused myself with pretty girls,
either through marriage or by whoring.

"And his verse:

I spent the night being her husband's substitute,
and of that woman's master too, and hers as well!

"And his verses:

I kept an eye on her, while he kept guarding her,
until, the darkness closing in, I too came close,
And, aiming for the moment that his eyes were heedless of his sheep,
I struck her in the depths of heart and spleen.

"There are more such verses of his that have been transmitted. Now there are two possibilities: either al-Aʿshā said all this merely to compose good poetry, according to the conventions of the poets, or he did actually do these things and he has been forgiven. «Say: O my servants, who have been profligate against themselves, do not despair of God's mercy! God forgives sins altogether. He is the Forgiving, the Compassionate.»[328] and «God does not forgive anything being associated with Him, but He forgives what is less than that to whomsoever He wishes. Whoever associates anything with God has gone far astray»."[329]

8.5.1 The Sheikh (may God make his voice sound loudly!) continues, addressing al-Nābighah al-Jaʿdī: "Abū Laylā, I like these verses of yours:

Lovely she smells, even when you see her without warning,
  in every situation, when she sleeps or when she breathes on you.
It is as if her mouth, when she is woken,
  with her sweet nose and her fine teeth,
Has been cleaned with aromatic wood[330]
  from Haylān or Barāqish or a slender stick of the wild olive tree:
Camomile flowers on a dune, set in
  a vein of silver ore and raisin wine, by light rain watered,[331]
With rain-cloud water from the well in Dawmah, which
  was poured down[332] on a cold night when the north wind blew,
Mixed with an old and potent,
  wormwood-flavored wine[333] that one has little cause to rue,
To which two doses have been added: one of Dārīn musk,
  and one of burning pepper,
Sent to the tawny-shouldered amphora, which is then sealed
  stored in the clay, and where the wine ferments,
Black like a donkey's back,[334] stripped by
  the farrier; not acid, and not whirring(?).[335]
In it, raging against it, the wine rumbles, like
  the repeated roaring of an agitated stallion.

"How could the sweet smell of the woman described in these lines be compared with the fragrance of these «loving, well-matched women»[336] that you see here? Impossible, by God! How can the familiar be compared with the novel and strange? How would her mouth, of which we have heard, compare with those mouths never sullied by a base word? The damsels surpass that girl just as a castaway pebble is surpassed by a safely kept pearl, or as blessings to be won are superior to accidental matters one should shun. I say, what is this 'vein of silver ore' of yours, and your 'raisin wine'? Your loved one in the Fleeting World is not so fine! A mouth that requires regular cleaning with twigs of the balsam tree[337] is to its owner quite a bit of a liability! If its teeth were not covered with plaque and filth, there would be no need for twigs of terebinth, much sought, or of branches of the wild olive tree from afar to these parts brought. And what makes this water from Dawmah that you describe excel, whereas there is nothing wrong with water from any other well? Does it not, if left standing, turn stale, to the drinker of no avail, if he tarries for a while? If the north wind stops making it cool, it becomes like the water in any stagnant pool, into which the wind blows dirt and what not, and which the shimmering afternoon heat makes piping hot. And what is this 'mixed potent wine,' even if the drinkers like pilgrims to it incline? May your wishes always be favored—but spare us your claret 'wormwood-flavored'! How often did you, with your friends get drunk and then repent, all your wealth having been spent! What is this 'old wine' of yours and your 'two doses?' May darkness be removed from your sight! If the musk of Dārīn were to enter the Garden of our Lord, given to those who do not stubbornly doubt, it would on its soil with its pleasant flavor be deemed the filth scraped off a foot or the stink of a cadaver! You said that the wine was spiced with pepper as a condiment, whereas another poet compared it to a whiff of carnation scent. But this place here where we dwell does so sweetly smell that it will excel, not tenfold but many, many times impossible to tell, the smell of the Perishable World. But let's hope this wine of yours will not be stored in a 'tawny-shouldered 8.5.2

amphora'! He who keeps it must be deemed misguided. Then it came to be 'marked[338] in its clay'; he who was watching it put marks on it. Then it became 'black like a donkey's back': may it not be kept in good order for the wine-merchant, its hoarder! It is not 'acid' but it is bad, condemned by any pious Muslim as well as one who sits in the courtyard of a monk's cell. The ruddy, pressed must 'rumbles' in it, close to giving birth, surely, like camel calves, not born prematurely! When it has reached the age it cuts its first teeth, it ceases its rumbling sound, and someone will make the cup go round."

9.1 *The singing of the damsels*

The Sheikh (may God cause all manner of benefaction to him and kindle all hearts with affection for him!) thinks of the singing girls in Fustat and the "City of Well-being," Baghdad. He remembers how they performed the poem rhyming on *m* by al-Mukhabbal al-Saʿdī.[339] Spontaneously those girls—those who by God's omnipotence were changed from the shape of pecking birds into shapely black-eyed girls—burst out intoning al-Mukhabbal's verses:

He thought of al-Rabāb—the thought of her was misery;
he longed for her, but he who longs lacks a firm will.[340]
Whenever her nightly phantom visits me
my eyes are hurt, my tear ducts overflow,
With tears like pearls let loose—strung on a string,
but now the string has let them down.

Any consonant, any vowel that passes gives delight such that if it was matched with all the delights of the people of the Fleeting World since God created Adam until the time He folded up his descendants on earth, it would exceed them just as the billows of the deep sea exceed a toddler's tear, or as a lofty mountain exceeds a speck of dust that one flicks off one's saddle blanket. He says to his drinking companions, "Listen to al-Mukhabbal al-Saʿdī's verses:

She who blames me says (she does not know
about tomorrow and of what comes after it):

'Wealth is the life eternal! Poverty
 will bring a man near to his death.'[341]
But even if you built for me the fort of al-Mushaqqar, on
 a mountaintop unscalable to ibex goat,
My doom would seek me out and find me there:
 there's no decree like God's decree.

"Poor man! He composed these verses while mankind lived in the abode of tribulations, careworn, their hands gripping afflictions' thorn. A mother feared for the life of her child, always grieving, terror in her heart never leaving. Poverty was feared and kept at bay; wealth sought and made to stay. Famine was found there, and burning thirst, and people blind from birth; feet chapped like truffles, rough. Jealousy reigned unbridled, and no one dwelled in a garden, pardoned and forgiven. «Praise be to God who removed from us all sorrow. Our Lord is truly forgiving and thankful; who, of His bounty, has made us dwell in the Lasting Abode, where no weariness touches us and where no fatigue touches us».[342] Blessed be God the Holy One! He has changed each girl who sings from a creature with wings into a woman with a bum that swings! Then He, with His wisdom, inspired them with the knowledge of poems they had never heard before, which they performed with perfection, with various tunes for every section, with musical melodies, free from vulgar linguistic and grammatical maladies. When in the Fleeting World a girl was perceived to be gifted and was given a teacher who taught her the rhythmical modes, the 'heavy' and the 'light,' her instruction being 'heavy' rather than 'light,' she would spend a full month with her before the girl could perform even one or two verses of love poetry (pure lies, all untrue!), and then she is taught at most a hundred or two! Praised, therefore, be He who is able to do anything that is arduous, and who by His grace distinguishes anything that is virtuous!" 9.2

An altercation in Paradise

Al-Nābighah of the Jaʿdah tribe, who has been sitting and listening, asks al-Aʿshā, "Abū Baṣīr, this Rabāb who is mentioned by al-Mukhabbal al-Saʿdī, and the Rabāb that you mention in your poem, 9.3.1

He[343] disobeys reproaching women and bestows
with open hands and generously gives, proud and relaxed.
No sooner crows the cock than I have filled
the cup of al-Rabāb for him,[344] and it goes round.
Whenever a radiant wine is poured amidst the servants,
is what they hand to one another silver or gold?

"Are they the same woman?"

Al-Aʿshā replies, "You have lived for too long, Abū Laylā! I think you have become old and dotty, and have remained thus until today.[345] Don't you know that there are innumerable women called al-Rabāb? Do you really think that this Rabāb is the same as the one in these verses:

Why is it, Rabāb, that your people are looking
askance, narrow-eyed, as if they were angry?
They have guarded you jealously. Why?
For around you lies nothing but desolate desert.

". . . or the same as the one mentioned by Imru' al-Qays:

An abode of Hind and al-Rabāb and Fartanā,
and of Lamīs, before Time struck with all its vagaries.

". . . or perhaps her mother is Umm al-Rabāb in another verse by Imru' al-Qays:[346]

And her neighbor, Umm al-Rabāb, in Ma'sal."

9.3.2 Al-Nābighah al-Jaʿdī replies, "How dare you talk to me like that, you bastard of Ḍubayʿah![347] You died as an unbeliever and you have confessed to immoralities; whereas I have met the Prophet (God bless and preserve him) and I have recited a poem to him, in which I say:

We, with our glory and splendor, have reached the sky;
but we desire a state that is still higher yet.

"The Prophet then asked, 'Where would you go, Abū Laylā?' And I answered, 'To Paradise, with you, Messenger of God!' Then the Prophet said, 'Well spoken, God bless you!'[348] Has it gone to your head that you have been ranked by some ignoramus as the fourth of the great poets?[349] In preferring you he has lied: I am more prolific than you, and more versatile too! I have composed more verses than any Arab before me; you merely amuse yourself with malicious stuff, slandering the women of your own tribe. Or, if you spoke the truth, shame on you and those who are with you! That woman from the tribe of Hizzān was fortunate that you got rid of her, having lived with a barking night-blind dog that prowled among the tribal tents seeking discarded bones and looking to dig up graves in lonely spots!"[350]

"How dare you say that!" says al-Aʿshā angrily. "But one verse composed by me is worth one hundred of yours. You may have been prolix, but a prolix poet is like someone who gathers firewood at night.[351] I am rooted in the tribe of Rabīʿat al-Faras whereas you are from Jaʿdah; and what is Jaʿdah but a party of ostrich hunters? Are you upbraiding me for eulogizing kings? If you had been capable of doing that, you fool, you would have left your wife and children for it. But you are a natural coward and a weakling. You are not one to set out in the dark night, you will not travel in the scorching midday heat. You mentioned my divorce from the woman of Hizzān; but she was sorry to part from me. And divorce is not shameful, neither to common people nor to kings."

"Shut up!" says al-Jaʿdī, "you nobody, son of nobody! I swear, 9.3.3
your entry into the Garden is an abominable thing. But divine decisions happen as God wills. You deserve to be in the lowest reach of the Fire, where better people than you now roast. If it were possible to think that the Lord of Might had made a mistake, I would say that a mistake was made in your case. Did you not say:

I entered when the watchman slept, and spent
the night, while no clothes were between us.

When, finally, she gave herself to sleep,
after her playfulness,
I turned my mind to her two halves,
each one desirable!
I bent a neck like that of an innocent creature[352]
and touched what was inside her underclothes:
Just like a scent box, pale,
its fragrance mixed with liquid perfume.
And see! she had a cup
raised to receive the wine![353]

"You despise the Banū Jaʿdah; yet one of their battle-days alone outweighs all the efforts of your tribe! You have asserted that I am a coward: you lied! I am braver than you and your father, I can better endure traveling on a freezing night, and I go further into the scorching midday heat."

9.3.4 Al-Nābighah al-Jaʿdī pounces upon Abū Baṣīr al-Aʿshā and strikes him with a golden beaker. The Sheikh (may God give peace through him, at his hands!) says, "No quarreling in Paradise! That is only known in the Perishable World, among the lower classes and the ignorant. You, Abū Laylā, are a hothead. There is a story about you: a man in Basra shouted 'Men of Qays!' whereupon you, al-Nābighah al-Jaʿdī, came with a little stick. You were apprehended by the constables of the governor, Abū Mūsā al-Ashʿarī, who had you flogged, because the Prophet (God bless and preserve him) has said, 'He who is patient in the manner of the pre-Islamic period is not one of ours!' Had it not been said in the Holy Book[354] about the wine in Paradise that «they will not suffer headache from it and not be intoxicated», we would have thought that you were out of your mind. As for Abū Baṣīr, he has drunk only milk and honey here.[355] He is dignified when he sits in a gathering; he is not unseemly quick when he unwraps, getting up.[356] His behavior with us is like that of Abū Nuwās, when he says:

You two, who censure me for drinking wine, go blame me!
I taste the wine by merely smelling it.
A caliph[357] has reproached me on account of it:
I do not think it right to disobey.
My share of it, when it goes round,
is only seeing it and smelling its bouquet.
Turn it away from me then, to another: I
shall only be a conversation partner.
I am in praising it, it seems, a Khārijite abstainer,
who speaks in favor of the arbitration:[358]
Incapable of carrying arms to war,
he orders others not to sit and stay behind."

Al-Nābighah al-Ja'dī replies, "In the days of the Deceptive World people often behaved foolishly when drinking milk, especially if they were lowly slaves. A *rajaz* poet said:

Ibn Hishām, milk has destroyed the people!
They all come in the morning with a sword and with a quiver.

"And another said:

What do the men of Ḍabbah want? Know this: it is defaming us!
Some stupid men among them got excited, drinking milk.

"Someone was asked, 'When should one be most afraid of the Banū So-and-So?' He answered, 'When they have plenty of milk.'"

The Sheikh (may God make him attain what he wants!) means to spread peace among the carousers and says, "One must beware of an angel who might pass by, see this gathering, and then report to the Omnipotent, the Almighty, which may bring about unpleasant consequences for you both. In fact, our Lord does not need reports to be brought to Him, but it happens just as it does with the recording angels in the Fleeting World.[359] Don't you know that Adam had 9.3.5

to leave Paradise for a trivial sin? Those born later cannot be sure that a like fate will not be theirs. I ask you, Abū Baṣīr, by God, do you not secretly long for wine?"

"Certainly not, by God!" replies al-Aʿshā. "To me it is like bitter aloes: even the thought of it never occurs to me. Praise be to God, who quenched my thirst with the oblivion of wine! I no longer care for another sip of 'Mother Iris.'[360]"

9.4 Al-Nābighah al-Jaʿdī, angry, stands up. The Sheikh (may God keep unpleasant things far from him!) does not want him to leave in this manner. "Abū Laylā," he says, "God, the Almighty, has granted us these black-eyed damsels, whom He transformed from geese. Choose one of them for yourself and take her home with you, where she will speak to you with the subtlest intimations and sing to you all kinds of intonations."

Then Labīd ibn Rabīʿah says, "If Abū Laylā takes a singing girl, and someone else takes another, will the news not spread throughout Paradise? Then these people will run the risk of being nicknamed 'goose spouses'!" So the whole company abstains from dividing the girls among themselves.

The conversation with Ḥassān ibn Thābit

10.1 Ḥassān ibn Thābit passes by.[361] "Welcome, Abū ʿAbd al-Raḥmān!" they all say, "Won't you talk with us for a while?" He sits down and they ask him, "How does this wine compare with the wine you bought and described in your verses:

It is as if a wine imported from Bayt Ra's,
  its mixture being honey and water,
Surrounds her teeth; as if the taste
  of apples freshly harvested
Were in her mouth, when fewer stars are visible
  at night, when darkness' cover takes the stars along.[362]
If ever all the wines on earth were listed, they
  would sacrifice themselves for that fine wine!

"Woe betide you! Are you not ashamed to mention this in your eulogy on the Messenger of God (God bless and preserve him)?"

"He was more tolerant than you think," replies Ḥassān, "I have said nothing but good things, I did not say that I drank wine, and I have not committed anything forbidden. I merely described the saliva of a woman who might have been my own wife after all;[363] I could also have said it by way of hypothesis. The Prophet (God bless him[364]) has interceded for Abū Baṣīr al-Aʿshā even after he boasted in his verse on many occasions and asserted that he traveled at night, either lying or being right. One has never heard of a more magnanimous man than the Prophet (God bless and preserve him). After I had lied and he had me flogged together with Misṭaḥ, he gave me the sister of Māriyah.[365] She bore my son ʿAbd al-Raḥmān. She is the aunt of the Prophet's son Ibrāhīm."[366]

The Sheikh (may God adorn belles lettres by granting him long life!) can think of many things he wants to ask Ḥassān and the others; but he is afraid they may be unable to give the right answers, so he refrains from asking, out of respect of his companions. 10.2

For instance, Ḥassān's verse "its mixture being honey and water": it occurs to him to ask, "What would you say, Abū ʿAbd al-Raḥmān, *mizājahā* ('its mixture,' accusative) *ʿasalun* ('honey,' nominative) *wa-māʾū* ('and water,' nominative)? Or *mizājuhā* (nominative) *ʿasalan* (accusative) *wa-māʾū* ('and water,' nominative)? Or rather *mizājuhā ʿasalun wa-māʾū* (all nominatives), assuming that this is a nominal sentence?"[367]

Or his verse:

He of you who lampoons the messenger of God
and praises him and helps him, are they equal then?[368]

Some believe that the word "who" is elided before "praises" and "helps," and that what follows it is a syndetic relative clause serving as an adjunct. Others say, however, that "who" is elided because it has an indefinite sense, in which case what follows it is a description of it, so that the asyndetic attributive relative clause takes the place of the thing that is described.[369]

One of those present asks Ḥassān: "What about this cowardice of yours, Abū ʿAbd al-Raḥmān?" Ḥassān replies, "Are you saying this to me, when my tribe is the bravest of all Arab tribes?[370] Six men of my tribe wanted to attack the heathen pilgrims with their swords and they protected the Prophet, agreeing to fight with him against any opponent. Then the tribes of Rabīʿah, Muḍar, and all the Arabs plunged their knives into our people and harbored hatred against them. If I have appeared to act with caution on some occasions, then it was merely a matter of being prudent. It is said in the Holy Book:[371] «He who turns his back to them on that day—unless withdrawing to fight again, or siding with another group—he will have to bear God's anger and his refuge will be Hell: an evil destiny!»"

10.3.1 *The five one-eyed men of Qays*

The company disperses, having spent a time equivalent to many earthly lifetimes. While he wanders through the meadows of Paradise, the Sheikh meets five men riding five she-camels. He says, "I have never seen people in Paradise with eyes as beautiful as yours! Who are you? May God give you eternal bliss!" They answer, "We five were the one-eyed men of the tribe of Qays: Tamīm ibn Muqbil al-ʿAjlānī, ʿAmr ibn Aḥmar al-Bāhilī, al-Shammākh ibn Ḍirār of the Banū Thaʿlabah ibn Saʿd ibn Dhubyān, ʿUbayd ibn al-Ḥuṣayn al-Numayrī nicknamed the Camel-herd, and Ḥumayd ibn Thawr al-Hilālī."[372]

The Sheikh addresses al-Shammākh: "I should like to ask you about a few things in your poem that rhymes in *-zū* and another poem rhyming in *-jī*; please recite them for me, may you be noble-hearted forever!" But al-Shammākh replies, "The perpetual bliss has made me forget these poems; I cannot remember a single verse from them." The Sheikh, with his exceeding love of literature and his eagerness to attribute virtue where it is due, says, "You have been neglectful, you true believer, and you have lost something precious! Don't you know that your two poems were more useful to you than your two daughters? By virtue of these poems you are mentioned in every place by name; travelers and those staying at home know your fame! Likewise, one of al-Nābighah al-Dhubyānī's poems was more useful to him than his daughter ʿAqrab, who may have brought him shame whereas the poem brought him fame; she could, in those heathen times, have been abducted and abused and her bride-price would have been greatly reduced! If you want me to recite your two poems to you, I could do so without difficulty." Al-Shammākh replies, "Recite them, may God's favors to you be plentiful!" The Sheikh recites:[373]

> No trace of Sulaymā is found in the valley of Qaww,
> nor in ʿĀliz, or Dhāt al-Ghaḍā, or the peaks of the highlands.

He finds that the poet is not knowledgeable about his own verse; he asks him about various things but he realizes that al-Shammākh does not understand them. "The delights of the eternal life," he explains, "have distracted me from being aware of these objectionable matters. «The god-fearing are amidst shade and springs, and such fruits as they desire: 'Eat and drink with relish, in return for what you did!'»[374] I accumulated my store of good deeds[375] merely in the hope of someone lending me a she-camel, or being given a year's ration of wheat for my family, as the *rajaz* poet says: 10.3.2

> If a dry bone stuck out from your head,
> A sturdy camel would come back from you;[376]
> A wretched old man would dole out for you a measure
> Of wheat like pebbles, amazing to him who touches it.[377]

"But now I am living in God's grace, scooping from the rivers of milk with golden mugs: camel's milk, cow's milk, or sheep's milk if I wish, all are abundant here; and goat's milk too. And if I feel like having a draught of ibex milk, there's many a river full, like the Tigris or the Euphrates. But often I saw[378] myself in the world of misery, milking dry the udders of sheep with little yield, without filling even a small pail."

10.4.1 Then the Sheikh (may he always speak for the sake of the good!) asks, "Where is ʿAmr ibn Aḥmar?" "Here I am," replies ʿAmr. "Recite for us," continues the Sheikh, "your poem that begins with

Youth has gone and *ʿamr* has failed us,
Friends and times have changed;

"for people have different opinions on the meaning of *ʿamr*. Some say you meant 'long life' but others say that you intended 'gums', the flesh between the teeth." ʿAmr replies with a proverb in verse:

"Take the road to Harshā or the other way:
Either side of Harshā is the road to go.[379]

"The horrors of the Resurrection have not left any place for reciting poetry. You must have heard the Qur'anic verse:[380] «On the day that you see it,[381] every suckling mother will be numb and forget the child she suckles, every pregnant woman will deliver what she carries, and you will think people drunk, yet they are not drunk. But God's torment is severe». You have been at the Standing Place;[382] it is a miracle that you can still recite poems!" The Sheikh explains: "Before I moved from that abode, I always prayed after the ritual devotions, imploring God to make me enjoy my literary erudition not only in this world but also in the Hereafter; and He has granted what I asked, praised be He!

10.4.2 "I like your poem:

I set out in the morning, not being afraid,
with nothing to fear or to dread,
In the prime of my youth; like a fresh, tender branch,
in the sacrosanct precinct of Mecca,
For a wine[383] like the wine of a *qayl*,[384] who has turned his mind
away from his mount[385] (everything has its time and its
measure).
His day was drawn out and his night has been long
and he had been longing for wine all the time.

There was also a low-lying, dark, gloomy one[386]
that was hanging, unmoving, a curtain let down this side of it,
And two locusts were singing to them,
while coral and gold beads were glittering;
And something made to resound, its peridot near to us,
its back with a hump like the back of a bee,
And two cymbals, their sound full of longing; between them
a string, sounding stridently, shawm-like its sound.
And their camel is quietly chewing the cud,
neither hunger nor fright has disturbed it;
When it is chewing the cud its firm teeth show,
when it listens to me it looks young like a calf.[387]
Abandon the way of fooling around, for the days
of your youth are now gone and you yourself have changed.

"What did you mean when you said 'the wine of a *qayl*'? Does it mean 'pre-Islamic king from Yemen'? Or does it refer to Qayl ibn 'Itr of the people of 'Ād?" 'Amr replies: "Both interpretations are conceivable."[388] The Sheikh continues (may God fulfill his wishes!), "An indication that Qayl ibn 'Itr is meant is where you say 'Two locusts were singing to them,' because the 'Two Locusts,' it is said, were two singing girls who sang for the deputation of 'Ād, in the presence of al-Jurhumī in Mecca. Thereby they were distracted from performing the circumambulation around the Kaaba and from asking God, praised and exalted be He, for rain, which is why they had come. Thus perished 'Ād, while they 'made merry'![389] I found, to my surprise, in some manuscript of the *Book of Songs*[390] a song text said to have been sung by the 'Two Locusts': 10.4.3

The summer resort is empty of people,
as is 'Ardah's valley and al-Gharīf.
Will I be brought to my people's dwellings
by a fast dromedary, stretching widely its legs?
O Umm 'Uthmān, let me obtain your favor!
—But what is the use of a trifling favor?

"This is an imitation of

Malḥūb is empty of people[391]

"—But who could possibly have transmitted to the singers in the time of Hārūn al-Rashīd or even later the information that this song was performed by the 'Two Locusts'? That is clearly preposterous; it must be a lie! As for your words 'a low-lying, dark, gloomy one,' what do you mean by them? And your words 'something made to resound, its peridot near to us'?"

Ibn Aḥmar replies, "That I mentioned the 'two locusts' does not prove that I especially meant Qayl ibn 'Itr, even though he was part of the deputation for whom the Two Locusts sang, for the Arabs came to call every singing girl 'locust,' because that term was used for a singing girl in ancient times. A poet has said:

Locusts sing to us while we are drinking,
and drinking once again, the wine with honey mixed.

"As for 'a low-lying, dark, gloomy one,' that is a cooking pot; and 'something made to resound, its peridot near to us,' that is a lute, 'its peridot' being the decorated part of it. And haven't you heard that one calls the various colors of a multicolored cloud *zibrij*, which is like *zabarjad*, peridot?[392] But if one reads 'resounding,' *mujaljil* instead of 'made to resound,' *mujaljal*, it refers to a thundercloud."

10.4.4 The Sheikh is amazed by these words. "It seems to me," he says, "that you, a true Arab whose expressions and verses are quoted as authoritative, assert that the word *zabarjad* is derived from *zibrij*! This supports what the author of *al-'Ayn* claims: that the letter *d* is secondary in the word *ṣalakhdam* ('strong camel'). But the Basran grammarians do not like this explanation."[393]

At this point God Almighty inspires Ibn Aḥmar with the knowledge of morphology, in order to prove to the Sheikh His omnipotence. "Why do you find it odd," replies Ibn Aḥmar, "that *zibrij* should be derived from the word *zabarjad*? It is as if a verb was derived from the noun *zabarjad*, in which not all its consonants could be used, for verbs cannot have roots of five consonants.[394] So one makes a verbal form '*yuzabriju*' and then one builds from this verb a noun: *zibrij*. Don't you see that when they make a diminutive of *farazdaq* ('piece of bread')[395] they say *furayzid*, and when they make a plural of it they say *farāzid*? This does not prove that the letter *q* is secondary."

The Sheikh (may God immortalize his utterances in the Register of Literature!) says, "You seem to assert that a verb can be derived from *zabarjad*, and that subsequently the noun *zibrij* is built on this. By this argument you are forced to maintain that verbs are prior to nouns!" Ibn Aḥmar replies, "I am not forced to say that, because I made *zabarjad* the original stem; it is possible that new branches are formed from it that should not be taken to be original stems. Don't you see that they say: a verb is derived from a verbal noun,[396] which is the stem. Furthermore, they speak of 'an attribute that is analogous to the verb,' meaning words such as 'striking' or 'noble' and the like.[397] But the fact that they make these statements does not prove that an attribute is derived from a verb, since it is a noun, and nouns deserve to be prior to verbs. Rather, what is intended is that many nouns can be spoken of in terms of a verb.[398] One could claim that a verb is derived from a verbal noun and thus a branch of it, while an attribute is another branch. Thus either branch could be prior to the other."

The Sheikh asks the poet some more questions about his poetry, but he finds him unable to answer them and unpersuasive; if he speaks he is evasive.

10.5 *The story of Tamīm ibn Ubayy ibn Muqbil*

"Which one of you is Tamīm ibn Ubayy?" asks the Sheikh. "That's me," says one of them. The Sheikh says, "Tell me about your verse:

> O Salmā's abode! I'll not charge anybody with seeking that lonely place,
> save al-Marānah, until she is bored with the custom.[399]

"What did you mean by al-Marānah? Some have said that it is a woman's name, others say it is the name of a camel. Yet others say it is a noun meaning 'habit.'"

Tamīm replies, "By God, from the moment I entered the gate of Paradise I cannot remember a line of verse, whether proper poetry or *rajaz*. That is because I have been severely taken to account. They said to me, 'You were among those who fought against 'Alī ibn Abī Ṭālib!'[400] Then al-Najāshī al-Ḥārithī came forward to speak against me, and I only escaped the flames of Hell after it had already scorched me a few times. Truly, your memory is still intact! It is as if you have not witnessed the horrors of the Reckoning, where the Herald of the Resurrection says, 'Where is So-and-so, son of So-and-so?' And then proud and mighty potentates are dragged to the Inferno by Hell's angels; women wearing crowns are pulled aside by means of tongues of ignited fuel that take them by their hair and their bodies, while they cry: 'Can't we buy ourselves out? Isn't there a good excuse?' Young sons of emperors are whimpering in their fetters of fire, saying, 'We have treasures, we are the lords of the Perishable World! We have performed good deeds and bestowed favors on the people! Will no one ransom us or help us?' But then a voice cried from the direction of God's Throne:[401] «Did We not give you a lifetime to reflect, for those who reflect, when the warner had come to you? Now taste! The wrong-doers have no helper.» Time after time have messengers come to you, who gave the security[402] that had been confirmed. It is said in the Holy Book:[403] «Beware of a day on which you will be returned to God. Then every soul will be paid in full what it has earned and they will not be wronged.» You were far gone in the pleasures of the world of mockery indeed, and to the works of the hereafter you paid no heed! Now the tiding is manifest. There is no injustice today; God has judged among the people."

The Sheikh's Story of his Resurrection, the Day of Judgement, and his Entry into Paradise

Then the Sheikh says (may God make him speak meritoriously when he says something, if his Lord will him to say something!): 11.1

The Sheikh's conversation with Riḍwān and Zufar, guards of the Garden

I'll tell you my own story. After I got up and rose from my grave and had arrived at the Plane of Resurrection ("plane" being like "plain," with a different spelling),[404] I thought of the Qur'anic verse, «To Him the angels and the Spirit ascend in a day the length of which is fifty thousand years. So be patient in a decent manner».[405] It did seem a long time to me; I got parched and torrid (meaning "very hot, without a puff of wind"), as your friend al-Numayrī says:

> The girls, in their wraps, are like ostrich eggs
> exposed by drizzle and the heat of a sultry night.

I am easily desiccated (that is, "quick to thirst"), so I thought about my situation, which I found quite unbearable for someone like me. There came an angel to me, the one that had recorded all the good deeds I had performed. I found that my good deeds were few, as few as tussocks of grass in a year of destitution (a tussock being a tuft of vegetation, destitution being a drought). But my repentance at the end shone like a light, bright like a lamp for travelers at night.

When I had stood there for one or two months, fearing I would drown in my sweat, I persuaded myself that I should compose a few 11.2.1

lines for Riḍwān, Paradise's Porter Angel. I composed them on the meter and rhyme pattern of

Stop, you two, for the memory of a beloved, and the recognition . . .[406]

In them I incorporated the name of Riḍwān. Then I jostled my way through the people until I stood where he could hear and see me, but he took no notice of me and I don't think he paid attention to what I said. I waited for a short while, perhaps ten days in earthly reckoning, and then I composed some lines on the pattern of

The gathered clans have parted. If I'd had my way,
they wouldn't have. They severed bonds of loving union.[407]

Again I mentioned Riḍwān in it; I approached him and did as before. But he did not appear to hear: it was as if I tried to move Mount Thabīr, or attempted to extract scent from cement ("cement" being a mixture of limestone and clay). Then I continued with all other metrical patterns that could accommodate "Riḍwān" until I had exhausted them; but still he did not help me and I don't think he even understood what I said. When I had tried everything without success I cried out as loud as I could, "Riḍwān, who are trusted by the Omnipotent Almighty, charged with guarding Paradise! Can't you hear me calling on you for help?"

11.2.2 He replied, "I heard you mention Riḍwān, but I had no idea that you meant me. What do you want, poor wretch?" I said, "I am a man who cannot endure to be dehydrated (that is, 'thirsty'); it is for the Reckoning that I have waited and waited. I've got my Document of Repentance, which cancels all my sins. I have composed numerous poems in praise of you, mentioning you by name!"

Riḍwān asked, "Poems, what's that? This is the first time I have heard that word." I replied: "'Poems' is the plural of 'poem', which is speech that is metrical and, on certain conditions, sounds pleasant. If the meter is defective, either by an excess or a shortfall, one notices it. People in the Temporal World used to ingratiate themselves with kings and lords by means of poems. So I composed some for you, hoping that you might let me enter Paradise by this gate. I think people have waited long enough now. I am only a weak, feeble person. Surely I am someone who may hope for forgiveness, and righly so, if God the Exalted wills." But Riḍwān said, "Do you expect me to allow you to enter without permission from the Lord of Glory, you dimwit? Forget it! Forget it! «How could they attain it from a remote place?»"[408]

So I left him and, expectantly, turned to a guard who was called Zufar. For him I composed a poem, mentioning him by name, on the meter of Labīd's line: 11.3

> My two daughters hope their father will live;
> but don't I belong to Rabīʿah or Muḍar?[409]

I approached him and recited the poem; but it was as if I was speaking to a mute and solid rock in the end, trying to get a wild ibex to descend.[410] I composed poems using the name Zufar in every possible meter and rhyme, but to no avail each time. I said, "God have mercy on you! In the Past World we would seek the favor of leaders and kings with two or three lines of verse and our wishes would be fulfilled; but for you I have composed enough to fill a tome of Collected Poems and still you don't seem to have heard one susurrus, i.e., a whisper!"

He replied, "I have no idea what you are expostulating (i.e., 'talking about'). I suppose all that jabbering of yours is the Qur'an of the Devil, that rebel! But the angels won't buy it! It belongs to the Jinn, who have taught it to Adam's children. Now what do you want?"

I explained what I wanted. He said, "By God, I can't help you in what you need; for humans I cannot intercede. What community are you from?" "The community of Muḥammad ibn ʿAbd Allāh ibn ʿAbd al-Muṭṭalib," I answered. "Ah, yes," he said, "the prophet of the Arabs. So that is why you have come to me with that poetry, because the accursed Devil spat it out in the lands of the Arabs, where women and men learned it. I'll give you some good advice: look for your friend and perhaps he will be able to let you have your way."

11.4 Thus I despaired of him. I worked my way through the multitude. Then I saw a man bathed in a glimmering of light, surrounded by others who shone with bright light. I asked, "Who is that man?" They said, "That is Ḥamzah ibn ʿAbd al-Muṭṭalib, the one who was killed by Waḥshī; those around him are those Muslims who died as martyrs at Uḥud." Inspired with false hope I said to myself: poetry will work better with Ḥamzah than with the Porter of Paradise, because Ḥamzah is a poet, as were his brothers and his father and his grandfather. It could well be that each and every one of his forefathers from Maʿadd ibn ʿAdnān on have composed verses. So I composed some lines after the model of Kaʿb ibn Mālik's elegy[411] on Ḥamzah, which opens with

> Ṣafiyyah, get up, don't be weak!
> Let the women weep for Ḥamzah!

I approached him and called out: "Lord of martyrs, uncle of God's messenger! Son of ʿAbd al-Muṭṭalib!" When he turned to me I recited the verses. But he said, "Shame upon you! Must you eulogize me here, of all places? Haven't you heard this Qurʾanic verse: [412] «Every man of them that day will have enough to preoccupy him?»" "Yes," I said, "I've heard it; and I've also heard what follows: «Some faces that day will be bright, laughing and expecting delight; other faces that day will be glum, by gloom overcome: these are the unbelievers, the sinners»!" He replied, "I can't do what you ask, but I will send a nuncio (meaning a 'messenger') along with you to my nephew ʿAlī ibn Abī Ṭālib, who can speak to the Prophet, God bless him, on your behalf."

He sent a man with me. When he had told my story to the Commander of the Believers,[413] the latter asked, "Where is your evidence?" He meant the document with my good deeds.[414] 11.5.1

The conversation with ʿAlī ibn Abī Ṭālib

At the assembling place I had seen an elderly man who used to teach us grammar in the Fleeting World. He was called Abū ʿAlī al-Fārisī. Some people had thrown themselves upon him to call him to account, saying "You have misinterpreted us and wronged us!" When he saw me he beckoned me with his hand, so I went over to him. There was a whole group with him, including Yazīd ibn al-Ḥakam al-Kilābī, who was saying, "Shame on you, you recited the following verse by me on my authority, the word 'water' (*al-māʾ*) in the nominative!"—He meant his verse

If only all your evil and your good deeds
were kept from me, for as long as a drinker drinks water to quench
his thirst

—"But I put 'water' in the accusative![415] Likewise, you asserted that I said *maqtawī* in my verse:

Take another friend instead of me, someone who looks like
you,
for I shall get myself a good and decent friend in your place!

"for I said *muqtawī*, with *u*!"[416]

There was a *rajaz* poet,[417] who said, "You have foisted on me a wrong reading of my verse:

Camels of mine, what is his crime that you should scorn him?
There is fresh water and tender thistles around him!

"for you read *taʾbayah*[418] instead of *taʾbayh* ('you scorn him'). By God, I have never said that, nor has any other Arab!"

There came another man, who said, "You have charged me with thinking that the pronoun 'it' refers to an implied 'studying' in my verse:

Here's this Surāqah: the Qur'an, he studies it,
whereas the man, with bribes if he can get them, is a wolf.

"Would I be so mad as to believe that?"[419]

A throng of such people came, all of whom blamed him for his interpretations; but I said: "People, these are trivial things! Don't be so hard on this learned old man. At least he can boast of being the author of his book on the Qur'an, *The Proof*.[420] It is not as if he has shed your blood or stolen your money!"

Then they left him and went their various ways.

11.5.2 Now while I was busy addressing them and discussing their complaints, I had dropped the writing that mentioned my repentance. I went back to look for it but could not find it!

I displayed much confusion and distress. But the Commander of the Believers said, "Don't worry. Did anybody witness your repentance?"[421] "Yes," I replied, "the qadi of Aleppo and his notaries." "What's his name?" "'Abd al-Mun'im ibn 'Abd al-Karīm, the qadi of Aleppo (may God guard it!) in the days of Shibl al-Dawlah."

He got a crier to stand up and call out: "'Abd al-Mun'im ibn 'Abd al-Karīm, qadi of Aleppo in Shibl al-Dawlah's time! Have you any knowledge of the repentance of 'Alī ibn Manṣūr ibn Ṭālib (ibn al-Qāriḥ), the Aleppine man of letters?"

But no one answered. I was dismayed and began to tremulate, i.e., to tremble. The man cried out a second time, and again nobody answered. I fell into a swoon, i.e., I fainted. Then he cried a third time, and someone spoke up: "Yes, I have witnessed the repentance of 'Alī ibn Manṣūr, in the nick of time![422] And a number of notaries were present at my place when he repented. I was then the qadi of Aleppo and adjacent districts. It is God whom we ask for succor!"

At that I got up and was able to breathe again. I told the Commander of the Believers (peace be upon him) what I wanted, but he turned away, saying, "You want something impossible. Follow the example of the other children of your forefather Adam!"

I wanted to get to the Basin[423] but had real trouble getting there. I drank a few gulps after which there would never be any thirst. The unbelievers also tried to reach the water, but the Angels of Hell drove them away with sticks that burned like fire, so that they retreated, with scorched faces or hands, wailing and squealing. I walked to the Chosen Progeny[424] and said, "In the Past World I always wrote at the end of any book of mine: 'God bless our lord Muḥammad, the Seal of Prophets, and his excellent and good descendants,'[425] to show my respect and hoping for a favor." They said, "What can we do for you?" I replied, "Our lady Fāṭimah (peace be upon her) entered Paradise ages ago. But from time to time she leaves it for twenty-four hours, by the reckoning of the Transitory World, to greet her father who is busy testifying for God's Judgment. Then she returns to her place in Paradise. Now when she appears as usual, please could you all ask her on my behalf? Perhaps she will ask her father to help me." 11.6.1

The conversation with Fāṭimah, the Prophet's daughter

When the time had come for her to emerge a crier called out: "Lower your eyes, people that stand here, until Fāṭimah, the daughter of Muḥammad (God bless him) has passed." A large number of men and women of Abū Ṭālib's family gathered, people who had never drunk wine or done evil things, and they came to meet her on her way. When she saw them she asked, "What is this crowd? Is anything the matter?" They answered, "We are fine; we enjoy the presents from those that dwell in Paradise. But we are being kept here because of the «word that preceded»;[426] we do not want to enter Paradise precipitously, before our time. We are safe and having a good time, on account of God's word:[427] «Those who have already been given the finest thing that came from Us, they shall be kept far from it, nor shall they hear any sound of it but they shall forever be in what their souls desire, the greatest distress shall not grieve them and the angels shall receive them: this is your day, that you have been promised!»" 11.6.2

'Alī ibn al-Ḥusayn and his two sons, Muḥammad and Zayd, were among them, with other pious and righteous persons. Next to Fāṭimah (peace be upon her) stood another woman, who resembled her in nobility and majesty. People asked, "Who is she?" The answer was: "That is Khadījah, daughter of Khuwaylid ibn Asad ibn 'Abd al-'Uzzā."

With her were some young men, riding horses of light. People asked, "Who are they?" They were told: "They are 'Abd Allāh, al-Qāsim, al-Ṭayyib, al-Ṭāhir, and Ibrāhīm, the sons of Muḥammad (God bless him)."[428] Then those whom I had asked said, "This man is one of our followers. His repentance is genuine and there can be no doubt that he will be among those in Paradise. He turns to you in supplication, God bless you, that he may be relieved from the terrors of this Place of Judgment, that he may enter Paradise and hasten to attain the triumph."

Thereupon Fāṭimah said to her brother Ibrāhīm (God bless him), "You look after this man!" He said to me, "Hold on to my stirrup." The horses then passed through the throng, whole nations and peoples making way for us. Where the crowd was too dense they flew up in the air, while I was holding on to the stirrup. They halted at Muḥammad (God bless him and give him peace).

11.7 *The Prophet's intercession*

The Prophet asked, "Who is this alien?" (meaning "stranger"). Fāṭimah replied, "This is a man for whom So-and-so and So-and-so have interceded." She named some of the Pure Imams.[429] He said, "First one must look at his works." He inquired about them and they were found in the Grand Register, sealed with Repentance. Then he interceded for me and I was permitted entrance. When Fāṭimah, the Resplendent (peace be upon her), returned I grabbed the stirrup of Ibrāhīm (God bless him).

11.8.1 *The crossing of the Bridging Path*

Having thus left the multitudes behind me I was told: "This is the Bridging Path, now cross it!"[430] I noticed it was empty, not one soul on it. I braced myself to cross but I found that I could not control myself. Fāṭimah, the Resplendent (God bless her), said to a servant girl of hers, "Girl, help him cross!" The girl began to push and pull me while I was tottering to the right and the left. "Girl," I said, "if you want me to arrive safely, then do with me as the poet put it in the Temporary World:

> Madam, if I'm tiring you,
> then let me ride you piggyback."

"Piggyback," she asked, "what is that?" " That is when you put your hands on someone's shoulders, who holds your hands and carries you, belly-to-back. Haven't you heard the line by al-Jaḥjalūl from Kafr Ṭāb,[431] when he says:

> My state improved backward
> until I began to move piggybackward."[432]

She replied, "I've never heard of piggyback, or al-Jaḥjalūl, or Kafr Ṭāb before!"

She picked me up and crossed like a bolt of lightning. When I reached the other side Fāṭimah, the Resplendent (peace be upon her), said, "I am giving you this girl. Take her and she will serve you in Paradise."

11.8.2 *The second conversation with Riḍwān; the entry into Paradise*

When I arrived at the gate of Paradise, Riḍwān asked, "Have you got your permit?" "No," I said. "Then you can't enter." I was desperate. I saw at the gate, just inside Paradise, a willow tree. I asked, "Can I have a leaf of that willow tree, so that I can go back to the Place of Judgment and get a permit, written on that leaf?" "I won't let anything leave Paradise without permission from the Most High, sanctified and blessed be He." I was at my wits' end at this new blow and said, "We belong to God and to Him we shall return! If Abū l-Murajjā, the Emir, had had a treasurer like you we would never have received a groat from his coffers." (A groat is a silver coin worth fourpence).

But then Ibrāhīm (God bless him) turned around! He saw me—I had stayed behind. Now he came back and he dragged me along with him and brought me into Paradise. I had spent six months, earthly reckoning, at the Place of Judgment. That is why my memory is still intact: the horrors have not depleted it, nor has the detailed Reckoning weakened it.

Paradise (II)

12.1 “So which one of you” (continues the Sheikh, addressing the five one-eyed poets) “is the Camel-herd?” “This is he,” they answer. The Sheikh greets him and says, “I hope I shall not find you like your friends, without any recollection or having lost your knowledge of the Arabic language!” The Camel-herd replies, “I hope so too. Ask me, but be brief!” The Sheikh asks him, “Is it true, as Sībawayh[433] says about you, that in your poem rhyming in *-lā*, in which you praise the caliph ʿAbd al-Malik ibn Marwān, you put the word ‘people’ in the accusative, in the verse:

The conversation with “the Camel-herd” and Ḥumayd ibn Thawr

In the days when my tribe and the people were like
one sitting firmly in the saddle, not letting it slip aside.”[434]

“It is true,” he answers.

12.2.1 The Sheikh turns from him straight to Ḥumayd ibn Thawr. “I say, Ḥumayd,” he says, “you composed some good poetry with your verses:

I see that my eyes, once healthy, are troubling me;
being healthy and sound is sufficient disease![435]
Before long the two times, day and night,
will have reached what they want and set out to achieve.

"How is your eyesight now?" Ḥumayd replies, "I could be in the western regions of the Garden and yet notice one of my friends in the eastern parts, with a traveling distance of thousands of solar years between us—you know how fast the sun moved in the Fleeting World! God, the Exalted One, is able to create any wonderful thing."

12.2.2 The Sheikh continues: "You also said well in your poem rhyming in *-dū*, that begins:

A noisy, clumsy female, who castrates her donkey[436]—
if one expects some good from her, one bites on stones!
She works, provides a living; girdle always tightly bound;
some youthful strength is left to her, but she is past childbearing.
Years upon years went by, emaciating her;
then came one year of plenty that reinvigorated people."

But Ḥumayd says, "I have become quite oblivious of any rhyme letter, whether *d* or *m*. I am too busy dallying with the black-eyed plump-legged damsels!" "Can one then renounce," says the Sheikh, "this poem, in which you also say:

An ill-tempered woman, who has still some strength;
her master is a man of diligence and good advice.
Whenever he calls: 'O noble creatures!' milk-rich camels come
without a driver leading them.
And then she brought a vessel to a filthy 'watering place,'
and her hands made the udder's milk ducts sprinkle into it.[437]

12.2.3 "In this poem there is a scene that al-Quṭāmī, I think, has taken over from you; or possibly he got to it before you, because you and he were contemporaries.[438] It is where you say:

Upon an evil, chilly night she had a visit from
my friend Abū l-Khashkhāsh. The night was cold.
When he tried to inveigle her, she said, 'Is it with food
you want to buy my favors? Ah, there's little chance of that!'[439]

When he said, 'Gently, please be kind to me!', she ogled him
with a blue eye,[440] to which no kohl-stick ever had been applied.
Her eyebrow bones were set as if in a black boulder,
made jagged by the steps of treading camels.

"This description is similar to the one by al-Quṭāmī:

I wrapped myself in dew and wind that coiled around me
in a dark night when no stars shone,
And went to an old crone who lit a fire
after Orion had begun to sink.
All of a sudden she perceived the groaning of a camel,
its sound exhausted and fatigued.
Then she went raving mad about a swift-paced camel, made
to kneel down, and a haggard man with fleshless fingers.
When I approached her with my saddle and my camel,
she said, 'Go away! Don't frighten my own animals!'

"These verses are well known. You, in your own poem, also said: 12.2.4

He came with something with two bags, made of an unshorn sheep,[441]
so ancient that they said, 'Has it life everlasting then?'
They seized it until they made it lean; it looked
like an old Turk that leaned over the trough.

"And butter is mentioned in it:

When night was cleared away, and distant shapes
were visible in morning's twilight,
His eye fell on a compact, yellow thing,
for which she suffered him and which seduced her."[442]

But Ḥumayd replies, "I am no longer concerned with butter, or with the hunting of shy ash-colored ostriches, because of the gifts from my Lord, the Generous One; I have no more fear nor grief.[443] People such as I used to rack their brain for a year or at least several months,[444] on behalf of some other man whom God had given honor and wealth, yet often meeting with total disappointment; and if the man gave something, it would be a paltry gift. But poetry happens to be that in which the Arabs excel."

12.3 *The second conversation with Labīd*

Labīd ibn Rabīʿah passes by them and invites them to his dwelling in the Qaysite quarter.[445] He adjures them to come with him. They walk a short distance and then find themselves at three houses that have no match in Paradise in their splendor and beauty. "Do you know, my erudite Aleppine friend, what these houses are?" asks Labīd.[446] "I don't know," replies the Sheikh, "by Him to whose Kaaba the tribes went on pilgrimage!" Labīd explains: "The first is my verse:

> Fear of our Lord is the best spoil;
> with God's permission is my tarrying and haste.

"The second is my verse:

> I praise God; He has no equal.
> His hands hold good things; what He wills He does.

"And the third is this verse of mine:

> He whom He guides on the paths of the good is guided well
> and is happy; but He leads astray whosoever He wills.

"My Lord, the Benevolent and Knowing One, has turned these verses into houses in Paradise, in which I shall dwell forever, enjoying eternal bliss."[447]

The Sheikh and all the others are amazed and say, "God is able to do what He wants!"

13.1.1 *A banquet in Paradise*

It occurs to the Sheikh (may God buttress his fame!) that he should give a banquet in Paradise, to be attended by as many poets as possible, those born in the pre-Islamic period who died as Muslims, or those born in Islam: those who consolidated the speech of the Arabs such as it is now preserved in books; in addition to some others with a measure of erudition who might be good company. He thinks it should be like a banquet of the Fleeting World; after all, the Creator (sublime is His glory) is not incapable of bringing them everything needed, without effort or delay.

Thus, mills are erected at the Kawthar stream, which noisily grind heavenly wheat, as superior to the wheat described by the poet of the Hudhayl tribe, who said:

May I not thrive if I regale their visitor
  on crusts and peelings while I have a store of wheat[448]

as Heaven is superior to earth.

He suggests (may the Omnipotent fulfill his suggestions!) that 13.1.2
some girls with black, lustrous eyes[449] come before him, to work the hand mills: one millstone is made of pearl, another of gold, others from precious stones never yet seen by dwellers in the Fleeting World. When he looks at the girls he praises God for His gift and is reminded of the words of the *rajaz* poet who describes a hand mill:

For guests and neighbors I've prepared
Two girls, hard-working, who cooperate,
Without compassion, though they feed us.[450]

He smiles to them and says, "Grind along! Sideways and contrary!" They ask him, "What are sideways and contrary?" " Sideways is to the right and contrary is to the left. Haven't you heard the words of the poet:

In the morning, having breakfast, we are fattest,
  but at dinner in the evening we are hollow-bellied.
We grind with hand mills, sideways and contrary;
  and if they gave us spindles we would not tire.

"They say these verses were written by a prisoner-of-war to his people."

In his mind the Sheikh (may God let him live long and joyously!) sees millstones being turned by animals. Before him appear all kinds of buildings, containing precious stones of Paradise. Some mills are turned by camels that graze on the paradisical thorn-bushes, she-camels that do not bend over their calves, and various kinds of mules, cattle, and wild asses.

13.1.3 When he thinks enough flour has been milled for the banquet his servants, the youths who live forever, disperse and return with yearlings, that is kids, various kinds of edible birds such as pigeon chicks, pea chicks, fat chickens of Mercy, and pullets of Eternity. Cows, sheep, and camels are driven to be slaughtered. There rises a loud camel-groaning, a goat-whickering, a sheep-bleating, and a cock-crowing, when they see the knife. Yet, God be praised, none suffers any pain: it is in earnest but like play.[451] There is no god but God, who creates marvelously out of nothing, without having to think about it, and shapes it without having a model.

Now when the chunks of meat lie on the meat planks, as they say in the dialect of Ṭayyiʾ instead of "blocks," he says (may God increase the efficacy of his intentions!), "Let the cooks of Paradise come, all those who have worked in Aleppo through the ages!"

A large crowd comes forward. He orders them to take the food: a delicious treat from God, sublime is His might, in accordance with His word:[452] «In it is what the souls desire and the eyes delight in; you shall dwell therein forever. That is Paradise, which you have inherited as a reward for what you used to do. Therein you shall have fruits in plenty of which you may eat.» When the dishes arrive his servant boys, who are like «well-kept pearls»,[453] disperse to collect the invited guests. Not one poet from the Islamic period did they leave behind, nor any of those who straddled the pre-Islamic and the Islamic periods, nor any scholar learned in various disciplines, nor any erudite person: they fetched them all. Thus a large throng, or many people, gathered.

(The word "throng" is used by a poet:[454]

Throngs flock at his doors
    from distress in years of famine.)

Golden tables are erected and silver trays are put down. The dinner guests sit down. Bowls are brought; and a bowl remains with them while they eat its contents for a time as long as the lifetimes of Kuwayy and Surayy, the two "vultures" among the stars.[455] When all have eaten their fill the cupbearers come with various potations and singing girls who produce sweet-sounding intonations.

The Sheikh (may he always say the right thing!) says, "Bring me all the singers, male and female, in Paradise, those who lived in the Fleeting World and for whom repentance was decreed!" A large crowd of men and women appears, among them al-Gharīḍ, Maʿbad, Ibn Misjaḥ, and Ibn Surayj, until finally Ibrāhīm al-Mawṣilī and his son Isḥāq arrive.[456] Someone among the crowd says, having seen the flocks of singing girls that have come, such as Baṣbaṣ, Danānīr, and ʿInān:[457] "It is strange that 'the two Locusts' are still in the most remote parts of Paradise." When the Sheikh hears this (may his ears always be struck by what delights him!) he says, "They must come too!" One of the servants mounts a she-camel of Paradise and goes to them, however far away they are. 13.2.1

The conversation with the two "Locusts"

They approach on two noble steeds, faster than flashing lightning. When they have arrived at the company the Sheikh greets them and gives them a friendly welcome. He asks them, "How did you manage to enter the Abode of Mercy, after having stumbled blindly in error?"[458] They answer, "Repentance was decreed for us and we died in the religion of the prophets sent by God." "God has been good to you both!", says the Sheikh. "Please recite for us some verses of the poem rhyming in *-āḥī*, that is sometimes attributed to ʿAbīd and by others to Aws!"[459] They have never heard of either ʿAbīd or Aws, but they are divinely inspired to sing what is requested.

They intone the following lines: 13.2.2

Bid Lamīs farewell, as a reproaching tender lover!
  She obstinately wronged me, though she was good before,
When captivating you with polished teeth,
  thin gums, sweet to the taste, and not unpleasant;

After her slumber her saliva tastes as if it had an evening draught
of a liquid from a dark skin in the tavern, richly flowing,
And of a strong, inebriating wine with water mixed;
or from the tubes of pomegranates and apples.[460]
She woke, full of reproach—it is no time for blame!
Why couldn't you have waited with reproach until I'd woken up?
God curse her! She rebukes me, though she knows
that it is up to me to waste or keep my wealth!
If I drink wine or buy it at a price,
one day I shall be sober, certainly, again.
We'll not escape a grave set in a winding wadi, or
a wasteland wide and flat like a shield's surface.

The girls enrapture those who hear them, stirring the hearts with joy. There is much thanking of God (praised be He) for the blessings He bestowed on those who believe and repent, saving them from the Abode of Misery and bringing them to the Place of Bliss.

13.3 There occurs to the Sheikh (may God make beauty perpetual by letting him live forever!) a longing to see a cloud such as was described by the poet in the same ode:

Sleepless I lay (you, my friend, were not lying awake!),
having spied a round cloud, very soon after falling asleep, which flashed,
You were asleep, but the lightning kept me awake all night,
like a Jew with a lamp, lucubrating.
The south wind is driving its front, while its hindermost parts,
bringing water, are tottering, heavily laden with rain.
Its opening rain, when it falls on Mount Shaṭib,
resemble the flanks of a back-kicking piebald horse, chasing horses.
It is as if she-camels, large and full-grown, are rumbling inside it—
recently they've given birth; they are gently nudging their calves with their heads.

Close down, with its fringe hanging only a little above the earth—
standing up, you could almost drive it back with your hand!
Those on the high ground and those on the low are alike;
he who seeks shelter at home is like he who walks on the bare plain.
In the morning the meadows and plains are verdant with herbage,
in all cracks and crevices, nooks and crannies.

Then God (exalted are His gifts) forms a cloud as beautiful as a cloud can be. Whoever looks at it will testify that he has never seen a more beautiful one, adorned as it is with lightning in the middle and at its extremities; it rains rosewater from Paradise, made with dew and drizzle, and it scatters pebbles of camphor like small hailstones. Mighty is our God, the Pre-existent, who is not incapable of giving shape to any wish and bringing into existence any surmised suggestion.

13.4 *The conversation with Jirān al-ʿAwd*

The Sheikh turns around and sees Jirān al-ʿAwd al-Numayrī.[461] He greets him and welcomes him. "Let us hear some verses of this master," he says to a singing girl, "such as these:

The women carried Jirān al-ʿAwd and laid him down
on a high spot, around which the jinn were humming.[462]
They guarded from me all those places where they wore
their underclothes, while their embroidered veils had fallen.
'Enjoy this night,' they said, 'before we part,
because tomorrow you'll be stoned or killed with swords!'"

(This last verse has also been attributed to Suḥaym).[463] The singing girl performs with complete mastery. When the company, amazed, admires her virtuosity, she says, "Do you know who I am?" They all say, "No, by God, praise Him!" She says, "I am Umm ʿAmr, of whom the poet says:

Umm ʿAmr withholds the cup from us;
but the cup should move to the right.

Your friend, Umm ʿAmr, whom you deny
    a morning drink, is not the worst of us three!"

They grow yet more amazed about her and honor her. "Who composed this poem," they ask, "is it ʿAmr ibn ʿAdī al-Lakhmī or ʿAmr ibn Kulthūm al-Taghlibī?"[464] "I have known the two drinking companions of Jadhīmah, Mālik and ʿAqīl. I gave them a morning drink of wine mixed with water. When they noticed ʿAmr ibn ʿAdī and I withheld the wine from him, ʿAmr said these two verses. Perhaps ʿAmr ibn Kulthūm wanted to adorn his poem with them and added them to his verses."

13.5 *The dance of the damsels*

The Sheikh (may God always remind him of good deeds!) is reminded of the verses that are ascribed to al-Khalīl ibn Aḥmad, who was among the company. It occurs to him that these verses are fit to be danced to. God, the Omnipotent, by the grace of His wisdom, makes a *Juglans regia* grow, i.e., a walnut tree,[465] which bears fruit immediately: it sheds a number of walnuts that can only be counted by God, praised be He. Each single walnut splits into four parts, disclosing four girls who delight the onlookers, nearby and far. They dance to the verses attributed to al-Khalīl, beginning:[466]

The gathered clans have split asunder:
    Fly up or fall with your love sickness!
If there were no pretty maidens,
    four, like oryx calves,
Umm al-Rabāb, Asmāʾ,
    al-Baghūm, and Bawzaʿ,
I'd tell the man who leads away the women in their litters:
    "Lead them, if you must, or leave them here!"

All regions of the Garden shake. The Sheikh (may he always be inspired to say the right thing!) asks al-Khalīl, "Whose verses are these, Abū ʿAbd al-Raḥmān?" "I don't know," replies al-Khalīl. "But in the Fleeting World we used to transmit them as yours." "I don't remember anything of that," answers al-Khalīl. "But it may be true what they say!" The Sheikh exclaims, "Have you then forgotten, Abū ʿAbd al-Raḥmān? You had the best memory of all Arabs in your time!" Al-Khalīl replies, "Crossing the Bridging Path has shaken out all that was stored in the mind."

13.6 *Beer, marinated peacock, and roast goose*

The Sheikh happens to think of beer, the kind that used to be made in the Deceptive World. Instantly God, in His omnipotence, lets rivers of it flow; one draught of it is nicer and more refreshing than all the delights of the Perishing World from God's creation of heaven and earth until the day that the last nations are wrapped up. He says to himself, "I know that God is omnipotent, but really I wanted the kind I used to see with the beer sellers in the Fleeting World!" No sooner has he said that than God gathers all beer sellers in Paradise, Iraqis, Syrians, and from other regions, preceded by the immortal youths,[467] who carry baskets to the company.

The Sheikh (may God preserve him for all lettered people!) asks the scholars that are present, "What are these baskets called in correct Arabic?" They are taciturn, i.e., silent. One of them says, "They are called 'hampers,' in the singular 'hamper.'" One of the others says, "And which lexicographer says that?" The Sheikh replies (may his learning never fail to reach his companions!), "It is mentioned by Ibn Durustawayh." He happens to be present. Al-Khalīl asks him, "Where did you find that word?" "In the writings of al-Naḍr ibn Shumayl," answers Ibn Durustawayh. Al-Khalīl asks, "Is that correct, Naḍr? You are a reliable source in my view." "I can't remember precisely," replies Naḍr, "but I think the fellow is quoting accurately, if God wills."

At that moment there comes along, past the throng, i.e., the assembled people, a paradisical peacock, a veritable feast for the eye. Abū ʿUbaydah would like to eat it marinated. Instantly it is like that, on a golden plate.[468] When he has had his fill the bones reassemble and 13.7

become a peacock as before. They all exclaim, "Glory to Him «who revives the bones after they have decayed»! It is just as it says in the Qur'an: «When Ibrāhīm said, 'My Lord, show me how Thou revivest the dead!' He said, 'Don't you believe me, then?' 'Yes, I do,' he said, 'but just so that my heart be reassured.' 'Then,' He said, 'Take four birds and cut them up, then put a piece of them on each hill, then call them and they will come running toward you! Know that God is all-mighty and all-wise!'»"

Then the Sheikh (may God delight mankind with his life!) asks, "What is the mood of 'be reassured'?" They reply, "Subjunctive, because it is dependent on the conjunction 'so that' in the sense of purpose." "Could there be another interpretation?" asks the Sheikh. (They answer,)[469] "We cannot think of anything." "It is possible," continues the Sheikh, "that it is a jussive, after the particle *li-* that denotes a command,[470] which here could express a prayer, as when one says, 'O Lord, forgive me!' As for 'Āzar's words that are quoted,[471] these have been recited either as «He said: I know (*aʿlamu*) that God is powerful over everything» or «He said: know (*iʿlam*) . . . !», the former as a statement and the latter as a command from God, mighty is His power. Abū 'Alī al-Fārisī thinks that 'know!' can be taken as addressed by 'Āzar to himself, because this is a well-known phenomenon. Someone will say, 'Woe unto you! What have you done?' meaning himself. Al-Ḥādirah al-Dhubyānī says:[472]

Sumayyah rose early this morning. Enjoy!
But she came in the morning like someone departing, not staying."

13.8 Then a goose comes along, big like a Bactrian camel.[473] One person wants it roasted, and thus it appears, on a table of emerald. As soon as he has had his fill, it returns, with God's permission, to its former winged state. Another prefers it as kebab, someone else wants it spiced with sumac, yet another with milk and vinegar, and so on, while the goose turns into whatever is desired. This process repeats itself for some time.

Then Abū ʿUthmān al-Māzinī says to ʿAbd al-Malik ibn Qurayb al-Aṣmaʿī, "I say, Abū Saʿīd, what is the morphological pattern of *iwazzah*, 'goose'?" Al-Aṣmaʿī replies, "Are you insinuating something, you scorpion? You were in my class in Basra for so long when nobody paid any attention to you. The pattern is factually *ifaʿlah* ('iC_1aC_2C_3ah) but originally *ifʿalah* ('iC_1C_2aC_3ah)."[474] Al-Māzinī asks, "What is your proof that the glottal stop ' is secondary and not an original root consonant, the pattern then being *fiʿallah* (C_1iC_2aC_3C_3ah)?" Al-Aṣmaʿī answers, "That the glottal stop is secondary is proved by the fact that people also say *wazz*." "But that does not prove that the glottal stop is secondary," counters Abū ʿUthmān, "for people say *nās* ('people'), the original form of which is *ʾunās*, and *mīhah*, for 'sheep pox,' which is in fact *ʾamīha*." Al-Aṣmaʿī says, "Don't you and your friends, the 'Analogists,'[475] assert that the pattern is *ʾifʿalah* ('iC_1C_2aC_3ah)? If they then build a noun from the root *ʾ-W-Y* ('to seek refuge') on the pattern of *ʾiwazzah*, they would say *ʾiyyāh*![476] And if the pattern were *fiʿallah* (C_1iC_2aC_3C_3ah), they would say *ʾiwayyah*; if it were *ʾifaʿlah* ('iC_1aC_2C_3ah), the *ʿayn* having no vowel, they would say *ʾiyayyah*, in which the *y* that follows the glottal stop—which is the original glottal stop of the root *ʾ-W-Y*—has been changed into a *y* because two glottal stops coincide here, and because a short *i* precedes it, while it has itself been vowelled with a short *a*. If you soften the glottal stop in *miʾzar* ('loin-cloth, wrap') you say *mīzar*, with a pure, long *ī*." Al-Māzinī says, "This is merely an arbitrary interpretation and claim of our colleagues, for it has not been established conclusively that the glottal stop in *ʾiwazzah* is secondary". Al-Aṣmaʿī says,

"The tribe of Jurhum feathered arrows; Jurhum then
was shot by notches and by tips of their own arrows![477]

"You followed them, deriving much benefit; then you came back and attacked what they said! You and they are like the ancient poet who said,

I taught him shooting, every day;
and when his arm was steady he shot me."[478]

Angrily, he gets up; the people of that session go their separate ways, having a blissful time.

14.1 *The conversation with the two damsels*

Thereupon he is alone (may God's beneficence never leave him alone!) with two black-eyed damsels of Paradise. Dazzled by their beauty he exclaims, "Alas, the poor Kindite, who perished![479] You remind me of his verses:

> As was your wont before her, with Umm al-Ḥuwayrith,
> and her neighbor friend, Umm al-Rabāb, in Ma'sal:
> When they rose the scent of musk would waft from them,
> like the eastern breeze, bringing the smell of cloves.

"and his verses:

> Just like two oryxes, ewes from Tabālah, bending tenderly
> toward their calves; or like some Hakir statues:
> When they rose the scent of musk would waft from them,
> of perfume from a flask, and odoriferous aloe wood.

"But his girlfriends are no match for you, no nobility, no treat for the eye! Sitting in your company for even one minute, of earthly reckoning, is better than the realm of Ākil al-Murār and his kin, or that of the Naṣrids in al-Ḥīrah, or the Jafnids, kings of Syria."

He turns to the two girls, sipping their sweet saliva, and says, "Imru' al-Qays is a poor, poor soul! His bones are burning in hell-fire, while here I am quoting his verse:

> It seems the coolness of her teeth,
> when birds at dawn are warbling, is
> infused with wine, with rain, the smell
> of lavender, the scent of aloe wood.

"or his verses:

> Days when her mouth, as I roused her from her sleep,
> would smell like musk, kept in its filter overnight,

Wine the color of gazelle's blood, kept for years,
vintage from 'Ānah or the vineyards of Shibām."

14.2 One of the girls begins to laugh uncontrollably. The Sheikh asks, "Why are you laughing?" "For joy," she replies, "because of the favor that God has bestowed on me, and the forgiveness that he showed to me! Do you know who I am, 'Alī ibn Manṣūr?" "You are one of the black-eyed damsels whom God has created as a reward for the god-fearing. He said of you: «It is as if they are rubies and pearls»."[480] She says, "Yes, I am indeed, through God Almighty's kindness. But in the Fleeting World I was known as Ḥamdūnah and I used to live in Iraq Gate in Aleppo, where my father worked a mill. A rag-and-bone dealer married me, but he divorced me because of my bad breath. I was one of the ugliest women in Aleppo. When I realized that I became pious and renounced this Delusive World. I devoted myself to religious worship and earned a living from my spindle. This made me what you see now."

The other one says, "And do you know who I am, 'Alī ibn Manṣūr? I am Black Tawfīq, who used to work in the House of Learning in Baghdad in the time of Abū Manṣūr Muḥammad ibn 'Alī al-Khāzin. I used to fetch the manuscripts for the copyists."

He exclaims, "There is no god but God! You were black and now you are more dazzlingly white than camphor, or camphire[481] if you like." "Do you find that odd?" replies the girl, "After all, the poet says of some mortal being:

One mustard-seed of light from him, with all
black people mixed, would whiten all the blacks."[482]

14.3 *The tree of damsels*

At that instant an angel comes along. The Sheikh asks him, "Servant of God, tell me about the damsels with black, lustrous eyes: doesn't it say in the Holy Book:[483] «We have raised them and made them virgins and loving companions for the people in the right»?" The angel replies, "There are two kinds. One kind has been created by

God in Paradise and they have never known otherwise, and there is another kind that God has transferred from the Temporary World because they have done pious deeds."

The Sheikh is stupefied, i.e., amazed by what he has heard. "Where are the ones that have never been in the Transitory World?" he asks, "And how do they differ from the others?" The angel answers, "Just follow me and you will see a wondrous example of God's omnipotence."

He follows the angel, who takes him to gardens the true nature of which only God knows. The angel says, "Take one of these fruits and break it open. This tree is known as the tree of the black-eyed damsels."[484]

The Sheikh takes a quince, or a pomegranate, or an apple, or whatever God wills, and breaks it open. A girl with black, lustrous eyes emerges whose beauty dazzles the other damsels of the Paradisical gardens. She says, "Who are you, servant of God?" He gives his name. She says, "I was promised I would meet you four thousand years before God created the world!" At that the Sheikh prostrates himself to magnify the omnipotent God and says, "Thus it says in the Hadith: 'I have prepared for my believing servants things no eye has heard—apart from what I have told them about it.'"[485] ("apart from" is used in the sense of "let alone and not to speak of").

14.4 It occurs to him, while he is still prostrate, that the girl, though beautiful, is rather skinny. He raises his head and instantly she has a behind that rivals the hills of ʿĀlij, the dunes of al-Dahnāʾ, and the sands of Yabrīn and the Banū Saʿd.[486] Awed by the omnipotence of the Kind and Knowing God, he says, "Thou who givest rays to the shining sun, Thou who fulfillest the desires of everyone, Thou whose awe-inspiring deeds make us feel impotent, and summon to wisdom the ignorant: I ask Thee to reduce the bum of this damsel to one square mile, for Thou hast surpassed my expectations with Thy measure!" An answer is heard: "You may choose: the shape of this girl will be as you wish." And the desired reduction is effected.

Between Paradise and Hell

Then it occurs to him that he would like to see the people in Hell and how things are with them, that his gratitude for his blessings be magnified. For God says,[487] «One of them said: I had a companion who would say, "Are you really one of those who believe that if we die and have turned to dust and bones we will be judged?" He said, "Won't you look down?" So he looked down and saw him in the midst of blazing Hell. He said, "By God, you had nearly let me perish; but for my Lord's blessing I would have been one of those brought there!"» 15.1

The Paradise of the demons

The Sheikh mounts one of the animals of Paradise and goes forth. He sees some towns unlike the towns of Paradise, without the glittering light; there are caves and dark, wooded valleys. He asks one of the angels, "What are they, servant of God?" He replies, "This is the Paradise of those demons[488] who believed in Muḥammad (God bless him), those that are mentioned in the Surah of the Sand Dunes and the Surah of the Jinnees.[489] There are lots of them." "I should like to pay them a visit," says the Sheikh, "I am bound to hear some wonderful stories from them!" 15.2.1

He turns toward them and sees an old person who is sitting at the mouth of a cave. He greets him and the other answers the greeting politely, asking, "What brings you to this place, human? You would deserve a better one; like you there is none!" The Sheikh replies, "I heard that you are the believing jinnees, so I've come to ask for some stories about the jinnees, and perhaps to hear some poems by the rebellious jinnees."[490]

The old jinnee says, "You've hit the bull's eye; you've found me like the moon in its halo in the sky, like someone who waits before pouring away the hot fat:[491] here am I! Ask whatever you like." The Sheikh asks, "What is your name, old man?" "I am al-Khaytaʿūr, one of the sons of al-Shayṣabān.[492] We are not descended from the devil: we belong to the jinnees that lived on earth before the children of Adam (God bless him)."

15.2.2 *The poetry of the demons*

The Sheikh says, "Tell me about the poems of the jinnees! Someone called al-Marzubānī has collected a fair number of them." The old man replies, "But that is all rubbish, wholly unreliable. Do humans know more about poetry than cattle know about astronomy and geodesy? They have fifteen different meters, and rarely transcend them;[493] whereas we have thousands of meters that humans have never heard of. Some naughty toddlers of ours happened to pass by some humans and spat some poetry at them, a trifle like a splinter from an arak tree of Naʿmān.[494] I myself have composed informal *rajaz* and formal *qaṣīd* poetry an eon or two before God created Adam. I have heard that you, race of humans, are rapturous about Imru' al-Qays's poem, 'Stop, let us weep for the remembrance of a loved one and a dwelling place,'[495] and make your kids learn it by heart at school. But if you wish I could dictate to you a thousand poems with the same meter and the same rhyme, *-lī,* a thousand such poems rhyming in *-lū,* a thousand in *-lā,* a thousand in *-lah,* a thousand in *-luh,* and a thousand in *-lih,* all composed by one of our poets, an unbeliever now burning in the depths of Hell."

The Sheikh (may God make him happy continually!) says, "You have got a good memory, old man!" The jinnee replies, "We are not like you, children of Adam, overcome by forgetfulness and moistness, for you have been created from «moulded mud»[496] but we have been created from «a fiery flame».”[497]

The Sheikh is moved by a desire for erudition and literature to ask the old man, “Will you dictate some of these poems to me?” “If you like,” says the jinnee, “I will dictate to you loads more than camels can carry and all the pages of your world can contain.”

The Sheikh has a mind (may his mind ever be lofty!) to take some dictation from him. But then he says to himself: in the Transitory World I was always wretched when I collected literature; I never profited from it. I tried to curry the favor of leading persons but I was milking the udder of a bad milk camel and was exerting myself with the teats of a slow cow. I’ll never be a success if I give up the pleasures of Paradise in order to copy the literature of the jinn. I’ve got enough erudition as it is, all the more so because forgetfulness is rife among the dwellers in Paradise, so that I have turned out to be one of those with the greatest erudition and the largest memory, thanks be to God!

He asks the old man, “How should I address you respectfully?”[498] 15.2.3
He answers, “As Abū Hadrash. I have fathered God knows how many children, whole tribes of them, some in the burning Fire, others in Paradise.” The Sheikh asks him, “Abū Hadrash, how come you are gray-haired? I thought those who dwell in Paradise would be young.”[499] He replies, “Humans have been given that privilege, but we have been denied it, because we could change shape in the Past World. Anyone of us could be a speckled snake if he so wished, or a sparrow if he wanted, or a pigeon. But in the Hereafter we are forbidden to change shape. We are left as we were created originally. The children of Adam have been given a beautiful appearance by way of compensation. As some human said in the World that Was: ‘We have been given make-shift, and the jinn have been given shape-shift.’”

The jinnee continues, “I have met evil at the hands of humans, but 15.2.4
they have met the like from me! Once I entered the house of some persons, wanting to strike a girl with fits.[500] I took on the shape of

Abū Hadrash al-Khayta‘ūr’s heroic deeds

a *Rattus rattus*, i.e. a rat; they called the cats, and when I was hard pressed by these I changed myself into a speckled viper and hid in a hollow tree trunk. When they found out they uncovered me. Afraid that they would kill me, I became a whizzing wind and clung to the rafters. They tore down the wooden beams but could not see anything. Then they were puzzled and said, 'There is no place here where it could be hiding!' While they were deliberating I went for the full-bosomed maiden in her mosquito net. When she saw me she had a fit. Her family came from all sides; they gathered exorcists and brought doctors and spent large sums. Every exorcist left no spell untried on me, but I did not react. The physicians kept giving her potions but I stayed put and did not budge. When death overtook her I looked for another girl, and so on, until God granted me repentance and rewarded me richly! I shall always be one of those who praise Him![501]

15.2.5 I praise Him who took my sinful burdens and destroyed them
for me! My crime has been forgiven now.
I had a close affair once with a pretty girl
from Cordova; and then, in China, with the daughter of an emperor.
I visited now one and then another, unconcerned,
at night, before I could discern the light of dawn.
And any animal or human I encountered
I would leave distraught and terrified.
I frightened Blacks, by visiting their womenfolk,
and Byzantines, and Turks, and Slavs, and Afghān Ghūr![502]
I'd ride an ostrich in the dark, haphazardly
or not; then a wild bull, who spent the night in freezing cold.
I'd be with drinkers, to afflict them with mishap perpetual,
while they played on their lute, their shawm, and their sitar.[503]
I would not part from them before they had performed
a deed that would make Satan glad.

I'd cheat a notary, make him betray the trust
they had in him, and give false testimony.
Many a woman middle-aged I cast into a blazing fire,
when she was working at a heated oven for her children.
And that man, Noah, drove me off his Ark
and beat me till my shin bone broke.
I flew up high into the sky during the Flood,
until I saw the waters in retreat.
I bothered Moses, when he had withdrawn alone
with sheep and goat that bore him lamb and kid,
And I kept talking to him with insinuating whispers,
until your Lord, who spoke to him, crumbled the mountain.[504]
I led the father of Sāsān astray, away from the right path,
and hid myself, marching in Shapur's army.
Bahrām then reigned, being my follower,
the days at least when he built Gūr.[505]
At times I am a viper with its wicked wiles,
at other times the eye will spy me as a bird.
Humans, because of me, will turn one-eyed or squint,
though they were never one-eyed or cross-eyed.
But then I took a warning; my repentance was exemplary,
after I'd lived a life notorious for disobedience.
And finally the world came to an end. A call was heard:
'Why don't you blow the trumpet, Isrāfīl?'[506]
God made me die for a short while and then He woke me up
and resurrected me. Then I was given life eternal, blessed!"

The Sheikh exclaims, "Wonderful, Abū Hadrash! And that after you practiced all these wicked and calamitous things!—But tell me about your languages: are there among you Arabs who do not understand the Byzantines, and Byzantines who do not understand the Arabs, as we find among the human nations?" The jinnee answers, "Far from it, may God have mercy on you! We are clever and intelligent 15.2.6

people. Everyone of us must have knowledge of all the human languages, and besides that we have a language unknown to humans. I am the one who warned the jinn that the Holy Book was being revealed.[507] One night I was traveling with some jinnee friends, on our way to Yemen. When we came past Yathrib (it was the time of fresh dates) «we heard a wondrous Recitation which leads to the right course; so we believed in it and we shall not associate anyone with our Lord.»[508] Then I returned to my people and told them about it. Some of them hastened to believe; they were moved to do this all the more because they had been pelted with scorching stars when they were eavesdropping."[509]

15.2.7 The Sheikh says, "Abū Hadrash, inform me (for you are well-informed): this pelting with stars, did it happen in the pre-Islamic period? For some people say that it happened in Islamic times." "That is wholly wrong," replies Abū Hadrash. "Have you not heard the verse by al-Afwah al-Awdī:

[An arrow(?)] like a shooting star thrown at you
by a horseman, with fire in his hand for the battle.

"And the verse by Aws ibn Ḥajar:[510]

Then it darted away, like a scintillating star, with in its wake
a dust cloud which one could imagine was a tent.[511]

"However, this pelting increased at the time of the Prophet's mission. There was a lot of lying among humans and jinn, and truthfulness was scarce. Good health, in the end, to those who have spoken the truth! Regarding the story of the pelting with shooting stars I composed the following poem:[512]

15.2.8.1 Mecca has been abandoned by the Banū l-Dardabīs:
no demon's sound is heard there now.
Its idol statues have been smashed to bits with force,
each idol, with an axe destroyed.
Among Hāshim's elite a brilliant man stood up,[513]
one never to neglect the rights of his companion.

He heard the revelation by his Holy Lord sent down,
sounding like metal basins being struck.
He flogged severely those who would drink wine,
and even drinking date wine he would not allow.
He stoned the married fornicator, not accepting
intercession from a tribal chief.[514]
Many a bride, guarded at night by guards 15.2.8.2
as strong as Jurhum or Jadīs,
Escorted to a tribal leader as his spouse
—no weakling or a dastard he—
I jealously assaulted, snatching her with a swift fit,
before her husband even touched her.
And I would go to a young girl, secluded in
her bower, or walking proudly 'midst her servant girls.
A lion might be stopped before he has his prey:
not even spells could stop me from attaining what I wanted.
I would set out in a dark night among
some jinnee friends, over a bare flat plain,
A trackless desert where the demons hum,
a wasteland, only by the bravest jinn inhabited,
White, mighty, heavy, like white clouds,
yet noble, speaking with a whispering.
At night horses with wings would carry us,
unlike the horses of mankind,
And female camels, faster than your eyes could see,
created from a cross of ostrich and of camel,
Which in one night would pace from ʿAlwah
to the hamlets of Tashkent, with only muffled sounds.[515]
There was no piety among us in those days: 15.2.8.3
religion suffered a relapse and we were not astute.
Sunday and Saturday were just like any Monday,
and Friday was like any Thursday.
We were no Zoroastrians, nor Jews,
nor Christians who go to church.

The Torah we would tear apart in scorn
 and we would shatter crosses like dry wood.
We battled against God as troops of Satan, friend
 of swindling, impure views.
To him we left the judgment when he weighed decisions
 and we consented to the error when it was decided.
Both young and old men we inveigled into emptying
 purse after purse for lecherous behavior.
The jinn of Solomon we followed, to set free
 those wicked ones that were detained,
Put into bottles sealed with lead,
 which left them with a mere last gasp.[516]

15.2.8.4 We let a pretty wife be driven from her house
 because of a suspicion, a mere guess,
'Don't be content with a revocable divorce,'[517] we tell
 the husband, 'do take our advice, it is no trick!'
Then, when she has become another's wife,
 his former passion, with a vengeance, will return to him,
While we remind him, though she's married to another, of
 her pearly teeth that bathe in wine.[518]
We used to cheat the priest at Easter, after he
 had filled himself with eel;
He had already drunk and drunk again, pure wine or mixed,
 but in the morning yearned for more delight.
He swore he would not drink to drunkenness,
 but 'teeth will follow after milk teeth!'
We said to him, 'Come on, just one more cup!
 That wouldn't do you any harm!
'T will warm you in this weather
 in which the oven's fire will be extinguished by the cold!'
And thus he gulped it down. His mind gave way
 and he was counted 'mongst the cursed and the disgraced;
And in the end his mouth spilled the regurgitated wine
 on his two pillows.

We would infuriate the king against his councillor,
so kind and full of good advice, whenever the realm was ruled.
And I would snatch an ogress's repast when she
held in her hands the sirloin of a skinny antelope.
I did not fear the terrors of the land
or traveling by sea when it was freezing cold.
I drank with Cain and Seth and Abel
an ancient vintage wine,
And the two friends of Lamech, while the lute
was played with touch unfaltering on the highest string.[519]
I was familiar with Luqmān and with his gambling friends[520]
having worn out the cloak of youth.
But subsequently I believed.[521] To whom belief is given 15.2.8.5
will gain what matters and is precious!
I fought at Badr for the Faith; at Uḥud I defended; and
I terrorized the foe's commander at the Ditch,[522]
Behind the angels Gabriel and Michael, in the thick of battle, we
would sever heads as blades of grass are cut.[523]
When the victorious hosts flew in the sky
and Satan's forces were undone and trampled down like plants,
Their heads were wearing, in the battle's dust clouds,
yellow turbans, as if dyed with *wars*.[524]
Even now I hear the neighing of Ḥayzūm still ringing in
my ears: ah, such a noble, blessed stallion![525]
He follows not the hunt, he knows no fetters, nor
does he complain of injuries or ulcers of his hooves.
No free-born woman, whether old or young and beautiful,
has given me a taste of love since my conversion.
Now Zaynab could be certain of my piety;
Lamīs would have no fear of my assaulting her.[526]
I told the jinn: 'Come on, prostrate yourselves 15.2.8.6
for God, and let yourselves be humbly led!
Your world has, for so long, been treacherous
both in its tolerance and in its harshness.

Bilqīs has died, her realm has gone from her,
and not a whisper in the ear is left of it.[527]
Al-Mundhir's dynasty in Ḥīrah: neither here nor there;[528]
each one of them is buried in the earth.
Know that we tried, like you before us, to attain
the highest heaven, but it was astir with evil things:[529]
It shoots the devils with its fires until
they look like ashes strewn about.'
A group of them obeyed me then, and gained salvation;
another party of them joined the overthrown.
15.2.8.7 At the Yarmūk a fleet horse flew with me,[530]
where men outwitted one another, striking, stabbing,
Until the war revealed me as
a burning ember in the battle's blaze.
And I have seen that wretched camel[531]
(ill-fated offspring of sturdy dam!),
While bravely I advanced among the Banū Ḍabbah;[532]
ignorance is a fatal illness in the world!
I visited Ṣiffīn,[533] riding a sleek and short-haired horse,
never by a peasant groomed,
Felling its heroes with my sword
and hurtling at them hard, smooth rocks.
I marched in front of 'Alī on the morning of
the battle of al-Nahrawān until the army's edge was blunted.[534]
Someone admonished me and found in me repentance:
'The fertile mare met with a virile male!'"[535]

The Sheikh is amazed (may he always be joyous and glad!) about what he has heard from the jinnee. He does not want to stay too long with him, so he bids him farewell.

16.1 *Animals in Paradise*

He urges on his mount. Suddenly he faces a lion, who is busy devouring cows and calves from the animal herds of Paradise—he is not content with scoring a century or two, i.e., one hundred or even two hundred animals. The Sheikh says to himself, this lion may have been used to devouring a skinny sheep, living on it for days on end without tasting anything else!

Thereupon God inspires the lion (who has understood the Sheikh's inner thoughts) with speech. "Servant of God!" says the lion, "Has nobody of you been presented, in Paradise, with a bowl of rice pudding with honey and fresh butter? And eaten it for as long the heavens and the earth last, enjoying what he consumes without ever being satiated, and the bowl never being exhausted? In the same way I devour God knows how many animals, yet without the prey being harmed by claw or tooth. Rather, they enjoy it just as much as I do, through the kindness of their almighty Lord. Do you know, handsome and amiable young man, who I am? I am the lion from al-Qāṣirah, a wadi on the way to Egypt! When 'Utbah ibn Abī Lahab[536] was traveling in that region, after the Prophet (God bless him) had said, 'O God, let one of Your dogs get him!' I was inspired to go hungry for his sake for several days. I came upon him when he was sleeping among some companions. I crept through the company toward him; and I was allowed entry into Paradise because of what I had done."

Then the Sheikh comes past a wolf who is busy catching gazelles. 16.2
He consumes herd after herd, but whenever he has finished a buck or a doe it returns, by God's might, to its former state. The Sheikh understands that it is the same with the wolf as with the lion. He asks, "What is your story, servant of God?" and the wolf replies, "I am the wolf who spoke to al-Aslamī[537] in the time of the Prophet (God bless and preserve him). For ten days or more I had not been able to catch even a hare, whether buck or doe. Whenever I set my eyes on a motherless kid the goatherd would set his dogs on me who attacked me madly, and I would get back to the wife with my hide torn badly. She would say, 'You were wrong in your guess! Going out in the morning was not a success!' Sometimes my flank was shot

at with an arrow that stuck in me, and I spent the night in agony, until my bitch pulled it out, while I was on my last legs. But then the blessing of Muḥammad reached me, God bless and preserve him!"

16.3 *In the furthest reaches of Paradise; a conversation with al-Ḥuṭay'ah*

The Sheikh moves on (may God acquaint him with joy on every path!). He sees, in the furthest part of the Garden, a dwelling that resembles the hut of a shepherd girl. In it is a man on whom the light of the dwellers of Paradise does not shine. Near him stands a stunted tree with poor fruit. "You, servant of God," he says, "are content with paltry things!" The man replies, "By God, I arrived here only after much hustle and bustle, a lot of sweat and tears, and the intercession of the tribe of Quraysh, which I wish had not happened!" "Who are you?" asks the Sheikh. The man answers, "I am al-Ḥuṭay'ah al-ʿAbsī." "How did you manage to receive intercession?" "Because of my truthfulness." "In which matter?" " Because I said:

> Today my lips refuse to utter anything but
> indecency—but I don't know to whom I'll speak.
> I see I have a face that is malformed by God's creation:
> shame on that ugly face and on its carrier!"

Then the Sheikh asks him, "What about your verse:

> He that does good will not lack his reward:
> kind deeds will not be lost between mankind and God.

"Why wasn't it this verse for which you were granted repentance?" Al-Ḥuṭay'ah replies, "Because pious people before me had already said the same. I may have composed it but I did not act accordingly; therefore I was denied a reward for it." The Sheikh asks, "And what about al-Zibriqān ibn Badr?"[538] "He was a leader in the former world and is one now in the Hereafter," answered al-Ḥuṭay'ah, "He benefited from my lampoons, whereas others did not benefit from my eulogies."

The Sheikh leaves al-Ḥuṭay'ah and goes on. He sees a woman in the furthest part of Paradise, close to the place from where one can look down into Hell. "Who are you?" he asks. She replies, "I am al-Khansā', of the tribe of Sulaym. I wanted to see my brother Ṣakhr, so I had a look and I saw him, like a lofty mountain, with a fire burning on his head. He said to me, 'What you said about me has come true!' He meant my verse: 16.4

The conversation with al-Khansā'

Truly, leaders follow Ṣakhr's example;
he's like a marker mountain with a fire on top."[539]

Hell

17.1 *The conversation with Satan* The Sheikh looks down and sees Satan[540] (God curse him!), writhing in fetters and chains, while Hell's angels have a go at him with iron cudgels. The Sheikh says, "Thanks be to God, who has got the better of you, enemy of God and of His friends! How many generations of Adam's children you have destroyed innumerable, only God can count." The devil asks, "Who is this man?" "I am ʿAlī ibn Manṣūr ibn al-Qāriḥ, from Aleppo," replies the Sheikh. "I was a man of letters by profession, by which I tried to win the favor of rulers." "A bad profession indeed!" says Satan. "You'll live on a minimum income, hardly enough to keep your family. It's a slippery business; many like you have gone to perdition because of it. Congratulations on being saved! «So beware, and again, beware!»[541] But I'd like you to do something for me. If you do I will be much obliged."

"I cannot possibly do anything to help you," replies the Sheikh, "for there is a Qur'anic verse already about those in Hell; I mean the words of the Exalted,[542] «Those in Hell will call to those in Paradise, 'Pour us some water or whatever God has given you!' They will reply, 'God has forbidden these things to the unbelievers!'»"

"I am asking you none of that," says Satan. "I am asking you to tell me something: wine is forbidden to you in the Temporal World but permitted in the Hereafter; now, do the people in Paradise do with the immortal youths what the people of Sodom and Gomorra did?" The Sheikh exclaims, "Damn you, haven't you got enough to distract you? Haven't you heard what the Exalted says:[543] «There they will have pure spouses and they will live there forever»?"

Satan says, "In Paradise there are many drinks apart from wine . . . ![544]—But tell me, what happened to Bashshār ibn Burd? I owe him something that I do not owe any other son of Adam: he, unlike all other poets, preferred me to Adam, for he said:

Satan is better than your father, Adam;
  you wicked people, understand this well!
His element is fire, and Adam is of mud:
  mud will never rise as high as fire!

"He spoke the truth; but those who speak the truth will always be hated!"

17.2.1 *The conversation with Bashshār ibn Burd*

No sooner does Satan fall silent than a man appears, plagued with various kinds of torment. He closes his eyes so as not to have to see the punishment that has come upon him; but then the Angels of Hell open them again with pincers of fire. This is Bashshār ibn Burd, who has been given eyes after having been blind from birth, to make him see the chastisement that has come over him.

The Sheikh (may God raise his rank!) says to him, "Abū Muʿādh, you were excellent as a poet but bad in your beliefs! In the Fleeting World I would often think of some of your verses and ask God's mercy for you, assuming that repentance might still come to you. I mean, for instance, these verses:

Return to an abode where you can live in comfort;
  The time has passed and now you are alone.
You hope for a tomorrow; but tomorrow is like a pregnant woman
  in the tribe: one does not know what she will bear.

"Or these:[545]

Woe for Asmā', the daughter of al-Ashadd!
She stood up to be seen and saw me, all alone.

She's like the sun that breaks through the thin clouds.
She was stingy with one cheek but revealed the other.
And then she turned away, just like a breath sighed inwardly.
—Many a 'friend' was like a suppurating boil,
(I feared his coming like a fit of fever),
A boil I had to carry on a patch of skin. . .
A free-born, noble man may be rebuked; sticks are for slaves.
There's nothing for the importune except rebuff.

17.2.2 "But now your situation is desperate!—Actually, in one rhyme of this poem you use the word *subd*.[546] Now, if you meant the plural of *subad*, which is a kind of bird,[547] you are mistaken because a word of this pattern cannot have such a plural. Or, if you simply left out the second vowel of *subad*, you have made a bad verse, because omitting the vowel *a* is not a recognized poetic license. You cannot use the argument that al-Akhṭal said:

Not everyone who is duped, when he's concluded (*salfa*, for *salafa*) a sale,
can return to rescind and get back what he lost;

"nor that someone else said:

They said: 'You dusty one!' I said, 'You're right!
My father is from dust, since God created (*khalqahu*, for *khalaqahu*) him an Adam.'

"For these are irregular forms. As for the verse by Jamīl:

There cried of parting from Buthaynah—the aim is a gathered tribe
at Dhāt al-Raḍm—a pure black (*ṣard*, for *ṣarad*), 'fettered' crow.[548]

"Those who recite it with *ṣurd*, meaning *ṣurad* ('shrike'?)[549] and then deleting the second vowel, are wrong, for correct is *ṣard*, i.e., 'pure,' as in the expression 'I love you with a *ṣard* (pure) love,' here meaning a black crow in which there is no white. The word *muḥajjal* ('fettered') is derived from *ḥijl*, an ankle-ring used as a fetter. 'Adī ibn Zayd says:

You, woman, you who blame me: I've encountered what holds back a man
and I've been hopping with two ankle-rings, like a shackled man.

"A crow is described as being 'shackled' on account of the shortness of its heel tendons.[550] A poet says:

Many a 'shackled one' that hopped between the dwellings, like
an Ethiopian under a deep-black cloud, now falling, now rising."[551]

But Bashshār replies, "Hey man, spare me your trivialities! I am busy with other concerns and have no time for you!"

17.3.1 *The conversation with Imru' al-Qays*

The Sheikh asks where he might find Imru' al-Qays ibn Ḥujr. "There he is, within hearing distance!" is the answer. He says to him, "Abū Hind, the transmitters in Baghdad recite, from your poem 'Stop, you two and let us weep,'[552] a few of the lines with the addition of an extra-metrical 'and' at the beginning. I mean these verses:[553]

And the peaks at al-Mujaymir's crest, the morning after,
[with debris from the flood, looked like a spindle's whorl.]

"Likewise:

And the songbirds of the valley, in the morning, [seemed
to have been made to drink a fine and spicy wine.]

And the wild beasts in the evening, lying drowned [in all
its furthest reaches, looked like wild uprooted onion bulbs.]"

Imru' al-Qays replies, "May God do away with those people! They have spoiled the transmitted text. If they do such things, then what difference is there between poetry and prose? This is something done only by people without any instinct for knowing about poetic prosody. And as a result later critics assume that this is allowed in principle in verse.[554] Wrong! Wrong!"

The Sheikh continues: "Tell me about your verse,

She's like the first-born one, the whiteness mixed with yellow
[nourished with pure water that has not been sullied].[555]

"What did you mean by 'first-born'? The commentators have different opinions. Some say it is an egg; others say it is a pearl; or a meadow; or a flower; or a papyrus plant. And is the word 'whiteness' a nominative, a genitive, or an accusative?"

Imru' al-Qays answers, "All these are good, but I prefer to read it as a genitive." The Sheikh says (may God free his mind so that he can devote himself to literature!) says, "You would be surprised if I explained to you what the grammarians had said about it! Now as for your verse:

. . . with debris from the flood, looked like a spindle's whorl,

"some scholar recites the word 'debris' as *ghuththā'*, with geminated *th*."[556] "That man is really ignorant!" replies Imru' al-Qays, "It is the opposite of what those do who add the word 'and' at the beginning of lines, for they wanted the text to cohere but spoiled the meter, and this wretch wanted to correct the meter but corrupts the word. Likewise, in my verse

I came when she had shed (*naḍat*), for sleep, her clothes,

"some read it with doubled *ḍ* (as *naḍḍat*), others recited it with a single one (as *naḍat*). Both mean 'to shed one's clothes,'[557] but if you double the *ḍ*, the verb looks as if it is from *naḍīḍ* ('small quantity'),[558] as when one says 'this is small quantity of rain (*naḍīḍah min al-maṭar*),' meaning 'light rain.' I prefer to read it with a single *ḍ*, but people have been moved to read it with double *ḍ* because they do not like the metrical shortening. But I do not dislike it myself."[559]

17.3.2 The Sheikh says (may he never cease to utter wise words), "Tell me about your poems that rhyme in *-ānī*, in *-īṣū* and *-īḍī*. The first begins with:

To whom do these remains belong that I can see, which made me sad:
like lines of script upon a palm leaf from the Yemen?[560]

"In this poem you say several things that are rejected by the ear, such as:

> Though I may be grieving in the evening, yet at many raids
> I have been present, on a lean, soft-chested horse.[561]

"It is the same with the poem on *-īṣū*:

> . . . On a tall ostrich male, which with its spouse has,
> at the sand dune's ridge, some heaped-up eggs.[562]

"And also your verse:

> I pray this rain may fall upon my sister, far away Ḍaʿīfah:
> too far to visit her myself, except in verse.

"There are more like these. Did you and the others not instinctively notice these irregularities? Or did these recondite ways of speech come to you naturally, while you were fully aware of its possibilities? There can surely be no doubt that Zuhayr knew the metrical irregularity he committed, when he said,[563]

> He seeks to surpass two men, who, before him, were of noble descent,
> who reached the status of kings and excelled above subjects.

"for one perceives it through one's inborn instinct; God be blessed, the best of creators!"

Imruʾ al-Qays answers, "As far as we know, the early Arabs did not mind at all about coming up with such things, and I do not know what stopped them. My contemporaries and I would just compose a verse from beginning to end, and when it failed, or almost,[564] then its quality would be clear to whoever heard it."

The Sheikh continues (may God steadily give him His benefi- 17.3.3
cence!), "Tell me about your verse[565]

> O yes, so many splendid days you had with them,
> one day (*yawm-*) at Dārat Juljul in particular!

"Do you read *laka* ('you had') with a shortened syllable at the end of the second foot, or do you recite it in the other transmitted version?[566] As for the word *yawm* ('day') in the second hemistich, it is possible to have it in the accusative, the genitive, and the nominative. The accusative, because this is required for adverbial adjuncts; the operator is here an implied verb. The nominative, if one takes the *-mā* in *siyyamā* to be the 'preventing' *mā*, which according to some Basran scholars is indefinite; if this is the case, then the pronoun *huwa* ('he, it') is implied after it.[567] Finally, if one reads *yawm* in the genitive, then *mā* is considered to be one of the 'redundant additions.'[568] Instead of *lā siyyamā* ('in particular') one can also read *lā siyamā*, with a single *y*. The former is standard, but some people use the lightened form, al-Farazdaq for instance.[569] It is said that he, being drunk, came past a pack of dogs. He greeted them and, not hearing an answer, he said:

The leaders of the tribe did not return my salutation
  when I came past at Postal Service Street,
and in partic'lar (*lā siyamā*) one who wore
  a purple woollen garment, sitting there."

"As for the metrical irregularity in 'so many splendid days you had,'" says Imru' al-Qays, "that is what I said in those pre-Islamic days. But the schoolteachers in the Islamic period changed it according to their taste, and there is no harm in their preference. The various opinions on the case of *yawm* ('day') are equally plausible. But *siyya-*, with doubled *y*, is better and more usual than *siya-*." "Certainly;" replies the Sheikh, "if you use the lightened form it would contain merely two consonants, one of which is a weak one.[570]

17.3.4 "But tell me about the stanzaic poem that is attributed to you: is it genuine?" He recites to him what some people have transmitted in his name:[571]

My friends, turn off the track and halt!
Then will the swift she-camels halt,

The Mahrī dromedaries, travelers at night,
Fast-footed in their march,
And used to lengthy journeying.
They all turned off the track and stopped,
Preoccupied with worrying,
Still carried by the ruddy mounts,
But not consoled by them;
The parties turned aside and stopped.
My fellow tribesmen! When
Love hits a youthful man
First in his heart, then rises up,
And wrecks his strength—
That man has fallen deeply down.

Imru' al-Qays exclaims, "No, I swear by God I have never heard this! It is a style I have never attempted. Truly, a lot of lies are being told. I think it must be by some poet in Islamic times. He has wronged me and done me a bad turn! After my poem that begins:

A happy morning to you, O decaying traces!
—But can be happy he who lived in bygone times?

"And my poem

Two friends of mine, let's pay a visit to Umm Jundub,
so that I can fulfill a need for my tormented heart!

"is it conceivable that such things are attributed to me? *Rajaz*[572] is among the weakest kinds of poetry and this meter is one of the weakest kinds of *rajaz*!"

The Sheikh (may God fill his heart with joy!) is amazed by what he hears from Imru' al-Qays. "How do you recite," he asks, "this verse: 17.3.5

She swayed,[573] to throw me off. 'Hold it!', I said to her,
'You are forbidden to throw down a man such as I am!'

"Do you say *ḥarāmū* ('forbidden,' nominative), making an imperfect rhyme, or do your say *ḥarāmī*, making it like Ḥadhām(i) or Qaṭām(i)?[574] For some scholars of the Second Dynasty[575] think so much of you that they think you could not have committed such a fault."

Imru' al-Qays answers, "In our view there is nothing amiss with this imperfect rhyme. Have you not heard this verse from the same poem:

> It is as if Badr were adjacent to Kutayfah,
> and as if Irmām were part of 'Āqil."[576]

The Sheikh says, "You are right, Abū Hind, because 'Irmām' is not an attribute here, so that it could take the genitive by adjacency,[577] since it is dependent on the word *ka-annamā* ('it is as if'). Adding the possessive pronominal suffix of the first person would weaken the intended effect.[578] Some people believe that such a possessive is found in the verse by al-Farazdaq:

> And you don't know, when she sits upon it,
> 'if Sa'd Allāh is more numerous or (my?) Judhām.'[579]

"They say that he used a possessive pronoun (*Judhāmī*, 'My Judhām'), as did Jarīr when he said:

> These are my Quraysh (*Qurayshiya*) and the Helpers are my
> helpers.'[580]

"And similarly when he said:

> And when I am angry the tribe of Māzin will be behind me, throwing,
> and the sons of my Jandalah ('Rock') are as the best of rocks.[581]

"Some recite it as 'the sons of Jandalah (*Jandalatin*) are as the best of rocks.' This Jandalah is the mother of Māzin ibn Mālik ibn 'Amr ibn Tamīm; she is one of the women of Quraysh.

17.3.6 "We also transmit a verse of yours that is not found in all recensions, and I suspect it is spurious, since it contains things that do not conform to your practice; it is this verse of yours:

When in the morning ʿAmr ibn Darmāʾ, the hero, comes
with his cutting sword, he walks like a lion."

Imruʾ al-Qays says, "God blast the wretch! He has forged a lie and did not rectify. To attribute something like this to me, I consider it a scandal! If he who did this lived in pre-Islamic times, he is one of those found roasting in the flames;[582] if he was a Muslim, he was stumbling in the dark." The Sheikh says,[583] " I disapprove of the elision of the ending *-ah* of *qaswarah* ('lion'), for it cannot be elided here. This happens very rarely in the poetry of the Arabs. As for the verse by a certain poet:[584]

Ibn Ḥārith,[585] whether I long to see him
or aim to praise him—people know!

"—this is different, for changing the form of personal names occurs more readily than changing indefinite nouns, for the indefinite noun is the original in this respect."[586]

17.4.1 *The conversation with ʿAntarah*

The Sheikh looks and sees ʿAntarah al-ʿAbsī,[587] wholly bewildered, in Hellfire. "What is wrong with you, my friend from ʿAbs?" asks the Sheikh, "It is as if you never composed your lines:

And I have drunk, after the midday heat slowed down,
some good old wine *bi-l-mashūfi l-muʿlam*,[588]
From a striped, yellow glass, paired, in my left
hand, with a gleaming pitcher fitted with a strainer.

"When I think of your line:

Have poets still left anything to patch?[589]

"then I say: this was said when the total amount of recorded poetry was still small and committed to memory. But now that 'for the hunter there are too many lizards' and 'ten thousand people have become wizards,'[590] if you heard all the poetry that was composed after the mission of the Prophet (God bless and preserve him), then you would blame yourself for what you said and you would realize that it is rather as Ḥabīb ibn Aws said:

If poetry could be exhausted, then it would already have been so
by the collected water in your cisterns, in past times.[591]
Rather, it is the rainfall of the mind: some clouds
may vanish, only to be followed by more clouds."

"Who is this 'darling' (*ḥabīb*) of yours?" asks ʿAntarah. "He is a poet who appeared in the Islamic period," answers the Sheikh; he recites some of his verse. "The root is Arabic," says ʿAntarah, "as for this branch of it, it is uttered by a dunce! This is not the style known to the Arab tribes." The Sheikh laughs, amused. "True, he was criticized for all these metaphors. Yet there are metaphorical expressions in many poems of the ancients; only they are not heaped together as in the poetry of Ḥabīb ibn Aws.

"But what did you mean by *bi-l-mashūf al-muʿlam*? A dinar or a garment?" ʿAntarah replies, "Whichever way you prefer. Both are good and unobjectionable." Then the Sheikh (may God make his ears the repository of all pious deeds!) says, "I find it hard to bear that someone like you has entered Hell. It is as if my ears still listen to the singing girls in al-Fusṭāṭ, warbling your verses:[592]

These tears, are they Sumayyah's, dripping from the eyes?
If only I had been aware of this from you before today!
She threw herself upon me when the stick fell down on me:
as if a young gazelle were in the tent, with tearful eyes.
This slave is *your* slave and this wealth is yours!
Your torment, will it be dispelled from me today?[593]

17.4.2 "I also like to quote this verse of yours:[594]

You have become to me—don't think it otherwise—
someone much loved and honored.

"You did right in using the word *muḥabb* ('loved'), for it is the word that is required by the form *aḥbabtu* ('I loved'), which is the form generally used by poets; but when they use a passive participle they turn to the form *maḥbūb*.[595] Zuhayr ibn Masʿūd al-Ḍabbī says:

With a bright white blaze, much loved (*maḥbūbah*):
a decent horse is loved indeed.

"Some scholar or other said that the word *muḥabb* is never heard, except in ʿAntarah's verse. Someone who says *aḥbabtu* ('I loved') must also say *muḥabb*; however, the Arabs chose to use *aḥabba* for the verb but they use *maḥbūb* for the passive participle. Sībawayh quotes this verse with the form *iḥibbu* ('I love'), with initial *i*:[596]

Because I love her I love black people: I even
love, for the love of her, black dogs.

"This is according to the view of those who say 'Mighīrah,'[597] with *i* after the *m*, for the sake of vowel harmony. But in his view this form is not from the verb *ḥababtu - aḥibbu* ('I loved - I love').[598] The form *ḥababtu* does in fact occur; a poet said:[599]

By God, but for his dates I would not love him (*mā ḥababtuhū*)
and he would not be beneath ʿUbayd and Murshaq.[600]

"It is said that Abū Rajāʾ al-ʿUṭāridī recited:[601] «So follow me and God will love you (*yaḥbibkumu*)». As a general rule verbs of geminate roots with a transitive meaning have *u* as vowel of the imperfect tense, as in *ʿadadtu - aʿuddu* ('I counted - I count') and *radadtu - aruddu* ('I sent back - I send back'); but there are some rare irregular cases, such as *shadadtu l-ḥabl* ('I fastened the rope'), with imperfect tense both *ashuddu* and *ashiddu*, *namamtu l-ḥadīth* ('I reported slanderous talk'), imperfect tense *anummu* or *animmu*, and *ʿalaltu l-qawl* ('I repeated the words'), imperfect tense *aʿullu* and *aʿillu*. If such a verb is intransitive it has *i* as the vowel of the imperfect as a general rule, as in *ḥalla ʿalayhi l-dayn* ('the debt became due for him'), imperfect *yaḥillu*, or *jalla l-amr* ('the matter became important'), imperfect *yajillu*. The imperfect vowel *u* occurs more often in intransitive verbs than the vowel *i* occurs in transitive verbs; for example in *shaḥḥa* ('to be stingy'), imperfect *yashuḥḥu* or *yashiḥḥu*, *shabba l-faras* ('the horse pranced'), imperfect *yashubbu* or *yashibbu*, *ṣaḥḥa l-amr* ('the matter was correct'), imperfect *yaṣiḥḥu* or *yaṣuḥḥu*, *faḥḥat al-ḥayyah* ('the snake hissed'), imperfect *tafiḥḥu* or *tafuḥḥu*, *jamma l-mā'* ('the water gathered'), imperfect *yajimmu* or *yajummu*, *jadda fī l-amr* ('he was serious about the matter'), imperfect *yajiddu* or *yajuddu*, and many other verbs."

17.5.1 *The conversation with ʿAlqamah*

The Sheikh looks up and sees ʿAlqamah ibn ʿAbadah. "How painful to see you in this place!" he exclaims. "Of no avail to you now are your two 'strings of pearl'!"[602] (He means his poem rhyming in *-ūbū*:

A heart by pretty girls enraptured carried you away,

and the other rhyming in *-ūmū*:

Is what you know, what you have been entrusted with,
concealed?[603])

"By Him who is able to release you, what did you mean by:

Do not equate me then, girl, with a callow youth—
may rain-filled clouds pour down their loads on you!
—But why's your heart still thinking of her, that Rabīʿah girl,
for whom a well is being dug in Tharmadā'?[604]

"By 'well' did you mean a well one goes to for water, or is it a grave? Both interpretations make good sense." ʿAlqamah replies, "You try to make laugh someone who would rather cry;[605] you want to pluck fruit when it is dry! Mind your own business, you who are saved!"

17.5.2 The Sheikh says, "If truthful verses could intercede for you, even though God, praised be He, is not mentioned in them, then your verses on women could; I mean your lines:

You ask me about women? I'm a specialist,
a doctor, knowing about women's ailments all![606]
When a man's hair turns gray, or when his wealth is scarce,
he has no share of their affection.

What women want is wealth, wherever they know it is;
men's bloom of youth is wonderful to them.

"If I found you in more comfortable circumstances I would ask you about your verse:

On every tribe you have conferred (*khabaṭṭa*) a benefit:
so Sha's, too, is entitled to a bucketful of boon.[607]

"Did you really pronounce it as *khabaṭṭa*, with doubled *ṭ*?[608] Or did some other Arab say it like that? After all, it is possible for a poet to say one thing in a poem after which the transmitters change it.—I also want to ask about your verse:

A cup of grape-wine of a powerful man, that was kept for ages
for some of its owners; it came from the wine shop, in plenty (*ḥūm*).[609]

"People have different views about your word *ḥūm*. Some say: he means *ḥumm*, i.e. 'black,' with one *m* changed into *w*;[610] but others say: he means *ḥawm*, meaning 'plenty,' with the *a* changed into *u*, as required by the rhyme. Yet others say that *ḥūm* means 'circulated (*yuḥām bihā*) for the drinkers,' i.e. 'passed round.' Likewise, your verse:

One with reddish-brown cheeks leads them, experienced (*mukhtabar*),
a camel stallion, thickly fleshed, bulky.

"This has been transmitted with *yahdī* ('he leads'), with *d*, and with *yahdhī*, with *dh*.[611] As for the word *mukhtabar*, it is said that it refers to finding out the difference between non-pregnant camels and those that have been impregnated; others say that it comes from *khabīr*, meaning 'foam at the mouth,' or, according to others, 'flesh,' or 'camel hair.'"

17.6.1 *The conversation with ʿAmr ibn Kulthūm*

The Sheikh muses, "I wonder what ʿAmr ibn Kulthūm is doing." He is told, "There he is, below you! If you wish you can have a chat with him." The Sheikh asks him, "How are you, 'drinker in the morning' from the bowl of the pretty woman, and 'drinker in the evening' in the Perishable World?[612] I wish you had not made a faulty rhyme in your verse:

> Their coats of mail were like the surfaces
> of ponds, when struck by skimming winds."[613]

ʿAmr replies, "You are happy and unaware of our misery! Rather keep yourself busy with glorifying God and let alone what is past, for it will never return. As for that rhyming defect of mine that you mention, well, it happens that among three or four brothers there is one who is lame or one-eyed, but they are not blamed for that. Let alone when their number reaches five score, or even more!"[614] "I am very sorry" says the Sheikh, "that now you drink nothing but water boiling hot,[615] because you sinned such a lot; and that after you used to purchase vintage wine from Khuṣṣ or elsewhere, standing before you, like saffron its hue![616]—They have two explanations of the word *sakhīnā*: one is that it is from *sakhāʾ*, 'generosity,' i.e., 'we were generous (with the wine),' and the other is that it derives from 'hot water' (*al-māʾ al-sakhīn*),[617] because al-Andarīn and Qāṣirīn[618] belonged to the Byzantines at that time, and they used to drink wine mixed with hot water, in summer or winter.

17.6.2 "Some lettered person in Baghdad was once asked about your verses:

> Such grief as mine has not been suffered by a camel mother who
> has lost her calf and lets resound her yearning moans,
> Nor by a gray-haired woman whose misfortune left to her
> of nine sons none who are not buried.

"Is it possible to read *shamṭāʾ* ('gray-haired woman') in the accusative? The man did not answer, but in my opinion this is possible on two grounds. One is that a verb is implied, to which the listener's knowledge guides him, as when one says, 'nor *shall I mention* a gray-haired woman,' namely that her yearning is strong. It is also possible that it is as when one says, 'And *do not forget* a gray-haired woman,' or some other verb.[619] This is like saying 'Ka'b ibn Māmah is generous, and not (*wa-lā*) Ḥātim,' that is, 'I shall not mention Ḥātim,' meaning 'he is extremely generous and I need not mention him since he is so famous.'[620]

"The other ground is that *walā* can be derived from *walāhu l-maṭar*, 'the rain irrigated it a second time'; meaning that this yearning concurs with my yearning, so it has become, as it were, its associate (*waliyy*). It is also conceivable that it is from the verb *waliya – yalī* ('to be near, to follow'), which has been changed into *walā*, according to the dialect of the tribe of Ṭayyi'."

17.7.1 *Al-Ḥārith ibn Ḥillizah*

The Sheikh has another look and sees al-Ḥārith al-Yashkurī.[621] He says to him, "You have given much trouble to the transmitters, with the explanation of your verse:

They claim that everybody who has 'beaten the wild ass'
is a vassal unto us and that we are their protectors.

"I think you must have meant a real wild ass.[622] And you made a bad mistake in the rhyme in that poem.[623] Perhaps in your dialect you do not pronounce the final vowel at the end of a verse; but when you do that rhymes ending in a vowel and rhymes ending on a consonant will get confused, and this ode of yours would be on a par with these verses of a *rajaz* poet:

An abode that belonged to Ẓamyā—but where is Ẓamyā?
Has she died or is she still among the living?[624]

"Some people recite this verse of yours:

So live (*fa-'ishan*) in good health; may foolishness not harm
you, as long as you will be granted good fortune,

"with a vowel after the *sh* of *'ishan* together with a shortening of the long *ī*, from the verb *'āsha - ya'īshu* ('to live'); and this is rare and ugly.[625] It is the same in the verse by another poet:

Whenever you wish (*tasha'ī*), O Umm ʿUthmān, sever the bond,
and I shall inform you like a parting friend.

"In normal speech one would say *tashā'ī*, for when *tasha'* is followed by a vowel, the vowel length is restored.[626] But this verse of yours is good:[627]

Don't stop the milk flow of your camels, leaving them with milk:
you don't know who may help them to give birth!

17.7.2 "In pre-Islamic days they used to tether a she-camel, its head turned, to the grave of its deceased owner, claiming that when the man was resurrected he would find it revived for him, so that he could mount it straight.[628] O, may he never break her shoulder with his weight! But they are wrong! Rather, people will be resurrected naked, barefoot, uncircumcised.[629]—This camel left to die is mentioned in your verse:

My mount is my pleasure on hot afternoons, when
each worrying man is a blind beast-of-death!"

17.8.1 *The conversation with Ṭarafah*

The Sheikh turns to Ṭarafah ibn al-ʿAbd[630] and asks him, "Ṭarafah, my friend,[631] may God lighten your suffering! Do you remember your verse:

I am a noble man who drinks his fill as long as he's alive;
when we have died you'll know who is the thirsty one of us!

"and

I see no difference between a grumbling miser's grave
and that of one who frivolously, rashly spends his wealth.

"and

Whenever you come to me I'll let you have a quenching morning drink;
and if you've had enough, then be content and more content!

"But how are your morning drink and evening drink now? Both consist of 'water boiling hot,' I think; forever condemned are those who take this drink!

"There is some dispute about the following verse: some people ascribe it to you and others attribute it to 'Adī ibn Zayd; but it resembles more your style: 17.8.2

From many a yellow, fire-scorched arrow I awaited a reply,
beside the fire, having entrusted it to an unlucky hand.[632]

"The grammarians strongly differ in their views on your verse:

O you who are rebuking me I'm present at the battle's din,
and that I attend pleasures: can you let me live forever?

"Sībawayh dislikes the subjunctive *aḥḍura* ('[that] I'm present'), because he believes that the particles that govern the modes cannot be hidden.[633] The Kūfan grammarians, however, read it as a subjunctive on account of the implied particle. This is corroborated by its presence in 'that I attend pleasures,' where you have 'that.' This is not more unusual than in the verse:

Ill-omened people, who do not make a tribe prosper,
and whose crow is croaking of naught but ill omen.[634]

"Al-Māzinī relates from 'Alī ibn Quṭrub that the latter had heard his father Quṭrub quote some Bedouin Arab who read *aḥḍura*, with a subjunctive.—You made a marvellous piece when you said:

If among us there were kings who bestow
upon us like what you are bestowing on us,
I would cross the two plains of Iraq[635] on a lean,
trusty she-camel, with flanks sloping down.
On the day of departure I was given pleasure with her,
by a branch selected by the arrow shafts . . . (?)[636]

"But you followed the ways of the Bedouin Arabs, doing what al-Muraqqish did in his poem beginning:

The abodes, are they deaf, since they do not reply?
If only they lived and had speech, they would speak!

"Or al-Aʿshā when he says:

Leave off! For everyone will become weary of what once he sought.

"But Muraqqish mixed meters[637] in his poem when he said:

Why should we be blamed if a raid has been made
by a king of the Jafnids, an unjust oppressor?

"This goes against the system of al-Khalīl.[638]

17.8.3 "Much has been speculated," continues the Sheikh, "about what happened to you. Some people assert that you were imprisoned during the rule of al-Nuʿmān, others say that it was ʿAmr ibn Hind who did these things to you. But if you had left no other trace in the Fleeting World than your ode rhyming on *-dī*,[639] you would have left your mark splendidly."

"I wish," replies Ṭarafah, "I had not uttered one single hemistich and I had not found, in the Transitory World, any rich pasturing ground, but instead had entered Paradise with the mob and the vulgar herd at least, without having been led forcibly with a halter like a beast. How could I get some quiet and some peace, whereby I find at least some release? «But those who are unjust are firewood for Hell»."[640]

17.9.1 *The conversation with Aws ibn Ḥajar*

The Sheikh turns his head in order to have a good look. There he sees Aws ibn Ḥajar. He says, "Aws! Your companions do not answer my questions. Will you give me an answer? For I want to ask you about your verse:[641]

She did not get the mange, but nearly did; a groom
has bought for her fresh clover for some coins.

"It is from your ode that begins:

Can any of the tribe's belongings still be seen,
or is, after our union, Dawmah's dwelling now deserted?

"But it has also been transmitted as a line in al-Nābighah's[642] ode that begins:

Say farewell to Umāmah—but saying farewell is so hard!
How can you bid farewell to one who is taken away by the caravan?

"It is the same with the line that precedes it:

For half a year, month after month, she was not ridden,
dust being blown upon her saddle in al-Ḥīrah by the wind.

"And also his verse:

The departure is to a tribe, though they are far,
who are now beyond Mount Thahlān and al-Nīr.

"Now both of you are counted among the great poets. So how can this confusion be explained?—Actually, I have always admired your poem rhyming in *-lū*, in which your mention a *jurjah*, which is a leather saddlebag. You said, after having described a bow:

Then I came back with what I'd bought; I'll give no more
for it (I shall, when pigs will fly!)[643]
Than three good cloaks, a saddle-bag,
and a dark skin filled with bees' honey."

Aws replies, "I heard that al-Nābighah of the Banū Dhubyān is in Paradise! Ask him whatever occurs to you and he may tell you. He is more likely to pay attention to these things than me. As for me, I have become oblivious of all that. A fire has been kindled, fingers have been crossed.[644] When I am overcome with thirst, something looking like a river is raised for me, but when I scoop up some of it to drink I find it to be a blazing fire. I wish I were Darim!—He is the one of whom it is said, 'Darim has perished'; one of the Banū 17.9.2

Dubb ibn Murrah ibn Dhuhl ibn Shaybān.[645]—Some worse people than I have entered Paradise! But it is not everybody's fortune to be granted forgiveness, it is like wealth in the Fleeting World."

17.9.3 The Sheikh replies (may his friends be obeyed and those fools who hate him be made afraid!), "I should like to quote these words of yours and present them to those who live in Paradise, saying, 'Aws said to me, Abū Shurayḥ told me!'—I intended to ask you about what Sībawayh says about your verse:

> Her hind legs (*rijlāhā*) keep pace with his forelegs (*yadāhu*); his head
> appears like a pack saddle mounted behind the saddle bag.[646]

"I do not think it is proper to put both 'hind legs' and 'forelegs' in the nominative; there is no metrical necessity that calls for this, because if you had said 'his forelegs (*yadāhu*, nominative) keep pace with her hind legs (*rijlayhā*, accusative),' the meter would not be impaired. Perhaps—if you really said it like this—you strove to achieve assonance; this would have a stronger effect if one read *yadāhā* ('her forelegs'), with a feminine suffix; but in this case, with a masculine suffix, it has no effect. And I really dislike this verse of yours:

> The horses emerge from the dust cloud (*qasṭāl*),

"where you changed the noun into a rare pattern, for CaCCāC is found only for reduplicate roots,[647] even though the expression 'a she-camel with *khaz'āl*,' i.e., 'with a limp' has been recorded."

17.10 *The conversations with the Hudhalī poets Abū Kabīr and Ṣakhr al-Ghayy*

The Sheikh sees a man in the Fire; he is unable to discern his identity. "Who are you, poor soul?" he asks. "I am Abū Kabīr al-Hudhalī 'Āmir ibn al-Ḥulays," replies the man. The Sheikh says, "You are one of the leading poets of Hudhayl! However, I do not like your words:

> Zuhayr! Is there no way to keep gray hair away?
> Is there no going back to one's first youth?[648]

"For in another poem you said:

Zuhayr! Is there no way to turn gray hair away?
    Is there no staying for a weak, much-burdened man?

"And in a third you said:

Zuhayr! Is there no way to keep gray hair at bay?

"—meaning 'to restrain.'—This shows the limitation of your poetic talents. Why did you not begin each poem in a different manner? Al-Aṣmaʿī transmitted only these poems of yours; it is said that a fourth poem is transmitted in your name, one rhyming in *-rī*, which begins:

Zuhayr! Is there no way to hold gray hair away?

"But these verses are very fine:

And I came to the well, where none had drunk
    between the winter and the months of spring,
Except fast-moving wolves like unfletched arrows,
    back at the well at night, where a lone coiling viper drinks,
A narrow path, on which the wolf keeps following his shadow,
    keeping his body at an angle as he goes.
I turned away from it, still thirsty, and I left it, while
    the duckweed rippled, as if it had not been cleared before."

Abū Kabīr al-Hudhalī replied, "How can I gnaw my way through heaps of burning coal, to arrive at a sweet-streaming water hole? The speech of the inhabitants of Hell is Woe and Wail, they have naught else that will avail! Go away, on your intended course, and take care you are not distracted from your horse!"

The Sheikh (may God make him reach the utmost of his hopes!) says, "How can I not be merry, since I have been guaranteed eternal mercy, by Him whose guarantee is true, and whose safeguard encompasses all those who fear Him, too?"

17.11 Then the Sheikh asks, "How is Ṣakhr al-Ghayy doing?" "You can see him there!" is the answer. The Sheikh asks him, "Where is your Dahmā' now, Ṣakhr al-Ghayy? You are not on the same earth or under the same sky! Once, in your time, her youth was blooming and bright, but then the love of her caused you a fright. That is why you said:

I suffer so badly because of Dahmā':
since I love her so much I have frequent visits of fright.

"And what has become of your son Talīd? Your eternal damnation has distracted you from him indeed! And you are justified in forgetting him, just as a wild animal pays no heed, if his heel tendon should bleed."[649]

17.12.1 *The conversation with al-Akhṭal*

Then he spots a man who is writhing with pain. "Who is this?" he asks. The answer is, "al-Akhṭal, of Taghlib." He says to him, "You always used to describe wine, but as a result you are doomed by hot embers to be consumed! How the lords were enraptured by your poem:[650]

They let their camels kneel and dragged skins full of wine,
the skins with stumps protruding, just like breechless blacks.
I said, 'Give me my morning drink, I say!'
and in no time they did so, having taken down their loads.
And then they poured into the jug a wine that, when they glanced
at it, was like an ember being consumed by fire.
They came with a Baysānī wine that, when the pourer poured
a second time, was even more delicious and more smooth.
Hands passed it round to right and left;
it was put down with 'Cheers!'[651] and taken up again.
At times the cups were stopped and we were interrupted by
the singing of a singer or by slices of roast meat.
Delightful was that wine for a relaxing man, delicious for a drinker; I
was tossed by it between hilarity and arrogance.
But instantly inebriation overcame us
from drinking in succession once and twice.

It crept into our bones like ants
that creep upon a dune of fine loose sand.
The vine grew where an expert vintner in the vineyard grew up too,
who sedulously plied his feet upon his spade.
Whenever he feared a thirst caused by a failing star[652]
he'd let a trickling channel flow to it.
I said, 'Kill her, that wine, by mixing her!
How loveable she is when killed!'"[653]

The Taghlibite says, "Yes, many a wineskin did I trail, and I met many a man armored in mail! I avoided any great sin, and I had hoped that my God-serving soul would be called in. But the divine decrees decided otherwise."

The Sheikh says (may God let perdition come over those who hate him!): "You erred in two things: you failed to embrace Islam when it came; and you were close to a man who behaved without shame: you were an intimate friend of Muʿāwiyah's son Yazīd and you obeyed your soul that misleads! You preferred that which perishes to that which will always be, so how could you hope to flee and be free?" 17.12.2

Al-Akhṭal utters a sigh that makes Hell's angels marvel. "Ah, those days with Yazīd!" he says, "With him I would smell ambergris; the supply of mint would never cease. I would jest with him as one jests with a friend; he tolerated me just as a noble man would condescend. So often would he dress me in robes embroidered with brocade, in which mornings and evenings I, trailing it, would parade! I can still see the singing girls when they played before him and sang his verses:

In Māṭirūn, when ants consume
what they have hoarded,
She gathers autumn fruits, but when at last
she comes, she dwells in churches near Damascus,[654]
Or in pavilions round a tavern,[655] with
around it olive trees with ripened fruit.

She stops to watch the rising of the moon;
but see! Already the full moon—she—has appeared!

"I was joking with him one day, being drunk and befuddled, and I said,

Be hale and healthy, Abū Khālid!
And may your Lord with fragrant mint revive you!
You've eaten chicken and consumed it all;
and what is wrong with eating piglets?

"But he only smiled and gave me an award, as fast as the quivering of a sword."

17.12.3 The Sheikh (may God empower him!) says, "That is why you were given what you deserve! Did you not know all that this obstinate man persisted in, who scaled the mountains of sin! What did you find out about his belief: was he a monotheist, or did you find him to be an apostate?" Al-Akhṭal replies, "He liked these verses:

O Khālidah, come here and tell me, let me know
your story (I shall not reveal[656] a confidential talk):
The story of Abū Sufyān, when he went up
to Uḥud, leaving wailing women standing![657]
And how 'Alī sought power, but he failed,
and fortune favored then Mu'āwiyah and gave it him.[658]
Stand up, pour me another cup of wine
pressed by a Christian from a Syrian vine!
When we consider things in bygone ages
we find that drinking it continually is allowed.
There's no dispute among mankind: Muḥammad, in
Medina, has been laid to rest forever in a grave!"

The Sheikh says (may God make all his moments happy!), "A curse upon you! The poets in Heaven and Hellfire have forgotten their panegyrics and love lyrics, but you have not been confused to the extent of being distracted from your unbelief and misdeeds!"

Satan, who has heard all this speech, says to his angels of Hell, "I have never seen creatures more impotent than you, brothers of Mālik!" "How can you say that, Father Bitterness?"[659] they answer. He continues, "Can't you hear this man speaking about things that do not concern him? He has distracted you and the others from your job! If there was anybody with guts among you he would jump up, seize him, and drag him to Hellfire!" They reply, "You can't do anything, Father Whirlwind! We have no power over those who dwell in Paradise." 17.12.4

When the Sheikh (may God make him hear the things he loves!) hears what Satan says he begins to scold and curse him, openly gloating. Satan (a curse be upon him!) replies, "Have you not been forbidden to gloat, children of Adam? But—God be praised!—whenever you were told not to do something you always did it!" The Sheikh (may God continue to favor him!) says, "You are the one who first gloated at Adam's misery; and he who starts is the more unjust one!" He turns to address al-Akhṭal again. "Is it you who said these verses:

I shan't obediently fast in Ramadan
  nor eat the sacrificial meat![660]
I shan't stand up like a wild ass and cry,
  just before dawn, 'Come to salvation!'[661]
Rather, I'll drink it, a chilled wine;
  I shall prostrate myself when dawn is breaking."

"Yes," says al-Akhṭal, "I am sorry and full of worry! But did repentance avail the man of the tribe of Kusaʿ?"[662]

The Sheikh is bored with talking to the inhabitants of Hell. He turns toward his lofty castle again. Having gone for a mile or two it occurs to him that he has not asked about Muhalhil al-Taghlibī, nor about the two called Muraqqish. He has also neglected al-Shanfarā and Ta'abbaṭa Sharrā. So he retraces his steps and stops at that same 18.1.1

The conversation with Muhalhil

place. "Where is ʿAdī ibn Rabīʿah?" he calls. They reply, "Be more specific!" He says, "The one whose verse is quoted as linguistic evidence by the grammarians:

She struck her breast and said to me:
'Adī, you have had strong protectors![663]

"And also this verse:

(The horses) struck down Yashkur's tents,
our uncles matrilineal, the sons of uncles patrilineal.[664]

"And his verse:

What can I hope for in my life, now that my friends
have all been given to drink the cup of Death?"

The answer is, "You describe your friend with things of which we have no knowledge. What are 'grammarians'? What is 'linguistic evidence'? What is all this drivel? We are the Guards of Hell. Say clearly what you want, and you may get a reply!"

The Sheikh says, "I want him who is known as Muhalhil al-Taghlibī, the brother of Kulayb of the tribe of Wāʾil, who has become proverbial." They reply, "There he is, listening to your speech. Say what you want."

18.1.2 The Sheikh says, "ʿAdī ibn Rabīʿah! I am grieved that you have entered this place! If I were sorry for you only on account of your ode that begins:

O, night of ours in Dhū Ḥusam, be bright!
When you are past, do not return![665]

"then this poem alone were worthy of causing lengthy grief for your sake. And whenever I recited your verses about your daughter, who married into the tribe of Janb, my eyes would brim over with tears. Now tell me, why were you called Muhalhil? It is said that this is because you were the first who 'finely wove' (*yuhalhil*) poetry."

"There are many lies that go round," says Muhalhil, "I had a brother called Imru' al-Qays. Zuhayr ibn Janāb al-Kalbī raided us; my brother followed him with some of his people. He composed verses on this:

When their half-bred climbed up the summit of the road I was
within
an inch (*halhaltu*) of vengeance for the deaths of Mālik and of
Ṣinbil.
He's like a goshawk of great age,
leading the vanguard with his weapons.

"The word *halhaltu* means: 'I almost did'; it is also said that it means 'I stopped.' By the 'half-bred' he meant Zuhayr ibn Janāb. Then he was nicknamed Muhalhil.[666] But when he died I was confused with him and I was called Muhalhil." The Sheikh replied, "Now at last I have stilled my thirst for knowledge with truth of certainty!

"But tell me about this verse that is attributed to you: 18.1.3

They thundered in the hour of turmoil and we flashed like lightning,
like stallions threatening stallions.

"Al-Aṣmaʿī thought it spurious and said it was not early Arabic, but Abū Zayd used it as linguistic evidence, declaring it to be authentic. " "Lubad lived a long life!"[667] says Mulhalhil, "I have forgotten what I said in the Perishable World. Why did he think it was spurious?" The Sheikh replies, "Al-Aṣmaʿī claimed that the verbs 'thunder' and 'flash' are not used for threats or for clouds." "That is an error," says Muhalhil, "This verse was said by a man who was rooted in the purity of language—whether it was me or someone else! So stick to that and pay no heed to the words of fools."

The Sheikh asks about al-Muraqqish the Elder; he spots him in the echelons of Hell's torment. "May God lighten your pain, you wronged young man," says the Sheikh, "for I always grieved, in the Fleeting World, because of what that man of the tribe Ghufaylah did 18.2

The conversation with the two poets called Muraqqish

to you, one of the Banū Ghufaylah ibn Qāsiṭ, God's curse be upon him![668]—Some people in Islamic times would scorn your ode rhyming in *-m*, which begins

> The abodes, are they deaf, since they do not reply?
> If only they lived and had speech, they would speak!

"I myself think it is a singularly good poem. Some literate person thought that this poem and the other poem rhyming in *m* by Muraqqish the Younger fall short of the quality of the other odes in the *Mufaḍḍaliyyāt*.[669] But whoever said so was wrong!—Someone has attributed the following verses to you:

> In Naʿmān I selected a piece of *arāk* wood[670]
> for Hind—but who will be able to take it to Hind?
> My two friends (may God bless you!), leave the road, visit Hind, even if
> it is not on your way to your land!
> And then tell her: We lost not our way when we swerved,
> but we turned from the road for the purpose of meeting with you!

"But I do not find them in your collected verse. Is the attribution to you correct?"

"I have said so many things," replies Muraqqish. "Some of it has been transmitted to you and other things have not. It is possible that I have composed these verses, but I have forgotten them because of the eternally long time. Perhaps you find it odd that they are about Hind, whereas my girl was Asmāʾ. But do not disapprove of this, for someone who composes love poetry may move from one name to another. At one stage of his life he may rave about one person and then he may turn to another. Haven't you heard this verse of mine:

> Stupid it is to remember Khuwaylah, now that the tops
> of Najrān's mountains stand in the way of a meeting with her!"

The Sheikh turns to Muraqqish the Younger and asks him about his affair with the daughter of al-Mundhir and the daughter of ʿAjlān,[671] but he does not find him very knowledgeable: he has forgotten the affair because of the epochs that have succeeded one another. "Don't you remember," he asks, "what Janāb did to you, the one of whom you say; 18.3

Janāb swore an oath; I obeyed him.
So blame yourself, if you must blame someone!"[672]

"What did he do?" asks Muraqqish. "I have encountered calamitous things and have been given to drink bitter drinks![673] I wish I could have the torment of the Fleeting World instead!"

Since the Sheikh does not find with him any useful information he leaves him. He asks about al-Shanfarā al-Azdī[674] and finds him to be someone who complains little about his sufferings. "I see you are not as troubled as your companions," says the Sheikh. "True," replies al-Shanfarā, "I made a verse in the Deceptive World and I intend to live up to it for all eternity. It is this: 18.4

The conversation with the two brigand poets, al-Shanfarā and Taʾabbaṭa Sharrā

He erred, they erred; but then he refrained, they refrained.
Forbearance, when complaining is of no avail, is best."[675]

And there he is joined by Taʾabbaṭa Sharrā, as he was in the Deluding World. The Sheikh (may God raise his share of forgiveness!) asks Taʾabbaṭa Sharrā, "Is it true what they tell about you, that you married female ghouls?" "In the pre-Islamic times of Ignorance," he replies, "we would spread all kinds of false reports and rumors. Common sense rejects those things that have reached you; they are all lies. It is the same with all history. What Maʿadd ibn ʿAdnān has witnessed is like what the youngest of Adam's descendants has witnessed." 18.5

The Sheikh says (may God give him abundant forgiveness!), "Some verses have been quoted to us that were attributed to you:

I'm he who married ghouls in a country
where no autumnal rain[676] gives dew or downpour,
Where no lion, hunting in the morning, overcomes his blindness (?)[677]
and where no ostrich is a-seeking bitter colocynths.
I've sported with a girl with polished teeth,
a virgin who tried to pinch my cup and bunch of dates.
My time with her is past and gone; and on its heels there came
the time of graying hairs. Of all good things, say: Gone!

"I have found indications that this poem is by you, for you speak of an ostrich 'a-seeking' colocynths, using the verbal noun *tihibbād*, so I said to myself, this is like when he says, using a similar word pattern in rhyme:

The apparition of the noble man's daughter—when we were together;
but then I went mad because of her, when a-drifting asunder (*tifirrāq*).

"The verbal noun pattern *tifirrāq* can be derived regularly from the verb *tafarraqa* ('to separate'), even though it is rare in poetry. Likewise, Abū Zubayd says:

The scolders raged; then he came ever more
a-nearing (*tiqirrāb*), and a wicked man met him."

But Ta'abbaṭa Sharrā gave no useful reply.

Return to Paradise

Having found few pearls of wisdom with them, the Sheikh leaves them in their neverending misery. He sets out for his dwelling in Paradise. On the way he meets Adam (peace be upon him). "Our father," he says, "May God bless you! There is some poetry that has been transmitted as being by you, such as this: 19.1.1 *A meeting with Adam*

> We are the sons of the earth and those who dwell on it:
> from it we've been created, and to it we shall return.
> Good fortune will not stay with those who have it, and
> bad fortune is obliterated by good fortune's nights."

"True words," says Adam, "They must have been uttered by some sage. But I have never heard them until this moment." The Sheikh says (may God given him an ample portion of reward!), "Perhaps, father, you composed these verses and then forgot about them. For you know that you were prone to forgetting quickly, which is sufficiently proved by the verse recited in the Revelation[678] of Muḥammad (God bless and preserve him): «We made a covenant with Adam before, but he forgot and We did not find constancy in him». Some scholar asserted that you were called *insān*, 'human being,' because of your forgetfulness, *nisyān*. The proof, he argued, is that the diminutive form, 'little man,' is *unaysiyān* and the plural, 'men' is *anāsīy*.[679] That 'human being' is derived from 'forgetfulness' is also transmitted on the authority of Ibn ʿAbbās, and the poet from the tribe of Ṭayyiʾ[680] said:

> Do not forget those pledges! You are called *insān* ('a man')
> because you are a *nāsī* ('someone who forgets').

"Someone read the Qurʾanic verse «Then move on from where the people (*al-nāsu*) move on»,[681] reading *al-nāsi*, meaning *al-nāsī* ('he who forgets'), shortening the *ī*, as it is shortened in «equally for him who stays in it and him who comes to it (*al-bādi*)».[682] The Basrian scholars, however, believe that *insān* ('human being') is derived from *uns* ('sociability') and that the diminutive form *unaysiyān* is irregular.[683] The plural form *anāsīy* was originally *anāsīn*, the *n* having been changed into *y*. But the former opinion is better."

19.1.2 *The snakes of Paradise*

Adam (God bless him) replies, "Must you always be insolent and hurtful? I spoke Arabic when I was in the Garden. When I fell down to earth my language changed into Syriac and I never spoke any other tongue until I died. But when God, praised and exalted be He, returned me to the Garden, I spoke Arabic again. So when am I supposed to have composed these verses, in the Fleeting World or the Latter World? The man who made them must have done so in the Deluding World. Look at his words: 'from it we've been created, and to it we shall return.' How could I have said this when my language was Syriac? And before I left the Garden I did not know about death, or that it was to be decreed for all men, made like a dove's neck ring,[684] not respecting anybody or anything! As for the time after my return, the words 'to it we shall return' would not make sense then, because it would be a plain untruth. We, dwellers in the Garden, are here forever, as immortals."

The Sheikh says (may he be destined for ultimate happiness!), "A certain historian asserts that Yaʿrub found the verses in some ancient folios, in Syriac, and then translated them into his language. This is not impossible.

19.1.3 "Likewise they transmit verses by you (God bless you), composed after Cain killed Abel:[685]

The lands have changed, their inhabitants too;
the face of the earth is dust-colored and ugly.
The abode of its people has fallen into ruin. They've gone,
and the handsome face[686] was left in earth.

"Some people recite the last half-verse as

and gone is the cheer of the handsome face,

"with a rhyme defect.[687] There is a story, which I summarize here, that a man, a descendant of yours known as Ibn Durayd, recited this poem, with the version

and gone is the cheer of the handsome face.

"The first thing he said was, 'He has made a faulty rhyme!' Among those present was Abū Saʿīd al-Sīrāfī, who said, 'But it is possible to read it as

and gone is, in cheerfulness, the handsome face,

"'with "cheerfulness" in the accusative of specification, with the indefinite ending shortened to avoid a cluster of three consonants,[688] just as in

'Amr, who made bread pudding for his people
when the men of Mecca were starving and skinny.'[689]

"But I say, Abū Saʿīd's suggestion is worse than ten cases of faulty rhyme in one poem!"

Adam says (God bless him), "I am sorry for you, all you dear children of mine! You are truly sunken deep into error. I swear, I have not composed this poem and it was not uttered in my lifetime. Some idle layabout must have made it. There is neither might nor power but through God! You have uttered lies first about your Creator and Lord,[690] then about Adam, your father, then about Eve, your mother; and finally amongst yourselves you would lie—but in the end it is in the earth that you will lie!"[691]

19.2.1 The Sheikh moves on apace through Paradise. Suddenly he sees a pretty meadow. He spots snakes in the water, playing and plunging, now lightly, then heavily lunging, "There is no god but God!" he exclaims. "What is a snake doing in the Garden?" Then God (great is His might) gives it speech, after having inspired it with knowledge of what was in the Sheikh's mind. "Haven't you heard in your lifetime," it says, "of She of the Rock, who was true to another as long as he was true? She lived in the fertile river valley, on the water of which she would thrive as long as she was alive. Her human partner she would decently pay whenever she went to drink at noon every other day[692]—someone who is ungrateful is not entitled to abuse a benefactor.[693] But when, through her affection, he made his wealth grow abundantly, and he hoped to perform what he had hoped to do, he thought again about avenging his brother's murder, and he was bent on taking the matter further. He reached for an axe, well-made, and sharpened for the unsuspecting one its blade. He stood himself next to a rock waiting for her to come along fast, and to wreak vengeance upon her at long last: for his brother was among those she had killed, either openly meeting him, or, as some said, from an ambush cheating him. So he hit her—it is easy to drink the cup of death, so bitter! But soon he felt his deed had gone to waste: he had lost a friend that could not be replaced. However, the axe's blow had not resulted in the snake's death, since his hatred had impeded his breath. He repented as strongly as anybody can repent—but who can undo such an event? He said to the snake, deceitfully concealing what he was really feeling, 'Shall we be friends again, ending our estrangement, and both swear to keep our former arrangement?' He invited her to a pact with foolish trickery, having drunk from the milk of treachery. But she replied, 'However long it may be, in all eternity, I shall never again be your mate! How many a back has been broken by fickle Fate! I have found you to be a sinner badly deluded, who in your "friendship" on my ruin has always brooded. I cannot be friends again, because I had to cope with a blow on my head that caused me great pain! A grave that has been dug [694] lies between your aim and me; but of good works there is an abundant quantity.'

"Al-Nābighah of the Banū Dhubyān described this and said, 19.2.2

From those who hold a grudge against me I shall meet
—no sleepless woman suffers in the morning such a worry—
Like what 'She of the Rock' encountered from her ally, though
she paid to him the wergild every other day at noon.
But when he saw that God increased his wealth
and he was happy now, God having stopped his poverty,
He then reached for an axe, the blade of which he sharpened,
a cutting implement of steel.
He stood upon a rock, above her hole,
to kill her; yet his hand, though quick, just failed to hit.
When God had saved her from the axe's blow—
the Kind One[695] has a watchful eye that never blinks—
He said, 'Come on, let's make a pact to God
about our money, till you've paid the sum in full!'
But she replied, 'No, God forbid that I should do this!
For I have seen you are deluded and your oath is false.
I am prevented by a grave that has been dug, always confronting me,
also a neck bone-breaking axe's blow upon my head!'"

Another snake says, "I used to live in the house of al-Ḥasan al-Baṣrī. 19.2.3
He would recite the Qur'an at night and thus I learned the Holy Book from him, from beginning to end." The Sheikh asks (may right guidance always be with him wherever he is!), "How did you hear him recite «He who splits the sky in the morning (*fāliqu l-iṣbāḥ*)»?[696] For some have transmitted that he read it with *a* instead of *i*, as if it were a plural: 'mornings (*aṣbāḥ*).' Likewise with «at evening and morn (*wa-l-ibkār*)»,[697] reading «morns (*abkār*)», as if it were a plural of *bakr*—one says, 'I met him in the morn (*bakaran*).' And if we argue that *anʿum* and *ashudd* are plurals of *niʿmah* and *shiddah*, and ignore the feminine ending, then it is also possible to think that

abkār is the plural of *bukrah*, just as *ajnād* (troops) is the plural of *jund*."

The snake replies, "I have indeed heard him recite it like this. I followed him for a while; but when he died (God have mercy on him) I moved to a wall in the house of Abū ʿAmr ibn al-ʿAlāʾ[698] and I heard him recite the Qurʾan. Then I turned away from the variant readings of al-Ḥasan, such as these two, or his reading 'godspell' (*anjīl*) instead of 'gospel' (*injīl*).[699] When Abū ʿAmr died I did not want to stay there and I moved to Kufa, where I became the neighbor of Ḥamzah ibn Ḥabīb. I heard him recite many readings that are rejected by experts in the Arabic language, such as the reading *arḥāmi* ('bonds of kinship'), in the genitive instead of the accusative (*arḥāma*), in God's word[700] «Fear God, through whom you make requests of one another, and bonds of kinship», or reading *muṣrikhiyyi* instead of *muṣrikhiyya* in «neither can you aid me»,[701] or reading *sayyiʾ* instead of *sayyiʾi* in «waxing proud in the land and plotting evil».[702] This means locking the door of Arabic, because in the Revelation there is no need for poetic license!

19.2.4 "Such things occur in verse, as has been transmitted from Imruʾ al-Qays, who said:

Today I'll drink (*ashrab*, instead of *ashrabu*) without incurring
sin with God, nor as an uninvited guest.[703]

"Some people read it as 'Today I'll be given a drink (*usqā*).' If one reads 'Today I'll drink (*ashrab*),' it is possible to have a hint of the elided *u*, which has no metrical value,[704] for Sībawayh asserts that they do this in the verse by the *rajaz* poet:

When shall I sleep and not be kept awake (*yuʾarriqᵘnī*) by the
donkey man
At night, not hearing the sounds of the beasts?

"This proves that they did not mind the omission of case endings. As for the following verse by another *rajaz* poet:[705]

Whenever the camels swerved I said, 'My frien' (*ṣāḥib*, for *ṣāḥibī*),
straighten them up!
There in the desert, just like ships that swim!'

"—this is very strange; the poet was too stupid to say *ṣāḥi*,[706] which would not affect the meter! But those who defend him assert that he wished to balance the meter of the two hemistichs, so that the meter of *-ḥib qawwimī* ('-n straighten') would be identical to *-ni l-ʿuwwamī* ('-ps that swim').[707] This resembles what they claim for the verse of the poet of the tribe of Hudhayl:[708]

I spent the night enjoying their luxurious naked bits;
covered with saffroned perfume, red as sacrificial blood.

"The grammarians assert that the poet said *maʿāriya* ('naked bits'), instead of *maʿārin*, because he disliked the metrical shortening.[709] However, this view is refuted by the fact that in the same poem rhyming in *-āṭī* there are many verses with such shortening, and it is the same with any long poem of the Arabs. Similarly, in his verse:

I recognized, in Ajduth and Niʿāf ʿIrq,
marks like patterns woven on carpets

"there are two shortenings of this kind;[710] and the same happens in all but a few of its verses. It has been transmitted that al-Aṣmaʿī heard the Arabs recite only *maʿārin* ('naked bits'); but this does not refute the view of the Partisans of Analogy, when they transmit the other version from people that are experts in the pure Arabic tongue."

The Sheikh is astounded (may God bring him near the pious and the god-fearing!) by what he has heard from this snake. She says, "Won't you stay awhile with us? If you wish I could shed my skin and take the form of the most beautiful of the girls in Paradise. If you sipped my saliva you would realize that it is more excellent than the elixir that is mentioned by Ibn Muqbil: 19.2.5

She gave me to drink a red wine, an elixir;
whenever it softened my bones, it[711] too would soften.

“Were I to breathe in your face you would know that ʿAntarah’s girl friend[712] suffers from bad breath and halitosis (which means ‘foul odor of the mouth’) compared with me.”—She meant ʿAntarah’s verse:

It was as if a whiff of musk, straight from a merchant’s pouch,
came from her mouth to you, before her teeth.

“And if I brought your pillow near to my pillow you would rather have me than the woman described in the words of the early poet:[713]

She slept all night; the caravan set off at nightfall.
But the women in our thoughts don’t truly travel.
Her sweet saliva is like musk with honey, mixed
with a red wine bought from the Syrians.
Lord, never rob me of her love!
God will have mercy on His servant when he says Amen!”

19.2.6 The Sheikh is frightened of her (continually safe may God make him, and may He thwart him who attempts to overtake him!). He scuttles off hurriedly through Paradise, saying to himself, “How can one trust a snake whose poison is her pride and glory, and whose concern is a murderous foray?” She calls after him, “Come to me if you want to have pleasure! I am better than that Ḥayyah (‘Snake’), Mālik’s daughter, who is mentioned by the man of the tribe of ʿAbs[714] when he says:

Ḥayyah, Mālik’s daughter, has not out of wedlock given birth to me,
nor do I speak the tales of one who lies.

“And I am better company than Ḥayyah, Azhar’s daughter, of whom a poet says:

When we have drunk clouds’ water mixed with wine,
we thereby think of Ḥayyah, Azhar’s daughter.

“If you stayed with us long enough to find out how affectionate and fair we are, you would be sorry you had ever killed, in the Fleeting World, a snake or a young viper!”[715]

But the Sheikh, hearing her enticing words, says, "May God close the lips of the fair black-eyed damsels for me if I bring myself to suck the lips of this snake!"

Passing through the fields of Paradise he meets the girl that had come out of the fruit. She says, "I have been waiting for you for some time. What has kept you from visiting me? Surely I have not been with you long enough yet to bore your ears with my conversation! I am entitled to preferential treatment from you like any newly wedded wife! A husband has to give her special attention, more than his other wives." 20.1

The Sheikh's return to his paradisical damsel

The Sheikh replies, "I felt like having a chat with the people in Hell and when I had done what I wanted I came back to you. Now follow me, between the Ambergris Hills and the Musk Dunes!"

They cross the hills of Heaven and the sands of Paradise, and she says, "Dear departed servant of God, I think you are imitating the deeds of the Kindite with me,[716] when he says:

Then I got up, taking her with me, as she trailed
over our tracks the train of an embroidered gown.
When we had crossed the clan's enclosure, turning to
a sandy coomb with twisting slopes,
I drew her temple-locks toward me and she leaned
to me, slender her waist but plump her calves."

The Sheihk replies, "God's omnipotence is truly marvellous! You have said precisely what I was thinking, too, in my heart of hearts. But how do you know about Imru' al-Qays? I thought you had grown up in a fruit, far from jinnees and humans?" She answers, "God is able to do everything."

He remembers the story of Imru' al-Qays at Dārat Juljul.[717] Instantly God, the Almighty, creates girls with black, lustrous eyes, who contend with one another in plunging into one of the rivers of Paradise, playing together. In their midst is one prettier than all the others, like Imru' al-Qays's girlfriend. They throw bitter, acid weeds to one another,[718] but they smell like the costliest perfume of Paradise. He slaughters for them his riding animal; he eats and they eat some of it, which is indescribably delicious and delectable.

20.2 *In the Paradise of the* rajaz *poets*

He passes by some houses that are not as lofty as the other houses in Paradise. He asks about them and is told that this is the Garden of the *Rajaz* poets, the dwelling place of al-Aghlab al-ʿIjlī, al-ʿAjjāj, Ruʾbah, Abū l-Najm, Ḥumayd al-Arqaṭ, ʿUdhāfir ibn Aws, and Abū Nukhaylah,[719] and all the others who received forgiveness.[720] [The Sheikh says,] "Blessed be the Almighty Giver! The tradition that has come down to us has come true: 'God loves that which is lofty and dislikes that which is lowly.'[721] *Rajaz* is really a lowly sort of poetry: you, people, have fallen short so you have been given short measure."

Ruʾbah appears on the scene. The Sheikh says to him, "Abū l-Jaḥḥāf! You were rather fond of unpleasant rhyme letters. You composed poetry on the letter *gh*, on *ṭ*, on *ẓ*, and other intractable consonants! And you have produced not even a single memorable saying nor a single sweet expression."

Ruʾbah says angrily, "Do you say this to me, though I am quoted by al-Khalīl and Abū ʿAmr ibn al-ʿAlāʾ! And, in the Past World, you yourself used to flaunt your knowledge of words that those scholars have taken from me and my colleagues!"

Seeing Ruʾbah's sense of his own self-importance, the Sheikh (may his opponent ever be defeated!) replies, "If your *rajaz* verse and that of your father were melted down you wouldn't get one single decent *qaṣīdah* out of it. I have heard that Abū Muslim was talking to you and spoke of the son of a 'slattern' and you did not know the word, so that you had to ask about it in your tribe! You have received rewards from kings without deserving them; others would have been more entitled to them."

Ruʾbah answers, "But surely your leader, in the past, whose views were accepted as normative,[722] used to quote my verses as evidence, making me a kind of authority!" The Sheikh, quick at repartee, says, "Being quoted is nothing to boast about.[723] For we find that they also quote any sluttish slave girl who brings brushwood to fan a fire that blazes on a cold morning when frost has shaken out its feathers and a hoary-headed man fashions firewood from his humble hut, flinging it into the flames so that he can huddle in its heat; to pick mushrooms and fungi is her most glorious day, or to follow a camel driven away. Her master is a brute who is stupid and doesn't care a hoot. And how often do grammarians quote any tiny tot, who knows of letters not a jot? Or any person of the female gender, in need of men to defend her?"

Ru'bah replies, "Have you come to my place only to quarrel with me? In that case, please be on your way! You criticize everything I say!" The Sheikh says (may God silence his opponent!), "I swear that your verses are not suitable for praising those that hear them:[724] they are no better than tar with which you besmear them! You hit your patrons' ears with verses like boulders; one would rather be pleased with the scent of mandal wood when it smoulders. When you pass on from describing the need of a long-suffering camel to describing a galloping steed, or barking hounds at full speed, then you are lost indeed!"

Ru'bah replies, "God, praised be He, has said,[725] «They hand one another cups; neither drivel is there nor recrimination». But what you say is complete drivel; it is neither fair nor civil!" After this lengthy exchange between him and Ru'bah, al-ʿAjjāj hears of it and approaches to separate the two.

20.3 *The joys of Paradise*

The Sheikh is reminded (may God remind him of pious deeds!) that those who drink old wine will reposefully recline. This is what he now chooses, but with a mind unbefuddled and a foot unstumbling.[726] And behold, he imagines the wine seeping through his relaxed limbs like ants creeping on a dune in the light of the moon. He hums the verse of Iyās ibn al-Aratt:

If you, fault-finding woman, would drink wine
  till all your fingers tingled,

You would forgive me, knowing I was right
to squander all my money.

He reclines on a silk mat, telling the damsels with their black, lustrous eyes to lift the mat and put it on one of the couches of the dwellers in Paradise. It is made of peridot, or of gold. The Creator has formed rings of gold, fixed on all its sides, that the immortal youths and the girls, who have been compared to pearls,[727] can take hold of a ring each. In this manner Ibn al-Qāriḥ is carried to the dwelling place that has been erected for him in the Eternal Abode. Whenever he passes a tree, its twigs sprinkle him with rose water mixed with camphor, and with musk though not from a musk rat's blood obtained, but by God the Almighty ordained.

The fruits call at him from every side, as he lies on his back, "Would you like me, Abū l-Ḥasan, would you like me?" Thus, if he wants a bunch of grapes, for instance, it is plucked from its branch by God's will and carried to his mouth by His omnipotence, while the people of Paradise shower him with various greetings: «Their final call will be: Praise be to God, Lord of all Beings!».[728] Thus he is employed, for aye and ever, blessed in length of time delectable, not to change susceptible.

* * *

I have been long-winded in this part. Now we shall turn to reply to the letter.[729]

On Hypocrisy

I have understood the Sheikh's words, "may God make me his ransom";[730] he does not intend to be a hypocrite in saying this. Mankind is far from being in agreement; yet this[731] is a natural trait by which the Sheikh is distinguished from others. People coexist by means of deceit; they have come to invent novel ways of lying. If Queen Shīrīn had said to Kisrā, "May God make me your ransom, whether you are staying here or traveling," she would be merely have been beguiling him and dissembling, no matter how much she pleased him with her unadorned beauty and appealed to him. He had taken her from a lowly state and brought her to resplendent luxury, while his close friends rebuked him for it. There are several stories and reports about them concerning this.[732] It is mentioned that they said to him—but only God knows who is to be blamed or blessed—"How can the King bring himself to approve of this prostitute, who has crept into the sewer?"[733] Thereupon the king gave them a parable of a wine cup (if a beautiful woman finds favor, she does not need magic beads[734]). He put some hair and blood in the cup and said to the person with him, unrepentingly, "Are you willing to drink the contents?" To correct him was his sole intention. "It is not nice," replied the man, "for it is mixed with filth!" Then the king emptied the cup and rinsed it. He cleaned the vessel,

21.1 *Hypocrisy in humans and animals*

sweetened it with honey, and filled it with wine. He offered it to his drinking companions. All now were happy to drink from it—who would loathe a vintage wine? "It is thus," he then said, "with Shīrīn. So do not rush into impudence!"[735]

21.2 Many a lion cub dissimulates towards a lion, secretly harboring rancor and envy. Many a lioness flatters the male, liberally displaying her affection but loath to touch him. Many a lion has vented his rage on a whelp, wishing he could bury it in a deep place ("whelp" is a lion's cub in the language of the tribe of Asad Shanū'ah).[736] But the Sheikh—may God cheer this region with his vicinity!—is above being in need of such explanations. However, I fear that this letter may fall into the hands of a young servant boy, who is not very quick of understanding, so some expressions may be like a foreign tongue to him and he will be as if fettered by it, unable to proceed swiftly or slowly.

Many wolves have been beguiled by she-wolves, while calamities were hidden in their hearts!

"Calamities" (*filaq*) means misfortunes; compare the verse by Khalaf:[737]

The death of the imam is a calamity (*filqatun mina l-filaq*).

The word *silaq* ("she-wolves") is the plural of *silqah*, meaning a female wolf.

Many a king has treated his queen with a gentle disposition, after which she prepared his perdition. Someone may say, "I would give my own father to ransom you, you have done well, you acted perfectly!" But if he could he would cut his jugular vein, for all he did was flatter and feign. A cockerel will sometimes spit out for a hen a grain of wheat, being friendly to her in the cold or the heat, while extraordinary rancor rankles his heart. *Manājīb* are many and few.

The word *manājīb* can here be interpreted in two different ways: firstly, it means "those who have noble sons," from *najābah* ("nobility"), and secondly it means "weaklings," as in the verse by the poet of the tribe of Hudhayl:[738]

> I sent him off into the blackness of the night, while he was
> watching me;
> for only weaklings would prefer to sleep and to keep warm.

What I mean is therefore: *manājīb* meaning "those who have noble sons" are few and *manājīb* meaning "weaklings" are many.

Perhaps that deceitful fowl wishes the mother-of-eggs to die, rather than wanting to protect her. He says to himself with his inner voice, "I wish the slaughterer would come in the morning to this cackling hen, for she is utterly hateful!" Or he will say, "If I were put into a cauldron or into an oven, so that I would meet my end for nothing,[739] then this hen would marry a cockerel in the prime of youth who would properly love her henceforth."

I shall remind the Sheikh of that expression that occurred (in his letter),[740] since he began with such friendly words, and distanced himself from the malicious wiles of mankind. 21.3

Is it not strange that the expression of the Bedouin Arabs *fidā'in laka* ("may I be your ransom!") has the ending *-in*?[741] The *rajaz* poet said:[742]

> Woe! May I be your ransom (*fidā'in laka*), Faḍālah!
> Stab him with your lance and take no heed of him (*lā tubālah*).

Another version that is transmitted has "do not fear him" (*lā tuhālah*).[743] Aḥmad ibn ʿUbayd ibn Nāṣiḥ, who is known as Abū ʿAṣīdah, mentions that in the expression *fidā'in laka*, with *-in*, this ending is not allowed if there is something that requires a nominative.[744] No doubt he adopted this view from the Kufan scholars. His specific evidence for this was the verse by al-Nābighah:[745]

> Gently—may all men be your ransom (*fidā'un laka*)
> and whatever wealth and children I may produce.

The Basran scholars, however, transmit this verse with the reading *fidā'in laka.*

21.4 How can my sincere friend, who is so reluctant to stay away, say that he yearns to meet me as a bereft she-camel yearns for her calf,[746] whereas she forgets it as soon as she is made to carry a load? She may moan three or four times,[747] after which she thinks of it no more! As for the bewailing dove, the Creator has given her wide-spread fame. She is widely characterized as grieving. She gets up to peck a grain and returns to her young with some food—but if she finds that it has been devoured by a peregrine (whoever sees its traces is not pleased!); the talons of a falcon have taken it away! Yet she, the wretch, will soon forget about it. She is but an animal, which is bored in the shortest time with being in the same state. Somebody has asserted—he should not be believed—that pigeons in the present time weep for an unfledged chick that perished in the time of Noah;[748] either the event was inauspicious or the strike was propitious. The fact that they are still doing it proves their loyalty. What can compensate for a sincere friend? Compensation and proper substitute can only be found in such a person. But how can one reproach Time for its cruel behavior? It is replete with evil and perfidy; it is predestined to be mighty in the divine decree.

The gazelle doe should not be described as yearning. She merely grazes with an unconscious mind. Who will give her a tender twig of the *arāk* tree? She will not say to the rider of the emaciated horses: "Reach!"[749] If someone's passion leaves his mind, then, when he longs for a (deceased) child,[750] the passage of time will make him forget, as if he never grieved. How scarce is the sincerity of intimate friends, even if they could be bought for thousands of gold, let alone silver coins!

My friend is never tired of me, nor will he,
if I'm absent, sell me for another friend.[751]

I think that Kuthayyir was inexperienced when he uttered this, unaware of how much evil exists. How could one aspire to the friendship of angels, or be raised to the celestial sphere?

As for what the Sheikh says about my situation (may his person be protected against Time's evil eye and be given prodigious wealth to enjoy!)—"prodigious" (*ḥiyar*) means "much." A *rajaz* poet says:[752] **22.1** *On Ibn al-Qāriḥ's excessive praise of Abū l-ʿAlāʾ*

O Lord of ours, if one is happy for him to grow old,
Then send to him, O Lord, prodigious (*ḥiyar*) wealth!

—how often has an idol been thought to bring good luck,[753] so that, when it actually happened, the ignorant thought it was what was promised![754] If I should enjoy vain praise, then I might as well be publicly exposed as drinking wine in gulps! The steadfast will be rewarded and praised; he who changes his abode will surely be destined to drink from a nearly dry waterhole.

I swear an oath like that of Imruʾ al-Qays, when he wished to stay with his beloved, unafraid of a woman spying or spied upon, and said,

I said, I swear an oath by God: I shall not leave but stay,
though they may cut my head off in your presence, and my limbs!

or another such as was sworn by Zuhayr,[755] when the north wind blew away the war that had risen; I mean his verses:

So I swore upon the Building[756] circumambulated by
the men who built it, of Quraysh and Jurhum,
An oath: How excellent you are, two chiefs, in every situation,
whether unraveled or entangled!

or the binding oath uttered by Sāʿidah,[757] who said, when his soul was ascending to its Lord:

(I swear) an oath of an honest man, whose pledge you're not familiar with;
anyone who governs is a man of experience.[758]

Further, I swear the pledge of al-Farazdaq,[759] when he was afraid of (God's) vengeance, and took the opportunity, standing between the Kaaba and the Standing Place,[760] to say, describing what he had done:

Have you not seen that to my Lord I've made a pledge, and that I stand
between the Kaaba's bolted door and the Standing Place,
Swearing an oath that I shall never vilify a Muslim,
and that false speech will never come out of my mouth.

(With these oaths I swear) that I am lied against, just as the Bedouin Arabs lie about the ghoul,[761] unconcerned with what is transmitted about her; just as what those slanderous proverbs say about the lizard,[762] who cleaves to the rough, hard ground like a lover to his beloved; and just as they put words into the mouth of the hyena though it is dumb,[763] its tongue never loosened, in broad daylight or the evening.

22.2.1 I am supposed to be a man of learning; but I am neither its master nor its fellow. It is, upon my life, an affliction in which one misses, despite one's learning, certain truth. The various kinds of learning require application and someone who "threshes" books assiduously.[764] It is also said that I am a man of religion; but if what lies behind the veil were to be revealed, those who describe my character could never find enough to their satisfaction to revile me and would be eager to make me drink poison mixed with vitriol. When a wild ass, which roams in lush, dark[765] pastures, brays at dawn, how could one claim that it produces metered verses like those that are heard by a damsel kept in her chamber?[766] And would any intelligent and astute person imagine that when a crow croaks he utters amatory poetry? Or that birds that fly with wings are like the "birds" of al-Mundhir that existed for the sake of being given away?[767] How could one think that any bird can produce the cooing of the dove even when it is in fact deaf as well as ugly? Far from the truth is he who claims that stones will speak and that they feel pain when struck, or who seeks to make a cloak of the foam on a camel's mouth! He will not find a model to follow.

If I were unaware of what is being said about me, I would be relieved of having to deny it and set things right. I would be like an idol, indifferent whether it is revered or laden with heavy loads, or like a salt swamp that does not care whether it is called a fertile pasture or one says, "what a bad crop!," or like a slaughtered young lamb that does not mind whether he who eats it says, "it is really fat!" or, when it is cut up, "it is stingy with its fat!" God is the one whose help one asks against false reports (*ilāqī*); the unmoving earth[768] is not weighed in ounces. 22.2.2

The word *ilāqī* is derived from *ilāq*, "false lightning."[769]

How could I be happy when people lie about me and when knowledge is attributed to me? I cannot be sure that, as a consequence, there will not be an unbecoming scandal. My situation, were I glad of this, is that of someone suspected of being rich, who then becomes convinced that the rumor will actually bear fruit.[770] He is happy when ignorant people say, "He is a man of ample means. Both his hands are full of gold!" But then some ruler demands that he bring him a large sum, and he finds it to be a lie, uttered as a sigh. The ruler has him beaten to make him confess, until he dies under torture and receives no mercy.

God is my witness that I am glad when someone finds fault with me, because he speaks the truth about his misgivings about me, and that I am worried by false praise, which leaves me like a hunted animal so thirsty it is unable to feed. If I were butted by a locust's antennae I would give up all volition.[771] A mountain goat could not head-butt me, because I would perish already by the horns of a gazelle. May God forgive him who thinks well of someone who does 22.2.3

evil and who performs his pilgrimage in the intercalary month![772] Were I not so reluctant to appear in people's company and would rather die like a gazelle in its covert, and then were those deluded people who think well of me to keep my company, it would soon turn out that they stray from the right course, the truth that had been obscured would shine bright for them, and those who grope around would grasp a thorny tragacanth(?).[773]

The Sheikh's Return to Aleppo

23.1 *Ibn al-Qāriḥ's arrival in Aleppo*

The Sheikh mentioned that he arrived in Aleppo—may God protect it! If it possessed reason it would have rejoiced at his arrival just as a bereaved crone who has lost her wits rejoices, a woman who has neglected the good management and care of her camels. Her only son has gone far away. He has not denied her what is due to her, and then returns after many years, and then she quenches, through him, her burning thirst. She was to him like a flat-nosed oryx cow grazing with her calf in the late afternoon. The calf was not yet doomed to die. When she saw that the place was safe and did not fear the lurking of limping wolves, she went out into the wide pasture ground and left her calf behind, giving it the difficult task of finding fresh herbage(?), and so that she could save for the calf the milk in her udders(?).[774] But there is no remedy after perdition. The poor thing returned and did not find him. "Do not cause him any pain," she said to the Everlasting, "if he has fallen into the claws of a wolf and suffering has been his lot! You are able to replace lost children; You know the outcome of all augury and prognostication!" While she was wavering between being benumbed and distraught, her lost young lowed softly to her from a curved sand dune where it had lain down, not having seen any hunter drawing his bow. It felt at ease, having eaten its fill. Fate had not done any evil to it and it had not become a predator's prey. Joy flooded her heart after the course of events had become clear to her.

If the acacia gatherer would return to his tribe of ʿAnazah,[775] the joy that would be evident in the tribe at his return and the providential end of their grief would be less than the delight that I harbor and hide in my breast at the Sheikh's approaching these parts and casting down his walking stick. God be praised! He returns the lightning to the clouds in spring![776] A bright flash has come to adorn the skies. Aleppo (may God give it victory!) really is in need of someone who has a little knowledge, in days of war and peace. So what does the Sheikh think? May God establish literary scholarship by adding to his lifetime! Because he is the right equipment for the marvels of literature(?).[777]

23.2 I am truly amazed that a society is colluding in something that is neither good nor pious; something that has no firm ground of certainty, but is polished and made to look good by a skilled artisan! I had almost joined the company of non-existence,[778] without sorrow or remorse, but I feared to appear before the Almighty without having set my palm grove in order by pollinating it. Someone said to a certain sage, "So-and-so has employed subtle means to kill himself; he was unable to detain himself in the Passing Abode, loath to commit novel deeds of evil, and wanted to move on to the Dwellings of Joy." Thereupon the sage spoke, saying words to the effect that this person, still in the prime of his life, committed a sin; it were better for him and his mother if she had lost him as a child. Why did he not suffer with fortitude the vagaries of Time, until Destiny would afflict him? He had no inkling of what he was recklessly undertaking. Every house will come to ruin. But for the wisdom of God (great is His omnipotence), and His holding back men from death through fear of its agony and of annihilation, then everyone who is on fire with anger, or whose sword[779] is too blunt to strike, would wish cups of death to be filled for him. God knows how He will recompense.

Abū l-Qaṭirān al-Asadī—which human being is ever set free from misfortunes?—was a poet of love lyrics and futile themes, dedicating himself to pretty maidens and idleness. I have no doubt that the Sheikh—May God delight literature by lengthening his life!—yearns more strongly for Aḥmad ibn Yaḥyā, in spite of his deafness, or for Abū l-Ḥasan al-Athram, in spite of his broken tooth, than al-Marrār ibn Saʿīd yearned, hoping for a promise and fearing a threat. That man was madly in love with Waḥshiyyah, though he had to forgo a soft bed, being separated from her. He thought of a mouth with teeth white like the flowers of a palm tree, a cheek that could be compared to the color of safflower. But the love of a beautiful woman is deceptive and delusive. In his passion he suffered ever-new miseries. If this woman had died while Marrār was still alive, he would have thought himself as carried upon her bier,[780] particularly in old age, with his soul's strength in decline. Perhaps, if Abū l-Qaṭirān had been able to enjoy this woman for a hundred epochs, without anxiety or being spied upon, it is possible that he would have tired of being united with her, knowing that his bond was lasting. If something had happened to her that had made her change her loyalty, he would have wished that she were cast into something other than a cradle,[781] because a human being is miserly and easily bored; a trusty, docile she-camel[782] will bring him to his death. If she had lost an eye, which once was black and lustrous, he would have thought this was an unforgiveable incident, beyond expiation. But how can someone who has been careless be rebuked, or revenge taken on the neglectful? God—glorified be He—has kept this away from someone who has forgotten and does not know, or from a sleeper who feels pain when perceiving something that hurts.[783] 23.3.1

How could the loyalty of this man from the tribe of Asad be compared with the great loyalty that God has bestowed on the Sheikh? If al-Samaw'al had known of it, he would have acknowledged that he had been a traitor; if al-Ḥārith ibn Ẓālim had known of it, he would have testified that he had been insouciant (*sādir*). This is from the 23.3.2

expression “he did such-and-such a thing insouciantly (*sādiran*),” i.e., not being concerned with anything.

Abū l-Qaṭirān lived among camel-herding slaves, male and female; when he looked at his heels he found them bleeding from treading on thorny shrubs. Who could give him *farās* dates in the grazing ground? *Farās* are black dates. The following verses are quoted in works on obscure expressions:[784]

When they eat *farās* you see black “moles”
  produced by them on the mud from the wells and the hollows.
Incessantly you hear rumbling claps
  like the sound of thunder in a year of abundance.

Perhaps, if he had found a woman prettier than Waḥshiyyah by even half a stone of a doom-palm date he would have forgotten about her and she would have caused him no more pain. It was the habit of this man and people of his kind merely to describe a she-camel or a campsite. The trees he planted were no *nabʿ* trees. When he gathered some truffles he would exult and imagine he had an excellent result! If he sat at tables such as those that the Sheikh sits at, he would end up just as the poet says:[785]

If you had an ʿUdhrite attachment you would not spend the night
  full-bellied: your passion would make you forget eating a lot.

23.3.3 The Sheikh (may God destine for him what he loves!) has sat with the kings of Egypt, about which Pharaoh says:[786] «Have I not the kingdom of Egypt and these rivers, flowing beneath me? Do you not see, then?» And he has stayed in Iraq for a long time, depending on his erudition, while Iraq was ruled by Persia.[787] They are noble and refined people. They spend on food more than one could possibly spend. There can be no doubt that he sat with the highest-ranking lords and experienced their characters in their company, while they handed him cups adorned with pictures,[788] after the custom of the Persian knightly margraves,[789] as al-Ḥakamī says:[790]

The cup[791] went round among us, held in a golden (vessel),
on which Persia had bestowed variegated pictures:
Chosroes on the bottom, and on its sides
wild cows, for which riders are lying in wait with their bows.

—whereas Abū l-Qaṭirān used to draw a drop of water by means of a rope made of palm fiber, putting it into his mug or leather pail. When he ate, who would serve him his broth?[792] In times of plenty he would embark on eating a *nahīdah.*

Nor do I doubt that if the Sheikh (may God give enjoyment to literature by granting him long life!) had been given the opportunity to have a conversation with Abū l-Aswad, in spite of his lameness, his miserliness attested in anecdotes, and his gruffness(?),[793] his affection for him would have been stronger than the affection of Mahdī for his Laylā,[794] not to mention that of Ru'bah for his Ubaylā.[795] If he had lived at a time in which he could have attended a lecture by Abū l-Khaṭṭāb, he would have been more passionate about the latter's weak eyesight than al-Ḥādirah about Sumayyah, or Ghaylān[796] about Mayyah, for he said: 23.4

Two eyes: God said, "Be!" and they were,
doing to minds what wine does too.

And the Sheikh would have admired the gaping mouth of Abū l-Ḥasan Saʿīd ibn Masʿadah more than Kuthayyir admired 'Azzah's white teeth, or the 'Udhrite poet[797] Buthaynah's dark-red lips. Even if Abū 'Ubaydah suffered from bad breath, I am sure that the Sheikh, what with his fondness of historical reports, would have kissed him "as one splits a fig," not feeling himself too grand for this.

In a hadith transmitted on the authority of 'Ā'ishah (God have mercy on her) it says: "The messenger of God (God bless and preserve him) would kiss me as one splits a fig." Someone transmits it as "as one splits a date." It means: taking the upper lip with one hand and the lower lip with the other hand, and then kissing the space between the lips.

23.5 As for the friends that the Sheikh missed when he entered Aleppo (may God protect it!), well, this is the habit of Time, which cannot be trusted to keep matters safe and sound: it replaces inhabited houses with graves and it will not allow a slip to be mended. The tomb of a deceased person is surely the true house, though it may bring the most troublesome misfortune. However, it makes its resident free from need, after his privation,[798] and it saves him from having to procure provisions, no matter how long he has been there(?).[799] The body is concealed from evil,[800] far from women or wine.[801] The poet from the tribe of Ḍabbah[802] said:

I have come to know that my end[803] will be a grave-pit,
after which there is for me neither fear nor privation.
I shall visit the house of truth for a permanent visit;
why should I care for things that fall into ruin and collapse?

The Arabs always speak of the grave as a "house," even if he who moves into it is dead. A *rajaz* poet said:[804]

Today a house will be built for Duwayd.
Many a respectable house have I built,
Many a wrist with a bracelet have I bent.
If Fate could be worn out, I would wear it out;
Or if my opponent were single, I would be more than his match.

23.6 In the paragraph in which the Sheikh mentions al-Khalīl the name is missing of the person that extols me so excessively,[805] pairing the stars with hard stones. Whoever it was—may God forgive his misdeeds and preserve for him for ever his noble qualities!—in his assertion he erred both against me and himself. He ascribed to me things I do not deserve. How often do I have to exculpate myself and justify myself for a sin that never occurred! Truly, I loathe—God be my witness—such false claims as much as the Messiah loathed those who turned him into the Lord Omnipotent, and who thus did not omit any opportunity to stir up religious temptation.[806] The proof is in the words of God the Exalted:[807] «And when God said, "O ʿĪsā son of Maryam, did you say to the people: Take me and my mother as two gods, rather than God?" He answered, "May You be glorified! It is not for me to say what I am not entitled to. If I said it You would know it: You know what is in my soul, whereas I do not know what is in Your soul. You are the one who knows all things that are hidden."»

24.1.1 *The stolen letter*

As for Abū l-Faraj al-Zahrajī, the fact that he knows the Sheikh testifies as if on oath that he has a close connection with erudition and is allied with a good natural disposition. I wished that the letter had reached me,[808] but that fellow traveler was a felon traveler[809]—away with him, for as long as doves sing![810] Could he not have been content instead with some cash or clothes, leaving the letter alone? May his hands drop from his body! May he not find the right path at night by the two stars of the Little Bear![811] If he had been one of the proverbial Arab robber-poets[812] spoken of by people wherever they go,[813] then I would not have forgiven him his deed, despite the poetry he composed, because he went too far and committed an enormity, i.e., a grave misdeed, and he destroyed a well-strung necklace.

24.1.2

Abū l-Faraj and his son[814] were fortunate! His little puddle of knowledge became like the sea's billows when he studied his books under the Sheikh's guidance and memorized what will be forever immutable. "He handed the ancient bow to the man of the tribe of al-Qārah, the musk pouch to the man of Dārīn, the long lance to Ibn al-Ṭufayl, and the reins to the riders that never quit the saddle."[815]

24.2

Though the Sheikh had to contend with contretemps,[816] he has renewed his former acquaintance with the river Quwayq. What a lovely river! It will not give whoever swims in it a drowning death, nor render him out of breath. Its fishy daughters sought by suitors are small and are taken from it unawares; it does not guard them jealously. It sustains them; Fate snatches them. They conceal themselves and do not show their charms, but they leave it reluctantly.

Their boudoirs are of water; the grabbed thing visits them with grabbing—"The grabbed thing" is the net. One says "he grabbed (*alma'a 'alā*) something" when he takes something in its entirety.—while poor Quwayq is not even aware whether Arabs or Byzantines have taken his children into captivity; it does not even care about their desires. Al-Buḥturī mentioned it, al-Ṣanawbarī described it;[817] but I imagine that the Sheikh's taste for it was spoiled by the Tigris and its tributary al-Ṣarāh, helped by its friend the Euphrates.

24.3.1 *Proverbs* As for Aleppo—may God protect her!—she is a devoted mother, joined with all joy. I do not think (if God wills) that she will ever display a blameworthy lack of maternal devotion or neglect the duties imposed on her. The Sheikh—may God please the humanities by granting him lasting life!—has probably made Waḥshiyyah a substitute for those friends he missed, and whose equals no longer exist. It is similar in the idioms of the Arabs: they allude with one particular name to all other names. Someone will say, for example,[818]

May a hand that murdered 'Amr not be lamed,
for you will no longer be humbled nor be wronged.

One man may see someone kill somebody called Ḥassān or 'Uṭārid, or some other name, and then quote this verse. Then "'Amr" stands for anybody for whom the verse is quoted.

24.3.2 It is the same with the verse by a *rajaz* poet:

Sa'd took them to the water, Sa'd being wrapped in his robe.[819]

This became a proverb for everyone who carries out a job but does not do it properly. It could be said about someone called Khālid or Bakr, or God knows what name. In the same vein one uses the feminine form for the masculine, or the masculine for the feminine; they will say to a man: "Woman, walk at the side of the path, for you have strong soles!"[820] or "This summer you, woman, spoilt the milk!"[821] or "You're doing well, woman, pour out!"[822] or "You, girl, say to them first: 'Sluts, may you be kidnapped!'"[823] If they want to tell that a woman used to do good but then died, so that whatever she did was discontinued, they could say: "The good has gone with ʿAmr ibn Ḥumamah."[824] They may say to someone, warning him against the proximity of women: "Don't spend the night close to a man of the tribe of Bakr" or "The man of Bakr is your brother, but do not trust him."[825] There are many similar cases.

25.1.1 *The plight of men of letters*

As for the Sheikh's complaint to me, we are both as it is said in the proverb: "One bereaved woman helps another."[826] This is how al-Aṣmaʿī interpreted the verse by Abū Duʾād:[827]

> And he listens sometimes, as someone who has lost an animal
> will listen to the call of another one who searches.

Both of us, God be praised,[828] have lost something. Whom should we attack, upon whom can we pounce? The riding animal is weak and slow, the provision bag is empty, the riders are in need of a pebble,[829] and all of them hurry longingly toward a palm branch.[830]

> My camel complains to me about the lengthy nightly journey.
> Decent fortitude! Both of us are suffering.[831]

If the thorny acacia tree complains about the adze of the woodsman to the thorny mimosa tree, then it complains of a mishap to another who complains.[832] Speaking truthfully is better than mendacity. I do not doubt that the Sheikh has retained these verses of the man of Fazārah in his memory for some fifty or more years:[833]

> ʿUyaynah, now that you are smitten with love for her,
> why did you seek assistance from someone who has lost his mind?
> You've tried to find support from a man,
> but the one whose help is sought has other things on his mind!

Men of letters have always complained of the vagaries of time, in every generation. They have been singled out by strange events in bucketfuls. The Sheikh knows the story of Maslamah ibn ʿAbd 25.1.2

al-Malik, who bequeathed part of his possessions to men of letters. "They are," he said, "people of a despised art." I think they and bad luck[834] were created as twin brothers. One of them may be successful for a short while, but then it does not take long before his foot slips and his skin is rent by Fate. The Sheikh has heard, in Egypt, the story of Abū l-Faḍl and Saʿīd, whose cases were similar.[835] Now if people with literary erudition were harshly treated already in Umayyad times, how could they be safe from harm during the reign of the Abbasids? If tribulations afflicted them in the prime of al-Rashīd's days, how could one hope for them to enjoy good fortune on a solid basis? Did Abū ʿUbaydah not come with al-Aṣmaʿī, while both of them were seeking good pastures, not wishing to return to Basra? But only ʿAbd al-Malik was made to stay and Maʿmar was sent back.[836] Who knows what is hidden in the bushes? And who would wish to earn a living with this profession? Who does so keeps his wine in a worn-out skin that cannot be relied upon to keep its deposit: it is to him a deceitful friend. It is reported that when Sībawayh[837] considered his situation and weighed it, he wanted to be appointed at the tribunal of torts[838] in Shiraz; and that al-Kisāʾī expressed grief about what he did to him and supported him, so as to surpass Sībawayh's expectations by far. Ḥabīb ibn Aws passed away while in Mosul, in charge of the postal service. A man of letters is always familiar with receiving too little.

25.2 Those the Sheikh mentioned who are guilty of misplacing the diacritical marks when they read are neither respectful nor just. A fox will always be keen to harm a lion; I don't think he is even aware that it is due to envy. When a fierce, softly treading lion goes out at night, ready to cause misery to a large-humped she-camel, or one whose fatness is palpable,[839] then the fox warns against him, as if he were a cautioner of the prey. But the lion does not think him worthy of rebuke and merely considers him one of those misfortunes that must be endured when they befall. How many a thick-necked lion stirred to a rage is kept awake by the singing of a mosquito! All night long it is humming while the bulky lion is suffering. However,

It does not harm the sea, when it is full to overflowing,
if a boy casts a stone at it.[840]

Or whenever a fly is buzzing, should I scare it away?
The fly would then be important to me![841]

The rabble never stop talking, always falling short of noble things and never excelling. They are too sluggish to grasp what is nobly rooted, whereas those who seek erudition will climb its mountains. He who, uniquely, has a noble virtue will advance with many excellent qualities, while those who envy someone who excels are truly as al-Farazdaq says:[842]

If you lampoon the clan of al-Zibriqān, then you
lampoon men who are tall and proud, of Yadhbul's hill.[843]
A dog may bark at the stars, while between them and it
are many miles[844] that wear out[845] the eye of the observer.

The envier's envy turns on himself: his body is worn away by the repression of his feelings.

Will striking the Byzantine provide you with
a forefather descending from Kulayb, or an ancestor like
Dārim?[846]

Heretics, Apostates, and Impious Poets

26.1.1 As for the Sheikh's quotation of Abū l-Ṭayyib's verse:

Al-Mutanabbī and the diminutive

I blame the little people of these times[847]

the man was fond of using the diminutive,[848] not being content merely with what a raider snatches away, as when he says:

Who can help me make the little people of these days understand,
who claim that a Bāqil among them can compute with Indian numerals?[849]

and:

Little darling of my heart! O my heart, my heart! Ah, Juml![850]

and:

. . . My addressing that little moron with "O wise one!"[851]

and:

That little servant slept at night, when we. . .[852]

and:

Must I carry a little poet under my arm every day?[853]

There is more of this in his collected verse. He should not be criticized for this: it is merely a habit that has become like second nature. The familiar abode has not become beautiful with this(?),[854] but it is to be forgiven in view of his many beautiful other things. Sometimes moles appear on noses!

With this verse that begins with 26.1.2

I blame the little people of these times

he addressed ʿAlī ibn Muḥammad ibn Sayyār ibn Mukrim in Antioch, before he composed panegyric poetry on Sayf al-Dawlah ʿAlī ibn ʿAbd Allāh ibn Ḥamdān. Poets are free to do so, for the Qurʾanic verse attests that they produce lies and speak idle words:[855] «Have you not seen that they[856] roam in every valley, and that they say what they do not do?»

Ahl ("people") is a word that conventionally refers to a group, originally.[857] One says: "The people of the house departed"; then the hearer knows that the speaker does not mean one person by his statement. Nevertheless, this word is also used for individual persons, as when one says: "So-and-so is *ahl* (someone doing) good" or "*ahl* (a man) of beneficence."[858] Ḥātim al-Ṭāʾī said:[859]

She kept blaming (me) because of a young camel I had generously
given (?).
(The loss of) Ibn Masʿūd is a great calamity to the world.
The men left him on the stony ground, thrown down;
he was a man (*ahl*) of liberality, prudence, and generosity.

It seems that this word was originally used for a plural and then also transferred to a singular, just as *ṣadīq* ("friend"), *amīr* ("commander"), and similar words were conventionally used only for individuals originally, but subsequently transferred to a plural, by way of making them similar. Thus people will say: "The sons of So-and-so are a brother to us." One says *ahl*, *ahlah*, and *ahalāt* in the plural. A poet says:[860]

They are people (*ahalāt*) standing around Qays ibn ʿĀṣim
when they set out at night, calling "O abundant giver!"

A certain grammarian[861] said about the diminutive form of *āl* ("the clan, family") of a man that it may be *uwayl* or *uhayl*. It seems that he believes that the *h* in *ahl* was replaced by a glottal stop, and that when two glottal stops came together the second was turned into an *alif*.[862] Something like this cannot be ascertained. The most likely thing is that the *āl* ("the clan") of a man is derived from the verb *āla – ya'ūlu* ("he went back – he goes back"), i.e., "he returned," as if to say that his clan returns to him, or that he returns to them.

26.2 *Al-Mutanabbī, the would-be prophet?*

As regards the story told by al-Quṭrabbulī and Ibn Abī l-Azhar, which the Sheikh mentions, such things happen.[863] It is not evident that the fellow was imprisoned in Iraq, whereas everyone knows that he was imprisoned in Syria. I was told that when he was asked about the true origin of this nickname[864] he said, "It is from *nabwah*," i.e., an elevated piece of land. He had aspired to something that lesser men than he had also aspired to. These things are divinely decreed, directed by a Director on high. Those favored with success will attain them, and those who strive earnestly should not be dismayed if they fail. Various things in his collected verse show that he was (generally) devout and (at times, however) bereft of reason,[865] like other people. Thus he says:

. . . Not accepting any judgment except from his Creator.[866]

And:

How all-powerful is God, to shame His creatures
and not to prove the truth of what some people maintain![867]

When one reverts to the facts, then what the tongue utters says nothing about a person's firm belief, for the world is formed with a natural disposition toward lying and hypocrisy. It is possible for a man to proclaim something openly, showing his religiousness, while he does this merely in order to adorn himself with a fine appearance, wishing to gain praise or some other intention of the deceptive world, "mother of extinction." Perhaps a number of people have come and gone who were outwardly devout but heretics inside.

26.3 *Other poets: Di'bil and Abū Nuwās*

I am not beset by any doubt that Diʿbil ibn ʿAlī had no religion. He made a show of being a Shi'ite but his only motive was mercenary. How many a lineage he established to lay claim to a false genealogy![868] I do not doubt that Diʿbil held the same views as al-Ḥakamī and his sort. Heresy became widespread amongst them and sprang up in their country.

People differ of opinion about Abū Nuwās. It has been alleged that he was pious and performed his missed daily ritual prayers at night. The truth is that he believed what other people of his time believed. The Prophet (God bless and preserve him) came to the Arabs while they were desirous of thick marrow and their concerns fell short of black pudding.[869] Some of them followed in his stride; «God knows well what they hide!»[870]

26.4 *Heretics in Islam: Quraysh*

When Islam established itself and its empire rested on its cornerstones in good order, the Arabs came to mix with other nations. They heard what was said by physicians, astronomers, and logicians, and a large group of them felt inclined towards them.[871] Unbelief has always existed among mankind throughout the ages, to the extent that historians maintain that when Adam (God bless him) sent for his children and warned them about the Hereafter, filling them with fear of torment, they called him a liar and rejected his words. And thus it continues until today. Some scholar says that the leaders of Quraysh were heretics. And it is very likely that they were, too! A poet of theirs said the following lines, lamenting those killed at Badr; they are attributed to Shaddād ibn al-Aswad al-Laythī:[872]

Umm Bakr paid a visit, greeting (us);
so return the greeting to Umm Bakr!

So many, in the brick-covered well, the well of Badr,
good reputations and noble men!
So many, in the brick-covered well, the well of Badr,
bowls that are crowned with camel-hump![873]
O Umm Bakr, do not hand to me, again,
the cup, after the death of Hishām's brother,
And of his father's brother. He was a leader
of men, drinkers of vintage wine.
Ah, who will bear my message to the Merciful
that I renounce the month of fasting![874]
When the head has left its shoulders
the cheerful companion has had his fill of food.
Does Kabshah's son promise us that we shall live?[875]
But what kind of life has a screech owl?[876]
Will you omit to hold death away from me
but revive me when the bones have decayed?

Assertions such as these are made only by someone who seeks nothing further than a reckless death in battle and who has no regrets about it when it happens.

26.5 *Stories about al-Mutanabbī*

I was told that, in the days when he had an estate in Ṣaff, Abū l-Ṭayyib[877] was seen to perform the ritual prayer at a place in Maʿarrat al-Nuʿmān, called "the Bedouins' Church," and that he performed two "bows," which was at the time of the afternoon prayer.[878] It is possible, therefore, that in his view he was traveling and that shortening was permissible.

A reliable person told me a story about him to the intent that when he had arrived at the Banū ʿAdī and attempted to raise a rebellion among them, they understood his claim and said to him:[879] "Here is a refractory she-camel. If you are able to ride her we will attest that you are sent by God." He went toward that camel as she was returning home in the evening with the other camels. Cleverly he managed to jump on her back. She bolted for a bit and resisted him for a moment. But then she stopped bolting and she began to walk like a docile animal. He rode her, it is said, to the tribal settlement. They were much amazed and this became one of his prophetic signs for them.

I was also told that he was in the administrative department in Latakia, when a pen-knife cut the hand of one of the scribes, wounding him severely. Abū l-Ṭayyib spat on it and bandaged it without delay. "Do not undo it today," he told the wounded man. He told him to wait a number of days and nights. The scribe accepted the advice and the wound healed. Then they started to form the strongest beliefs about Abū l-Ṭayyib, saying, "It is as if he can revive the dead!"

A man at whose place Abū l-Ṭayyib had been hiding in Latakia, or some other place on the coast, told that he wanted to go from one place to another. He left at night, in the man's company. They came across a dog that pestered them with its barking and then went away. Abū l-Ṭayyib said to that man as he was returning, "You will find that that dog has died." When the man returned he found that it was as he had said. It is not impossible that he had prepared some poisoned food and thrown it to the dog, hiding his action from his companion. Hellebore is a well-known poison for dogs.

26.6 *On collaborative authorship*

It is extraordinary that al-Quṭrabbulī and Ibn Abī l-Azhar wrote a book together: such a thing is little known. A similar case is the story of the two Khālidī brothers who lived in Mosul, both being poets.[880] They were attached to Sayf al-Dawlah's court but left after a quarrel. Their collected poetry is in both their names and only very few pieces are by one of them individually. This is a thing that is very difficult to achieve among humans, because human nature tends to contrariety and a lack of agreement. It is easier to understand that one man produces a piece of writing which is then completed by another, than that two men collaborate. The people of Baghdad relate that Abū Saʿīd al-Sīrāfī[881] wrote his book known as *The Sufficient*, or *The Sufficiency*, as far as the chapter on the diminutive. Then he died and his son Abū Muḥammad completed it after his death. Such a thing is possible, people do not doubt it. A reliable person told me that Abū ʿAlī al-Fārisī mentioned that Abū Bakr ibn al-Sarrāj wrote the first half of his *The Concise [Book on Syntax]* for a cloth merchant, after which he asked Abū ʿAlī to complete it. This part, however, cannot be said to have been "written" by Abū ʿAlī, because the subject matter of *The Concise* is taken from Ibn al-Sarrāj's own words in his *The Principles [of Syntax]* and *The Sentences*, so it is as if Abū ʿAlī merely copied them and did not produce anything original himself.

26.7.1 *Al-Mutanabbī on Time*

Those who transmit the collected verse of Abū l-Ṭayyib relate about him that he was born in the year 303,882; he went to Syria in the year 321,883 and stayed there for a while. Then he returned to Iraq, but he did not remain there for any length of time. That this report is correct is proved by the fact that his panegyric odes composed during his younger years are all on Syrians, except his poem that begins:[884]

> Woman, stop! [My worries] have made your blaming (woe unto you!) look more blameworthy to me.

With his complaint, to Time, of the people living in it he followed the path of the ancients. So much has been said in condemnation of Time that there is even a hadith: "Do not revile Time, because God is Time."[885] The meaning of these words is well known, but the hidden sense is not like the superficial meaning; for none of the prophets (peace be upon them) held the view that Time is the Creator or is to be worshipped. In the Noble Book it says:[886] «Nothing but Time destroys us». What some people say, that time is the movement of the celestial sphere,[887] holds no truth. In Sībawayh's book there is an indication that in his view time is the passing of night and day, an expression that has been glossed by commentators. I[888] have given a definition that very likely has been given before, but I have not heard it: namely, that "time" is something the smallest part of which contains all things that can be comprehended. In this respect it is the opposite of "space," because the smallest part of it cannot contain a thing in the manner that circumstances can contain it. As for "being," it is necessarily attached to what is little or large in quantity.

As for those who said «Nothing but Time destroys us» and similar things, such as the verse attributed to al-Akhṭal (Ḥabīb ibn Aws quotes it as if by Shamʿalah al-Taghlibī):[889] 26.7.2

The Commander of the Believers and his deeds
are like Time—there is no shame in what Time does.

or the verse by another:[890]

Time brought our companionship harmoniously together;
likewise Time has separated us.

or Abū Ṣakhr's verse:[891]

I was amazed at the mischief that Time did between us;
but when what existed between was at an end, Time was quiet.

One cannot maintain that any of them used to offer sacrifices to the celestial spheres, or claimed that these spheres are rational beings. It is merely a motif that communities have inherited successively from one time to another. There was a poet called "Time's Reviler" in the tribe of ʿAbd al-Qays, who said:[892]

When I saw how rough was the path of Time
and that it showed us a shaggy face with the nose cut off,
And a monkey's forehead, as narrow as a shoe-strap,
and a nose,[893] while it twisted its neck-veins with its beard,[894]
I was reminded of the noble departed, the generous ones,
and I said to ʿAmr and al-Ḥusām:[895] Ah, leave it!

As for the Sheikh's anger with the heretics and apostates, may God reward him for it, as He may reward him for his being thirsty on the road to Mecca, for being burned by the sun at ʿArafah, and his 27.1

More heretics and apostates

spending the night at al-Muzdalifah. No doubt he prayed humbly to God, praised be He, during the appointed, known days,[896] asking Him to fortify the hills of Islam, and to erect beaming beacons for its followers.[897] However, heresy is an old disease by which people have so often been afflicted![898] One legal scholar is of the opinion that when a man openly professes heresy and then repents, merely because he is afraid of being executed, his repentance cannot be accepted, unlike other unbelievers, for an apostate is accepted if he returns to Islam.

There is no religion that has no heretics, who give their co-religionists the appearance of siding with them, whereas they secretly oppose them. A deceiver like this must be exposed and the first buds of evil must be laid bare. The kings of Persia used to execute people for heresy.

27.2.1 The heretics are those that are called "Eternalists."[899] They believe neither in prophethood nor in scripture. Bashshār[900] adopted this belief from others. It is said that a note was found among his papers. The phrase "I wanted to lampoon So-and-so, the Hāshimite, but I forgave him because of his kinship with the Messenger of God, God bless and preserve him" was written on it.[901] They assert that he was hostile to Sībawayh and that one day he attended the circle of Yūnus ibn Ḥabīb, where he said, "Is there anyone here who will inform on me?" They replied, "No." Then he recited to them:

Umayyads, wake up from your slumber!
　　The caliph is Yaʿqūb ibn Dāwūd!
The caliph is not to be found, so seek
　　God's caliph between flute and lute![902]

Sībawayh was present in the circle, and one of the people claimed that Bashshār had slandered him.[903] But Sībawayh, I think, would have been above entering into such lowly matters; he aimed at higher things. It is related that he criticized Bashshār's verse:

To the flirteous one (*al-ghazalā*) from me a greeting! So often
have I amused myself with her in the shade of a bright
green spot!

Sībawayh said, "The true Arabs do not use 'flirteous.'" Thereupon Bashshār replied, "But this is like when they say 'courteous' and 'righteous' and the like."[904]

Bashshār also used the word *nīnān* in his verse, the plural of *nūn*, "fish." Sībawayh is said to have disapproved of this.[905] But these are unconfirmed reports; it is transmitted in *Sībawayh's Book*[906] that the word *nūn* has a plural *nīnān*, which contradicts the report. The person who transmitted the reports about Bashshār mentions that he threatened Sībawayh with making lampoons, so the latter placated him by citing his poetry as linguistic evidence. It is possible that he cited his poetry in this manner just as people do when quoting things in sessions and gatherings. The partisans of Bashshār transmit this verse as being his: 27.2.2

Not every intelligent man will provide you with his advice;
nor is everyone who gives his advice intelligent.

In *Sībawayh's Book* the second hemistich of this verse is found in the chapter on assimilation, without mention of the poet. Others say that it is by Abū l-Aswad al-Du'alī.[907]

Ya'qūb ibn Dāwūd, the vizier of al-Mahdī, is said to have intrigued against Bashshār until he was executed. People differ about his age: it is said that at the time he was eighty years old, others say he was older. God knows best the truth of the matter.

I shall not say categorically that he is one of the people of hellfire.[908] I said what I said previously because I connected it with God's will;[909] but God is forbearing and munificent.

The author of *The Folio Book*[910] mentions a number of poets of the generation of Abū Nuwās and before, describing them as heretics. 27.3.1

People's inner thoughts are hidden and only He who knows all hidden things knows them. At that time such beliefs were concealed, for fear of the sword, whereas now people's hidden secrets have become evident and the abandoned ostrich-shell has broken to reveal the ugliest chick! In that period there was a man who had friends who were Shi'ites and another friend who was a heretic.[911] One day he invited the Shi'ites; then the heretic arrived, knocked on the door, and said:

"This morning my breast is full of perturbations,
jointly beset with various anxieties and thoughts."

The master of the house said to him, "Mercy on you! Why is that?" But the heretic left him and went away. Afterward the man who had given the banquet met him and said to him, "Did you want to get me into trouble?"—afraid that his friends would think he was a heretic himself. The other replied, "Invite them again and let me know where they will be." When they had arrived at his place the heretic came and said,

"This morning my breast is full of perturbations,
jointly beset with anxieties and thoughts."

They all said, "Mercy on you! Why is that?" and the man continued:

Because of the crime committed against Ḥasan's father
by ʿUmar and his fellow, Abū Bakr.[912]

Then he left. The Shi'ites were delighted by this. The master of the house met him and said, "May God recompense you for the good that you have done me! You have saved me from suspicion!"

27.3.2 A number of scholars used to sit in a gathering in Basra. Among them was a heretic who had two swords, one of which he called "Welfare" and the other "Prosperity." Whenever a Muslim greeted him he would reply,

Welfare to you in the morning, Prosperity to you in the evening!

Then he would turn to his companions, who knew about the two swords, and say:

Two swords like lightning when the lightning flashes!

Take the verse by al-Ḥakamī:[913]

The conceitedness of a singer and the sophistication of a heretic.

He was criticized for this motif.[914] It is said that he meant a man of the tribe of Banū l-Ḥārith who was well known for his heresy and his sophistication; he held a favored position with the ruler.[915]

As for the first hemistich of this verse:

A prince's boon companion, on speaking terms with a king,[916]

this is like the verse by Imru' al-Qays:[917]

Today I'll drink without incurring
sin with God, nor as an uninvited guest.

One cannot consider it analogous to the use of the pausal form *-ah*, as in:

O Baydharah, O Baydharah, O Baydharah![918]

Or as someone else said:[919]

Over many a leaping white-footed ibex, fair-sized,
The shadows contracted and then shrank together;
When it saw there was no chance to rest (*daʿah*)[920] or eat its fill,
It turned aside to an *arṭā* tree on a sand dune and lay down,

because here it is good to make the *h* distinct, since the utterance is complete and it is good to pause there, whereas in *muḥaddithuh malikin* one has a pre-genitive and a genitive,[921] where such a thing is not good, for the two nouns are like one noun.

27.4 *Ṣāliḥ ibn ʿAbd al-Quddūs*

Ṣāliḥ ibn ʿAbd al-Quddūs[922] was notorious for his heresy but he was not killed—God knows best—until statements came to light from him that made it inevitable. The following lines are attributed to his father, ʿAbd al-Quddūs:

How many visitors has Mecca brought to perdition!
May God destroy it and its houses!
May the Merciful not give sustenance to its quarters
and may His mercy pass over its dead!

Ṣāliḥ had a son who was imprisoned for a long time because of heresy. The following lines are attributed to him:[923]

We left the world when we belonged to it;
and now we are neither living in it nor dead.
Whenever a visitor comes seeking us
we rejoice and say, "This man comes from the world!"

Ṣāliḥ's recanting from heresy when he thought he would be executed was merely deception. God bless Muḥammad, who is reported to have said, "I have been sent with the sword. There is good in the sword and there is good through the sword." And in another hadith: "My community will be well as long as it carries swords." The sword made Ṣāliḥ assent to the truth and renounce his heresy. This is one of God's signs when it becomes evident to an unbelieving soul, whose time has come to an end, no doubt about it! For at this stage its belief will not be accepted. «It has not believed before».[924] Folly comes as drizzle and as a downpour!

27.5.1 *The Fuller, the Box-Maker, and others*

Al-Qaṣṣār, "the Fuller"[925] was altogether full of folly. Had he followed an old camel, its flanks aching, he would have been spared the poison-taking![926] But one's natural dispositions are one's enemies, and one cannot escape the appointed hour.

The one connected with "box"[927] is to be considered a heretic, unorthodox. I think he was known as al-Manṣūr. He appeared in the year 999;[928] he stayed for a while in Yemen. In his day, singing girls used to play the tambourine and sing:

Girl, pick up the tambourine and play!
Proclaim the virtues of this prophet!
Gone is the prophet of the Banū Hāshim[929]
and the prophet of the Banū Yaʿrub[930] has arisen.
We no longer want to run at Ṣafā
or to pay a visit to the tomb in Yathrib.[931]
If they perform the ritual prayer, don't stand up;
if they are fasting, eat and drink!
Don't hold yourself taboo to the believers,
whether close kin or strangers!
For why should you be free to marry any stranger
but be forbidden to your father?
Doesn't a plant belong to him who reared it
and who watered it in a year of drought?
And what is wine but like the water of the clouds,
permitted? Hallowed be you as a faith!

May the adherents of this doctrine be cursed by all who pray!

People like this—God curse them!—use various methods to enslave the common people. When they are eager to claim divinity they are not ashamed to make a proclamation and they balk at no abomination; but when they know somebody has discernment they show him that the good is their preferment. There was a man in Yemen who had secluded himself in a castle he owned. His only contact with other people was a black servant, whom he called Jibrīl.[932] One day the servant killed him and ran off. Some irreverent jester quipped: 27.5.2

Blessed be God on high!
Jabraʾīl has fled from his depravity,
And he that you maintained was Lord
lies murdered on his throne.

It is said that the depravity his master would impose on him moved him to commit this deed.

When one of this lot is ambitious he is not content with being an imam or even a prophet but mounts higher still in his lies. His drink will be foul water from under the scum (i.e., the pondweed).

27.5.3 The Arabs, in pre-Islamic times, did not commit such enormities and irregularities. On the contrary, their minds tended toward the opinion of the sages and the books of the ancients from the past. Most philosophers did not believe in a prophet and considered anyone who asserted prophethood to be a fool. There was an incident involving Rabīʿah ibn Umayyah ibn Khalaf al-Jumaḥī and Abū Bakr al-Ṣiddīq (may God have mercy on him!),[933] whereupon Rabīʿah joined the Byzantines. It is related that he said:

I went to live in the land of the Byzantines, not minding
  my giving up the evening or the midday prayer.
But don't leave me without a morning draught of wine,
  for God has not forbidden choicest wine!
If Taym ibn Murrah rules among you,
  then there's no good in the land of the Hijaz or Egypt.
My Islam may have been Truth and Right Guidance,
  but I hereby leave it to Abū Bakr!

There are many different ways in which people have gone astray, even to the point of thinking it possible to claim divinity. This was unbelief most thorough and refined, a piling of disobedience into bags of the amplest kind! The people of the time of Ignorance merely rejected prophethood and went no further. When ʿUmar ibn al-Khaṭṭāb (God have mercy upon him) expelled the adherents of the protected religions[934] from the Arabian Peninsula, the displaced were distressed. It is said that a man of the Jews of Khaybar known as Sumayr ibn Adkan said on this:[935]

Abū Ḥafṣ attacks us with his leather whip.
  Gently does it! A man now surfaces, now sinks.
It seems you never followed a loaded camel of a beating driver[936]
  to get a bellyful. Provision is a much-loved thing!

Had Moses spoken the truth you would not have had the upper
hand
against us. But a dynasty may come and go again.
We were liars before you. Know therefore that we have
the honor of being first and thus the worst!
You merely walked in our tracks, on our path;
your wish is to rule and be feared.

For as long as it has existed, Yemen has been a breeding ground of people who through religion earn their livelihood, and by fair pretense contrive to get ill-gotten good. Someone who traveled there told me that to this very day a group of people live there, each of whom claims to be the expected messiah[937] and they never fail to receive money through a taxation, for their base ambitions' gratification. I have been told that the Carmathians in al-Aḥsā keep a house from which, as they claim, their imam will come forth. They have a horse, saddled and bridled, standing at its door and say to the common people and the vulgar herd: "This horse is destined for the stirrup of the Mahdi, who will mount it when he appears with unprecedented Truth." Their only object in this is quite simply deceit and specious argumentation, to lead people astray and gain domination. 27.5.4

One of the strangest things I have heard is that long ago, when one of the leaders of the Carmathians was on his deathbed and felt death approaching, he gathered his followers and began to say, "I am resolved to migrate. I have already sent Moses, Jesus, and Muḥammad; now I must send someone else." A curse upon him! He committed the gravest kind of unbelief, at the moment when it is incumbent on the unbeliever to believe and on the traveler to return to his final destination. 27.5.5

Al-Walīd ibn Yazīd

Al-Walīd ibn Yazīd[938] he had the intelligence of an infant indeed, though he had reached the age of solid maturity. A firm(?)[939] intention did not avail him, nor was the vessel(?) of any use to him. He 28.1.1

was distracted from the wine pitcher by the sin of his erring soul.[940] He was driven into Hellfire, where he does not ladle cups of wine! Some poems are attributed to him that bring him disgrace, such as:[941]

Bring me, you two, my friend
'Abdal without his loin-cloth,[942]
For I am certain I shall not
be resurrected and be sent into a Fire.
Let those who seek Paradise
waste their efforts!
I'll train those people until
they follow the religion of a donkey.[943]

It was an amazing time that made someone like him the leader of the community and brought him to the brimful well of power! It may well be that other rulers held identical or similar beliefs, but kept them hidden and feared being upbraided. The following is also transmitted as being by him:[944]

I, al-Walīd, am the imam, and proud of it.
I trail my mantle and listen to love poetry.
I drag my robe's hem to her dwellings,[945]
not caring about who censures or reproaches me.
The good life is nothing but listening to a skilled singing girl
and wine that leaves a man intoxicated.
I do not expect to meet black-eyed damsels in the eternal abode.
Does any sensible person hope for the houris of Paradise?
When a pretty girl grants you her favors, reward her
liberally, as someone who bestows a present.[946]

28.1.2 It is said that when he was besieged[947] he entered his palace, shut the door, and said:[948]

Leave me Hind, al-Rabāb, and Fartanā,[949]
and a singing girl: that is all the wealth I need!

Take your kingdom—may God not establish your kingdom!—
for after this it isn't worth a camel's hobble!
Let me go free before the blinking of an eye
and do not begrudge me a death from starvation!

How he was chased from that high estate! His head was seen being carried in the mouth of a dog, as some relate. God punishes the reprobate. People are helpless in this world, "Mother Stink," which renders powerless those who stay at home and those who travel alike. The office of being a caliph should by rights come to somebody known for his piety, who is not turned from the right path by time's adversity. However, affliction was created together with the sun. Will those who dwell in the grave be set free?

28.2 *Abū ʿĪsā, the son of al-Rashīd*

Abū ʿĪsā, the son of al-Rashīd,[950] is neither seeking nor sought.[951] If the reports about him are true, he set himself apart thereby from his ancestors and showed his opposition to religious people. The Lord does not care whether His servants keep the fast through fear or break it; but people have been warned(?).[952] Sometimes an ignoramus, or someone pretending to be so, will utter a statement though in his heart he is well aware that the opposite is true. I say this in the hope that Abū ʿĪsā and his likes did not follow those who lead into error, and that, having pondered it at night, they think differently from what was said openly. Certainly, the dead taught them a lesson.

Somebody dreamed he saw ʿAbd al-Salām ibn Raghbān, who is known as Dīk al-Jinn, looking fine. He mentioned to him the lines rhyming in *-āfī*, including the following:[953]

This is the [real] world, though they are happy with [the thought of] another:
to fix one's thoughts on things to come is fell.

("Fell" means "deadly.") The poet replied, "I said that only in jest; I did not really believe it." Perhaps many of those who are notorious for saying such ignorant things upheld the shariah in their innermost thoughts, staying within its bounds and grazing in its rich pasture-grounds. For the tongue is full of avidity and will yield to error and stupidity.

The poems consisting of two or three lines by the aforementioned Abū ʿĪsā were admired. Al-Ṣūlī, in his *Anecdotes*, quotes the following poem of his:[954]

My tongue keeps its secrets hidden,
  but my tears betray my secret and divulge it.
But for my tears I would have hidden my passion;
  but for my passion, I would not have shed tears.

Even though he fled from the month-long fasting, he may perhaps [not][955] fall into everlasting torment. «Only unbelieving people despair of God's comfort».[956]

28.3 *Al-Jannābī*

As for al-Jannābī,[957] if a town were punished for its inhabitants, then it would be possible for Jannābah to be punished because of him and its repentance not be accepted. But the judgment of the revealed Book is more apt and more appropriate: «That no burdened soul shall bear the burden of another».[958] There are different versions of the story about him and the cornerstone of the Kaaba. Some who claim they were well acquainted with him assert that he took it in order to worship and glorify it, because he had heard that it was the hand of the idol that was made in the likeness of Saturn.[959] Others say he used it as a footstep in a privy. These stories contradict each other, but whatever was the case, a curse be upon him, for as long as Mount Thabīr stands and rain from white clouds falls.

28.4.1 *The leader of the Zanj*

Someone reported that before the ʿAlid from Basra[960] came out in rebellion he used to say he belonged to the tribe of ʿAbd al-Qays, more specifically to Anmār. His name was Aḥmad, but when he rebelled he called himself ʿAlī—there is a lot of lying!—as if he were a lofty mountain in terms of profound insight. Truth was to him like pebbles, to be trodden underfoot by the feet of rebels! The following well-known lines are attributed to him:[961]

O trade of the chronically ill,[962] may perdition come upon you!
Is there no escape for me from you, not even when the assembled people gather?[963]
If my soul is content to teach young children forever,
I would surely be content with being humiliated.
Would a free man take pleasure in teaching children
when it is thought that there are ample means of subsistence on earth?

I do not hold it for impossible that love of the world's vanity moved him to the point of drowning in an overflowing sea, where he will swim «as long as the heavens and the earth endure, unless your Lord wills otherwise. Your Lord carries out whatever He wishes».[964]

Some verses are transmitted as being by him indicating that he 28.4.2
was pious, but I will not deny that these lines may have been put into his mouth, for those with experience of this world pronounce it to be full of immorality and falsehood, with a character far from beautiful. The lines are these:

I have killed people, anxious
to keep myself alive;
I have laid hands on property by the sword
that I might be happy and not wretched.
Whoever sees my last resting place,
let him not wrong any creature!
Woe unto me when I die,
before God, what will happen to me?
Will it be eternal life in God's protection,
or will I be thrown into His fire?

Someone recited to me some verses attributed to ʿAḍud al-Dawlah[965] in a long meter[966] with the same rhyme letter as in the preceding lines. It is said that one day, having recovered from an illness, he wrote them on the wall of the room he was in. They are modeled on the lines by the man from Basra. However, I testify that they are contrived, fabricated by some shameless person, and that ʿAḍud al-Dawlah had never heard of them.

28.5.1 As for the story about the Hadith scholars who misspelled Rakhamah as *raḥmah* ("mercy"), I do not believe anything of the kind happened. Untruthfulness will have the upper hand and be evident, truth is hidden and feeble. «We belong to God and to Him we shall return.»[967] It is the same with the claim of those who assert that ʿAlī (peace be upon him) said, "Basra will perish at the hands of the Zanj" and that the Hadith scholars then misspelled it as "through the wind."[968] I believe none of this. The knowledge of the unseen[969] was not revealed to ʿAlī (peace be upon him) or to anyone else. As it says in the Holy Book:[970] «Say: None in the heavens or on earth know the unseen except God.» And in a transmitted hadith it is said that the Prophet once heard girls sing the following verses at a wedding:[971]

He gave us rams
  that occupy the middle of the pen;
And your spouse sits in a gathering
  and knows what will happen tomorrow.

Thereupon the Prophet said, "No one but God knows what will happen tomorrow!"

Nor is it possible that somebody would have announced one hundred years ago that the Emir of Aleppo (may God protect it!) in the year 1,153 would be called So-and-so, son of So-and-so, and would look like this.[972] If someone were to make this claim he would be a confirmed liar.

28.5.2 The stars merely hint and do not state explicitly. It is related that al-Faḍl ibn Sahl often quoted the following lines by a *rajaz* poet:

If I escape and my mounts escape
From Ghālib and the band of Ghālib,
I surely will escape from all adversities!

Someone called Ghālib was in fact among those who killed him.[973] Such things do happen, although it is more likely that this story was invented. It is not implausible that he used to quote the verses, and perhaps it happened that at the time some people were called this.[974] It is possible for a meaning to be joined with an expression.[975] Strange things may happen in the course of time; but above any man of knowledge is the All-Knowing. It is related that Iyās ibn Muʿāwiyah, the judge, would surmise things which then happened just as he had surmised. It is for that reason that one speaks of a man as being "sharp-witted" or "brilliant." Aws said:[976]

A brilliant mind, who surmises something
as if he saw and heard it.

He also said:

A sharp-witted man, who speaks of unseen things.

29.1.1 *Al-Ḥallāj*

The ignorance of al-Ḥusayn ibn Manṣūr knew no bounds. If a whole nation sometimes worships a stone, how could a judicious man be safe from defects?[977] He wanted to turn error on its axis[978] and therefore left dealing with cotton.[979] If only he had applied himself to cotton, his name would have remained unmentioned on any page and forgotten! But these are the workings of Fate that occur, whereby the eye is covered with a blur. It were better for a human being to be a pebble or a rock than be made a laughingstock. People hasten to whatever is vain; they turn their eyes to every temptation.

29.1.2 So many trumped-up stories have been invented about al-Ḥallāj! Falsehood often attracts. All the extraordinary things that are attributed to him are lies pure and simple; I would not believe them even if in my sleep. One of the stories fabricated about him is that he said to those who executed him, "Do you think it is me you are killing?

Rather, you are killing al-Mādharāʾī's[980] mule!" This mule, it was said, was found killed in its stable. Even today there are still some mystics who exalt him and rank him with the stars. I have heard that some people in Baghdad expect his emergence and that they stand where he was crucified, on the bank of the Tigris, anticipating his appearance. This is not a new instance of people's ignorance. One might as well worship a gazelle in its covert![981] A monkey that reached a most honored position once had a similar fortune. The common people said, "Prostrate yourselves to the Monkey in his Heyday!"[982] I shrink from mentioning the monkey that, so it is said, the army commanders used to visit and greet in the time of Zubaydah, and that Yazīd ibn Mazyad al-Shaybānī came amidst those who came to greet it, and ki..ed(?) it.[983] It is related that Yazīd ibn Muʿāwiyah had a monkey that he mounted on a wild she-ass, which he made to race with the horses in the racecourse.[984]

29.1.3 As for the verses rhyming in *-ayy*:[985]

O secret secret, subtle to the point of being
  exalted above description by any living being;
Outwardly, inwardly, you manifest yourself
  in every thing to every thing.
O sum of All, you are none other than I,
  so why excuse myself then to myself?

—there is nothing wrong with composing this, potentially.[986] But the word *ilayy* ("to myself") is a technical defect in these verses, for a rhyme ending in a consonant is not allowed in a meter like this according to some, and if he read it as *ilayyī* it would be a bad and ugly blemish.[987] Specialists in the Arabic language unanimously disapprove of Ḥamzah's reading:[988] «neither can you aid me», reading *muṣrikhiyyi* with *-i*.[989] It is related that Abū ʿAmr ibn al-ʿAlāʾ was asked about this and that he said, "It is fine, now up, now down!" meaning *muṣrikhiyya* and *muṣrikhiyyi*.[990] Those who transmit this story use it to vindicate Ḥamzah and argue that Abū ʿAmr allowed the ending *-i* here in order to avoid a cluster of two unvoweled consonants.[991] If this report about him is authentic, then he said it only by way of sarcasm, meaning in fact the opposite, as when al-Ghanawī, i.e., Sahm ibn Ḥanẓalah, said:[992]

People will not deny me what I want, nor shall I
give them what they want. Such good manners!

—meaning "they are not good." This is like what a man may say to his son when he has seen him do something bad: "That's a fine thing!" while he means the opposite. Such an ending in *-i* is not found in verse composed in the correct literary language. Al-Farrā' criticized a line that he recited:[993]

He said to her, "You there, do you fancy me?"
she said to him, "I do not like you."

I have heard *ilayyi* ("to me"), *ʿalayyi* ("on me"),[994] and similar forms in the poems of the moderns; it is a sign of a weak poetic gift and a feeble talent.

It is the same with al-Ḥallāj's word *al-kull* ("All"), for using this with the definite article is disapproved. Abū ʿAlī deemed it permissible against Sībawayh. In ancient speech[995] the words *kull* ("all") and *baʿḍ* ("some; a certain") are not found with the definite article. But they quote a line by Suḥaym:[996]

I have seen the rich and the poor, both of them,
all gone to death. Death comes to visit all.

The following lines are quoted, attributed to a young man in al-Ḥallāj's time: 29.2.1

If the doctrine of incarnation is true,
then my god is in the glassmaker's wife.
She appeared in a thin embroidered dress
between the perfumer's house and that of the ice vendor.
They declared something to me. It is not true:
it is one of the lies of our master al-Ḥallāj.

These doctrines are ancient. They migrate from one epoch to another. It is said that Pharaoh adhered to the doctrine of the incarnationists, and that it was therefore that he claimed to be the Lord Almighty. It is said that one of them used to say when praising God:

> Praised be Thou! Praised be I! Thy forgiveness! My forgiveness![997]

This is rampant madness. Whoever says this is to be counted among the beasts without sense, never aware of the essence of God's beneficence. Someone else said,

> I am Thou, no doubt about it;
>   Therefore, praise be to Thee, praise be to me!
> Making Thee angry is making me angry,
>   Thy forgiveness is my forgiveness.
> Why should I be flogged, O Lord,
>   when they say, "He is a fornicator"?

Mankind has no sense. This is something that a child grasps from an adult's instruction, something that, as sure as the layered white cloud gives rain, will lead to destruction![998] «Or do you think that most of them hear or understand? They are but like beasts; no, they are even further astray from the path».[999]

29.2.2 The following lines are attributed to one of the adherents of this sect:

> I saw my Lord walking with shoes on[1000]
>   in Yaḥyā's Market.[1001] I nearly burst out of my skin!
> I asked him, "Would you be eager to join us?"[1002]
>   "Out of the question!" he replied, "Caution prevents me."
> If God had decreed loving concord
>   there would have been nothing but prostration and gazing.

This sect propagates the idea of metempsychosis, which is an ancient belief held by the Indians. It has also become common among a group of Shi'ites. We ask God for success and protection.

The following verse is attributed to a man of the Nuṣayriyyah sect:

Marvel, mother of us, at the vagaries of the Nights:
our sister Sukaynah has been turned into a mouse!
So drive these cats away from her
and let her have the contents of the straw sack.

Another said:

Blessed be God, who relieves afflictions,
for He has shown us the marvels of Time.
The donkey of Shaybān, our town's Sheikh:
our neighbor Abū l-Sakan has been turned into it.
Instead of walking in his robe
he now walks with a girth and a halter.

They see sinister and dubious things, formed by their corrupt opinions. They walk in a valley of darkness[1003] and its deceptive paths.

I have been told that there was once a king of the Indians, a hand- 29.2.3
some young man, who was stricken with smallpox. He looked at his face in a mirror and on seeing how badly it had changed he burned himself, saying, "I want God to change me into a more beautiful image than this."

Some jurisprudents related to me—and they are not telling a lie with this story, nor are they in any way connected with heterodox sects—that they were in the country of Maḥmūd. There were a number of Indians in his retinue. He had come to trust their sincere friendship and he bestowed gifts on them for their loyalty. They were his closest soldiers wherever he resided or traveled. One of them was traveling in an army equipped by Maḥmūd. The news arrived that this man had died, either of natural causes or having been killed. So his wife gathered a large quantity of firewood, lit an enormous fire, and threw herself into it while people were watching. It turned out that the news was not true. Upon his return the man lit a blazing fire in order to burn himself, so that he could join his spouse. A large crowd gathered to watch him. His Indian friends came and gave him all kinds of advice and messages to convey to their dead relatives, one to his father and another to his brother. One man brought a rose and said, "Give this to So-and-so," meaning some dead relative of his. Then the man threw himself into the fire.

Those who have witnessed Indians practice self-immolation tell that when they feel the fire burning they want to get out, but those present push them back with sticks and sharpened swords. There is no god but God; «You have done a monstrous thing!».[1004]

29.2.4 There are some people who openly profess a belief without holding it to be true, thereby seeking gain in the perishable world, which is more treacherous than Warhā' the whore.[1005] There was such a man in the West, known as Ibn Hāni', one of their excellent poets. He used to compose very exaggerated eulogies on al-Mu'izz Abū Tamīm Ma'add,[1006] to the point of addressing the royal parasol-holder thus:

You who turn it wherever he goes round: how closely
  you rub shoulders, under his stirrup, with Gabriel!

He also said about him when he had stopped at a place called Raqqādah:[1007]

The Messiah has alighted at Raqqādah,
  where Adam and Noah alighted too.
God, the Lord of Glories, alighted there,
  save whom everything is but wind.

A poet known as Ibn al-Qāḍī ("the Judge's son") recited an ode in the presence of Ibn Abī 'Āmir, the ruler of al-Andalus, which began thus:[1008]

Whatever you wish—not whatever Fate wishes—
  so rule, for you are the One, the Subduer.

He went on to say similar things; but Ibn Abī 'Āmir disapproved and gave orders for him to be flogged and banished.

Al-Ḥallāj, evidently, has to be ranked as a swindler, not as a man of penetrating understanding or quick wit. Nevertheless, he is revered by a sect of mystics, who do not perceive his true nature.[1009]

30.1 *Ibn Abī ʿAwn*

Ibn Abī ʿAwn[1010] went from one thing to another. The poor man was beguiled by that Abū Jaʿfar of his and he "did not put his milk in a perfect skin." Sometimes a man is skilled in his craft and has a high degree of insight and reason, but when he turns to religion he is found to be like a wild donkey made tractable, that simply follows what it is accustomed to.

30.2 *Various forms of belief*

Being devout is instinctive in human nature; it is considered a safe refuge. As a young child grows up he learns what he hears from adults and it stays with him forever. All who dwell in monks' cells and worship in mosques accept their conditions and ideas just as any report that is transmitted, without distinguishing between the truthfulness and the falsehood of the interpreter. If somebody were to find that his kin were Zoroastrians, he would become a Zoroastrian himself; or, if they belonged to the Ṣābians, he would join them likewise. When someone who exercises his own judgment rejects the uncritical acceptance of authority, he will only succeed in becoming weak.[1011] When one lets oneself be guided by common sense it will quench the thirst of someone who is parched. But where is he who can bear to submit to the rulings of reason and who thoroughly polishes his understanding? Alas, this is to be found neither among those upon whom the sun rises nor among those who lie as corpses in their graves—save when there is an exceptional man in the world who is characterised by complete excellence.

Several times we have met people who have looked into the books of the philosophers and studied some of the works of the ancients. But then we found that they would approve of ugly things and soon enough their minds are overwhelmed.(?)[1012] If they are able to commit an abomination they will do it, if they recognize a duty they will shrink from it, as if the whole world strives to deprive them. (?)[1013] But their beliefs are the worst possible. If they are entrusted with a deposit they will be dishonest, if they are asked to testify they will lie, if they prescribe a remedy for a sick person they do not care whether they will kill him with their advice or merely double his trouble.[1014] Their only concern is to earn their fee, whereas they lay claim to wisdom and philosophy! Often those who mock religious people for their ignorance are themselves afflicted inwardly with an even more disastrous defect. Humans are truly as the Holy Book says:[1015] «each party rejoicing in what is theirs».

30.3 The Imami Shi'ites seek God's favor by rubbing their faces with dust,[1016] which some pious people consider an unforgivable sin. Some gatherings are attended by godless people who seem to be seekers of the true path; but these (God knows) are heretical and sly innovators. But who will provide you with Zanj for the game? (?)[1017]

How many a one pretends to be a Muʿtazilite, battling with his opponent, asserting that his Lord will cast people into everlasting Hell for an atom's weight [of evil], let alone a dirham or dinar's weight![1018] But of burdening himself with monstrous crimes he never tires, for which he will fall into blazing fires. He is wholly preoccupied with whoring and depravity, departing with the heaviest cargo of mortal sins. He is submissive toward the Predestinarians but bases himself on ʿAbd al-Jabbār.[1019] He is busy all day and all night long; secretly he believes that the leading authority of the Muʿtazilites is foul from the hem of his sleeve to the train of his robe. He has made a snare out of disputation and with it he composes an ode of error and temptation.

I have been told the following story about one their leaders, who was revered and had followers, even though he seemed like the first-born of Ignorance. Whenever he was sitting with others, drinking wine as the intoxicating liquid went round among them, flowing lavishly, and the cup would come to him, he would drink it and empty it, and then made those present testify that he had repented of what he had done.

If an Ashʿarīte is examined he will appear to be of base alloy. The unmovable earth and the heavens will curse him. He resembles a shepherd who maltreats his flock. He plods on in the pitch dark and does not care if he drives his sheep to mishap and damage, or brings them to tasty herbage. As likely as not he will lead them to wolves, guaranteed to annihilate the lot! The man with even the least intelligence seems to have been placed in darkness, apart from the man whom God has kept from error by making him follow the forefathers and impose upon himself the burdens of the law. 30.4

Truly, we are—this is no unbelief in God our Lord—
like fat sacrificial animals, who do not know when they will die.[1020]

If somebody is an Ashʿarite[1021] the wretch follows the authority of someone else; he trusts only those who lead him astray. If he inquires into a mystery and ponders it, he fails to grasp the message and falls short.

The Shi'ites assert that ʿAbd Allāh ibn Maymūn al-Qaddāḥ,[1022] of the Bāhilah tribe, was one of the prominent followers of Jaʿfar ibn Muḥammad—peace be on him—and transmitted much material from him. Subsequently he became an apostate. One of their leading authorities related to me that they transmit things on his authority, saying "ʿAbd Allāh ibn Maymūn al-Qaddāḥ related to us, when he was in his prime," that is, before his apostasy. They transmit the following lines as being by him: 30.5 *Shi'ite beliefs*

Come, give wine to drink, you clever boy,[1023]
for I do not believe that I shall be resurrected.
Don't you see that the Shi'ites are infatuated,
beguiled by Jaʿfar to abandon their religion?
For a while I too was beguiled by him;
but then a hidden message appeared to me.

Also attributed to him is the following:

I joined Jaʿfar for some time
but I found him a beguiling deceiver,
Who draws supreme power to himself,
pulling everyone to his snare.[1024]
If your cause were "true"[1025]
your murdered ancestor[1026] would not have been dragged along,
And neither would the Old Man have slighted your people,
nor would ʿUmar have risen above you, preaching![1027]

30.6 The incarnationists are close to the doctrine of metempsychosis. I was told a story about one of the leading astronomers of Ḥarrān, who stayed in our town for some time. Once he went on an outing with some people. They went past an ox that was ploughing and he said to his companions, "I am sure that this ox is a man who was known as Khalaf in Ḥarrān!" He began to shout, "Hey, Khalaf!" As it happened, the ox lowed. "You see," the man said to his friends, "I told you the truth!"

I was also told that another man, who believed in metempsychosis, said, "I dreamed of my father. He said, 'Dear son, my soul has been transferred to a one-eyed camel in So-and-so's herd. I would like a watermelon!' So I got a watermelon, asked about the herd, and found a one-eyed camel there. I approached him, holding the watermelon, and he took it as if he really wanted it and had an appetite for it."

My master, the Sheikh, surely sees the lack of understanding that has afflicted these people, and how they are drawn to things to which they should not be drawn!

31.1 *Ibn al-Rāwandī's books*

Ibn al-Rāwandī[1028] was not divinely guided to salvation. His *Crown* is not even fit to be a sandal. He has not found a covert from chastisement, i.e., a refuge.

Dhū l-Rummah said:[1029]

At last, when it does not find a covert and it holds back its mate
for fear of the hunter's bow, until they are all mad with thirst . . .

His *Crown* can be changed into scorpions;[1030] for he was no good, not nearly! How would he be if he were crowned with scorpion stings:[1031] would it not have hindered him from committing these follies? Is his *Crown* not like what the sorceress[1032] said: "Pshaw and phew,[1033] Sock and Shoe!"? They asked her, "What are 'sock and shoe?'" She replied, "Two wadis in Hell!"

His *Crown* is not royal: rather, it is called fatal. It is not made of gold but will be formed of flames. It is not strung with pearls but has come home to roost in misery.

One says "it has come to roost" when something has fallen into place, usually in a negative sense. The poet says:[1034]

> They (*viz.* the camels) hope for it, though they've come home to roost,
> as ʿAtīb[1035] hopes for its young children.

He was not crowned with silver, nor can he be pelted enough with pebbles. It is not like the crown of Chosroes: it has taken an evil road. Nor is it like the crown of King Anūsharwān, for it weighed him down and brought him humiliation. It is a crown that has broken a neck; one thinks it would infuriate anyone crowned with it. It is not like the crown of al-Mundhir:[1036] it is a disgraceful calamity for someone who errs though he has been warned.[1037] It is not like the crown jewels of al-Nuʿmān, but a shameful crime that will be stored till the end of time! The like of it need not be declared null and void: along with its author[1038] it has already been destroyed.

As for *The Brain-Basher*, I imagine that it bashed only the brains 31.2.1
of him who composed it and it took his place in a bad succession. Among the Arabs there was someone known as Damīgh al-Shayṭān, "the one whose brains are bashed by the devil." This man (*viz.* Ibn al-Rāwandī) is now like faded threads,[1039] but the awful thing, that he is still mentioned through the ages, proves that he who wrote the book was soft in the brain. Would one listen to the sound of a mewing cat?[1040]

This is from the verb *maghā*, said of a cat when it cries out loud.

He threw at me something of which I and my father
were innocent; and it was from the inside wall of the well that he threw at me.[1041]

May his stones fall on his own head and may his griefs and misfortunes be lasting in the hereafter! What a bad man has been named after Rāwand! Has he struck fire in Dabāwand? He has rent his own shirt and exposed his lean, hungry belly to every onlooker.

31.2.2 Apostate and rightly guided believer alike, he who who deviates from the straight path and he who follows it, all are agreed that the Book brought by Muḥammad—God bless him—is a book that dazzles by being inimitable and made his enemies tremble. It did not follow any model and did not resemble rare maxims;[1042] it is neither metrical *qaṣīd* verse nor the smooth or rough-and-ready *rajaz*. It resembled neither the oratory of the Arabs nor the rhymed prose used by the soothsayers for their purposes.[1043] It came like the shining sun, a light for those who keep or reveal secrets . If an unmoving mountain could understand it, it would crack; if white-footed[1044] mountain goats could, it would delight them old and young. «These parables: we make them for people, so that they may reflect».[1045] A verse from it, or part of a verse, may occur in the course of the most eloquent speech that mankind is capable of, and then it shines like a brilliant shooting star in a dark night, or a prettily arranged desert flower in a barren land. «Blessed be God, the best of creators.»[1046]

31.3.1 As for the *The Rod* (*al-Qaḍīb*), he who composed it made a worse deal than Qaḍīb.[1047] It would have been better for him if he had mounted an untamed she-camel (*qaḍīb*) at nightfall and had been thrown into a thorn-bush, dislocating his joints like tent pegs.

Al-Ṭirimmāḥ lampoons me, hoping I'll revile him:
No way, no way! May improvised poems (*quḍub*) be taken away from him![1048]

How could the life of someone who utters such things be cut short[1049] when he is a young man, with no one to intercede to save him from punishment! He would have wished he were a stick,[1050] or that a mountain had closed over him, so that he might have avoided resembling the poet's words:[1051]

> Many an evening journey in the world(?)[1052] I made between two tribes,
> driving an untrained she-camel (*ʿarūḍ*), or an untamed she-camel (*qaḍīb*) that I tame.

Qaḍīb is a wadi where a battle took place in pre-Islamic times between Kindah and the Banū l-Ḥārith ibn Kaʿb. How would it have been for that dolt[1053] to have been killed in Qaḍīb, and to have fallen there, his skin dyed with blood! For that would have been worse for him than a branch (*qaḍīb*) of a tree chastizing a fornicating slave girl. Who could see to it that his death is announced by the women?[1054] How would it be for him if his nose were cut off by an Indian sharp sword (*qaḍīb*), and he were to be clothed, for what he uttered, as someone to be redeemed. God has sent down such exemplary punishment on him as cannot be expiated by being loaded with fetters. He is as an early poet says:[1055] 31.3.2

> I have never seen two defeated men who accomplished what we accomplished,
> nor how that sword struck, with the stroke of a cutting sword (*qaḍīb*).

This line is quoted as linguistic evidence, as the Sheikh knows, because the poet uses the singular *yafrī* after the dual subject, whereas he should have used the dual, *yafriyāni*. He treats the dual as if it were a plural, like the verse by a *rajaz* poet:[1056]

> Like chicks whose crops have become full.

As for *The Unique One* (*al-Farīd*),[1057] he kept it alone, with no bosom friend, and clothed it for eternity in the mantle of the 31.4

despised. There is a tribe within Kindah that is known as "the lone tribe (*al-ḥayy al-farīd*)."

They are the Banū l-Ḥārith ibn ʿAdī ibn Rabīʿah ibn Muʿāwiyah the elder ibn al-Ḥārith the younger ibn Muʿāwiyah ibn al-Ḥārith the elder ibn Muʿāwiyah ibn Thawr ibn Murattiʿ ibn Muʿāwiyah ibn Thawr, who is Kindah.[1058] The genealogists say that he is Kindī ibn ʿUfayr ibn ʿAdī ibn al-Ḥārith ibn Murrah ibn Udud ibn Zayd ibn Yashjub ibn ʿArīb ibn Zayd ibn Kahlān ibn Saba'. They were called "the lone tribe" because the Banū Wahb formed an alliance with the Banū Abī Karb and the Banū l-Mithl, but the Banū l-Ḥārith joined neither them nor the Banū ʿAdī, so they were called "the lone tribe."[1059]

Some people are unique in glory on account of their dignity; but the "unique one" of that unbeliever is unique in its despicability. It is like a mangy camel,[1060] when smeared with camel urine, whose proximity is avoided by everyone who detests infamy. A pretty woman may be glad with a solitaire, a unique pearl, but for him it is a necklace of grave sins. Abū ʿUbaydah mentions that in a horse's spine there is a vertebra called "the solitary," which is the largest of the vertebrae.[1061] But if that rebel's "solitaire" were loaded on the back of a noble horse it would crush its "solitary" vertebra; or if a lover adorned with it a beautiful girl he would kill his precious virgin pearl.

31.5 As for *The Coral* (*al-Marjān*), if it is said that *marjān* rather means "small pearls,"[1062] then God forbid that his *marjān* should be (anything but)[1063] "small pebbles," for they are too vile to be mentioned and selected. If, on the other hand, it is said that they are this red substance that comes from the west,[1064] then this has some value; but the baseness of his book is lasting. It is called *marjān*, from the verb *maraja*, "to let (horses) pasture freely with one another," leaving them unattended on the earth. Or perhaps it is from *murr jānⁱⁿ*, "the bitter (fruit) of a plucker," i.e., from a tree; or from *marra jānn*, "a demon passed by," i.e., one of the brazen satans, or a "demon," which is a kind of snake that is easily killed, and which is loathed by all and sundry, i.e., everybody.

32.1 *Ibn al-Rūmī and his superstition*

Ibn al-Rūmī is one of those whose erudition is said to be greater than their intellect. He dabbled in philosophy. Once he borrowed a book from Abū Bakr ibn al-Sarrāj and when the latter asked it back, Ibn al-Rūmī said, "If Jupiter were a young man he would be hasty(?)."[1065] The people of Baghdad claim that he was a Shi'ite. The evidence they adduce is his ode rhyming on *-jū*.[1066] But I think he merely followed what other poets said.

Those obsessed with evil omens do not see any good in them. No, it is an evil that comes quickly, whereas all souls have a term that is fixed. All this comes from being wary of death, a noose round the necks of living beings, something they could be destined to meet at any moment. There are some people who believe that once something is said, it may possibly come true. That is why the common people say, "A rumor is the beginning of it coming true." It is also said that the Prophet—God bless and preserve him—quoted the following verse as a proverb, without completing it:[1067]

> See favorable omens of what you wish, and it will be! It rarely happens
> that when it is said of something "it occurred" it does not come true.

Whatever astute people believe, the good in this world is very little and evil outweighs it innumerable times. How godfearing people resemble sinners, all driven to perdition! They will meet with what is loathed and will not be held back. Perhaps God—exalted is His omnipotence—will make a distinction between them at the Overturning, and grant him who seeks what he wants![1068]

'Alqamah[1069] said,

> He who comes across crows and scares them away,
> thinking himself to be safe and sound, will have bad luck without fail.

Ibn al-Rūmī was notorious for his superstition. But who is free to choose? There are many reports about the Prophet—God bless and preserve him—that demonstrate his dislike of names that are not beautiful, such as Murrah ("bitter"), Shihāb ("blaze, shooting star"), as well as al-Ḥubāb ("love" or "beloved"), because he interpreted it as "snake."

32.2 A story similar to that about Ibn al-Rūmī that al-Nājim relates is the one about an Arab woman who said to another woman, "My father called me Ghāḍiyah, which means 'fire burning brightly with euphorbia wood.' Praise be to God for what He has decreed! And I married, from the tribe of Jamrah ('ember'), a man who made hotpot,[1070] whose stew, however, was not up to much. His name was Tawrab, which is the same as *turāb* ('dust'). All the other women gloated. His father was called Jandalah ('boulder'), and by being with him I was biting on a boulder and not smelling the scent of mandal wood. His mother's name was Sawwārah ('assaulter') and she never stopped assaulting me in a dispute; she never helped me with as little as a water-skin strap!"[1071]

The other woman said, "But my father called me Ṣāfiyah ('pure'), and I was free of all impurity and kept away from harmful places. He married me to someone of the tribe of Saʿd ('good fortune') ibn Bakr, and good fortune came to me early (*bakara ʿalayya*) and the promise was fulfilled for me. My husband's name is Muḥāsin ('kind'), may he be rewarded handsomely, for he treated me kindly and did not revile me. His father's name is Waqqāf ('bestower'), may God keep him, for he has bestowed on me his goods and provided me amply with provision. His mother's name is Rāḍiyah ('pleased'); she was pleased with my character and was not bent on my divorce."

32.3 If a man is superstitious he will always be chewing grit.[1072] If he sees a mountain swallow (*samāmah*) he thinks of swallowing poisons (*simām*) and if he sees a pigeon (*ḥamāmah*) he is afraid of perdition (*ḥimām*), as the Ṭāʾite poet[1073] has said,

> They are doves (*ḥamām*); but if their Ḥ is read with an I,
> by way of augury they are death (*ḥimām*).

If he comes across a flat-nosed woman (*khansāʾ*) he will not feel safe from evil, saying to himself, "I fear that a companion will turn up his nose at me (*yakhnis*),[1074] that something will stain my honor." If it is a flat-nosed animal his heart shies away from the land of the demons (?).[1075] Even if he sees it crossing from the right,[1076] his body trembles with fright, saying, "The people of abundant intellect among those who possess camels' soles and horses' hoofs see crossing from the right as a bad omen and are frightened that their luck[1077] has left them." If, by the workings of Fate, it crosses from the left, he beholds in it (a portent of) a gaping wound and says, "Did not those who own horses and saddles fear evil from the signs of the zodiac?" If he meets someone called Akhnas[1078] it is as if he has met with a strutting lion. He says, "How can I be sure he will not be like al-Akhnas, the 'Back-slinker' of the Banū Zuhrah tribe,[1079] who deserted with his allies from the multitude (?),[1080] while the slain were thrown into the well?" And if someone besotted with this superstition encounters a dust-colored gazelle he expects to be rolled in the dust.[1081] If he sees a brown (*admāʾ*) gazelle he is certain that blood (*dimāʾ*) will be shed.[1082] If he is confronted by an animal with a long tail he is like a proud lion and says, "I shall very soon humble and rebut the words of those who reproach me!"[1083] If, with a company of travelers in the desert, he spots an ostrich (*naʿāmah*) he does not connect it with bliss (*naʿīm*) but takes it as a harbinger of perdition and, being feeble-minded and inarticulate, says, "It begins with *naʿā*, which means 'to announce someone's death!'" If in a wasteland he comes across a male ostrich (*ẓalīm*), this is «a painful torment»[1084] and he says, "I wonder who will wrong me (*yaẓlimunī*)? Will they take my wealth or wound me?" If he sees a small bird (*ʿuṣfūr*) he says, "A storm plentiful (*ʿaṣf bi-wufūr*) of misfortunes!" Thus he is perpetually miserable, but still he must perish in the end.

Such considerations made Ibn al-Rūmī take "Jaʿfar" as being 32.4
"hunger" (*jūʿ*) and "fleeing" (*firār*). If he had been rightly guided

he would have linked it with a flowing river, because *jaʿfar* means "a stream with much water." But people of this disposition do not take things as they are in reality. One of them wanted to travel at the beginning of the year. "If I travel in Muḥarram,"[1085] he said, "I would deserve to be deprived (*uḥram*). But if I depart in Ṣafar I fear I shall be empty handed (*taṣfar*)." So he postponed his journey until the month of Rabīʿ; but when he traveled he fell ill and failed to achieve anything. "I thought *rabīʿ* meant 'spring,'"[1086] he said, "but it turned out to derive from *ribʿ*, 'quartan fever!'"

That Ibn al-Rūmī had some ice-cooled water ready was merely pretense; a burning thirst is not slaked by tricks. Keeping a dagger at his side is the precaution of a coward. The decisions one wants to carry out are foiled, as is what the builder has built. Many a man digs his grave in Syria, and then Destiny makes him undertake a far and troublesome voyage and he dies in Yemen or India! Death comes in lowlands and in the mountains. «No soul knows in which land it will die. God is all-knowing, all-informed.»[1087] Just as the soul is ignorant where its bones will be buried, it is ignorant of what will bring an end to its coherence. Many who expected to perish by the sword died by a boulder falling from a slope; many who were certain they were destined to die in their beds were slain by spears somewhere in a ravine.

The two verses by Ibn al-Rūmī that al-Nājim transmitted have a rhyme ending in a consonant. But as far as I know nobody skilled in using correct literary language has ever used a rhyme ending in a consonant in this meter, except in one verse quoted time after time by the lexicographers:[1088]

> It is as if the men have been fed on a dinner of mutton:
> they have indigestion and their necks are bent.

In this verse the penultimate syllable has a long *ā*, unlike the verse by Ibn al-Rūmī.

Al-Nājim did not know—but perhaps he conjectured in his thought—whether the old poet went to heaven or hell. How heavy are the caravan's loads![1089]

Abū Tammām did not hold on to the halter of religion. The story told by Ibn Rajā'[1090] is well known. A soul is (sometimes) overcome by its vices. If Ḥabīb (Abū Tammām) is thrown into the fire of hell his eulogies and his love poems will not avail him. If odes possessed knowledge and could grieve for the suffering of a friend, his two poems rhyming in *-ā'* at the beginning of his *Collected Poetry*[1091] would hold a funeral celebration for him that would be amazed at its distressed one,[1092] and they would lament him like the two daughters of Labīd.[1093] They drank a drink of bereavement as bitter as colocynth, and they said what Labīd, of the tribe of Kilāb, said in his own verses: 33.1.1 *Abū Tammām*

Say, you two: "He, the deceased, did not neglect his womenfolk[1094]
and he did not betray nor cheat his friend,"
(Lament) for a whole year; and then farewell, you two!
He who has wept a whole year long is excused.

I imagine that if this were God's decree, all other poems rhyming in *-ā'* would join these two poems, just as wailing[1095] women would come from all around, having agreed to attend the gathering one after the other. And if they did this, the poems rhyming on the letter B would vie with them and make a funeral celebration even more resounding and more plaintive in the dark, as al-'Abqasī said:[1096]

Every dawn they answer the dogs;
their throats are hoarse from wailing.

If there are one hundred poems on *-ā'* assisting and supporting one another at a funeral, there must be several thousand poems rhyming in the letter *B*, speaking out openly and loudly, because 33.1.2

rhyming with the letter *B* is a smooth road, easy to master; whereas rhyming on *-ā'* is a path beset with disaster.[1097] The poems that Abū Tammām composed rhyming on *T* will be able to contribute too. The two poems rhyming in *Th* will come, each like al-Jawn's daughter,[1098] hurrying, dressed in black: if they were given the form of humans, they would outdo the sight of the two singing girls of Ibn Khaṭal.[1099] The *Th* is a rare rhyme-letter in the poetry of the Arabs, but they can find support from the poem by Kuthayyir:[1100]

The bonds with Salāmah have become frayed;
  may rain fall on them, whether they are new or worn

and the *rajaz* poems by Ru'bah and similar forced rhymes and labored, license-ridden poems. They have assistance, sooner or later, from the compositions of Ibn Durayd.[1101] As for the poems rhyming on the letters *D* and *R* and those built on the easy consonants such as *M*, *'ayn*, and *L*,[1102] even if each category of them gathered—virgins as they are[1103]—the place for entering and exiting would be too narrow.[1104] They would number more than the men and women reported to have gathered at the funeral of Aḥmad ibn Ḥanbal. It is said that more people gathered at the death of Aḥmad than ever did in pre-Islamic times or in Islamic times, an estimated one million men and six hundred thousand women. God knows what is certain.

33.2.1 If Ḥabīb Abū Tammām neglected his ritual prayers he was lost in his lonely wastes. The ploys of one's enemies cannot achieve what ignoring a morning prayer does.[1105] How many an opponent withdrew from him, being out of breath![1106] The midday prayer is not like that.[1107] If he omitted it, it will testify, making an effort to complain. How many a lofty mansion is built in Paradise as reward for the afternoon prayer, how much musk is wafting fragrantly in Paradise for those who perform the sunset prayer without restraint, how many black-eyed damsels are freshly created from nothing for those who observe the evening prayer!—According to the Prophetic

Tradition it is forbidden to call this "first darkness prayer":[1108] "Do not be deceived about the name of your prayer; 'first darkness' is only used for the time camels are milked." Another Tradition has: "First Darkness is the name of the Devil's daughter."

He who is too lazy[1109] to perform those prayer sequences truly harbors an insolent intention. Would that Ḥabīb had combined two prayers, making them like those in the following verse:[1110] 33.2.2

He paired the midday with the afternoon prayer, as
a mature she-camel is paired with a male.

But I would be sparing with such "joints," to save the body from being roasted at the kindled fire,[1111] because he had an original style, with motifs like a succession of pearls, which he brought up from the dark depths of the seas, disclosing them by breaking their closed oyster shells.

If Mālik's servants[1112] were quick to get at him he has been hurled into perdition. If only he had been like al-Nābighah al-Jaʿdī, or had walked the path of ʿAdī, or had followed the road of Ḥātim![1113]—For Ḥātim was pious and godfearing to distraction. He said,

I shall be rewarded for what I do
and a roofed dwelling, Māwiyyah, will house me![1114]

Or would that he had joined Zayd ibn Muhalhil,[1115] who went in a delegation to the Prophet (God bless him) and cast aside the cloak of ignorance.

Al-Māzyār and Bābak

Al-Māzyār[1116] was a fool whether he settled or moved afar. He has plenty to swallow of the scalding water of Hell and enough ugly words to endure. Writings on him preserve for posterity things that demand he be cursed until Doomsday. Why shouldn't he be turned into something like a damp, soft piece of skin! God have mercy on Ibn Abī Du'ād! He quenched people's burning thirst for retribution and exposed al-Afshīn's doings, so that it became known that he was in league with disgrace and opposed to good sense and decorum. 34.1.1

Bābak opened the gate of tyranny and was found to be an evil shepherd.[1117] I believe that the holy war against him (may perdition be upon him!) was the best holy war ever known, and his crime the greatest crime ever committed. Perhaps, in the Hereafter, he would like to have his throat cut one hundred times for all who were killed during his day of power, when he begins to drink his salt water, and then to escape from utter torment and save his neck from the noose!

34.1.2 *Abū Muslim* And how strange that Abū Muslim tumbled along blindly in a dark night, thinking that he was on to something, but he was like someone who supports his weight on a shadow. He himself gathered the firewood for a fire that consumed him; he killed obediently for rulers who in turn killed him. He was not the first to work assiduously for others but was then misled by striving toward those who misled him. He devoted his waking hours to the base world, "Mother Stink," he chased after a mirage in the desert, and finally found that his sin was not forgiven by the ruler of the dynasty, Abū Jaʿfar.

34.2.1 *The vanity of worldly things* Everyone who strives after gain in the perishable world will necessarily come to regret it, at the time of separation and the moment of non-being. Our censure of the world is reckoned to be an error, just as when a frugal person wishes for contentment! This adds to our plight; the man who picks up the stick wins the race.[1118] We condemn the world although she has committed no crime against us. She is not concerned with anyone in particular. No, all her sons are alike in suffering afflictions: their whims will not avail them. Many a man who carries a load of firewood, whose household goods are a jumble, is unable to pay for his food with the price he gets for it and lives a life of loathsome poverty. His foot is penetrated by thorns, a spike[1119] dyes him with blood; yet he has fewer worries than someone who is seated[1120] on a throne, enjoying the company of a young, inexperienced "gazelle," while gold of unlawful provenance has been amassed for him, by oppressing nations and angering his relations. When he has filled his belly with food and swims in a foaming sea of opulence, then for these blessings and his pleasures he will suffer harm and Fate will strike him unawares. The destination of travelers is a homecoming![1121]

A sensible person, when he reflects, does not know which is better: a pampered child given a crown to wear from birth, or a speckled snake whose great delight it is to suck the earth.[1122] Both achieve their goals: one eats dust just like any beast, and the other drinks wine while great efforts are made to make his life a feast. 34.2.2

We know that religious rites are neither a protection nor something that leads to higher things. People act according to a predestined decree; what they hope for escapes them and I am not sure that the Hereafter . . . (?), so that the . . . will arrive at the Basin (?)[1123] But the secret is hidden and we all are thwarted in what we seek. An ignoramus—in fact, a person more ignorant than an ignoramus—is he who claims to have knowledge of the end of the days' journey. A curse upon those who lie!

34.3.1 *Claims of extremist Shi'ites*

As for those who make those claims for ʿAlī (peace be his!),[1124] this is an ancient way of going astray, a perpetual shower upon shower of error. It is transmitted that ʿAlī had ʿAbd Allāh ibn Sabaʾ burned for openly proclaiming this.[1125] The beliefs of the Kaysānites about Muḥammad ibn al-Ḥanafiyyah are strange and no honorable person should believe such things to be true. It is transmitted that a fire was lit for Abū Jaʿfar al-Manṣūr on the road to Mecca on the night he died, and that he said, "May God curse al-Ḥimyarī! If he saw this fire he would think it was the fire of Muḥammad ibn al-Ḥanafiyyah!" ʿAlī has precedence and numerous splendid qualities. Likewise, the noble qualities of Jaʿfar ibn Muḥammad cannot be exhausted.[1126]

I have heard that a man in Basra known as Shābāsh[1127] is claimed by many people to be the Lord Almighty. A great quantity of money is levied for him, a large part of which he hands to the authorities so that he can achieve what he seeks. But if he is scrutinized he is found to be base and vile: a serf is superior to him (a "serf" is someone who can be hired and moved from one place to another).[1128] I have been told that a similar claim is made for a woman in Kufa. 34.3.2

34.3.3 I have heard someone tell me that Ibn al-Rāwandī has followers who say that divinity dwells in him and empowered him with knowledge. They falsely attribute virtues to him which the Creator and all reasonable persons attest to be unpolished lies. But in all this he is one of the unbelievers and not to be reckoned among the noble and the pious. Someone recited the following verses by him—and whoever is godly and guides to the right path, it is not he!

Thou hast apportioned people's means of livelihood
like a drunk, plainly in error!
Had any man divided means of subsistence like this
we should have said to him, "You're mad, take an enrhine!"[1129]

If these two verses could stand up erect they would be taller in sin than the two great pyramids of Egypt.

If an intelligent person were to die of grief he could not be blamed! For where can a rational man find a refuge from misery that is ordained? Whenever some impostor deceives, bolts of unbelief are shot ("bolts" means "arrows"). Whenever black bile[1130] overcomes an impudent man and makes him satisfied with his own claim, he will come across some ignorant person to egg him on (i.e., to incite).

34.3.4 In the village known as al-Nayrab, near Sarmīn, a man emerged known as Abū Jawf,[1131] who did not even sport a *ḥawf* to hide his ignorance (a *ḥawf* is a small loincloth made of leather, split at the lower edges, worn by young girls). He claimed to be a prophet and told ridiculous things. He was stubborn in his schemes like any obstinate quarrelmaker. He possessed a store room full of cotton of which he said, "My cotton will not burn!" He told his son to hold a lighted lamp close to it; promptly it consumed the cotton! The women screamed and the neighbors gathered, intending to extinguish the fire. An eyewitness it told me that Abū Jawf used to laugh a lot for no particular reason, without an incident to marvel at. When they asked him "Why are you laughing?" he replied with a statement the gist of which is: If a person may be merry about a trivial, small matter, how much more so he who has received a sublime gift! He was plainly mad; his lunacy was not hidden. Stupid people followed him. He said that other prophets were liars. In the end the governor of Aleppo (may God protect it!) had him executed. This happened after the patrician[1132] known as the Duke[1133] was killed at Afāmiyah. Abū Jawf's assassination had been instigated by Jaysh ibn Muḥammad ibn Ṣamṣāmah who had received a report about him. He sent a message to the ruler of Aleppo (may God protect it!), saying, "Kill him, or else I shall send someone to kill him!" The ruler despised him because he was a man of humble stock. But many a ewe brings forth a flock (i.e., a herd of sheep)!

Some Shi'ites relate that Salmān the Persian and some other people came to see ʿAlī ibn Abī Ṭālib (God's peace be upon him!). They did not find him at home and while they were looking for him there was a flash of lightning followed by thunder, and there was ʿAlī, who had descended on the roof of his house, holding a blood-stained sword in his hand! "There was an argument," he said, "between two parties of angels. So I went up to heaven to make peace between them." Those who say this believe that al-Ḥasan and al-Ḥusayn are not ʿAlī's sons. May a painful torment encompass them! Consider this community: how manifold are its ways of error, just as Spring produces various kinds of herbage, or as grazing animals raise various kinds of young in the wild! For lies, unlike truthfulness, there is a market that turns a lion into a lamb among the flock. 34.3.5

Old Age, Grave Sins, Pilgrimages, and Sincere Repentance

35.1 *Old age* As for the Sheikh's reference to his old age,[1134] God (praised be He!) has created gall as well as honey, a desire for the Fleeting World as well as abstemiousness from it. When an intelligent person looks at it closely he sees that life only draws him to harm and drives his body onward on its course. Even he who stays in one place is like a traveler: divine decrees never confirm him in one state. A morning smiles or an evening, but he does not abide with either for long. Day and night are like rapacious wolves, and one's life is a herd on the move; they raid the shepherd and annihilate and destroy his grazing flock.

If the Sheikh (may God enable him to tread in the paths of erudition, by letting him live!) has put his youth behind him, at least he has spent it in the pursuit of knowledge and belles-lettres and[1135] made his quest his most pressing habit. If these things could abide for any living person, they would cling to his precious soul. But they are merely accidental attributes and do not experience life or its extinction.

If we agree in blaming this stage and are resolved to part from it, why should we regret leaving this treacherous world behind? A small palm tree comes from a large one.[1136]

Ashā'ah means "small palm tree," *ʿawānah* means "large palm tree."

When someone who has been negligent sincerely repents, his repentance leaves no transgression behind. It washes his sins just as a washerwoman washes the wool shorn from a lamb in water that has poured profusely from a cloud, even though the wool was full of filth and dirt. People wanted to rinse it, since it had been taken from the backs of white sheep, superior to all grazing flocks. Then it turned as white as camphor, the aromatic substance (*kāfūr*), or palm-blossom's fresh "camphor" that discloses[1137] its white spathe (*kāfūr* is the inflorescence of the palm tree; some say it is the integument of the spathe).

For pretty women after one has passed the age of seventy, a gray-haired man is like a hurrying wolf making for the white oryx cows. 35.2.1 It is said that Abū ʿAmr ibn al-ʿAlāʾ used to dye his hair. One day he fell ill and a friend came to visit. "You'll be back on your feet again," he said, "if God wills." Abū ʿAmr replied, "What can I hope for,[1138] at eighty-six?" The friend visited him again after he had recovered. "Don't tell people what I said to you earlier!" said Abū ʿAmr. This is a nice anecdote: he wanted to cheat by dying his hair and he hid his age from all his friends![1139]

A certain student of literature told us that the Sheikh (may God always adorn gatherings with his presence!) thought of marrying, so as to have someone to serve him. I was pleased to hear it, because it showed that he intended to stay in the country. Any intelligent person would be glad to have him near, for he is like a tree whose luxuriant foliage provides shade on hot afternoons, cool air in summer, sweet fruit for whoever tastes it, and a fragrant soft breeze for whoever inhales it. The Sheikh will know the story of what al-Khalīl quotes the Bedouin Arabs as saying: "When a man has reached sixty, let him beware of young women." There is no good in decrepit old men. But a middle-aged person has been described:[1140] «Neither too old nor too young, but middling, in between; so do as you are commanded.»

Don't marry an old woman if she's brought to you;
wash your hands clean of her and flee far away!
And if they come to you and say, "She's merely middle-aged!"
—Yes, but the better half of her has gone![1141]

35.2.2 But perhaps the Sheikh will be destined to marry someone like Umm ʿAmr, the wife of Abū l-Aswad. There is many a good thing found under veils![1142]

Like the robe of a Yemeni merchant, old and tattered,
its patches making it appear as you wish to eye and hand.[1143]

Or as another poet said,[1144]

A woman with a plump behind, well-preserved,[1145] whose coevals
have grown old and worn like rags, while she is as new.

It is related that Abū Ḥātim Sahl ibn Muḥammad once recited before al-Aṣmaʿī some poetry by Ḥassān ibn Thābit. When he reached the following line:[1146]

She yields in nothing to the daytime sun;
but youth won't last forever,

al-Aṣmaʿī said, "By God, he has described her as an old woman!" It is possible that it is as he said, but it is more likely that the poet said it when she was a young woman, regretfully, meaning that things will not last, just as another poet said:[1147]

You are a joy! If only you could last—
but human beings cannot last.

35.2.3 If the Sheikh actively pursued the matter, women old and in the prime of life would vie to have him, marriage proposals of women in their dotage[1148] would resound! A clever woman of sound judgment will be inclined to seek the company of a fair-minded man. It is as the early poet said:[1149]

ʿAzzah, would you like an old man who is ever youthful?
Some youngsters are no manly youths.

The Sheikh would not be the first to seek fulfillment(?)[1150] and marry an old woman despite her age, as the poet said:[1151]

Now that young women shun me,
isn't there an old one who will help me?
(Her jawbones, joined, when she unveils her nose,
are like a mug).

The following verses are attributed to al-Ḥārith ibn Ḥillizah,[1152] although I have not found them in his collected poetry:

They asked, "What kind of woman did you marry?"[1153] I replied,
"I married well:
an old woman from the tribe of ʿUraynah, a wealthy one!"
I married an old woman and gained[1154] wealth.
Such is trade: things come cheap or dear.

And may God protect me from what another poet said:[1155]

An old woman who, if water could (only) be drunk from
her hand,
would not let us pass and drink[1156] the waters.

The Bedouin Arabs have always praised old crones and mature women; they were not averse to middle-aged women still in the bloom of life. The Prophet (may God bless him!) married Khadījah, the daughter of Khuwaylid, when he was a young man while she was advanced in years. Umm Salamah, the daughter of Abū Umayyah, said to him, "Messenger of God, I am an old woman and I could not stand being jealous of your other wives!" He replied, "Yes, you are old, but I am older than you. And your jealous nature I shall pray to God that He may relieve you of."

A poet said,[1157]

I am not Ruhm's son, as you know, nor the son
of the woman from the tribe of ʿĀmilah; so beware of me!
But I was born under an ill-tempered star
to an old crone with gray locks.

35.2.4 I have no doubt that when the Sheikh was in Egypt he made use of the services of various kinds of female servants, who hasten[1158] to fulfill one's desires. Were it not that an aged man needs someone to help him, it would be prudent to content oneself with drinking from the spring on the surface.[1159] The Sheikh knows what a poet said: [1160]

A good life is nothing but a lock and key,
And a room through which cool winds blow,
Without loud noise or screaming.

36.1 *Servants, slaves, or freemen*

Ibn al-Qinnasrī, the Qurʾan reciter,[1161] told me that he had heard the Sheikh ask about a slave-boy servant. Employing freemen may prevent them from staying. Abū ʿUbādah said,[1162]

I am descended from Yāsir, Yusr, and Nujḥ,
not from ʿĀmir or ʿAmmār.[1163]
Is there, O people, no freeborn man in Iraq
who can absolve me from employing freemen?

It is better for a single man to be his own servant than having slaves enter his house. Often they compel their owner to beat them or to guard himself against them by being active and alert(?).[1164]

36.2.1 Often a man of letters, who is himself neither perfidious nor mistrusted, stays in an inn and is waited on by a boy freed from slavery, who serves him with theft and misery. If he sends him with a few coins, fractions of a dirham, to bring him a watermelon, when watermelons are available in plenty and their steep[1165] price has become affordable, he runs off with the coins on the way and goes to great lengths to betray his master. Then he stops at the fruit-seller, who swindles him in slicing the melon.[1166] He takes a small piece of watermelon, which does not strike the eye as something daubed with a dirty yellow dye. Then he runs off with it, playing, as if leading a full-breasted bride to her groom. He runs with it and does not stop. Then he drops it on the road amid a group of people and it breaks; the pips get mixed with pebbles: all sensible people would abstain from getting anywhere near it. It may, on the other hand, also happen that he carries the watermelon intact, and then goes swimming with other lads. When he is in the water some naughty little boy snatches it and eats it while the servant is watching him, not caring about the skin when he cuts it off. Or perhaps his master sends him with a large bowl to fetch milk; but he is cheated by his ill judgment. When the sour milk is in the bowl he stumbles and finds the milk clotted in lumps on the desert earth, and the earthenware dish has become potsherds that nobody wants, pious ascetics and unbelieving rebels alike would give it away for nothing. If his master has the same beliefs as Ibn al-Rūmī he would think that the breaking of the bowl (*ghaḍārah*) means the termination of his life of opulence (*ghaḍārah*). He would cry "Alas and alack!" and be distraught on account of his loss. What can he do with the sour milk when the time has come to depart to the final resting place?

In our town there lived a servant who belonged to a soldier and who asserted—truthfully—that he had been a slave soldier[1167] belonging to Abū Usāmah Junādah ibn Muḥammad al-Harawī, in Egypt. He regretted having to leave him[1168] and admired his good character. He had been bought, he said, because he could swim: a good reason to drive up the price![1169]—I only mention this because the Sheikh (may God make the time odoriferous, i.e., perfumed, with his life!) knew this Junādah and experienced his qualities. 36.2.2

As for the people of my town[1170] (may God protect them!), if I have been fortunate enough to have strangers entertain a good opinion of me, it is not impossible that the people near me also grant me this status. However, they are to me as those who seek a sermon from a mute person, or the heat of a summer month in a severe winter. 36.2.3

My lord Abū l-ʿAbbās al-Mumattaʿ is a child in age, a brother in affection, a grandfather or father in excellence. In his erudition he is truly as the Exalted says:[1171] «And to no one does he confer a favour merely to be recompensed».

37.1.1 *On drinking wine and other sins*

The Sheikh's anxieties[1172] (may God fill his mind with gladness and relieve his ears of all blame!) are natural to any civilized human being, not confined to a coward to the exclusion of a gallant hero. It is unjust to be affected by despondency:[1173] «Say: O my servants who have been excessive against themselves,[1174] do not despair of God's mercy». So many lettered people have drunk wine and were merry but then repented, responding to their critics. A guide may go astray in the full light of the moon but then God shows him the right path by means of some landmark or other. Many a drowning man has been saved from the waves, escaping unharmed and getting dry in the sun.[1175] Al-Fuḍayl ibn ʿIyāḍ used to pasture in the most pernicious meadows, but afterward he came to be counted among the renunciants and was turned into one of those who piously exert themselves. Many a profligate when a young man has become prominent when he grew older, or even a mufti! Many a singer playing the sitar[1176] or the lute came, by divine decree, under the influence of lucky stars and ascended a pulpit to preach, after sending out glances(?).[1177] The Sheikh may have looked at the biographies[1178] of singers and seen among them ʿUmar ibn ʿAbd al-ʿAzīz[1179] and Mālik ibn Anas,[1180] according to Ibn Khurradādhbih—if he is lying, his lies will be be on his head!

37.1.2 There is a well-known story about Abū Ḥanīfah,[1181] who used to drink wine in the company of Ḥammād ʿAjrad. Afterwards Abū Ḥanīfah became pious, whereas Ḥammād persisted in his errant ways. On being told that Abū Ḥanīfah had criticized and denounced him, Ḥammād wrote to him:

If, to make your piety complete,
you must scold and detract from me,

Get yourself into a state about me, if you must,
telling people near and far!
So often have you called me honest,
while I persisted in sinning,
The days you would hand me and take from me
what was contained in the lead pitchers!

Were not all the Prophet's Companions (God's pleasure be upon them) once in error, before the Almighty and Glorious One made them mend their ways? There is a report that ʿUmar ibn al-Khaṭṭāb once left his house intending to join some people who had gathered somewhere in order to gamble.[1182] Not finding anybody there, he said to himself, "I'll go to the wine seller; perhaps he'll have some wine." But he found that the man had nothing in store. Then he said, "I'll go and become a Muslim!"[1183] 37.1.3

Success comes from God, praised be He, through compulsion.[1184] Among God's words addressed to the Prophet (God bless and preserve him) is[1185] «And did He not find you going astray and guide you?» Abū Maʿshar al-Madanī[1186] mentions in his *Book of (the Prophet's) Mission* a story according to which the Prophet (God bless and preserve him) slaughtered a sacrificial animal for the idols. He took some, which was cooked for him. Zayd ibn Ḥārithah carried it and together they went off to eat it in some mountain pass or other, where they met Zayd ibn ʿAmr ibn Nufayl, who was one of the godly men of the pre-Islamic period. Muḥammad invited him to partake of the food, but Zayd inquired about it. "It is some of what we sacrificed to our gods," answered Muḥammad. Then Zayd ibn ʿAmr said, "I will not eat anything that has been sacrificed to the idols! I follow the religion of Abraham, God bless him." Thereupon the Prophet (God bless and preserve him) told Zayd ibn Ḥārithah to throw away what he had with him. 37.1.4

According to another hadith, which I heard together with its chain of transmitters, Tamīm ibn Aws al-Dārī (al-Dār being a branch of the tribe of Lakhm) used to present the Prophet (God bless and preserve him) every year with a skin of wine. One year he brought it after wine had become forbidden, so the Prophet poured it away (or "spilled it," according to some lexicographer).[1187]

37.2.1 Boiled wine, if intoxicating, counts as ordinary wine. Nevertheless, many legal scholars have drunk "popular"[1188] wine, *vin cuit*,[1189] and "half-wine."[1190] In a session with Aḥmad ibn Yaḥyā Thaʿlab someone mentioned Aḥmad ibn Ḥanbal and asked if he had ever drunk date wine (date wine is not the same as "wine" according to the legal scholars).[1191] Thaʿlab replied, "I gave him some with my own hand, at a circumcision feast given by Khalaf ibn Hishām al-Bazzāz."[1192] As for "syrup,"[1193] ʿUmar ibn al-Khaṭṭāb stipulated[1194] that the Syrian Christians gave it to the Muslim soldiers. But as the proverb has it,[1195]

> It is grape wine, nicknamed "syrup"
> just as the wolf is nicknamed "Woolly."

This verse, as the Sheikh knows, is transmitted incomplete[1196] and is attributed to ʿAbīd ibn al-Abraṣ. It can be found in some though not in all copies of his collected verse. In fact, I believe that this verse was composed in the Islamic period, after wine had been forbidden.

37.2.2 A drinker's pleasure is only due to the intoxication that affects him. But for this, other drinks would be sweeter and more warming. Al-Taghlibī says,[1197]

> Give me again, you two, a drink of syrup,
> such a blessed comforter in a sharp frost!

The following verse is attributed to Diʿbil:[1198]

> Give me again, you two, some music and syrup,
> and a hungry guest who wants a meal!

This is an indication that "syrup" is intoxicating. The following verse is attributed to a Hudhalī poet:[1199]

And when I wish, I enjoy in the morning something fresh,[1200]
and a wineskin containing wine, unboiled or boiled.

Another said:[1201]

Don't pour me wine except when it is unboiled, aged,
sealed: the worst wine is wine that has been boiled.

If the Sheikh (may God provide him with all he loves!) has drunk 37.2.3
unboiled wine and his drinking companions said "Cheers!" to him, then he has a model in Muḥammad ibn al-Ḥasan,[1202] the learned scholar of the tribe of Azd, when he said:

No, many a night I spent, from beginning to end,
with an eighty-year old girl, a bride unveiled.

At the end of the poem he says:

If I die, at least my pleasure was extreme.
Everything that has reached the limit must end.

I would not[1203] like the Sheikh to follow the words of al-Ḥakamī:[1204]

They said, "You are too old!" I replied, "My hand is not too old
to raise the glass to my mouth!"

And the Sheikh will know this verse:[1205]

They did not boil it, but their servant
toiled all night long in its vineyard with a lamp.

And the verse by ʿAbd Allāh Ibn al-Muʿtazz:[1206]

The infidel said that they boiled it,
and we agreed to have it, if only with a toothpick.[1207]

In the past drinking companions, both young and old men, would 37.2.4
ask for "boiled wine," dissembling and hiding their true intent with this term, without mentioning the old reddish wine. The verses by al-Ḥusayn ibn al-Ḍaḥḥāk, "the Profligate," but also attributed to Abū Nuwās, are well-known:[1208]

To one with a mischievous tongue, inventive in
denigrating others, who mixed libertinism with piety,
Who spent the night in Ghummā[1209] in search of "one that had been
warmed at the fire," alluding to it as "the king's daughter,"
I surreptitiously handed a "red one" shining like a meteor,
got from the hand of a fraudulent wine seller in a tavern,
Who swore by his Creator, by the Lord of Moses and
the builder of the Ark,[1210] that it had been boiled.
It was as if a moon was standing before the cup,
sipping some of the stars of the firmament.[1211]

One is a hypocrite if one makes a show of drinking what some jurist or other has pronounced to be permitted, while in fact intending to drink "the one that makes you forget your food."[1212] Al-Ḥakamī[1213] put it well:

But if you renounce your error, let this renunciation be
for God, not for the people.

37.3.1 Now the time has come for the Sheikh to renounce the ways of Ḥumayd and turn away from the path of Abū Zubayd.[1214] I mean Ḥumayd al-Amajī,[1215] who composed the following verses:

I have drunk wine and have not given it up;
I have been reproached for it but did not mend my way.
Ḥumayd, whose home is Amaj,
wine's friend, with gray hair, balding:[1216]
Gray hair came over him, in spite of his love of wine;
he was generous and did not give it up.

Someone else said:[1217]

An aged mother scolds me because of wine;
but her words are not, I think, correct.
She says, "Will you not shun wine? We have
sustenance: dates close at hand and raisins!"

I answered, "Wait! Raisins cannot make me merry
and dates do not creep into my bones.
Ḥumayd was regaled with wine in his youth
and did not sober up from it when gray hair appeared."

When word goes round among people's get-togethers that the Sheikh has repented, people will flock to him: young men in the prime of life, middle-aged men of letters, and even gray-haired men who have as little time left as the interval between two waterings of a donkey.[1218] Likewise all kinds of people will gather to enjoy a nightly conversation and to derive benefit from his erudition. They will prick up their ears to hear his oration. He will have a session for them in some mosque or other in Aleppo (may God protect it!), for after the death of Abū ʿAbd Allāh ibn Khālawayh it has been made bare of anklet and bracelet and has been extremely shy of erudition.[1219] 37.3.2

Now if that happens, with God's grace, he shall have ready a dagger like Ibn al-Rūmī's dagger, or the one that Ibn Harmah refers to when he says,[1220]

I will not let the camel mares enjoy their newborn calves
and I will not buy except what will soon meet its appointed time.
My sheep's lives will not be stretched
beyond a meal for a guest; likewise my camels.
So many a she-camel have I stabbed in the throat,
letting the blood gush forth, or a camel stallion!

Then, when the Sheikh sits in his gathering where those present pluck the flowers of dawn, or rather pearls from the sea, that dagger shall be near him. When it is decreed that there passes by his door a middle-aged one cut off at the neck,[1221] such as meant by the one who said,[1222]

When the middle-aged one who is cut off at the neck is nearly empty
we go for a second one like it from the vat.[1223]

The armless one,[1224] in bonds, looks like
a man of al-Daybul,[1225] stripped of his arms.

—then the Sheikh shall leap as a leopard leaps on the straggler of a large herd, or he shall order one of his companions to jump at it, and stab it with the dagger, so that it sheds its contents that are like blood or pure brazilwood.[1226] He shall recite this verse from the Qur'an:[1227] «Good deeds make bad deeds disappear. That is a reminder for the mindful.» When the owner of the wineskin goes to the ruler to complain and appeal, and the ruler asks, "Who has done this to you?" and your name is mentioned to him, then the ruler shall say, if God wills, "There is no free man in 'Awf's wadi![1228] What can I do with him who is the root of all erudition and the best of its people? He has trodden them underfoot and considers them his base underlings!"[1229]

37.3.3 As soon as the Sheikh has done this once or twice, those who carry armless skins will avoid that place, just as Abū Sufyān ibn Ḥarb avoided his normal route out of fear for the Prophet (God bless and preserve him), as Ḥassān said:[1230]

If they descend on Ḥawrān via the Sands of 'Ālij,
then say to them: "There's no road there!"

There is no harm if the prepared weapon is a cutlass, carried up one's sleeve. If he strikes an armless wineskin with it, those who have looked into *The Book of the Beginning*[1231] will be reminded of the story of Saul, when he ordered his daughter, the wife of David (may God bless him!), to let him enter David's apartment while he was asleep, so that he could kill him. But she foisted a wineskin into his bed. When she let Saul enter he struck it with his sword; the wine flowed and he thought it was blood. Then he was sorry and full of regret. He moved his sword so as to kill himself in his daughter's presence, but she stayed his hand and told him what she had done. Then he thanked her for that.

37.3.4 Whenever a drunken person visits that mosque he shall be manhandled and shaken about,[1232] as in the story in the Hadith, and they shall sniff the smell of his mouth. If his condition demands that he be flogged, he shall be flogged, and the Sheikh (may God incite him to command what is right and forbid what is wrong![1233]) need not limit himself to forty strokes as the prescribed punishment for him, as is the custom of the Hijazis;[1234] rather, he should whip him with eighty lashes, according to the way of the Iraqis, for that is more painful and grievous. It is said that the Prophet (God bless and preserve him) set forty lashes as the punishment, but when ʿUmar ibn al-Khaṭṭāb (peace be upon him) ruled he found it too few and, having consulted ʿAlī (peace be upon him), they decided on eighty.

Reports have been transmitted that the people in the Hereafter know about the people of the Fleeting World. If true, the Sheikh's black-eyed damsels who are readied for him in the Eternal Abode will ask the virtuous people whom they meet about him. They will hear that he is now in Fusṭāṭ, now in Basra, then in Baghdad, and sometimes in Aleppo. If it becomes widely known that he has repented and some pious person from Aleppo dies and tells them, they will be glad and rejoice; their neighbors will congratulate them. No doubt the Sheikh has heard the story connected with the two verses that are found in the *Book of Contemplation*:[1235] 37.4.1

May God bless the eyes of the two apparitions[1236]
and your nightly visit, Umaymah, to us!
How strange that you are not frightened by the desolation
of the tomb and the darkness of the graves that cover us!

I seek refuge with God against people who are incited by their gray hair to drink a lot of "Mother Iris,"[1237] as if it will save them from calamity,[1238] as Ḥātim says:[1239] 37.4.2

The tribes know that if Ḥātim wished for wealth
he would have had it in abundance;
But he ransoms with it captives and provides tasty food,
and the gambling arrows do not strip him of it.[1240]

O Māwiyyah, if my screech owl[1241] calls one morning
in a wasteland without water, without wine,
You'll see that what I have spent has not harmed me
and that my hand is empty of anything I withheld.

And Ṭarafah said:[1242]

Since you cannot prevent my fated death,
let me spend without delay, before I meet my fate, what I possess.

And ʿAbd Allāh ibn al-Muʿtazz said:[1243]

Don't tarry with the wine cups, don't hold them back from me!
Today, my friend, is not like yesterday!
Don't ask me, but ask my gray hair about me:
since I was fifty I don't know myself.

This man was urged by his advanced age to drink a lot of wine; but he failed to keep his caliphate. It is strange that he was desirous to succeed as caliph, as if he had turned wan and decrepit by constant worship! But it was as someone said to Muʿāwiyah ibn Yazīd:[1244]

Yazīd took the reign from his father;
now take it, Muʿāwiyah, from Yazīd!

37.4.3 Muḥammad ibn Yazīd al-Mubarrad used to be al-Buḥturī's[1245] drinking companion, but he gave it up. I should not like the Sheikh (may God make the heart of his enemy burst with rage![1246]) to be like Abū ʿUthmān al-Māzinī: he was reproached for drinking wine and replied, "When it becomes my worst sin I'll give it up."

Ibrāhīm ibn al-Mahdī did wrong when he suggested to Muḥammad ibn Ḥāzim that he should take a cup of wine.[1247] But someone who trifles with the lowest and highest strings of the lute is not to be chastised in matters of religion.[1248] It is transmitted that al-Muʿtaṣim once invited Ibrāhīm, as was his custom. Ibrāhīm sang to him the two lines that gave rise to the saying "He sang the song of Shiklah's son."[1249] Then Ibrāhīm cried. Al-Muʿtaṣim asked him,

"Why are you crying?" He answered, "I had pledged to God that when I would be sixty years old I would repent. I am sixty now." Then al-Muʿtaṣim exempted him from singing and attending drinking sessions.

37.4.4 If repentance is not sincere,[1250] old and threadbare repentance will not be mended. There was a man in our town who was addicted to wine. When he was old he took a liking to boiled wine. He would meet with his drinking companions, with some boiled wine in a *khurdādhī*[1251] in front of him. They had one cup between them; he would drink from the boiled wine and his friends would drink from the uncooked wine. Whenever it was his turn to drink he would rinse the traces of wine from the cup and drink from it. But when the *khurdādhī* with the boiled wine was empty he would drink from his friends' wine.

38.1 *Repentance*

As for the Sheikh's addressing someone else while meaning himself,[1252] this is as the proverb says, "It's you I mean, woman, and listen, neighbor!"[1253] One cannot abandon one's nature. Someone trying to be devout may want to turn away from his love of the Fleeting World, but he is as unable to do so as a gazelle is to turn into a lioness, or a pebble to be transformed into a pearl. «Joseph, turn away from this! And you, woman, ask forgiveness for your misdeed! You are one of the sinners.»[1254] To pray and say, "O God, make my sparrow a hawk!" would be equivalent to foolishness.

You know—and I shall not forbid any of your traits—
that a man cannot be other than how he has been created.[1255]

We may find a man convinced of the Hereafter, sincerely believing in the Resurrection, and acknowledging God's oneness, withhold a bone from a barking dog or refuse a girl the loan of a necklace, as if he would live on earth forever, even though the earth, easy and hard ground alike, perishes. Many of those who recite the Qur'anic verse:[1256] «The likeness of those who spend their wealth in the way of God is that of a grain that brings forth seven ears, each ear containing one hundred grains. God gives a multiple to whom He wishes. God is all-embracing and all-knowing», who believe it to be true and who are anxious out of fear of their God, are nevertheless stingy with paltry, insignificant things and give neither to beggar nor to churchwarden.[1257] So what can one expect from those who deny divine requital and do not accept the excellent solace of the Perishing World?

38.2 The Sheikh will have come across the story of Abū Ṭalḥah, or Abū Qatādah, about how he appealed to the Prophet (God bless and preserve him), litigating against a Jew. Abū Ṭalḥah had a palm grove and they had an argument about one palm tree. The Prophet (God bless and preserve him) said to the Jew, "Will you give him the tree if I guarantee you a tree in Paradise?" The messenger of God (God bless and preserve him) described it with all the attributes of the trees of Paradise, but the Jew replied, "I will not sell something in hand for something in the future." Then Abū Ṭalḥah said, "Will you give me the same guarantee, messenger of God, as you did him, if I give him the whole grove?" The Prophet said, "Yes." Abū Ṭalḥah was happy with that. He took the Jew with him and went to his grove, where he found his wife and his children, eating from its fruits. He stuck his finger into their mouths, taking out the dates. His wife asked, "Why are you doing that to your children?" He replied, "I have sold the grove." She said, "If you have sold it for something transitory in this world, you have struck a bad bargain!" But then he told her what happened and she rejoiced.

If one said to one of the worshippers of this age: "Give me a gravelly mud brick and you'll be given a silver brick in the Future World," he would not agree. If he were asked to give a one-eyed slave girl in exchange for a black-eyed damsel in the Hereafter, he would not do it, even if he is one of those who believe. So what can one expect from someone who has been nurtured on disbelief[1258] and who denies the truth of divine torment?

As for Fādhūh,[1259] he met his bird of doom while swaggering to and fro. There is no god but God! The mortar was not made especially to crush his skull, but «there is something written for every term».[1260] Evil comes early and strikes; his soul made him hope he would repent, but it was like the girl friend of Imruʾ al-Qays when he said to her,[1261] 38.3

> You've made me hope for one tomorrow after another,
> but in the end you were a miser of the worst kind.

It is related that Abū l-Hudhayl al-ʿAllāf used to go along the market streets, riding a donkey, and saying, "People, be warned by the repentance of my servant!" He had a servant who had made a promise to himself that he would repent. But a brick fell on his head and killed him. The Deluding World had cheated him.

39.1

The author's acquaintance with Ibn al-Qāriḥ

The first thing I heard about the Sheikh (may God perpetuate the consolidation of excellence by keeping him alive!) was from a man from Wāsiṭ[1262] who busied himself with the science of poetic prosody. He mentioned that he had seen the Sheikh in Nisibis, where there was a man known as Abū l-Ḥusayn al-Baṣrī,[1263] teacher of some descendant of ʿAlī. A servant called Ibn al-Dān would often visit him. The Sheikh passed by our town at a time when this man from Wāsiṭ was there too. When I was with Abū Aḥmad ʿAbd al-Salām ibn al-Ḥusayn, known as al-Wājikā (may God have mercy on him, for he was a noble man) I saw some books on which there was an endorsement of audition[1264] for "a man from Aleppo" who was the Sheikh, without any doubt—may God support his person with success, for he is a *rara avis*[1265] and does not need to be made known in verse: rather, his eminence is loudly proclaimed, no need for any hints. Al-Bakrī, the genealogist,[1266] said to Ruʾbah, "Who are you?" and Ruʾbah replied, "Al-ʿAjjāj's son." Al-Bakrī said, "You've said it briefly and informatively!" The Sheikh's fame is as widespread as the light of day, just as the Ṭāʾite poet says:[1267]

His brilliancy or his sharp mind protects him from being
humbled by "Who are you?" or "Who's that man's father?"

If it is possible that people can reincarnate through the ages, then he is the ʿAlī ibn Manṣūr whom al-Juʿfī[1268] eulogizes when he says (the Creator is trustworthy):[1269]

Having a rank that people on earth are kept from attaining,
he is exalted, so they called him "ʿAlī the Keeper."

The Sheikh has kept students of literature from reaching that rank and has settled on the peak rather than the slope of the hill.

39.2.1 As for the scholars he has met,[1270] these are all saving luminaries, stars in the darkness. Merely to look at them is an honor; all the more so if one scoops a handful from every sea of knowledge that one finds! I express myself with restraint, but perhaps the Sheikh has in fact drained their seas dry with his pen and his understanding, and they opened for him the locks of recondite things—"recondite" means what is stowed away and cannot be found again.—and he may have learned from al-Kattānī the Suras of the Revelation, acquiring an ample reward; it is as if he had been taught by the Messenger himself—but the goal can be reached without this step—or as if he took them from Gabriel, without alteration or substitution. Those teachers leveled for him the difficult heights of the Arabic language, so that the rough ground of Sībawayh's *Book*[1271] became to him even and soft, as it were, and he did not need to board a raft to sail across the depths of its seas.

39.2.2 As for the Sheikh's association with Abū l-Ḥasan (God have mercy on him), that man was a true master, a supporter of men of letters if they were weak, affectionate to those who were strong, counteracting adversities. He was as the poet says:[1272]

When you see his full brother and his friend
you would not know which of them is his kin.

Or as al-Ṭāʾī says:[1273]

Every mountain path where you are, family of Wahb,
is also my path and the path of every lettered man.

The proverb says: "Barāqish wrongs her own people."[1274] Al-Ṣūlī mentions that he once entered the presence of Caliph al-Muttaqī, after the Banū Ḥamdān had killed Muḥammad ibn Rāʾiq. The caliph asked him about the verses of Nahshal ibn Ḥarrī:[1275]

A master disobeyed me and was obstinate in his opinion,
just as Qaṣīr was disobeyed in al-Baqqah.[1276]
When he saw what would come of me and him,
and when matters took a turn for the worse,[1277]
He wished—post-maturely—he had obeyed me,
now that events had followed upon events.

One says "he did it post-maturely," i.e., too late, after the opportunity had gone. A poet said:[1278]

You, Quṭayn, not being one of them, are truly
the basest ruler, in offspring and wealth.
The tribe of ʿUdus ibn Zayd has moved away from you
and only came to know you post-maturely (*naʾīshā*).

Young men who feel an urge to rise always desire any position of 39.2.3
eminence. But how can they be safe from something that tramples them underfoot? A current saying has it that "The opinion of an old man is better than the testimony of a young man."[1279] Often someone who strives to climb finds that his assault meets with an adverse fate. If one has the bare minimum to live on, one has no need to build and feather one's nest with wealth and finery. But there is no refuge from the ordained decision. Alas for a life that is sealed with perdition!

Many an ascent to knowledge was ill-directed and has turned,
without dispute, into an ascent to ignorance.[1280]

40.1.1 *Pilgrimages* As for the Sheikh's five pilgrimages,[1281] the first will be enough for him when, with God's will, he congregates with others at the Resurrection. Let him have a look among the recent scholars; no doubt he will find some who have not been on pilgrimage. He can give them the other four as a charitable donation!

I can imagine him, together with the scattered parties of pilgrims, loudly proclaiming the formula "Here I am for Thee!"[1282] while thinking about similar invocations of the Arabs and how they came in three kinds: unmetrical but rhymed, the dimeter, and the trimeter.[1283] An example of the first is:

Here we are for Thee, our Lord, here we stand!
All that is good is in Thy hand!

The dimeter comes in two forms, one in *rajaz* and the other in *munsariḥ*.[1284] An example of *rajaz* is the following:[1285]

I'm here for Thee, praise be to Thee!
Thine is the kingdom, no partner to Thee,
Except a partner who belongs to Thee,
One whom you own, and eke all property
Of Fadak's idol, "Daughters' Father" he.[1286]

This is one of the invocations of the pre-Islamic period. At the time there were idols in Fadak. Another example is:

Giver of plenty, we are here for Thee,
From the Namir tribe[1287] we're here for Thee.
We've come to you in a year of scarcity
Hoping for rain to pour in quantity,
Striking in the watercourse covered by shrubbery.[1288]

40.1.2 The kind in *munsariḥ* meter is of two types. One has a rhyme that ends in an overlong syllable,[1289] as in the following:

Lord of Hamdān, for Thee we're here,
We've come to Thee from far and near

For Thy beneficence this year,
On sturdy mounts easy to steer,
To Thee the plains we cross and clear,
Hoping for Thy forgiveness dear.

The other type does not have an overlong syllable, as in the following:

We're from Bajīlah, here for Thee,
A tribe of proud solidity,
A fine and splendid tribe are we!
We come to bring a gift to Thee,
In hope of generosity.

Sometimes they come with more than one rhyme, as does the invocation of the tribe of Bakr ibn Wā'il:

In truth, in truth, we're here for Thee,
In worship and in slavery.
We come to Thee for counsel[1290] plain;
We have not come for trade and gain.

The trimeter also comes in two kinds. One is considered a form of *rajaz* by al-Khalīl, as is the invocation of the tribe of Tamīm as it is transmitted:[1291] 40.1.3

We're here for Thee! If Bakr did not stand in the way of Thee(?)
People would thank Thee or be ungrateful(?) to Thee.
Crowds of us have always come to Thee.

The other kind is in the meter *sarīʿ*. It comes in two forms. One ends with an overlong syllable, as in the invocation of Hamdān that is transmitted as follows:

We're here for Thee, and all tribes do the same:
Hamdān, the sons of kings, invoke Thy name.
They left their idols and to Thee they came.
So hear our prayer, 'midst all Umlūk of fame.[1292]

The form *labbūka* is derived from the verb *labbā*, "to obey, be at someone's service." Those who, in the preceding invocation, transmit the form *labbawk* produce an ugly rhyme defect.[1293]

The trimeter form without an overlong syllable is as in the following:

> We're here for Thee, Sa'd and their sons, aligned;
> Also their womenfolk, behind.
> They've come to reap Thy mercy kind.

All metrical *labbayka* ("Here I am for Thee") invocations must be in *rajaz* according to the Arabs; they do not come in the *qaṣīd* meters,[1294] or perhaps they did make such invocations but they have not been transmitted.

40.2 I can imagine the Sheikh, resolved to touch the Corner,[1295] having thought of the two lines that al-Mufajja' cites in his book *On the Definition of Desinential Inflection*:[1296]

> If they had ever greeted departing women before them,
> the Wall and Zamzam Well would have greeted their faces.[1297]
> But it is dumb and does not answer those
> who circumambulate around it.

Al-Mufajja' was struck by the change from masculine to feminine.[1298] It is not too far-fetched to think that a noun is implied, the adjective of which has taken its place.

Likewise the Sheikh will have remembered the verses of another poet:[1299]

> I thought of you while the pilgrims were shouting
> in Mecca and hearts were throbbing,
> And I said, while we were in a sacred place,
> where hearts were devoted solely to God:
> I shall repent unto Thee, O Lord, from what
> I have committed, for my sins are evident.

But from my passion for Laylā and my love
of visiting her I shall never repent.

Then he will say: Don't the Basran scholars say that the "*H* of lament" is not preserved in non-pausal forms? The *H* in *rabbāh* ("O Lord!") is like that *H*; there is no difference![1300] But it is possible that they refer only to prose in this connection; versification allows licenses that are not tolerated elsewhere.

And perhaps the Sheikh was reminded of the following verses, on circumbulating the Kaaba:[1301] 40.3

I go around the Kaaba with all who go around,
lifting my loin-cloth that hangs down.[1302]
At night I pray, prostrated, till the morning,
reciting from the clear, revealed Book.
Perhaps that He who relieved Joseph's misery
will give me power over that woman in the camel litter!

And he will have said, "How easy, the diction of these verses! If only the poet had not added 'that' after 'perhaps.'"[1303]—Praise be to God! "A beautiful woman will not lack blame,"[1304] and, "Which man is perfectly polished?"[1305]

And at the Dispersal,[1306] when people go their several ways, the Sheikh will have remembered the following verses:[1307] 40.4

Say farewell to my heart, Quraybah, and be generous
to a lover whose departure is imminent!
There's nothing between life and death but
their camels' being returned and their being reined.

And the verses by Qays ibn al-Khaṭīm:[1308]

Abodes of her who nearly stayed with us when we were
at Minā,[1309] had the camels not been so swift.

I saw her only on the three days at Minā,
where I knew her as a virgin with plaited locks.
She appeared to us as the sun from under a cloud;
one of her eyebrows showed, but she was stingy with the other.

The Sheikh will have distinguished between the two interpretations of the words "she stayed with us," for it is possible that it means "she stayed among us" but it could also be that the poet intends "she made us stay," just as one says "stop with us here!" meaning "make us stop." It is the same in,[1310]

". . . as a smooth pebble slides off anything that settles on it."

40.5.1 If the Sheikh lived in Mecca for pious purposes[1311] between the pilgrimages that he performed he must have become more knowledgeable about the town than a crow about its nest, or a sand grouse about its hollow, or a chameleon about its thorny tree.[1312] But if he traveled to Yemen or some other place, making a pilgrimage every year, he will have a yet greater reward and will be all the more entitled to reach the status of a true penitent.[1313] Perhaps he has stood at al-Mughammas, praying to God to have mercy on Ṭufayl al-Ghanawī when he says:[1314]

Is the bond with Shammā' still attached, after parting?
Or are you, dwelling far from her, occupied with other matters?
She is darker than a gazelle born in spring, brow
and eye made up with kohl, made of antimony from al-Ḥīrah,[1315]
Which[1316] grazes in the well-rained valley bottoms with vegetation that offers
itself to it in the bend where the elephant disobeyed its masters.

I spoke of "praying to God to have mercy on Ṭufayl" because some transmitter asserts that he was still alive at the coming of Islam, and his verses in praise of the Prophet (God bless him) have been transmitted, even though I have not heard them in his collected verse:[1317]

By your father, a better man![1318] The camels of Muḥammad
are defenseless,[1319] lamenting when the north wind blows.
When they see a strange camel near the forecourt
bucketfuls of tears stream forth from them!
And in severe winter you see on the ground, waiting for them,
the vultures; none of their calves will live.

And the Sheikh will have recited the verses by Ibn Abī l-Ṣalt al-Thaqafī:[1320] 40.5.2

The signs of our Lord are evident:
only an unbeliever will dispute them.
He detained the elephant in al-Mughammas until
it had to crawl as if hamstrung.
To God every religion, on the Day of Resurrection,
—except the True Religion—is worthless.

And these verses of Nufayl will not have failed to occur to him:[1321]

Greetings from us, Rudaynah!
May our eyes be pleased to see you in the morning!
For if you had seen (but may you not see it!),
what we saw near al-Mughammas
You would have forgiven me and be pleased with me,
and not be sorry for what is past and gone.
I praised God when I saw the birds
and the stoning with pebbles that were cast upon us.[1322]
Everybody is asking about Nufayl,
as if I owed a debt to the Abyssinians![1323]

I wish I knew if the Sheikh said "Here I am for Thee" while combining the pilgrimage with the lesser pilgrimage[1324] or performed only the former. And I hope that in Mecca he did not meet a middle-aged woman who suggested to him that he should follow the fatwa of Ibn ʿAbbās,[1325] swearing to him that there was nothing wrong in that! Then the Sheikh will have thought of the following words of a poet:[1326] 40.6

She said, after I had circumambulated her Kaaba seven times,
"How about the fatwa of Ibn ʿAbbās, old man?
How about a woman with tender, soft limbs
who'll be your bed-fellow until the people separate?"

40.7 As for those relations of Jawhar,[1327] even after attaining good fortune a "jewel" will change and be shattered. Many a pearl in the crown of a king, when he was overthrown by the Destroyer,[1328] was crushed out of grief by his concubines. Could his squadrons have prevented his death? And many's the pearl on the throat of a full-breasted girl far from pollution and vice that was afflicted with defect or blemish,[1329] so that her mother put it in a mortar.

41.1 *The Sheikh's thoughts in Antioch and Malatya*

I imagine I can see the Sheikh coming past Antioch and thinking of the words by Imru' al-Qays:[1330]

The women mounted inside camel litters draped with Antioch
cloth on top of red embroidered cloth,
like a lopped-off date palm branch or Yathrib's garden.[1331]

It will have occurred to him that the word *naṭk,* from which "Antioch" would have to be derived if it were Arabic, is not used; it is not mentioned by any well-known and reliable authority.[1332]

When he came past Malatya he will have frowned at the odd morphological form and said, "The pattern is $C_1aC_2aC_3yah$, one that is not listed.[1333] If we assume it is derived from an Arabic root the Y must be secondary, because it is preceded by three root consonants."

41.2.1 As for the Sheikh's friend whose friendship turned barren upon examination:[1334] the Sheikh knows the proverb, "Let the one in the grave alone."[1335] When a person is covered by earth all ambitions are at an end. He who was blamed when alive is entitled to pardon when dead. But perhaps the Sheikh was not completely serious when he spoke as he did, or rather was rash with his words. If one forgives a living person the sin he has committed and the damage one has suffered thereby, how could one not forgive him after he has died and can no longer do any harm? A cursory blessing on a tomb equals one thousand blessings at people's gatherings. The Sheikh knows what they said about the meaning of the following verse:[1336]

I go to my friend where he said farewell,

i.e., I visit his grave.

As for the improvisation that this man found suspicious,[1337] my lord the Sheikh's name is repeated in the world of letters as the names of al-Ḥasan and al-Ḥusayn are repeated among the descendants of Hāshim,[1338] or as a tattoo is repeated by the hand of the tattooer.[1339] Should one be amazed at the cooing of a turtledove, or at the first drop that falls from a cloud rich in "milk"?[1340] If the Sheikh confronted the lavender of ʿĀlij with the fine odor of his speech, it is possible that he would surpass even its fresh scent; or if he confronted the lightning, it is possible that he would precipitate its flash. There are some people who are by nature cantankerous, who will annoy their companion and often cheat them; but the Sheikh knows he is virtuous and that no one can beat him in a shooting match. 41.2.2

Improvisation[1341] comes in several categories; in order to be declared the winner one can think of diverse ways. One of them is "extemporizing"; the Sheikh is perhaps faster in this than Sabal, or he is the *sabal*! (By Sabal a famous mare is meant; *sabal* means "rain.") Another kind is "capping."[1342] But a large cooking pot is not generous with olive oil(?).[1343] Finally there is "constraint":[1344] this is something that wakes one from slumber; it comes in different forms and a simpleton is not up to it.

As for Abū ʿAbd Allāh ibn Khālawayh, who had manuscripts brought to him for his studies, he was not incapable or amnesic (i.e., forgetful): a prudent man will want to adduce corroborating evidence and backing from a second testimony:[1345] 41.3

I see that one's needs from Abū Khubayb
are in distress, and there is no Umayyah in the land.

Where is the like of ʿAbd Allāh ibn Khālawayh? Syria is bereft of him. It was like Mecca when Hishām was sorely missed—I mean Hishām ibn al-Mughīrah—because the poet lamented him, saying,[1346]

Now Mecca's valley shudders
as if there is no Hishām in the land.
He was always thin like the bends of a whip.
but on his bowls there were piles of fat.
The elderly could eat as much as they liked
and the young could carry and collect.

41.4 Abū l-Ṭayyib al-Lughawī is ʿAbd al-Wāḥid ibn ʿAlī. He is the author of a small book called *Rhyming Pairs*,[1347] arranged alphabetically. It is current among the people of Baghdad. He also wrote a book known as *Permutation*,[1348] in which he followed the method of Yaʿqūb in his book *Phonemic Conversion*,[1349] and a book known as *The Pearl Tree*,[1350] in which he followed the path of Abū ʿUmar in his *Concatenation*.[1351] Also a book on *Difference*,[1352] in which he wrote much and at length. No doubt many of his books and systematic works are lost, because he and his father were killed by the Byzantines at the fall of Aleppo.[1353] Ibn Khālawayh used to give him the nickname "Beetle Pill,"[1354] referring to a scarab's dung ball, because he was so short.

A reliable person told me that he once was in the gathering of Abū ʿAbd Allāh ibn Khālawayh. A messenger had just arrived from Sayf al-Dawlah, summoning him to his presence and saying to him, "A lexicographer has arrived," meaning this Abū l-Ṭayyib. "I got up and left Ibn Khālawayh," said the man who told the story, "and I went to al-Mutanabbī and told him about it. 'Now he will ask that man,' said al-Mutanabbī, 'about the meaning of *shawṭ barāḥ*, of *ʿillawḍ*,[1355] and such words!' meaning he would give him a hard time."

Abū l-Ṭayyib al-Lughawī and Abū l-ʿAbbās ibn Kātib al-Baktimurī were intimate friends. The latter said to him,

ʿAbd, you are Paradise to my heart
  in love, and you are the pupil of my eye.
You are resolved to go; say whatever you must,
  and mention to him who keeps his passion what you must:
I shall not complain of lying awake for a long stretch:
  the night knows that I shall be forever sleepless.

By "ʿAbd" he means ʿAbd al-Wāḥid, just as ʿAdī ibn Zayd said in his verses rhyming on the letter *ṣād*, quoted earlier:[1356]

May you be far from me, ʿAbd, when the times
  are bad, and kept away when times are difficult!

He meant ʿAbd Hind.

Abū l-Ṭayyib also dabbled in making verse.

41.5 *Ibn al-Qāriḥ's praise of al-Maʿarrī*

God knows that I am "neither in the caravan nor in the troop"![1357] And who would be ungrateful to him who feeds his family?[1358] Whenever I tried to remain obscure I was destined to see my hopes thwarted. If the Sheikh were to stay in Maʿarrat al-Nuʿmān for a whole year he should not have heard my name mentioned or have thought of me at all. Now his gracefulness has engulfed me and the leafy branches of his erudition, not his lotus tree,[1359] have shaded me. Unique pearls came from him to me; if one of them appeared as a silver bead it would not be hidden on the pages of his letter, and a whole tribe would be rich with its price. People would fill the road toward it, to look at the precious jewel, bright like Venus, as the *rajaz* poet said,[1360]

When Tuzmurah saw her it was as if he saw gold in a mine,[1361]
And he said, "People, I've seen something incredible!
It was a gold nugget in a wadi, when I saw Venus!"

Instead of Tuzmurah, some transmit the name as Turmulah, which is the more frequent version, in spite of the rhyme defect.[1362]

The Sheikh (may God perpetuate literature's glory by keeping him alive!) has a generous nature, and a generous man is easily deceived. He who hears something may imagine something. A rock does not give birth to lambs!

42.1 *Pleasure and Wine*

The Sheikh mentioned that in Egypt he had inclinations toward certain pleasures.[1363] He knows the hadith: "Relieve your hearts, then they will be mindful of God!"[1364] Uḥayḥah ibn al-Julāḥ said,[1365]

I've sobered up from foolish love. Pleasure is a fickle demon
and a man's soul gets bored sometimes.

The Sheikh should at that time have acquired the erudition available to him from studying with those he studied under; for at a young age one is necessarily receptive to influence and able to aim at much with little effort. But a single drop of the Sheikh's knowledge will make one drown and his breath, even when cold, will burn. A man of Quraysh said,[1366]

How excellent I am when decrepitude overtakes me!
Should I regret anything time's vicissitudes bring?
Have I not unveiled a white-skinned woman with glittering anklet,
with a pure skin and a fine-featured face?[1367]
Or haven't I had, before chiding women could stop me, a morning drink
of wine mixed with water, an old wine like blood?

Perhaps the Sheikh has had his fill of all these desires; but all things come to an end and the Fleeting World is a mocking mirage. He has been intimate with kings and viziers, he has lacked nothing and there is nothing degrading or contemptible in that. He will have heard the story about al-Nuʿman the Elder, who abdicated in the guise of a hairy beast, taking haircloth instead of silk, and who wanted to wander as an anchorite. It is to him that the ʿIbādī poet[1368] refers when he says,

Remember the lord of al-Khawarnaq,[1369] who pondered
one day—one may well ponder about True Guidance!
He was pleased with his kingdom and his many possessions,
with the river, showing its width, and al-Sadīr.
But then his ignorance[1370] converted and he said,
"What is the happiness of a living being bound to die?"

Being drunk is forbidden in every religion. It is said that the Indians never make a man king if he drinks alcohol, because they consider it abominable. It is possible, they say, that some news arrives in the kingdom while the king is intoxicated, and then the king, who should be obeyed, is sleeping off his hangover! Cursed be the wine![1371] How many a company because of it went into decline! There is no good at all in alcohol. It makes one tread as if on burning coal. He who drinks wine in the morning is walking on the road to catastrophe; he who drinks "Mother Night" in the evening is trailing his skirt in vanity. Whoever is infatuated with "Mother Iris"[1372] has given in to his ruined mind. To carry a cheering wine in one's hand is quickly to let good conduct slip. Enjoyment of the company of a vintage wine strips off the robe of dignity. He who is addicted to a pungent wine will not stand on the clear road.[1373] To be besotted with heady wine is to revert to the state of a newly weaned child. Habitually drinking ʿĀnah wine prevents one from attaining one's desires. Failure because of wine bought to be drunk extracts every hidden secret. There is no profit in bay-red wine that makes the living as good as dead. He who is afflicted with a Ṣarkhad wine cannot be redeemed from scandal. How treacherous are wine's promises: it breaks the strongest oaths. Wine makes one whine.[1374] So many a lad from the tribe of Kilāb[1375] died in his prime, not having attained happiness in this world: addiction to aged, deceitful wine struck him with a fatal consumption. Someone who hurries to strong, chilled wine[1376] sees 42.2

as if with blinded eyes. A lion roaring in its den is less dangerous than a lute-playing singing girl. Many a wooden lute has wreaked havoc with the stingy and the generous; many a skin-bellied lute[1377] has caused a sleeper sleeplessness.

The Sheikh knows the verses by al-Mutanakhkhil:[1378]

Of what shall I die? A man's destiny is to
the hyenas,[1379] or gray hair, or to be killed.
If one evening he is intoxicated with unmixed wine,
drinking his fill of it, with meat raw or from the cooking pot,
His precautions will not protect him from death:
that is written for him since his mother was pregnant with him.

42.3 Something that ought to make the Sheikh abstemious from the limpid reddish wine is the fact that his noble drinking companions ended up in graves now obliterated. So often has he sat with young men who have now been swept away by Time, so that it was as al-Jaʿdī said:[1380]

I remembered—remembering stirs my passion,
and a sad man needs to remember—
My drinking friends with al-Mundhir, al-Muḥarriq's son;
the surface of the earth is now devoid of them.

And he knows the verses that begin:[1381]

My two friends, get up, you've slept long enough!
Will you seriously not end your slumber?[1382]

Is the Sheikh unable to be as another poet said?

As for "syrup,"[1383] I will not taste it
until I meet, after death, an Omnipotent One.

It is as if this poet was the Sheikh's companion in drinking "syrup"; when ruin struck him unheroically[1384] he made drinking it forbidden to himself, until the solid earth would give him lodging in its soil.

The Stolen Dinars and the Number Eighty

I was pleased that the Sheikh's dinars were returned to him.[1385] They are helpers; their various kinds resemble one another. People have duties toward them; they can be devoted if (other people's) disobedience is feared. ʿAmr ibn al-ʿĀṣ said to Muʿāwiyah: "I dreamed that the Resurrection had begun; you were brought while sweat was 'bridling' you!"[1386] Muʿāwiyah replied, "Did you see there any of the dinars of Egypt?"[1387] 43.1.1

Ibn al-Qāriḥ's eighty stolen dinars

No doubt these dinars of the Sheikh were from "the dinars of Egypt" that did not come from the common people but from princes and they were not the bride-price for a harlot.[1388] Praise be to God, who delivered them into the Sheikh's hands until this time; they were not like gold that was stored but ended up with a taverner together with the weighed coins, as the poet said:[1389]

There was a female taverner, daughter of Zoroastrians,
in whose house you see the wine-skin being raised;
We weighed for her solid gold
and she measured out for us liquid gold.

Nor was the following verse made into a riddle alluding to them:

Our "dinars" come from the horn of an ox, not
from gold minted between stone slabs.[1390]

If al-Muraqqish saw them he would realize that they are prettier than the faces of his girlfriends, when the camel litters departed with the women in the morning:[1391]

Their fragrance is musk, their faces are
dinars, and their fingertips are *ʿanam* berries.[1392]

And they are more beautiful than the faces mentioned by al-Jaʿdī, who asserted that their beauty was unprecedented:[1393]

Among young men with noses proudly held high,
like dinars that have been polished with a weight.[1394]

43.1.2 They were taken from awards granted by noble, proudly men, now for a service, now for an ode. They were not paid in advance[1395] for camels of the Banū ʿĪd, nor considered feeble (?)[1396] when needed, as Raddād al-Kilābī said:[1397]

Ibn Salmā traverses the lands with it, mounted on camels
of the ʿĪd tribe, for which dinars were paid in advance.[1398]

Whether one is stupid or clever,[1399] they are better than the seal mentioned by Ibn Qays when he said,[1400]

When she uses her seal the clay of her seal is widely accepted
just as precious ʿAbdite dinars are accepted.

With "ʿAbdite dinars" those of the caliph ʿAbd al-Malik ibn Marwān are meant; he is said to have been the first to mint dinars in Islam.[1401]

And they are superior to the coins of a money changer; they weigh heavily in a true scale. God forbid that they be as al-Farazdaq said:[1402]

Her forelegs reject the pebbles on every hot afternoon,
as the testing of money changers rejects dinars.

(This verse is recited in two versions, with "dinars" and "dirhams."[1403]) Nor do they belong to the dinars of Aylah, with which someone bought a small palm tree.[1404] They speak of "dinars of

Aylah" because it was Byzantine territory and dinars came to it from Syria. A poet said,[1405]

A gold dinar from Aylah
in the hands of the adorners, shining, glowing,[1406] is not . . .

The "adorners" are the engravers that adorn it.[1407]

And if Muḥriz al-Ḍabbī saw them he would have sworn that when viewed they are superior to those "countenances," even if they appeared on faces with fine features. He said:[1408] 43.1.3

It is as if there are dinars on their countenances,
even though an encounter has wizened their faces.

God forbid that they should be compared to the crowfoot of a wadi that has been watered by rain clouds in the evening and the morning, but when the summer is ablaze with heat, the plants that clothe the wadi are tattered and shriveled. A poet said,[1409]

And into many a wadi watered by a blessed star,[1410]
where wild animals roamed and dust-colored gazelles,
Have I descended while the sun was rising in the morning,
where the crowfoot flowers resembled dinars.

If someone who regretted the sale of his bay horse got dinars like them they would bring splendor to his heart and home. He would not be sorry that he was given a donkey in exchange for a horse, and would be found silent, uncomplaining. He would not say:[1411]

I regret the sale of the bay;
a man's life brings nothing but worry and loss.
When he who had negotiated with me brought the dinars
Nawār[1412] listened and was delighted by the sale.
"Complete the sale," she said, "and buy something else!
Around you in our winter dwelling there are young children!"
So I spent on them what I had earned; I always
had drink available and the smell of cooked food with me,

Until the army rallied for a campaign
and the abundant rains of winter had gone.
Then I needed a colt that could take its place:
it was as if there weren't any colts in the whole world.
My companions went on fleet horses
and I went with under me, to my misery, a donkey!

43.2.1 It is due to God's grace that with His decree He saved the Sheikh's dinars from an early morning visit to the tavern—he who goes there early in the morning, carrying the dinars with him, should not be thanked! He will not seek the company of pinchfists (i.e., misers) but he will stay with them in the tavern for days, intoxicated, whether awake or sleeping, and wine cups will exhaust the gold as if it were a camel slaughtered for the gambling game, and the cups the arrows.[1413] Al-Jaʿdī said,[1414]

To many a tavern, whose door creaked
like the sound made by those who draw water with a large bucket,[1415]
I came early, before the cocks crowed
and the church-clappers[1416] had not yet been struck.

Another said,[1417]

Often I went in the morning, with a handful of dinars,
to the taverner, surrounded by generous young men,
And there he kept pouring wine for us, taking the coins,
until the cup had taken all that had been in the purse.

If the Sheikh had lived in the times of the ancient kings each one of his dinars would have been like that described by the poet:[1418]

A yellow one struck in the palace of kings,
with Jaʿfar shining on its face,
More than one hundred by one;[1419]
when people obtain it they are rich.

The Sheikh's dinars are, by God's permission, sanctified, not encumbered by anything forbidden. Prudence is part of his nature and character; so he will lend none of his electables, i.e., his choice possessions, to anyone who trades on his behalf for a share in the profit. In the Noble Book it says,[1420] «There are some people of the Scripture[1421] who, if you entrust them with a hundredweight,[1422] will pay it back to you; and there are some who, if you entrust them with one dinar, will not pay it back to you.» This was said to the Messenger of God (God bless and preserve him) in a period when there were scrupulous people, who anointed and perfumed themselves with piety. Today, however, if a person of the Scripture is entrusted with a penny, suspicions would rush to him as quickly as rain from a cumulonimbus (a cumulonimbus is a cloud that quickly clears away); as the poet of the tribe of Hudhayl said:[1423] 43.2.2

Those men: if you[1424] invited them there would come
from them men like rain from summer cumulonimbus clouds.

When I mentioned a "person of the Scripture" I did not exclusively refer to the Torah and the Gospel, but also to the Noble Qur'an. But trustworthiness surely needs to be widespread on earth and be inherited by any virtuous person; in the Hereafter it is yet nobler and cleanses away more sins one has committed. Therefore let the Sheikh look after the remnant of his money as an astute and intelligent man would do. For every single one of his dinars is a "dinar of mighty men" that would move any mature young man to elation, as Suḥaym said:[1425]

She shows you, the morning of departure, a hand and a wrist,
and a face bright like a dinar of mighty men.

If Qays ibn al-Khaṭīm[1426] looked at it he would not compare the face of his Kanūd to it, he would make it the most helpful of his supporters and he would not allow himself to say: 43.2.3

Today you severed your bond with Kanūd,
in order to have a new tie instead of with her.
That evening, when she appeared and showed you,
briefly, some of her splendid charms, her neck,
And a face that I imagined to be, when it appeared to me
on the morning of departure, a sound dinar coin . . .

Rabīʿah ibn al-Mukaddam[1427] had it in mind when he was certain that his premature death was impending, saying,

Bandage me, Umm Sayyār;
you are bereaved of a knight like a dinar!

Or, if Mālik ibn Dīnār had owned it, despite his indifference to worldly matters and his efforts to achieve the utmost piety, it is possible that he would have kept it for himself, withholding it from his father Dīnār.

But one may lie when making similes. Every one of these blessed yellow gold coins goes further in realizing one's need than the man called Dīnār, chosen for a purpose by the one who said the following verse:[1428]

Have you sent Dīnār on behalf of us,
or ʿAbd Rabb, the brother of ʿAwn ibn Mikhrāq?

This verse is often quoted by grammarians. A recent scholar asserts that it is fabricated, and well it might be![1429]

43.2.4 As for al-Farazdaq's line:[1430]

I have seen Dīnār's son Yazīd, whom a "goat's day" [1431]
brought to his end in Syria, God being his killer![1432]

If the Dīnār mentioned here had been one of the Sheikh's dinars, Yazīd would have tried to trace his descent to him. How could the "working cattle's dinar" be compared with them? On one of the former someone says:[1433]

My uncle is the one who held back the dinar, openly,
the "working cattle's dinar" of the Jarm tribe; it is attested.

The "working cattle's dinar" is the dinar that the alms distributor takes after he has completed his tax collection.

Every engraved one of the Sheikh's dinars, that returned after they were despaired of, is more fit to quench the burning thirst of a parched man than the Dīnār that the rider in the desert called upon to pour him water, when seated upon the saddle of a bulky camel mare, saying,[1434]

I say to Dīnār, while our camel mares are milkless,[1435]
like ostriches seeking their chicks,
"Damn you! Reach me a drink of brackish
water, a liquid drinkable even if not fresh!"
And Dīnār, with a drop, in the nick of time came to support
the dying breath of a soul about to expire.

Nor is such a dinar like al-Akhṭal's dinar, mentioned in the following 43.2.5
verse by him:[1436]

Bay-red wines, three years in their clay vessels,
until a Christian from al-Ḥīrah[1437] bought them for a dinar.

If one of the Sheikh's dinars came into the possession of a Christian from al-Ḥīrah he would not readily give it to a wine merchant, even if he could buy on credit. Nor is it like the dinar in the verse quoted by Abū 'Umar al-Zāhid:[1438]

In the letter there are some lines that are scratched out.
The *kārūkah* has no share in the dinar.

He asserts that *kārūkah* means "bawd."

What a wonder! They fled from the thief's fingers just as the dinars of the shining sun described by Abū l-Ṭayyib when he said,[1439]

The rising sun cast from the branches on my clothes
dinars that flee from the fingers.

If Kuthayyir ʿAzzah had seen them he would have sworn a most solemn oath that they were more beautiful than the "Heraclian" ones, to one of which he compared himself:[1440]

He pleases the eyes of those who look at him, as if he were
a dinar of Heraclian weight, of red gold, heavy.

43.3.1 *The number eighty* If they are more than eighty[1441] they surpass the number of Moses' companions, about whom the Qur'an says,[1442] «And Moses chose his people, seventy men for Our appointed time»; and the number of times of asking forgiveness mentioned in God's word:[1443] «If you ask forgiveness for them seventy times, God will not forgive them»; and the number of cubits in the chain in the words of God the Exalted:[1444] «Then in a chain with a length of seventy cubits throw him!»

Even if someone were in a well eighty fathoms deep, these yellow coins might be able to rescue him without pain and put an end to his predicament. I mention this because of al-Aʿshā's verse:[1445]

Even if you were in a pit of eighty fathoms
and made to climb the ropes to heaven[1446] with a ladder . . .[1447]

And if the years of Zuhayr's life[1448] had been like them he would not have described himself as bored with life and they would have been his most energizing aides.

"Aides" (*qāmah*, plural of *qā'im*) means "helpers." A *rajaz* poet said:[1449]

My aides are the tribe of Rabīʿah ibn Kaʿb:
You have enough with their aid and so have I.

And if ʿUrwah ibn Ḥizām[1450] had lived until the time of the Sheikh—he is the poet who said,

My uncle has demanded eighty camel mares from me,
but, ʿAfrāʾ, I have merely eight—

it is possible that the Sheikh would have pitied him, helping him out with a few of these dinars or even granting them all, because he has a generous nature and he is made of the right stuff! If these eighty had ended up in ʿUrwah's hand he would have achieved his desire, because in those days a camel mare could sometimes be bought for ten dirhams.[1451] In one of the stories about al-Farazdaq an Umayyad ruler gave him one hundred camels from the alms tax revenue.[1452] He sold them for 2,229 dirhams, having taken care of the matter and the price had been raised. And the Sheikh will have come across the story mentioned by historians, about a camel sold in the time of Abū Jaʿfar al-Manṣūr for one dirham, and that when the caliph confiscated the property of some of his companions they sold the sheep they had, eight for one dirham. This is found in the *History* of Ibn Shajarah,[1453] in al-Marzubānī's[1454] handwriting.

The Sheikh's dinars are also more helpful than those eighty mentioned by the ʿAlid of Basra,[1455] who said: 43.3.2

I crossed toward them amid eighty horsemen
and achieved my aim and my desire of them.

If I were not afraid of exaggeration I would add: more helpful than the eighty thousand mentioned by al-Sinbisī,[1456] who said:

Eighty thousand; I have not counted them
but their number reaches my estimate, or surpasses it.

And how would it have been for Hammām ibn Ghālib[1457] if he had been "struck" by events with these eighty, instead of with years, as he says:

The nights and days[1458] have struck me with eighty years;
Time's arrow is the deadliest of any archer's arrows.

If they had been owned by the "shepherd of eighty," mentioned in the proverbial saying "more stupid than the shepherd of eighty sheep,"[1459] they would have given him a sound mind and an ample robe of comfort. The proverb says, "Finding comfort and cash dispels the dullness of the dullard"[1460] (it is also transmitted as "covers the dullness of the dullard").

A silver dirham[1461] is not as noble as these shining shapes. Gold is superior to silver in value, and noble qualities have a good scent.

43.3.3 The Sheikh will know the story of al-Ḥuṭay'ah[1462] and Sa'īd ibn al-'Āṣ.[1463] When the latter asked him, "Who is the best poet?" he replied, "The one who said (meaning Abū Du'ād al-Iyādī):[1464]

I do not deem poverty a lack; but the loss
of those of whom I am bereaved is utter destitution."

"And who next?" asked Sa'īd. Al-Ḥuṭay'ah replied: "He who said (meaning Ḥassān ibn Thābit):[1465]

Often knowledge is wasted by a want of money
and ignorance hid by being well-to-do."

"And who next?" "The one who said (meaning al-A'shā of the tribe of Qays):[1466]

A woman white-skinned in the morning, yellow
in the evening, like oxeye flowers."

"And who next?" "Look no further than me, when I put one foot on the other and then bleat in search of verses, as a weaned camel calf bleats, searching for the herd!"

A poet says,[1467]

I found the turd-woman's sons to be lowly people;
he who does not despise them is a despicable scoundrel,
And more stupid than the "shepherd of eighty" that pasture
at al-Sitār,[1468] on the herbs of a meadow of spring-grass.

Those eighty dinars—may they yield interest, each carat[1469] becoming a hundredweight, and may they all be odoriferous ever, i.e., with a good odor, not lacking in fasting or fast-breaking!—are more praiseworthy than those mentioned by the man from Ḥarrān, of the Sulaym tribe, Abū l-Muḥallim ʿAwf ibn al-Muḥallim, who said,[1470] 43.3.4

Eighty years (may you be made to reach them!)
have made my hearing need an interpreter
And gave me, in exchange for being tall and erect, a bent body,
though once I was like a straight lance shaft under a lance tip.

For the eighty he mentions make one weak, whereas the Sheikh's dinars revive and support. The former make a man who once was like a lance, like a bow in the hands of bowyers; the latter straighten what is bent and gladden the heart. The following verse attributed to Abū l-ʿItrīf[1471] is well known:

An Abyssinian who has eighty "eyes"
that lend him awe and respect.

Perhaps the Sheikh has traveled in the region of Mosul, passing by a village called "Eighty"[1472] which lies near Mount al-Jūdī. The village of "Eighty" may be the homestead of people, but the Sheikh's dinars would be as friendly a place to live in, as someone said:[1473]

Poverty in our homelands is being in a foreign land,
wealth in a foreign land is being home.

Gold is such a good friend! It provides protecting shade; if it is buried it is no matter: it does not decay like other things. It is given a precious status and its high position is not in danger of sinking. If pearls break their value vanishes; even a very precious pearl is not preserved when shattered. But often the gold of a bracelet will remain for ages, never hidden from sight, and is then turned into an anklet, worn by a woman with a pretty mole, striding proudly,[1474] 43.3.5

then transformed into a bowl or a cup, still clothed in beauty, unchanged by the touch of fires, not betraying loyal partners. Perhaps the gold of these eighty has already been around in the time of Qārūn, or God's messenger Moses and his brother Aaron, never perishing, never separated from glory, revered in Sind and India!

44.1.1 *The Sheikh's naughty niece*

The daughter of the Sheikh's sister (may God always keep her safe!) took liberties with her maternal uncle, for the uncle is a second father. She intended to "eat with two hands"[1475] and she was not a sister of the man about whom a poet said,[1476]

And ready for my revenge there is a sister's son that is me,
a strong warrior, whose knots cannot be untied.[1477]

But do not make her a sister of al-Hijris,[1478] for he sought revenge on his mother's brother, although it was not an ugly thing that he did. Rather, she seems to be a sister of Ibn Muḍarris,[1479] if she cannot be a sibling of al-Hijris. He is known as al-Khinnawt though his proper name is Tawbah. He had a brother called Ṭāriq, who was killed by the kinsmen of his mother's brother. So he decided to kill his uncle, and said,

My mother, Rumaylah, wept, distressed, when she saw
her brother's blood that was visible on the Indian sword.
I said to her, Don't grieve! Ṭāriq
was my friend, a devoted soulmate.
Though they offered me two thousand noble camel mares[1480]
and their calves that do not count, driven, and a herdsman,
I would not accept a blood-price from them without
seeing blood of the Banū ʿAwf flow on my sword.
Whatever blood of ʿAwf I shed, it would not
fully make up for Ṭāriq's death, except my uncle's!

He also said,[1481]

Let the wailing women weep for Ṭāriq,
and weep for Mirdās, killed by Qanān,[1482]

Two murdered men for whom the parturient camels do not weep,
having eaten their fill from thornless trees and tender ones.[1483]

It is possible that some of the good qualities of the mother's family got entangled in the character of the Sheikh's niece. Let him therefore be on his guard against the scandal of her eloquence more than against the stealth of her hand. He will know that Zuhayr inherited his poetic talent from his maternal uncle Bashāmah ibn al-Ghadīr, for there was not any poetry worth mentioning in the tribe of Muzaynah. Zuhayr was present when he died and wanted him to give him some of his possessions. Bashāmah replied, "Is it not enough for you that I left you an inheritance of wonderful odes?" 44.1.2

Perhaps there are some poets among the women of Aleppo (may God protect it!), in which case the Sheikh cannot be sure that she is not one of them.

Often women are more talented than men. A blind man of Āmid, who knew the Qur'an by heart and who was familiar with various kinds of knowledge, told [me] that he had a wife when he was young, who was a lady's maid; she would deck out women for weddings. He himself practiced astrology on the road. He had a leather portfolio that contained poems of the kind that is found in leather portfolios.[1484] He intended to memorize these poems and study them at home, but he had no talent for poetic meters, so he would make mistakes in scansion. His wife, the hairdresser, would say to him, "O dear, that is not right!" Then he would insist that she was wrong. The following morning he would leave and ask some knowledgeable person, who told him that she was right and pointed out to him what it should be. Having thus been instructed, he would return the following evening and recite the corrected version. Then the hairdresser wife would say, "Now it's all right!" 44.2.1

I had a donkey driver, a Bedouin called ʿAlwān. He had a wife who claimed to belong to the tribe of Ṭayyiʾ. He could not tell a metrical verse from a non-metrical one, whereas the woman would 44.2.2

notice the difference. She mourned for a young son, called Rajab, who had died. She used to recite this verse:

You may, on account of your loved one, be grieving;
however, one day one must part from a loved one.

One day she said,

You may, on account of Rajab darling, be grieving;

but she realized that the meter was wrong,[1485] so she said,

You may, on account of Rajaby darling be grieving,

putting a vowel after the name. But this seemed unnatural to her.[1486] Then she said,

You may, on account of Rajab, your darling, be grieving.

She had added a possessive pronoun and thereby both the meter and the grammatical form were correct.

In the Holy Book it says,[1487] «O you who believe: among your spouses and children there are enemies to you, so beware of them! But if you pardon and forgive, then God is forgiving and merciful.»

44.3 As for Abū Bakr al-Shiblī (may God have mercy on him!), there is no doubt that he was one of the virtuous. I hope he was kept clear of the doctrines of the incarnationists. Someone recited to me the following lines by him:[1488]

The madman of the tribe of ʿĀmir revealed his passion
but I concealed it and thus gained ecstatic love.
When, at the Resurrection, it will be cried out:
"Where are the people of passion?" I shall come forth, alone.

This is how it was recited to me, *nūdī* ("it will be cried out") instead of *nūdiya*; I do not like this even though it is permitted.[1489] It is only found among the poems of weak "modern" poets. If these two verses are actually by him it is not impossible that someone will object and say, "Whoever asserts that he is pure should not be biased: people will not concede his claim of being the only one in the whole world. Whether his passion was for human creatures or the Creator—one cannot be certain—there are, in any case, many like him among the various nations."

I apologize to my lord the noble Sheikh for being so tardy with my reply. The obstacles of time prevented me from dictating the rough draft, more black than white, like the Sawdā' ("black one") meant by the one who said,[1490] 45 *Finis*

I was informed that Sawdā' is far from me, though I follow her;
our two shapes have moved far apart and do not come near.
I found her when I was young, but she did not give me what I sought:
Now that my head has become black and white, how can it be that she will help those who seek?

Also, I am able only with the help of others. If my scribe is absent I cannot dictate. Let the Sheikh not condemn my tardiness. Often the purest gold is bought for many times its weight in silver. How would it be if the price was expressed in base coins that are found cast on the road?

To His Honor, the noble Sheikh, greetings whose young camels follow the old stallions and the calves join the mares![1491]

(The Epistle is completed, praise be to God, the Lord of all beings. God is sufficient to us and He is the best guardian. God bless and preserve our master, the prophet Muḥammad, and his good, pure family.)[1492]

* * *

Notes

1 The English-language synopses have been supplied by the translators and are not part of the original Arabic text.

2 Reading (with Kurd ʿAlī and Dechico) *qibalahu* instead of Bint al-Shāṭiʾ's *qablahu*.

3 The author uses, in what seems a rather unscientific fashion, four technical terms: *ustuquṣṣāt* (derived from Greek στοιχεῖα), *ʿanāṣir*, *arkān*, and *jawāhir*. Professor Hans-Hinrich Biesterfeld (Bochum), in a private communication to the translators, characterized this passage as "*terminologisches Geklingel*" ("terminological jingling").

4 Reading *aḥmada* (with Kurd ʿAlī and Dechico) instead of Bint al-Shāṭiʾ's *uḥmida*.

5 A play on words: *ṭabʿ* means both "imprint, seal" and "natural talent."

6 This and the following two poetic quotations are printed as prose in all editions and translations; it is a hemistich (minus the first word) by al-Mutanabbī; see *Dīwān*, p. 253.

7 Another hemistich by al-Mutanabbī; *Dīwān*, p. 494.

8 A verse by al-Ṣanawbarī (d. 334/945); *Dīwān*, p. 414.

9 Literally, "from his (own) skull, or brain."

10 The sense is not wholly clear and the translation uncertain.

11 Q Qamar 54:29, on the man from the people of ʿĀd who killed the God-sent camel.

12 Or "who wallows in the dust."

13 From a famous poem by the pre-Islamic poet al-Aʿshā.

14 Ample hips and buttocks are regularly compared to a sand dune. The syntax is not wholly clear.

15 Reading *murratan* (Dechico), "bitter," instead of *marratan*, is less likely, despite the parallel with *taṭību*.

16 There is a lacuna in the text here, found in all manuscripts, and al-Maʿarrī received the epistle with the same lacuna, for in the second part of *Risālat al-Ghufrān* he notes that "in the section where he mentions al-Khalīl the name of the extolled person—me—is lacking." Apparently, Ibn al-Qāriḥ arrives at a gathering where someone speaks; the subject of "and [someone] said" is unknown.

17 *Taṣḥīf*, a common kind of mistake in Arabic, is to err in assigning the proper dots that distinguish different consonants (such as *r*/*z*, *ḥ*/*j*/*kh*, *b*/*n*/*t*/*th*/*y*); for two examples, see below, Ibn al-Qāriḥ §3.6.1.

18 Bint al-Shāṭiʾ thinks that something may be missing here, because the connection with the following is somewhat tenuous. Ibn al-Qāriḥ picks up the theme of "belittling" (*taṣghīr*) again, a term also used for the diminutive.

19 For the hemistich see his *Dīwān*, p. 298.

20 Echoing the saying of the pious ʿUbayd Allāh ibn ʿAbd Allāh (d. 97/716), when blamed for making verse: "He who suffers from phthisis must needs expectorate" (see, e.g., al-Jāḥiẓ, *Bayān*, i, 357, ii, 97, iv, 46; see also below, *IQ* §3.13).

21 Q Nisāʾ 4:143. The odd phrase «between this» is explained as "between belief and unbelief."

22 Identified by Bint al-Shāṭiʾ as Abū l-Ḥasan Aḥmad ibn ʿAbd Allāh al-Quṭrabbulī, mentioned in Ibn al-Nadīm, *al-Fihrist*, which was composed in 377/987–88.

23 Abū Bakr Muḥammad ibn Aḥmad Ibn Abī l-Azhar (d. after 313/925), also mentioned in *al-Fihrist*. Nothing is known about a book written by him and al-Quṭrabbulī.

24 The sources do not confirm the historicity of the following encounter. See Heinrichs, "The Meaning of *Mutanabbī*."

25 Since the names Aḥmad and Muḥammad are similar in sense ("most praiseworthy"), and the Prophet Muḥammad is sometimes called Aḥmad, al-Mutanabbī, saying this, seems to identify himself with the Prophet.

26 The Prophet Muḥammad is said to have had a mark (called "the seal of prophethood") between his shoulder blades.

27 i.e., the reproachful reminder of gifts.

28 The poet complains to Sayf al-Dawlah, reproaching him for being angry after his former generosity.

29 *Zanādiqah*, pl. of *zindīq*: someone professing Islam but having heretical (often Manichaean) beliefs.

30 *Mulḥidīn*, a somewhat vague term for heretics, atheists, and all those who deviate from orthodoxy (the technical term for an apostate from Islam is *murtadd*).

31 A hemistich by Abū Nuwās, see Abū Nuwās, *Dīwān*, i, 210 and v, 463.

32 He is Bashshār's rival, the poet Ḥammād ʿAjrad (d. between 155/772 and 168/784), who was also accused of Manichaeism.

33 Poet unidentified.

34 He is known as al-Muqannaʿ ("the veiled one"); his real name is not known. His rebellion, which began around 160/777, was suppressed after a siege in 166/783. Reports on his doctrine are somewhat vague; it seems to have been inspired by Mazdakism. See *EI2*, vii, 500 ("al-Muḳannaʿ").

35 The report is obviously exaggerated.

36 Reading *yudkhilu l-rijāla ʿalayhinna* (with Qumayḥah and al-Iskandarānī/Fawwāl); Dechico has *yadkhulu l-rijālu*, Bint al-Shāṭiʾ has *yudkhilu ʿalayhinna*.

37 The verses are not found in the collected verse published by Francesco Gabrieli, "Al-Walīd ibn Yazīd: il califfo e il poeta." With "tales of Ṭasm" he refers to the legends about the pre-Islamic Arab tribe of Ṭasm. Nothing is known about Umm al-Ḥunaykil ("mother of the little dwarf").

38 With a variation on the traditional exclamation pilgrims utter when entering the sacred area of the Hajj.

39 Bint al-Shāṭiʾ reads *bunābijah* (earlier editions *bunāyijah*), an unknown word. One could think of a corruption of Persian *piyālah* ("cup, goblet"), with middle Persian ending *-ag* or even the diminutive ending *-čah* (a suggestion by Professor Ludwig Paul, Hamburg).

40 It is not clear who is speaking. The word *ʿilj*, here translated as "lout," is sometimes applied to non-Muslims or non-Arabs, but also to uncouth persons in general.

41 cf. the version in al-al-Zamakhsharī, *Rabīʿ al-abrār*, iv, 81.

42 Al-Walīd uses the Persian word *haftajah*.

43 "Stinkmouth," on account of a malodorous lake in the neighborhood (thus, rather than "al-Baḥrā," as in Bint al-Shāṭi'''s edition). Instead of being "in the environs of Damascus," it was located south of Palmyra; see H. Kennedy in *EI2*, xi, 128a, and Hamilton, *Al-Walīd and his Friends*, p. 154.

44 Reading *jamal*, with Bint al-Shāṭi', ninth edition and Dechico, instead of *ḥml*.

45 i.e., the "Black Stone;" the "place of attachment" (*al-multazam*) is the part of the Kaaba between its door and the corner that contains the stone, so called because the pilgrims press themselves against it.

46 A waterspout mounted on top of the Kaaba, also called "the spout of mercy."

47 The speaker cannot be Ibn al-Qāriḥ.

48 An example of *taṣḥīf* (see above, §2.6.1): Rakhamah (which means "vulture") and Raḥmah ("mercy") differ only by one diacritical dot. The tradition is likely to have been one with eschatological content.

49 The words *rīḥ* ("wind") and *zanj*, when written, differ only in their diacritical dots. The Zanj were blacks originally from East Africa; widely exploited as slaves on plantations in southern Iraq, they revolted several times, most dangerously between 255/869 and 270/883, when they defeated several caliphal armies and sacked Basra. Their leader was, or called himself, ʿAlī ibn Muḥammad; he claimed descent from ʿAlī ibn Abī Ṭālib.

50 Unidentified; Warzanīn, a place near al-Rayy (close to present-day Tehran in Iran), is where the leader of the Zanj is said to have been born.

51 Perhaps ʿAlī ibn Abī Ṭālib is meant.

52 In fact a Qur'anic quotation (Q Āl ʿImrān 3:97), and thus by Muslim standards not a saying of the Prophet.

53 This seems to be the sense, but it is not clear which religious duty is meant.

54 Q Baqarah 2:228, continuing «for three monthly periods», i.e., before remarrying.

55 Taking *ḥill* as the opposite of *al-ḥaram*; it could also be "a non-sacred state" (*iḥlāl*, opposite of the *iḥrām* of the pilgrim).

56 Q ʿAnkabūt 29:67.

57 Surely a synecdoche, meaning "I."

58 Al-Ḥallāj "followed the ways of the Sufis in his mad speech and often spoke of the 'glittering light'" (al-Tanūkhī, *Nishwār al-muḥāḍarah*, i, 169). Ibn al-ʿArabī explains this "glittering light" as the light that takes vision away when God reveals Himself, cf. Louis Massignon, *Essay on the Origins of the Technical Language of Islamic Mysticism*, pp. 29–30. See also §15.2.1.

59 There is a lacuna in the text.

60 Adopting Bint al-Shāṭiʾ's emendation: *khashyatahū*. The manuscript readings *khashabah* and *khashabatahū* ("[his] piece of wood") could refer to the gibbet, gallows, or crucifixion cross on which al-Ḥallāj was executed, but the lacuna makes it impossible to decide and the translation is conjectural.

61 This seems to refer to a theory of vision, going back to Empedocles, according to which both object and eyes emit rays.

62 Unidentified.

63 It was the caliph al-Muqtadir, who (after initial reluctance) eventually signed the death warrant.

64 He was executed in Baghdad in 322/934.

65 In Shi'ite theology a prophet has a legatee (*waṣī*) who must uphold the law given by the prophet.

66 Quoting al-Khalīl ibn Aḥmad's verdict on Ibn al-Muqaffaʿ (who said the reverse of the former); see, e.g., Ibn Khallikān, *Wafayāt*, ii, 151.

67 Muḥammad ibn Yasīr al-Riyāshī (d. early third/ninth century).

68 *Al-Dāmigh* could also be rendered as *The Refutation*; graphic titles of invective poems or polemic treatises are not uncommon (cf. al-Ḥātimī's treatise of poetry criticism *al-Mūḍiḥah*, *Laying Bare the Bone*).

69 Ibn al-Qāriḥ's list is in fact copied from (Ibn) al-Nadīm's *Fihrist*, see ed. R. Tajaddud, Tehran: Marvi Offset printing, 1971, p. 216 (personal communication from Professor Josef van Ess). When al-Maʿarrī discusses this passage later in *Risālat al-Ghufrān* another work is listed: *al-Farīd* (*The Unique One*), said to be an attack on the Prophet. The editions by Kaylānī and Kurd ʿAlī (followed by Dechico) have "*al-Farīd, fī l-ṭaʿn ʿalā l-nabiyy ʿalayhi l-ṣalāh wa-l-salām.*"

70 In view of the somewhat abrupt transition to the following there may be a lacuna in the text.

71 Unlike the preceding etymologies, this one is wholly fanciful. The connection made next, between *shimāl* and *shuʾm*, has some support in historical linguistics.

72 The original connects it with *siyāq*, "agony."

73 Ibn al-Rūmī, *Dīwān*, p. 1889.

74 For the following anecdote see al-Masʿūdī, *Murūj al-dhahab*, v, 367 and compare al-Ṣūlī, *Akhbār Abī Tammām*, p. 172.

75 cf. Q Ghāfir 40:39.

76 This expression occurs in several sources that relate this episode; in one of them it is explained as "Zoroastrianism" (*al-Majūsiyyah*); see al-Dhahabī, *Tārīkh al-Islām, Ḥawādith* 221–30, p. 18. "White" may have been chosen in opposition to black, the official color of the Abbasid Dynasty.

77 From a famous poem by Abū Tammām, composed only a few years before, on al-Muʿtaṣim's victory over the Byzantines at Amorium in 223/838. In other sources it is Māzyār who tries to save his life with his wealth, see, e.g., al-Masʿūdī, *Murūj*, iv, 360.

78 Much in this passage is very unclear and the text seems corrupt. Bint al-Shāṭiʾ has the ungrammatical *ithnayn qatalū* (changed to *qatalā* in the editions of Qumayḥah and al-Iskandarānī/Fawwāl). The "two (men)" could be Bābak and Māzyār (if *ithnayn* is a corruption of Afshīn, one misses the article that it normally has). "Three million and five hundred" may be either a mistake for "two and a half million" or for the rather more plausible "three thousand five hundred." It is unclear what *dhabbāḥ* (lit. "slaughterer") means here.

79 A proverb (usually with *jarā* instead of *atā*).

80 The text is lacunose.

81 Apparently Jaʿfar, called al-Ṣādiq, the sixth imam of the Twelver Shīʿah (whose father was in fact called Muḥammad).

82 The sense is not clear. Perhaps: "I would be sent to prison, because I would have to incriminate powerful people (all of them heretics!)." See the verse quoted above, §3.2.

83 Lines by Abū Ḥamzah al-Mukhtār ibn ʿAwf, a Khārijite rebel (d. 130/748).

84 Not identified.

85 See his criticism of al-Mutanabbī, above, §2.7.1.

86 Ibn al-Rūmī, *Dīwān*, p. 1506.

87 A line by Ibn al-Rūmī (*Dīwān*, p. 1419); the interpretation follows Ibn Rashīq, *ʿUmdah*, i, 323.

88 Quoted anonymously in several sources (which have, more appropriately, "flew up" instead of "was agitated"); the vulture and crow stand for white and black hairs, respectively, the two nests are probably hair and beard; see Ibn Abī l-Iṣbaʿ, *Taḥrīr*, p. 274; Ibn Ḥijjah, *Khizānah*, iv, 86, first hemistich in *Lisān al-ʿArab*. s.v. *Gh-R-B*.

89 The verses are nos. 3, 26, 27, and 24 of a vaunting ode, which explains the incoherence of the quotation (*Dīwān*, pp. 590, 593). "Its days:" viz. of youth; in the second verse "they" refers to the poet's fellow tribesmen of Ṭayyiʾ.

90 There is an untranslatable play on words: *ḥaddatha* "to talk to" and *ḥādatha* "to furbish (a sword)."

91 The Hejaz, part of the traditional territory of Ṭayyiʾ (the poet himself grew up in Syria).

92 The words *mā khalā* cannot mean "except" here; "to say nothing of" is apparently to be taken in the sense of "especially."

93 The profusion of third person singular pronouns causes the usual confusion; it is somewhat unclear whether it is Abū l-ʿAbbās or Abū l-ʿAlāʾ who is doing the praising.

94 Bilāl, born as a slave, was the first black Muslim and on account of his powerful voice became the first muezzin; ʿAmmār ibn Yāsir was the son of a freedman; Ṣuhayb ibn Sinān was called al-Rūmī, "the

Byzantine," because he had been taken captive by the Byzantines as a child. A freedman (*mawlā*) was associated with a tribe without having a proper tribal descent.

95 All were leading figures in Quraysh, ancestors of the Prophet, except ʿAbd Shams, an ancestor of the Umayyads.

96 *Al-Jāhiliyyah*, literally "ignorance," is the normal term for the pre-Islamic period.

97 Abū Ṭālib died without converting to Islam but protected his nephew during the difficult early stages of his preaching. See Ibn Hishām, *Sīrah*, i, 266, trans. Guillaume, p. 119.

98 Literally, "for a few *qīrāṭ*," a *qīrāṭ* ("carat") being the twenty-fourth part of a dinar.

99 The campaign to the Byzantine outpost at Tabūk, in northwestern Arabia, in 9/630 achieved rather little.

100 i.e., motionless (the expression is found in early poetry).

101 Reading *mūbiq*, "pernicious, noxious," instead of *mūniq* as in the various editions.

102 The editions by Kurd ʿAlī and Dechico add "and its joy having mixed with my mirth, my spirit, and my friends."

103 Verses by Abū l-ʿAtāhiyah; see *Dīwān*, p. 117.

104 The same verse as above, §4.2.

105 Poet unidentified.

106 Boiling down wine to reduce or eliminate its alcohol content made it permissible to drink it according to some jurists.

107 In the following rambling passage it is not always clear who is speaking, nor is it clear where the passage ends.

108 Quoting Ibn al-Sammāk; see Ibn Qutaybah, *ʿUyūn al-akhbār*, ii, 368.

109 Translation tentative, reading *alā mutaʿalliq bi-adhyāl dalīlihī* (cf., e.g., Ibn Abī Yaʿlā, *Ṭabaqāt al-Ḥanābilah*, ii, 160: *alā mutaʿalliqun bi-adhyāli ayimmatih*; al-Ḥātimī, *al-Risālah al-Mūḍiḥah*, p. 142: *mutaʿalliqan bi-adhyāli l-adab*). The editions of Qumayḥah and al-Iskandarānī & Fawwāl both have *alā mutaʿalliqun wa-l-adhyālu adhyālu dalīlihī*, which does not seem better.

110 viz. Ibrāhīm/Abraham; cf. Q Nisā' 4:125 «God took Abraham as a friend».

111 Or "when you remember them"?

112 Q Baqarah 2:186.

113 Q Isrā' 17:83 and Fuṣṣilat 41:51.

114 cf. Q Infiṭār 82:6 («What has deceived you about your generous Lord?»).

115 The meaning is not quite clear.

116 From a poem by Abū 'Uyaynah ibn Muḥammad ibn Abī 'Uyaynah (d. during the reign of Hārūn al-Rashīd). In line 3, "world of mine (*dunyāya*)" could also be translated "my Dunyā" (the name given to his beloved, who was in fact called Fāṭimah); see, e.g., al-Mubarrad, *al-Kāmil*, ii, 62; al-Iṣfahānī, *al-Aghānī*, xx, 87–88.

117 The Pharaoh who oppressed Mūsā (Moses) and the Israelites, and who was drowned; see Q Ṭā Hā 20:78; Gabriel (Jibrīl) is the archangel.

118 ". . . but through God," a very common phrase.

119 The sentence puns on several grammatical terms: *ta'rīf* "making acquainted/making definite," *tankīr* "making unknown/making indefinite," *khafḍ* "lowering/genitive," *raf'* "raising/nominative," *furādā* "single/singular forms," *jam'* "gathering/plural."

120 Printed as prose in previous editions, it is in fact a proverb in *rajaz* verse, found with many variants in several sources, see, e.g., al-'Askarī, *Jamharah*, ii, 219; Ibn 'Abd Rabbih, *al-'Iqd al-farīd*, iii, 77; al-Tanūkhī, *Nishwār al-muḥāḍarah*, iii, 135; al-Maydānī, *Majma' al-amthāl*, ii, 359; Abū 'Ubayd, *Faṣl al-maqāl*, p. 461.

121 i.e., 397/1007.

122 In present-day Lebanon.

123 Khawlah is called "*al-māyisṭiriyyah*."

124 A proverb (al-Maydānī, *Majma'*, ii, 495; al-'Askarī, *Jamharah*, ii, 337).

125 Quoted, anonymously, by al-Jāḥiẓ, *al-Ḥayawān*, iii, 109 and vi, 243.

126 The Arabic word for mad, *majnūn*, literally means "possessed by jinn."

127 i.e., by a mangy camel. This and the following expression are used for a person on whom one can rely.

128 *Ṭārimah* can be the cabin on a boat.

129 *Al-farqadān*: the two major stars of the Little Bear (α and β Ursae Minoris), including the Pole Star.

130 In popular psycho-physiology the liver was thought to be the seat of passions and emotions.

131 Taking *ʿawd* as a synonym of *ʿāʾidah*; alternatively, "one does not hope to see him again."

132 The tortuous style, here and elsewhere in the epistle, reflects that of the original (which is, admittedly, less verbose).

133 Not, as Bint al-Shāṭiʾ says, a verse from the famous poem attributed to al-Shanfarā called *Lāmiyyat al-ʿArab* ("the poem of the Arabs rhyming in L;" cf. its third verse, which resembles it). The verse is in fact by Maʿn ibn Aws (born in the pre-Islamic period, d. 64/684 or some years later) and is found in the celebrated anthology by Abū Tammām, *al-Ḥamāsah* (see al-Marzūqī's commentary, *Sharḥ Dīwān al-Ḥamāsah*, p. 1129).

134 i.e., he does not feather arrows nor trim wood for them, an expression meaning "he is neither useful nor harmful."

135 With this money he financed an unsuccessful rebellion against the Fatimids, in the name of a Meccan *sharīf* set up as a counter-caliph.

136 The words *maʿānīhi wa-mabānīhi* have been taken to refer to the content and style of al-Maʿarrī's works (cf. Ḥāzim al-Qarṭājannī's work on poetics, *Minhāj al-bulaghāʾ*, where the major sections are entitled *al-mabānī* and *al-maʿānī*).

137 Not identified.

138 Both are lexicographical works, the former (*al-Faṣīḥ*) by Thaʿlab (d. 291/904) and the latter (*Iṣlāḥ al-manṭiq*) by Ibn al-Sikkīt (d. ca. 244/857).

139 Iyās ibn Muʿāwiyah, judge in Basra under Caliph ʿUmar ibn ʿAbd al-ʿAzīz (r. 99–101/717–20), proverbial for his sagacity; Bāqil, an obscure figure said to have been a member of the tribe of Iyād, proverbial for his inarticulateness.

140 In joke collections the unreliable keeper is a muezzin (al-Ābī, *Nathr al-durr*, vii, 311; al-Ibshīhī, *al-Mustaṭraf*, Cairo, 1952, ii, 273).

141 Reading *ṭarīf* instead of *ẓarīf*.

142 Apparently a proverb; it scans as a hemistich in *khafīf* meter. On *harīsah* see above, §6.5. In a note in the edition by al-Iskandarānī and Fawwāl the word *zabūn* is taken to mean "(she-camel) who kicks a lot," and the saying is interpreted as "Be amazed at the one that I feed and that kicks me with her foot or kills me." But feeding a camel with *harīsah* seems unlikely.

143 This verse has been attributed (in al-Baghdādī, *Khizānat al-adab*, ii, 265) to ʿAbd Allāh ibn al-Zabīr al-Asadī (second/eighth century), in praise of the poet Asmāʾ ibn Khārijah (d. 66/686 or some years later); but it is also found in the *Dīwān* of Abū Tammām in praise of Caliph al-Muʿtaṣim (*Dīwān*, iii, 29).

144 From a poem by the pre-Islamic poet Zuhayr ibn Abī Sulmā in praise of Ḥiṣn ibn Ḥudhayfah, a leader of the Fazārah tribe.

145 For the anecdote, compare Ibn ʿAbd Rabbih, *al-ʿIqd al-farīd*, iii, 164.

146 *Usfitta* does not really make sense; it is not about "drinking a lot without quenching one's thirst" but about not being able to urinate (one would expect a form of the verb *ḥaqana*); the version in *al-ʿIqd* is clearer: *fa-law ḥubisa ʿanka khurūjuhā*.

147 The "shirt" is apparently used figuratively for his material circumstances; but the measures given here, if taken literally, are odd: "two cubits" seems rather too long for a newborn child. In the following, "twelve cubits" is also too long (and would still be even if one assumes that the author confuses *dhirāʿ* with *shibr*, "span of the hand").

148 Q Shuʿarāʾ 26:79; the following "he" is Ibrāhīm/Abraham.

149 Q Shuʿarāʾ 26:80.

150 One would expect, e.g., "promise a reward," but *tawaʿʿada* normally has a negative sense. The acts listed are involuntary or automatic and thus beyond our control, and so we cannot be punished for them.

151 Q Insān 76:7; its continuation is «. . . a day whose evil will fly up».

152 Emendation suggested by Bint al-Shāṭiʾ.

153 By ʿUbayd ibn Ayyūb al-ʿAnbarī, a "brigand poet" from the Umayyad period (see al-Jāḥiẓ, *al-Bayān wa-l-tabyīn*, iv, 62), adopting the reading *qaddama* instead of *dhammama* as in Bint al-Shāṭiʾ's edition.

154 Untranslatable play on two meanings of the word *al-sawdā'* ("the black one"), the former apparently used for *musawwadah* ("draft, rough copy"), the latter short for *al-mirrah al-sawdā'*, "melancholy." Abū l-ʿAlā' picks up the theme of "blackness" in the beginning of his epistle.

155 Anonymous in al-Farrā', *Maʿānī l-Qur'ān*, i, 262; al-Baghdādī, *Khizānat al-adab*, viii, 486 and 514.

156 *Ḥamāṭah* is (a) a tree, or (b) its fruit, said to resemble the wild fig or a peach. Other meanings are (c) "heartburn" (the sensation of acridity in throat or chest) and (d) "blackness or bottom of the heart" (which "dwells" in the writer and which is his intended meaning here). The whole preamble is an exercise in such double entendre (*tawriyah* in Arabic).

157 Snakes are said to live on the *afāniyah* tree on which the *ḥamāṭah* fruits grow.

158 Ibn al-Qāriḥ.

159 In Arabic usage a day of twenty-four hours begins at sunset.

160 Either "the mother of the little babe," or "the mother of little al-Walīd;" probably referring to the poet's wife.

161 A tribe; the reference is unclear.

162 Translation uncertain.

163 The rest of the verse, with the crucial word, is lacking.

164 It is likely that with the "two robes" the author means his body and his real clothes.

165 Another double entendre: *ḥiḍb* is said to mean a kind of snake; it also means "the sound made by a bow," and, as the author will explain, "heart."

166 i.e., whether she is a snake or human.

167 Ru'bah ibn al-ʿAjjāj.

168 *Aswad*, "black (thing)," here standing for the "black bottom" of the heart, also means "large snake."

169 The masculine word *aswad* (literally, "black") and its feminine equivalent *sawdā'* both can mean "bottom of the heart," as does the diminutive of the latter, *suwaydā'*.

170 In the following many personal names (Aswad, Suwayd, Sawdah, Sawādah, Suḥaym) refer to "blackness."

171 viz. a "black thing" or "heart." In the following, "it" always means "the heart."

172 The verse is from his most famous poem, one of the seven celebrated long pre-Islamic poems called *Muʿallaqāt*.

173 *Bi-l-aswadayn* is ambiguous; some commentators believe, with al-Maʿarrī, that two men called al-Aswad are meant, but most think it means "the two black things," here standing either for "dates and water" or "night and day" (in Arabic a dual is sometimes used for complementary pairs, such as "the two fathers" for "parents"). A variant has *bi-l-abyaḍayn* "with the two white things," also variously explained.

174 The identity of this Abū l-Aswad is not known; he may be his cousin Abū l-Aswad Yazīd mentioned in the Glossary s.v. Aswad ibn Maʿdīkarib.

175 Elsewhere the lines are attributed to al-Akhyal ibn Mālik al-Kilābī (*Ḥamāsat al-Buḥturī*) or Muzarrid (al-Nushshābī al-Irbilī, *Mudhākarah*).

176 Literally, "(his) desire did not turn away from it;" probably referring to the fact that she dissuaded him from divorcing her (Q Nisāʾ 4:127 alludes to this).

177 "The two white things (*al-abyaḍān*)" also stand for water and flour.

178 Another version of these lines (Ibn Qutaybah, *Maʿānī*, p. 425) has "two black things," explaining that *faththth* is an inferior grain from which "black" bread is made.

179 The poet is Hudhayl ibn ʿAbd Allāh al-Ashjaʿī; here "the two white things" are water and milk.

180 The common female name Rabāb stands for any woman who, as so often in poetry, will only love a healthy young man (see also below, the passage on the various Rabābs, §9.3.1).

181 Wine, meat, and gold, or a kind of perfume made with saffron, according to the lexicographers. There are other interpretations.

182 The eye is followed by the heart.

183 Q Fāṭir 35:10.

184 Q Ibrāhīm 14:24–25.

185 The Arabic for "sky" used here is the same as that for "heaven."

186 Weapons were suspended from it.

187 He will appear later in the text.

188 The following lines are found in al-Iṣfahānī, *al-Aghānī*, xx, 330.

189 This verse is quoted in the famous grammar by Sībawayh, where it is attributed to Abū ʿAṭāʾ al-Sindī.

190 Traditionally only three variants are recognized (ending in SLLL, SLSL, and SLL, where S stands for a short and L for a long syllable); if Abū l-Hindī's verses end on a consonant (*-zubd*, *-raʿd*), the fourth variant would end in SLO, where O stands for an overlong syllable.

191 Again, the strainer is described (see Ibn Manẓūr, *Lisān al-ʿarab*, s.v. *Kh-N-F*; in the entry *B-R-Q* the verse is ascribed to ʿAdī ibn Zayd).

192 With untranslatable play on obscure additional meanings of *abārīq* ("jugs").

193 The expression "sipping (the beloved's) saliva," which sounds somewhat odd in modern English, is a recurrent motif in classical Arabic love poetry; cf. below, §§10.1, 13.2.2, 14.1, 19.2.5.

194 "Modern" refers to the Abbasid period, from the middle of the second/eighth century.

195 Said to be a wine merchant in al-Ṭāʾif in Arabia, only known from the following line by the first/seventh-century poet Abū Dhuʾayb.

196 Q Muḥammad 47:15.

197 The poet means: "to me;" he is imagining or dreaming of his beloved.

198 The "nightly phantom" (*khayāl*) of the beloved, either her image in a dream or a fantasy, is an extremely common motif in Arabic poetry.

199 The rare word *lamṣ* is explained with the common word *fālūdh*, the same as *fālūdhaj*, a sweet made of flour and honey.

200 This is indeed what the author does, at some length, suggesting alternative rhyme words with all the other letters of the alphabet in their proper order. Not content with this, he ensures that most of the following rhymes are "rich rhymes," involving two consonants instead of one, just as he did in his extensive collection of verse called *Luzūm mā lā yalzām* (loosely translated as *The Self-Imposed Constraint*).

201 The glottal stop (ʾ).

202 In Sībawayh's grammar the verse is quoted with *al-khamr* ("wine") instead of *al-nashʾ*.

203 The last sentence, found as a marginal addition, may have been part of the main text.

204 In other words, a rhyme in *-ā* (called *alif maqṣūrah*, spelled with either *alif* or *yāʾ*, the only rhyme that is not based on a "true" consonant) hides an unvoweled "virtual consonant" ($\bar{a} = a^0$); it cannot immediately follow an unvoweled consonant, though the meter requires this here.

205 The Bedouins had a kind of popular meteorology based on the stars; some stars and constellations were associated with rain.

206 In the pre-Islamic gambling game called *maysir*, forbidden in Islam (cf. Q Baqarah 2:219, Māʾidah 5:90–91), portions of a slaughtered camel were divided by shuffling marked arrow shafts. The implication is that her family is wealthy.

207 *Alladhī qāla lāna kulluh*: the word *qāla* ("he said") is either a mistaken insertion or refers to an unnamed lexicographer.

208 The verse is possibly corrupt and rather unclear. Bint al-Shāṭiʾ's suggestion of reading *mimman laqū* instead of *man laqū*, is unmetrical. Al-Iṣfahānī, *Aghānī* xii, 136 has *fa-Bahratun* (for *fa-Bahrāʾu*, a tribe); rejected by the editor of Ibn Sallām, *Ṭabaqāt*, p. 513, who emends to *muntahizan man laqū* and gives a lengthy explanation.

209 *Muwallad*, here meaning "not found in the 'pure' Arabic of pre- and early Islamic Arabs."

210 On the seven readings of the Qurʾanic text generally recognized as "canonical," see below, notes 420 and 696.

211 They are quoted in Sībawayh's grammar, attributed to "a man from Oman;" elsewhere they are attributed to al-ʿUmānī.

212 The issue is whether the accusatives of *ṭūlan* and *ʿarḍan* are to be explained as adverbial qualifications of place or adverbial specifications ("qua length and breadth").

213 All rhymes in this digression end in *-ī*, the pausal genitive ending, which has been left out in the translations, where the normal prose

forms are given; but Mubghī cannot be shortened in the same manner.

214 This explanation is not given by most sources, which say that *ḥaww* and *laww* in this expression mean "truth" and "falsehood," respectively, or "yes" and "no" (see e.g. *Lisān al-ʿArab*, *Ḥ-W-W/Y*; al-ʿAskarī, *Jamharat al-Amthāl*; *WKAS* II, iv, 1901, 1903; Lane, *Lexicon*, p. 681b). Al-Maʿarrī's source is unknown.

215 Or: that has become (too) longwinded (the use of the imperfect tense, in that case, is unusual but not impossible: see Reckendorf, *Arabische Syntax*, p. 12, par. 8, 2a).

216 After using various near synonyms (*ṣāb*, *habīd*, *ḥadaj*) the more usual word, *ḥanẓal(ah)* is used here.

217 The poet is Ru'bah ibn al-ʿAjjāj. The verse is quoted by Sībawayh and other grammarians because of the unusual *kahū* and *kahunna*, here imitated in the translation.

218 *Diflā*; poisonous, used to kill or repel vermin.

219 Bint al-Shāṭi''s edition has *ṣalāḥ*, but according to the grammarians and lexicographers the correct reading is *ṣilāḥ*, alternative of *muṣālaḥah* (hence the feminine suffix of *fīhā*); see, e.g., *Lisān. al-ʿArab* s.v. *Ṣ-L-Ḥ*, al-Akhfash, *al-Ikhtiyārayn*, p. 601.

220 Khālid ibn Zuhayr al-Hudhalī (a contemporary of the Prophet), in response to a poem by his uncle Abū Dhu'ayb. The verse is not by Abū Dhu'ayb himself as Bint al-Shāṭi' says (see al-Sukkarī, *Sharḥ ashʿār al-Hudhaliyyīn*, pp. 212, 215).

221 The quoted line, on a gift including a fish made of sugar and almonds "swimming" in honey, is uncharacteristic of the poet, who despised trifles and who excelled in sonorous and rhetorical eulogy, vaunting, and invective.

222 The meaning of *khawwārah* is not clear ("mild, weak" seems incompatible with what follows).

223 The famous grammarian al-Mubarrad (d. 285/898) belonged to Thumālah; the lexicographer Ibn Durayd (d. 321/933) belonged to Daws.

224 Q Ḥijr 15:47.

225 The former is better known as Thaʿlab (d. 291/904), grammarian from Kufa, bitter rival of al-Mubarrad of Basra (here called Muḥammad ibn Yazīd).

226 Jadhīmah, a legendary pre-Islamic king of Iraq, killed his two inseparable friends while drunk, bitterly repenting afterward; later killed by Queen al-Zabbāʾ of Palmyra, who may be (partially) identified as Zenobia.

227 Al-Kisāʾī, who was the tutor of Hārūn al-Rashīd's sons, and Sībawayh discussed a point of grammar in a session arranged by Yaḥyā al-Barmakī; al-Kisāʾī apparently instructed Bedouin Arabs to support his (incorrect) view, thus defeating Sībawayh.

228 Labīd, famous pre- and early Islamic poet, lamented his brother's death in several elegies. Al-Maʿarrī's protagonist Ibn al-Qāriḥ will meet the poet in Paradise (see §8.3.1). Mutammim ibn Nuwayrah and his brother Mālik were both poets of the pre- and early Islamic periods; Mutammim composed elegies on his brother after his death in 13/634. Ṣakhr and Muʿāwiyah are lamented in numerous poems by their famous sister, al-Khansāʾ (d. ca. 23/644); Ibn al-Qāriḥ meets her later (§16.4).

229 Q Raʿd 13:23–24.

230 Maymūn ibn Qays, known as al-Aʿshā. Ibn al-Qāriḥ will meet him soon (below, §5.2).

231 Quraysh, the Prophet's tribe but still opposed to him when al-Aʿshā sought to visit him, bribed the poet into changing his mind, thus preventing his conversion to Islam, even though he had already composed an ode on the Prophet (see below). But according to another version, told by Ibn Qutaybah (d. 276/889), al-Aʿshā, on his way to convert, had second thoughts when he was told that the Prophet forbade drinking wine and committing adultery. He decided to enjoy himself for one more year, but died before the year was over.

232 According to Nicholson (p. 654), "And the wine bowl conveyed from hand to hand long-used cups of glass (i.e., the drinkers filled their cups from it in turn, by means of the *ibrīq*), while those who drew

therefrom mixed their draught with water)", adding, "This seems to be the sense if the reading is correct."

233 These five persons were tribal leaders on whom al-Aʿshā composed panegyric odes. ʿĀmir ibn al-Ṭufayl, a bitter enemy of the Prophet, was himself a poet.

234 i.e., al-Aʿshā; the verses are not found in his *Dīwān*. Yāqūt, in his geographical dictionary, lists al-Ṣaybūn, merely saying that "it is mentioned in al-Aʿshā's verse" and quoting the two lines.

235 The word *hātif* (lit., "shouting, calling") is often used for an invisible being such as a demon (*jinnī*) inspiring a poet or a mysterious prophetic voice bringing messages.

236 One cannot help thinking that with this mocking description of the Arab nomads (not unusual in refined urban circles) the author is also casting some doubt on the process of transmission and the reliability of the chain of authorities (*isnād*), a method ubiquitous in Islamic disciplines. Curdled milk and dates are part of the normal Bedouin diet; here they are described as too poor and destitute even for this.

237 The genealogy in al-Iṣfahānī's *al-Aghānī* (ix, 108) is almost identical and traces it even further back, to Nizār, the legendary ancestor of the "North Arabs."

238 Muslims believe that the Prophet Muḥammad will intercede on behalf of his community on Judgment Day. According to popular belief his cousin and son-in-law ʿAlī (who became the fourth Caliph) will assist him there.

239 For another English translation of these verses (a longer version of the poem) see A. Guillaume's translation of *Sīrāt Rasūl Allāh*, the second/eighth-century biography of the Prophet (Ibn Isḥāq, *The Life of Muhammad*, pp. 724–25), where the story is told in the additions by Ibn Hishām (third/ninth century).

240 He addresses his camel. Hāshim was in fact the Prophet's great-grandfather.

241 Here, of course, the poet addresses his audience (a few lines have been omitted by Abū l-ʿAlāʾ).

242 Muslims may eat only ritually slaughtered animals (with some exceptions in connection with hunting and shooting).

243 This refers to the practice of bleeding cattle to drink the blood or prepare dishes from it such as *majdūḥ* (a kind of black pudding); Muslims are forbidden to consume blood. The translation combines the readings *li-tuqṣidā*, "to stab it" (found in all MSS) and *li-tufṣidā* "to bleed it" (found in the *Dīwān* and many other sources).

244 The book mentioned here is lost; it is mentioned in the early treatise on figures of speech by Ibn al-Muʿtazz (d. 296/908) when he speaks of *tajnīs* (paronomasia).

245 Or: "that, even when held back, runs fast." The verb *zajara* ("to hold back"), when applied to camels, can mean "to spur on."

246 Here the second foot, normally SLLL, is SLSL, which is not uncommon in early poetry but very rare in later periods.

247 i.e., LL instead of SLL here, a feature called *kharm* and only found in early poetry at the beginning of a whole verse (and in fact only in the first line of a poem).

248 From an ode in praise of Qays ibn Maʿdīkarib, a famous tribal leader.

249 A nearly literal quotation of Q Ghāfir 40:7: «Our Lord, Thou embracest everything in mercy and knowledge».

250 This is from his most famous poem, one of the seven celebrated pre-Islamic odes called *al-Muʿallaqāt*.

251 Not found in the ode of the same meter and rhyme in his *Dīwān*, but ascribed to Zuhayr in *al-Muʿammarūn* (*Long-lived People*) by Abū Ḥātim al-Sijistānī (d. 254/868).

252 Between the two prophets Jesus and Muḥammad.

253 See Q Āl ʿImrān 3:103 («Hold fast to the rope of God, all together») and cf. 112.

254 See Q Insān 76:17–18 («And they are given to drink a cup whose admixture is ginger; a spring therein called Salsabīl»).

255 The verses are found elsewhere ascribed to the pre-Islamic poet ʿAdī ibn Zayd; the designation al-Sarawī (probably referring to the Arabian mountain range called al-Sarāh) is not clear.

256 Reading *ta'bīd* (as in Bint al-Shāṭi''s ninth edition) instead of *ta'yīd*, found in other editions.

257 The verse is sometimes found in ʿAbīd's most famous poem, but it is lacking from many versions, and its authenticity is therefore rather suspect.

258 Q Fāṭir 35:34.

259 The path (*al-ṣirāṭ*, from Latin *strata*, via Greek and Syriac) that bridges Hell toward Paradise is not mentioned in the Qur'an but found in the Hadith. It can only be crossed by the believers; in due course (see below, §11.8.1) the Sheikh will tell how he crossed it.

260 ʿAdī was famous for his descriptions of wine.

261 All lines of a classical Arabic poem have the same rhyme; the basis of the rhyme is a consonant, very often (but not here) followed by a long vowel. The letter *ṣ* is a very rare rhyme consonant.

262 Identified by the editor as ʿAbd Hind ibn Lakhm, a mistake for ibn Lujam (see al-Kalbi / Caskel, *Ǧamharat an-nasab*, Tab. 175, Register p. 124).

263 Either wineskins made of gazelle hides (thus the dictionary *Lisān al-ʿArab*) or large pitchers (thus Ibn Qutaybah, *al-Maʿānī*, p. 449).

264 Attractive women are often described as moving slowly, because of their plumpness.

265 Another interpretation of this verse is: "On a high spot, chilled by the wind, for us is poured | a dark wine mixed with water from a cloud."

266 A victim of intrigues at the court of King al-Nuʿmān in al-Ḥīrah, the poet was imprisoned and later put to death.

267 According to Bint al-Shāṭi' *nīq* ("mountain top") could mean "a wooden plank on which a person subjected to torture is carried"; we were unable to verify this. The "ostrich" is a metaphor (instead of the more usual simile) for a camel.

268 This line is difficult to understand; a more comprehensible version is found in Ibn Qutaybah, *al-Shiʿr*, p. 239: *au murtaqā nīqin ʿalā markabin | adfara ʿawdin* ("Or being raised on top of an old animal [i.e., mule or donkey], stinking . . .").

269 Perhaps the reading in Ibn Qutaybah's *al-Shiʿr* (*lā yuḥsinu l-mashya*, "It cannot walk well") is to be preferred.

270 Not only in the same meter (*sarīʿ*, not uncommon) but also with the same, very unusual rhyme (*-ī/ūṣ*).

271 The word *anā* ("I") very often scans as *ana*, with a short second syllable (here it is necessary because of the meter). If, however, the first syllable is elided, only *na* would remain, in which case it can no longer count as a true word according to Arabic grammarians.

272 i.e., turning *wa-ana* (with a "half-realized" glottal stop) into *wāna*.

273 The verse is discussed in Sībawayh's *Kitāb*, i, 70–71 and many subsequent works on grammar. In *al-Aghānī* (ii, 152) a variant without the puzzling "you" is quoted and paraphrased as "Shall we say goodbye to you in the evening or in the morning? Which do you want?"

274 Several interpretations are supplied in Ibn Manẓūr, *Lisān al-ʿArab* (on a similar verse by Qays ibn al-Khaṭīm): the animal has been ridden to exhaustion, or it has fine features.

275 The translation of this verse is based on the paraphrase in Ibn Qutaybah, *al-Maʿānī*, p. 70.

276 The last word, *yafan*, is explained as "rapid pace" in a marginal gloss; the dictionaries only give "old man." Ibn Qutaybah has a different interpretation: "It makes a good run, with rapidity, let loose like a downpour, just as a mature cloud (reading *muzn* instead of *marr*) is filled with rain."

277 Interpretation based on Ibn Qutaybah.

278 On the "rain stars" see above, §3.8.2. The Arabic for Aquarius *al-Dalw*, means "bucket"; the "bucket handles" are rain stars associated with Aquarius.

279 This is meant ironically, praise in the form of blame, according to Ibn Qutaybah, *Maʿānī*, p. 360.

280 The meaning of *zawāʾid* ("additions") is unclear; cf. Ibn Qutaybah, *Maʿānī*, p. 339: "perhaps they are on its feet, like people with extra fingers, or the *zawāʾid* of a lion."

281 From a poem by Kaʿb ibn Maʿdān al-Ashqarī (d. ca. 95/714); see, e.g., al-Iṣfahānī, *al-Aghānī*, xiv, 299.

282 The wife of the pre-Islamic King al-Nuʿmān ibn al-Mundhir, subject of stories and poems. Al-Mutajarridah is a nickname and means "she who stripped [herself], the denuded woman." The king's horse was called al-Yaḥmūm ("Black Smoke"). Jalam is mentioned in al-Zabīdī's dictionary *Tāj al-ʿarūs* as Jalam ibn ʿAmr, where it is said "there is a story about him with al-Nuʿmān ibn al-Mundhir," but the story itself is not found.

283 See al-Iṣfahānī, *Aghānī*, ii, 154.

284 *Aghānī*, ii, 153.

285 The preceding line and the following piece are in *sarīʿ* meter, but the fact that the opening hemistich of the first line and all hemistichs of the second piece end in SSL rather than LSL makes them unusual.

286 The Arabs assumed, with Aristotle, that the head of a bee colony could only be male.

287 Q Aʿrāf 7:43.

288 The word "brisk" (*fārih*) is appropriate for donkeys and packhorses but not for a noble horse.

289 The particle *layta* ("if only, would that") should be followed by a noun or pronoun, not by a verb.

290 The ʿIbād (lit., "servants") is the name of the Christian Arabs that lived in al-Ḥīrah in the pre-Islamic period. The philologists had reservations about their language (including the poetry of ʿAdī) because they were sedentary and exposed to Persian influence.

291 Q Ṭūr 52:19, Mursalāt 77:43.

292 The pronunciation of *j* as [g] is mentioned by the early grammarians (they, like Abū l-ʿAlāʾ here, spell it with *k*, since standard Arabic has no letter for [g]).

293 Q Rūm 30:18.

294 The nickname al-Nābighah ("the copious genius") was given to at least eight early poets, the two most famous being al-Nābighah al-Dhubyānī (sixth century AD) and al-Nābighah al-Jaʿdī (d. ca. 63/683).

295 Birds may not be killed in Mecca, which was already a sanctuary and a holy place before Islam.

296 He addresses ʿAdī ibn Zayd and the two Nābighahs. With the "ʿIbādī poet" he means ʿAdī.

297 Literally "Chosroan wine," after Chosroes/Khusraw, the name of several Sasanian emperors in the pre-Islamic period.

298 He refers to al-Aʿshā, whom he has met before.

299 Q Shūrā 42:29.

300 Al-Nābighah's poem from which the following lines (on the king's spouse al-Mutajarridah) are quoted lost him the king's favor; he fled and composed a number of famous apologetic odes, eventually becoming reconciled to the king.

301 This refers to some verses in the same meter and rhyme that describe, in hardly veiled terms, the queen's private parts engaged in sexual intercourse, not quoted by Abū l-ʿAlāʾ but found in several sources (e.g. Ibn Qutaybah, *al-Shiʿr*, p. 166, Ahlwardt, *The Divans of the six ancient Arabian poets*, p. 11). Their attribution to al-Nābighah may well be spurious.

302 In unvoweled Arabic script *naẓartu* and *raʾaytu* etc. (first person singular) could also be read as *naẓarta* and *raʾayta* (second person singular), which is in fact how the lines are usually read. The following lines, not quoted, are already so improper, irrespective of the grammatical person being used, as to make the poet's (or rather al-Maʿarrī's) defense rather feeble.

303 ʿAbd al-Malik is normally known as al-Aṣmaʿī.

304 See for instance Q Maryam 19:40, where God says «We shall inherit the earth and all those who are on it».

305 Q Naml 27:33; the Queen of Sheba is addressed by her counselors.

306 The dual refers to the traditional motif, very often found at the beginning of odes, of the "two companions"; they are supposed to accompany the poet-persona on his desert journey, stopping with him when he wants to reminisce at an abandoned site.

307 i.e., I did not compose this poem.

308 The verses are not found in al-Nābighah's collected poems.

309 Thaʿlabah ibn ʿUkābah was a tribe associated with al-Ḥīrah in the sixth century AD. There are several clans called Thaʿlabah ibn Saʿd, but

they are unimportant and it is likely a mistake, put into al-Dhubyānī's mouth, who subsequently seems to admit this.

310 The letter *Sh* is another very rare rhyme consonant.

311 A Qur'anic quotation (see Q Fuṣṣilat 41:8, Qalam 68:3, Inshiqāq 84:25, Tīn 95:6).

312 Babel and Adhriʿāt are often mentioned for their wine.

313 The poet refers to horses who have suffered in battle (see the complete poem in al-Qurashī, *Jamharat ashʿār al-ʿarab*).

314 Q Baqarah 2:156.

315 The opening line of the poem in which he describes al-Mutajarridah, mentioned above. On the various rhythmical modes (not to be confused with the poetical meters), see, e.g., O. Wright, "Music," pp. 450–59.

316 *Burahīn*: explained by the dictionaries as "calamities," but here obviously meaning "terribly good things."

317 Q Yā Sīn 36:78.

318 There is a report, probably spurious, that Labīd did not compose any poetry after his conversion to Islam.

319 The problem is the jussive of *yartabiṭ*: does it still depend on *lam*, or is it a poetic license for *yartabiṭa*, subjunctive after *aw*, with the force of "unless"? See, e.g., Alan Jones, *Early Arabic Poetry*, ii, 188, who prefers a third interpretation, making the verb dependent on *idhā* ("when") but not on *lam* ("not"): "and if [I feel that their] fate may attach itself to a certain soul." This and the following line are from the *Muʿallaqah* and have therefore often been the subject of grammatical analysis.

320 Arabic grammarians normally derive forms from a verb in the base stem (I) or from a noun (as below), whereas a more modern way would be to derive them from an abstract consonantal root (here *'-W-L*). No doubt the grammarians are right in terms of historical linguistics: the roots are themselves derived from concrete words.

321 The former reading should be connected with the word *ālah* "instrument"; the latter assumes that *ta'tā* is an irregular shortening of *ta'attā*, itself a normal shortening of *tata'attā*; the meaning would be "which her thumb handled easily."

322 Al-Fārisī was known to the "Sheikh," ʿAlī ibn Manṣūr Ibn al-Qāriḥ.

323 Common but irregular variants of *istaḥyā* and *yastaḥyī* (root *Ḥ-Y-W/Y*).

324 A reconstructed form, not attested, in which the root is treated as a "hollow root" (i.e., a root with *W* or *Y* as middle root consonant) rather than as a geminate root (where the second and third consonants are identical); something similar applies to the following **iʾtāya*, in which the *W* is "weakened," instead of the normal *iʾtawā* (root *ʾ-W-Y*).

325 Oddly, form VIII of the root *ʿ-W-N* is in fact the irregular *iʿtawana*, rather than the "normal" *iʿtāna*.

326 Normally called "present" or "imperfect" tense (*al-muḍāriʿ*).

327 The reasoning is as follows: form VIII of the root *ʾ-W-Y*, if treated (irregularly) as a "hollow root," is **iʾtāya*; the imperfect third person feminine would be **taʾtāyu* and elision of the final root consonant would give *taʾtā*, as in the poem.

328 Q Zumar 39:53.

329 Q Nisāʾ 4:116.

330 The syntax and the sense of the passage are somewhat problematic.

331 According to a commentator (Abū ʿUbayd al-Bakrī, *Simṭ al-laʾālī*, p. 432) her teeth are compared to white camomile, her dark gums to silver ore, and her saliva with wine made from raisins.

332 The interpretation of *jurrida* ("was despatched"?) is not wholly clear and here it has been taken as a possible mistake for *juwwida*, cf. *jāda jawdan* "to be copious (rain)."

333 *Qarqaf*, as a word for wine, is usually explained as "making the drinker shiver," apparently a recommendation; "potent" will do. *Isfanṭ* is derived from "absinthe," i.e., wormwood.

334 This verse is rather obscure; cf. Lyall, *The Mufaḍḍalīyat*, ii, 98, 100, on line 75 of an ode by ʿAbdah ibn al-Ṭabīb, ("the flagon was a mixing bowl, like the middle of a wild ass"), where it is suggested that "the bowl is compared to the belly of a wild ass because it is constantly being refilled," the animal having to drink frequently. Perhaps the color is what is meant: the amphora is coated with black pitch.

335 The meaning of the word *hazim* is unclear; it seems to denote a kind of sound; the noise of the fermenting wine is often described in Arabic wine poetry, as it is in the following line. In that case it apparently is a different kind of noise to that in the next line. It is also somewhat odd that the words *nāqis* and *hazim* are masculine, whereas wine is usually feminine in Arabic, as in the rest of the passage.

336 Q Wāqiʿah 56:37.

337 Arabs traditionally clean the teeth and the gums with brushes made of twigs of aromatic wood.

338 Bint al-Shāṭiʾ's edition has *mawsūman*; we read *marsūman*, as in the poem.

339 The poem is found in the celebrated second/eighth century anthology *al-Mufaḍḍaliyyāt* (see Lyall's translation and commentary, pp. 73–78).

340 Al-Rabāb is a woman's name often found in early Arabic love poetry. The poet speaks about himself, shifting to the first person singular in the next line.

341 The female reproacher, a stock figure in many poems, represents the voice of reason, warning the poet-hero against reckless spending or engaging in hazardous ventures.

342 Q Fāṭir 35:34–35.

343 The poet seems to be speaking about himself here (perhaps quoting someone else). There is a confusing shift of pronouns in the complete poem.

344 Presumably his guest, implied in the first line.

345 According to Islamic belief, those in Paradise are restored to the prime of their life physically and mentally.

346 The verse is from the most celebrated of the *Muʿallaqah* odes.

347 The word *khalīʿ*, in al-Maʿarrī's time, normally meant "shameless, profligate, depraved," but here its older sense of "repudiated (e.g., a son by his father)" is certainly relevant.

348 Literally, "May God not break your mouth!"

349 The early critic Ibn Sallām al-Jumaḥī (d. ca. 232/846), in his *Ṭabaqāt fuḥūl al-shuʿarāʾ* (*The Categories of the Master Poets*) lists

in his first class Imru' al-Qays, al-Nābighah al-Dhubyānī, Zuhayr, and al-Aʿshā.

350 Al-Aʿshā, "the night blind," married this woman but did not like her and divorced her. His parting poem addresses her as a chaste and blameless woman (see al-Iṣfahānī, *Aghānī*, ix, 121–22).

351 A common idiom for someone who indiscriminately produces or accepts good and bad.

352 Perhaps the word *gharīrah* "innocent, inexperienced" implies a comparison of the girl to a gazelle or oryx cow.

353 The sense is possibly obscene: her pale belly is like a scent box (possibly made of ivory) and he is about to (re)fill her "cup."

354 Q Wāqiʿah 56:19.

355 Compare above, §5.4 (al-Aʿshā was allowed to enter Paradise on condition that he would not drink any wine there).

356 This refers to the way a Bedouin Arab sits, with legs drawn up and wrapped in his garment.

357 The caliph al-Amīn (r. 193–8/809–13).

358 The "arbitration," a key moment in Islamic history, was between ʿAlī ibn Abī Ṭālib, the fourth caliph, and his opponent Muʿāwiyah (who became the first Umayyad caliph). The Khārijites ("Seceders"), fervent partisans of ʿAlī at first, became fierce opponents because he consented to the arbitration; but some abstained from fighting.

359 Just as in the Christian tradition, Islam has its recording angels, who keep account of good and bad deeds (see Q Anʿām 6:61). As the Sheikh says, God, being Omniscient, does not really need them (and this being so, there is no reason why they should especially fear a passing angel. Is the author mocking orthodox belief?).

360 One of the many appellations of wine, perhaps because of its fragrance or its color.

361 The following lines are from the "amatory introduction" of a poem that satirizes Abū Sufyān, the leading Meccan adversary of the Prophet.

362 Interpretation uncertain: is *al-ghiṭāʾ* the "covering" of the woman or the darkness of the night? Does the suffix *-hā* refer to the woman or the stars?

363 The masculine form of the verb (*yakūnu*) is odd; but it could refer to "saliva" rather than the woman.

364 Here and on several other occasions Bint al-Shāṭiʾ has completed the customary formula after a mention of the Prophet by adding *wa-sallama* ("and give [him] peace"). We have given the original text.

365 Ḥassān and others had accused ʿĀʾishah, the Prophet's young wife, of improper behavior with a young man who had picked her up after she had inadvertently been left behind by the caravan with which she was traveling. The Prophet's initial doubts were repelled by a revelation from God and the accusers were flogged. Māriyah and her sister Sīrīn were Coptic slaves, given to Muḥammad by the Byzantine governor of Egypt; Muḥammad took Māriyah as his concubine and gave Sīrīn to Ḥassān.

366 Ibrāhīm died before he was two years old.

367 The verse is discussed by Sībawayh and later grammarians. The predicate after *yakūnu* ("is") should take the accusative; since the nominative ending of *māʾū* ("water") is secured by the rhyme, this must be the subject (with *ʿasalun*, "honey"), and *mizājahā* must be the predicate, taking the accusative. It is unusual to have an indefinite subject and a definite predicate like this, and a poetic license is assumed. In the second version a rather contrived explanation for the odd nominative *māʾū* has been given: it is a shortening of a sentence such as "and water (is also mixed with it)." It has also been argued that *yakūnu* is "superfluous" here, in which case "its mixture being honey and water" is a nominal, verbless sentence in which all nouns have the nominative.

368 The verse (from the same poem) is cast as a statement, but a rhetorical question is surely intended (as is found in other sources that have *a-man* instead of *fa-man*).

369 Arabic grammar distinguishes between two kinds of relative clause: one attached to a definite antecedent, in which case a relative pronoun is needed, and another attached to an indefinite antecedent, in which case a relative pronoun is not used (as in English "a man I know"). The problem is whether the relative pronoun *man* should be interpreted as "he who" (definite) or "one who" (indefinite).

370 He belonged to Khazraj, one of the two leading tribes settled in Medina. He was accused of cowardice during the "Battle of the Ditch" at Medina and the subsequent raid against the Banū Qurayẓah (5/627) when the Meccans attacked the Muslims (see, e.g., *al-Aghānī*, iv, 164–66 and Ibn Isḥāq, *The Life of Muhammad*, trans. A. Guillaume, p. 458).

371 Q Anfāl 8:16,

372 All were poets. The "Camel-herd" died ca. 96/714; the others were born in the pre-Islamic period and died after the coming of Islam.

373 The beginning of the poem rhyming in *-zū* (a rare rhyme), famous for its description of a bow. The poem opens with the customary motif of the deserted places where the poet reminisces about his meeting with the beloved and her tribe.

374 Q Mursalāt 77:41–43.

375 Literally, "things." Perhaps he refers to his poetry, made for the sake of gain.

376 Meaning unclear.

377 The sense of these lines is obscure.

378 Or "I see."

379 Harshā is a mountain pass near Mecca. The sense is "either way leads to Mecca" or, in English, "All roads lead to Rome"; Ibn Aḥmar means that both interpretations are valid. The line is by ʿAqīl ibn ʿUllafah, a younger contemporary of Ibn Aḥmar.

380 Q Ḥajj 22:2.

381 viz. the "earthquake of the Hour" at the Resurrection.

382 The place where mankind will be gathered after the Resurrection (see below, §11.1).

383 The words "For a wine" have been added; it seems that something is missing; or perhaps the wine (with its effects) serves as another *secundum comparationis* for "the prime of youth."

384 This word and subsequent enigmatic descriptions in the poem will be discussed later.

385 We follow the interpretation of this line by Ibn Qutaybah, *Maʿānī*, p. 463: *anā fī sukri shabābī ka-dhālika idh lahā ʿan maṭiyyatih.*

386 The poem seems to describe a rain cloud (but see the poet's explanation, below). Such metonyms, instead of straightforward nouns, are extremely common in early Arabic poetry.

387 Bint al-Shāṭi' has another interpretation: "When its tongue is split (to prevent it from sucking), it is a *bāzil* (camel whose first teeth have come through)." Here the interpretation of early commentators has been followed. Another interpretation is given by Ibn Qutaybah, *Maʿānī*, p. 463: "when it is chewing the cud its eye-teeth appear"; it means the animal looks healthy and young.

388 Another possible interpretation of *sharāb qayl* in line 3 is "a drink (of wine) at midday." That the poet does not mention it is understandable, in view of his diminished memory; but one would have expected the Sheikh to do so.

389 See Q Najm 53:61: «while you make merry».

390 The great *Kitāb al-Aghānī* by Abū l-Faraj al-Iṣfahānī (d. ca. 363/972), devoted to singers, musicians, and especially poets. For the verses, with some variants, see viii, 326. There, the "two locusts of ʿĀd" are said to belong to ʿAbd Allāh ibn Judʿān, who lived shortly before the coming of Islam; they cannot have been identical with the two singers from ancient times and "locust" was obviously a general nickname for singers, as ʿAmr will explain.

391 The opening of a famous poem by the pre-Islamic poet ʿAbīd ibn al-Abraṣ.

392 The poet makes a spurious connection between *zabarjad* (peridot, or chrysolite) and *zibrij* ("ornamentation"); the words are not related (*zabarjad* is to be connected with *zumurrud*, Targumic Hebrew

zᵉmargad, Greek *smaragdos*, English "emerald," ultimately probably from Sanskrit).

393 The author of *al-ʿAyn* is said to be al-Khalīl ibn Aḥmad. He will appear later in the text. The word *ṣalakhdam* ("strong camel") is connected here with *ṣalkham* ("big and strong").

394 There are nouns, such as *zabarjad*, that have five consonants, but verbal roots always have either three or four. In the present example the last consonant of *zabarjad* is ignored in *yuzabriju* (which can be translated as "he peridots"). The same happens with the formation of so-called "broken" plurals.

395 A word taken from Persian, it is also the name under which a famous and very Arab poet is known (see below, §17.3.3).

396 The Arabic term, *maṣdar*, literally means "place from which something proceeds, place of origin."

397 The corresponding verbs are *ḍaraba* ("to strike") and *karuma* ("to be noble"). Thus, e.g., *al-rajulu ḍāribun* ("the man is striking") = *yaḍribu l-rajulu* ("the man strikes"), *al-rajulu karīmun* ("the man is noble") = *yakrumu l-rajulu*.

398 Translation uncertain.

399 One wonders if Abū l-ʿAlāʾ chose this line because the words *ḥattā tasʾama l-dīnā* could also be interpreted (wrongly) as "until she is bored with religion." The known versions of this famous poem (e.g., in the anthologies *Jamharat ashʿār al-ʿarab* and *Muntahā l-ṭalab*) have *taʿrifa* ("she knows") instead of *tasʾama* ("she is bored with").

400 Nothing is known about Ibn Muqbil's active participation in the conflicts between ʿAlī ibn Abī Ṭālib and his various opponents.

401 Q Fāṭir 35:37.

402 Reading *al-amān*, as in Bint al-Shāṭiʾ's ninth edition (earlier editions had *al-aymān*).

403 Q Baqarah 2:281.

404 The Sheikh (or rather the author) has an irritating habit of using unusual words and explaining them himself; it has been imitated in the translation.

405 Q Maʿārij 70:4–5. For eloquent descriptions of the arid plain where the waiting humans, naked and barefoot, crowding together, are tormented by heat and thirst, see, e.g., al-Ghazālī (d. 505/1111), *Iḥyāʾ ʿulūm al-dīn*, iv, 512–15: "the place of assembling and its people," "the sweating," "the length of the Day of Resurrection," all of it supported with relevant quotations from Qurʾan and Hadith.

406 The beginning of a *qaṣīdah* by the pre-Islamic poet Imruʾ al-Qays; not his famous *Muʿallaqah* but another, with a near-identical opening line. The rhyme is *-ānī*, which accommodates the name Riḍwān in the genitive.

407 The opening of a poem by the famous poet Jarīr (d. 111/729), rhyming in *-ānā*, which suits the name Riḍwān in the accusative.

408 Q Sabaʾ 34:2.

409 Rabīʿah and Muḍar are two ancient ancestors of the Arabs, giving their names to large tribal confederations. Labīd's father was also called Rabīʿah.

410 A common image for something impossible.

411 For this and other elegies on Ḥamzah, see Guillaume's translation of Ibn Isḥāq's *al-Sīrah al-nabawiyyah*, *The Life of the Prophet*, p. 420 (with several other elegies composed after the battle, pp. 404–26).

412 Q ʿAbasa 80:37, on the Day of Judgment.

413 Customary phrase for addressing or speaking of caliphs, in particular ʿAlī.

414 cf., e.g., Q Ḥāqqah 69:18–23, «On that day you will be exposed, not one secret of yours will be concealed. Then as for him who is given his writ in his right hand, he will say, "Here it is, read my writ! I thought that I should meet my reckoning." He will be in a pleasing life, in a lofty Garden, its clusters within reach».

415 The syntax of this verse has been discussed extensively by the grammarians (see, e.g., ʿAbd al-Qādir al-Baghdādī, *Khizānat al-adab*, x, 472–84). It is not clear why *al-māʾ* could be nominative.

416 *Muqtawī* is derived from the root *Q-W-Y* (form VIII: "to appropriate"); there is some confusion with the root *Q-T-W*, giving *muqtawī* "taking as a servant" and *maqtawiyy* "servant."

417 Al-Zafayān al-Saʿdī (fl. ca. 80/700).

418 Or *taʾbiyah*; see e.g. Ibn Manẓūr, *Lisān al-ʿArab* s.v. *ʾ-B-Y*.

419 The verse is quoted anonymously in Sībawayh's grammar on account of the word order (normal would be *al-marʾu dhiʾbun in yalqa l-rushā* or *al-marʾu ʿinda l-rushā in yalqahā fa-huwa dhīb*); later grammarians argue that the suffix in *yadrusuhū* "he studies it" cannot refer to *qurʾān*, because it is not compatible with the preposition *li-* in *lil-qurʾān*, which already has the function of defining the direct object, and therefore the suffix must refer to an implied verbal noun *darsan* "studying." Al-Maʿarrī clearly thinks this reasoning is faulty.

420 In full: *The Proof Concerning the Seven Variant Readings (of the Qurʾan)*. The consonants of the Qurʾanic text can be read in several ways; seven versions are recognized as equally valid and canonical. See also below, n. 696.

421 In Islamic law written documents are considered valid and legally binding only when two or more witnesses can testify to their validity.

422 Some Islamic scholars are of the view that repentance shortly before one's death will not save one from Hell.

423 The place where the believers will meet the Prophet on the Day of Judgment; see, e.g., A. J. Wensinck, entry "Ḥawḍ" in *EI2*, III, 286.

424 The Prophet's descendants.

425 This is a customary formula written by copyists at the end of a manuscript.

426 See, e.g., Q Yūnus 10:19, Hūd 11:110, Fuṣṣilat 41:45: «but for a word that preceded from your Lord» (to postpone Judgment).

427 Q Anbiyāʾ 21:101–03; "it" refers to Hell.

428 They all died young, without issue.

429 The word "imam" has several meanings; here it refers to ʿAlī and his male descendants mentioned before.

430 See above, n. 259.

431 Al-Jaḥjalūl (if he is a real person at all) has not been identified.

432 The sense is rather obscure. The words *ilā l-warā* are (possibly intentionally) ambiguous: "toward people" and "backward" (as a poetic license for *ilā l-warāʾ*).

433 In his famous book, the first and most authoritative Arabic grammar.

434 i.e., in the days when things were all right. One would expect "the people" to be in the nominative, but the particle *wa-*, usually meaning "and," sometimes means "together with," in which case it is followed by the accusative.

435 Since man is mortal and subject to decay, even being healthy implies sickness.

436 i.e., she is shameless and does not mind doing unpleasant things.

437 i.e., she took a pail to an udder decked with muck.

438 Visiting women at night is an extremely common theme in Arabic poetry; but visiting old women is a rarity.

439 A variant (Ibn Qutaybah, *al-Shiʿr*, p. 393) has *zubd* ("butter") instead of *zād* ("food"). Buttermaking is described in the poem (see below); the precise meaning of some verses is rather obscure.

440 Traditionally blue eyes are considered inauspicious.

441 He is carrying a pair of skins filled with milk, presumably on a yoke.

442 As is made clear by additional verses in another source (Ibn Qutaybah, *Maʿānī*, pp. 599–600), the woman tastes the milk approvingly and then churns it to make butter. This seems to be the meaning; but several things remain unclear. Ibn Qutaybah has *fa-ghuṣṣat tarāqīhī bi-ṣafrāʾa jaʿdatin | fa-ʿanhā tuṣādīhī wa-ʿanhā turāwidū*. In *ʿalayhā tuʿānīhī*, *ʿalā* may have the same function as in the earlier phrase *turīdunī ʿalā l-zādi/zubdi*: "for the sake of it (the butter) she (the woman) suffered (or: kept herself busy with) him (the man)."

443 An allusion to the common Qurʾanic expression, on the people in Paradise: «there is no fear upon them, nor will they grieve», e.g. Q Baqarah 2:35, 62, 112, Āl ʿImrān 3:170.

444 Making a panegyric poem.

445 Apparently the Arabs in Paradise live according to their tribal affiliations. Labīd's tribe, ʿĀmir ibn Ṣaʿṣaʿah, is part of the large federation called Qays, a major branch of the "North Arabs."

446 The passage exploits an untranslatable play on words: the Arabic word *bayt* means not only "tent" or "house" but also "line of verse."

447 The verses seem to demonstrate that the Lord is more concerned with piety than with good poetry.

448 The verse is by al-Mutanakhkhil.

449 *Al-ḥūr al-ʿīn*: the paradisial damsels or "houris" (see Q Dukhān 44:54, Ṭūr 52:20, Wāqiʿah 56:22).

450 The two merciless "girls" are the two grinding millstones.

451 Abū l-ʿAlāʾ, exceptionally in Islam, was a vegan who preached abstinence from meat, fish, eggs, milk, and honey, in order not to harm animals.

452 Q Zukhruf 43:71–73.

453 Q Ṭūr 52:24.

454 Kaʿb ibn Mālik, a contemporary of the Prophet, in a boasting poem (the original has "our shelters" instead of "his doors").

455 A vulture (*nasr*) is proverbial in Arabic for its longevity. Surayy has not been identified; on Kuwayy see *WKAS* I, 582b; it is called "one of the rain stars" in the dictionary *Lisān al-ʿArab*. *Nasr* is also the name of two stars: *al-nasr al-ṭāʾir* (Altair, or alpha *Aquilae*) and *al-nasr al-wāqiʿ* (alpha *Lyrae*). Perhaps these two stars are called Kuwayy and Surayy, and here used for longevity because they are both "vultures." In al-Maʿarrī, *al-Fuṣūl wa-l-ghāyāt*, p. 148, Kuwayy is also used to denote longevity.

456 All of them famous male singers.

457 Famous female singers from the early Abbasid period. They started their careers as highly trained and educated slave girls, bought for large sums by caliphs, viziers, and others. Several of them, such as ʿInān (for a time a girl friend of the poet Abū Nuwās) were also poets.

458 i.e., lived in the pre-Islamic period of "ignorance" (*jāhiliyyah*).

459 The Sheikh will see Aws in Hell (below, §17.9.1). There is much confusion in the sources not only about the ascription but also concerning the text of this poem. For an English translation of one version, see Lyall, *The Dīwāns of ʿAbīd ibn al-Abrāṣ of Asad, and ʿĀmir ibn aṭ-Ṭufail, of ʿĀmir ibn Ṣaʿṣaʿah*, pp. 59–60.

460 The "tubes" or "pipes" (*anābīb*) puzzled the critics. The use of the word is criticized in al-ʿAskarī, *Ṣināʿatayn*, p. 79. He suggests that "it

could mean the ducts in the pomegranate;" al-Zamakhsharī, *Asās al-balāghah* (s.v. *N-B-B*) says that *anābīb* is "figurative (*majāz*)" here.

461 Jirān al-ʿAwd is a nickname, meaning "leather whip made from an old camel stallion," an expression he used in a poem in which he threatens his two wives with a whipping. He refers to himself by this nickname in the present poem, in which he describes a nocturnal adventure.

462 Poets often mention the "humming of the jinn," apparently the "singing sands," a well known phenomenon of desert lands. It has been shown that the sound of "the singing dunes," when it is real and not caused by one's imagination in the stillness of the desert, may be the result, under particular circumstances, of the friction of sand grains against one another. See Hogan, "Dunes Alive with the Sand of Music"; Merali, "Dune Tune: The Greatest Hits."

463 This verse is not found in the poem of the same meter and rhyme in his *Dīwān*.

464 ʿAmr ibn ʿAdī, pre-Islamic king of al-Ḥīrah, is connected with the famous ancient legend about Jadhīmah, "the Leprous" and al-Zabbāʾ, the Arabian queen in whom memories of Queen Zenobia survive. Jadhīmah had two drinking companions, Mālik and ʿAqīl. ʿAmr ibn Kulthūm (sixth century AD) was also connected with al-Ḥīrah. The lines are from his only famous poem, one of the seven *Muʿallaqāt* but are not found in all versions.

465 The author again uses a very rare word and immediately explains it.

466 Ibn Qutaybah, in his book on poetry and poets, condemns these lines as "obviously constrained and badly composed." It is perhaps the meter (with its eight syllables per hemistich, much shorter than average) that makes it suitable for dancing.

467 See Q Wāqiʿah 56:17 and Insān 76:19.

468 Compare hadiths quoted by al-Ghazālī, *Iḥyāʾ ʿulūm al-dīn*, iv, 540: "Ibn Masʿūd said, The messenger of God, God bless and preserve him, said: Truly, you will merely look at a bird in Paradise and desire it, and it will fall before you, roasted." "Ḥudhayfah said, The messenger of God, God bless and preserve him, said: There are birds in Paradise like Bactrian camels. Abū Bakr, may God be pleased with

him, asked: Are they nice, messenger of God? He answered: Nicer than they are those who eat them, and you, Abū Bakr, will be among those who eat them!" The following Qur'anic quotations are Q Yā Sīn 36:78 and Baqarah 2:260.

469 The parenthesis is an editorial addition.

470 The conjunction *li-*, when followed by a subjunctive, means "so that, in order that"; when followed by a jussive (which in this case has the same form as the subjunctive) it expresses an order or invitation ("let my heart be reassured"). Since God cannot be commanded, it functions as a prayer.

471 Q Baqarah 2:259; according to most commentators the speaker (not named in the Qur'an) is ʿUzayr (sometimes identified as Ezra) or the "Green Man", al-Khaḍir. God made him die for a hundred years and then brought him back to life; ʿĀzar is one of the Arabic names for Lazarus (cf. John 11:1–46).

472 The verse is from a poem in the famous collection *al-Mufaḍḍaliyyāt*.

473 The Central Asian, "Bactrian" camel has two humps and is bigger than the Arabian, one-humped camel.

474 Morphological patterns in Arabic are expressed by means of the "dummy" root *F-ʿ-L* (of the verb *faʿala* "to do"); prosodists do the same for metrical feet (e.g., *faʿūlun* is short-long-long). Here the three root consonants are given, alternatively, as C_1, C_2, C_3. The pattern of *iwazzah* is discussed, e.g., by Ibn Jinnī (d. 392/1002), *al-Khaṣāʾiṣ*, iii, 6–7.

475 The grammatical "school" of Basra (to which al-Māzinī belongs) traditionally accords a greater role to analogy in formulating grammatical rules than the rival "school" of Kufa, which is more tolerant of irregularities sanctioned by actual usage.

476 ʾiC_1C_2aC_3ah would give **ʾiʾwayah*; Arabic phonotactic rules would automatically change *ʾiʾ* into *ʾiy*, the sequence *yw* into *yy*, and *aya* into *ā*, giving *ʾiyyāh*.

477 A verse from a famous poem by al-Afwah al-Awdī; the authenticity of the poem is dubious (see al-Jāḥiẓ, *Ḥayawān*, vi, 275, 280).

478 A verse often quoted as a proverb, attributed to several poets (Maʿn ibn Aws, Mālik ibn Fahm al-Azdī, or ʿAqīl ibn ʿUllafah), on being shot by one's own son.

479 The great poet Imru' al-Qays (first half of sixth century AD). The first quotation is from his *Muʿallaqah*; the poet (addressing himself) reminisces about his amorous adventures.

480 Q Raḥmān 55:58.

481 The Sheikh uses two Arabic forms of the word, the usual *kāfūr* and the rare *qāfūr*.

482 By al-Ḥusayn ibn Muṭayr (d. ca. 179/786), on the Abbasid caliph al-Mahdī.

483 Q Wāqiʿah 56:35–38.

484 The English word "houri," now no longer well known, goes back, via Persian, Turkish and French, to Arabic *ḥūr* (plural of *ḥawrā'*), the word used in the Qur'an and here for the "black-eyed damsels" in Paradise.

485 Compare 1 Cor. 2:9 (which is not about damsels). We thank Professor Christian Lange for his help with this sentence.

486 Heavy posteriors are part of the ideal beauty in classical Arabic love poetry, whether on women or boys; the standard poetic simile is that of the sand hill or dune.

487 Q Ṣāffāt 37:51–57.

488 *ʿAfārīt*, plural of *ʿifrīt* ("afreet, afrit"), a demon of the more malicious kind; the general word for demons is *jinn* (singular *jinnī*, "jinnee, djinnee, genie").

489 See Q Aḥqāf 46:29–32 and Jinn 72:1–16, respectively.

490 The *maradah* (sg. *mārid*), an evil kind of jinn, who rebelled with Satan against God.

491 All editions have *lā ka-l-ḥāqin min al-ihālah*; the negative particle *lā* is problematical, because without it the idiom refers to a person with skill and experience: "someone who retains the melted fat (waiting to pour it until it cools down, so as not to burn the vessel)"; see the identical explanations in Abū ʿUbayd al-Bakrī, *Faṣl al-maqāl*, 298;

al-ʿAskarī, *Jamharat al-amthāl*, ii, 135; al-Maydānī, *Majmaʿ al-amthāl*, i, 76. Apparently, the word *lā* is a mistake, perhaps a misreading of *anā* "I am," on the part of the author or a scribe. However, an interpretation that retains the word *lā* has been proposed by Gregor Schoeler and Tilman Seidensticker: "(You have found) someone who (in relation to the question, or the questioner) is like the moon to the halo, not like someone who suffers from strangury and cannot pass urine" (meaning that the jinnee's knowledge pours forth freely).

492 Thus, instead of "al-Khaythaʿūr" as found in the manuscripts. *Khaytaʿūr* is an unusual word for "mirage" or "fata morgana"; *shayṣabān* is said to mean "male ant" or perhaps "termite mound."

493 This refers, of course, to Arabic. Al-Khalīl ibn Aḥmad was the first to describe and systematize the meters (some of which are hardly ever found but were constructed for the sake of his system).

494 Twigs of the *arāk* tree were used as toothbrushes or toothpicks.

495 The first half of the opening line of the *Muʿallaqah* by Imruʾ al-Qays, probably the most famous verse in Arabic.

496 Q Ḥijr 15:26, 15, 33.

497 Q Raḥmān 55:15.

498 He asks for the *kunyah*, a name beginning with Abū/Umm ("father/mother of"), usually followed by the name of the eldest son.

499 It is said in the Hadith (see, e.g., al-Zamakhsharī, *Kashshāf*, ad Q Wāqiʿah 56:37) that everyone in Paradise will always be thirty-three years old.

500 It was believed that epilepsy was caused by a jinnee entering the body.

501 The following poem (obviously by al-Maʿarrī himself) is a parody of a vaunting poem, in which a poet boasts of the virtues and heroic exploits of himself and his tribe; it is the most important poetic genre of pre- and early Islamic poetry. See Bürgel, "Les deux poèmes autobiographiques du démon Khaytaʿūr."

502 Ghūr, here used for the people living in the region of that name, a mountainous territory in present day Afghanistan.

503 The Arabic *ṭunbūr* is a long-necked stringed instrument. The word entered Europe as "pandore," "pandora," or "bandora"; "sitar"

was chosen because it will be more familiar to most readers than "pandore."

504 A reference to Q A'rāf 7:143, where Mūsā (Moses) at Mt. Sinai expresses a desire to see God, which a human being cannot aspire to.

505 References to the Persian Sassanids, who ruled from AD 224 until they were overthrown by the early Muslim conquests. Sāsān was the eponymous founder of the dynasty. Shapur (Shāhpur in Middle Persian, Sābūr in Arabic) was the name of several Sassanian kings; the reference could be to Shapur II, who led punitive actions against the Arabs in the fourth century AD, acquiring the nickname "Shoulder-man" (Dhū l-aktāf) because of his habit of dislocating or piercing the shoulders of captives. Bahrām V (Middle Persian Vahrām, r. 420–38) was called Bahrām Gūr "the Onager" (Jūr in Arabic) on account of his vigor. In the poem Gūr/Jūr is mistaken for the Persian town of that name.

506 Isrāfīl, one of the archangels, will blow the trumpet on the Last Day. The blast on the trumpet is often referred to in the Qur'an (without Isrāfīl being mentioned).

507 See Q 72, Sūrat al-Jinn (the "Surah of the Jinn").

508 Abū Hadrash literally quotes the Qur'anic text (Q Jinn 72:1–2); the Arabic for "recitation" is *qur'ān.*

509 As is told in the Qur'an and the relevant exegesis (Q Ḥijr 15:18, Jinn 72:8–9), some jinn were eavesdropping on God's High Council, whereupon they were pelted by angels with meteors or shooting stars.

510 The line describes an oryx bull.

511 This follows James Montgomery's interpretation (*The Vagaries of the Qaṣīdah*, pp. 120, 123–24, with several parallels); *ṭunub* ("tent-rope") should therefore be taken as *pars pro toto*, standing for a tent.

512 This long poem is again a parody with self-praise as its main theme. It alludes to numerous common motifs, such as the abandoned abodes at the beginning. It contains some rather abrupt transitions, wholly in the style of early poetry.

513 The Prophet belonged to Hāshim, the leading clan of the tribe of Quraysh.

514 The stoning of married fornicators is not mentioned in the Qur'an but mentioned in the Hadith.

515 The text has Shās, said to be a road near Mecca. Other manuscripts have Shāsh, i.e., the town better known as Tashkent, which is better suited to the hyperbolical vaunting (compare the broad geography in the preceding poem). It is slightly odd, however, that it should be linked with the obscure ʿAlwah instead of, e.g., Mecca.

516 Sulaymān (Solomon) is the master of demons in Islamic lore; the motif of the jinnee in a bottle is familiar from the *Thousand and One Nights*.

517 Literally "a single divorce," which is easily revoked, unlike a triple divorce, after which the husband can only remarry the same woman after she has been married to someone else first.

518 In Arabic poetry the mouth of the beloved is often said to taste like wine.

519 According to Arabic lore the lute (*al-ʿūd*) was invented by Lamak (Lamech), a few generations after Cain; there is a grisly story that the construction was inspired by the decomposing body parts of a young son of his. The two companions are presumably Lamak's son Tūbal (cf. Biblical Jubal or Tubal), the inventor of the drum and tambourine, and his daughter Ḍilāl (cf. Biblical Zillah, who is Lamech's wife), who invented stringed instruments. Compare Gen. 4:21–22.

520 Legendary long-lived pre-Islamic sage, associated with ʿĀd; he is mentioned in the Qur'an (Q Luqmān 31:12 ff.) in the Sura that bears his name. Many maxims and fables were later attributed to him. Other sources, including a verse by the pre-Islamic poet Ṭarafah, mention Luqmān (the same?) as a famous player of *maysir*, an ancient Arab gambling game.

521 A reference to the motif often found in early Arabic poems in which the poet renounces his youthful follies once he is old.

522 The three main battles between the unbelieving Meccans and the Muslims led by the Prophet, which took place in 2/624, 3/625, and 5/627, respectively.

523 According to Muslim tradition angels fought on the Muslim side at the battle of Badr.

524 This refers to a well-known tradition according to which the angels who intervened in the battle of Badr wore yellow turbans.

525 Ḥayzūm is said to be the horse of Jibrīl (Gabriel).

526 Zaynab and Lamīs are typical women's names found in early Arabic poetry; see above, §9.3.1.

527 Bilqīs is the Arabic name of the Queen of Sheba.

528 Al-Mundhir's dynasty is the Lakhmid Dynasty.

529 A reference to the jinn who had listened to God's high council (see above, §15.2.6). Abū Hadrash had apparently done the same, from his lowly place in Paradise.

530 In a crucial battle the Muslims defeated a Byzantine force at the river al-Yarmūk, south of Damascus, in 15/636.

531 At the "Battle of the Camel" (36/656) ʻAlī, the fourth caliph, defeated his rivals al-Zubayr and Ṭalḥah, who were supported by Muḥammad's widow, ʻĀʼishah; she witnessed the fight seated on a camel.

532 The Banū Ḍabbah were a tribe that fought on the losing side at the Battle of the Camel.

533 The protracted Battle of Ṣiffīn (37/657), on the upper Euphrates, between the caliph ʻAlī and his rival Muʻāwiyah (who was to be the first Umayyad caliph a few years later), ended in stalemate.

534 On the heels of the Battle of Ṣiffīn, ʻAlī had to fight his former partisans who had been disappointed about his assent to arbitration and had become fierce opponents. He defeated them at al-Nahrawān (here shortened to al-Nahr, "the river") in Iraq in 38/658.

535 A proverb; i.e., with a similar metaphor, the admonition fell on fertile ground.

536 ʻUtbah ibn Abī Lahab married Ruqayyah, a daughter of the Prophet, before the latter's mission, but divorced her when Muḥammad began to preach Islam. In spite of ʻUtbah's later conversion to Islam, the curse seems to have worked. His father Abū Lahab, an uncle of Muḥammad, is the object of a curse in Q 111, Sūrat al-Masad.

537 Uhbān ibn al-Akwaʿ (or ibn Aws), nicknamed Mukallim al-Dhiʾb ("Spoke with Wolf"). One day, while Uhbān is herding his sheep, a wolf grabs one of them. Uhbān goes after the wolf, who stops and speaks: "Why do you want to rob me of the livelihood God has given me?" Uhbān is amazed that the wolf can speak, but the wolf replies, "Yet more amazing is that God's messenger is preaching in Mecca!" Then Uhbān converts to Islam.

538 He and al-Ḥuṭayʾah exchanged a series of lampoons; a complaint by al-Zibriqān to the caliph ʿUmar led to al-Ḥuṭayʾah's imprisonment in Medina.

539 The word here rendered as "marker mountain," *ʿalam,* is any sign, a post or natural feature such as a hill or mountain, that may serve as a road marker. The word *raʾs* ("head") can also mean "mountaintop." Unfortunately for Ṣakhr, the metaphor has been taken literally in Hell.

540 In English, "Satan" is the devil's name; Arabic reverses this, for al-Shayṭān ("the Satan," or the devil) is the more general designation, whereas his name (used here) is Iblīs (possibly derived from Greek *diabolos* and cognate with "devil").

541 Q Qiyāmah 75:35; the interpretation of the verse is uncertain. It could also mean "nearer to you and nearer."

542 Q Aʿrāf 7:50.

543 Q Baqarah 2:25.

544 Possibly he suggests that in addition to the "pure spouses" (i.e., wives) the "immortal youths" would also be available to the male believers. The question whether homosexual intercourse with them would be possible in the hereafter was seriously discussed by the theologians; for arguments pro and contra, see, e.g., al-Ṣafadī, *al-Wāfī,* ii, 84–85.

545 The following lines are discontinuous fragments from a lengthy ode on a governor, composed in *rajaz* meter (hence the shorter lines).

546 "On a morning before the *subd* were up."

547 The dictionaries identify it, not very convincingly, as "wild swallow," "a bird like the eagle," and "a bird with water-repellent feathers" (apparently a water fowl). The editor of Bashshār's poetry,

Muḥammad al-Ṭāhir ibn ʿĀshūr, explains *subd* as the plural of *asbad*, "long-haired," referring to oryxes, but this is not confirmed by other attestations.

548 The crow, bird of ill omen, is often described as announcing the separation of lovers.

549 Identification uncertain: *ṣurad* has been translated as "shrike" (*EI2*, vii, 906b, 951b s.v. "naḥl" and "naml"), "magpie" (*EI2*, iii, 307a, s.v. "ḥayawān"), "sparrow hawk" and "green woodpecker" (both in Hava, *al-Farāʾid al-durriyyah*).

550 A strange explanation of the hopping of crows, perhaps forgivable in a blind man.

551 The translation follows that of Ullmann, *Der Neger*, p. 50: "einen, der . . . einem Abessinier im Dauerregen gleicht." The verse is not found elsewhere.

552 See above, *Gh* §§15.2.2 and 14.1 and below, §20.1.

553 The Arabic text only gives the beginnings of the lines, which have here been given in full.

554 Writers on poetic metrics mention such extra-metrical irregularities in early poetry; but they would never allow it in later verse.

555 This line, describing a beautiful woman, has received much commentary. One notes that the poet fails to settle the question, unless the answer is subsumed in his words "all these are good."

556 This reading would make the meter more regular.

557 Root *N-Ḍ-W*, forms II and I, respectively.

558 Root *N-Ḍ-Ḍ*.

559 In early poetry the second and sixth feet of *ṭawīl* are sometimes SLSL (as in *wa-qad naḍat*) instead of SLLL (as in *wa-qad naḍḍat*); in later, urban poetry this is extremely rare.

560 According to the commentators the Yemenis used to write deeds and covenants on palm leaves.

561 The sixth foot of this verse is again SLSL instead of SLLL; moreover, the penultimate foot is SLL, which is highly unusual in this shortened form of *ṭawīl*, which almost always ends with SLS SLL. The two following lines have the same irregularity.

562 The poet, riding his dromedary, compares it to sitting on an ostrich.

563 The metrical irregularity is found in the third foot (SLSL instead of LLSL, extremely unusual in the *basīṭ* meter). The "two men" are father and grandfather of the addressee, Harim ibn Sinān.

564 A tentative translation of the somewhat obscure *idhā faniya wa-qāraba*.

565 From the famous *Muʿallaqah*; for the story connected with this verse, see below, §20.1.

566 As quoted, *alā rubba yawmin laka minhunna ṣāliḥin*, has a second foot SLLS, instead of SLLL, which is extremely rare. An alternative version, *alā rubba yawmin ṣālihin laka minhumā* (with a pronominal suffix referring to only two women instead of more), is probably an attempt by a transmitter to remedy the fault.

567 The particle *mā* has many functions; sometimes it is considered *zā'idah*, "redundant," in which case it may be "preventing" (*kāffah*) the influence of a preceding particle. Thus one finds *innamā huwa* (nominative), even though the particle *inna* normally governs the accusative.

568 If *mā* is *zā'idah* but not *kāffah*, it has no influence at all, and in this case *yawm* would take the same genitive case as the word *yawm* in the first hemistich.

569 In the quoted line, the lightened form *siyamā* ("partic'lar") is the only possible reading, whereas both forms scan correctly in Imru' al-Qays's line.

570 The consonants *w* and *y* are considered "weak" because in various circumstances they change into the long vowels *ū* and *ī*, or disappear altogether.

571 The great majority of classical Arabic poems have monorhyme (*aaaaaa. . .*). Stanzaic or strophic forms (with rhyme schemes such as here: *aaaab ccccb ddddb*) do not occur until later in Islamic times, notably in the Hispano-Arabic *muwashshaḥ* ("girdle poem") and *zajal*, with their hotly debated similarity to the Provençal poetry of the troubadours. It is utterly unlikely that Imru' al-Qays should have composed the present poem.

572 The Sheikh will later meet some *rajaz* specialists in a less posh part of Paradise, see below, §20.2.

573 The poet's camel.

574 The poem rhymes in *-āmī*, so that *ḥarāmū* would not give a proper rhyme. Ḥadhām and Qaṭām are women's names; they are among a number of names and nouns of the pattern $C_1aC_2āC_3$ that are indeclinable and end in *-i* (omitted in pausal forms in prose but in poetry usually lengthened to *-ī*). In a list of all these forms (al-Suyūṭī, *Muzhir*, ii, 131–34) the form *ḥarāmi* does not occur.

575 The Abbasids (from 132/750).

576 The poet says that his camel is so fast that that there seemed to be hardly any distance between places remote from one another. The verse ends in *irmāmū*, again with the rhyme defect called *iqwāʾ*.

577 "Adjacency" (linguists would speak of "attraction") happens in Arabic when an adjective receives an improper case ending "attracted" from an immediately preceding word, rather than from the word it qualifies; a well-known example from Imru' al-Qays's *Muʿallaqah* is *kabīru unāsin fī bijādin muzammalī* ("an elder tribesman wrapped in a striped cloth"), where *muzammal* ("wrapped") has attracted the genitive case of *bijād* ("cloth") although it qualifies *kabīr* ("elder tribesman"), nominative.

578 *Irmāmī*, "my Irmām," would rhyme perfectly but sound strange.

579 A verse from an obscene passage in a longer poem; the sense is not wholly clear. Saʿd Allāh and Judhām are names of tribes; the words are a proverb. The syntax would require a nominative *Judhāmū* but the rhyme demands *Judhāmī*, either genitive or, oddly, "my Judhām."

580 The Helpers (*al-Anṣār*) are those Medinans who supported the Prophet after the Hijra.

581 A play on words: *jandal* means "rock, stone."

582 A near-quotation of Q Maryam 19:70; one must assume that the pre-Islamic Imru' al-Qays has heard some Qur'an in Hell.

583 The words "The Sheikh says," have been added, for it is unlikely that the poet is still speaking: not only is what follows more characteristic of the Sheikh than of the poet, it is also difficult to explain how the

sixth-century AD poet could know a verse by a poet who lived much later (see the next note). Instead of *ankara* "he disapproved" (Bint al-Shāṭiʾ's edition) we read *unkiru*.

584 al-Mughīrah ibn Ḥabnāʾ (d. 91/710); the verse is quoted in Sībawayh's grammar.

585 Instead of Ḥārithah.

586 Personal names, even if indefinite in form, are syntactically definite; personal names are normally derived from (indefinite) nouns, which are therefore original; e.g., *muḥammadun*: "a much-praised person," *ḥārithatun*: "someone who cultivates much land," giving the personal names Muḥammad(un), Ḥāritha(tu).

587 The following two quotations have been taken from his *Muʿallaqah*.

588 The meaning of these words (literally, "a marked, bright thing") is uncertain; the commentators generally seem to prefer to interpret them as "(wine I bought) for minted cash" but also give "(which I drunk) from a polished cup," "(bought) for a camel treated with tar (i.e., protected against mange)," and "in a decorated garment" as possible meanings. Below, the poet shows his indifference to the matter.

589 The opening hemistich of the *Muʿallaqah*.

590 The reading and interpretation of the last sentence is rather obscure and the editor gives several possibilities.

591 The lines are from a eulogy on Abū Dulaf, a general and patron of literature. The meaning is that the patron's noble ancestors would already have "exhausted" panegyric poetry; there may also be an allusion to the fact that Abū Dulaf was himself an able poet.

592 It is said that ʿAntarah composed this poem when still a slave. His father had beaten him when Sumayyah, his wife, had claimed that ʿAntarah had tried to seduce her; but then she pitied her stepson, shedding tears.

593 It is assumed that in the first half of this line the father is addressed. If, in the second half, one reads *ʿadhābuki*, as given by the editor, the poet addresses Sumayyah (whose "torment," is to see ʿAntarah as a beaten slave); if one reads *ʿadhābuka* (as, e.g., in al-Baṭalyawsī, *Sharḥ al-ashʿār al-sittah al-jāhiliyyah* and Ahlwardt's *The Divans*) the whole

verse is addressed to the father, in which case *ʿadhābuka* means "the punishment coming from you."

594 From the *Muʿallaqah*; the poet addresses his beloved, ʿAblah.

595 The normal verb for "to love" uses form IV of the root *Ḥ-B-B*, the passive participle of which is *muḥabb*; nevertheless, the common word for "loved," *maḥbūb*, is derived from the base stem (I) of the verb even though this is seldom used.

596 The form *iḥibbu*, for *uḥibbu*, is irregular; the prefix vowel *i* (instead of *u*) is found in some ancient forms, remains of old Arabic dialect forms (and common in modern Arabic dialects). *Pace* the author, the verse is not quoted in Sībawayh's grammar; it is found, anonymously, in various other sources, e.g., Ibn Qutaybah, *ʿUyūn*, iv, 43; Ibn Yaʿīsh, *Sharḥ al-Mufaṣṣal*, ix, 47; al-Baghdādī, *Khizānat al-adab*, vii, 273, xi, 459.

597 Instead of Mughīrah, a common man's name.

598 In other words, the form *iḥibbu* in the quoted verse is a variant of *uḥibbu* (form IV), not of a non-existent **aḥibbu* (form I).

599 The verse has been attributed to Ghaylān ibn Shujāʿ al-Nahshalī.

600 Or "nearer than ʿUbayd and Marshaq;" the sense is not clear. Other sources (al-Mubarrad, *al-Kāmil*; Ibn Manẓūr, *Lisān al-ʿArab* s.v. *Ḥ-B-B*) have Mushriq instead of Murshaq.

601 Q Āl ʿImrān 3:31, the normal form being *yuḥbibkum*; according to other sources (e.g., al-Mubarrad, *al-Kāmil*), Abū Rajāʾ read *yaḥibbakum*. Abū Rajāʾ ʿImrān ibn Taym al-ʿUṭāridī died 105/723–24.

602 A poem is very often compared to a string of pearls; the Arabic for "stringing," *naẓm*, also means "versifying, making poetry."

603 He speaks of his love. Both poems are found in the old anthology *al-Mufaḍḍaliyyāt* (see Lyall's annotated translations, *The Mufaḍḍalīyāt*, ii, 327–41).

604 These lines and the following four lines are from the first-mentioned poem. Rabīʿah is the beloved's clan; Tharmadāʾ, its location uncertain, is apparently far away. Several pre-modern commentators suggest this could mean that the "well" is a grave: she will never come back and die in Tharmadāʾ.

605 Literally, "frown."

606 Instead of "their ailments" one could interpret it as "diseases caused by women." A medieval commentator glosses it as "women's characters."

607 The poem was composed on the occasion of a battle (the Battle of 'Ayn Ubāgh) that took place in AD 554 between the Ghassānid king al-Ḥārith al-Aʿraj and the Lakhmid king al-Mundhir ibn Māʾ al-Samāʾ of al-Ḥīrah. The poet's brother Shaʾs had been taken prisoner and the poem closes with an appeal to al-Ḥārith to free him. The petition was successful.

608 In *khabaṭṭa* the *t* of the suffix has been assimilated to the *ṭ* of the root; it would be difficult to do otherwise, although the Sheikh seems to take a different view. Here the word is spelled with *ṭṭ*, although the usual spelling would be *khabaṭta*.

609 For yet another interpretation, see Sells, *Desert Tracings*, p. 18: "It'll take you up and spin you around."

610 The long vowel *ū* is analyzed (and written) as *uw*.

611 All available sources have *yahdī*, which makes sense, unlike *yahdhī* ("he raves[?]").

612 An allusion to the opening of his *Muʿallaqah*: "Wake up girl, get your bowl, give us our morning drink!" (what follows makes it clear that wine rather than milk is intended).

613 The rhyme word, *jaraynā*, jars; all other lines end correctly in *-īnā* or *-ūnā*.

614 The number of verses in 'Amr's *Muʿallaqah*, in the current redactions, fluctuates between 93 and 115.

615 See, e.g., Q Anʿām 6:70, Yūnus 10:4 and passim.

616 Referring to the second line of 'Amr's *Muʿallaqah*: "(Wine) mixed, as if containing saffron, / when the water mingles with it; hot."

617 The former explanation derives *sakhīnā* from the root *S-Kh-Y*, with a pronominal suffix *-nā*, the latter from the root *S-Kh-N*.

618 Line 1 mentioned "the wines of al-Andarīn"; Qāṣirīn (not mentioned in the poem) is also said to be a place in Syria. The often-discussed ambiguity of the word *sakhīnā* is surely unintentional and it is obvious that it means "hot."

619 Such as “forget.”

620 Kaʿb ibn Māmah and the poet Ḥātim al-Ṭāʾī, both pre-Islamic, are proverbial for their generosity. On this idiomatic use of *wa-lā* in comparisons, which acquires the sense of “even more than,” see, e.g., Wright, *Grammar,* ii, 333.

621 The following verse is from his *Muʿallaqah.*

622 Some commentators think that the “wild ass” is an allusion to a particular tribe; they also think that the words “vassal” and “protectors” (both from the root *W-L-Y*) here stand for “kinsmen.”

623 The poem rhymes in *-āʾū,* but one verse ends in *samāʾī.*

624 The rhyme words are *Ẓamyā* and *aḥyā,* although strictly speaking they should both end in *-aʾ,* with glottal stop (a consonant). A final glottal stop, when not followed by a vowel (as in al-Ḥārith’s poem) tends to disappear.

625 The imperative *ʿish* (“live!”) has a short *i* because a long vowel in a closed syllable is not normally allowed in Arabic phonology. With the addition of the emphatic suffix *-an* the long *ī* should be restored; but this would be unmetrical here.

626 The second vowel in *tashaʾ* (of the verb *shāʾa - yashāʾu*) is short only because of the closed syllable. With the addition of the feminine suffix the length should be restored, which, again, would not scan here.

627 Leaving a she-camel with some milk in the udder was supposed to make them conceive. Rather, says the poet (in a following verse), the milk should be offered to guests; after all, the animal might be stolen from you before it gives birth.

628 Letting a camel die in this manner may have been a kind of sacrifice; it was seen as an indication that the pre-Islamic Arabs believed in the Resurrection.

629 The word *buhm* is explained in the text as meaning *ghurl,* “uncircumcised (pl.).” This is a mistake on the part of al-Maʿarrī, based on a misinterpretation of a hadith in the collection of Aḥmad ibn Ḥanbal, according to which the Prophet said that people at the Resurrection will be “naked, uncircumcised, and *buhm,*” a word he then explains as “without having anything with them.” This explanation, in its turn,

is not confirmed by the dictionaries (the singular *abham* meaning "speaking a foreign language").

630 With Ṭarafah the Sheikh completes his series of meetings with the seven poets of the *Muʿallaqāt*. The *Muʿallaqah*, from which the five following lines are taken, is famous for its long and detailed description of the poet's camel.

631 Or more literally "nephew," *ibn akhī*. Does this mean that Ibn al-Qāriḥ and Ṭarafah are somehow related, belonging to the same tribe (Ḍubayʿah, Qays ibn Thaʿlabah)? The Sheikh's family seems to have been obscure (Blachère, *Analecta*, p. 432). Or is *akh* simply "friend," with *ibn* added because Ṭarafah died so young?

632 The *maysir* game is played with marked arrow shafts. The poet hopes for his arrow to "reply," i.e., to come out winning. "Scorched": to harden the shafts; "beside the fire": they are playing in winter.

633 Since the particle *an* ("that") is absent, Sībawayh reads *aḥḍuru*, indicative rather than subjunctive.

634 By al-Akhwaṣ al-Yarbūʿī (or al-Riyāḥī; d. ca. 50/670). The point is that the genitive *nāʿibin* ("croaking") can only be justified by an implied *laysa bi-* "is not."

635 This expression is unclear.

636 The meaning of the last line of this fragment (not found in Ṭarafah's collected verse) is unclear; there is a reference to the game of *maysir*.

637 Bint al-Shāṭiʾ is mistaken in thinking it was about a matter of rhyme (a form of *sinād*: in a poem with a rhyme ending in a consonant the preceding short vowels *i* and *u* may be freely used, but they should not be mixed with *a*, even though this is not uncommon in early poetry). Rather, it is about meter: the mixing, in the last foot of a verse or hemistich, of LL (*taʿṣir, kallam, murghim*) and SSL (*-ḥu yasar, -ba ṣamam, malikun*); cf. Ibn Qutaybah, *Shiʿr*, pp. 72, 102–3, on the *mīmiyyah* by al-Muraqqish.

638 Needless to say, the poets lived long before al-Khalīl.

639 i.e., his *Muʿallaqah*.

640 Q Jinn 72:15.

641 The verse is about a she-camel; it is said to contain three loan words from Persian or Greek.

642 See above, §7.3.

643 Literally, "when al-Munakhkhal will return," a proverbial expression for something that one does not expect to happen. Al-Munakhkhal al-Yashkurī, a pre-Islamic poet, was suspected by king al-Nuʿmān of al-Ḥīrah of having an affair with his wife, al-Mutajarridah (see above, §6.5). Al-Munakhkhal disappeared and was never seen again; perhaps he was buried alive.

644 Literally, "knotted." The sense is not wholly clear. Perhaps there is a connection with *ḥisāb al-ʿaqd/ʿuqad*, dactylonomy; or the origin has to be sought in magic or superstition, as the English "keeping one's fingers crossed."

645 The proverb is explained in different ways: either Darim was killed but his death was not avenged; or he was taken prisoner to be killed at the orders of al-Nuʿmān, but he died on the way.

646 The verse describes a pair of onagers; the male is so closely behind the mare that his head looks like a pack-saddle on her croup.

647 The normal form is *qasṭal*; lengthening the second produces a pattern normally found only for roots of the type $C_1C_2C_1C_2$, such as *zalzāl* ("earthquake").

648 Zuhayr is said to be short for Zuhayrah, a woman's name.

649 A play on words (*nasiya* "to forget", *nasā* "heel tendon").

650 From a long supplicatory ode addressed to an Umayyad prince; for a translation of the complete poem see Stetkevych, *The Poetics of Islamic Legitimacy*, pp. 121–28.

651 Literally, "O God, give (us) life!"

652 On the "rain stars" see above, *Gh* §3.8.2.

653 Wine (*khamr*) being feminine in Arabic, such metaphors are rife in Bacchic verse.

654 "She" is an amour of the caliph, a Christian girl.

655 The word *daskarah* can mean "village, hermit's cell, tavern"; the last has been chosen in view of the caliph's character.

656 *Asarra* has two opposite meanings: "to keep secret" and "to divulge, reveal." The former does not make sense here (but the speaker may be intentionally equivocal).

657 Abū Sufyān (Yazīd's grandfather) led the victorious anti-Muslim forces at the Battle of Uḥud.

658 See above, *Gh* §15.2.8.7 on the undecided battle of Ṣiffīn and its aftermath, which brought Yazīd's father to power.

659 A common nickname of the devil, as is the one that follows.

660 Animals are slaughtered at the Muslim "Feast of Sacrifice" (*ʿīd al-aḍḥā*) or "Major Feast" (*al-ʿīd al-kabīr*).

661 Part of the Muslim call to prayer. The motionless standing of wild asses or onagers and the braying of the male are often depicted in Bedouin poetry.

662 A proverb, explained with the story of a man who angrily broke his new bow, thinking he had repeatedly missed his target in the dark, only to discover the next morning that he had killed five onagers. To spite himself he cut off his thumb.

663 The grammarians have discussed the unusual accusative used for the vocative, and the form *awāqī* (from **wawāqī*).

664 The verse is quoted in Sībawayh's grammar; as the commentaries explain, the subject of "knocked down" is an implied "the horses," meaning "our cavalry." The second half may indicate the closeness of kinship (inbreeding as a reason for boasting of nobility).

665 The beginning of a lament on the death of his brother.

666 Several early poets were nicknamed after a rare or striking word they used.

667 A proverb. Lubad was the name of the last of the seven long-lived vultures of the legendary sage Luqmān, who was promised a lifetime spanning the consecutive lives of the birds.

668 Muraqqish was promised marriage to his cousin Asmāʾ, but during his absence she was married to another. Upon his return he was told she had died. Having found out the truth he went on his way to her, together with a servant of Ghufaylah. Too weak to proceed, he was

left in a cave and the man told others that Muraqqish had died. Asmāʾ, in her turn, discovered the truth and found her lover, who soon afterward died in her presence.

669 A famous collection of pre- and early Islamic odes (126 in one recension), compiled by al-Mufaḍḍal al-Ḍabbī (d. 164/780 or a few years later). A complete, richly annotated translation was published by C. J. Lyall.

670 Twigs of the *arāk* tree (for which Naʿmān, not far from Mecca, was famous) were used to clean the teeth and massage the gums.

671 The younger Muraqqish was the lover of Fāṭimah, daughter of King al-Mundhir ibn al-Nuʿmān of al-Ḥīrah. She ordered Hind bint ʿAjlān, her servant, to bring him to her.

672 Janāb ibn ʿAwf, a friend of Muraqqish, insisted on secretly taking his place with Fāṭimah one night. When Muraqqish gave in at last, and Fāṭimah became aware of the matter, she broke with Muraqqish.

673 "The two bitter things" have been explained as "poverty and old age," or "old age and disease," or "poverty and nakedness."

674 The following line is taken from the famous ode attributed to him called *Lāmiyyat al-ʿArab*, although the second/eighth-century poet and transmitter Khalaf al-Aḥmar is said to have fabricated it; opinions are still divided.

675 The line is from a passage about a wolf answered by other wolves; the standard version has "He complained, they complained; and then he turned, they turned . . ."

676 *Simākī* is apparently rain "caused" by the rain stars called al-Simāk, which are associated with the sign of Libra (September/October).

677 Translation uncertain.

678 The Qurʾanic word *al-furqān* (of uncertain meaning, see R. Paret, entry "Furḳān" in *EI2*) is here used for the Qurʾan itself. The following verse is Q Ṭā Hā 20:115.

679 The roots are different (*ʾ-N-S* "human", *N-S-Y* "forget") but especially in some derived forms they can be confused.

680 Abū Tammām.

681 Q Baqarah 2:199.

682 Q Ḥajj 22:55. Standard Arabic would be *al-bādī* (the word has also been interpreted as "Bedouin, dweller in the desert").

683 One would expect it to be *unaysān*, which could not be confused with the root *N-S-Y*. Obviously, the Basrians are correct in rejecting the etymological connection between "human" and "forgetting," even though the Sheikh does not follow them.

684 An image for something that cannot be gotten rid of.

685 These lines are often quoted and ascribed to Adam, theologians being on the whole more gullible than philologists.

686 Presumably Abel's.

687 *Malīḥī* instead of *malīḥū* produces a faulty rhyme.

688 i.e., reading *bashāshata l-wajhu l-malīḥū* (even though normal syntax requires *bashāshatan*).

689 *ʿAmru lladhī* should in normal syntax be *ʿAmrun-i lladhī*. This ʿAmr is better known as Hāshim, "the bread crumbler;" he was the Prophet's great-grandfather. The epithet "Hāshimī" has been used through the centuries until today by those claiming descent from him. In most sources the verse is attributed to Ibn al-Zibaʿrā.

690 cf. Q Zumar 39:32: «But who does greater wrong than he who lies against God and denies truth when it comes to him?»

691 cf. Q Nūḥ 71:17–18, «And God has made you grow from the earth; then He will make you return to it.»

692 There is a pre-Islamic tale about a snake ("She of the Rock") who killed a man but afterward struck a deal with his brother, agreeing to pay him a dinar every other day as blood money. Al-Nābighah al-Dhubyānī refers to the story in the poem quoted below, which is paraphrased by al-Maʿarrī.

693 This seems to be the sense; the normal meanings of *man kafara* and *mu'min* are "he who is an unbeliever" and "believer," respectively, and probably play a part here as well.

694 The brother's grave.

695 Taking *al-barr* to refer to God; alternatively, "for a righteous person there is a watchful eye."

696 Q An'ām 6:96. Variant readings crept in as a result of the early transmission of the Qur'an, aurally or in a script originally without diacritical dots (distinguishing between particular consonants) or vowel signs, which were introduced later. To put a halt to the proliferation of variants a limited number (seven or ten) of versions were recognized as canonical. The differences are mostly insignificant, without any serious consequences for the interpretation.

697 Q Āl 'Imrān 3:41.

698 Unlike al-Ḥasan's version, Abū 'Amr's is one of the canonical seven.

699 Through Ethiopian from Greek *euangelion* ("evangel"); it occurs twelve times in the Qur'an.

700 Q Nisā' 4:1.

701 Q Ibrāhīm 14:22.

702 Q Fāṭir 35:43.

703 Imru' al-Qays, *Dīwān*, p. 122; having revenged his father's murder he is no longer bound to the oath of abstention that he had sworn.

704 Pronouncing it as *ashrab*ᵘ, with a furtive vowel, the word counting as two long syllables rather than one long followed by two short.

705 The verses, also found in Sībawayh's grammar, are attributed to Abū Nukhaylah (second/eighth century).

706 *Ṣāhi*, though going further in shortening *ṣāḥibī* ("my friend"), is common and allowed, unlike *ṣāḥib*.

707 The meter does not require this balance and the final foot may be LLSL or SLSL.

708 Al-Mutanakhkhil.

709 In this meter SLSS (*ma'āriya*) is considered a fuller form than SLL (*ma'ārin*), but both are allowed.

710 In this opening verse of the poem *'alāmātin* ("marks") and *ka-taḥbīri l-* ("like woven patterns of") are both SLLL instead of SLSSL.

711 Or possibly "she," taking the woman to be the subject of *talin* rather than the wine.

712 The verse is from his *Mu'allaqah*.

713 Bint al-Shāṭi' ascribes them to Majnūn Laylā but they are not in his collected verse. The third line is found in the *Dīwān* of Ibn Muqbil.

714 Unidentified, as is the following one.

715 With the last, rare word (*ʿuthmān*) the author no doubt alludes to the killing of the third caliph ʿUthmān in 35/656, an event that lies at the root of serious rifts in early Islam.

716 Imruʾ al-Qays; the lines are from his *Muʿallaqah*.

717 In the story connected with the poem the poet sees some girls, including his beloved ʿUnayzah, bathing in a pool; he takes away their clothes and returns them only after they have let him admire their charms. Then he slaughters his camel and regales them on the meat.

718 In the *Muʿallaqah* the girls throw chunks of raw meat to one another, after the poet has slaughtered his camel. The rare word *tharmad*, a bitter herb, may have been chosen because the verb *tharmada* means "to undercook meat."

719 All of them *rajaz* poets from the first/seventh and second/eighth centuries.

720 There is a short lacuna in the text; the following words between square brackets must be supplied.

721 This saying of the Prophet is found in the Hadith.

722 The "leader" could be al-Khalīl or else Sībawayh (d. ca. 177/793), in whose *Kitāb* Ruʾbah is often quoted.

723 In the following purple passage the Sheikh employs rhymed prose and again displays his fondness of obscure words, not imitated here.

724 The Sheikh apparently condemns the use of the lowly meter for the lofty genre of eulogy and for the *qaṣidah* form (in which praise of the patron is often preceded by a camel description).

725 Q Ṭūr 52:23.

726 cf. Q Wāqiʿah 56:18–19, in a description of Paradise: «a cup from a spring; their brows will not be throbbing, to them no befuddling».

727 cf. Q Wāqiʿah 56:23.

728 Q Yūnus 10:10.

729 i.e., Ibn al-Qāriḥ's letter; the reply follows in *Gh* §21.1 and beyond.

730 At the beginning of Ibn al-Qāriḥ's letter, after the doxology.

731 i.e., an aversion to hypocrisy.

732 For the story of the cup, see Firdawsī's *Shāhnāma* (Abolqasem Ferdowsi, *Shahnameh: The Persian Book of Kings*, trans. by Dick Davies, 812–13). An Arabic version that may have been known to al-Maʿarrī is found in al-Thaʿālibī, *Ghurar akhbār mulūk al-Furs wa-siyarihim*, 691–94.

733 The precise meaning of the word *al-mughammas* (*nomen loci* of *ghammasa*, "to plunge into water") is unclear here. Bint al-Shāṭi' (who reads it as the active participle, *al-mughammis*) suggests "filth," because a location with this name near Mecca was used to relieve oneself (see Yāqūt, *Muʿjam al-buldān*, s.v.). If correct, such a reference would be somewhat odd, coming from the mouth of a pre-Islamic Iranian courtier. It is supported, however, by the expression used in al-Thaʿālibī's text (see preceding note) describing Shīrin as "a green plant of a dung-heap" (*khaḍrā' dimnah*, a well-known phrase for a beautiful woman of ill repute, see, e.g., al-Maydānī, *Majmaʿ al-amthāl*, 1:64–65: *iyyākum wa-khaḍrā' al-diman*). Nicholson translates "who will enter Hell-fire" (*JRAS* 1902, 88); one could connect it with *ghamūs* (Ibn Manẓūr, *Lisān al-ʿArab*: "false oath" because "it plunges the swearer into sin and then into the Fire"). The verb *walaja*, used by al-Maʿarrī, fits this interpretation (cf. *walaja l-nār*, "entering Hell-fire," see A. J. Wensinck et al., *Concordance et indices de la Tradition Musulmane*, s.v. *W-L-J*).

734 To entice her lover.

735 Taking *musīrīn* to be derived from *asāra*, "to set in motion"; one would have expected a direct object.

736 Asad (which means "lion") was the name of several tribes; the one mentioned here is not the most famous of them, but a division of the south Arabian tribe of Shanū'ah. In this passage several of the many Arabic words for "lion" are used.

737 See al-Mubarrad, *Kāmil*, 1:163.

738 The poet is the pre-Islamic Khuwaylid ibn Murrah, known as Abū Khirāsh, see *Dīwān al-Hudhaliyyīn*, 1233 (in *Lisān al-ʿArab* (*N-J-B*), the poet is called ʿUrwah ibn Murrah).

739 The meaning of *laḥiqtu bi-l-hidr/hadr* is not wholly clear; it could also be connected with *hadara* "to be shed without retaliation (blood), be unavenged."

740 The following makes it clear that he refers to Ibn al-Qāriḥ's words *jaʿalanī fidāʾahū* (*IQ* §2.1).

741 This ending marks the genitive of an indefinite noun. In such expressions one would expect an accusative (*fidāʾan*); a genitive not dependent on a preceding noun or preposition is odd.

742 Anonymously in *Lisān al-ʿArab* (*F-D-Y*, which has *fidāʾan*, with an accusative; and *H-W-L*).

743 The forms *tubālah* and *tuhālah* are somewhat irregular; see *Lisān al-ʿArab* (*H-W-L*). The latter is found in Bint al-Shāṭiʾ's and other editions and also in Ibn Manẓūr, *Lisān al-ʿArab*, s.v. *H-W-L*, but under the root *F-D-Y* one finds *tahālah*.

744 Tentative translation; *murāfiʿ* has been connected with *rafʿ*, "nominative," but the form is unusual.

745 The verse is discussed in, e.g., al-Baghdādī, *Khizānat al-adab*, 6:181–82, where also some explanations are offered for the reading *fidāʾin*.

746 See Ibn al-Qāriḥ's letter, in *IQ* §2.1.

747 Or perhaps "for three or four days" (the word *layālī* , "nights" being understood).

748 Arabic Nūḥ. For this belief, often mentioned, see, e.g., *Lisān al-ʿArab* (*H-D-L*).

749 The passage is somewhat obscure. The author seems to say: a gazelle doe may be yearning for leaves of the *arāk* tree but does not tell the rider to give her some.

750 The context seems to require the addition of "being bereaved".

751 A verse by Kuthayyir. Kuthayyir, *Dīwān*, 279.

752 Quoted in dictionaries (Ibn Durayd, *Jamharah*, 526, 1049; Ibn Manẓūr, *Lisān al-ʿArab*, *Ḥ-Y-R*) as being recited (perhaps composed) by a woman while making her little son dance. On this genre, see Wiebke Walther, "Altarabische Kindertanzreime."

753 Literally, "how often was an idol given good luck."

754 Al-Maʿarrī compares Ibn al-Qāriḥ's excessive praise of him with the adoration of idols by pagans.

755 The verses are from his *Muʿallaqah,* an ode in which he praises two men, al-Ḥārith ibn ʿAwf and Harim ibn Sinān, for their peacemaking efforts between the tribes of ʿAbs and Dhubyān.

756 The Kaaba. Before Quraysh was the dominant tribe in Mecca, according to legend the ancient tribe of Jurhum controlled the sanctuary. In the Islamic tradition the Kaaba was first built by Ibrāhīm/Abraham and his son Ismāʿīl/Ishmael.

757 See al-Sukkarī, *Sharḥ ashʿār al-Hudhaliyyīn,* 1102. There are no indications that the poet was about to give up the ghost when he uttered the verse, as al-Maʿarrī suggests; perhaps he could not resist the rhyme of Sāʿidah and *ṣāʿidah.*

758 Reading (with the edition of al-Iskandarānī and Fawwāl) *wa-la-kullu*; the version in al-Sukkarī has *wa-li-kulli mā tubdī l-nufūsu mujarrabū*; see also Ibn Manẓūr, *Lisān al-ʿArab* (*S-R-F*). Bint al-Shāṭiʾ refrains from deciding between the two readings.

759 The following verses are from a poem composed in old age. He did not, however, keep his promise (see Abū ʿUbaydah, *Naqāʾiḍ Jarīr wa-l-Farazdaq,* 126–27).

760 The place near the Kaaba where Ibrāhīm is supposed to have stood when building the Kaaba.

761 The *ghūl* is a dangerous demon, either male or female, described by several early poets.

762 Proverbially they are bad parents, supposedly eating their offspring when they hatch, thinking them to be predators; see, e.g., al-Maydānī, *Majmaʿ al-amthāl,* 2:56–57 (*aʿaqq min ḍabb*). Other negative sayings are *akhabb min ḍabb* and *akhdaʿ min ḍabb* (both meaning "more deceitful than a lizard"); cf. al-Ābī, *Nathr al-durr,* 6:195–96, 201–2.

763 There are many beliefs, usually negative, about the hyena (see F. Viré, entry "ḍabuʿ" in *EI2, Supplement,* 173–76), but it is unclear what is meant here. Possibly it alludes to the saying *aḥādīth al-ḍabuʿ istahā* ("the hyena's stories to its arse"), explained as its habit to wallow in

the dirt, then squat and "sing" incomprehensible things (al-Maydānī, *Majma'*, 1:262).

764 There is a play on the two unrelated meanings of the root *D-R-S*: "to learn" and "to thresh."

765 Literally "Abyssinian," dark meaning lush with vegetation.

766 Reading *al-makhzūnah*, following Nicholson (*JRAS* 1902, 815), which seems to make more sense than *al-maḥzūnah* ("a sad woman"), found in all other editions.

767 These "birds" were noble black camel mares belonging to the pre-Islamic king al-Nuʿmān ibn al-Mundhir (thus, instead of al-Mundhir), who, it is said, gave the poet al-Nābighah al-Dhubyānī one hundred of them. See, e.g., al-Jāḥiẓ, *Ḥayawān*, 3:418, 5:233; al-Iṣfahānī, *Aghānī*, 9:29, 39; Ibn Manẓūr, *Lisān al-ʿArab* (*ʿ-Ṣ-F-R*).

768 Bint al-Shāṭiʾ interprets *al-rākidah* as referring to one of the three stones that hold up a cauldron. The word *al-rākidah* can also refer to the cauldron itself (al-Marzūqī, *Sharḥ Dīwān al-Ḥamāsah*, 1679). But the sense is not wholly clear. More likely, it means "the unmoving (earth)," for whenever al-Maʿarrī uses the word it seems to have this sense (*Ghufrān*, §2:: *min al-arḍ al-rākidah ilā l-samāʾ*; §30.4: *talʿanuhū l-arḍ al-rākidah*; §42.3: *ḥattā tuskinahū l-rākidah turbahā*; *Risālat al-Malāʾikah*, 54: *aʿazz sukkān al-rākidah*; *Risālat al-Hanāʾ*, 241: *abnāʾ al-rākidah jamīʿan*).

769 i.e., not followed by rain.

770 i.e., those who, notwithstanding, make an attempt to ascertain that I am a wise man, will make the bitter experience that I am not.

771 Apparently meaning, as Nicholson says, "the feeblest attack reduces me to helplessness."

772 In pre-Islamic times the lunar year was, it seems, prolonged periodically with an extra month, in order to fix the pilgrimage (*ḥajj*) in a suitable season; this practice was abolished in Islam. See A. Moberg, "nasīʾ," in *EI2*, 7:977. Here the expression is apparently used figuratively for doing something inappropriate.

773 i.e., those who, notwithstanding, make an attempt to ascertain that I am a wise man, will make the bitter experience that I am not. Instead

of *qatād* ("tragacanth," a thorny bush), as in all editions and tentatively adopted here, Nicholson has *qiyād* ("leading rope"), which perhaps deserves consideration.

774 The meaning of *takallafat'hu* and *li-tujirra (. . .) mā fī l-akhlāf* is not clear.

775 "When the acacia gatherer returns" is one of the many expressions meaning "never." A certain Yadhkur ibn Asad of ʿAnazah became proverbial because he went out gathering acacia leaves (used for tanning) but never returned; he fell into a well and his companion let him perish because Yadhkur refused to let him marry his daughter. See, e.g., al-ʿAskarī, *Jamharat al-amthāl*, 1:103–4.

776 Promising rain.

777 The phrase is rather obscure; the word *gh.rāb* is either *ghirāb*, "marvels" or, read as *ghurāb*, "boat, galleon," as Bint al-Shāṭiʾ suggests. But this post-classical word is unlikely to be used by al-Maʿarrī. If, however, *al-ʿuddah* ("equipment") is emended to *al-ʿuqdah*, one has an allusion to the proverbial expression *ālaf min ghurāb ʿuqdah*, "as attached as a crow to a palm grove," meaning a crow finding himself in a lush palm grove, unwilling to leave it (see, e.g., al-Maydānī, *Majmaʿ al-amthāl*, 1:126, al-Thaʿālibī, *Thimār al-qulūb*, 458). Here it would suggest that the Sheikh is a treasure-trove of literary scholarship. A major problem with this emendation is the fact that al-Maʿarrī consistently uses a "double" rhyme involving two consonants (*luzūm*) in his *sajʿ* in this epistle (*muddah* would therefore rhyme with *ʿuddah* but not with *ʿuqdah*). Yet another possibility, suggested by James Montgomery, is to take *ghurāb* in the sense of "edge (of a sword)," i.e., "he is like a tool (a whet-stone) for sharpening its edge."

778 i.e., I had almost killed myself.

779 Literally, "sword hilt," taken here as *pars pro toto*.

780 The word *naʿīsh* is ambiguous; here it has been taken as a synonym of *manʿūsh*, "raised upon a bier." It also could mean "revived, reinvigorated," but this seems to fit the context less easily.

781 *Mahd* means "cradle, bed; smooth ground." "Something else" may be a grave (cf. the expression *min al-mahd ilā l-laḥd*, "from the cradle to the grave").

782 The camel is metaphorical.

783 Translation and interpretation uncertain. Possibly *mā ʿalima* has to be be taken as standing for *ʿammā ʿalima*: "(who has forgotten) what he once knew."

784 *Abyāt al-maʿānī* means "verses with meanings or motifs (*viz.*, that need explanation)," as in works by Ibn Qutaybah (*Kitāb al-maʿānī l-kabīr*) and al-Ushnāndānī (*Maʿānī l-shiʿr*), where the present verses are not found, however. The first is quoted anonymously in Ibn Manẓūr, *Lisān al-ʿArab*, (*F-R-S*); both verses are quoted in al-Maʿarrī's *al-Fuṣūl wa-l-ghāyāt*, 463. The poet apparently mocks the unsavoury habits of the date-eaters.

785 The verses have been attributed to Jamīl; see al-Mubarrad, *Kāmil* (Hindāwī), 2:306 (*li-aʿrābī*); al-Washshāʾ, *Muwashshā*, 51 (Jamīl); al-Qālī, *Nawādir*, 207 (anon.); Ibn Jinnī, *Khaṣāʾiṣ*, 1:79 (Jamīl); Gabrieli no. CX.

786 Q Zukhruf 43:51.

787 Iraq and with it the Abbasid Caliphate were dominated by the Daylamite (Iranian) dynasty of the Būyids since the middle of the fourth/tenth century, until the Seljuk (Turkish) takeover in 447/1055, a few years before al-Maʿarrī's death. The Būyids were generally patrons of (Arabic) literature.

788 Wine cups with pictures of Persian scenes are often described in Arabic Bacchic poetry.

789 Arabic *marāzibah*, plural of *marzubān*, from Persian *marz-bān* ("march-holder").

790 For the verses, see his *Dīwān* (ed. Wagner), 3:184.

791 Wagner's edited text has *rāḥ* ("wine") instead of *ka's* ("cup"), but according to the critical apparatus of the edition the more reliable manuscripts all have *ka's*, as in the present version. Perhaps the glass cup is held in a gold container. The verse is often quoted in other sources, always with *rāḥ* (e.g., al-Mubarrad, *Kāmil*; Ibn Qutaybah, *Shiʿr*; Ibn al-Muʿtazz, *Ṭabaqāt*; Ibn Ṭabāṭabā, *ʿIyār*; al-Zajjājī, *Amālī*; Yamūt ibn al-Muzarraʿ, *Amālī*; al-Ḥātimī, *Mūḍiḥah*; al-Raqīq al-Qayrawānī, *Quṭb al-surūr*).

792 *Lahīdah*, described as "a soft kind of gruel, neither a soup that could be drunk nor thick so that it could be swallowed" (Ibn Manẓūr, *Lisān al-ʿArab*).

793 *Jaraj* ("rough ground") could be a corruption of *ḥaraj* ("narrowness" or "sin").

794 Majnūn Laylā.

795 Ru'bah ibn al-ʿAjjāj (d. 145/762) is one of the *rajaz* poets with whom Ibn al-Qāriḥ has a conversation in Paradise, see *Gh* §20.2. A certain Ubaylā ("little Ablā" or "sweet Ablā"), perhaps the poet's wife, mocks him for his old age, as described in a poem by Ru'bah (*Dīwān*, 13). Ru'bah's alleged love for her is not famous (he mentions several names in his love poetry but not her) and Ubaylā merely provides a suitable rhyme here.

796 The following verse is found in his *Dīwān*, 578.

797 Jamīl.

798 *ʿAdam*, "privation," is often used for "destitution, poverty." It can also mean "non-existence," but even with al-Maʿarrī's reputation for heresy this interpretation (as if a human soul did not exist between dying and resurrection) is probably to be rejected; however, it could possibly mean "death" here.

799 Tentative translation; the meaning of *maʿa l-qidam* is uncertain.

800 Bint al-Shāṭi' has changed her initial reading *min sharri khabī'in*, "(the body is truly) an evil thing when concealed," to *min sharrin khabī'un*, ("hidden from evil") which seems to fit the context better. There is a problem with this: even though the pausal forms of *khabī'un* and the following *sabī'in* would rhyme, al-Maʿarrī normally ensures that the rhymes have matching inflectional endings, as if in poetry, which means that *khabī'in* would be expected here.

801 There are allusions to the motifs often celebrated in heroic early poetry: capturing enemy women (*saby*) and drinking expensive wine (*sabī'*); al-Maʿarrī abhorred both women and wine.

802 The lines are by ʿĀmir ibn Ḥawṭ, an obscure poet of the tribe of ʿĀmir ibn ʿAbd Manāh ibn Bakr ibn Saʿd ibn Ḍabbah; they are found in Abū Tammām's celebrated anthology *al-Ḥamāsah* (see al-Marzūqī, *Sharḥ*

Dīwān al-Ḥamāsah, 1676; also al-Jāḥiẓ, *Burṣān*, 107). But the first hemistich is incorrectly quoted and al-Maʿarrī mistakenly substitutes a hemistich from a poem by ʿAbdah ibn al-Ṭabīb (d. after 20/641), see *al-Mufaḍḍaliyyāt*, 148. It should have been *wa-la-qad ʿalimtu la-taʾtiyanna ʿashiyyatun* ("I have come to know that surely an evening will arrive . . .").

803 Taking *qaṣrī* to mean "my palace" is not supported by the commentators, who do not see a play on words here. A Bedouin poet such as ʿAbdah ibn al-Ṭabīb would probably not refer to a palace.

804 The poet is Duwayd ibn Zayd ibn Nahd, said to have been a very early poet who lived for 456 years. In a Bedouin context, *bayt* means "tent" rather than "house." The lines are often quoted, see, e.g., Abū Ḥātim al-Sijistānī, *Muʿammarūn*, 16; Ibn Sallām, *Ṭabaqāt*, 28; Ibn Qutaybah, *Shiʿr*, 104.

805 See *IQ* §2.4–5.

806 The word *fitnah* (pl. *fitan*) can mean "charm, temptation, sedition, dissension, civil strife."

807 Q Māʾidah 5:116.

808 As Ibn al-Qāriḥ had explained in his *Epistle* (*IQ* §2.6.1), Abū l-Faraj al-Zahrajī, the state secretary, had asked him to deliver a letter from him to al-Maʿarrī; but the letter was stolen on the way by his traveling companion.

809 The Arabic puns with *ʿadīl* "traveling companion" and *mā ʿadala* "was unjust."

810 One of the many idioms for "for ever and always."

811 *Al-farqadān*: the two major stars of the Little Bear (α and β Ursae Minoris), including the Pole Star.

812 A remarkable number of early Arab robbers made poetry, see, e.g., the collection by ʿAbd al-Muʿīn al-Mallūḥī, *Ashʿār al-luṣūṣ wa-akhbāruhum.*

813 Literally, "going to highlands or lowlands."

814 Ibn al-Qāriḥ had pointed out to them that their library was full of heretical works; see *IQ* §2.6.2.

815 Proverbial expressions meaning "he put things in the right places." Al-Qārah was a tribe famous for their skill with bow and arrow, Dārīn

was a port in Eastern Arabia, where Indian musk was imported, and ʿĀmir ibn al-Ṭufayl was a poet and hero, a contemporary of the Prophet.

816 Ibn al-Qāriḥ (*IQ* §2.4) had used similar outlandish expressions (translated as "catastrophe, calamity, and casualty") to describe his misfortunes.

817 Al-Buḥturī mentions the river in four poems (*Dīwān*, 1074, 1135, 1230, 2267). Al-Ṣanawbarī wittily connects the name of the river with the croaking (*quwayqu, quwayq!*) of frogs (*Dīwān*, 385; for other poems on the river see 221, 357–59, 396, 465).

818 Poet unknown. The line is quoted anonymously in Ibn Hishām, *Mughnī l-labīb*, 1:411 and ascribed to a pre-Islamic man from the tribe of Bakr ibn Wāʾil in Abū Zayd al-Anṣārī, *Nawādir*, 153.

819 i.e., Saʿd took the camels to the well, but then, instead of helping them to drink, wrapped up and lay down to sleep; a proverb (see Abū ʿUbayd al-Bakrī, *Faṣl al-maqāl*, 347–48; al-ʿAskarī, *Jamharah*, 1:79–80) for not completing a job (but some say: for doing something effortlessly). The poet is said to be Saʿd's brother, Mālik ibn Zayd Manāh ibn Tamīm.

820 Abū ʿUbayd al-Bakrī, *Faṣl al-maqāl*, 169–70; al-Maydānī, *Majmaʿ*, 1:539. Another interpretation is ". . . for you are wearing sandals."

821 Abū ʿUbayd al-Bakrī, *Faṣl al-maqāl*, 357–58; al-ʿAskarī, *Jamharah*, 1:473.

822 Abū ʿUbayd al-Bakrī, *Faṣl al-maqāl*, 306; al-ʿAskarī, *Jamharah*, 2:207.

823 See, e.g., Ibn Manẓūr, *Lisān al-ʿArab* (*ʿ-F-L*); cf. Abū ʿUbayd al-Bakrī, *Faṣl al-maqāl*, 92; al-Maydānī, *Majmaʿ al-amthāl*, 1:145–46. Said by a woman to Ruhm bint al-Khazraj, her daughter, when she was scolded by the fellow wives of her husband and called *ʿaflāʾ* ("slut," literally "woman with a large clitoris," i.e., uncircumcised).

824 ʿAmr ibn Ḥumamah al-Dawsī, occasionally mentioned for his wisdom, as one of the pre-Islamic Arab "arbiters" and "soothsayers." The saying, also used by al-Maʿarrī in other works (*Risālat al-Ṣāhil wa-l-shāḥij*, 86–87, *al-Fuṣūl wa-l-ghāyāt*, 111), is not found in the standard collections of proverbs.

825 The second saying only in al-ʿAskarī, *Jamharah*, 1:146.

826 Ibn Qutaybah, *Maʿānī*, 753 and al-Maydānī, *Majmaʿ*, 1:205 have "One bereaved woman loves another."

827 For the verse and al-Aṣmaʿī's commentary ("It is like the saying 'One bereaved woman loves another,' as if he hears his voice and finds consolation in it"), see Ibn Durayd, *Jamharah*, 652 and cf. Ibn Qutaybah, *Maʿānī*, 753.

828 It is common in Islam to praise God also for one's misfortunes.

829 A pebble in a cup was used to divide the available water equally if it was scarce; see, e.g., al-Baṭalyawsī, *Sharḥ al-ashʿār al-sittah al-jāhiliyyah*, 91, on a verse by Zuhayr, and Jones, *Early Arabic Poetry*, 2:129.

830 To use as a strap or girth, see al-Fīrūzābādī, *Qāmūs*, s.v. *W-Ṣ-Y*: *al-waṣāh . . . jarīdat al-nakhl yuḥzamu bihā.*

831 Anonymously quoted in Sībawayh's *Kitāb* (1:162) and many other works; the poet is by some said to be al-Mulbid ibn Ḥarmalah al-Shaybānī (al-Sīrāfī, *Sharḥ abyāt Sībawayh*, 1:317). For the expression *ṣabr jamīl* cf. Q Yūsuf 12:18.

832 *Shākin* has been interpreted as "someone who complains," but there must be a connection with the expression *shākī l-silāḥ* (or *shākk al-silāḥ, shāʾik al-silāḥ, shawk al-silāḥ*—there is much confusion here) "armed to the teeth," since both trees are thorny.

833 The poet is Mālik ibn Asmāʾ ibn Khārijah (d. after 95/714), of the tribe of Fazārah. He addresses his brother ʿUyaynah, who, as he himself was, was in love with a slave-girl belonging to their sister, Hind.

834 Bint al-Shāṭiʾ has *al-ḥirfah*, as have al-Iskandarānī and Fawwāl, who gloss it as "*al-mihnah ay ḥirfat al-adab* (occupation, i.e., the profession of being a man of letters)"; but the context demands reading it as *ḥurfah*, "bad luck," though a pun with *ḥirfah* is probably intended.

835 These two persons are unknown and the reference is unclear.

836 Abū ʿUbaydah, like al-Aṣmaʿī, was summoned from Basra to Baghdad by Hārūn al-Rashīd; but his rival criticized him in the caliph's presence and Abū ʿUbaydah left angrily.

837 The following report alludes to his public humiliation by another grammarian, al-Kisāʾī (d. 189/805), see *IQ* §2.4 and *Gh* §4.1. Al-Kisāʾī, some say, then paid Sībawayh a large sum of money.

838 *Maẓālim*, "torts, grievances," refers to special extra-judicial tribunals set up by the rulers to investigate complaints of alleged wrongs.

839 The dictionaries define *lamūs* as "one of whose fatness one doubts" or "whose hump has to be felt (in order to check how fat it is)." The context, however, suggests something less negative than either of these. See Ibn Qutaybah, *Maʿānī*, 505, where the word is given a positive sense.

840 Anonymously in al-Jāḥiẓ, *Ḥayawān*, 1:13; al-Iṣfahānī, *Aghānī*, 14:349; al-Washshāʾ, *Muwashshā*, 6, etc.

841 Anonymously quoted in Thaʿlab, *Majālis*, 345; Ibn Dāwūd al-Iṣbahānī, *Zahrah*, 696; attributed to Khiyār al-Kātib in al-Ṣūlī, *Akhbār Abū Tammām*, 50.

842 The following verses are from one of his many invective poems on his main rival, Jarīr; see Abū ʿUbaydah, *Naqāʾiḍ Jarīr wa-l-Farazdaq*, 713.

843 All editions have *min āli Yadhbulī*, as if Yadhbul were a clan; but it is a mountain and the standard texts have *min haḍbi Yadhbulī*, "of the hills of Yadhbul" (e.g., Abū ʿUbaydah, *Naqāʾiḍ*, 713, also al-Farazdaq, *Dīwān*, 2:177 and other sources). It is hard to imagine that Abū l-ʿAlāʾ did not know that Yadhbul is a mountain.

844 Literally, "parasangs" (*farāsikh*, sg. *farsakh*, a distance of between three and four miles).

845 The reading *tuqṣī*, found in all previous editions of *al-Ghufrān*, has been emended to *tunḍī*, as found in the *Naqāʾiḍ* and the *Dīwān*.

846 From another, long poem by al-Farazdaq against Jarīr (Abū ʿUbaydah, *Naqāʾid*, 383), alluding to an incident in which al-Farazdaq and Jarīr were ordered by caliph Hishām ibn ʿAbd al-Malik to execute Byzantine prisoners-of-war. Jarīr carried out the order but al-Farazdaq, who had been given a blunt sword, bungled the execution.

847 Abū l-ʿAlāʾ greatly admired his poetry.

848 Arabic has special forms for the diminutive, all involving the sequence *-u-ay-*, as in *uhayl*, from *ahl* ("people") or *ḥubayyibah*, from *ḥabībah* ("beloved").

849 See al-Mutanabbī, *Dīwān*, 270. Bāqil is the name of a proverbial paragon of inarticulateness; when asked how much he had paid for

a gazelle he was carrying, he spread out his fingers and stuck out his tongue, meaning "eleven dirhams," thereby letting the gazelle escape. Indian numerals were adopted by the Arabs, greatly facilitating arithmetic, in the early third/ninth century.

850 Reading, with the *Dīwān*, 67, *ḥubayyibatā qalbā fu'ādā* instead of *ḥubayyibatā qalbī fu'ādī* as in Bint al-Shāṭi''s edition. They are two exclamations (*ḥubayyibatā* standing for *ḥubayyibatī* + suffix *ā*), as the commentators explain.

851 *Dīwān*, 691; the "little moron" is Kāfūr, the ruler of Egypt with whom the poet had fallen out. He says that he was forced to praise him in earlier poems.

852 *Dīwān*, 702, from another invective poem on Kāfūr, referring to the poet's nocturnal flight from Egypt.

853 *Dīwān*, 540. He represents himself as in a wrestling match with his weak poetic rivals.

854 The meaning of *mā ḥasuna bihā ma'lūfu l-rabʿ* is unclear. Perhaps he means that the frequent use of diminutives detracts from the customary high standard of the poet's verse, or (as James Montgomery suggests) that ordinary phrases are not rendered attractive by his use of the diminutive which might excuse its proliferation.

855 Q Shuʿarā' 26:225–26.

856 The poets.

857 Formally it is a singular, although syntactically it can be construed as a plural.

858 *Ahl* followed by the preposition *li-* or (as here) a genitive often means "worthy, deserving of," but the following quotation shows that this does not apply here.

859 The following lines are not found in his collected verse, or anywhere else; the modern editor quotes the two verses in the addenda (Ḥātim al-Ṭā'ī, *Dīwān, sharḥ Abī Ṣāliḥ Yaḥyā ibn Mudrik al-Ṭā'ī*, 102–3), without giving the source (they are probably taken from al-Maʿarrī's work). The identity of Ibn Masʿūd is unknown and the sense of the opening hemistich is unclear in the context.

860 A verse by al-Mukhabbal al-Saʿdī, who is said to have died at a great age during the reign of ʿUmar ibn al-Khaṭṭāb (23–35/644–56). It is quoted in Sībawayh's grammar (2:191) and many other sources. Qays ibn ʿĀṣim (d. 47/667) was a celebrated tribal leader famous for his magnanimity and wisdom.

861 Al-Kisāʾī, see, e.g., al-Marzūqī, *Sharḥ Dīwān al-Ḥamāsah*, 452.

862 In other words, *ahl* became *aʾl* (which is strictly *ʾaʾl*, with two glottal stops) and subsequently *āl*. Al-Maʿarrī prefers to derive *āl* from the root *ʾ-W-L*. See, e.g., the discussion in Ibn Manẓūr, *Lisān al-ʿArab* (*ʾ-H-L*). It is not impossible that there is an ancient etymological connection between *ahl* and *āl*.

863 See Ibn al-Qāriḥ's *Epistle* (*IQ* §2.7.2) about al-Mutanabbī ("that man"), imprisoned in Baghdad and claiming to be a prophet.

864 *viz.* al-Mutanabbī, usually interpreted as "the would-be prophet." See Heinrichs, "The Meaning of *Mutanabbī*." The following derivation from *nabwah* is no doubt fanciful but morphologically possible.

865 The word *mutadallih* is prompted mainly by the rhyme, but it is rather odd, as if he says that al-Mutanabbī and most people are bereft of reason when they are pious. To soften this, the translation has added "(generally)" and "(at times, however)." It is also possible that instead of *mutadallihan* one should read its near-synonym *mutawallihan* ("distracted," by the fear of God); the rhyming pair *mutaʾallih*/*mutawallih* is used below, §33.2.2.

866 Al-Mutanabbī, *Dīwān*, 263, describing himself.

867 *Dīwān*, 689. God "shamed His creatures" by letting them be ruled by a worthless man (Kāfūr); "some people" are heretics mentioned in the preceding verse ("the materialist, the agnostic and the atheist," in Arberry's translation, *Poems of al-Mutanabbī*, 116).

868 For different views on his lineage, see the editor's introduction to the *Dīwān*, 17–21.

869 In other words, the Prophet came when the Arabs were ripe for greater things. *Qaṣīd* does not have its *prima facie* meaning ("poems, odes") here. *Faṣīd* is blood tapped from a camel's neck and made

into a kind of black pudding, eaten when other food is scarce; see, e.g., *Mufaḍḍaliyyāt*, trans. Lyall, 318, 320 (no. 114 vs. 19); consuming blood is not allowed in Islam. Compare the expression (given in al-Zamakhsharī, *Asās al-balāghah*, *F-Ṣ-D*): *iqnaʿ bi-l-faṣīd wa-lā taqnaʿ bi-l-qaṣīd*, "Be content with black pudding and don't be content with thick marrow" (this is either meant to be a paradox or a corruption, *faṣīd* and *qaṣīd* having changed places).

870 Q Inshiqāq 84:23.

871 i.e., to their "heretical" ideas inspired by Greek philosophy and science.

872 The poem, with many differences, is quoted in Ibn Isḥāq's biography of the Prophet, *al-Sīrah al-nabawiyyah*, 2:29; see the translation by Guillaume in Ibn Ishaq, *The Life of Muhammad*, 352–53; and compare Nicholson in *JRAS*, 1902, 93. The poet is said to have converted to Islam but then apostatized.

873 The "bowls," as Bint al-Shāṭi' explains, probably are a metaphor for the Meccans slain and thrown into the well, here described as generous hosts.

874 In some late sources (Ibn Shākir, *Fawāt al-Wafayāt*, 4:257; al-Ṣafadī, *al-Wāfī*, 28:14) this verse, not in Ibn Isḥāq, is attributed to the Umayyad caliph al-Walīd ibn Yazīd (d. 126/744). Al-Maʿarrī, in a letter quoted in Yāqūt, *Muʿjam al-udabāʾ*, 3:187–88, quotes the poem and adds: "God curse the poet! It is said he is al-Walīd ibn Yazīd ibn ʿAbd al-Malik."

875 "Abū Kabshah's son" (here shortened to "Kabshah's son") was a derisive nickname of the Prophet among his opponents; Abū Kabshah is said to be a pre-Islamic worshipper of Sirius (Ibn Ḥabīb, *al-Muḥabbar*, 129).

876 The pre-Islamic Arabs believed that the spirit of someone whose death was unavenged appeared over his grave in the form of a kind of owl (*ṣadā* or *hām*). See Homerin, "Echoes of a Thirsty Owl: Death and Afterlife in Pre-Islamic Arabic Poetry."

877 He is al-Mutanabbī. Sayf al-Dawlah had granted him an estate near al-Maʿarrah, entitling him to its revenue.

878 A "bow" (*rakʿah*) stands for a sequence of movements in the course of the ritual prayer (*ṣalāh*), including a bowing of the body. The afternoon prayer should consist of four *rakʿah*s; allowances are made for exceptional circumstances such as travel.

879 He claimed to be a prophet.

880 Abū Bakr Muḥammad al-Khālidī (d. 380/990) and Abū ʿUthmān Saʿīd (or Saʿd) al-Khālidī (d. ca. 390/1000), poets and anthologists; some of their poetry and all of their prose works were composed in collaboration. They were employed as Sayf al-Dawlah's librarians.

881 The work mentioned here is not extant. His son Abū Muḥammad Yūsuf died in 385/995.

882 AD 915–16.

883 AD 933.

884 *Dīwān*, 17; he addresses a female censurer, a stock figure in poetry. The name of the real addressee of the poem is unknown.

885 The word *dahr* is "(infinite) Time," "Eternity," and often has the connotation "Fate." The hadith is found in standard collections such as those of al-Bukhārī and Muslim.

886 Q Jāthiyah 45:24; the words are said by unbelievers.

887 Here the word *zamān* is used, which is "time" that is not infinite. "Some people" includes Ibn al-Qāriḥ (see his *Epistle*, *IQ* §2.7.1) but he was not the first: the idea goes back to Aristotle. See, e.g., D. Mallet, entry "Zamān," in *EI2*, 9:434–38.

888 Bint al-Shāṭiʾ, in her fourth edition (followed by al-Iskandarānī and Fawwāl) reads *ḥadadtahū ḥaddan*, "You have given a definition," but there are no indications that he is addressing anybody, certainly not Ibn al-Qāriḥ (who is never addressed directly with the second person singular). The crucial vowel has been omitted in her ninth edition, and we read *ḥadadtuhū*, following Nicholson's translation (95) and Kaylānī's edition (224).

889 The line is not found in his *Dīwān*. Ḥabīb ibn Aws is Abū Tammām, who does not (*pace* Bint al-Shāṭiʾ) quote this line in his famous anthology *al-Ḥamāsah*. It is quoted anonymously in Ibn Qutaybah,

'Uyūn, 1:104, attributed to Sham'alah ibn Fā'id al-Taghlibī in al-Āmidī, *Mu'talif*, 141, and to al-A'shā al-Taghlibī (d. 92/710) in al-Iṣfahānī, *Aghānī*, 9:282 (about an incident involving Sham'alah). The caliph is said to be Hishām ibn 'Abd al-Malik. The misattribution to al-Akhṭal may go back to al-Ḥātimī (d. 388/998), see *al-Risālah al-Ḥātimiyyah*, 282.

890 A line quoted in Abū Tammām's *Ḥamāsah* (see al-Marzūqī, *Sharḥ Dīwān al-Ḥamāsah*, 1052), by Munqidh ibn 'Abd al-Raḥmān al-Hilālī, an early Abbasid poet from Basra, suspected of "heresy" (*zandaqah*).

891 On Abū Ṣakhr al-Hudhalī, see al-Sukkarī, *Sharḥ ash'ār al-Hudhaliyyīn*, 958 and Dmitriev, *Das poetische Werk des Abū Ṣaḫr al-Huḏalī*, 231. This book also contains a chapter (129–48) on time and *dahr* in early Arabic poetry and Abū Ṣakhr in particular.

892 See, e.g., Abū Tammām, *Waḥshiyyāt*, 220; al-Āmidī, *Muwāzanah*, 1:258; al-Jurjānī, *Wasāṭah*, 430; al-'Askarī, *Ṣinā'atayn*, 112. The name of the poet is unknown.

893 This seems to contradict "with the nose cut off" in the preceding (other versions do not have this contradiction). The motif of Time having a mutilated nose is known from other poems (Ibn Manẓūr, *Lisān al-'Arab*, *J-D-'*).

894 The sense of *wa-lawwā bi-l-'athānīni akhda'ā* is not wholly clear. Other sources have *wa-lawnan bi-l-'athānīni* (or *dhā 'athānīna*) *ajda'ā*, which, if anything, is even less clear.

895 Or possibly "to 'Amr and (my) sword." Al-Ḥusām is found as a proper name, though rarely.

896 cf. Q Baqarah 2:203: «Remember God during the appointed days.»

897 An *'alam* (pl. *a'lām*) is (among other things) a landmark, a mountain, a beacon, or an elevated place where rites and ceremonies are performed.

898 Literally, "by which the skin has so often been pierced (as if by ticks)"

899 In Arabic, *al-Dahriyyah*, those who believe in *dahr*, eternal time, and therefore deny the existence of a creator; the term is sometimes translated as "Materialists."

900 On the poet Bashshār ibn Burd's heresy, see *IQ* §3.1 and *Gh* §17.2.1–2.

901 cf. al-Iṣfahānī, *Aghānī*, 3:249.

902 See al-Iṣfahānī, *Aghānī*, 3:243, 245. Yaʿqūb ibn Dāwūd (d. ca. 186/802) was vizier under the caliph al-Mahdī. It is said that al-Mahdī had Bashshār executed because of these verses; other reports assert that he was killed because of his alleged heresy.

903 For a lampoon by Bashshār on Sībawayh, see *al-Aghānī*, 3:210, al-Marzubānī, *Nūr al-qabas*, 96.

904 Bashshār's verse uses the unattested word *ghazalā*, of a rare pattern found in the words he adduces in support: *bashakā* ("nimble") and *jamazā* ("fast").

905 See al-Iṣfahānī, *Aghānī*, 3:209; al-Marzubānī, *Nūr al-qabas*, 95–96. The plural used by Bashshār is in fact in the dictionaries (with *anwān*) and analogous with, e.g., *ghūl* ("ghoul") pl. *ghīlān*, *ʿūd* ("piece of wood, lute") pl. *ʿīdān*, and *ḥūt* ("large fish") pl. *ḥītān*.

906 The extremely influential grammar by Sībawayh is simply known as *Sībawayh's Book*. For the plural *nīnān* see 2:188.

907 The verse is more firmly attributed to him, see al-Jāḥiẓ, *Ḥayawān*, 5:601; al-Iṣfahānī, *Aghānī*, 12:305. The verse (not merely its second half) is quoted in Sībawayh's *Kitāb*, 2:409.

908 *Gh* §17.21–2 Bashshār is found in Hell.

909 As Bint al-Shāṭiʾ explains, al-Maʿarrī qualifies the imagined adventures of Ibn al-Qāriḥ with the phrase "if God wills" at the beginning of his *Epistle* (*IQ* §3.1).

910 Muḥammad ibn Dāwūd ibn al-Jarrāḥ (d. 296/908) is the author of *Kitāb al-Waraqah*, on early Abbasid poets, so named because each entry takes one folio or less. In the published edition no poet is explicitly called a heretic (*zindīq*).

911 The heretic friend was the libertine poet Muṭīʿ ibn Iyās (d. 169/785), boon companion of al-Walīd ibn Yazīd; see al-Iṣfahānī, *Aghānī*, 13:294–95. The host is not named.

912 According to the Shi'ites ʿAlī ibn Abī Ṭālib, the fourth caliph, father of al-Ḥasan and al-Ḥusayn, should have been the first, but his rightful succession was usurped by Abū Bakr and ʿUmar, the first and second caliphs.

913 cf. Ibn al-Qāriḥ's *Epistle, IQ* §3.1 and see Abū Nuwās, *Dīwān*, 1:210, 5:463.

914 The criticism concerns the expression "the sophistication of a heretic." See Abū Nuwās, *Dīwān*, 1:211: "Abū Bakr [al-Ṣūlī] said: 'By God, someone who does not believe in God Almighty has neither reason nor sophistication!'"

915 He is identified as the poet Yaḥyā ibn Ziyād al-Ḥārithī (d. between 158/775 and 169/785), see Abū Nuwās, *Dīwān*, 1:210–11; Sezgin, *Geschichte*, 2:467–68.

916 The verse sins against grammar. Bint al-Shāṭi' reads *muḥaddithuh malikin*, apparently considering it a lengthening (for the sake of the meter) of *muḥaddithu malikin* ("someone who speaks with a king"). The *Dīwān* has *muḥaddithah malikin*, as has Ibn Qutaybah, *Shiʿr*, 818 (perhaps one should rather read *muḥaddithat malikin*). Both have *waṣīf* ("servant," either male or female) instead of *nadīm*; the verse describes a girl.

917 Imru' al-Qays, *Dīwān*, 122; instead of *ashrabu* ("I'll drink") the verse has *ashrab*. The verse has been quoted before, *Gh* §19.2.4.

918 The verse has *Baydharah* three times, even though strictly this is possible only in rhyme position; the first and second should have been *Baydharatu*. This *rajaz* verse is quoted in Ibn Durayd, *Jamharah*, 63 (*B-T-T*) and 275 (*Ḥ-B-R*); the poet is unknown. Baydharah is apparently a name (see al-Maʿarrī, *Fuṣūl*, 354, for a man with this name; called Baydarah in al-Maydānī, *Majmaʿ*, 1:323); it may be a variant of *baydhārah* ("great talker").

919 The lines are found, anonymously, in Ibn Manẓūr, *Lisān al-ʿArab* (*Ṣ-D-ʿ* and *'-R-Ṭ*), in both instances with *dhi'b* ("wolf") instead of *ẓill* "shadow" (cf. Nicholson, in *Journal of the Royal Asiatic Society*, 1902, 101: "Often the wolf crouched and gathered himself to spring upon a gamesome buck . . .").

920 Again a pausal form, *daʿah*, instead of correctly *daʿata* or *daʿatun*.

921 Or an "added term" (*muḍāf*) followed by a "term added to" (*muḍāf ilayh*). This "possessive construction" forms a syntactic unit and the

first term can never be given a pausal form (which would in this case not be *muḥaddithuh* but *muḥaddith*).

922 See *IQ* §3.2.

923 The lines have also been attributed to Ṣāliḥ and to Abū l-ʿAtāhiyah, see al-Sharīf al-Murtaḍā, *Ghurar*; 1:145, Ibn Khallikān, *Wafayāt*, 4:34–35.

924 Q Anʿām 6:158: «On the day when one of the Lord's signs comes, belief will not avail a soul that has not believed before.»

925 See *IQ* §3.3.

926 If, instead of rebelling as a heretic, he had been a camel-herd he would not have had to kill himself, as he did after his defeat in 166/783, either with poison or by throwing himself, with family and followers, onto a large pyre.

927 Al-Ṣanādīqī ("the box maker"); see *IQ* §3.4.

928 AD 883–84.

929 Muḥammad.

930 Yaʿrub and his father Qaḥṭān are legendary ancestors of the "South Arabs"; the prophet Muḥammad belonged to the "North Arabs."

931 Running between al-Marwah and al-Ṣafā (two mounds at Mecca) forms part of the rites of the Hajj or pilgrimage, as does visiting the Prophet's tomb at Medina (originally called Yathrib).

932 Jibrīl and Jabrāʾīl (shortened in the following poem to Jabraʾīl for the sake of the metre) are the Arabic forms of Gabriel, the angel who serves as an intermediary between God and men.

933 According to other sources it was not he but his successor ʿUmar ibn al-Khaṭṭāb who had Rabīʿah ibn Umayyah flogged for drinking wine (al-Iṣfahānī, *Aghānī*, 15:21; al-Balādhurī, *Ansāb al-ashrāf*, 5:312–13, 382, 439). However, the poem quoted here mentions Abū Bakr.

934 "The people of protection" (*ahl al-dhimmah*) are Christians, Jews, and Zoroastrians, who are free to practice their religions in Islamic lands (with the exception of the Arabian Peninsula) on certain conditions, such as acknowledging Muslim suzerainty and paying a special tax.

935 Khaybar was a settlement some 150 km north of Medina, inhabited by Jewish tribes, taken by the Prophet in 7/628. ʿUmar (called by his

kunyah Abū Ḥafṣ in the poem) expelled them from Arabia in 20/641; see *EI2* s.v. "Khaybar" (L. Veccia Vaglieri). Sumayr ibn Adkan is not known from other sources. Yāqūt, who quotes this passage (*Muʿjam al-udabāʾ*, 3:165–66) suspects that the verses are in fact by al-Maʿarrī himself and adds that if they are not by him, the quotation is evidence of bad faith.

936 *Māqiṭ* can mean, among other things, "slave freed by a freedman" or "someone who hits with a stick."

937 Literally, "he who stands up," a term used by Shiʾites and other sectarians for a figure who will rise at the end of the world to restore justice on earth, not unlike the Mahdi (*al-mahdī*, "the rightly guided one").

938 *Walīd* means "infant."

939 Nicholson's translation, "a haughty will," is based on his reading *nāfijah*, and derided by Bint al-Shāṭiʾ. It is true that the rich rhyme consistently used by al-Maʿarrī requires accepting the reading *sābijah* as found in the manuscripts. Bint al-Shāṭiʾ refers to *sabābijah*, given in *Lisān al-ʿArab* as a plural and explained as "strong men from Sind [part of present-day Pakistan] and India who accompany the captain of a seafaring ship as its guards; sometimes they say *sābij*," the last word apparently meaning "strong." This reading assumes that the following obscure rhyme-word (on which see *IQ*, §3.5.1) is correctly read as *bunābijah*, which is not wholly certain. If the earlier suggestion *biyālajah* (from Persian *piyāla*, "goblet") is correct, the rhyme requires changing *sābijah* into, e.g., *sālijah* ("sucking, swallowing").

940 Unclear; Nicholson comments, "i.e., his sins in this world deprived him of the joys of Paradise" (but there is nothing to suggest that the "wine pitcher" is a heavenly one). Monteil interprets it as "he only left the wine pitcher in order to commit other sins."

941 Al-Walīd ibn Yazīd, *Dīwān*, 64–65. Lines 2–4 are found in al-Iṣfahānī, *Aghānī*, 7:46; al-Murtaḍā, *Ghurar*, 1:129; Gabrieli, "Al-Walīd ibn Yazīd," 48. The first line, with some differences, is found in Ibn Qutaybah, *Ashribah*, 57.

942 Nicholson, followed by al-Iskandarānī and Fawwāl, reads *khalīlay*, as a license for the vocative *khalīlayya* ("O my two friends"); here it has been taken as the object of the imperative. Nicholson believes *ʿabdalā* to mean "a slave" and oddly thinks that *izār* ("loin-cloth") means "cheek-down" (confusing it with *ʿidhār*) . Bint al-Shāṭiʾ and other Arab editors think it must be the name of a girl. However, ʿAbdal is a man's name (cf. the early Umayyad poet al-Ḥakam ibn ʿAbdal).

943 *Ḥattā yarkabū dīna l-ḥimārī*, found also in Ibn Qutaybah, *Ashribah*, 57; al-Murtaḍā, *Ghurar*, 1:129; and Yāqūt, *Muʿjam al-udabāʾ*, 3:188; but perhaps the original version was the one found in *Aghānī* and Gabrieli: *ḥattā yarkabū ayra l-ḥimārī* ("until they are mounted on a donkey's prick"). Compare Hamilton, *Al-Walīd and his Friends*, 122.

944 *Dīwān*, 92. Lines 1 and 2 (with different readings) in al-Mubarrad, *Kāmil*, 2:296; al-Iṣfahānī, *Aghānī*, 7:44; Gabrieli, "Al-Walīd," 57.

945 The pronoun "her" refers to a preceding line (not found here) mentioning his beloved Sulaymā (i.e., "sweet Salmā").

946 There is an untranslatable word-play on *wiṣāl* ("lovers' union") and *waṣala* ("to join; to give a present").

947 A broad coalition of opponents besieged al-Walīd in his palace al-Bakhrāʾ, where he was killed in 126/744.

948 Compare the versions in his *Dīwān*, 94–95; al-Iṣfahānī, *Aghānī*, 7:79; Gabrieli, "Al-Walīd ibn Yazīd", 52–53; and see the translation in Hamilton, *Al-Walīd and his Friends*, 157.

949 Three traditional Arabic female names often used in love poetry; cf. *Gh* §9.3.1

950 For his poem against fasting in Ramadan, see *IQ*, §3.5.2.

951 Meaning unclear; perhaps "he is wholly unimportant." It seems to echo Q Ḥajj 22:73, «*ḍaʿufa l-ṭālibu wa-l-maṭlūb* (Weak are the seeker and the sought)».

952 The base manuscript has *muḥẓirīn*, which does not make much sense; Bint al-Shāṭiʾ thinks the passive form (*muḥẓarīn*) may be better. However, "people have become being forbidden" does not seem satisfactory either. We propose to read either *mukhṭirīn* ("in

danger") or *mukhṭarīn* ("warned"), which also gives a better "rich" rhyme with *mufṭirīn*.

953 See also Yāqūt, *Muʿjam al-udabāʾ*, 3:189 (where Ibn Raghbān wrongly appears as Ibn Raʿyān); anonymous in Ikhwān al-Ṣafāʾ, *Rasāʾil*, 2:444 (with *wuʿidū bi-ukhrā*, "they are promised another," which looks more logical, and *mina l-sawāmi* instead of *mina l-suwāfi*).

954 He quotes the following lines in his *Kitāb al-Awrāq* (*Book of Folios*, here called *al-Nawādir*, *Anecdotes*), in the volume entitled *Ashʿār awlād al-khulafāʾ wa-akhbāruhum* (*The Poems of the Sons of the Caliphs and the Reports on Them*), 90.

955 The negative particle is not in the manuscripts; Bint al-Shāṭiʾ seems justified in arguing that the context demands it.

956 Q Yūsuf 12:87.

957 See *IQ*, §3.6. He came from Jannābah, a small town on the coast of southern Persia (Yaqūt, *Muʿjam al-buldān*, s.v.).

958 Q Najm 53:38.

959 There is a report that in pre-Islamic times the Kaaba was one of seven sacred buildings dedicated to the sun, the moon, and the five traditional planets (al-Masʿūdī, *Murūj*, 2:381); however, most reports connect the Kaaba with several pagan gods rather than one god or planet.

960 See *IQ*, §3.6.1, on the leader of the revolt of the Zanj, who claimed to be a descendant of ʿAlī.

961 These "well-known" lines and the following five lines have not, in fact, been found elsewhere.

962 It is not clear what he means by this. Were invalids and the chronically ill employed as schoolteachers? Or did schoolteachers suffer from chronic stress caused by their pupils' behavior?

963 The last expression, *wa-l-shamlu jāmiʿ*, possibly refers to the Last Day, as Nicholson thinks. It occurs in a famous poem by Qays ibn Dharīḥ (e.g., al-Iṣfahānī, *Aghānī*, 9:218), but without any eschatological connotation.

964 Q Hūd 11:107.

965 Some poetry of his is quoted by al-Thaʿālibī in his *Yatīmah* (2:217–18), but not the poem referred to here.

966 *Ṭawīlat al-wazn* would be an unusual expression for "of *ṭawīl* meter"; presumably it refers to either *ṭawīl* or *basīṭ*, both having lines of eight feet in their standard forms.

967 Q Baqarah 2:156.

968 See *IQ*, §3.6: Rakhamah and *raḥmah* differ only by one diacritical dot; likewise *bi-l-Zanj* and *bi-l-rīḥ* only differ by their dots.

969 i.e., of future events.

970 Q Naml 27:65.

971 See, e.g., Ibn Manẓūr, *Lisān al-ʿArab*, (*B-Ḥ-B-Ḥ*).

972 The year 424 began on 7 December 1032. The Mirdāsid ruler at the time in Aleppo was Naṣr ibn Ṣāliḥ Shibl al-Dawlah.

973 See al-Yaʿqūbī, *Tārīkh*, 2:452; cf. al-Marzubānī, *Muʿjam al-shuʿarāʾ*, 183.

974 i.e., "the band of Ghālib."

975 Ghālib means "someone who vanquishes or overpowers."

976 Aws ibn Ḥajar (see *Gh* §13.2.1). The line is from a famous elegy on Faḍālah ibn Kaladah (see al-Iṣfahānī, *Aghānī*, 11:72–73); the following hemistich is from a different elegy on the same person.

977 The word *bujar* literally means "swellings of the navel," but it is used in idiomatic expressions in the sense of "defects."

978 The image is possibly that of the destructive, grinding action of a quern or stone handmill.

979 Al-Ḥallāj means "the cotton carder" (which may have been his father's trade).

980 Al-Mādharāʾī was a friend of al-Ḥallāj; his uncle Abū Zunbūr had presented the caliph with a mule. Some people believed that the mule was substituted for al-Ḥallāj before his execution; see Louis Massignon, *The Passion of al-Hallāj, Mystic and Martyr of Islam*, 1:415, 592. See also al-Tanūkhī, *Nishwār*, 1:164 and 6:91–92 (= al-Khaṭīb al-Baghdādī, *Tārīkh Baghdād*, 8:141).

981 The sense is not wholly clear.

982 See the *rajaz* lines by al-ʿAttābī: "Prostrate yourselves to the evil monkey in its heyday (. . .) | And flatter him as long as you are in his power!," al-Jāḥiẓ, *Ḥayawān*, 1:355, cf. 7:166; Ibn ʿAbd Rabbih, *ʿIqd*,

2:443; al-Damīrī, *Ḥayāt*, 2:205; as a proverb: al-Maydānī, *Majmaʿ*, 1:452. Abū Nuwās said of the Barmakid family of viziers, "This is the time of monkeys, so submit: | Listen to them and obey!" (*Dīwān*, 2:51).

983 The word "(he) ki..ed it" is undotted in the base manuscript; in other manuscripts it appears as *qatalahū* ("he killed it"), a reading preferred by Kaylānī and Bint al-Shāṭiʾ, as does Monteil, whereas Nicholson, al-Iskandarānī/Fawwāl and Qumayḥah read *qabbalahū* ("he kissed it").

984 For the monkey, called Abū Qays, see al-Masʿūdī, *Murūj*, 3:265–66; al-Jāḥiẓ, *Ḥayawān*, 6:66.

985 See *IQ*, §3.8.1.

986 We take *fī l-quwwah* in the sense as used by the philosophers; both Nicholson ("the composition does not lack power") and Monteil ("dans sa force poétique") interpret it as referring to poetic quality.

987 The last foot of this meter (*mukhallaʿ al-basīṭ*) should be SLL, whereas *ilayy* would result in SL. The meter would be rectified by reading *ilayyī*, which is, however, a bad solecism (correct would be *ilayyā*, which would not rhyme with the other lines).

988 The verse is Q Ibrāhīm 14:22.

989 Instead of *muṣrikhiyya*.

990 In Arabic script, the signs indicating a short *a* and *i* are written above and underneath a consonant, respectively.

991 Such a cluster is impossible in Arabic, except in pausal forms; but even though pausal forms are observed in Qur'anic recitation, the orthography does not recognize them and the reading *muṣrikhiyy* is therefore impossible.

992 The line is from a poem in the ancient collection *al-Aṣmaʿiyyāt*. Grammarians have discussed the line and whether to read it as (self-) praise or amazement (i.e., irony or sarcasm), see, e.g., al-Baghdādī, *Khizānat al-adab*, 9:431–35.

993 They are two *rajaz* lines by al-Aghlab al-ʿIjlī (d. 21/641), see Hämeen-Anttila, *Five Rağaz Collections*, 168. Al-Farrāʾ objects to *fiyyī*, which

should normally be *fiyya*, or *fiyyā* in rhyme; see his *Maʿānī l-Qurʾān*, 2:76 (on Q Ibrāhīm 14:22).

994 Instead of *ilayya* and *ʿalayya*; presumably the incorrect forms occur in rhyme position (and should accordingly be read *ilayyī* and *ʿalayyī*).

995 i.e., in pre-Islamic and early Islamic Arabic until around the middle of the second/eighth century, which forms the basis on which Arabic grammar was codified by the grammarians.

996 The line is in his *Dīwān*, 41, but with *yaʾtī minhumā l-mawtu* instead of *yaʾtī l-mawtu li-l-kull.*

997 Printed as prose in most editions and as poetry in Bint al-Shāṭiʾ's edition; it could be scanned as the exceedingly rare *mutadārik* meter. As Nicholson notes, the words are reminiscent of the mystic Abū Yazīd (or Bāyazīd) al-Bisṭāmī (d. 261/874 or 264/877–78), who said "Praise be to me, how great am I!"

998 The meaning of *fa-yakūnu bi-l-halakah awfā ṣabīr* is not wholly clear. *Ṣabīr* means "layered white cloud"; it is sometimes described as a cloud that rarely gives rain, but in *al-Fuṣūl wa-l-ghāyāt* (97–98, 346–47) al-Maʿarrī associates it with giving rain rather than withholding it.

999 Q Furqān 25:44.

1000 *Lālakah*, from Persian *lālak* or *lālakā*, "shoe, slipper." See Hellmut Ritter in *Oriens*, 6 (1951): 190 and Dozy, *Supplément*, 2:508.

1001 A market in Baghdad.

1002 Or, as the context strongly suggests, "Art Thou eager to be united with us?"

1003 The unusual form *tughullis* (or *tughallis*) is found in the expression *wādī tughullis*; the root *Gh-L-S* means "darkness at the end of the night" (a time suitable for raids). This and the following expressions are metaphors for things that are vain or disastrous.

1004 Q Maryam 19:89.

1005 See a line by al-Kumayt on a woman called Warhāʾ ("Clumsy") who used to cheat her husband and was punished in a manner similar to what happened to Alison in Chaucer's *Miller's Tale* (Abū ʿUbayd al-Bakrī, *Faṣl al-maqāl*, 500; al-Maydānī, *Majmaʿ al-amthāl*, 2:119).

1006 For the following verse, see Ibn Hāni', *Dīwān* (al-Yaʿlāwī), 275.

1007 These verses are not found in al-Yaʿlāwī's edition of the *Dīwān*, but they are in the edition of Būlāq, 1274, 26.

1008 The verse is in fact the opening of a long ode by Ibn Hāni' dedicated to al-Muʿizz (*Dīwān*, ed. al-Yaʿlāwī, 181). The expression "the One, the Omnipotent" occurs six time in the Qur'an, always referring to God. With "the judge's son" apparently ʿAbd al-ʿAzīz ibn al-Khaṭīb is meant, a poet attached to Ibn Abī ʿĀmir; he is said to have composed the verse and is flogged, imprisoned and subsequently banished on account of it, as related in Ibn ʿIdhārī, *al-Bayān al-mughrib*, 2:293.

1009 The words *mā hiya li-amrihī shā'ifah* remain somewhat obscure. A derivation from *shāfa*, "to polish, make shine" does not make much sense. We have hesitantly relied on Dozy, *Supplément*, which has "*apercevoir, penser*" (which seems to foreshadow the modern vernacular *shāf*).

1010 On him and Abū Jaʿfar al-Shalmaghānī, see *IQ*, §3.9.

1011 The words *mā yaẓfaru bi-ghayr al-tablīd* are not wholly clear. Perhaps "he will only succeed in becoming sick to death with his efforts," meaning that trying to escape from blindly following authority saps one's energy; or perhaps it means that he only finds that *other* people remain apathetic and inert when he wants to change things.

1012 A tentative translation. Bint al-Shāṭi' derides Nicholson's attempts to understand *yabtakiru bi-lubbin maghmūr* (*JRAS*, 1902, 351) but her own gloss does not make things any clearer : "The problem is simpler than all that: one says *ibtakara*, i.e., 'to come early (*bukratan*)' and *ibtakara l-fākihah*, i.e., 'eating its first fruits.'" James Montgomery suggests reading *yatakabbaru*, "acts haughtily."

1013 Again, Bint al-Shāṭi' says it is clear but we fail to understand it. Even Monteil says he finds it obscure and guesses ("*comme si le monde les poussait à leur perte*"). Perhaps, "as if the whole world caused them to disregard it."

1014 Studying the ancient Greek philosophers and medicine often went hand in hand.

1015 Q Mu'minūn 23:53 and Rūm 30:32.

1016 Or "kiss the earth"; See Dozy, *Supplément*, s.v., "*ʿaffara wajhahū*." It is deemed objectionable perhaps because it refers to Shi'ites approaching the imams, as Nicholson thinks (*Journal of the Royal Asiatic Society*, 1902, 352).

1017 The expression *man laka bi-zanjin fī dikr* (thus, following the dictionaries, rather than *dakr* as in Bint al-Shāṭi''s text), translates literally as "Who (will be responsible) for you (to provide you) with Zanj (East African blacks) in (an African game called) *dikr*?" This is wholly obscure to us, *pace* Bint al-Shāṭi', who says that the sense is clear.

1018 A *dharrah* is a tiny particle of dust or a very small ant; it also stands for the smallest appreciable quantity (here, metaphorically, of sin or evil, as in Q Zalzalah 99:8). Dirham and dinar are silver and gold coins, respectively, but also stand for weights.

1019 As a Muʿtazilite he would be opposed to the Predestinarians.

1020 Anonymously in al-Jāḥiẓ, *Bayān*, 3:181, spuriously attributed to Labīd in some other sources (e.g., Ibn Manẓūr, *Mukhtaṣar tarīkh Dimashq*, 3:153).

1021 Bint al-Shāṭi' is no doubt right in rejecting Nicholson's translation of *in shaʿara* as "If such a one makes verses." She thinks that *shaʿara* here means "to be an Ashʿarite"; this seems unlikely, but if one emends *shaʿara* to *tashaʿʿara*, as we have done, this is a possible interpretation, although such a verb is not attested as far as we know. It is not impossible that al-Maʿarrī is playing on words.

1022 The following verses attributed to him have not been found elsewhere.

1023 The rare word *sanbar* is explained as "knowing, proficient"; it may be a personal name here.

1024 All editions have *kullun*, whereas one would expect it to be the object of Jaʿfar's pulling, hence the emendation to *kullan*. "Pulling to his snare (or rope)" remains odd.

1025 A reference to Jaʿfar's epithet, al-Ṣādiq ("the True One").

1026 His great-grandfather Ḥusayn ibn ʿAlī ibn Abī Ṭālib, the chief Shi'ite martyr, killed at Karbala in 61/680.

1027 The "Old Man" is Abū Bakr, who was some sixty years old when he became the first caliph (r. 11–13/632–34); his successor was ʿUmar ibn al-Khaṭṭāb (r. 13–23/634–44). The Shi'ites believe that they usurped the positions that should have been held by ʿAlī and his descendants.

1028 See *IQ*, §3.9.

1029 The line (*Dīwān*, 442) is from a passage on a pair of onagers.

1030 Or "can be bejeweled with scorpions." Scorpions stand metaphorically for misery (cf. *ʿaysh dhū ʿaqārib*, " a life with scorpions," i.e., a miserable life); but a pun is involved: *ʿaqrab al-naʿl* means "sandal strap."

1031 Again a play on words connecting scorpions and sandals: *shabwah* is "stinger of a scorpion" and "side of a sandal." The connection of "crown" with "scorpion" may also be inspired by the expression *iklīl al-ʿaqrab* ("the scorpion's crown"), which are three stars at the top of the constellation Scorpio.

1032 Unidentified.

1033 The words *uff* and *tuff* are interjections; but the lexicographers tell us that as nouns they mean "earwax" and "dirt under the fingernails," respectively, which fits the context too.

1034 ʿAdī ibn Zayd; for the poem see al-Iṣfahānī, *Aghānī*, 2:118.

1035 ʿAtīb ibn Aslam was a clan all of whose men were killed by a raiding king; the women hoped in vain that their children would avenge their death (Yāqūt, *Muʿjam al-buldān*, s.v. ʿAtīb).

1036 Several of the pre-Islamic Lakhmid kings of al-Ḥīrah were called al-Mundhir or al-Nuʿmān. Probably the third or the fourth is meant, grandfather and father of al-Nuʿmān ibn al-Mundhir, the last king of the dynasty, who reigned ca. AD 580–602).

1037 Bint al-Shāṭi' and al-Iskandarānī/Fawwāl have *ḥadhir*, "cautious," which seems strange here. Reading *ḥudhdhira* makes better sense, although normally the case endings in rhyme are observed even in pausal forms, which would mean that *ḥudhdhir(a)* and *Mundhir(i)* are not perfect. But the patterns of *ḥudhdhir*/*Mundhir* are a better fit, prosodically, than *ḥadhir* and *Mundhir*.

1038 Taking *bihī* to refer to Ibn al-Rāwandī.

1039 Bint al-Shāṭī' is surely right in reading *dhāwī* (other editions have *dāwī*), but there is no reason to think, as she does, that *khīṭān* means "strings of ostriches" here. Nicholson's "gossamer," followed by Monteil ("fil aérien d'araignée"), makes more sense, but in that case one would have expected *khīṭān al-shayṭān* (or *mukhāṭ al-shayṭān*, or *luʿāb al-shams*), not just *khīṭān*.

1040 Another of the many instances where a difficult rhyme (here on *-māgh*) forces the author to use contrived imagery.

1041 A verse attributed to Ibn Aḥmar in Sībawayh, *Kitāb*, 1:38 and to al-Azraq ibn Ṭarafah in other sources, see, e.g., al-Sīrāfī, *Sharḥ abyāt Sībawayh*, 1:248–49.

1042 *Amthāl* are maxims, proverbs, or parables.

1043 A moot point, for some of the earliest revealed parts of the Qur'an strongly resemble precisely this rhymed prose or *sajʿ* of the pre-Islamic soothsayers.

1044 Taking *muʿṣim* to be a synonym of *aʿṣam*, a standard epithet of mountain goats; one could perhaps also interpret it as "seeking refuge in inaccessible places."

1045 Q Ḥashr 59:21.

1046 Q Mu'minūn 23:14. This eulogy on the Qur'an did not prevent Abū l-ʿAlā' from being accused of attempting to surpass it with his *al-Fuṣul wa-l-ghāyāt*, nor did his attack on Ibn al-Rāwandī stop later authors from yoking them together as arch-heretics (see, e.g., Ibn al-Jawzī, *Talbīs Iblīs*, 63, 99–100).

1047 A date merchant called Qaḍīb sold some baskets of dried dates to a Bedouin, forgetting that he had put a purse with one thousand dinars in one of them. When he remembered he followed the buyer and retrieved the purse. He told the Bedouin that he had brought a knife and that he would have slit his belly if he had not found the money. The Bedouin asked to see the knife, took it from him, and slit his belly (al-ʿAskarī, *Jamharat al-amthāl*, 2:184, al-Maydānī, *Majmaʿ al-amthāl*, 2:293, in explanation of the proverb *alhaf min Qaḍīb*, "A bigger loser than Qaḍīb").

1048 Al-Ṭirimmāḥ (d. ca. 110/728) made satires on his contemporary al-Farazdaq. The line is attributed to the latter in Ibn Qutaybah, *Maʿānī*, 813 and Ibn Rashīq, *ʿUmdah*, 1:110, on poets who refrain from lampooning others because they despise them too much; but it is not found in his *Dīwān*. *Quḍub*, plural of *qaḍīb*, is explained as "improvised poems" (*qaṣāʾid muqtaḍabah*).

1049 *Uqtuḍiba*, word play with the root of *qaḍīb*. It is not known when Ibn al-Rāwandī died or how old he was. Abū l-ʿAlāʾ continues with more, rather insipid and virtually untranslatable punning on the root *Q-Ḍ-B*.

1050 *Qaḍbah*: stick, stalk of edible vegetable, or an arrow shaft, or (read as *qiḍbah*) a herd of camels or sheep.

1051 Anonymously in al-Maʿarrī, *al-Ṣāhil wa-l-shāḥij*, 549; attributed to ʿAmr ibn Aḥmar in Ibn Manẓūr, *Lisān al-ʿArab* (*ʿ-R-Ḍ*) and to Ziyād ibn Ribʿī al-Qutabī al-Bāhilī (otherwise unknown) in al-Aṣmaʿī, *Ibil*, 106. Someone interprets it as "reciting two *qaṣīdah*s" instead of riding two camels. It is not clear why this verse is quoted.

1052 *Wa-rawḥati dunyā*: sense unclear. Perhaps "a nearby evening journey," with construct phrase standing for noun plus adjective (just as *samāʾ al-dunyā*, "the lower Heaven," is found instead of *al-samāʾ al-dunyā*, see, e.g., Ibn Manẓūr, *Lisān al-ʿArab*, *D-N-W*).

1053 viz. Ibn al-Rāwandī.

1054 Literally, "Who could help him to gain the speech of a woman announcing a death?," apparently a roundabout way of inviting people to kill him.

1055 Poet not identified; the line has not been found elsewhere.

1056 Poet unidentified. The point of citing this verse (quoted in Thaʿlab, *Majālis*, 1:103) is that a plural subject is followed by a verb in feminine singular. The interpretation of *nataqat* (thus in Thaʿlab, *Majālis*) or *nutiqat* (as in Bint al-Shāṭiʾ's edition) is uncertain.

1057 See *IQ* §3.9, note 69. The word *farīd* could also be translated as "solitary, isolated."

1058 On the tribal group called Kindah, see "Kinda," in *EI2*, 5:118–20 (I. Shahīd and A. F. L. Beeston). For the genealogical tree of Kindah, see al-Kalbī/Caskel, *Ǧamharat an-nasab*, I, table 176 (upward) and tables 233–43 (downward); for al-Ḥārith ibn ʿAdī, see table 235.

1059 According to some, it should be *al-ḥayy al-ḥarīd*, "the angry tribe" (see al-Kalbī/Caskel. *Ǧamharat an-nasab*, 2:302). The Banū Wahb, Banū ʿAdī, and Banū l-Mithl were all tribes within Kindah (see al-Kalbī/Caskel, *Ǧamharat an-nasab*, I, table 235).

1060 Perhaps a human sufferer is mentioned; but the treatment of mangy camels is often described in ancient poetry; cf. Muzarrid, in *al-Mufaḍḍaliyyāt*, 79: "They suffer from mange, and they have been anointed all over with *ghalqah*, a stinking ointment, and the urine of women whose monthly courses have ceased" (trans. Lyall, 45).

1061 He is the author of a book on horses, *Kitāb al-khayl* (see 133–34 for the vertebra called *al-farīdah*).

1062 The word *marjān*, often meaning "coral," occurs in the Qur'an (Q Raḥmān 55:22, 58) joined with *luʾlu'* ("pearls") and exegetes and lexicographers have sometimes explained the former as "small pearls" and the latter as "large pearls" (e.g., al-Farrāʾ, *Maʿānī l-Qurʾān*, 3:115). *Marjān* is obviously related to Aramaic *margenītā* or *margālītā*, "pearl, jewel," which is derived from Greek μαργαρίτης, "pearl" (which may be of Indian origin). Abū l-ʿAlāʾ supplies his own, preposterous etymologies.

1063 This addition seems to be required by the sense.

1064 In Arabic sources coral is often said to be procured at a place in present-day Algeria, or to be "Frankish," i.e., European (see A. Dietrich, entry "Mard̲j̲ān" in *EI2*, 6:556–57).

1065 Translation uncertain and meaning unclear. Apart from "Jupiter," *al-mushtarī* can also mean "the buyer." Ibn al-Rūmī, obsessed with omens, is more likely to think of planets, Jupiter being a particularly favorable one. Perhaps he means that Jupiter is now old and no longer quick (which would contradict the common opinion that planets do not age); or that if Jupiter were newly created (instead of having existed from all eternity, *qadīm*, as the philosophers say), he would be quick. The owner (who was the buyer, *al-mushtarī*), like Jupiter, should not be hasty. We thank Professor Ewald Wagner for his suggestion (personal communication).

1066 His elegy of 111 lines on Abū l-Ḥusayn Yaḥyā ibn ʿUmar ibn Ḥusayn ibn Zayd ibn ʿAlī, an ʿAlid rebel who was killed in 250/864; see Ibn al-Rūmī, *Dīwān*, 2:492–500. His strong Shi'ite leanings are beyond doubt, *pace* Abū l-ʿAlāʾ.

1067 The poet is unknown. The anecdote is quoted in al-Baghdādī, *Tārīkh Baghdād*, 10:180, ending in *kāna illā taḥaqqaq*, which is unmetrical, because the penultimate foot is SLL instead of SLS, as it should be in this form of *ṭawīl* meter. The shortening is said to have been deliberate, "lest it become poetry" (cf. Q Yā Sīn 36:69: «We have not taught him [viz. the Prophet] poetry: that is not proper for him.»). This implies that the Prophet is supposed to have composed the verse, although al-Maʿarrī seems to say that the Prophet quoted some existing line. The version in al-Rāghib al-Iṣfahānī, *Muḥāḍarāt*, 1:90, ending in *illā takūnā*, is unmetrical for the same reason.

1068 The Day of Judgment, cf. Q Shuʿarāʾ 26:227.

1069 See for an English translation of the poem *al-Mufaḍḍalīyāt*, trans. Lyall, 333–41 (see l. 37). "Scaring away birds" (*zajr*) is often a form of prognostication, depending on the direction of flight taken by them (see T. Fahd, entry "ʿIyāfa," *EI2*, 4:290–91).

1070 Literally, "who made a broth or gruel called *ḥarīqah* or *ḥarūqah*" (from the root *Ḥ-R-Q*, "burning"). It is food consumed in hard times. Al-Iskandarānī and Fawwāl gloss *aḥraq* as an adjective: "whose hair has fallen out," or "with short hair"; but the dictionaries only give *ḥariq*, for someone with little hair on the cheeks, not *aḥraq*.

1071 The word *ʿiṣām* can also mean "collyrium, kohl."

1072 Compare the imprecation, "May there be grit in your mouth!" (Ibn Manẓūr, *Lisān al-ʿArab*, *K-Th-K-Th*).

1073 Abū Tammām; see his *Dīwān*, 3:152.

1074 Literally, "who will slink back."

1075 cf. Ibn Manẓūr, *Lisān al-ʿArab* (*Ḥ-W-Sh*).

1076 *Sāniḥ*, usually taken as a propitious sign, the opposite of *bāriḥ*; but there is considerable confusion about the precise meanings of the terms.

1077 Literally, "the (arrow shaft called) *manīḥ*," as used in the pre-Islamic gambling game called *maysir*, considered to be of good omen (see T. Fahd, "al-Maysir," *EI2* 6:923–24).

1078 "Pug-nosed," an epithet of the lion; it can also be interpreted as "back-slinker."

1079 Al-Akhnas, nickname of Ubayy ibn Sharīq (d. 13/634), of the tribe of Thaqīf, an ally of the Banū Zuhrah, a subdivision of Quraysh (see al-Kalbī/Caskel, *Ǧamharat an-nasab*, Tafeln, 118, Register, 564), an opponent of the Prophet Muḥammad. At the Battle of Badr (2/624) he deserted his fellow Meccans and thus escaped being killed (see Ibn Hishām, *al-Sīrah al-nabawiyyah*, 1:619, trans. Guillaume, 296); the slain were thrown into a well (Ibn Hishām, *al-Sīrah al-nabawiyyah*, 1:638–40, trans. Guillaume, 306–7).

1080 i.e., of Meccans. The meaning of *ʿan wafr* is not wholly clear; it does not mean "abandoning his riches" (as the note in al-Iskandarānī/Fawwāl seems to suggest), because he says he wants to save the property of his allies. Monteil does not translate it. Nicholson (359) has "though he had nothing to complain of," suggesting in a note that it could be synonymous with *ʿan qudrah*, "while he had the opportunity."

1081 "To throw someone in the dust" often stands for felling an opponent.

1082 The words are not etymologically related.

1083 Connecting *dhayyāl* ("long-tailed") and *idhālah* ("humbling"), from the same root.

1084 An expression very frequently found in the Qur'an.

1085 The first three months of the Islamic year are Muḥarram, Ṣafar, and Rabīʿ al-Awwal.

1086 The noun *rabīʿ* usually means "spring" or "spring herbage"; originally the season in which rain brings vegetation (in fact autumn). The third and fourth months of the Islamic calendar are called "First Rabīʿ" and "Second Rabīʿ," respectively, but due to the Islamic lunar year they are no longer connected with a particular season.

1087 Q Luqmān 31:34.

1088 Attributed to Dhū l-Rummah by lexicographers such as Ibn Durayd, *Jamharah*, 486; Ibn Manẓūr, *Lisān al-ʿArab*, (*N-ʿ-J*), but not found in his regular *Dīwān* (see his *Dīwān*, appendix, 3:1907).

1089 Presumably a metaphor for people's sins.

1090 See *IQ* §3.11.

1091 See Abū Tammām, *Dīwān*, 1:7–39.

1092 i.e., the poet in the fire. If one emends *yaʿjabu li-aswānihī* to *yuʿjibu aswānahū* one gets a more natural sense: "which would amaze their distressed author" (as suggested by James Montgomery). The personification of the poems may have been inspired by Abū Tammām's comparison (in prose and verse) of his poems to children, see al-Ṣūlī, *Akhbār Abī Tammām*, 114–15 and Abū Tammām, *Dīwān*, 3:331.

1093 It is said that his two daughters lamented him in elegies for a full year (al-Iṣfahānī, *Aghānī*, 15:389); the story is apparently inspired by Labīd's poem addressing his two daughters shortly before his death, from which the two following lines are taken. See his *Dīwān* (Beirut: Dār Ṣādir, 1966, 79) and see *Gh* §11.3.

1094 The *Dīwān* has "his bosom friend."

1095 Reading *muʿaddidāt* instead of *maʿdūdāt* found in all editions.

1096 Al-ʿAbqasī, viz. a man of the tribe ʿAbd al-Qays. The line is from a pre-Islamic poem attributed to al-Mufaḍḍal al-Nukrī (i.e., of the tribe of Nukrah, which is part of ʿAbd al-Qays) in *al-Aṣmaʿiyyāt* (202) and to ʿĀmir ibn Maʿshar, also of Nukrah, in al-Akhfash, *Ikhtiyārayn* (250) and al-Khālidiyyān, *Ashbāh*, 1:150. It is one of the three poems called "fair" (*munṣifah*) because they do justice to the poets' opponents.

1097 It is true that *B* is a popular rhyme consonant; but the rhyme on *-āʾ* is not particularly rare or difficult. Al-Maʿarrī takes the rhyme letters in the order of the Arabic alphabet, *-āʾ* representing both the letter *alif* and the consonant ʾ (the glottal stop, called *hamzah*).

1098 A woman proverbial for her lamenting, mentioned in a verse by the pre-Islamic poet al-Muthaqqib al-ʿAbdī; see al-Khālidiyyān, *Ashbāh*, 1:189; Ibn Manẓūr, *Lisān al-ʿArab* (*J-W-N*); and al-Maʿarrī, *Siqṭ al-zand*, 32.

1099 ʿAbd Allāh ibn Khaṭal and his two singing girls, who had lampooned the Prophet, were executed in 8/630 after the conquest of Mecca (see Ibn Hishām, *al-Sīrah*, 2:409–10, trans. Guillaume, 550–51).

1100 Kuthayyir, *Dīwān*, 87.

1101 His *Dīwān* (ed. al-Asmar) contains a poem of forty-five lines rhyming in *-īṭū*, one of ninety-seven lines on *-ā.ithū*, and one of eleven lines on *-āẓū*, all uncommon rhymes.

1102 The most common rhyme consonants are *R, L, M, N, D, B,* and *ʿayn.*

1103 The meaning of *wa-huwa khirād* (thus in all manuscripts) is uncertain. *Khirād* could be the plural of *kharūd,* "virgin" or "unbored pearl," a common metaphor for a poem with original motifs and expressions. Bint al-Shāṭiʾ suggests reading *ḥirād* (plural of *ḥarid* or *ḥarīd*), "apart, on one's own." In either case, one would expect *hiya* instead of *huwa.*

1104 Translation uncertain; more literally, "the watering hole would be too narrow to accommodate them all." *Al-ṣadar wa-l-īrād* literally means "returning from a watering place and bringing (cattle) to the water"; the terms are used in various idiomatic expressions. The words *ḍāqa . . . l-ṣadar* evoke the expression *ḍāqa . . . l-ṣadr* ("to be annoyed, oppressed").

1105 For *ghadāh* in the sense of "morning prayer," see *EI2* 8:926b (entry "Ṣalāt").

1106 Presumably Abū Tammām's rivals despair of attaining his level (but the connection with the context is obscure). The implication seems to be that this triumph will not help him because he omitted his prayers.

1107 It is uncertain what precisely is the implied difference with the morning prayer. Perhaps: the morning prayer is harder for the believer, who has to get up early; one's absence at the midday prayer is more conspicuous.

1108 The term *ʿatamah* specifically refers to the first third of the night.

1109 The verb *ʿajiza* normally means "to be incapable, too weak," but one cannot be condemned for being unable to perform one's religious duties. See Dozy, *Supplément*, s.v. *ʿajiza*: "*Etre paresseux, manquer, faire faute, manquer à ses engagements.*"

1110 In certain circumstances, such as travel or sickness, one is allowed to combine two consecutive prayers. The poet of the following line is al-Uqayshir (on him see *Gh* §3.5), see Ibn Durayd, *Taʿlīq min amālī Ibn Durayd*, 112; al-Iṣfahānī, *Aghānī*, 11:268.

1111 "Joints" (*awṣāl*) is apparently a play on words (joining two prayers; and joints or limbs of the body).

1112 Mālik, an angel, is the chief guardian of Hell; see *Gh* §17.12.4.

1113 Ibn al-Qāriḥ met the first two of these poets in Paradise; see *Gh* §§7.3 (al-Nābighah al-Jaʿdī), 6.2.1 (ʿAdī ibn Zayd).

1114 Māwiyyah is the poet's wife. The verse is a conflation of two hemistichs from a poem by Ḥātim, see his *Dīwān* (*Sharḥ Abī Ṣāliḥ Yaḥyā ibn Mudrik al-Ṭāʾī*), 74.

1115 Zayd ibn Muhalhil (d. between 9/630 and 23/644), a tribal leader and poet, known as Zayd al-Khayl ("Zayd of the Horses") converted to Islam in 9/630.

1116 On him, Ibn Abī Duʾād, al-Afshīn, and Bābak see *IQ* §3.12.

1117 It is said that Bābak was a shepherd in his youth; cf. Ibn al-Nadīm, *Fihrist*, 343.

1118 Literally, "who gains the cane of victory." A cane or reed was placed at the end of the race course.

1119 *Shāʾik* means both "thorny" and "someone armed to the teeth."

1120 *Wathaba* normally means "to jump" but can also mean "to sit" (see, e.g., Ibn Manẓūr, *Lisān al-ʿArab*).

1121 The word *qufūl*, verbal noun meaning "homecoming, returning," could perhaps also be taken as a plural of *qufl* "lock," i.e., "his journey will end behind bars."

1122 Literally, "whose shade in sucking earth is dense." "Dense shade" (*ẓill ẓalīl*) is mentioned in Q Nisāʾ 4:57 as something desirable.

1123 An impenetrable passage. Literally the text seems to say: "I am not sure that the Hereafter will be with kinds of sustenance, so that the preponderant one will arrive at the basin." Bint al-Shāṭiʾ suggests that "the one that weighs more (*al-rājiḥah*, feminine) is the soul whose sustenance of forgiveness is preponderant." The basin (*mihrāq*) is presumably the apocalyptic Basin (*al-ḥawḍ*), see *Gh* §11.6.1. One notes that *arzāq* and *mihrāq* do not form a rich rhyme, contrary to the author's habit; but reading *mihzāq* ("frivolous, laughing a lot") does not help.

1124 Various sects claimed some kind of divinity for ʿAlī ibn Abī Ṭālib, the fourth caliph.

1125 The story of his execution is probably an invention by Shi'ites wanting to discredit extremist views.

1126 Literally, "is not a puddle that dries up in summer."

1127 All editions have Shābās.

1128 Al-Maʿarrī uses the rare word *māqiṭ*, defined in dictionaries either as "freedman of a freedman" or "hireling, employed from one household to another."

1129 Medicine administered through the nose was used for several diseases. See, e.g., al-Anṭākī, *Tadhkirah*, 183–84, s.v. *saʿūṭ*. *Pace* Bint al-Shāṭiʾ and other editors, the "snuff" mentioned here was not made of tobacco, which was unknown in al-Maʿarrī's time.

1130 "Melancholy," in the sense of madness.

1131 Abū Jawf is not found in other sources.

1132 *Biṭrīq*, from the Graeco-Latin *patrikios/patricius*, here means local governor or military commander.

1133 The Arabic has *al-Dūqas*, from Latin *dux*. The invading Byzantines were defeated at the battle of Afāmiyah (ancient Apamea, not far from Ḥamāh in Syria) in 388/998, when their commander, Damianos Dalassenos, Duke of Antioch, was killed by a Muslim warrior.

1134 See *IQ* §§4.2–3.

1135 Reading *wa-ṣayyara* instead of *ṣayyara*, found in all editions.

1136 The point of this maxim is not clear in this context.

1137 Literally, "laughs (disclosing)"; the white spathe is compared to teeth.

1138 Or possibly "I don't expect it."

1139 Dying one's hair black is frowned upon in Islamic law; there is no objection to dying it red with henna (the Prophet himself is said to have done this).

1140 Q Baqarah 2:68; the reference is to a cow, to be sacrificed by Moses/Mūsā.

1141 These lines are found only in the margin of some manuscripts and it is not certain that they belong to al-Maʿarrī's original text. The verses (with variants) are attributed to "a Bedouin" in Ibn Qutaybah, *ʿUyūn al-akhbār*, 4:43 and quoted in many later sources, including Ibn ʿAbd Rabbih, *ʿIqd*, 6:113; al-Thaʿālibī, *al-Tamthīl wa-l-muḥāḍarah*, 219; and al-Rāghib, *Muḥāḍarāt al-udabāʾ*, 2:118. In al-ʿAskarī, *Dīwān al-maʿānī*, 2:240 they are ascribed to al-Ḥirmāzī (possibly the Basran philologist and poet of the first half of the third/ninth century).

1142 Bint al-Shāṭiʾ vowels it as *khamir* ("place full of trees") in her ninth edition and mentions several alternatives: *khamar*, "thicket" and *khum(u)r*, pl. of *khimār*, "veil"; correct is no doubt *khumr*, since *khamar* or *khamir* does not give a good rhyme with ʿAmr.

1143 The verse, anonymously in Abū Tammām's *Ḥamāsah* (see al-Marzūqī, *Sharḥ*, 1344) is attributed to Abū l-Aswad in Ibn Qutaybah, *ʿUyūn al-akhbār*, 4:43 and al-Iṣfahānī, *Aghānī*, 12:296, 326. In the preceding verse he mentions his love for one of his wives, called Umm ʿAwf al-Qushayriyyah, who is described as "an old woman" (*ʿajūz*). She was good to him in his old age, unlike another, younger wife.

1144 Attributed in al-Zamakhsharī, *Asās al-balāghah* (*N-Y-R*) to Ḥumayd; it is not clear whether this is Ḥumayd ibn Thawr (on whom see *Gh* §10.3.1, 12.2.1) or the Umayyad poet Ḥumayd al-Arqaṭ. See Ḥumayd ibn Thawr, *Dīwān*, ed. ʿAbd al-ʿAzīz al-Maymanī, Cairo: Dār al-Kutub, 1951, 65.

1145 Literally, "double-threaded (cloth)," i.e., made to last.

1146 Ḥassān ibn Thābit, *Dīwān* (ed. Sayyid Ḥanafī Ḥasanayn), 81, (ed. ʿArafāt), 1:40.

1147 By Mūsā ibn Yasār, called Mūsā Shahawāt (Umayyad period), addressing Ḥamzah ibn ʿAbd Allāh ibn al-Zubayr, see Ibn Qutaybah, *al-Shiʿr wa-l-shuʿarāʾ*, 578; idem, *ʿUyūn al-akhbār*, 2:17; al-Iṣfahānī, *Aghānī*, 3:360; Ibn ʿAbd Rabbih, *ʿIqd*, 4:425.

1148 The form *munhabilāt* has tentatively been connected with *habala* "to dote, rave"; perhaps it has the same force as *muhtabilāt* "scheming, intriguing (women)," or *hiball* "corpulent and old" (said of people and camels).

1149 A single verse (*yatīm*) by an unidentified poet, used as song lyrics by the famous female singer ʿArīb (d. 277/890), see al-Iṣfahānī, *Aghānī*, 21:83–84; cf. Ibn ʿAbd Rabbih, *ʿIqd*, 3:12. In al-Thaʿālibī, *Yatīmah*, 3:83 the line is attributed to Kuthayyir, but it is not found in his *Dīwān*.

1150 The word *nujūz* is not in the dictionaries; here it has been taken as a synonym of *najz* or *najāz*.

1151 Quoted anonymously in al-Ḥātimī, *Ḥilyat al-muḥāḍarah*, 2:236 and al-ʿAskarī, *Dīwān al-maʿānī*, 2:240.

1152 The verses are attributed to a certain al-Ḥārith ibn Zuhayr ibn Taym in al-Kalbī, *Nasab Maʿadd wa-l-Yaman al-Kabīr*, 2:556 and to al-Ḥārith ibn Zuhayr ibn Wadham ibn Wahb in al-Wazīr al-Maghribī, *al-Īnās*, 131.

1153 *Mā nakaḥta* could also be "haven't you got married?"; the particle *mā* "what"—instead of the expected *man* "who(m)"—has been taken to refer to the kind of marriage rather than the person married.

1154 The text of Bint al-Shāṭiʾ, *wa-gharimtu mālan* "and I lost wealth" does not make sense. The version in *al-Īnās* has *wa-nuqidtu alfan*, "and I was paid one thousand (dirhams) in cash." We have adopted an emendation suggested by James Montgomery.

1155 Quoted anonymously in Ibn Qutaybah, *ʿUyūn al-akhbār*, 4:44; al-Askarī, *al-Awāʾil*, 200 (which has ". . . if she held all the water in the world in her hand").

1156 For the verb *jāza*, compare the expression *ajāza* "to let (someone) water his camels," or *jāʾiz* "someone who, being thirsty, passes by some people" (*Lisān al-ʿarab*).

1157 Unidentified.

1158 Bint al-Shāṭiʾ suggests deriving *mawār*^{in} from the root *W-R-Y*, as if the servants are "women who can strike fiery sparks." This is attractive, but we believe it is more likely to be a plural of *māriyah* (root *M-R-Y*), see al-Zamakhsharī, *Asās*: *al-nāqah tamrī fī sayrihā: tusriʿu, wa-nūq*^{un} *mawār*^{in}.

1159 Apparently a contrast is meant between what is readily available (spring on the surface) and what is not (water from a deep well).

1160 According to al-Khaṭṭābī, *al-ʿUzlah*, 126, the traditionist and legal scholar Sufyān al-Thawrī (d. 161/778) used to quote these lines.

1161 Not found elsewhere, unless he is identical with the father of "Abū ʿAbd Allāh Muḥammad ibn Sindī al-Qinnasrī, the judge," who is said to have met al-Maʿarrī according to Ibn al-ʿAdīm (*Taʿrīf al-qudamā'*, 560).

1162 The lines are from a poem in which he asks a patron for the gift of a slave-boy servant and complains about freemen servants; see his *Dīwān*, 988.

1163 Yāsir, Yusr, and Nujḥ (or Saʿd, as in the *Dīwān*) are names of slaves, unlike ʿĀmir and ʿAmmār. Al-Buḥturī was in fact descended from a respectable Arab tribe.

1164 Translation uncertain; perhaps instead of *bi-l-ʿarb* one should read *bi-l-gharb*, "with the edge of the sword."

1165 The word *mushtaʿil* (literally "flaming, burning"), glossed as *murtafiʿ* by Bint al-Shāṭi', is somewhat strange; perhaps one should read *mustaʿlī* ("rising, towering").

1166 All editions have *ghabn al-rā'iʿ*, which does not make any sense. The correct reading is no doubt *al-zā'iʿ*, "someone who cuts a slice of melon."

1167 Arabic *mamlūk*, denoting a white slave trained for military service.

1168 Perhaps because Junādah had been killed by al-Ḥākim.

1169 This seems to be the most likely interpretation of the somewhat obscure passage.

1170 See *IQ* §4.4.

1171 Q Layl 92:19.

1172 See *IQ* §6.

1173 Q Zumar 39:53.

1174 This is usually explained as "who have harmed themselves by their sinning."

1175 *Tashrīq* has several meanings; here it has tentatively been connected with the expression *sharraqa l-laḥm fī l-shams* "to let meat dry in the sun."

1176 Arabic *ṭunbūr*; cf. *Gh* §15.2.5.

1177 Perhaps the gestures of singers are meant, or the behavior in general of lascivious youths.

1178 *Ṭabaqāt* is usually translated as "classes," but the reference is obviously to the genre of biographical compilations called "Classes of . . . ," which rarely classify anything; *ṭabaqāt* can also mean "generations."

1179 ʿUmar ibn ʿAbd al-ʿAzīz (r. 99–101/717–20), singled out by historiographers as the only truly pious Umayyad caliph; there are, however, also some reports of his delight in the luxuries of courtly life. Al-Iṣfahānī mentions him as a composer of music and singer, see *Aghānī*, 8:207 (on the authority of Ibn Khurradādhbih), 8:250, 253, 268.

1180 Mālik ibn Anas (d. 179/796), famous traditionist of Medina, who gave his name to the Mālikites, one of the four major legal schools in Sunnite Islam. There is a report (al-Iṣfahānī, *Aghānī*, 2:238) that he was heard to sing at the wedding of a man called Abū Ḥanẓalah in Medina.

1181 On his being a drinking companion of the libertine poet Ḥammād ʿAjrad, see al-Iṣfahānī, *Aghānī*, 14:333–34, where also the following verses are quoted.

1182 All forms of gambling are prohibited in Islam. See Rosenthal, *Gambling in Islam*, where this report is not found. ʿUmar's predecessor, Abū Bakr, however, was involved in a bet before it became forbidden (*Gambling in Islam*, 27–30).

1183 The "standard" accounts of his conversion (see, e.g., al-Suyūṭī, *Tārīkh al-khulafāʾ*, 128–34) do not include this story.

1184 The word (*ijbār*) has connotations of "predestination" (*jabr*).

1185 Q Ḍuḥā 93:7.

1186 His *Kitāb al-Maghāzī* (*Book of [the Prophet's] Campaigns*), known only from later recensions (e.g., Ibn Hishām's *Sīrah*), is presumably identical with the book mentioned here.

1187 The two verbs, *arāqa* and *baʿʿa*, are near synonyms, the latter meaning "pour out in quantity."

1188 "Popular (wine)" (*jumhūrī*) is a kind of boiled wine mentioned by Abū Ḥanīfah; it is made by returning to *bukhtaj* (see next note) the water that has been distilled from it and boiling the mixture again and it is said to be intoxicating but also permitted. It is called *jumhūrī* because the masses (*jumhūr*) drink it (Ibn Manẓūr, *Lisān al-ʿArab*, *J-M-H-R*).

1189 The French renders *bukhtaj* (from Middle Persian *pokhtag*, "boiled, cooked"), a kind of boiled wine.

1190 "Half-wine" (*munaṣṣaf*) is grape wine that has been reduced to half its volume by boiling it; it is forbidden, unlike *muthallath*, i.e., wine reduced to one third.

1191 *Khamr* is grape wine, *nabīdh* is wine made of various other substances such as dates or honey, which according to some scholars is not forbidden as long as it does not cause intoxication. See, e.g., the entries "Khamr" and "Nabīdh" in *EI2*, 4:994–98 and 7:840, respectively.

1192 He used to drink *nabīdh* for many years but relinquished it, see, e.g., Ibn Khallikān, *Wafayāt*, 2:242–43.

1193 *Ṭilā'* (also "tar, fluid pitch, oil") is a thickened kind of wine, grape juice boiled down to one third, or merely another word for grape wine. See, e.g., the discussion in Ibn Manẓūr, *Lisān al-ʿArab* (*Ṭ-L-Y*).

1194 The word, unclear in the manuscripts, has been read as *rattabahū* following Bint al-Shāṭi'.

1195 By ʿAbīd ibn al-Abraṣ. See his *Dīwān*, 3; al-Iṣfahānī, *Aghānī*, 22:91.

1196 The first half has only three feet instead of four.

1197 See his *Dīwān*, 135, which has *kumayt* "reddish (wine)" instead of *ṭilā'*.

1198 The line is found in his *Dīwān*, 97.

1199 Al-Aṣmaʿī quotes this line anonymously (Ibn Manẓūr, *Lisān al-ʿArab*, *N-Y-'*); see also Ibn Qutaybah, *Maʿānī*, 456. The collected poetry of the tribe of Hudhayl does not contain this line; al-Maʿarrī probably confused it with a different verse ending with the same words: *nī'un aw naḍījū*, by the Hudhalī poet al-Dākhil ibn Ḥarām, see al-Sukkarī, *Sharḥ Ashʿār al-Hudhaliyyīn*, 619.

1200 *Gharīḍ* is anything fresh (meat, dates, water, milk) and could also be applied to a "fresh" song, which would fit the context.

1201 Not identified.

1202 The verse is from his famous *Maqṣūrah*, see his *Dīwān* (ed. ʿUmar ibn Sālim), 136. The "eighty-year old girl" is an aged wine; or "daughter of eighty" refers to the eighty lashes as punishment for drinking wine (see below).

1203 Taking *mā* to be the relative particle rather than a negative, the text could also be read (more provocatively) as: "What I would like the Sheikh to do is to follow . . ."

1204 Abū Nuwās; see his *Dīwān*, 3:186.

1205 Unidentified; cf. the similar verse said by a man met by Abū Nuwās: "No fire has touched it, apart from the fact that this infidel of theirs | has toiled all night in the region of its vineyard with a lamp" (Ibn Ḥamdūn, *Tadhkirah*; 8:405, al-Zamakhsharī, *Rabīʿ al-abrār*, 4:55). Possibly al-Maʿarrī misquoted this line.

1206 See his *Dīwān* (ed. Muḥammad Badīʿ Sharīf), 2:296.

1207 The word *ʿilj* can mean "loutish person" but it often refers to non-Muslims, here presumably a Christian or Jewish wine seller. "With a toothpick": jokingly, meaning as little as possible; Abū Nuwās uses the same expression elsewhere (*Dīwān*, 2:61).

1208 See Ibn al-Muʿtazz, *Ṭabaqāt*, 269–70; al-Iṣfahānī, *Aghānī*, 7:155–56; Abū Nuwās, *Dīwān*, 3:226.

1209 Ghummā ("Gloom") is a village near Baghdad associated with wine. See Yāqūt, *Muʿjam al-buldān*, s.v., where Bacchic poems by Wālibah ibn al-Ḥubāb and Jaḥẓah al-Barmakī are quoted.

1210 Noah/Nūḥ is invoked, partly for the rhyme, but also because he is traditionally associated with wine.

1211 The stars are the bubbles arising from the mixing of wine with water, a standard topos of wine poetry; the moon is the attractive recipient of the cup.

1212 The word *iqhāʾ* ("reducing one's appetite") is cognate with *qahwah*, one of the words for "wine" (and the origin of "café" and "coffee").

1213 Abū Nuwās, see his *Dīwān*, 3:187. The verse is the last line of the wine poem of which another line was quoted above, §37.2.3.

1214 See *Gh* §3.3, where he is mentioned and quoted as a poet of wine poetry.

1215 Amaj is a place near Medina; see Yāqūt, *Muʿjam al-buldān* s.v., where the three lines by the very obscure Ḥumayd are quoted. For the story, involving the Umayyad caliph ʿUmar ibn ʿAbd al-ʿAzīz, see Ibn ʿAbd al-Barr, *Bahjah*, 1:107 (quoting lines 2–3); a different version in Ibn ʿAbd Rabbih, *ʿIqd*, 6:352 (where the poet is Ḥumayd's uncle).

1216 This line is quoted anonymously by grammarians (e.g., al-Mubarrad, *Kāmil*, 1:318; Ibn al-Shajarī, *Amālī*, 1:382, 2:182; al-Baghdādī, *Khizānat al-adab*, 9:376) because the correct *Ḥumaydun-i lladhī* is contracted to *Ḥumaydu lladhī*. Moreover, it contains either a rhyme defect (if one reads the correct *al-aṣlaʿū*) or a syntactical error (reading *al-aṣlaʿī*). For once, Abū l-ʿAlāʾ does not interrupt himself with these matters.

1217 Not identified; he apparently alludes to Ḥumayd al-Amajī in the last line.

1218 *Ẓimʾ* means "thirst" or "time that elapses between two waterings (of an animal)"; Abū l-ʿAlāʾ alludes to the idiom *ẓimʾ al-ḥayāh*, explained (*Lisān al-ʿarab*, *Ẓ-M-ʾ*) as "what lies between the birth of a child and his death."

1219 Aleppo (grammatically feminine, as are most Arabic placenames) is described as a woman without ornaments. For the grammarian Ibn Khālawayh, see below, §41.3 and Glossary.

1220 See the verses and the story in al-Iṣfahānī, *Aghānī*, 5:259–65, where despite his own boasts he turns out to be a miser.

1221 A wine-skin is meant. Al-Maʿarrī uses the expression *al-kahl al-muraqqab* also in his *al-Fuṣūl wa-l-ghāyāt*, 104 and explains it.

1222 Not identified. Al-Maʿarrī also quotes the lines in his *Fuṣūl*, 104 and the first only *ibid.* 370; the second line is quoted anonymously in al-Zabīdī, *Tāj al-ʿarūs* (*D-B-L*).

1223 *Qarw*, explained in dictionaries as "basin, tank" or "cup," is defined by al-Maʿarrī as "something in which a wineskin is put" (*Fuṣūl*, 104) and "container in which the wine is pressed" (*Fuṣūl*, 161).

1224 A *dhāriʿ* is a smaller goat skin used for wine, cut not from the neck but from the forelegs. Comparisons of wineskins with bodies of slain blacks (or Indians, as here) are common; see, e.g., *Gh* §17.12.1.

1225 The form ending in *-ān* is probably a poetic license.

1226 *ʿAndam*, brazilwood, is a reddish wood used for dyeing.

1227 Q Hūd 11:114.

1228 A proverb (see al-Maydānī, *Majmaʿ*, 2:279), meaning that someone's authority is undisputed. It is said that a pre-Islamic Arab king demanded ʿAwf ibn Muḥallim, a tribal leader, to give up a man who enjoyed his protection; but ʿAwf refused, whereupon the king uttered these words. According to another version (which would be appropriate here) ʿAwf used to kill his captives.

1229 Literally, "the appendages of his skin"; *zaʿānif* can mean "fringes, fins," often used for lowly and base things or persons in general.

1230 See his *Dīwān* (ed. Ḥasanayn) 164, (ed. ʿArafāt) 1:85; Ibn Hishām, *Sīrah*, 2:51, 211, trans. Guillaume, 364, 448. In the line he is taunting the Meccans for sending their trading caravans to Syria via the Iraq road, avoiding Medina and the Muslims.

1231 Books with this title, containing pre-Islamic history from the Creation to the time shortly before the prophet Muḥammad, were written by Wahb ibn Munabbih (d. ca. 114/732) and Ibn Isḥāq (d. 150/767). Both works (the latter being the more scholarly one, and perhaps intended here) transmitted much material from Jewish and Christian sources; both are known only through quotations. The story of Ṭālūt/Saul and his daughter Michal, wife of Dāwūd/David, goes back to I Samuel 19, which has instead of the wineskin "an image in the bed, with a pillow of goats' hair for his bolster." For the Muslim version see, e.g., al-Thaʿlabī, *Qiṣaṣ al-anbiyāʾ*, 242.

1232 The unusual verbs *tartara* and *mazmaza* are from a story about Ibn Masʿūd (d. 32/652), a famous Companion of the Prophet, who gives orders for a drunken man to be thus treated, to find out if he smells of alcohol; see, e.g., Ibn Manẓūr, *Lisān al-ʿArab*, (*T-R-R* and *M-Z-Z*).

1233 A reference to a recurring Qur'anic phrase.

1234 The "Hijazis" and "Iraqis" refer to two of the main legal schools in Sunni Islam, more usually called the Mālikites (after the founder, Mālik ibn Anas) and the Ḥanafites (after the founder, Abū Ḥanīfah), respectively.

1235 Several works with this title are mentioned in the sources, among them *al-Iʿtibār fī aʿqāb al-surūr wa-l-aḥzān* by Ibn Abī l-Dunyā (ed.

Najm ʿAbd al-Raḥmān Khalaf, Amman, 1993); it does not contain the verses and Abū l-ʿAlāʾ's source is not known. The first verse is found in an anecdote in which al-Aṣmaʿī relates how he hears it (with a different second verse) in a graveyard, uttered by an invisible speaker (al-Washshāʾ, *Muwashshā*, 87; al-Anṭākī, *Tazyīn al-aswāq*, 1:271).

1236 On the topos of the nightly apparition or phantom of the beloved, see *Gh* §3.7. Occasionally poets imagine how both his and the beloved's phantom meet, see Jacobi, "The *Khayāl* Motif" and "*Al-Khayalāni*."

1237 One of the many appellations of wine, perhaps because of its fragrance or its color.

1238 The expression *bint ṭabaq* is variously explained as "tortoise" ("daughter of a shield") or "snake" ("daughter of coils"); metaphorically it means "calamity."

1239 See Ḥātim al-Ṭāʾī, *Dīwān* (ed. Schulthess), 14.

1240 See Glossary, *maysir*.

1241 A reference to the ancient Bedouin belief that the spirit of someone whose death is unavenged appears on his grave in the form of a screech owl that calls "*usqūnī* (give me to drink)!" See *EI2* s.v. "ṣadā" (T. Fahd) and Homerin, "Echoes of a Thirsty Owl."

1242 The verse is from his *Muʿallaqah*; he addresses someone who blames him for revelling and risking his life in battle.

1243 The verses are attributed to Ibn al-Muʿtazz in al-Thaʿālibī, *Aḥsan mā samiʿtu*, 83, but are not found in his *Dīwān*. When Ibn al-Muʿtazz was killed, after a caliphate of little more than one day, he was not yet fifty.

1244 The line is attributed to ʿAbd Allāh ibn Hammām al-Salūlī (d. ca. 99/717) in al-Balādhurī, *Ansāb*, 4/1:291; Ibn Sallām, *Ṭabaqāt fuḥūl al-shuʿarāʾ*, 524; al-Masʿūdī, *Murūj*, 3:247; and to ʿAlī ibn al-Ghadīr al-Ghanawī in *Naqāʾiḍ Jarīr wa-l-Akhṭal*, 3.

1245 See, e.g., al-Buḥturī's poem in which he invites al-Mubarrad to a drinking session, al-Marzubānī, *Nūr al-qabas*, 326.

1246 cf. Q Mulk 67:8.

1247 See *IQ* §6.3.

1248 *Taʿzīr* is "censure, rebuke" and "discretionary punishment," less than the *ḥadd* or prescribed punishment (which in theory should be applied, in the form of flogging, for drinking wine).

1249 Shiklah (also read Shaklah) was Ibrāhīm ibn al-Mahdī's mother. For the lines (beginning "I have gone from the world and the world has gone from me") and the story, see al-Ṣūlī, *Awrāq (Ashʿār awlād al-khulafāʾ)*, 22; for "He sang the song of Shiklah's son" as a proverbial expression for something old and worn, see al-Ṣafadī, *Wāfī*, 6:112.

1250 For the expression *tawbah naṣūḥ* ("sincere repentance"), see Q Taḥrīm 66:8.

1251 *Khurdādhī* is said to be a kind of wine (al-Fīrūzābādī, *Qāmūs*), but it is also used for a kind of bottle; for a crystal *khurdādhī* see al-Tanūkhī, *Nishwār*, 1:336, 8:253. *Khurdādh* is the name of the third month (May–June) of the Persian calendar.

1252 See *IQ* §6.4.1.

1253 A line of *rajaz* by the pre-Islamic Sahl (or Nahshal, or Sayyār) ibn Mālik al-Fazārī, used as a proverb. He had fallen in love with a woman but, being too shy to address her, he had made love poetry on another woman. See al-ʿAskarī, *Jamharat al-amthāl*, 1:30; al-Maydānī, *Majmaʿ al-amthāl*, 1:83–84; Abū ʿUbayd, al-Bakrī, *Faṣl al-maqāl*, 76–77.

1254 Q Yūsuf 12:29; Potiphar (al-ʿAzīz in the Qurʾan) addresses Joseph and his wife.

1255 Not identified.

1256 Q Baqarah 2:261.

1257 The only reason to use this unusual word (*wāfih*) is to provide a rich rhyme with *tāfih* ("insignificant").

1258 Or "deception."

1259 See *IQ* §6.5.

1260 Q Raʿd 13:38.

1261 *Dīwān* (ed. Muḥ. Abū l-Faḍl Ibrāhīm), 236.

1262 See *IQ* §3.8.

1263 Perhaps he is Muḥammad ibn ʿAlī ibn al-Ṭayyib Abū l-Ḥusayn al-Baṣrī (d. 436/1044), a Muʿtazilite scholar; see, e.g., Ibn Khallikān, *Wafayāt*, 4:271.

1264 A *samāʿ* (literally, "hearing" or "audition") is a certificate written by a teacher testifying that someone has studied a text with him and is licensed to transmit it.

1265 Literally, "more famous than a pregnant piebald stallion," a proverb (al-ʿAskarī, *Jamharah*, 1:459; cf. al-Maydānī, *Majmaʿ*, 1:478: "more famous than a piebald horse"). One also finds "he seeks a pregnant piebald (male animal)", i.e., something impossible (Ibn Manẓūr, *Lisān al-ʿArab*, *ʾ-N-Q* and *B-L-Q*), and "harder to find than a pregnant piebald stallion" (Ibn Manẓūr, *Lisān al-ʿArab*, *ʿ-Q-Q*, al-Damīrī, *Ḥayāt al-ḥayawān*, 1:202, in the entry on *jamal*, "camel.") The *ablaq* is certainly not a bird here, as Bint al-Shāṭiʾ thinks; nevertheless *rara avis* seems appropriate.

1266 His name is given incompletely, as "al-Bakrī the genealogist," in Ibn al-Nadīm, *Fihrist*, 89, where he is said to have been a Christian. The anecdote is found in Ibn Qutaybah, *ʿUyūn al-akhbār*, 2:118, idem; *Maʿānī*, 478, 506, and many later sources.

1267 Abū Tammām, see his *Dīwān*, 3:15, from an ode addressed to the caliph al-Muʿtaṣim.

1268 al-Mutanabbī, see his *Dīwān*, 175, from a poem eulogising ʿAlī ibn Manṣūr al-Ḥājib ("the Chamberlain"); Ibn al-Qāriḥ was also called ʿAlī ibn Manṣūr. The line puns on the verb *ḥajaba* "to screen, keep out"; a *ḥājib* was a doorkeeper or chamberlain, often a very important functionary at court.

1269 The only point of this parenthesis is the rhyme it provides.

1270 See *IQ* §7.2.

1271 Sībawayh's famous grammar (which has no title but *Sībawayh's Book*) is notoriously difficult to read and consult.

1272 Muḥammad ibn Bashīr al-Khārijī (d. after 120/738), a poet from the Hijaz. Al-Khārijī refers to his tribe, Khārijah, not to the rebel sect known as Khārijites. The verse is one of three quoted in Abū Tammām's famous anthology *al-Ḥamāsah*, see al-Marzūqī, *Sharḥ Ḥamāsat Abī Tammām*, 809. In al-Marzubānī, *Muʿjam al-shuʿarāʾ*, 75 (followed by Ibn Khallikān, *Wafayāt*, 6:340) the verses are attributed to Abū Balhā' 'Umayr ibn 'Āmir (second/eighth century), and also to Muḥammad ibn Bashīr (*Mu'jam al-shu'arā'*, 343).

1273 See Abū Tammām, *Dīwān*, 1:125, from a poem in praise of Sulaymān ibn Wahb (d. 272/885), a member of a family of high officials.

1274 See Abū 'Ubayd al-Bakrī, *Faṣl al-maqāl*, 459–60; al-Maydānī, *Majma' al-amthāl*, 2:18–19. Barāqish ("Many-colored") was the name of a bitch belonging to some raiders, whose barking gave them away to their pursuers. According to another story, Barāqish was the wife of the legendary sage Luqmān; she turned her son and husband from vegetarians into lovers of camel meat, to the detriment of her own and her tribe's livestock. The point of quoting this proverb here is not wholly clear.

1275 The verses are found in al-Buḥturī, *Ḥamāsah*, 206–7, also Ibn Manẓūr, *Lisān al-'Arab* (*N-'-Sh*). For the encounter of al-Ṣūlī with the caliph, see al-Ṣūlī, *Awrāq (Akhbār al-Rāḍī wa-l-Muttaqī)*, 38–40, where also these and the following verses are found.

1276 A reference to the famous story of the pre-Islamic queen of Tadmur/Palmyra, al-Zabbā' (partly based on Queen Zenobia). She had killed Jadhīmah, king of al-Ḥīrah, who had ignored the advice of his faithful counsellor Qaṣīr. Qaṣīr avenged his death, having deceived al-Zabbā' by mutilating himself and claiming that this had been done by 'Amr ibn 'Adī, Jadhīmah's nephew. The figure of Qaṣīr is apparently based on Zopyros, in a story told by Herodotus, see Muth, "Zopyros bei den Arabern." The Arabic version is found in many sources, see, e.g., al-Ṭabarī, *Tārīkh*, 1:613–27, trans. by Moshe Perlmann, *The History of al-Ṭabarī*, 4:129, 132–49. Baqqah (or al-Baqqah, here with a "poetic" dual ending) is a place near al-Ḥīrah; the proverb "In Baqqah the matter was decided" is connected with the story.

1277 This seems to be the sense; literally: "When the front parts (beginnings) where weighed down by the hind parts (ends) of the affairs."

1278 The second line is quoted anonymously by al-Ṣūlī. It is not clear to which events the lines refer. Quṭayn may be a diminutive of Qaṭan, perhaps the pre-Islamic Qaṭan ibn Nahshal, who belonged to the tribe of Dārim, as did the subtribe ʿUdus ibn Zayd.

1279 Attributed to ʿAbd al-Malik ibn Marwān in al-Jāḥiẓ, *Risālah fī l-jidd wa-l-hazl*, in his *Rasāʾil*, i, 273; anonymously in Ibn Qutaybah, *ʿUyūn*, i, 15; and attributed to ʿAlī ibn Abī Ṭālib in al-ʿAskarī, *Jamharah*, 1:409 and al-Maydānī, *Majmaʿ*, 1:374.

1280 Unidentified.

1281 See *IQ* §7.3.

1282 Pilgrims, on entering Mecca while in the appropriate ritual state, pronounce this old invocation, *labbayka* ("Here I am for Thee" or "At Thy service!"). As al-Maʿarrī goes on to say, the formula is pre-Islamic. See, e.g., T. Fahd, entry "Talbiya," *EI2*, 10:160–61; Kister, "*Labbayka, allāhumma, labbayka*: On a monotheistic aspect of a Jāhiliyya practice"; Tilman Seidensticker, "Sources for the History of Pre-Islamic Religion."

1283 Most of these are in the simplest meter, *rajaz*, with a basic foot of XXSL (i.e., four syllables, the third of which must be short and the fourth long). See also index s.v. "*rajaz*."

1284 The *munsariḥ* meter, in its full form, is distinct from *rajaz*, but in the shortened forms given below there is some confusion with *rajaz*; the same with the meter *sarīʿ* (see below).

1285 To preserve the monorhyme some minor liberties have been taken in this and the following translations.

1286 It is not clear who is meant by "Father of Daughters"; the word "idol" has been added in the translation on the basis of al-Maʿarrī's commentary. Nicholson, in *JRAS* 1902, p, 360, thinks (without giving sources) that the "daughters" are female children buried alive as a sacrifice to the idols. Rather, one should think of a god with daughters, just as al-ʿUzzā, Manāt (more correctly Manāh), and Allāt were sometimes called "*banāt Allāh*."

1287 The pre-Islamic invocations often include tribal names, such as al-Namir, Hamdān, and Bajīlah.

1288 Translation tentative.

1289 An overlong syllable ends either in two consonants or, more commonly, a long vowel followed by a consonant. Such rhymes, rare in Arabic poetry, can only occur in some meters. The following lines rhyme in *-ān*; their meter is XLSL XLO (where O stands for an overlong syllable).

1290 Lane translates "We have come to Thee for the purpose of sincere worship" (*Lexicon*, s.v., *N-Ṣ-Ḥ*, p. 2801), but this meaning of *naṣāḥah* is not supported by the Arabic dictionaries.

1291 The invocation is said to be to the goddess Manāh in Ibn Ḥabīb, *Muḥabbar*, 313 (and see Kister, "Labbayka," 52), even though the present text has masculine forms. The translation is uncertain and the interpretation unclear. Tamīm and Bakr were on hostile terms; apparently the latter stood in the way of Tamīm, preventing them from worshipping. The version in Ibn Manẓūr, *Lisān al-ʿArab* (*ʿ-Th-J*) has *yaʿbuduka l-nāsu wa-yafjurūnakā*; the version in Ibn Ḥabīb, *Muḥabbar*, 313, quoted with variations in Kister, is *labbayki lawlā anna bakran dūnak(ī) | yabarruki l-nāsu wa-yahjurūnak(ī) (. . .).*

1292 Al-Umlūk and Hamdān both belonged to the larger tribe of Ḥimyar, according to Ibn Durayd (*Jamharah*, *R-D-M* and *M-L-K*).

1293 The grammatically correct form, *labbawk,* must be changed to *labbūk* to make for a correct rhyme.

1294 This seems to contradict the identification of some quoted invocations as being in *munsariḥ* or *sarīʿ*, meters that, being non-*rajaz*, count as *qaṣīd*. It confirms the confusion, noted above, between the shorter forms of these two meters and *rajaz*. Al-Maʿarrī probably refers to the fact that all invocations make use of short lines of two of two or three feet, whereas *qaṣīd* meters normally consist of longer lines containing two hemistichs.

1295 The eastern corner of the Kaaba, where the Black Stone is encased.

1296 The first verse is attributed to "someone from Quraysh" in al-Mubarrad, *Kāmil*, 1:355; to ʿUmar ibn Abī Rabīʿah in al-Baṣrī, *al-Ḥamāsah al-Baṣriyyah*, 2:157; to al-ʿArjī or ʿUmar ibn Abī Rabīʿah in al-Khālidiyyān, *Ashbāh*, 2:138–39; and to ʿUrwah ibn Udhaynah in various other sources, including al-Qālī, *Amālī*, 3:125; al-Iṣfahānī, *Aghānī*, 1:277, 281, 18:332; al-Marzubānī, *Muwashshaḥ*, 331. Both lines are attributed to ʿUmar ibn Abī Rabīʿah in al-Sarrāj, *Maṣāriʿ*, 2:124; they are not found in his *Dīwān*.

1297 The Wall is a semi-circular marble wall near the Kaaba; its name (*al-Ḥaṭīm*) is variously explained: either "broken," because unfinished, or because people used to trample one another (*yataḥaṭṭamu*) when praying there, etc. (see Ibn Manẓūr, *Lisān al-ʿArab*, *Ḥ-Ṭ-M*). Zamzam is a well near the Kaaba, the water of which is drunk by pilgrims. "It" in the second line is apparently the Kaaba or possibly the Black Stone.

1298 In the second line masculine forms are used for the subject whereas part of the predicate, "dumb" (*ṣammāʾ*), is feminine. Al-Maʿarrī's suggestion is that the predicate could be thought of as "dumb rock" (*ṣakhrah ṣammāʾ*), shortened to *ṣammāʾ* "a dumb (thing)," which is grammatically correct.

1299 Majnūn Laylā. See his *Dīwān*, ed. Zakī ʿAdnān, Beirut, 1994, 38–39.

1300 The ending *-ā*, used in exclamation, lament, or address, has a form *-āh* that is normally used only in pausal position (Wright, *Grammar*, 1:295); if, as here, it occurs in mid-sentence a short vowel (here *u*) has to be added for prosodical reasons.

1301 Not by ʿUmar ibn Abī Rabīʿah, as Bint al-Shāṭiʾ maintains; quoted anonymously in an anecdote about the famous Meccan singer Ibn Jāmiʿ (fl. late second/eighth century), see al-Mubarrad, *Kāmil*, 2:272–73; Ibn Qutaybah, *ʿUyūn*, 4:91–92; al-Iṣfahānī, *Aghānī*, 6:293; al-Balādhurī, *Ansāb*, 5:228–29; Ibn ʿAbd Rabbih, *ʿIqd*, 6:9–10.

1302 "Lifting one's loin-cloth" is a metonymy for "exerting oneself in worship" (Ibn al-Athīr, *al-Nihāyah fī gharīb al-ḥadīth*, *R-F-ʿ*).

1303 The Arabic has in fact the reverse: the particle *an* ("that") is missing after *ʿasā* ("perhaps"), which is unusual.

1304 A proverb, see al-ʿAskarī, *Jamharah*, 2:310 and al-Maydānī, *Majmaʿ*, 2:252. It is found, perhaps already as an existing proverb, in a verse by the pre-Islamic poet al-Aʿshā (*Dīwān*, ed. Beirut, 190).

1305 From a poem by the pre-Islamic poet al-Nābighah al-Dhubyānī (*Dīwān*, ed. Ahlwardt, *The Divans*, 5), often quoted as a proverb.

1306 The "Dispersal" from Minā to Mecca takes place at the end of the rites of the pilgrimage.

1307 By ʿUmar ibn Abī Rabīʿah. For the lines see his *Dīwān*, 205.

1308 The lines are from a poem included in the fourth/tenth-century anthology by al-Qurashī, *Jamharat ashʿār al-ʿarab*, see 227. For a translation of the whole poem see Lichtenstadter, *Introduction to Classical Arabic Literature*, 184–87.

1309 A place some five miles east of Mecca, where the last three days of the pilgrimage are spent with several rites, including the great sacrifice. The poet died a few years before the Hijra, but the Hajj is older than Islam.

1310 A hemistich from the famous *Muʿallaqah* by Imruʾ al-Qays. There are several interpretation of this verse (see also Jones, *Early Arabic Poetry, II: Select Odes*, 76). The grammatical point is that in Arabic an intransitive verb of motion (e.g., *ḥalla*, "stop") can have a transitive function when combined with the preposition *bi-* "with" or "at," so that *ḥalla bi-* can mean "stop at (a place)" as well as "make (someone) stop."

1311 See the entry "Mu<u>dj</u>āwir" in *EI2*, 7:293–94 (W. Ende).

1312 The *tanḍubah* is described as a large thorny tree that grows in the Hijaz, with big white branches, looking dry and dusty even when alive (Ibn Manẓūr, *Lisān al-ʿArab*, *N-Ḍ-B*).

1313 The word *awwāb*, literally "someone who returns," is found several times in the Qur'an in the sense of "penitent" (Q Isrāʾ 17:25, Ṣād 38:19, 30, 44, Qāf 50:32).

1314 The poet addresses himself. For the second and third lines see Ṭufayl al-Ghanawī, *Dīwān*, 55–56; for the third line, see also al-Jāḥiẓ, *Ḥayawān*, 7:197. The first line is in fact from a poem by ʿAbdah ibn al-Ṭabīb (*Mufaḍḍaliyyāt*, no. 26, the following line also mentions an elephant, which may have caused the confusion).

1315 For this line, see Sībawayh, *Kitāb*, 1:230, with an explanation why *makḥūl* ("made up with kohl") is masculine even though it qualifies the feminine *ʿayn* ("eye").

1316 Again there is some pronominal confusion: *tarʿā* is feminine, whereas *ribʿī* is masculine; the *Dīwān* and al-Jāḥiẓ, *Ḥayawān*, 7:197 have *tarʿā* but *lahū* instead of *lahā*, Abū ʿAlī al-Qaysī, *Īḍāḥ shawāhid al-Īḍāḥ*, 506 has *yarʿā* and *lahū*.

1317 The first two lines are quoted anonymously in Ibn Rashīq, *ʿUmdah*, 2:103 and Ibn Abī l-Iṣbaʿ, *Taḥrīr*, 287; the third in al-Maʿarrī, *Ṣāhil*, 391.

1318 Some other editions (Qumayḥah, al-Iskandarānī/Fawwāl) have *wa-abīka khayran*, but *khayrin* is correct. Compare *wa-abīka khayrin minka* (in a verse by Shumayr ibn al-Ḥārith al-Ḍabbī), explained as "by your father, a better man than you," al-Baghdādī, *Khizānah*, 5:179–81. Ibn Rashīq and Ibn Abī l-Iṣbaʿ have *ḥaqqan*.

1319 The editions of al-Yāzijī and Bint al-Shāṭiʾ have *ghuzulun*, which is meaningless. The correct reading is doubtless *ʿuz(u)lun* (as in Qumayḥah, al-Iskandarānī/Fawwāl, Ibn Rashīq, and Ibn Abī l-Iṣbaʿ), "unarmed" or "defenseless," meaning that their owner generously slaughters them for guests (who arrive on a "strange camel"), something done especially in cold winters.

1320 For the verses, see al-Jāḥiẓ, *Ḥayawān*, 7:198; Ibn Hishām, *Sīrah*, 1:60, trans. Guillaume, 29–30.

1321 Nufayl ibn Ḥabīb al-Khathʿamī was taken prisoner by Abrahah; offering himself as his guide he led them to al-Mughammas, where he told the elephant to stop since it was sacred territory. The animal obeyed and knelt down toward Mecca. For the story and the verses, see Ibn Hishām, *Sīrah*, 1:46–53, trans. Guillaume, 23–27; also al-Jāḥiẓ, *Ḥayawān*, 7:199.

1322 The invaders were killed or driven away by birds that cast stones, sent by God; see the story in Ibn Hishām and the Surah of the Elephant. The fate of the elephant (called Maḥmūd) is not known.

1323 Abrahah had been set on the throne by Abyssinians (or Ethiopians) who had remained after an Abyssinian invasion of Yemen.

1324 The *ʿumrah* or "lesser pilgrimage" is a shortened form of the Hajj that, unlike the Hajj, can be performed at any time of the year. When one combines them one has to enter into the appropriate state of ritual purity (*iḥrām*) only once. See R. Paret and E. Chaumont, "ʿUmra" in *EI2*, 10:864–66. The verb *ahalla* can mean either saying the *talbiyah* (the formula "Here I am for Thee!") or the *basmalah* ("In the name of God, the Merciful, the Compassionate"); the context suggests the former.

1325 An allusion to the controversial matter of the "temporary marriage" (*mutʿah*, literally "enjoyment"), a marriage contract for a fixed period. The Qur'anic verse «The wives that you enjoy thereby, give them their wages (or: dowries)» (Q Nisāʾ 4:24) had a variant adding "until a specific time," which was by some exegetes seen as confirmation of this practice. Among them was the famous cousin of the Prophet, ʿAbd Allāh ibn ʿAbbās (d. 68/687). The Sunnites do not recognize this kind of marriage (which could be seen as a form of prostitution) but it exists in Shiʾite Islam. See W. Heffening, "Mutʿa" in *EI2*, 7:756–59.

1326 Unidentified. "Circumambulating her Kaaba" is probably a somewhat risqué sexual metaphor. The verses are quoted anonymously (with a variant *ḥattā taṣdura l-nāsū*, with a rhyme defect) in al-Subkī, *Ṭabaqāt al-Shāfiʿiyyah*, 3:141, and said to be by a contemporary of Ibn ʿAbbās. See also al-Rāghib al-Iṣbahānī, *Muḥāḍarāt*, 2:125 (a woman says, in verse: "Old man, how about the fatwa of Ibn ʿAbbās?").

1327 Jawhar ibn ʿAbd Allāh al-Ṣiqillī. The word *jawhar* means "jewel."

1328 i.e., by Death, or God.

1329 The two words used here are more appropriate to camels than pearls: *niqābah* is "foot ulcer" (also "first signs of mange" and "rust"), *nuḥāz* is a coughing disease of camels.

1330 Imruʾ al-Qays, *Dīwān*, 43. Lane, *Lexicon* (s.v., *J-R-M*) translates *bi-Anṭākiyyatin* as "at Antioch," but all commentators (e.g., al-Baṭalyawsī, Abū ʿAmr al-Shaybānī, and Yāqūt in *Muʿjam al-buldān*) interpret it as "with cloth from Antioch," because the correct form of Antioch in Arabic is *Anṭākiyah*, with single *y*, according to most authorities.

1331 The colors and patterns of the hangings are compared to dates.

1332 Needless to say, "Antioch" is not Arabic. Some lexicographers mention under the imaginary root *N-Ṭ-K* that Anṭākiyah (Antioch) is "probably Greek" (see al-Azharī, *Tahdhīb al-lughah*, 10:62; Ibn Manẓūr, *Lisān al-ʿArab*).

1333 On Arabic morphological patterns, see *Gh* §§3.8.4 and 13.8. The "derivation" assumes that Malaṭyah (Malatya) is from a root *M-L-Ṭ*, with a "secondary" *Y* followed by the feminine ending *-ah*. The name is not Arabic and probably not even Semitic.

1334 Abū l-Qāsim al-Maghribī, see *IQ* §7.4 and following sections.

1335 In other words, *De mortuis nil nisi bonum*. Ibn Durayd, *Jamharah*, 1287: "The Arabs say 'Let the one in the grave alone,' when someone blames a dead person."

1336 From a fragment included in Abū Tammām's *Ḥamāsah* (see al-Marzūqī, *Sharḥ*, 1740–41) by a certain Muzaʿfar, probably the early Islamic Maʿn ibn Ḥudhayfah al-Muzaʿfar al-Murrī (al-Marzubānī, *Muʿjam al-shuʿarāʾ*, 323).

1337 See *IQ* §7.5: Abū l-Qāsim could not believe that Ibn al-Qāriḥ's extemporized verses were not prepared in advance.

1338 Hāshim was the Prophet's grandfather, many of whose descendants are called al-Ḥasan or al-Ḥusayn, after the two sons of ʿAlī ibn Abī Ṭālib and Muḥammad's daughter Fāṭimah.

1339 The renewal of faded tattoos is found as a motif in poetry.

1340 Rainclouds are often compared to camels.

1341 See S. A. Bonebakker, "Irtid̲j̲āl," in *EI2*, 4:80–81.

1342 In English, "capping" can mean to supply a verse that somehow corresponds with a given verse; here (*tamlīṭ* in Arabic) it means to complete a line of which the first hemistich is given, observing the correct meter and rhyme; see Ibn Ẓāfir al-Azdī (d. 613/1216 or 623/1226), in his monograph on improvisation, *Badāʾiʿ al-Badāʾih*, 167–235.

1343 Meaning unclear; *rāsiyah* is either "lofty mountain" or "large cooking pot."

1344 *Iʿnāt* is not a term especially connected with improvisation. In literary criticism it is used as a synonym of *luzūm mā lā yalzam* (see Introduction, xxvi, xxxvi), the "rich rhyme" so beloved by al-Maʿarrī in his verse and prose. See Ibn al-Muʿtazz, *Badīʿ*, 74 and several later works such as al-Tibrīzī, *Wāfī*, 295.

1345 The verse, which is quoted in Sībawayh's *Kitāb* (1:355) as being by ʿAbd Allāh ibn al-Zabīr al-Asadī (early Umayyad period), has also been attributed to Faḍālah ibn Sharīk al-Asadī (d. 64/683); see al-Sīrāfī, *Sharḥ abyāt Sībawayh*, 1:569, and to Faḍālah's son ʿAbd Allāh, see al-Iṣfahānī, *Aghānī*, 12:72, from a poem in which he attacks Ibn al-Zubayr as being stingy and praises the Umayyads. Abū Khubayb is the "anti-caliph" ʿAbd Allāh ibn al-Zubayr who was defeated by the Umayyad caliph ʿAbd al-Malik and killed in 72/692; Umayyah, the pre-Islamic ancestor of the Umayyads, stands here for the Umayyads in general.

1346 Line one is often quoted anonymously, e.g., in al-Mubarrad, *Kāmil*, 2:165, and al-Iṣfahānī, *Aghānī*, 16:187; the third line in Ibn Durayd, *Jamharah*, 430 (*Q-Th-M*), all three in Ibn Manẓūr, *Lisān al-ʿArab* (*Q-Th-M*). The first line is attributed to al-Ḥārith ibn Khālid ibn al-ʿĀṣ al-Makhzūmī (d. after 96/715) in his *Dīwān*, 93; to al-Ḥārith ibn Asad al-Aṣghar in al-Marzubānī, *Muʿjam al-shuʿarāʾ*, 482; and to Buḥayr (or Bujayr) ibn ʿAbd Allāh ibn ʿĀmir ibn Salamah in Ibn Ḥabīb, *Muḥabbar*, 139.

1347 *Itbāʿ*, conventional rhyming pairs, the second element of which differs only in one letter, usually the first, but is often meaningless, as in *ḥasan basan* "very good" (a more demotic English equivalent would be "okey-dokey"). See M. Bencheikh, "Muzāwadja," *EI2*, 7:823–24.

1348 *Ibdāl* is the term for the various mutations undergone by phonemes as a result of phonotactic rules; it also concerns lexicographical variation between nearly identical forms, e.g., *rifall/rifann*, "long-tailed (horse)." Abū l-Ṭayyib's book deals with the latter kind; it is preserved and has been edited. See *EI2*, 3:665.

1349 As a technical term in linguistics *qalb* has two meanings (1) "conversion," related to *ibdāl*, the change of a phoneme, specifically the "weak" consonants *w* and *y*, and the glottal stop, in certain circumstances; and (2) metathesis, such as the variants *jadhaba* and *jabadha*, "to attract."

1350 The book deals with a peculiar, playful way of making chains or branched strings (hence the tree and pearls) of homonyms, using one meaning that links a word with a predecessor and another meaning that links it with the following word. A limited English example would be "adhere: stick; stick: stake; stake: post: post: mail; mail: armour." See, e.g., al-Suyūṭī, *Muzhir*, 1:454–59 (where it is called *al-mushajjar*).

1351 Brockelmann, *Geschichte*, Suppl. I, 183, mentions his *al-Madākhil wa-l-ziyādāt* (or *al-Madākhil wa-gharīb al-lughah*); the correct reading is *al-Mudākhil*, or possibly *al-Mudākhal*, see al-Suyūṭī, *Muzhir*, 1:454, quoting the opening of Abū l-Ṭayyib al-Lughawī's *Pearl Tree*: "This book is about how speech interferes with meanings (*mudākhalat al-kalām li-l-maʿānī*)."

1352 The subject is unknown; it could be on distinguishing the meanings of nearly identical words. See al-Suyūṭī, *Muzhir*, 2:288–301, on *furūq* (e.g., the difference between *ḥaththa* and *ḥaḍḍa*, both meaning "to incite," or *ʿiwaj* and *ʿawaj*, "crookedness").

1353 In 352/962 the Byzantines under Nicephorus II Phocas (called *al-dumustuq*, "the *domesticus*" by the Arabs) took Aleppo by storm, pillaged the town, and killed many inhabitants.

1354 The text has *qurmūṭat al-kabarthal*. Ibn Manẓūr, *Lisān al-ʿarab* has *kabawthal* and *kabartal*, but not *kabarthal*.

1355 *Shawṭ barāḥ* (difficult to translate, perhaps "course of the open land") is an unexplained name for the jackal (normally called *ibn āwā*) "or some other animal" (Ibn Manẓūr, *Lisān al-ʿArab*, *Sh-W-Ṭ*); *ʿillawḍ* also means "jackal."

1356 On his poem rhyming on *-ī/ūṣ* see *Gh* §§3.3–4, 6.2.

1357 A proverb, see al-ʿAskarī, *Jamharah*, 2:311; al-Maydānī, *Majmaʿ*, 2:261–63, said to refer to the trading "caravan" of Abū Sufyān and the "troop" setting out to fight the Prophet at Badr. It is applied to someone unfit for something and al-Maʿarrī means that he is unworthy of Ibn al-Qāriḥ's extolling him.

1358 Translation uncertain. Al-Maʿarrī uses the phrase *jārimat ʿiyāl* in his *Fuṣūl* (171) and explains it as *kāsibuhum* "he who earns their sustenance" (using the masculine singular); the context (*ḍaraba ʿunuq jārimat ʿiyāl*) also suggests a man rather than a female or a collective;

cf also his *Risālat al-Ṣāhil wa-l-shāḥij*, 96 (*aw jārimat ʿiyāl mithl al-dhiʾb*).

1359 The only reason for mentioning this tree (*ḍāl*) seems to be the rhyme with *ifḍāl* ("graciousness").

1360 Quoted anonymously in Ibn al-Sikkīt, *Iṣlāḥ al-manṭiq*, 317; Ibn Manẓūr, *Lisān al-ʿArab* (*Dh-H-B*, *Sh-Dh-R*, and *Th-R-M-L*). Tuzmurah, in other sources Thurmulah (or, as below, Turmulah, which is probably an error), is an unusual man's name.

1361 The dictionaries give the unusual verb *dhahiba* (derived from *dhahab*, "gold"), meaning "to be amazed by the riches of a gold mine."

1362 The second and third line end in *-rah*; *-lah* would be a serious rhyme defect.

1363 See *IQ* §9.2.

1364 Attributed not to the Prophet but (as *rawwiḥū hādhihi l-qulūb taʿi l-dhikr*) to the early Islamic Qasāmah ibn Zuhayr in al-Jāḥiẓ, *Bayān*, 1:326, idem, *Risālah fī nafy al-tashbīh*, in his *Rasāʾil*, 1:291; see also al-Zamakhsharī, *Rabīʿ al-abrār*, 1:39.

1365 The verse is the opening line of a poem included in al-Qurashī, *Jamharat ashʿār al-ʿarab* (231–33, with some variants).

1366 Unidentified.

1367 This hemistich is found as a (non-rhyming) first hemistich in a poem by Mālik ibn Zughbah (pre-Islamic), see al-Akhfash, *Ikhtiyārayn*, 148.

1368 ʿAdī ibn Zayd al-ʿIbādī. For the verses, see al-Akhfash, *Ikhtiyārayn*, 715; al-Buḥturī, *Ḥamāsah*, 106; Ibn Qutaybah, *Shiʿr*, 226; al-Iṣfahānī, *Aghānī*, 2:139.

1369 Before his abdication, al-Nuʿmān the Elder built the legendary castles al-Khawarnaq and al-Sadīr at al-Ḥīrah (near al-Najaf in Iraq, close to the Euphrates) for his Sassanid suzerain; al-Khawarnaq was still used by the Abbasids.

1370 The usual reading found in the sources is "his heart."

1371 In the following passage of prose in rich rhyme many different words for "wine" are used; it would be anachronistic to attempt an imitation by means of modern European words such as claret, rosé, Burgundy, Beaujolais, Sauterne.

1372 See above, §37.4.2.

1373 Or perhaps "will not be informed of evident truth."

1374 The Arabic puns on *sulāfah* ("choice wine, made of juice flowing from unpressed grapes") being *sull* ("consumption") and *āfah* ("bane, ruin, ailment").

1375 It seems that this tribe is singled out merely in order to supply a rhyme with "youth" (*shābb*).

1376 There are several explanations of the epithet *shamūl*, derived either from *shamila* "to envelop" or from *shamāl* "north wind": "wine that envelops those present with its aroma," "wine as strong as (or cooled by) the north wind," or "wine that envelops the mind and takes possession of it" (al-Marzūqī, *Sharḥ*, 1259; al-Zamakhsharī, *Asās*, *Sh-M-L*; Ibn Manẓūr, *Lisān al-ʿArab*, *Sh-M-L*).

1377 The author uses two different words for "lute" (but not the most common one, *ʿūd*): *barbaṭ* and *mizhar*; the latter had a belly made of skin rather than wood. See H. G. Farmer, "ʿŪd," *EI2*, 10:768a.

1378 For the verses see al-Sukkarī, *Sharḥ ashʿār al-Hudhaliyyīn*, 1261; Ibn Qutaybah, *Maʿānī*, 1198; Ibn Manẓūr, *Lisān al-ʿArab* (*Ḥ-B-L*).

1379 i.e., hyenas will dig up his grave.

1380 The lines are from a poem attributed to al-Nābighah al-Jaʿdī, included in al-Qurashī, *Jamharat ashʿār al-ʿarab*, 275. On the basis of the second verse it has been claimed, implausibly, that the poet, called "long-lived" (e.g., Ibn Qutaybah, *Shiʿr*, 290; al-Iṣfahānī, *Aghānī*, 5:5–6), was a drinking companion of the pre-Islamic Lakhmid king al-Nuʿmān ibn al-Muḥarriq, father of al-Nuʿmān ibn al-Mundhir at whose court another Nābighah, al-Dhubyānī, lived. Al-Jaʿdī died ca. 60/680 or some years later (Sezgin, *Geschichte*, 2:245–46, Arazi, "al-Nābigha al-Djaʿdī," *EI2*, 7:842–43).

1381 The verse is the first of five found in Abū Tammām's *Ḥamāsah* (al-Marzūqī, *Sharḥ*, 875–78), attributed to "al-Asadī." In al-Iṣfahānī, *Aghānī*, 15:245, 248 the lines are attributed to Quss ibn Sāʿidah, a legendary orator from pre-Islamic times, but a longer version of eleven verses is attributed, on the authority of Ibn al-Sikkīt, to ʿĪsā ibn Qudāmah al-Asadī (*Aghānī*, 15:248–49), who is otherwise unknown. The lines have also been ascribed to the equally obscure Naṣr ibn Ghālib (see al-Baghdādī, *Khizānah*, 2:87–88; Yāqūt, *Muʿjam al-buldān*, s.v. Rāwand).

1382 The relevant verses are not quoted by al-Maʿarrī: "I'll stay standing at your graves and will not leave (. . .)"

1383 See above, §37.2.1, where it is said that "syrup" (*ṭilā'*) is used as a euphemism for wine. The poet of this line has not been identified.

1384 Or perhaps "pitilessly"? The meaning of *min ghayr balā'* is not wholly clear; compare the words of Arwā bint al-Ḥārith, accusing Muʿāwiyah: "You have taken what is not your due *bi-ghayr balā'* on your and your ancestors' part" (Ibn Abī Ṭayfūr, *Balāghāt al-nisā'*, 40).

1385 See *IQ* §9.3.

1386 For this eschatological image see, e.g., Wensinck et al., *Concordance*, s.v. *L-J-M*; Ibn Manẓūr, *Lisān al-ʿArab (L-J-M)* explains: "sweat will reach their mouths, becoming like a bridle that prevents them from speaking on the Day of Resurrection."

1387 "Out of an annual Egyptian revenue of three or five million *dīnār*s, Muʿāwiya is said to have received a balance of only 600,000 *dīnār*s" (M. Hinds, "Muʿāwiya," *EI2*, 7:266a). For the anecdote, cf. Ibn Qutaybah, *ʿUyūn*, 1:318, and compare the version in Abū ʿUbayd al-Bakrī, *Muʿjam mā staʿjam* (ed. al-Saqqā), 2:445.

1388 i.e., it was not a trifling amount.

1389 Ibn al-Muʿtazz; see his *Dīwān* (ed. Muḥammad Badīʿ Sharīf), 2:297.

1390 The beginning can be read as *danānīrunā*, "our dinars," or as *danā nīrunā*, "our yoke has approached." The verse is quoted anonymously in al-Khalīl, *ʿAyn* (*Q-S-Ṭ-R*), Ibn Manẓūr, *Lisān al-ʿArab* (*N-Y-R* and *Q-S-Ṭ-R*), in both cases with a different ending (*ʿinda l-qasāṭirī* or *ʿinda l-qasāṭirah*, both meaning "at the money-changers"). Al-Maʿarrī's reading, *bayna l-ṣafā'iḥī*, "between slabs," not found elsewhere, is unclear (this usually refers to the slabs or stones on a grave).

1391 The verse is from a poem in *al-Mufaḍḍaliyyāt*, 238 (see Lyall's translation, 181). The word used by al-Maʿarrī, *rabā'ib*, strictly means "stepmothers," "foster-mothers," or "allied women"; but there is nothing in Muraqqish's poem that suggests they are anything but the women of the tribe and it seems that *rabāʾib* was chosen merely for the sake of the rhyme.

1392 *ʿAnam* is a parasitic plant of uncertain identity; Lyall (183) thinks of a kind of mistletoe, a species of *Loranthus*; see also Ghaleb, *Dictionnaire*, s.v. Its berries are red and mentioned by poets describing henna'd fingers.

1393 al-Nābighah al-Jaʿdī, *Dīwān*, 142.

1394 *Bi-l-mithqāl* ("with a weight") is unclear; one is tempted to read *bi-l-miṣqāl* "with a polishing tool," but this word is not well attested (in a poem by al-Ḥuṣayn ibn al-Ḥumām, in al-Ṣafadī, *Wāfī*, 13:90, it seems to mean "polished sword") and it is difficult to imagine that *miṣqāl* could become corrupted to *mithqāl* (unless someone with a lisp intervened at some stage in the transmission of the text).

1395 The word is vowelled as *murahhanāt* by Bint al-Shāṭiʾ and al-Iskandarānī/Fawwāl, but this form is not attested elsewhere as far as we know and we read it as *murhanāt*. For the sake of a better rhyme, we also read *mūhanāt* rather than *muwahhanāt*.

1396 Meaning unclear.

1397 The line is quoted anonymously in Ibn Manẓūr, *Lisān al-ʿArab* (*R-H-N*); with a different first hemistich it is attributed to "Radhādh al-Kalbī" in Ibn Manẓūr, *Lisān al-ʿArab* (*ʿ-W-D*); nothing is known about the poet. The second hemistich is quoted anonymously in several sources.

1398 The word *urhinat* is variously explained as "paid in advance" (*salafan*) and "prepared" (*uʿiddat*); see, e.g., Ibn Durayd, *Jamharah*, 807 (*R-H-N*). The epithet *ʿīdiyyah* is usually explained as referring to the tribe of ʿĪd, but another interpretation connects it with the legendary pre-Islamic people of ʿĀd. If instead of *buʿuran* ("camels") the reading of *Lisān al-ʿArab* (*buʿudan*, "far and wide") is adopted, *ʿīdiyyah* is better rendered as "a she-camel of the Banū ʿĪd."

1399 This otherwise pointless clause only serves a rhyme.

1400 For the verse, see Ibn Qays al-Ruqayyāt, *Dīwān*, 71, and al-Iṣfahānī, *Aghānī*, 12:181–82, where the words "the clay of her seal is widely accepted" is interpreted as "she has influence with the ruler," "she" being Umm al-Banīn, wife of Caliph al-Walīd ibn ʿAbd al-Malik (r. 86–96/705–17).

1401 One of the many important measures of the Umayyad caliph ʿAbd al-Malik ibn Marwān (r. 65–86/685–705) was the reform of the coinage. The first Islamic dinars were struck from ca. 72/692, modeled on Byzantine coins that had hitherto been used.

1402 Sībawayh, *Kitāb,* 1:10, al-Mubarrad, *Kāmil,* 1:319, and many later works; not found in al-Farazdaq's *Dīwān,* ed. Dār Ṣādir; in the edition of ʿAbd Allāh al-Ṣāwī, 570, it is given after Sībawayh. The verse describes a speeding she-camel.

1403 As, e.g., in al-Mubarrad, *Kāmil,* 1:319.

1404 The allusion is not clear. Bint al-Shāṭi' and al-Iskandarānī/Fawwāl have *nakhīlah,* but a proper rhyme with Aylah requires the diminutive *nukhaylah.*

1405 The line is quoted anonymously in Ibn Manẓūr, *Lisān al-ʿArab* (*H-B-R-Z* and *W-Sh-Y*) and attributed to Uḥayḥah ibn al-Julāḥ in Yāqūt, *Muʿjam al-buldān* s.v. Aylah; it is from an elegy on his son. The following line is ". . . more beautiful than he was when he appeared in the morning; | hasty Death made me sigh for him."

1406 Literally, "consuming itself," used for "being enraged" and "gleaming," said of lightning or swords; for the same image, see the verse on a sword by Aws ibn Ḥajar quoted in al-Qālī, *Amālī,* 2:220; Ibn Manẓūr, *Lisān al-ʿArab, '-K-L.*

1407 It is not, of course, the gold coin itself that is engraved but the stamp used for minting it. The commentary in Yāqūt and Ibn Manẓūr more correctly glosses *al-wushāh* as *al-ḍarrābūn* ("the minters").

1408 The verse, which describes the beaming faces of warriors in battle, is quoted, e.g., in al-Khalīl, *ʿAyn* (*Q-S-M*); it is from a poem included in Abū Tammām's *Ḥamāsah* (al-Marzūqī, *Sharḥ,* 1457), by Muḥriz ibn al-Mukaʿbir al-Ḍabbī (pre-Islamic but may have lived at the beginning of Islam).

1409 The poet is unknown and the lines have not been found elsewhere.

1410 On the "rain stars," see *Gh* §3.8.2.

1411 Poet unidentified.

1412 Presumably the speaker's wife.

1413 There is a play on words (*aqdāḥ*, "cups," and *qidāḥ*, "arrows")

1414 The two lines by al-Nābighah al-Jaʿdī are quoted in Abū ʿUbayd al-Bakrī, *Muʿjam mā staʿjam* (ed. Wüstenfeld), 1:300; the second line or parts of it are quoted in several sources.

1415 A reference to the creaking of the pulley.

1416 Wooden clappers in eastern churches serve like bells in the west.

1417 Unidentified; the lines have not been found elsewhere.

1418 The two lines are said to have been inscribed on the two sides of four thousand outsize dinars found in a pond belonging to the famous Barmakid vizier Jaʿfar ibn Yaḥyā (executed by Hārūn al-Rashīd in d. 187/803), see al-Jahshiyārī, *Wuzarāʾ*, 241 and cf. al-Washshāʾ, *Muwashshā*, 193. Elsewhere (al-Khaṭīb al-Baghdādī, *Tārīkh Baghdād*, 7:156) it is told how Jaʿfar had them struck, every coin weighing three hundred *mithqāl*s (equivalent to three hundred normal dinars) and bearing an image of his face; the verses (duly mentioning "a weight of three hundred" here) are said to have been composed afterward by Abū l-ʿAtāhiyah; they are not found in his *Dīwān*.

1419 Al-Jahshiyārī says that each coin weighed 101 "dinars" (a *dīnār* also being a weight of some 4.25 grams).

1420 Q Āl ʿImrān 3:75.

1421 Jews or Christians (but see al-Maʿarrī's comment, below).

1422 *Qinṭār*, ultimately from Latin *centenarium*, has been translated in this passage as "hundredweight," "talent," and "heap of gold." The commentators connect it with a story involving 1,200 ounces of gold.

1423 Abū Jundab al-Hudhalī, pre-Islamic (but may have reached the Islamic period); see al-Sukkarī, *Sharḥ ashʿār al-Hudhaliyyīn*, 363 (where it is said that al-Aṣmaʿī attributes the poem from which the verse is taken to another poet of Hudhayl, Abū Dhuʾayb).

1424 The Hudhalī *Dīwān* has masculine forms (*daʿawta, atāka*); Bint al-Shāṭiʾ has feminine forms (*daʿawti, atāki*), perhaps because the poem begins with addressing a woman (*Aqūlu li-Ummi Zinbāʿin aqīmī*). But women do not invite men; *daʿawta* is probably the "neutral" form ("if one invited them").

1425 See his *Dīwān*, 18.

1426 See his *Dīwān*, 89–90.

1427 With the following *rajaz* verses he addresses his mother, having been wounded during a fight with an opponent called Nubayshah ibn Ḥabīb. See al-ʿAskarī, *Jamharah*, 1:330; al-Maydānī, *Majmaʿ*, 1:286.

1428 The line is quoted and discussed anonymously in Sībawayh, *Kitāb*, 1:87 and many other works, e.g., al-Baghdādī, *Khizānah*, 8:215–19 (where it is said that some attribute it to Jarīr, or Jābir ibn Raʾlān al-Sinbisī, or Taʾabbaṭa Sharrā). The two men mentioned in the line are unknown.

1429 The verse is discussed because of the accusative in *ʿAbda Rabbin akhā ʿAwn*, even though it seems to continue the genitive in *bāʿithu Dīnārin*.

1430 The line is found in an ode in praise of Caliph Sulaymān in his *Dīwān* (2:90, which wrongly has Dhubyān instead of Dīnār).

1431 A "goat's day" is an allusion to a violent death; see, e.g., Ibn Qutaybah, *Maʿānī*, 876, 1028; Abū ʿUbayd al-Bakrī, *Faṣl al-maqāl*, 455; al-Thaʿālibī, *Thimār*, 379–80. The allusion is to a proverb, "like the one who searched for the knife," i.e., a goat that happened to find the knife that would be used to slaughter it. On this saying, originally Greek, and its many forms in Arabic, see Ullmann, "Αἴξ τὴν μάχαιραν."

1432 Instead of "his killer" (*qātiluh*), the *Dīwān* and other versions have "one who will keep him busy" (*shāghiluh*); al-Thaʿālibī has "one who will abandon him" (*khādhiluh*).

1433 The line is quoted anonymously in Ibn Manẓūr, *Lisān al-ʿArab* (*N-Kh-Kh, Ḍ-Ḥ-W*), mentioning another tribe (Kalb). The word *nakhkhah* (or *nukhkhah*) is variously explained: "male or female slaves," "donkeys," or "cattle put to work." The Prophet is reported to have said "There is no alms tax (*ṣadaqah*) on *nakhkhah*."

1434 Poet unidentified; the lines have not been found elsewhere.

1435 Literally, "raise their tails" (to receive a male), which means they have no milk.

1436 The line is from a poem in praise of Caliph Yazīd ibn Muʿāwiyah (*Dīwān*, 143; Ibn Sallām, *Ṭabaqāt*, 433; al-Qurashī, *Jamharah*, 329, all with a wholly different first half: "A virgin [wine] the brilliance of which is not discerned by the suitors . . . ," and with "discerned it" (*ijtalāhā*) instead of "bought it" in the second half).

1437 The Arabic *ʿibādī* is the term for Christians of al-Ḥīrah.

1438 The poet of the two rather obscure *rajaz* lines is unknown; the second is quoted in Ibn Manẓūr, *Lisān al-ʿArab* (*K-R-K*), who also mentions Abū ʿUmar al-Zāhid as his source. The rare word *kārūkah* is from Aramaic *kārōḵā*.

1439 A line from al-Mutanabbī's famous ode praising the Būyid ruler ʿAḍud al-Dawlah (*Dīwān*, 767); he describes his journey to the patron, passing by the wooded Valley of Bawwān. For an English translation of the poem, see Arberry, *Poems by al-Mutanabbī*, 143–41.

1440 Kuthayyir ʿAzzah, *Dīwān*, 1:83. The words *ʿuyūna l-nāẓirīna* ("the eyes of the onlookers") in the present text is an error for *al-ʿuyūna l-nāẓirāti* ("looking eyes") found in all other sources (e.g., al-Iṣfahānī, *Aghānī*, 12:187). "Heraclian" refers to the Byzantine emperor Heraclius who ruled AD 610–41; for the use of Byzantine dinars (the *solidus* of Heraclius) by the early Muslims, see above, §43.1.2.

1441 Ibn al-Qāriḥ speaks of eighty-three.

1442 Q Aʿrāf 7:155; cf. Num. 11:16–24.

1443 Q Tawbah 9:80.

1444 Q Ḥāqqah 69:32, describing the unbeliever in Hell.

1445 The line (al-Aʿshā, *Dīwān*, ed. Rudolf Geyer, London: Luzac, 1928, 94, Beirut: Dār Ṣādir, 1994, 182) is from a poem mocking a certain ʿUmayr ibn ʿAbd Allāh ibn al-Mundhir.

1446 See Q Ghāfir 40:36–37: «Pharaoh said, "O Haman, build me a high building, so that I may reach the ropes, the ropes of the heavens"»; the pre-Islamic poet Zuhayr also uses the expression in his *Muʿallaqah* (". . . even if he ascended the ropes of heaven with a ladder," al-Tibrīzī, *Sharḥ al-qaṣāʾid al-ʿashr*, 64).

1447 The following verses are "Then your words would surely disquieten you | until you will hate them and know that I shall not hold your blood sacrosanct. || And you will choke on the words you have spread

| as a lance-tip chokes on blood." See Ibn Manẓūr, *Lisān al-ʿArab* (*S-B-B, D-R-J*).

1448 Zuhayr ibn Abī Sulmā is said to have lived for one hundred-twenty years (Abū Ḥātim al-Sijistānī, *Muʿammarūn*, 73), but al-Maʿarrī is thinking of the verse in Zuhayr's *Muʿallaqah*, "... he who lives eighty years, dammit, gets bored" (Lyall, *Sharḥ al-qaṣāʾid al-ʿashr*, 65).

1449 Anonymously in Ibn Manẓūr, *Lisān al-ʿArab* (*Q-W-M*).

1450 For the verse, see al-Qālī, *Amālī*, 3:160 and (with rhyme-word *thamāniyā*) al-Baghdādī, *Khizānah*, 3:375 (cf. 379).

1451 A dinar was theoretically ten or twelve dirhams, in practice some twenty or considerably more.

1452 See Ibn Sallām, *Ṭabaqāt*, 33; al-Iṣfahānī, *Aghānī*, 8:85, 9:335–36: when al-Farazdaq needed one hundred camels as a bride-price for Ḥadrāʾ bint Zīq, a Christian woman, he appealed to the Umayyad governor al-Ḥajjāj, who refused at first; through the intercession of ʿAnbasah ibn Saʿīd he received one hundred "of the inferior camels of the alms tax revenue (*min ḥawāshī ibil al-ṣadaqah*)." The sale is mentioned only in the more detailed version of Abū ʿUbaydah, *Naqāʾiḍ Jarīr wa-l-Farazdaq*, 819–21.

1453 His *History* is not preserved and the story has not been found elsewhere.

1454 Perhaps Abū ʿAbd Allāh Muḥammad ibn ʿImrān al-Marzubānī (d. 384/993) is meant, author of various books on poetry, poets, grammarians, and other topics.

1455 ʿAlī ibn Muḥammad. The line has not been found elsewhere.

1456 With the following verse, the last of seven included in Abū Tammām's *Ḥamāsah* (see al-Marzūqī, *Sharḥ*, 602), he boasts of the number of men in his tribe, Sinbis.

1457 The line is from a poem in praise of Caliph Hishām ibn ʿAbd al-Malik (al-Farazdaq, *Dīwān*, 2: 291).

1458 Literally, "the nights," often used meaning "Fate" or "(destructive) Time."

1459 There are several explanations and discussions of this proverb and its variants; see al-Maydānī, *Majmaʿ*, 1:289; al-ʿAskarī, *Jamharah*,

1:314–15: the number is too large to handle; or it goes back to a Bedouin who was offered a reward by the Sasanian emperor for bringing him good tidings and who thought that eighty sheep was all he needed.

1460 Al-Maydānī, *Majmaʿ*, 2:432; al-ʿAskarī, *Jamharah*, 2:268.

1461 The word *riqah* has two meanings, "lush pasture" and "(silver) dirham," deemed inferior to the gold dinar.

1462 See *Gh* §16.3.

1463 For the anecdote, see, e.g., Ibn Qutaybah, *Shiʿr*, 238, 325–26; al-Iṣfahānī, *Aghānī*, 2:167, 16:378–79, 17:226.

1464 The verse is from a poem in the ancient anthology *al-Aṣmaʿiyyāt* (187).

1465 See his *Dīwān* (ed. ʿArafāt), 1:40 (ed. Ḥasanayn) 89, both having *ḥilm* ("wisdom") instead of *ʿilm* ("knowledge")

1466 See his *Dīwān*, (Beirut, 1994), 75. The woman is "yellow" in the evening, having put on saffron-based makeup.

1467 Unidentified; the lines are quoted anonymously in Yāqūt, *Muʿjam al-buldān*, s.v. al-Sitār. The Banū l-ʿAnbar tribe were nicknamed Banū l-Jaʿrāʾ ("the turd-woman's sons") after a woman called Dughah, proverbial for her stupidity (she gave birth to a child thinking she was defecating).

1468 Yāqūt explains *al-sitār* as "the gaps between the boundary stones of the sacred area (*ḥaram*), serving as a border between the profane and the sacred area (of Mecca)"; see also al-Zabīdī, *Tāj al-ʿarūs* (*S-T-R*). Here it has apparently been taken as a place name (see, e.g., poems by ʿAlqamah and Imruʾ al-Qays, in Ahlwardt, *The Divans*, 103, 150).

1469 A "carat" (*qīrāṭ*), originally a grain of the carob-tree, is also the twenty-fourth part of a dinar.

1470 The verses are from a poem in praise of Abd Allāh ibn Ṭāhir, the governor of Khurāsān. See Ibn al-Muʿtazz, *Ṭabaqāt*, 187.

1471 Abū l-ʿItrīf is unidentified; the line (with a different second hemistich but with the same rhyme in *-ālā*) is attributed to an unidentified Abū l-Miqdām in dictionaries (al-Khalīl, *ʿAyn*; Ibn Manẓūr, *Lisān al-ʿArab*) s.v. ʿ-*Y-N*, where "eyes" is explained as "dinars." All earlier editions of *al-Ghufrān* have *ʿayban*, an error for *ʿaynan*.

1472 Thamānūn, "Eighty," called thus because it was there according to legend that the eighty people in Noah's ark disembarked after the Flood. They all died of the plague except Noah and his family (Yāqūt, *Muʿjam al-buldān*, s.v.). Mount al-Jūdī is mentioned in the Qur'an (Q Hūd 11:44); see M. Streck, entry "Djūdī," *EI2*, 2:573–74.

1473 Quoted anonymously in Ibn al-Marzubān, *al-Muntahā fī l-kamāl*, 168, attributed to the grammarian Abū Bakr Muḥammad ibn al-Ḥasan al-Zubaydī (d. 379/989) in al-Thaʿālibī, *Yatīmah*, 2:71, whereas Ibn Khallikān, *Wafayāt*, 4:373 merely says that al-Zubaydī "often recited" the verses. In al-Rāghib al-Iṣfahānī, *Muḥāḍarāt*, 1:306 the verse is attributed to al-Mubarrad.

1474 The mole (*khāl*) not only serves rhyme and word play (*khalkhāl*, "anklet," *takhtālu* "being proud") but is very often mentioned in erotic verse.

1475 A proverb, meaning that someone who is too greedy ends up with nothing; see al-Maydānī, *Majmaʿ*, 1:371–72 (we thank Professor Tilman Seidensticker for this reference).

1476 A verse from the famous ode attributed to the pre-Islamic poet Ta'abbaṭa Sharrā (al-Marzūqī, *Sharḥ Dīwān al-Ḥamāsah*, 828); the authenticity has been contested already by early commentators. For an annotated translation see Jones, *Early Arabic Poetry*, 1:229–47. The poet refers to a dead kinsman, mentioned in the opening line, "whose blood is not yet avenged."

1477 Probably meaning that his acts or decisions cannot be undone.

1478 Al-Hijris, posthumous son of Kulayb ibn Rabīʿah; his mother was the sister of Jassās ibn Murrah, who, by shooting a camel belonging to Kulayb, started the legendary and protracted "War of Basūs" between the tribes of Bakr and Wā'il in pre-Islamic times (see, e.g., Nicholson, *A Literary History of the Arabs*, 55–60). Al-Hijris sought revenge for the killing of his father by Jassās. See, e.g., al-Iṣfahānī, *Aghānī*, 4:150–51.

1479 Tawbah ibn Muḍarris, nicknamed al-Khinnawt ("choked [by tears or anger]"), of uncertain period, avenged the death of his two brothers, Ṭāriq and Mirdās (al-Āmidī, *Mu'talif,* 68–69). The following piece has not been found elsewhere.

1480 Paying a blood price (*diyah*) was a peaceful alternative to retaliation (*qiṣāṣ*) in pre-Islamic customary law; it was incorporated in Islam and the usual price for homicide was one hundred camels of specified ages.

1481 See al-Mubarrad, *Kāmil*, 3:264, al-Qālī, *Amālī*, 2:26.

1482 Translation uncertain. Al-Qanān (with the article) is also the name of a mountain in the territory of the tribe of Asad (Ibn Manẓūr, *Lisān al-ʿArab*, *Q-N-N*); there are, however, fifteen persons named Qanān (without the article, as here) in al-Kalbī, *Ǧamharat an-nasab*.

1483 The camels will not lament the death of the deceased, because they were generous men who slaughtered their camels for guests. The Arabic has *qarmal* ("a weak, thornless shrub") and *afānī* (cf. *afāniyah* in *Gh* §1.1).

1484 The author is perhaps ironical here.

1485 *Rujaybin* ("of Rajab darling") is prosodically SLL, one syllable short (it should be SLLS or SLLL)

1486 The Arabic has *Rujaybina,* for *Rujaybin*, a grave breach of grammar, since the ending for the indefinite (*-n*) cannot be followed by a vowel in this position.

1487 Q Taghābun 64:14.

1488 The verses are sometimes ascribed to Laylā, beloved of Qays ibn al-Mulawwaḥ, nicknamed Majnūn Laylā (Laylā's Madman) of the tribe of ʿĀmir (al-ʿĀmilī, *Kashkūl*, 126, 423); anonymously in Ibn Abī Ḥajalah, *Dīwān al-ṣabābah*, 100; Dāwūd al-Anṭākī, *Tazyīn*, 2:143.

1489 Using a pausal form (*nūdī*) is normally allowed in rhyme position; it is allowed but frowned upon as a poetic licence.

1490 The verses have not been found elsewhere.

1491 Presumably meaning "continuously renewed greetings."

1492 This envoi may be a copyist's addition.

Glossary of Names and Terms

(Names are given as they appear in the text. Where necessary, a fuller version of them is given in parentheses).

abārīq pl. of *ibrīq* (q.v.).

ʿAbd Allāh ibn (al-)ʿAbbās see Ibn (al-)ʿAbbās.

ʿAbd Allāh ibn Jaʿfar (d. 80/699 or some years later) nephew of the fourth caliph, ʿAlī, known for his generosity; friends with several famous singers, including Budayḥ, who was his *mawlā* ("client").

ʿAbd Allāh ibn Maymūn al-Qaddāḥ a transmitter of traditions from Jaʿfar al-Ṣādiq ibn Muḥammad (d. 148/765), the last imam recognized by both "Twelver" and Zaydī Shi'ites; opponents of the Ismāʿīlīs, the third important branch of the Shi'a, maintain that ʿAbd Allāh founded the Ismāʿīlī sect, claimed to be a prophet, and committed various other enormities.

ʿAbd Allāh ibn al-Muʿtazz see Ibn al-Muʿtazz.

ʿAbd Allāh ibn Saba' a rather obscure figure said to be the "founder" of the Shi'ah, or at least some of its more extreme forms, by exalting ʿAlī, proclaiming that he was not dead and would return, or even asserting his being divine.

ʿAbd al-Jabbār (ʿAbd al-Jabbār ibn Aḥmad; d. 415/1025) judge and important Muʿtazilite theologian, author of the voluminous *al-Mughnī*, a work on dogmatics.

ʿAbd al-Malik ibn Marwān (r. 65–86/685–705) Umayyad caliph.

ʿAbd al-Malik ibn Qurayb (d. ca. 216/831) famous philologist better known as al-Aṣmaʿī; specialist in ancient Arabic language, lore, and poetry; rival of Abū ʿUbaydah.

ʿAbd al-Munʿim ibn ʿAbd al-Karīm ibn Aḥmad (Abū Yaʿlā) judge known as al-Qāḍī al-Aswad ("the black judge") who lived in Aleppo in the author's time.

ʿAbd al-Salām ibn al-Ḥusayn (Abū Aḥmad, nicknamed al-Wājikā; d. 405/1014) a lexicographer from Basra who worked as librarian in Baghdad (see, e.g., al-Khaṭīb al-Baghdādī, *Tārīkh Baghdād*, 9:57–58; al-Qifṭī, *Inbāh*, 2:175–76; al-Ṣafadī, *Wāfī*, 18:419–20); the nickname al-Wājikā appears as al-Wajkā in al-Qifṭī, *Inbāh*, 2:176, whose editor plausibly suggests as its origin the Persian *awj-gāh* ("Whose throne or power is as exalted as the zenith," see Steingass, *Persian-English Dictionary*).

ʿAbd al-Salām ibn Raghbān see Dīk al-Jinn.

ʿAbīd ibn al-Abraṣ (ʿAbīd ibn al-Abraṣ al-Asadī; first half of the sixth century) famous pre-Islamic poet.

Abū "father of."

Abū l-ʿAbbās Aḥmad ibn Khalaf al-Mumattaʿ (Abū l-ʿAbbās Aḥmad ibn Khalaf ibn ʿAlī al-Maʿarrī, known as al-Mumattaʿ, dates unknown) a man of letters and poet from Aleppo; a pupil of Abū l-ʿAlāʾ, who composed elegies on his death (Ibn al-ʿAdīm, *Bughyat al-ṭalab*, pp. 725–30).

Abū l-ʿAbbās ibn Kātib al-Baktimurī probably identical with Abū l-Fatḥ al-Baktimurī (or al-Buktumurī, after a Turkic name of uncertain voweling), called Ibn al-Kātib al-Shāmī ("son of the Syrian state secretary"), mentioned in al-Thaʿālibī, *Yatīmah*, 1:104–6 as one of the poets connected with the Ḥamdānid court.

Abū l-ʿAbbās al-Mumattaʿ (Abū l-ʿAbbās Aḥmad ibn Khalaf ibn ʿAlī al-Maʿarrī, known as al-Mumattaʿ) a man of letters and poet from Aleppo; a pupil of Abū l-ʿAlāʾ, who composed elegies on his death (Ibn al-ʿAdīm, *Bughyat al-ṭalab*, 725–30).

Abū ʿAbd Allāh al-Ḥusayn ibn Jawhar (executed in 401/1011) Fatimid general; son of Jawhar, the conqueror of Egypt for the Fatimids.

Abū ʿAbd Allāh ibn Khālawayh see Ibn Khālawayh.

Abū ʿAbd Allāh ibn Muḥammad ibn Rizām al-Ṭāʾī al-Kūfī (fl. 340/951) anti-Ismāʿīlī polemicist.

Abū Aḥmad ʿAbd al-Salām ibn al-Ḥusayn see ʿAbd al-Salām ibn al-Ḥusayn.

Abū ʿAlī al-Fārisī (d. 377/987) important grammarian born in southern Iran, active in Aleppo and Baghdad.

Abū ʿAmr ibn al-ʿAlāʾ (d. ca. 159/776) philologist from Baṣra, one of the earliest scholars who systematically collected early poetry; also a famous Qur'an reciter; one of the seven Qur'an readings goes back to him.

Abū ʿAmr al-Shaybānī (d. ca. 213/828) a lexicographer from Kufa.

Abū ʿAṣīdah (Aḥmad ibn ʿUbayd ibn Nāṣiḥ; d. 273/886) grammarian and lexicographer, of Daylamite (Persian) origin.

Abū l-Aswad al-Duʾalī (d. ca. 69/688) a minor poet famous as the alleged founder of Arabic grammatical studies in Basra; the report is probably spurious.

Abū l-ʿAtāhiyah (d. 210/825) a poet famous for his ascetic, world-renouncing poetry.

Abū Bakr (r. 11–13/632–34) one of the earliest converts, the father of ʿĀʾishah who became the Prophet's favorite wife; he is often given the epithet al-Ṣiddīq ("the truthful", or "trustworthy"); the first caliph.

Abū Bakr ibn Durayd (Muḥammad ibn al-Ḥasan ibn Durayd; d. 321/933) an important lexicographer as well as a poet; he died at a very advanced age.

Abū Bakr ibn Mujāhid (Aḥmad ibn Mūsā ibn Mujāhid; d. 324/936) influential Baghdadi specialist in the Qurʾanic textual variants.

Abū Bakr ibn al-Sarrāj see Ibn al-Sarrāj.

Abū Bakr Muḥammad ibn ʿUbayd Allāh al-ʿArzamī (d. after 133/750) minor poet from Kufa.

Abū Bakr al-Shiblī (d. 334/945 in Baghdad) early mystic; a follower of al-Ḥallāj for a while, but turned against him at the latter's trial.

Abū Bakr al-Ṣiddīq see Abū Bakr.

Abū Bakr al-Ṣūlī see Ṣūlī, Abū Bakr al-.

Abū Dhuʾayb poet of Hudhayl; a younger contemporary of the Prophet who participated in the early conquests.

Abū Duʾād (or Duwād) (Abū Duʾād al-Iyādī, Jāriyah ibn al-Ḥajjāj; d. probably between AD 540 and 550) an early pre-Islamic poet, active in al-Ḥīrah.

Abū l-Faraj al-Zahrajī nothing is known about him; the text notes that he was the state secretary at the court of Naṣr al-Dawlah.

Abū Ḥafṣ see ʿUmar ibn al-Khaṭṭāb.

Abū Ḥafṣ al-Kattānī (Abū Ḥafṣ ʿUmar ibn Ibrāhīm al-Kattānī; d. 390/1000) Qurʾanic scholar from Baghdad.

Abū Ḥanīfah (d. 150/750) famous Kufan jurist and theologian, who gave his name to the Ḥanafites, one of the four major legal schools in Sunnite Islam.

Abū l-Ḥasan see Abū l-Ḥasan al-Maghribī.

Abū l-Ḥasan ʿAlī ibn ʿĪsā (d. 334/946 at an advanced age) a vizier under the caliphs al-Muqtadir and al-Qāhir, known for his righteousness and learning.

Abū l-Ḥasan ʿAlī ibn ʿĪsā al-Rummānī see Rummānī, ʿAlī ibn ʿĪsā al-.

Abū l-Ḥasan al-Athram (ʿAlī ibn al-Mughīrah; d. 232/846–47) lexicographer from Baghdad; *athram* means "missing a tooth" or "having a broken tooth."

Abū l-Ḥasan al-Maghribī (ʿAlī ibn al-Ḥusayn; killed in 400/1009) the father of al-Wazīr al-Maghribī, who held offices under Sayf al-Dawlah in Aleppo and later in Cairo.

Abū l-Ḥasan Saʿīd ibn Masʿadah see Akhfash al-Awsaṭ, al-.

Abū Ḥātim Sahl ibn Muḥammad (Abū Ḥātim al-Sijistānī; d. 255/868) Basran philologist, author of several works on lexicography and early poetry; al-Aṣmaʿī' was one his teachers.

Abū l-Hindī (d. ca. 132/750) poet from the late Umayyad period known for his Bacchic verse.

Abū l-Hudhayl al-ʿAllāf (Muḥammad ibn al-Hudhayl ibn ʿUbayd Allāh, Abū l-Hudhayl al-ʿAllāf; d. 226/840 or a few years later) speculative theologian, a prominent representative of the "rationalist" Muʿtazilah school.

Abū l-Ḥusayn al-Khayyāṭ see Khayyāṭ, Abū l-Ḥusayn al-.

Abū ʿĪsā (d. 209/824–25) a son of Hārūn al-Rashīd; he was something of a rake and composed a poem against fasting in Ramadan.

Abū Jaʿfar al-Manṣūr see Manṣūr, al-.

Abū Kabīr al-Hudhalī, ʿĀmir ibn al-Ḥulays (d. probably early seventh century AD) poet of Hudhayl; little is known about him. Apart from some fragments only four odes of his have been preserved, all with the same opening words.

Abū l-Khaṭṭāb see Akhfash al-Akbar, al-.

Abū Manṣūr Muḥammad ibn ʿAlī al-Khāzin (d. 418/1027) librarian of the *Dār al-ʿilm* ("House of Learning"); Abū l-ʿAlāʾ knew him during his sojourn in Baghdad and addressed an ode to him.

Abū Maʿshar al-Madanī (Abū Maʿshar Najīḥ ibn ʿAbd al-Raḥmān al-Sindī al-Madanī; d. 170/787) Medinan author of *Kitāb al-Maghāzī* (*Book of [the Prophet's] Campaigns*), known only from quotations.

Abū l-Muḥallim ʿAwf ibn al-Muḥallim (ʿAwf ibn Muḥallim (thus, without the article) al-Ḥarrānī al-Khuzāʿī (thus, rather than of Sulaym); d. ca. 220/835) poet and man of letters from Ḥarrān (ancient Carrhae, in northern Mesopotamia).

Abū l-Murajjā apparently a benefactor of the Sheikh or the author; perhaps he is Sālim ibn ʿAlī ibn Muḥammad al-Amīr Abū l-Murajjā al-Ḥamawī, mentioned in Ibn al-ʿAdīm's *Bughyat al-ṭalab*.

Abū Muslim (d. 136/754) the propagandist and organizer of the revolution that brought the Abbasids to power in 132/749–50; his former employers had him murdered in 136/754; after his death he became the focus of messianic beliefs of heretical sects in Khorasan and Iran.

Abū Nuwās (al-Ḥasan ibn Hāniʾ al-Ḥakamī; d. ca. 200/814) one of the great and most versatile poets, famous especially for his Bacchic poetry and love lyrics (mostly on boys); associated with the caliph al-Amīn, Hārūn al-Rashīd's son, and died shortly after him.

Abū l-Qāsim al-Maghribī (Abū l-Qāsim al-Ḥusayn ibn ʿAlī al-Maghribī; d. 418/1027) known as al-Wazīr al-Maghribī (his family came from North Africa, but it seems he was born in Aleppo), a man of letters, the only one to escape the massacre of his family (a line of high officials and viziers under the Fatimids) in 400/1009, during the reign of the "mad" caliph al-Ḥākim; he held several offices; Ibn al-Qāriḥ had been his tutor but after the family fell from grace he satirized and criticized al-Maghribī in a poem.

Abū Qatādah (Al-Ḥārith ibn Ribʿī Abū Qatādah al-Anṣārī; d. 54/674 or earlier) early Medinan convert nicknamed Fāris al-nabī, "The Prophet's Knight."

Abū l-Qaṭirān al-Asadī see al-Marrār ibn Saʿīd.

Abū Saʿīd al-Sīrāfī (Abū Saʿīd al-Ḥasan ibn ʿAbd Allāh; d. 368/979) judge and grammarian born in Sīrāf (Persia), active in Baghdad; author of a commentary on Sībawayh's grammar.

Abū Ṣakhr al-Hudhalī a poet of the Umayyad period, known mostly for his love poetry.

Abū Sufyān ibn Ḥarb (Abū Sufyān ibn Ḥarb ibn Umayyah; d. ca. 32/653) the leader of the Meccan opposition against the Prophet; he converted to Islam after the conquest of Mecca; he was the father of Muʿāwiyah, founder of the Umayyad dynasty (called after Abū Sufyān's grandfather).

Abū Ṭālib (d. AD 619) the Prophet's paternal uncle and the father of ʿAlī; he looked after Muḥammad when he became an orphan in early childhood and protected him when Muḥammad's preaching evoked opposition and persecution, even though he himself did not convert to Islam.

Abū Ṭalḥah (Zayd ibn Sahl, Abū Ṭalḥah al-Anṣārī; d. 32/652 or 34/654) one of the leading Muslim converts from Medina.

Abū Tammām (Ḥabīb ibn Aws al-Ṭāʾī; d. ca. 231/846) a very important poet from the Abbasid period who composed odes on leading personages including Caliph al-Muʿtaṣim but also excelled in other genres; noted for his often difficult, rugged diction and a highly rhetoricized style full of rather far-fetched metaphors, plays on words, and "intellectual" conceits; he compiled a very influential, thematically arranged anthology of pre- and early Islamic poetry, called *al-Ḥamāsah* (*Zeal*, after the first, "heroic" chapter).

Abū l-Ṭayyib al-Mutanabbī see Mutanabbī, al-.

Abū l-Ṭayyib al-Lughawī (ʿAbd al-Wāḥid ibn ʿAlī Abū l-Ṭayyib al-Lughawī, i.e., "the lexicographer"; d. 351/962) lexicographer and grammarian.

Abū ʿUbādah see Buḥturī, al-.

Abū ʿUbaydah (Maʿmar ibn al-Muthannā; d. 210/825) famous philologist from Basra; a specialist in ancient Arabic language, lore, and poetry; rival of al-Aṣmaʿī.

Abū ʿUmar al-Zāhid (Muḥammad ibn ʿAbd al-Wāḥid al-Zāhid; d. 345/957) lexicographer and devoted pupil of Thaʿlab, hence known as Ghulām Thaʿlab, "Thaʿlab's servant;" he was also known as al-Zāhid ("the Ascetic").

Abū Usāmah Junādah ibn Muḥammad see Junādah ibn Muḥammad al-Harawī.

Abū ʿUthmān al-Māzinī (Abū ʿUthmān Bakr ibn Muḥammad al-Māzinī; d. 248/862 or some years later) a philologist from Basra.

Abū ʿUthmān al-Nājim (Abū ʿUthmān Saʿd (or Saʿīd) ibn al-Ḥasan al-Nājim; d. 314/926) minor poet, friend of Ibn al-Rūmī.

Abū Zayd (Abū Zayd al-Anṣārī; d. 214 or 215/830–1) grammarian and lexicographer.

Abū Zubayd (d. first half of the seventh century) Christian poet who died without converting to Islam; composed wine poetry.

ʿĀd mentioned in the Qur'an as an Arab tribe who, in ancient times, disobeyed the prophet Hūd; God consequently destroyed them by means of a "roaring wind" or a drought. They are traditionally located in Hadramawt; the historical background is obscure.

Adhriʿāt place in Syria.

ʿAdī ibn Rabīʿah better known by his nickname Muhalhil ("he who weaves [poetry] finely)", he is one of the earliest known poets and credited with producing the first *qaṣīdah*s or odes; said to be an uncle of Imru' al-Qays. His poems deal mostly with the protracted feud between the tribes of Taghlib and Shaybān known as the "War of Basūs," caused by the murder of his brother Kulayb (see, e.g., Nicholson, *Literary History of the Arabs*, pp. 55–60).

ʿAdī ibn Zayd al-ʿIbādī (d. ca. AD 600) pre-Islamic Christian poet from al-Ḥīrah famous for his descriptions of wine.

ʿAḍud al-Dawlah (r. 338–72/949–83) the most powerful ruler of the Būyid dynasty, in Iraq and southern and western Persia.

afāniyah a tree.

Afshīn, al- (d. 226/841) commander under al-Muʿtaṣim, of Iranian extraction, who had suppressed a dangerous revolt by Bābak; having been in secret correspondence with Māzyār, he was accused of apostasy in a show trial in Sāmarrā and left to starve to death.

Afwah al-Awdī, al- (d. ca. AD 570) a pre-Islamic poet.

Aḥmad ibn Ḥanbal (Aḥmad ibn Muḥammad ibn Ḥanbal; d. 241/855) very famous and popular scholar of Prophetic Tradition and Islamic law, founder of the Sunnite law school called Ḥanbalite after him; large crowds gathered at his funeral in Baghdad.

Aḥmad ibn al-Ḥusayn see Mutanabbī, al-.

Aḥmad ibn Kāmil (Abū Bakr Aḥmad ibn Kāmil ibn Khalaf Ibn Shajarah [al-Shajarī]; d. 350/961) author of works on history, the Qur'an, Islamic law, and other subjects.

Aḥmad ibn Khalaf al-Mumattaʿ see Abū l-ʿAbbās Aḥmad ibn Khalaf.

Aḥmad ibn ʿUbayd ibn Nāṣiḥ see Abū ʿAṣīdah.

Aḥmad ibn Yaḥyā al-Rāwandī (d. probably in the middle of the fourth/tenth century) he turned from the "rationalist" Muʿtazilah to "heresy" (*zandaqah*) and skepticism, rejecting the idea of prophethood and attacking the Qur'an; there are reports that he renounced this at the end of his life. Parts of his works have been preserved.

Aḥmad ibn Yaḥyā see Thaʿlab.

Aḥsā', al- one of the Carmathian strongholds in eastern Arabia, from where they attacked southern Iraq and the Hijaz in the first half of the fourth/tenth century.

Ahwāz, al- town in Khuzistan (now in Iran) close to Basra; it had extensive sugar plantations.

ʿAjjāj, al- (d. after 99/717) poet famous for his poems in *rajaz* meter; the first to use *rajaz* for longer poems and odes; on account of his extremely rich diction he is quoted very often by lexicographers.

Akhfash al-Akbar, al- (Abū l-Khaṭṭāb; d. 177/793) a grammarian from Basra, called "the older" al-Akhfash to distinguish him from two later philologists with the same nickname (meaning "weak-sighted" or "hemeralopic"), called al-Awsaṭ ("the middle") and al-Aṣghar ("the younger").

Akhfash al-Awsaṭ, al- (Saʿīd ibn Masʿadah Abū l-Ḥasan,; d. ca. 215/830) philologist; the sources say that his lips were unable to close properly (see, e.g., al-Qifṭī, *Inbāh*, 2:39).

Akhṭal, al- (al-Taghlibī; d. ca. 92/710) with Jarīr and al-Farazdaq, one of the three great poets of the Umayyad period; even though he was associated with the court of several caliphs, eulogising ʿAbd al-Malik and others, he was a Christian, like many other of his tribe, the Taghlib, in early Islam; he also excelled in Bacchic scenes; in the protracted poetic battle between Jarīr and al-Farazdaq he sided with the latter.

Ākil al-Murār ancestor of Imruʾ al-Qays and name of a pre-Islamic Arab dynasty in Central Arabia.

ʿAlī see ʿAlī ibn Abī Ṭālib.

ʿAlī ibn al-ʿAbbās ibn Jurayj al-Rūmī see Ibn al-Rūmī.

ʿAlī ibn Abī Ṭālib (killed in 40/661) cousin and son-in-law of the Prophet, the husband of the latter's daughter Fāṭimah; he became the fourth caliph and was murdered after a reign of five years; various sects claimed some kind of divinity for him.

ʿAlī ibn al-Ḥusayn son of al-Ḥusayn, the principal martyr of Shiʿite Islam (he died in 61/680 at Karbala) and one of the sons of ʿAlī and Fāṭimah; ʿAlī, like his father, is a Shīʿite imām.

ʿAlī ibn ʿĪsā, Abū l-Ḥasan see Abū l-Ḥasan ʿAlī ibn ʿĪsā.

ʿAlī ibn ʿĪsā al-Rummānī see Rummānī, ʿAlī ibn ʿĪsā al-.

ʿAlī ibn Muḥammad the leader of the revolt of the Zanj, who claimed to be a descendant of ʿAlī; the Zanj were blacks originally from East Africa; widely exploited as slaves on plantations in southern Iraq, they revolted several times, most dangerously between 255/869 and 270/883, when they defeated several caliphal armies and sacked Basra.

ʿĀlij a sandy place in Arabia; its location is controversial.

ʿAlqamah (ʿAlqamah ibn ʿAbadah; sixth century AD) pre-Islamic poet connected with the court of the Arab Lakhmid rulers in al-Ḥīrah.

ʿAlwah a place in Najd (Central Arabia).

Āmid now called Diyarbakır, in S.-E. Turkey.

ʿAmr ibn Aḥmar al-Bāhilī (first/seventh century) poet born in the pre-Islamic period who died after the coming of Islam; he is said to have died at a very advanced age, perhaps during the caliphate of ʿAbd al-Malik (65–86/685–705).

ʿAmr ibn al-ʿĀṣ (d. ca. 42/663) one of the great leaders of the early Islamic conquests; conqueror of Egypt; ally of Muʿāwiyah ibn Abī Sufyān in the conflict with ʿAlī ibn Abī Ṭālib; when Muʿāwiyah became the first Umayyad caliph ʿAmr remained governor of Egypt.

ʿAmr ibn Ḥumamah (ʿAmr ibn Ḥumamah al-Dawsī) occasionally mentioned for his wisdom, as one of the pre-Islamic Arab "arbiters" and "soothsayers."

ʿAmr ibn Kulthūm (sixth century AD) poet of one of the seven *Muʿallaqāt*, which is his only famous poem.

ʿĀnah place on the Euphrates in Northern Mesopotamia associated with wine production.

Anmār a sub-tribe of ʿAbd al-Qays.

ʿAntarah (ʿAntarah ibn Shaddād, ʿAntarah al-ʿAbsī; d. ca. AD 600) famous pre-Islamic poet and warrior, son of an Arab of the tribe of ʿAbs and a black slave mother called Zabībah, therefore considered a slave according to pre-Islamic custom, until he acquired his freedom by his courage in battle; the author of one of the seven *Muʿallaqāt*. Later he became (as ʿAntar) the hero of a vast, fantastic, and extremely popular epic in sub-standard Arabic, recited by oral narrators; ʿAntarah, Sulayk, and Khufāf are known as the "Ravens."

Antioch (Anṭakiyah, Turkish Antakya) town in Northern Syria (today Turkey), situated on the Orontes river.

Anūsharwān (r. AD 531–79) Sasanid emperor.

Arafah or ʿArafāt a plain east of Mecca that plays an important role in the ceremonies of the Hajj.

ʿArzamī, al- see Abū Bakr Muḥammad ibn ʿUbayd Allāh.

Aʿshā, al- (Maymūn ibn Qays) Al-Aʿshā means "the Night-blind, Nyctalopic"; of the tribe of Bakr, one of the great pre-Islamic poets; he was probably a Christian.

Ashʿarītes Abū l-Ḥasan al-Ashʿarī (d. 324/935–36) turned against the Muʿtazilites after having been one of them; his school of theology (which preserved some of the rationalist elements and methods of the Muʿtazilah) became the dominant one in Sunni Islam.

Aṣmaʿī, al- (ʿAbd al-Malik ibn Qurayb al-Aṣmaʿī; d. ca. 216/831) famous philologist from Basra; a specialist in ancient Arabic language, lore, and poetry; rival of Abū ʿUbaydah.

Aswad ibn ʿAbd Yaghūth, al- a contemporary of the Prophet.

Aswad ibn Maʿdīkarib, al- possibly a mistake for Abū l-Aswad Yazīd, son of Maʿdīkarib, one of the leaders of the Kindah tribal confederation.

Aswad ibn al-Mundhir, al- a hero eulogized by the poet al-Aʿshā, the brother of the last king of the Lakhm dynasty.

Aswad ibn Yaʿfur, al- (d. toward the end of the sixth century AD) poet; only a few of his odes have been preserved.

Aswad ibn Zamʿah, al- a contemporary of the Prophet, whose son was killed at Badr in AD 624.

Athram, al- see Abū l-Ḥasan al-Athram.

ʿAwf ibn Muḥallim see Abū l-Muḥallim.

Aws (Aws ibn Ḥajar; said to have died shortly before the Hijra (AD 622)) a pre-Islamic poet admired for his hunting scenes and descriptions of arms and manly virtues.

Awzāʿī, al- (d. 157/774) Syrian jurist, founder of a school of Islamic law superseded by other schools.

Aylah (Hebrew Elath/Eilat) located at the north end of the Gulf of Aqaba.

Bāb al-Ṭāq a large quarter, named after the arch (*ṭāq*) of the palace of Asmāʾ, the daughter of the founder of Baghdad, Caliph al-Manṣūr.

Bābak (Pāpak in Persian; d. 223/838) leader of the anti-Islamic and anti-Arab Khurramī movement in Azerbaijan, active since 201/816–17 and finally defeated by al-Afshīn in 222/837; he was cruelly executed in Sāmarrā the following year.

Badr the site of a minor battle of great importance in 2/624, when the Muslims defeated a superior force of Meccan opponents of Islam.

Bāhilī, al- see ʿAmr ibn Aḥmar.

Bakrī, al- see al-Aʿshā.

Banū ʿAdī a tribe in Syria, near Homs.

Banū l-Dardabīs a fanciful name of a tribe of the jinn; the word *dardabīs* is given various meanings by the lexicographers ("calamity," "old man," "old woman," "love charm," and "penis").

Banū Zuhrah a subdivision of Quraysh (see al-Kalbī/Caskel, *Ǧamharat an-nasab*, Tafeln, 118, Register, 564).

Barāqish place in Yemen.

Barmakids or *Barmecides* (descendants of Barmak) a family of very powerful viziers in the early Abbasid period; they fell spectacularly from power during the reign of Hārūn al-Rashīd.

Bashāmah ibn al-Ghadīr (or Bashāmah ibn ʿAmr) Zuhayr's maternal uncle who belonged to the tribe of Sahm; two of his poems are included in the ancient anthology *al-Mufaḍḍaliyyāt*.

Bashshār ibn Burd (Abū Muʿādh; executed 167/783–84) an important Arabic poet, called the "father of the modern poets"; proud of his Persian descent; the first great Arabic poet who was not an Arab; he excelled in many poetic genres; though famous for his "courtly" love poems, he was notorious for his suspected heretical, Manichaean beliefs, which may have led to his execution at the orders of the caliph al-Mahdī.

Basīl presumably Basil (Basileos) II Bulgaroctonos ("Bulgar-slayer," r. AD 976–1025).

Battī, al- (Abū l-Ḥasan Aḥmad ibn ʿAlī al-Battī; d. 403/1013) *kātib* ("state secretary") at the court of Caliph al-Qādir, man of letters and wit.

Baysān (adj. Baysānī) a town in the Jordan Valley, famous for its wine.

Bayt Ra's place in Syria, near Aleppo.

Bishr (Bishr ibn Abī Khāzim) a pre-Islamic poet, some eight hundred of whose verses are preserved.

Buḥturī, al- (Abū ʿUbādah; d. 284/897) important Abbasid poet.

Camel-herd, The see ʿUbayd ibn al-Ḥuṣayn al-Numayrī.

Carmathians or Qarmaṭians (Arabic: al-Qarāmiṭah) called after their founder Ḥamdān Qarmaṭ (third/ninth century), the Carmathians were a branch of the Ismāʿīlī Shi'ites, who rebelled in various parts of the Middle East; one of their strongholds was al-Aḥsā' (also known as al-Ḥasā) in eastern Arabia, from where they attacked southern Iraq and the Hijaz in the first half of the fourth/tenth century; during their notorious raid on Mecca in 317/930 they carried off the Black Stone of the Kaaba.

Chosroes (Persian Khusraw, Greek Chosroes, Arabic Kisrā) the name of several Sasanian emperors in the pre-Islamic period, and often standing for any Sasanian king, just as Qayṣar/Caesar stands for any Roman or Byzantine emperor.

colocynth a plant with pungent and very bitter fruit, used as a laxative and for various other medical purposes.

Dabāwand (or Dubāwand, more commonly Damāwand) the highest place in the mountains south of the Caspian Sea; it plays a part in the legends of ancient Persia.

Dahnā', al- a very long (some thousand kilometers) strip of sand desert in Arabia, connecting the Nafūd in the northwest with the "Empty Quarter."

Damīgh al-Shayṭān he is mentioned, without further particulars, in lexicons (e.g., Ibn Durayd, *Jamharah*, Ibn Manẓūr, *Lisān al-ʿArab*, *D-M-Gh*).

Dardabīs, Banū l- see Banū l-Dardabīs.

Dārīn port in Eastern Arabia, where Indian musk was imported.

Dawmah or *Dūmah* probably Dūmat al-Jandal, an oasis between Medina and Damascus.

Daybul, al- (also Daybul, without article) a town on the coast of Sind (approx. modern Pakistan); al-Maʿarrī calls it, oddly, "a well-known mountain" (*Fuṣūl*, 104).

ḍaymurān a kind of tree.

Dhāt al-Raḍm a place in northern Arabia.

Dhū Ḥusam a wadi in Najd.

Dhū l-Rummah (Ghaylān ibn ʿUqbah; d. ca. 117/735) one of the last great Bedouin poets who entered the traditional canon, famous for his desert descriptions and his love poetry on Mayyah.

Diʿbil ibn ʿAlī (al-Khuzāʿī; d. 245/859 or 246/860) poet from Kufa, known especially for his lampoons; he was murdered at an advanced age.

Dīk al-Jinn (ʿAbd al-Salām ibn Raghbān; d. ca. 235/850) a poet from Homs (Syria), who, suspecting his wife of infidelity, killed her, after which he repented and lamented her death in many poems; otherwise, he is known for his frivolous lifestyle.

dinar (*dīnār*, from Latin *denarius*) a gold coin.

dirham (from Greek *drachmē*) a silver coin.

doom-palm The doom palm or doum palm (*Hyphaene thebaica*, Arabic *daum*) has fan-shaped leaves and an edible fruit.

Duʾalī, Abū l-Aswad al- see Abū l-Aswad al-Duʾalī.

Ḍubayʿah a branch of the tribe of Qays ibn Thaʿlabah; the name means "little hyena."

Dūmah see Dawmah.

Duwayd (Duwayd ibn Zayd ibn Nahd) said to have been a very early poet who lived for 456 years.

Fadak a village in the northern Hijaz.

Faḍl ibn Sahl, al- (Al-Faḍl ibn Sahl ibn Zadhānfarūkh; d. 202/818) a Zoroastrian convert to Islam, vizier to al-Maʾmūn (who may have been behind his murder); also made *amīr*, his honorific title was Dhū l-Riʾāsatayn, "He with Two Commands."

fālūd, fālūdhaj from Pahlavi (Middle Persian) *pālūdag* ("strained"), a sweet made of flour and honey.

Faqʿasī, al- see Abū l-Qaṭirān al-Marrār.

Farazdaq, al- (Hammām ibn Ghālib; d. ca. 110/728) usually called al-Farazdaq ("Bread Morsel"); was with al-Akhṭal and Jarīr one of the great poets of the Umayyad period, famous for his many panegyric poems on caliphs and others, and feared for his satire; he and Jarīr exchanged a lengthy series of lampooning poems (*naqāʾiḍ*).

Fārisī, al- see Abū ʿAlī al-Fārisī.

Farrāʾ, al- (Abū Zakariyyā Yaḥyā ibn Ziyād al-Farrāʾ; d. 207/822) important grammarian of the "school of Kufa."

Fartanā traditional Arabic female name often used in love poetry.

Fāṭimah the Prophet's daughter and ʿAlī's wife, the mother of al-Ḥasan and al-Ḥusayn, through whom all descendants of the Prophet trace their descent.

Fuḍayl ibn ʿIyāḍ, al- (d. 187/803) an ascetic and early Sufi; in his youth he was a highwayman.

Fūrah, al- Yāqūt, *Muʿjam al-buldān* has al-Qurrah (s.v. al-ʿUmayr and al-Qurrah); it is said to be a monastery.

Fustat (Al-Fusṭāṭ) the "Old Cairo" of today, founded by the Arab conquerors in the first half of the seventh century.

Gabriel (Jibrīl, Jabrā'īl) the angel who conveyed the Qur'an, God's word, piecemeal to the Prophet.

ghalwā a perfume.

Ghanawī, al- see Sahm ibn Ḥanẓalah.

Gharīḍ, al- (d. ca. 92/716–17) a famous singer from the Umayyad period.

Ghayl, al- (or al-Ghīl, according to some). Location near Mecca.

Ghaylān ibn ʿUqbah see Dhū l-Rummah;.

Ghulām Thaʿlab see Abū ʿUmar al-Zāhid.

Ghumayr al-Luṣūṣ Yāqūt calls it ʿUmayr al-Luṣūṣ in his *Muʿjam al-buldān* s.v. al-ʿUmayrah and al-Qurrah, where it is said to be a village near al-Ḥīrah or al-Qādisiyyah.

Ḥabīb ibn Aws see Abū Tammām.

habīd explained as "colocynth" or its seeds.

Ḥādirah, al- (Quṭbah ibn Aws ibn Miḥṣan; d. early seventh century) pre-Islamic poet who was known as al-Ḥādirah ("the broad shouldered," i.e., "the frog").

Ḥakamī, al- see Abū Nuwās.

Ḥākim, al- (r. 386–411/996–1021) the controversial Fāṭimid caliph who at some stage claimed divinity; he was notorious for his capricious behavior and bloodshed. After his disappearance (apparently having been murdered) the cult of his person gave rise to the Druze religion.

Hakir (or *Hakr*) according to the sources, a place, or a palace, or a monastery; it is located in Yemen, or forty miles south of Medina, or a Roman name . . . in other words, nobody knows.

Ḥallāj, al- (al-Ḥusayn ibn Manṣūr; d. 309/922 in Baghdad) very famous early mystic, cruelly executed, accused of blasphemy and heresy.

ḥamāṭah 1. a tree; 2. its fruit; 3. heartburn; 4. blackness or bottom of the heart.

Ḥāmid ibn al-ʿAbbās (d. 311/923) vizier during the trial of al-Ḥallāj.

Ḥammād ʿAjrad (Ibn Nihyā; d. between 155/772 and 168/784) a poet, Bashshār's rival; he was accused of Manichaeism.

Hammām ibn Ghālib see Farazdaq, al-.

Ḥamzah ibn ʿAbd al-Muṭṭalib (d. 3/625). The Prophet's uncle; he was killed at the battle against the Meccans at Uḥud.

Ḥamzah ibn Ḥabīb (d. 156/772) established one of the seven canonical readings of the Qur'anic text.

harīsah a dish of minced meat and crushed wheat, pounded together.

Ḥārith ibn Hāniʾ ibn Abī Shamir ibn Jabalah al-Kindī, al- distinguished himself at the battle of Sābāṭ (a place near Ctesiphon) during the early conquests, in 16/637.

Ḥārith ibn Ḥillizah, al- (al-Ḥārith ibn Ḥillizah al-Yashkurī; d. ca. AD 570) of the tribe of Yashkur; a pre-Islamic poet, author of one of the *Muʿallaqāt*, an ode he extemporized, so the story goes, in the presence of ʿAmr ibn Hind, the ruler of al-Ḥīrah.

Ḥārith ibn Kaladah, al- the oldest known Arab physician; he studied at Gondeshapur in Iran and was a contemporary of the Prophet, surviving him by a few years. The sources ascribe to him a series of recommendations on medicine, diet, and hygiene.

Ḥārith al-Yashkurī, al- (al-Ḥārith ibn Ḥillizah al-Yashkurī; d. ca. AD 570) of the tribe of Yashkur; a pre-Islamic poet, author of one of the *Muʿallaqāt*, an ode he extemporized, so the story goes, in the presence of ʿAmr ibn Hind, the ruler of al-Ḥīrah.

Ḥārith ibn Ẓālim, al-Murrī, al- a pre-Islamic tribal leader expelled by his tribe, proverbial for his loyalty (al-Maydānī, *Majmaʿ*, 2:444); when his help was invoked by someone claiming to be his *jār* ("neighbor," entitled to protection), he responded even though he had merely once, in the past, lent his well-rope to the man.

Hārūn al-Rashīd (r. 170–93/786–809) the fifth Abbasid caliph.

Ḥarrānī al-Sulamī, al- see Abū l-Muḥallim Awf ibn al-Muḥallim.

Ḥasan al-Baṣrī, al- (al-Ḥasan ibn Abī l-Ḥasan Yasār) (d. 110/728) a famous theologian and Qur'an reciter from Basra frequently quoted with approval by almost all later schools, especially the Sufis.

Ḥasan ibn ʿAlī al-ʿAskarī, al- (d. 260/874) the eleventh of the twelve imams of the Twelver Shi'ah (all being descendants of the Prophet through his daughter Fāṭimah, her husband ʿAlī ibn Abī Ṭālib being the first).

Ḥasan ibn Rajā', al- (al-Ḥasan ibn Rajā' ibn Abī l-Ḍaḥḥāk) an official in Baghdad and Khorasan (now in Eastern Iran and Afghanistan) under the caliphs al-Ma'mūn and al-Muʿtaṣim.

Ḥasanī, al- apparently a local governor.

Hāshim the Prophet's grandfather.

Ḥassān ibn Thābit (d. probably before 40/661) converted to Islam around the time of the Hijra (AD 622) and forcefully supported Islam with eulogies on the Prophet and invective against his opponents; his pre-Islamic and even some "Islamic" poems contain passages describing wine.

Ḥātim al-Ṭā'ī a pre-Islamic poet, proverbial for his generosity.

Ḥawrān a region in southern Syria.

Haylān place in Yemen.

hazaj 1. a meter; 2. a rhythmical mode.

ḥiḍb male snake; other meaning: bottom of the heart.

Ḥimyarī, al- see Sayyid al-Ḥimyarī, al-.

Ḥimyar pre-Islamic kingdom in Yemen, overthrown by the Christian Ethiopians in the sixth century AD.

Hind traditional Arabic female name often used in love poetry.

Hishām ibn Mughīrah a leading member of Quraysh, the Prophet's tribe, in the pre-Islamic period.

Hudhayl a tribe that produced many poets; their poetry was collected in the third/ninth century and forms the only preserved instance of a collective, tribal *dīwān* (a *dīwān*, or collected verse, is normally of an individual poet); a recurrent theme in their poetry is honey gathering.

Ḥujr ibn ʿAdī al-Adbar distinguished himself at the battle of Sābāṭ (a place near Ctesiphon) during the early conquests, in 16/637.

Ḥumayd ibn Thawr al-Hilālī (d. ca. 90/709) poet born in the pre-Islamic period who died after the coming of Islam, apparently at an advanced age; he is famous especially for his animal descriptions.

Ḥusayn ibn al-Ḍaḥḥāk al-Khalīʿ, al- (d. 250/864 at an advanced age) poet, friend of Abū Nuwās.

Ḥusayn ibn Jawhar see Abū ʿAbd Allāh al-Ḥusayn ibn Jawhar.

Ḥusayn ibn Manṣūr, al- see Ḥallāj, al-.

Ḥuss, al- a place in Syria, near Homs; cf. Yāqūt, *Muʿjam al-buldān*, s.v. and mentioned in a well-known Bacchic epigram by Abū Miḥjan al-Thaqafī; but ʿAdī's verse is quoted in the entry "al-Khuṣṣ," said to be a place near al-Qādisiyyah.

Ḥuṭay'ah, al- (Jarwal ibn Aws of the tribe of ʿAbs; first/seventh century) a younger contemporary of the Prophet; a major poet notorious for his invective skills (which he used for extortion); also noted as a miser and a lukewarm Muslim; nicknamed al-Ḥuṭay'ah (a word with several meanings but usually interpreted as "the dwarf" or "the ugly runt").

Ibn (al-)ʿAbbās, ʿAbd Allāh (d. 68/687) a cousin of the Prophet and ancestor of the Abbasid caliphs (the dynasty having been named after him); he is considered the founder of Qur'anic exegesis.

Ibn Abī ʿĀmir (often called al-Manṣūr, or, in Europe, Almanzor; d. 392/1002) chamberlain of the Andalusian Umayyad caliph; the virtual ruler of al-Andalus from 368/978 to his death.

Ibn Abī ʿAwn (executed in 322/934) a man of letters, the author of a work on comparison in poetry, usually called *Kitāb al-Tashbīhāt* (*The Book of Similes*).

Ibn Abī Du'ād (Aḥmad Ibn Abī Du'ād; d. 240/854) judge of great power under al-Ma'mūn and al-Muʿtaṣim.

Ibn Abī l-Ṣalt al-Thaqafī see Umayyah ibn Abī l-Ṣalt.

Ibn Aḥmar see ʿAmr ibn Aḥmar al-Bāhilī.

Ibn Durayd see Abū Bakr ibn Durayd.

Ibn Durustawayh (d. 347/958) grammarian and lexicographer.

Ibn Ḥājib al-Nuʿmān (d. 423/1031) civil servant and anthologist.

Ibn Ḥanbal see Aḥmad ibn Ḥanbal.

Ibn Hāni' (Muḥammad ibn Hāni' al-Andalusī; d. ca. 362/973) born in Seville, active in North Africa and Egypt, as panegyrist of the Fāṭimid rulers, who were Ismāʿīlī Shi'ites.

Ibn Harmah (Ibrāhīm ibn ʿAlī; d. ca. 176/792) a poet straddling the Umayyad and Abbasid periods; counted among the last of the "classical" or the first of the "modern" poets.

Ibn Jawhar see Abū ʿAbd Allāh al-Ḥusayn ibn Jawhar.

Ibn al-Kātib al-Shāmī see Abū l-ʿAbbās ibn Kātib al-Baktimurī.

Ibn Khālawayh (Abū ʿAbd Allāh al-Ḥusayn ibn Aḥmad; d. 370/980 in Aleppo) lexicographer, grammarian, and Qur'anic scholar from Hamadhān.

Ibn Khurradādhbih (ʿUbayd Allāh ibn ʿAbd Allāh Ibn Khurradādhbih; sometimes spelled Khurdādhbih; d. ca. 300/911; earlier dates are also given) besides being an important geographer, he was the author of mostly lost works on cookery, wine, and music, and the boon companion of the caliph al-Muʿtamid; see al-Masʿūdī, *Murūj*, 5:126–31, where he addresses the caliph on music.

Ibn Misjaḥ (d. ca. 96/715) the Meccan singer was the founder of the new "art song" modeled on Byzantine and Persian music.

Ibn Mujāhid see Abū Bakr ibn Mujāhid.

Ibn Muqbil see Tamīm Ibn Ubayy.

Ibn al-Muʿtazz (ʿAbd Allāh)(d. 296/908) Abbasid prince, man of letters, and important poet; he was made caliph in a coup but was killed the following day.

Ibn Qays al-Ruqayyāt (ʿUbayd Allāh ibn Qays; d. 80/699) a poet especially famous for his love poems on women, at least one of whom was called Ruqayyah; there are several explanations of his odd nickname ("Qays of the Ruqayyahs"), see, e.g., al-Baghdādī, *Khizānah*, 7:278–84.

Ibn Rāʾiq see Muḥammad ibn Rāʾiq.

Ibn Rajāʾ (al-Ḥasan ibn Rajāʾ ibn Abī l-Ḍaḥḥāk) an official in Baghdad and Khorasan (now in Eastern Iran and Afghanistan) under the caliphs al-Maʾmūn and al-Muʿtaṣim.

Ibn al-Rāwandī (Aḥmad ibn Yaḥyā al-Rāwandī; d. probably in the middle of the fourth/tenth century) he turned from the "rationalist" Muʿtazilah to "heresy" (*zandaqah*) and skepticism, rejecting the idea of prophethood and attacking the Qur'an; there are reports that he renounced this at the end of his life; parts of his works have been preserved.

Ibn Rizām see Abū ʿAbd Allāh ibn Muḥammad ibn Rizām al-Ṭāʾī al-Kūfī.

Ibn al-Rūmī (ʿAlī ibn al-ʿAbbās ibn Jurayj al-Rūmī; d. 283/896 in Baghdad) one of the most important Abbasid poets; his grandfather Jurayj ("George") was a Byzantine (Rūmī); his superstition is often mentioned.

Ibn al-Ṣāmit (d. probably shortly before the Hijra) pre-Islamic tribal leader and poet in Medina.

Ibn al-Sammāk (Abū l-ʿAbbās Muḥammad ibn Ṣabīḥ; d. 183/799) ascetic and preacher from Kūfa.

Ibn al-Sarrāj (Abū Bakr Muḥammad ibn al-Sarī; d. 316/928) grammarian from Baghdad, one of Abū ʿAlī al-Fārisī's teachers.

Ibn Shajarah see Aḥmad ibn Kāmil.

Ibn al-Sikkīt (Abū Yūsuf Yaʿqūb ibn Isḥāq; d. 244/858 or perhaps some years earlier) famous philologist and lexicographer, several of whose books are preserved, including his *al-Qalb wa-l-ibdāl* (*Conversion and Mutation*).

Ibn Surayj (d. 96/714 or some years later) famous singer of the early Islamic and Umayyad periods.

Ibrāhīm ibn al-Mahdī (d. 224/839) son of the caliph al-Mahdī; a gifted musician, poet, and cook.

Ibrāhīm al-Mawṣilī (d. 188/804) a leading musician, composer, and courtier in the time of Hārūn al-Rashīd; of Persian origin.

ibrīq (pl. abārīq) 1. jug; 2. "radiant" (graceful) girl; 3. shining sword.

Ilāl (read by some as Alāl or Ulāl) watering place on the pilgrims' route to Mecca.

Imami Shi'ites ("Twelver Shi'ites") the Imami Shi'ites recognize twelve successive imams (leaders of the Muslim community, beginning with ʿAlī ibn Abī Ṭālib and ending with the "occultation" of Muḥammad al-Mahdī in 329/940); they are the dominant branch of the Shi'a in the present day.

Imruʾ al-Qays (d. in the middle of the sixth century) son of a prince of a tribal federation led by the tribe of Kindah; the most famous pre-Islamic poet and also the poet of the most famous of the *Muʿallaqāt*.

ʿĪsā the Muslim name of Jesus (the Christian form in Arabic being Yasūʿ).

Isḥāq ibn Ibrāhīm (d. 235/850) son of Ibrāhīm al-Mawṣilī who followed in his father's footsteps; in addition to being the leading singer and composer of his time he wrote books on music and was also a poet.

Iyās ibn al-Aratt (Iyās ibn Khālid al-Aratt) rather obscure poet, quoted a few times in Abū Tammām's famous anthology *al-Ḥamāsah.*

Iyās ibn Muʿawiyah (d. 121/739 or the following year) *qāḍī* of Basra, who became proverbial for his insight and shrewdness.

jaʿdah described as "a curly plant growing on river banks" or "a green herb growing in mountain passes in Najd," etc.

Jadhīmah a legendary pre-Islamic king of Iraq who killed his two inseparable friends while drunk, bitterly repenting afterward; later killed by Queen al-Zabbā' of Palmyra, who may be (partially) identified as Zenobia.

Jadīs legendary Arab tribe.

Jaʿfar ibn Muḥammad (d. 148/765) the sixth imam of the Twelver Shīʿah, called al-Ṣādiq ("the trustworthy").

Jafnids pre-Islamic Arab dynasty in Syria.

jāhiliyyah "ignorance", pre-Islamic period.

Jamīl (Jamīl ibn Maʿmar al-ʿUdhrī; d. 82/701) poet of the ʿUdhrah tribe; famous for his love poetry on Buthaynah, who was forced to marry another; he and several other poets of this tribe became famous for their passionate, chaste, self-effacing, and usually unfulfilled love; the adjective *ʿudhrī*, "ʿUdhrite," is often used to describe such love.

Jannābī, al- (Abū Ṭāhir al-Jannābī; d. 332/943–44) the leader of the Qarmaṭī movement in eastern Arabia, from where he raided southern Iraq and, notoriously, Mecca, where he killed pilgrims and took away the Black Stone in 317/930; it was returned only after some twenty years; he came from Jannābah, a small town on the coast of southern Persia (Yaqūt, *Muʿjam al-buldān*, s.v.).

Jarwal ibn Aws see Ḥuṭay'ah, al-.

Jawhar ibn ʿAbd Allāh al-Ṣiqillī the conqueror of Egypt for the Fatimids.

Jayfar the Splendid nothing is known about him; perhaps he is the same as Jayfar ibn al-Julandā, the "king of Oman," who converted to Islam at the time of the Prophet.

jinn (sg. jinnī, jinnee) jinnees, "genies" demons (good or evil).

Jirān al-ʿAwd al-Numayrī (ʿĀmir ibn al-Ḥārith) a poet of the tribe of Numayr, said to have lived in early Islamic and early Umayyad times; Jirān al-ʿAwd is a nickname, meaning "leather whip made from an old camel stallion," an expression he used in a poem in which he threatens his two wives with whipping them.

Juʿfī, al- see Mutanabbī, al-.

Junādah ibn Muḥammad al-Harawī (Abū Usāmah; d. 399/1009) lexicographer, executed by the Fatimid caliph al-Ḥākim, who blamed him for the shortfall in the rise of the Nile because he used to teach in the building known as the Nilometer (al-Miqyās); see Yāqūt, *Muʿjam al-udabāʾ*, 7:209–10; Ibn Khallikān, *Wafayāt*, 1:372.

Jurhum legendary Arab tribe.

Jurhumī, al- (Muʿāwiyah ibn Bakr) of the ancient Arabian tribe Jurhum, who according to traditional lore reigned in Mecca in the time of the Arabian prophet Hūd.

Kaʿb ibn Māmah pre-Islamic Arab of the tribe of Iyād famous for his generosity.

Kaʿb ibn Mālik (d. c. 50/670) one of the poets who supported the Prophet Muḥammad.

Kaʿb ibn Zuhayr contemporary of the Prophet, who opposed Islam at first. To save his life he composed a celebrated ode in praise of the Prophet, which came to be known as the "Mantle Ode," after the mantle that Muḥammad gave him as a sign of his favor. He converted before the Hijrah.

Kafr Ṭāb a town between Maʿarrat al-Nuʿmān and Aleppo.

Karkh, al- the part of Baghdad west and south of the original "Round City" founded by Caliph al-Manṣūr.

Kattānī, al- see Abū Ḥafṣ.

Kawthar, al- a river in Paradise whose name means "Abundance."

Kaysānites, or al-Kaysāniyyah named after Abū ʿAmrah Kaysān, a commander of the Kufan Shiʾite rebel al-Mukhtār (d. 67/687); they claimed that Muḥammad ibn al-Ḥanafiyyah (d. 81/700), a son of ʿAlī by a slavegirl, was the true *imām* (leader of the community of Islam) and the Mahdi.

Khadījah (d. AD 619) the first wife of Muḥammad, who was her third husband; mother of Fāṭimah; the Prophet's first supporter; she is said to have been forty when she married Muḥammad, who was between twenty-one and twenty-five years old.

Khalaf al-Aḥmar (Khalaf ibn Ḥayyān; d. ca. 180/796) poet and *rāwī* ("transmitter") of early poetry.

Khalaf ibn Hishām al-Bazzāz (or al-Bazzār; d. 229/844) a specialist in the Qur'anic text from Baghdad.

Khalīl ibn Aḥmad, al- (d. 160/776, 170/786, or 175/791) one of the founders of Arabic grammar and lexicography; the discoverer of the science of prosody; the author, or rather the *auctor intellectualis* or instigator, of the first Arabic lexicon, called "the letter *ʿayn*," after the first letter in his rearrangement of the alphabet; teacher of Sībawayh.

Khansāʾ, al- (b. between AD 580 and 590 and d. after 23/644, having converted to Islam) generally considered the greatest female poet in Arabic; her fame rests on her numerous elegies for her two brothers, Ṣakhr and Muʿāwiyah, the former having died before the coming of Islam.

Khayyāṭ, Abū l-Ḥusayn al- (ʿAbd al-Raḥīm ibn Muḥammad al-Khayyāṭ; d. prob. before 300/912) Muʿtalizite theologian and jurist from Baghdad.

Khāzin, al- see Abū Manṣūr Muḥammad ibn ʿAlī.

Khufāf ibn Nadbah al-Sulamī (died during the caliphate of ʿUmar (between 13/634 and 23/644)) called Ibn Nadbah after his mother who was a black slave; poet and warrior. ʿAntarah, Sulayk, and Khufāf are known as the "Ravens."

khurdādhī said to be a kind of wine (al-Fīrūzābādī, *Qāmūs*), but it is also used for some kind of bottle; for a crystal *khurdādhī* see al-Tanūkhī, *Nishwār*, 1:336, 8:253; Khurdādh is the name of the third month (May–June) of the Persian calendar.

Khuṣṣ, al- said to be a place in Syria famous for wine; or a place near al-Qādisiyyah (in Iraq); or a noun meaning "wine shop."

Khuṣūṣ, al- a place near al-Ḥīrah, on the Euphrates.

Kindah a large tribal confederation that dominated central Arabia in the fifth and early sixth centuries AD.

Kisā'ī, al- (d. 189/805) grammarian and specialist in the Qur'anic text; like many other Arabic grammarians, he was of Persian descent.

Kisrā Abarwīz (the Arabic form of Persian Khusraw Parwīz, r. AD 592–628) pre-Islamic Sasanian king.

Kuthayyir (d. 105/723) poet famous for his love poetry on ʿAzzah, and therefore often called Kuthayyir ʿAzzah ("Kuthayyir of ʿAzzah").

Labīd (d. ca. 41/661) a famous pre-Islamic poet who converted to Islam.

Lakhm, Lakhmids a pre-Islamic Arab dynasty ruling in al-Ḥīrah in Iraq (ca. AD 300–600), vassals of the Persian Sassanids.

Laṣāf watering place on the pilgrims' route to Mecca.

Maʿadd ibn ʿAdnān the legendary ancestor of the North Arabs.

Maʿarrat al-Nuʿmān the town in Syria where Abū l-ʿAlāʾ was born and died, and which gave him the epithet al-Maʿarrī.

Maʿbad (d. ca. 125/743) famous singer of the early Islamic and Umayyad periods.

Maghribī, al- see Abū l-Ḥasan al-Maghribī and Abū l-Qāsim al-Maghribī.

Mahdī see Majnūn Laylā.

Mahdī, al- (r. 158–69/775–85) Abbasid caliph whose reign was marked by the persecution of "heretics" (*zanādiqah*).

Maḥmūd (Maḥmūd ibn Sebüktegin; r. 388–421/998–1030) sultan of the Ghaznawid dynasty, based in Ghaznah (eastern Afghanistan); conquered a large part of northern India.

Majnūn Laylā ("Laylā's madman";first/seventh century) the semi-legendary poet and hero of the most famous Arabic love romance; often identified as Qays ibn al-Mulawwaḥ but sometimes given other names, including Mahdī ibn al-Mulawwaḥ.

Malatya place in eastern Anatolia.

Mālik an angel, the chief guardian of Hell.

Mālik ibn Anas (d. 179/796) famous jurist of Medina, who gave his name to the Mālikites, one of the four major legal schools in Sunnite Islam.

Mālik ibn Dīnār (d. 131/748–49) often-quoted preacher of Basra.

Maʿmar see Abū ʿUbaydah.

mandal wood a kind of wood from India, used as incense; Mandal is said to be a place in India (perhaps Mandal in Rajasthan, India).

Mani (Mānī, Manes, Manichaeus; executed AD 274 or a few years later) the founder of the dualist religion called Manichaeism after him, which enjoyed great popularity in the Sassanian empire and beyond.

Manṣūr, al- (Abū Jaʿfar al-Manṣūr; r. 136–58/754–75) the second Abbasid caliph.

maradah (sg. marīd) an evil form of jinn.

Marrār ibn Saʿīd, al- (Abū l-Qaṭirān al-Asadī; second/eighth century) a poet who was in love with a woman called Waḥshiyyah, who was married to another.

Marw al-Rūdh place in Khurāsān (modern Afghanistan).

Marzubānī, Abū ʿAbd Allāh al- (Muḥammad ibn ʿImrān al-Marzubānī; d. 384/994) prolific literary scholar and anthologist from Baghdad; wrote a (lost) book on the poetry of the jinn, said to have contained over one hundred folios. Several of his other works about poetry have been preserved.

Maslamah ibn ʿAbd al-Mālik (d. 121/738) son of the Umayyad caliph ʿAbd al-Malik (r. 65–86/685–705); a general famous for his siege of Constantinople in 98–99/716–8.

Māṭirūn a place near Damascus.

Maymūn ibn Qays see Aʿshā, al-.

Mawṣilī, al- see Ibrāhīm al-Mawṣilī.

maysir an ancient Arab gambling game forbidden in Islam (cf. Q Baqarah 2:219, Māʾidah 5:90–91), in which portions of a slaughtered camel were divided by shuffling marked arrow shafts.

Mayyāfāriqīn town in eastern Anatolia.

Māzinī, al- see Abū ʿUthmān al-Māzinī.

Māzyār, (al-) (d. 225/840) Qārinid ruler of a principality in Ṭabaristān; became a Muslim when he sought the help of Caliph al-Maʾmūn; involved in a rebellion during the reign of al-Muʿtaṣim; he was defeated and executed in 225/840.

Minā a place some 5 miles east of Mecca, where the last three days of the pilgrimage are spent with several rites, including the great sacrifice.

Muʿallaqah (plur. Muʿallaqāt) an old collection, made in the second/eighth century, of seven celebrated long odes (*qaṣīdah*s) from the pre-Islamic period, among them odes by Imru' al-Qays, ʿAntarah, Ṭarafah, Zuhayr, and Labīd, who was the youngest and who died at an advanced age in the early Islamic period; the term *al-muʿallaqāt* seems to mean "the suspended (poems)" but the true meaning is obscure and the story that they were hung in the Kaaba is a later fiction.

Muʿāwiyah ibn Yazīd (d. 64/684) the third Umayyad caliph, who died after a reign of only twenty days, being between 17 and 23 years old.

Mubarrad, Muḥammad ibn Yazīd al- (d. 285/898) famous grammarian from Basra; bitter rival of Thaʿlab of Kufa.

Muḍar one of the two most important confederations within the "North Arabian" tribes according to the genealogists; also the ancient ancestor of the Arabs for whom the confederation was named.

Mufajjaʿ, al- (Abū ʿAbd Allāh Muḥammad ibn Aḥmad ibn ʿUbayd Allāh al-Mufajjaʿ; d. 327/939) grammarian and poet from Basra, author of numerous works.

Mughammas, al- a place near Mecca, said to be the place where the Meccans encountered the elephant, brought by the South Arabian king Abrahah during his failed attack on Mecca, the year the Prophet was born (ca. AD 570), an episode alluded to in the Surah of the Elephant (105) in the Qur'an.

Muhalhil, al- see ʿAdī ibn Rabīʿah.

Muḥammad ibn ʿAlī al-Khāzin see Abū Manṣūr Muḥammad ibn ʿAlī al-Khāzin.

Muḥammad ibn al-Ḥanafiyyah (d. 81/700) a son of ʿAlī by a slavegirl, claimed by the Kaysānites as the true imam and the Mahdi.

Muḥammad ibn al-Ḥasan see Abū Bakr ibn Durayd.

Muḥammad ibn Ḥāzim al-Bāhilī (end of the second/eighth and the beginning of the third/ninth century) poet notorious for his satire; the sources maintain that his professed frugality and abstinence were feigned.

Muḥammad ibn Rāʾiq (d. 330/942) chief of police, then chamberlain under al-Muqtadir, and finally "commander-in-chief" (*amīr al-umarāʾ*) in 324/936; he was assassinated by al-Ḥasan ibn ʿAbd Allāh, also called Nāṣir al-Dawlah (d. 358/969), a member of the powerful Ḥamdānid family, who ruled as *amīrs* in northern Mesopotamia and Syria.

Muḥammad ibn al-Sarī see Ibn al-Sarrāj.

Muḥammad ibn Yazīd al-Mubarrad see Mubarrad, al-.

Muḥassin al-Dimashqī, al- probably al-Muḥassin ibn al-Ḥusayn ibn ʿAlī Kawjak (d. 416/1026), copyist, man of letters, minor poet.

Muʿizz Abū Tamīm Maʿadd, al- (r. 341–65/953–75) Fāṭimid caliph at first based in Ifrīqiyah (present-day Tunisia); he conquered Egypt in 358/969, where he founded Cairo.

Mukhabbal al-Saʿdī, al- (d. ca. AD 640) a poet of the early Islamic period from central Arabia.

mulḥid a somewhat vague term for heretics, atheists, and all those who deviate from orthodoxy (the technical term for an apostate from Islam is *murtadd*).

Mumattaʿ, al- see Abū l-ʿAbbās al-Mumattaʿ.

Muqannaʿ al- ("the veiled one"; also called al-Qaṣṣār; his real name is not known) he inspired a rebellion that began around 160/777 and was suppressed after a siege in 166/783; reports on his doctrine are somewhat vague; it seems to have been inspired by Mazdakism; see *EI2*, vii, 500 ("al-Muḳannaʿ").

Muraqqish, al- (al-Muraqqish al-Akbar ["the Elder"]) both the proper name (ʿAmr, or ʿAwf, or Rabīʿah) and the nickname (Muraqqish or al-Muraqqish) of this early pre-Islamic poet are disputed; the younger Muraqqish was his nephew; both became the hero of a love romance.

Mushaqqar, al- a fortress in eastern Arabia, held by a Persian governor in pre-Islamic, Sassanian times.

Mutajarridah, al- the wife of the pre-Islamic king al-Nuʿmān ibn al-Mundhir; al-Mutajarridah is a nickname and means "she who stripped [herself], the denuded woman."

Mutanabbī, al- (Abū l-Ṭayyib Aḥmad ibn al-Ḥusayn al-Juʿfī; d. 354/965) nicknamed al-Mutanabbī; though controversial in his own day, is by many considered to be the greatest Arabic poet of Islamic times; also highly regarded by al-Maʿarrī; he excelled in panegyrics, often skillfully combined with self-praise; Al-Mutanabbī earned his sobriquet, “the would-be prophet,” when, in his late teens, he was involved in a kind of revolutionary movement, which led to his arrest in Homs (Syria) in 322/933.

Mutanakhkhil, al- pre-Islamic Hudhalī poet.

Muʿtaṣim, al- (r. 218–27/833–42) Abbasid caliph.

Muʿtazilites a school of Muslim theologians influenced by Greek logic and rationalism, dominant for a while in the early third/ninth century.

Muttaqī, al- (r. 329–33/940–44) Abbasid caliph who was deposed; he died in 357/968.

Muzdalifah, al- a place between ʿArafah and Mecca, where pilgrims spend a night during the Hajj.

nabʿ tree used for making arrows.

Nabhān ibn ʿAmr ibn al-Ghawth ibn Ṭayyiʾ ancestor of a clan of the tribe of Ṭayyiʾ, called Banū Nabhān after him.

Nābighah, al-Dhubyānī, al- (sixth century) poet active at the court of the Lakhmid kings of al-Ḥīrah and the Ghassānid rulers in Syria; he is considered one of the greatest Arabic poets.

Nābighah al-Jaʿdī, al- (d. ca. 63/683) poet born in the pre-Islamic period; a supporter of ʿAlī ibn Abī Ṭālib, he was banished in old age to Isfahan by ʿAlī’s rival and successor as caliph.

Nadbah the mother of Khufāf al-Sulamī.

Naḍr ibn Shumayl, al- (d. ca. 204/820) expert in grammar and lexicography.

nahīdah a dish made of colocynth seeds cooked with flour.

Nahshal ibn Dārim a tribe belonging to the large tribe of Tamīm.

Nahshal ibn Ḥarrī (al-Nahshalī; d. between 41/661 and 60/680) poet.

Najāshī al-Ḥārithī, al- (Qays ibn ʿAmr nicknamed al-Najāshī, “the Negus,” on account of his dark color or because his mother was Ethiopian) a contemporary of Ibn Muqbil; he composed invective poetry on the latter. He fought with ʿAlī at the Battle of Ṣiffīn (37/657).

Najd the central Arabian plateau.

Nājim, al- (Abū ʿUthmān Saʿd (or Saʿīd) ibn al-Ḥasan al-Nājim; d. 314/926) minor poet, friend of Ibn al-Rūmī.

Najrān place in northern Yemen.

Naʿmān a wadi in the Hijaz between Mecca and al-Ṭāʾif.

Namir ibn Tawlab al-ʿUklī, al- (d. before 23/644) a poet who was born in the pre-Islamic period and who converted to Islam; he was praised for the purity of his language and style.

Naṣr al-Dawlah (Abū Naṣr Aḥmad ibn Marwān, r. 401–53/1011–61) Marwānid ruler of Mayyāfāriqīn and Diyār Bakr, in northern Syria and northern Mesopotamia.

Naṣr ibn Ṣāliḥ Shibl al-Dawlah see Shibl al-Dawlah.

Naṣrids pre-Islamic Arab dynasty in Iraq.

Nisibis, Nasibis, or Naṣībīn modern Turkish form Nusaybin; an ancient town in Northern Mesopotamia, now in Turkey.

Nuʿman the Elder, al- (al-Nuʿmān ibn Imriʾ al-Qays) the pre-Islamic (early fifth century) Lakhmid king of al-Ḥīrah, nicknamed al-Aʿwar (the One-Eyed), or al-Sāʾiḥ (the Wanderer), or al-Zāhid (the Ascetic); not to be confused with the later king al-Nuʿmān ibn al-Mundhir, mentioned several times in the text.

Nuʿmān ibn al-Mundhir, al- (r. ca. AD 580–602) the last king of al-Ḥīrah, subject of stories and poems.

Numayrī, al- see ʿUbayd ibn al-Ḥuṣayn al-Numayrī.

Nuṣayb (Nuṣayb ibn Rabāḥ; d. ca. 111/729) son of a black slave woman, a poet; he composed eulogies on Umayyad caliphs and princes.

Nuṣayriyyah named after the third/ninth-century founder Muḥammad ibn Nuṣayr, a Shiʾite sect that survives until today in Syria (they are now known as the Alawites); they are considered "extremists" (*ghulāh*) because they revere ʿAlī ibn Abī Ṭālib to the point of deifying him; they also believed in metempsychosis.

parasang the ancient Greek form of a Persian measure of length, between three and four miles (Parthian *frasakh*, Middle Persian *farsang*, Arabic *farsakh*).

Qafūṣ said to be a place (location unknown) from which incense is imported.

Qārūn mentioned in the Qurʾan as a very wealthy and unjust man in the time of Moses (Q Qaṣaṣ 28:76–79, Q ʿAnkabūt 29:39, Q Ghāfir 40:24); in the Old Testament (Num. 16) he is called Korah (Hebrew Qōraḥ).

qaṣīd high-status verse in any meter except *rajaz*, which is the simplest meter.

qaṣīṣ. a plant described in *Lisān al-ʿArab*, not very helpfully, as "a plant at whose stems truffles are found."

Qaṣṣār, al- see Muqannaʿ, al-.

Qayl ibn ʿItr (or ibn ʿUnuq) said to have been among ʿĀd's deputation to Mecca, where they had gone to pray for rain.

Qays ibn al-Khaṭīm (d. AD 620) a poet from Medina.

Quraysh the tribe of the Prophet Muḥammad.

qurūf (sg. qarf) described by the dictionaries as a leather container tanned with bark of the pomegranate tree, in which meat is stored that has been boiled with aromatic herbs.

Quṭāmī, al- (d. ca. 101/719) a poet from the Umayyad period.

Quṭrub (d. 206/821) a grammarian from Baṣra.

Quwayq river in Aleppo.

Rabāb, al- traditional Arabic female name often used in love poetry.

Rabīʿah one of the two most important confederations within the "North Arabian" tribes according to the genealogists.

Rabīʿah ibn al-Mukaddam legendary pre-Islamic hero.

Rabīʿat al-Faras ("Rabīʿah of the Horse") the eponymous ancestor of Rabīʿah acquired his nickname because he inherited his father Nizār's horses, as legend has it.

Rāʿī, al- see ʿUbayd ibn al-Ḥuṣayn.

rajaz the simplest and presumably oldest poetic meter; it resembles the Greek or Latin iambic meter and is considered to be of lower status; many specialists in *rajaz* studded their verse with rare words; as a consequence their verses are very often quoted as lexicographic evidence.

ramal 1. a meter; 2. a rhythmical mode.

Ramlah a major town in Palestine.

Raqqādah a place not far from Qayrawān (modern Tunisia).

Rashīd, al- see Hārūn al-Rashīd.

Rāwand a place near Isfahan, in Iran.

Ru'bah ibn al-'Ajjāj (d. 145/762) with his father al-'Ajjāj among the most famous *rajaz* poets; on account of their extremely rich diction they are quoted very often by lexicographers.

Rummānī, 'Alī ibn 'Īsā al- (Abū l-Ḥasan 'Alī ibn 'Īsā al-Rummānī; d. 384/994) grammarian, Qur'anic scholar, and literary theorist from Baghdad.

Ṣābians the term Ṣāb'iah ("immersers" or "baptists") or Ṣābians refers to two distinct groups: (1) the syncretistic, planet- and star-worshipping gnostics of Ḥarrān in Mesopotamia (this is the group that al-Ma'arrī refers to), and (2) a sect mentioned in the Qur'an that was once identified as the Mandaeans but appears to have been the "Judaeo-Christian" Elchasaites (followers of Elchasai, ca. AD 100).

Sa'd (Sa'd ibn Abī Waqqāṣ; d. between 50/670–71 and 58/677–78) early convert and conqueror of Iraq.

Sa'd al-Dawlah (r. 356–81/967–91) Ḥamdānid ruler of Aleppo; son of Sayf al-Dawlah.

Ṣafā, al- ("the Stony Ground") a low mound at Mecca, which plays a role in the rituals of the Hajj.

Sahm ibn Ḥanẓalah (Sahm ibn Ḥanẓalah al-Ghanawī; d. during the reign of 'Abd al-Malik (65–86/685–705)); a poet, born in the pre-Islamic period.

Sa'īd ibn al-'Āṣ (Sa'īd ibn al-'Āṣ ibn Umayyah; d. 59/678–79) member of the Umayyad clan; became governor of Kufa and Medina. He was known for his generosity and eloquence.

Sa'īd ibn Mas'adah see Akhfash al-Awsaṭ, al-.

Sā'idah (Sā'idah ibn Ju'ayyah; a contemporary of the Prophet) a poet of the tribe of Hudhayl.

Ṣāliḥ ibn 'Abd al-Quddūs (executed ca. 167/783) preacher and poet from Basra.

Salmān al-Fārisī ("the Persian") a Persian slave in Medina in the time of the Prophet Muḥammad, he became the first non-Arab to convert to Islam; some extremist Shi'ite sects consider him second only to 'Alī.

Ṣakhr al-Ghayy (Ṣakhr ibn ʿAbd Allāh) pre-Islamic poet of Hudhayl, counted among the *ṣaʿālīk* or "outcast, brigand" poets; he acquired his epithet al-Ghayy ("going astray") because of his dissolute nature.

Ṣāliḥ ibn ʿAbd al-Quddūs (executed ca. 167/783) preacher and poet from Basra.

Samawʾal, al- a pre-Islamic Jewish-Arab poet proverbial for his loyalty; having been entrusted with the weapons of the famous poet Imruʾ al-Qays, he refused to give them up to his friend's enemy, a Ghassanid king, even when the latter threatened to kill al-Samawʾal's son and carried out his threat.

Sanad, al- location near Mecca.

Ṣanādīqī, al- (al-Manṣūr; rebelled in 270/883–84) al-Ṣanādīqī means "the box maker"; he was possibly identical with Abū l-Qāsim al-Najjār ("the carpenter"), a Shiʾite extremist who is elsewhere named as Rustam ibn al-Ḥusayn ibn Ḥawshab; see *EI2*, vi, 438–39, "Manṣūr al-Yaman" (W. Madelung).

Ṣanawbarī, al- (d. 334/945) Syrian poet famous for his poetry on gardens, flowers, and spring.

Ṣarīfīn (or *Ṣarīfūn*) see Yāqūt, *Muʿjam al-buldān*, s.v.; a place in Iraq.

Ṣarkhad place in Syria.

Sarmīn a place near Aleppo.

Sawādah ibn ʿAdī the son of the pre-Islamic poet ʿAdī ibn Zayd; the word *sawādah* means "black patch."

Sawdah bint Zamʿah ibn Qays she was Muḥammad's second wife and survived him by thirty-two years; the word *sawdah* means "patch with black stones."

Sayf al-Dawlah (ʿAlī ibn ʿAbd Allāh ibn Ḥamdān; r. 333–56/944–67) Ḥamdānid ruler of Northern Syria, renowned for his campaigns (not always successful) against the Byzantines and the literary splendor of his court in Aleppo; he owes his fame for a large part to a series of odes by al-Mutanabbī.

Sayyid al-Ḥimyarī, al- (Ismāʿīl ibn Muḥammad; d. between 171/787 and 179/795) a prominent poet and an adherent of the Kaysāniyyah; he also composed panegyric poems on al-Manṣūr.

Shābāsh the Banū Shābāsh were Qarmaṭians, extreme Shi'is, who were active from ca. 380/990 until 480/1090; two of them were viziers to the Būyid governor of Baṣra; see L. Massignon, entry "S̲h̲ābās̲h̲iyya" in *EI2*, 9:159.

Shajarī, al- see Aḥmad ibn Kāmil.

Shalmaghān village between Basra and Baghdad.

Shammākh ibn Ḍirār, al- poet of the Banū Thaʻlabah ibn Saʻd ibn Dhubyān born in the pre-Islamic period who died after the coming of Islam.

Shanfarā al-Azdī, al- a pre-Islamic poet, one of the *ṣaʻālīk* or "outcast, brigand poets"; the famous ode called *Lāmiyyat al-ʻArab* is attributed to him, although the second/eighth-century poet and transmitter Khalaf al-Aḥmar is said to have fabricated it; opinions are still divided.

Shaybānī, Abū ʻAmr al- see Abū ʻAmr al-Shaybānī.

Shibām place in North Yemen associated with wine production (not to be confused with the more famous town of that name in South Yemen).

Shibl al-Dawlah (Naṣr ibn Ṣāliḥ; r. 420–29/1029–38) Mirdāsid ruler of Aleppo at the time al-Maʻarrī wrote his *Epistle of Forgiveness*.

Shiblī, al- see Abū Bakr al-Shiblī.

Shīrīn the wife of the pre-Islamic Sasanian king Kisrā Abarwīz; in Persian literature they are described as devoted lovers and spouses.

Sībawayh (d. 177/793) author of the first and by far the most important Arabic grammar; like many other Arabic grammarians, he was of Persian descent.

Sinbisī, al- (al-Akhram al-Sinbisī) an obscure poet of uncertain period.

Sīrāfī, al- see Abū Saʻīd al-Sīrāfī.

storax (lubnā) a vanilla-scented resin used as incense, medicine, or perfume.

Suḥaym (killed ca. 40/660) known as ʻAbd Banī l-Ḥaṣḥāṣ ("the slave of the tribe of Banū l-Ḥaṣḥāṣ"), of Ethiopian descent (Suḥaym means "Blacky"); a poet who was killed for his too explicit verses.

Sulakah, al- the mother of Sulayk.

Sulamī, al- see Khufāf ibn Nadbah al-Sulamī.

Sulayk (or al-Sulayk) called Ibn al-Sulakah after his mother, a black slave, he was a pre-Islamic "outcast, brigand poet"; ʻAntarah, Sulayk, and Khufāf are known as the "Ravens."

Ṣūlī, Abū Bakr al- (d. ca. 335/946) courtier, famous chess player, and man of letters; author of several works on poets and poetry.

Suwayd ibn Abī Kāhil a poet, a contemporary of the Prophet; Suwayd literally means "little black one."

Suwayd ibn Ṣumayʿ a minor poet.

Taʾabbaṭa Sharrā (Thābit ibn Jābir) one of the legendary "outcast, brigand poets"; friend of al-Shanfarā. His strange nickname ("He took evil under his arm") is explained in various anecdotes.

Tabālah said to be a place in Yemen.

Taghlibī, al- see al-Akhṭal.

Ṭāʾī, al- see Abū Tammām.

Tamīm ibn Aws al-Dārī (d. 40/660 or earlier) a Companion; said to have been a wine merchant before Islam; he is said to have been responsible for several Islamic customs originating in Christianity; see M. Lecker, "Tamīm al-Dārī," *EI2*, 10:176.

Tamīm ibn Muqbil see Tamīm ibn Ubayy.

Tamīm ibn Ubayy ibn Muqbil al-ʿAjlānī (d. after 35/656) poet born in the pre-Islamic period who died after the coming of Islam.

Ṭarafah poet attached to the court of ʿAmr ibn Hind at al-Ḥīrah; he died young; having angered the king he was sent with a "letter of Uriah" containing his own death warrant (cf. 2 Sam. 11).

Taym ibn Murrah Abū Bakr's clan within the tribe of Quraysh.

Ṭayyiʾ an important Arab tribe.

Thabīr a mountain near Mecca.

Thabrah watering place on the pilgrims' route to Mecca.

Thaʿlab (Aḥmad ibn Yaḥyā; d. 291/904) grammarian from Kūfa, bitter rival of al-Mubarrad of Basra; his deafness in old age caused him to be struck down by a horse while he was walking, reading a book; he died the following day (see, e.g., Yāqūt, *Muʿjam al-udabāʾ*, 5:105–7; Ibn Khallikān, *Wafayāt*, 1:104).

Thamūd frequently mentioned in the Qur'an, is a legendary Arabian tribe or people who were destroyed because they disobeyed God and his messengers; often mentioned in connection with ʿĀd.

Tinnīs a town (now in ruins) in Egypt, on a small island near the eastern part of the Nile Delta.

Ṭufayl al-Ghanawī (Ṭufayl ibn Kaʿb (or ʿAwf) al-Ghanawī; d. early seventh century) pre-Islamic poet.

ʿUbayd ibn al-Ḥuṣayn al-Numayrī (d. ca. 96/714) poet nicknamed al-Rāʿī al-Numayrī, the "Camel-herd," for his many descriptions of camels and other animals.

ʿUdhrī, al- see Jamīl ibn Maʿmar.

Uḥayḥah ibn al-Julāḥ pre-Islamic wealthy merchant and poet from Yathrib (later called Medina).

Uḥud place not far from Medina; also the location of a battle between the Muslims and the Meccans, who were victorious; it was only a temporary setback for the Muslims.

ʿUmānī, al- (Muḥammad ibn Dhuʾayb al-ʿUmānī; d. during Hārūn al-Rashīd's caliphate (170–93/786–809)) poet; he did not come from Oman, as his name would suggest, but acquired his nickname on account of his sallow complexion (perhaps a result of jaundice).

ʿUmar ibn ʿAbd al-ʿAzīz (r. 99–101/717–20) singled out by historiographers as the only truly pious Umayyad caliph.

ʿUmar ibn Abī Rabīʿah (d. 93/712 or 103/721) poet active in Mecca and Medina, famous for his love poetry, often boastful, about numerous women; he frequently describes scenes of the pilgrimage.

ʿUmar ibn al-Khaṭṭāb (r. 13–23/634–44) the second caliph; he is normally described as a paragon of strictness.

Umayyah (ibn ʿAbd Shams) (pre-Islamic) ancestor of the Umayyads.

Umayyah Ibn Abī l-Ṣalt al-Thaqafī a poet and contemporary of the Prophet, whose poetry (some of which is of dubious authenticity) contains accounts of Biblical stories and parallels with the Qurʾan.

Umm Salamah (d. 59/679 or shortly afterwards) married Muḥammad in 4/626, having been widowed after her husband died at the Battle of Uḥud.

Umm "mother (of)."

Uqayshir al-Asadī, al- (first/seventh century) poet from Iraq known for his bohemian behavior and love of wine.

ʿUrwah ibn Ḥizām (first/seventh century) poet of the ʿUdhrah tribe; famous for his love for his paternal cousin ʿAfrā' who was married by her parents to someone else, richer than he.

ʿUrwah ibn Masʿūd al-Thaqafī (d. 9/630) one of those who brokered the truce between the Prophet and the Meccans in 6/628 at al-Ḥudaybiyah, a village near Mecca.

ʿUrwah ibn al-Ward (second half of the sixth century AD) pre-Islamic poet.

ʿUtbah ibn Ghazwān (d. 17/638) an early convert to Islam, founder of the city of Basra.

ʿUthmān ibn Ṭalḥah al-ʿAbdarī a member of Quraysh, who held the hereditary office of guarding the Kaaba in pre-Islamic times.

Waḥshī ("Savage") an Abyssinian slave fighting with the Meccans at Uḥud.

Waḥshiyyah cousin and beloved of al-Marrār ibn Saʿīd (q.v.).

Wajj another name of al-Ṭā'if.

Walīd ibn Yazīd, al- (r. 125–26/743–44) Umayyad caliph notorious for his dissolute behavior; a good poet.

wars a yellow dye.

Warsh (ʿUthmān ibn Saʿd; d. 197/812) transmitted one of the seven canonical readings of the Qur'an from his teacher Nāfiʿ al-Laythī (d. ca. 169/785).

Wazīr al-Maghribī, al- see Abū l-Qāsim al-Maghribī.

Yabrīn place in central or eastern Arabia.

Yaʿqūb (Abū Yūsuf) see Ibn al-Sikkīt.

Yaʿqūb ibn Dāwūd (d. ca. 186/802) vizier under the caliph al-Mahdī.

Yaʿrub the son of Qaḥṭān, ancestor of the South Arabs; his name is etymologically connected with ʿArab, and he is said to have been the first to speak Arabic (there are different views).

Yashkur a tribe in al-Yamāmah.

Yashkurī, al- see Ḥārith al-Yashkurī, al-.

Yathrib the Pre-Islamic name of Medina.

Yazīd ibn Abī Muslim (Dīnār) al-Thaqafī (d. 102/720–21) notoriously cruel secretary of the governor al-Ḥajjāj, dismissed after his death by Sulaymān; later appointed governor in North Africa where he was killed.

Yazīd ibn al-Ḥakam al-Kilābī (d. ca. 105/723) poet from the Umayyad period; he should have been called al-Thaqafī ("of the tribe Thaqīf") rather than al-Kilābī.

Yazīd ibn Mazyad ibn Maʿn ibn Zāʾidah (d. 185/801) a general and governor under Hārūn.

Yazīd ibn Muʿāwiyah (r. 60–64/680–83) the second Umayyad caliph, known for his hedonism and love of wine; among Shiʾites his reputation is particularly bad because al-Ḥusayn, their principal martyr, was killed during his reign; he favored the arts and composed poetry.

Yūnus ibn Ḥabīb (d. 182/798) grammarian from Basra.

Zabībah the mother of ʿAntarah.

Zāhid, Abū ʿUmar al- see Abū ʿUmar al-Zāhid.

Zahrajī, al- see Abū l-Faraj al-Zahrajī.

Zanj blacks originally from East Africa; widely exploited as slaves on plantations in southern Iraq.

Zayd ibn ʿAmr ibn Nufayl a *ḥanīf* ("seeker of the true religion") of Quraysh, the same tribe as Muḥammad, and in some ways his predecessor; he traveled in quest of the true religion but died some years before Muḥammad began his mission; according to another report he returned toward Mecca having heard of Muḥammad's mission, intending to join him, but was killed on the way.

Zayd ibn Ḥārithah (d. 8/629) the Prophet's adopted son, originally a slave; he is the only Companion mentioned in the Qurʾan (Q Aḥzāb 33:37), in connection with the affair of Muḥammad's somewhat controversial marriage with Zaynab bint Jaḥsh, who had been Zayd's wife.

Zayd ibn Muhalhil (d. between 9/630 and 23/644) a tribal leader and poet, known as Zayd al-Khayl ("Zayd of the Horses"); converted to Islam in 9/630.

Zibriqān, al- (al-Ḥuṣayn [or al-Ḥiṣn] ibn Badr; d. between 41/661 and 60/680) poet; the husband of a paternal aunt of al-Farazdaq.

zindīq (pl. zanādiqah) someone professing Islam but having heretical (often Manichaean) beliefs.

Zubaydah (d. 216/831–32) a daughter of al-Manṣūr; Hārūn al-Rashīd's principal wife.

Zuhayr ibn Abī Sulmā al-Muzanī (said to have died at an advanced age in AD 609, just before the Prophet began to preach his message) famous pre-Islamic poet; father of Kaʿb, poet of the famous "Mantle Ode."

Zuhayr ibn Masʿūd al-Ḍabbī a pre-Islamic poet, not to be confused with Zuhayr ibn Abī Sulmā.

Bibliography

al-ʿAbbāsī, ʿAbd al-Raḥīm. *Maʿāhid al-tanṣīṣ*. 2 vols. Cairo: al-Maṭbaʿah al-Bahiyyah, 1316/1898–9.

ʿAbd al-Qādir. *See* al-Baghdādī.

ʿAbd al-Raḥmān Bint al-Shāṭiʾ, ʿĀʾishah. *Abū ʾl-ʿAlāʾ al-Maʿarrī*. Cairo: al-Muʾassasah al-Miṣriyyah al-ʿĀmmah, [1965, date of preface].

———. "Abū ʾl-ʿAlāʾ al-Maʿarrī." In *ʿAbbasid Belles-Lettres*, edited by Julia Ashtiany et al., 328–38. Cambridge: Cambridge University Press, 1990 (The Cambridge History of Arabic Literature).

———. *Qirāʾah jadīdah fī Risālat al-Ghufrān*. Cairo: Jāmiʿat al-Duwal al-ʿArabiyyah, 1970.

al-Ābī, Abū Saʿd Manṣur ibn al-Ḥusayn. *Nathr al-durr*, edited by Muḥammad ʿAlī Quranah *et al.* 7 vols. Cairo: al-Hayʾah al-Miṣriyyah al-ʿĀmmah, 1980–90.

ʿAbīd ibn al-Abraṣ. *Dīwān*. – *The Dīwāns of ʿAbīd ibn al-Abraṣ, of Asad, and ʿĀmir ibn aṭ-Ṭufail, of ʿĀmir ibn Ṣaʿṣaʿah*, edited by Charles Lyall. Cambridge: E. J. W. Gibb Memorial Trust, 1911.

Abū l-ʿAtāhiyah. *Dīwān*, edited by Shukrī Fayṣal. Damascus: Dār al-Mallāḥ, n.d.

Abū l-Faraj al-Iṣfahānī. *See* al-Iṣfahānī.

Abū Ḥātim al-Sijistānī. *Al-Muʿammarūn*, edited by Ignaz Goldziher. In Ignaz Goldziher, *Abhandlungen zur arabischen Philologie*, 2. Theil. Leiden: Brill, 1899.

Abū Nuwās al-Ḥasan ibn Hāniʾ. *Dīwān*, edited by Ewald Wagner. 5 vols. + 2 vols., index (vol. 4 edited by Gregor Schoeler). Wiesbaden: Franz Steiner; Berlin: Klaus Schwarz, 1958–2006.

Abū Tammām Ḥabīb ibn Aws al-Ṭāʾī. *Dīwān Abī Tammām bi-sharḥ al-Khaṭīb al-Tibrīzī*, edited by Muḥammad ʿAbduh ʿAzzām. 4 vols. Cairo: Dār al-Maʿārif, 1976.

———. *Al-Ḥamāsah. See* al-Marzūqī.

———. *Al-Waḥshiyyāt, wa-huwa al-Ḥamāsah al-ṣughrā*, edited by ʿAbd al-ʿAzīz al-Maymanī al-Rājakūtī and Maḥmūd Muḥammad Shākir. Cairo: Dār al-Maʿārif, 1987.

Abū ʿUbayd al-Bakrī. *Faṣl al-maqāl fī sharḥ al-amthāl*, edited by Iḥsān ʿAbbās and ʿAbd al-Majīd ʿĀbidīn. Beirut: Dār al-Amānah, 1983.

———. *Muʿjam mā staʿjam*, edited by Ferdinand Wüstenfeld. 2 vols. Göttingen/Paris: Dieterichsche Buchhandlung, 1876–77.

———. *Muʿjam mā staʿjam*, edited by Muṣṭafā al-Saqqā. 4 vols. Cairo: Maṭbaʿat Lajnat al-Taʾlīf wa-l-Tarjamah wa-l-Nashr, 1945–51.

———. *Simṭ al-laʾālī fī sharḥ Amālī al-Qālī*, edited by ʿAbd al-ʿAzīz al-Maymanī. 3 vols. Beirut: Dār al-Kutub al-ʿIlmiyyah, 1997 (repr. of ed. Cairo, 1936).

Abū ʿUbaydah Maʿmar ibn al-Muthannā. *Al-Khayl*, edited by Muḥammad ʿAbd al-Qādir Aḥmad. Cairo: Maṭbaʿat al-Nahḍah al-ʿArabiyyah, 1986.

———. *Naqāʾiḍ Jarīr wa-l-Farazdaq*, edited by Anthony Ashley Bevan. 3 vols. Leiden: Brill, 1905–12.

Abū Zayd al-Anṣārī. *Al-Nawādir*, edited by Muḥammad ʿAbd al-Qādir Aḥmad. Beirut: Dār al-Shurūq, 1981.

Ahlwardt, Wilhelm, ed. *The Divans of the Six Ancient Arabic Poets*. London, 1870. Reprint, Osnabrück: Biblio Verlag, 1972.

al-Akhfash al-Aṣghar. *Al-Ikhtiyārayn*, edited by Fakhr al-Dīn Qabāwah. Damascus: Majmaʿ al-Lughah al-ʿArabiyyah, 1974.

al-Akhṭal. *Dīwān al-Akhṭal*, edited by Mahdī Muḥammad Nāṣir al-Dīn. Beirut: Dār al-Kutub al-ʿIlmiyyah, 1994.

al-Āmidī, Abū l-Qāsim al-Ḥasan ibn Bishr. *Al-Muʾtalif wa-l-mukhtalif fī asmāʾ al-shuʿarāʾ*, edited by F. Krenkow. Reprint, Beirut: Dār al-Kutub al-ʿIlmiyya, 1982.

———. *Al-Muwāzana bayna shiʿr Abī Tammām wa-l-Buḥturī*, edited by Aḥmad Ṣaqr and ʿAbd Allāh Ḥamad Muḥārib. 4 vols. Cairo: Dār al-Maʿārif, 1961–65 and Maktabat al-Khānjī, 1990.

al-ʿĀmilī, Bahāʾ al-Dīn. *Al-Kashkūl*. Beirut: Dār al-Kitāb al-Lubnānī, 1983.

al-Anṭākī, Dāwūd. *Tazyīn al-aswāq*, edited by Muḥammad al-Tūnjī (Altūnjī). 2 vols. Beirut: ʿĀlam al-Kutub, 1993.

Arberry, A. J. *Poems of al-Mutanabbī: A Selection with Introduction, Translations and Notes*. Cambridge: Cambridge University Press, 1967.

———. *The Seven Odes: The First Chapter in Arabic Literature*. London: Allen & Unwin, 1957.

al-Aʿshā [Maymūn ibn Qays]. *Dīwān*, edited by Rudolf Geyer. London: Luzac, 1928.

———. *Dīwān*. Beirut: Dār Ṣādir, 1994.

Asín Palacios, M. *La Escatología musulmana en la Divina Comedia*. Madrid: E. Maestre, 1919.

———. *Islam and the Divine Comedy*, translated by H. Sutherland. London: J. Murray, 1926.

al-ʿAskarī, Abū Hilāl al-Ḥasan ibn ʿAbd Allāh. *Al-Awāʾil*. Beirut: Dār al-Kutub al-ʿIlmiyyah, 1987.

———. *Dīwān al-maʿānī*. 2 vols. Cairo: Maktabat al-Qudsī, n.d.

———. *Jamharat al-amthāl*, edited by Aḥmad ʿAbd al-Salām. 2 vols. Beirut: Dār al-Kutub al-ʿIlmiyyah, 1988.

———. *Kitāb al-ṣināʿatayn al-kitābah wa-l-shiʿr*, edited by ʿAlī Muḥammad al-Bajāwī. Cairo: ʿĪsā al-Bābī al-Ḥalabī, 1971.

al-Aṣmaʿī, Abū Saʿīd ʿAbd al-Malik ibn Qurayb. *Al-Ibil*, edited by Ḥātim Ṣāliḥ al-Ḍāmin. Damascus: Dār al-Bashāʾir, 2003.

al-Aṣmaʿiyyāt, edited by Aḥmad Muḥammad Shākir and ʿAbd al-Salām Hārūn. Cairo: Dār al-Maʿārif, 1979.

Aubrey's Brief Lives, edited by Oliver Lawson Dick. Harmondsworth, Middlesex: Penguin, 1974.

al-Azharī. *Tahdhīb al-lughah*, edited by Muḥammad ʿAwaḍ Murʿib et al. 15 vol. Beirut: Dār Iḥyāʾ al-Turāth, 2001.

al-Badīʿī, Yūsuf. *Awj al-taḥarrī ʿan ḥaythiyyat Abī l-ʿAlāʾ al-Maʿarrī*, edited by Ibrāhīm al-Kīlānī. Damascus: al-Maʿhad al-Ifransī bi-Dimashq, 1944 (Majmūʿat al-nuṣūṣ al-sharqiyyah, 4).

al-Baghdādī, ʿAbd al-Qādir ibn ʿUmar. *Khizānat al-adab wa-lubāb lisān al-ʿarab*, edited by ʿAbd al-Salām Muḥammad Hārūn. 13 vols. Cairo: Dār al-Kātib al-ʿArabī / al-Hayʾah al-Miṣriyyah al-ʿĀmmah, 1967–86.

al-Bākharzī. *Dumyat al-qaṣr*, edited by ʿAbd al-Fattāḥ al-Ḥulw. 2 vols. Cairo: Dār al-Fikr al-ʿArabī, 1968, 1971.

al-Balādhurī. *Ansāb al-ashrāf.* Vols. 4/1 and 5, edited by Iḥsān ʿAbbās, Beirut/Wiesbaden: Steiner, 1979, 1996.

al-Baṣrī, Ṣadr al-Dīn ibn Abī l-Faraj. *Al-Ḥamāsah al-Baṣriyyah,* edited by Mukhtār al-Dīn Aḥmad. 2 vols. Hyderabad: Dāʾirat al-Maʿārif al-ʿUthmāniyyah, 1964.

al-Baṭalyawsī, Abū Bakr ʿĀṣim ibn Ayyūb. *Sharḥ al-ashʿār al-sittah al-jāhiliyyah,* edited by Nāṣīf Sulaymān ʿAwwād. 2 vols. Beirut/Berlin: Klaus Schwarz, 2008 (Bibliotheca Islamica, 47).

Blachère, Régis. "Ibn al-Qāriḥ et la génèse de *l'Épître du Pardon* d'al-Maʿarrī." *Revue des Études Islamiques,* (1941–46): 5–15; also in his *Analecta*, Damascus: Institut Français, 1975, 431–42.

Brockelmann, Carl. *Geschichte der arabischen Litteratur*, 2. Aufl. 5 vols. Leiden: Brill, 1937–47.

al-Buḥturī. *Dīwān*, edited by Ḥasan Kāmil al-Ṣayrafī. 5 vols. Cairo: Dār al-Maʿārif, 1972–78.

———. *Ḥamāsah,* edited by Muḥammad Riḍwān Dayyūb. Beirut: Dār al-Kutub al-ʿIlmiyyah, 1999.

Bürgel, J. C. "Les deux poèmes autobiographiques du démon Khaytaʿūr dans 'l'Épître du pardon' (*Risālat al-ghufrān*) d'Abou l-ʿAlāʾ al-Maʿarrī." *Arabic and Middle Eastern Literatures,* 2 no. 1 (1999): 109–54.

Cerulli, Enrico. *Il «Libro della Scala» e la questione delle fonti arabo-spagnole della Divina Commedia.* Vatican City, 1949.

Continente Ferrer, J. M. "Consideraciones en torno a las relaciones entre la *Risālat al-Tawābiʿ wa-l-Zawābiʿ* de ibn Šuhayd y la *Risālat al-Gufrān* de al-Maʿarrī." In *Actas de las jornadas de cultura árabe e islámica,* 1978. Madrid: Instituto Hispano-Árabe de Cultura, 1981: 124–35.

al-Damīrī, Kamāl al-Dīn Muḥammad ibn Mūsā. *Ḥayāt al-ḥayawān al-kubrā*. 2 vols. Cairo: Muṣṭafā al-Bābī al-Ḥalabī, 1970.

Dechico, Michel. "La Risāla d'Ibn al-Qāriḥ: traduction et étude lexicographique," Thèse pour le Doctorat de 3e Cycle. Paris: Université de Paris III, Sorbonne Nouvelle, 1980 [also contains an edition of the Arabic text].

al-Dhahabī. *Tārīkh al-Islām: Ḥawādith wa-wafayāt 221–30*, edited by ʿAbd al-Salām al-Tadmurī. Beirut: Dār al-Kitāb al-ʿArabī, 1991.

———. *Tārīkh al-Islām: Ḥawādith wa-wafayāt 441–50, 451–60*, edited by ʿAbd al-Salām al-Tadmurī. Beirut: Dār al-Kitāb al-ʿArabī, 1994.

Dhū l-Rummah Ghaylān ibn ʿUqbah. *Dīwān Dhī l-Rummah*, edited by ʿAbd al-Quddūs Abū Ṣāliḥ. 3 vols. Beirut: Muʾassasat al-Īmān, 1982.

Diʿbil ibn ʿAlī al-Khuzāʿī. *Dīwān*, edited by ʿAbd al-Ṣāḥib ʿImrān al-Dujaylī. Beirut: Dār al-Kitāb al-Lubnānī, 1972.

Dmitriev, Kirill. *Das poetische Werk des Abū Ṣāḫr al-Huḏalī. Eine literaturanthropologische Studie*. Wiesbaden: Harrassowitz, 2008.

Dozy, R. *Supplément aux dictionnaires arabes*. 2 vols. Leiden: Brill, 1927.

EI2 = *Encyclopaedia of Islam*, New [= Second] edition. Leiden: Brill, 13 vols. 1960–2009.

al-Farazdaq. *Dīwān*, edited by ʿAbd Allāh al-Ṣāwī. Cairo: al-Maktabah al-Tijāriyyah al-Kubrā, 1936.

———. *Dīwān*. 2 vols. Beirut: Dār Ṣādir, n.d.

al-Farrāʾ, Abū Zakariyyāʾ Yaḥyā ibn Ziyād. *Maʿānī l-Qurʾān*, edited by Aḥmad Yūsuf Najātī et al. 3 vols. Cairo: al-Dār al-Miṣriyyah, 1955–72.

Firdawsī's *Shāhnāma* – Abolqasem Ferdowsi. *Shahnameh: The Persian Book of Kings*, translated by Dick Davies. New York – London: Penguin Books, 2007.

al-Fīrūzābādī, Muḥammad ibn Yaʿqūb. *Al-Qāmūs al-muḥīṭ*. 4 vols. Cairo: Maktabat Muṣṭafā al-Bābī al-Ḥalabī, 1952.

Gabrieli, Francesco. "Al-Walīd ibn Yazīd: il califfo e il poeta." *Rivista degli Studi Orientali*, 15 (1935): 1–64.

Ghaleb, Edouard (Idwār Ghālib). *Dictionnaire des sciences de la nature (al-Mawsūʿah fī ʿulūm al-ṭabīʿah)*. 3 vols. Beirut: al-Maṭbaʿah al-Kāthūlikiyyah, 1965–6.

al-Ghazālī. *Iḥyā' 'ulūm al-dīn*. 5 vols. Cairo: Maktabat al-Mashhad al-Ḥusaynī, n.d.

Gibb, H. A. R. *Arabic Literature: An Introduction*, second (revised) ed. Oxford: Clarendon Press, 1963.

Hämeen-Anttila, Jaakko. *Five Rağaz Collections: Materials for the Study of Rağaz Poetry II*, compiled and edited. Helsinki: Finnish Oriental Society, 1995.

Hamilton, Robert. *Walid and his Friends: An Umayyad Tragedy*. Oxford: Oxford University Press, 1988 (Oxford Studies in Islamic Art, VI).

al-Harrās, 'Abd al-Salām. "*Risālat al-Tawābi' wa-l-zawābi'* wa-'alāqatuhā li-*Risālat al-Ghufrān*." *Al-Manāhil*, 9 no. 25 (1982): 211–20.

Ḥassān ibn Thābit. *Dīwān*, edited by Walīd 'Arafāt. 2 vols. London: Luzac, 1971.

———. *Dīwān*, edited by Sayyid Ḥanafī Ḥasanayn. Cairo: Dār al-Ma'ārif, 1983.

Ḥātim al-Ṭā'ī. *Dīwān*, edited by Friedrich Schulthess. Leipzig: J. C. Hinrichs'sche Buchhandlung, 1897.

———. *Dīwān, sharḥ Abī Ṣāliḥ Yaḥyā ibn Mudrik al-Ṭā'ī*, edited by Ḥannā Naṣr al-Ḥittī. Beirut: Dār al-Kitāb al-'Arabī, 1994.

al-Ḥātimī, Abū 'Alī Muḥammad ibn al-Ḥasan ibn al-Muẓaffar. *Ḥilyat al-muḥāḍarah fī ṣinā'at al-shi'r*, edited by Ja'far al-Kattānī. 2 vols. Baghdad: Dār al-Rashīd, 1979.

———. *Al-Risālah al-Ḥātimiyyah*. In Abū Sa'd Muḥammad ibn Aḥmad al-'Amīdī. *Al-Ibāna 'an sariqāt al-Mutanabbī*, edited by Ibrāhīm al-Dasūqī al-Bisāṭī, 271–90. Cairo: Dār al-Ma'ārif, 1961.

———. *Al-Risāla al-Mūḍiḥah*, edited by Muḥammad Yūsuf Najm. Beirut: Dār Ṣādir, 1965.

Heinrichs, Wolfhart. "The Meaning of *Mutanabbī*." In *Poetry and Prophecy: The Beginnings of a Literary Tradition*, edited by James L. Kugel, 120–39, 231–39. Ithaca: Cornell University Press, 1990.

Heller-Roazen, Daniel. *Echolalias: On the Forgetting of Language*. New York: Zone Books, 2005 (see ch. 20, on language in Paradise).

Hogan, Jenny. "Dunes Alive with the Sand of Music." *New Scientist*, 18 (Dec. 2004): 8.

Homerin, Th. Emil. "Echoes of a Thirsty Owl: Death and Afterlife in Pre-Islamic Arabic Poetry." *Journal of Near Eastern Studies*, 44 (1985): 165–84.

Ibn ʿAbd al-Barr, Abū ʿUmar Yūsuf ibn ʿAbd Allāh. *Bahjat al-majālis wa-uns al-mujālis*, edited by Muḥammad Mursī al-Khūlī. 2 vols. Beirut: Dār al-Kutub al-ʿIlmiyya, 1981–2.

Ibn ʿAbd Rabbih, Abū ʿUmar Aḥmad ibn Muḥammad. *Al-ʿIqd al-farīd*, edited by Aḥmad Amīn, Aḥmad al-Zayn, and Ibrāhīm al-Ibyārī. 7 vols. Beirut: Dār al-Kitāb al-ʿArabī, 1983 (repr. of ed. Cairo, 1948–53).

Ibn Abī l-Iṣbaʿ. *Taḥrīr al-taḥbīr fī ṣināʿat al-shiʿr wa-l-nathr wa-bayān iʿjāz al-Qurʾān*, edited by Ḥifnī Muḥammad Sharaf. Cairo: Lajnat Iḥyāʾ al-Turāth al-Islāmī, 1963.

Ibn Abī Ṭayfūr, Aḥmad. *Balāghāt al-nisāʾ*. Beirut: Dār al-Ḥadāthah, 1987.

Ibn Abī Yaʿlā. *Ṭabaqāt al-Ḥanābilah*, edited by Muḥammad Ḥāmid al-Fiqī. 2 vols. Cairo: Maṭbaʿat al-Sunnah al-Muḥammadiyyah, 1952.

Ibn al-ʿAdīm. *Bughyat al-ṭalab fī tārīkh Ḥalab*, edited by Suhayl Zakkār. 10 vols. Damascus: no publ., 1988.

———. *Al-Inṣāf wa-l-taḥarrī fī dafʿ al-ẓulm wa-l-tajarrī ʿan Abī l-ʿAlāʾ al-Maʿarrī*. In *Taʿrīf al-qudamāʾ bi-Abī l-ʿAlāʾ* [q.v.], 483–578.

Ibn al-Anbārī, Abū l-Barakāt. *Nuzhat al-alibbāʾ fī ṭabaqāt al-udabāʾ*, edited by Ibrāhīm al-Sāmarrāʾī. Beirut: Maktabat al-Manār, 1985.

Ibn al-Athīr, Majd al-Dīn al-Mubārak ibn Muḥammad. *Al-Nihāyah fī gharīb al-ḥadīth wa-l-athar*. 4 vols. Cairo: al-Maṭbaʿah al-ʿUthmāniyyah, 1311/1893–1894.

Ibn Dāwūd al-Iṣbahānī, Abū Bakr Muḥammad. *Al-Zahrah*, edited by Ibrāhīm al-Sāmarrāʾī. Al-Zarqāʾ (Jordan): Maktabat al-Manār, 1985.

Ibn Durayd, Abū Bakr Muḥammad ibn al-Ḥasan. *Dīwān*, edited by ʿUmar ibn Sālim. Tunis: al-Dār al-Tūnisiyyah, 1973.

———. *Taʿlīq min Amāli Ibn Durayd*, edited by Muṣṭafā al-Sanūsī. Kuwait: al-Majlis al-Waṭanī li-l-Thaqāfah, 1984.

———. *Jamharat al-lughah*, edited by Ramzī Munīr Baʿlabakkī. 3 vols. Beirut: Dār al-ʿIlm li-l-Malāyīn, 1988.

———. *Dīwān*, edited by Rājī Ibn al-Asmar. Beirut: Dār al-Kitāb al-ʿArabī, 1995.

Ibn Ḥabīb, Muḥammad. *Al-Muḥabbar*, edited by Ilse Lichtenstädter. Hyderabad: Dā'irat al-Ma'ārif al-'Uthmāniyyah, 1942.

Ibn Ḥamdūn, Muḥammad ibn al-Ḥasan ibn Muḥammad. *Al-Tadhkirah al-Ḥamdūniyyah*, edited by Iḥsān 'Abbās and Bakr 'Abbās. 10 vols. Beirut: Dār Ṣādir, 1996.

Ibn Hāni' al-Andalusī, Muḥammad. *Dīwān*. Būlāq: al-Maṭba'ah al-Mīriyyah, 1274.

———. *Dīwān*, edited by Muḥammad al-Ya'lāwī. Beirut: Dār al-Gharb al-Islāmī, 1994.

Ibn Ḥijjah al-Ḥamawī. *Khizānat al-adab wa-ghāyat al-arab*, edited by Kawkab Diyāb. 5 vols. Beirut: Dār Ṣādir, 2001.

Ibn Hishām, Abū Muḥammad 'Abd al-Malik. *Al-Sīrah al-nabawiyyah*, edited by Muṣṭafā al-Saqqā, Ibrāhīm al-Abyārī and 'Abd al-Ḥafīẓ Shalabī. 2 vols. Cairo: Muṣṭafā al-Bābī al-Ḥalabī, 1955.

Ibn Hishām, Jamāl al-Dīn 'Abd Allāh ibn Yūsuf al-Anṣārī. *Mughnī l-labīb 'an kutub al-a'ārīb*, edited by Ḥ. al-Fākhūrī. 2 vols. Beirut: Dār al-Jīl, 1991.

Ibn 'Idhārī al-Marrākushī. *Al-Bayān al-mughrib*, edited by G. S Colin and É. Levi Provençal. 2 vols. Leiden: Brill, 1948, 1951.

Ibn Ishaq. *The Life of Muhammad: A Translation of Ishāq's* [sic] Sīrat Rasūl Allāh, translated by A. Guillaume. Oxford: Oxford University Press, 1955.

Ibn al-Jawzī, Jamāl al-Dīn Abū l-Faraj 'Abd al-Raḥmān. *Al-Muntaẓam*, edited by Muḥammad 'Abd al-Qādir 'Aṭā and Muṣṭafā 'Abd al-Qādir 'Aṭā. Beirut: Dār al-Kutub al-'Ilmiyyah, 1992.

———. *Talbīs Iblīs*. Beirut: Dār al-Fikr, 1999.

Ibn Jinnī, Abū l-Fatḥ 'Uthmān. *Al-Khaṣā'iṣ*, edited by Muḥammad 'Alī al-Najjār. 3 vols. Cairo: Dār al-Kutub al-Miṣriyyah, 1952–56.

Ibn al-Kalbī *see* al-Kalbī.

Ibn Khallikān, Abū l-'Abbās Shams al-Dīn Aḥmad ibn Muḥammad. *Wafayāt al-a'yān*, edited by Iḥsān 'Abbās. 8 vols. Beirut: Dār al-Thaqāfah, 1968–72.

Ibn Manẓūr, Muḥammad ibn Mukarram. *Lisān al-'Arab*. 20 vols. Cairo: al-Dār al-Miṣriyyah li-l-Ta'lif wa-l-Tarjama, n.d. (repr. ed. Būlāq, 1308).

———. *Mukhtaṣar Tārīkh Dimashq li-Ibn ʿAsākir*, edited by Riyāḍ ʿAbd al-Ḥamīd Murād et al. 19 vols. Beirut: Dār al-Fikr, 1988–9.

[Ibn al Marzubān, *al-Muntahā*] Salem M. H. al Hadrusi. *Al Muntahā fī l kamāl des Muḥammad Ibn Sahl Ibn al Marzubān al Karḫī (gest. ca. 345/956). Untersuchung und kritische Edition von Bd 4–5 und 9–10.* Berlin: Klaus Schwarz, 1988.

Ibn al-Muʿtazz, ʿAbd Allāh. *Al-Badīʿ*, edited by Ignatius Kratchkovsky. London: Luzac, 1935.

———. *Ṭabaqāt al-shuʿarāʾ al-muḥdathīn*, edited by ʿAbd al-Sattār Aḥmad Farrāj. Cairo: Dār al-Maʿārif, 1968.

———. *Dīwān*, edited by Muḥammad Badīʿ Sharīf. 2 vols. Cairo: Dār al-Maʿārif, 1977–78.

Ibn al-Nadīm. *al-Fihrist*, edited by Gustav Flügel. 2 vols. Leipzig: F. C. W. Vogel, 1871–2.

Ibn Qays al-Ruqayyāt, ʿUbayd Allāh. *Dīwān*, edited by Muḥammad Yūsuf Najm. Beirut: Dār Ṣādir, 1958.

Ibn Qutaybah, Abū Muḥammad ʿAbd Allāh ibn Muslim. *ʿUyūn al-akhbār.* 4 vols. Cairo: Dār al-Kutub, 1925–30.

———. *Kitāb al-Maʿānī l-kabīr fī abyāt al-maʿānī.* Hyderabad: Dāʾirat al-Maʿārif al-ʿUthmāniyyah, 1949.

———. *Al-Shiʿr wa-l-shuʿarāʾ*, edited by Aḥmad Muḥammad Shākir. Cairo: Dār al-Maʿārif, 1966–7.

———. *Al-Ashribah wa-khtilāf al-nās fīhā*, edited by Yāsīn Muḥammad al-Sawwās. Beirut: Dār al-Fikr al-Muʿāṣir, 1998.

Ibn Rashīq, Abū ʿAlī al-Ḥasan al-Qayrawānī. *Al-ʿUmdah fī maḥāsin al-shiʿr wa-ādābihi wa-naqdih*, edited by Muḥammad Muḥyī l-Dīn ʿAbd al-Ḥamīd. 2 vols. Reprint, Beirut: Dār al-Jīl, 1972.

Ibn al-Rūmī. *Dīwān*, edited by Ḥusayn Naṣṣār. 6 vols. Cairo: Dār al-Kutub, 1973–81.

Ibn Sallām al-Jumaḥī. *Ṭabaqāt fuḥūl al-shuʿarāʾ*, edited by Maḥmūd Muḥammad Shākir. Cairo: Dār al-Maʿārif, 1952.

Ibn al-Shajarī. *Al-Amālī.* Hyderabad: Dāʾirat al-Maʿārif al-ʿUthmāniyyah, 1349.

Ibn Shākir al-Kutubī. *Fawāt al-Wafayāt*, edited by Iḥsān ʿAbbās. 5 vols. Beirut: Dār Ṣādir, 1973–4.

Ibn Shuhayd. *The Treatise of Familiar Spirits and Demons by Abū ʿĀmir ibn Shuhaid al-Ashjaʿī, al-Andalusī*, Introd., transl., and notes by James T. Monroe. Berkeley etc.: University of California Press, 1971.

Ibn al-Sikkīt. *Iṣlāḥ al-manṭiq*, edited by Fakhr al-Dīn Qabāwah. Beirut: Maktabat Lubnān, 2006.

Ibn Yaʿīsh. *Sharḥ al-Mufaṣṣal*. 10 vols. Cairo: Maktabat al-Mutanabbī, n.d.

Ibn Ẓāfir al-Azdī. *Badāʾiʿ al-badāʾih*, edited by Muḥammad Abū l-Faḍl Ibrāhīm. Cairo: Maktabat al-Anglo al-Miṣriyyah, 1969.

Ikhwān al-Ṣafāʾ. *Rasāʾil Ikhwān al-Ṣafāʾ*. 4 vols. Beirut: Dār Ṣādir, 1957.

Imruʾ al-Qays. *Dīwān*, edited by Muḥammad Abū l-Faḍl Ibrāhīm. Cairo: Dār al-Maʿārif, 1969.

al-Ibshīhī. *Al-Mustaṭraf fī kull fann mustaẓraf*. 2 vols. Cairo: Muṣṭafā al-Bābī al-Ḥalabī, 1952.

al-Iṣfahānī, Abū l-Faraj. *Al-Aghānī*. 24 vols. Cairo: Dār al-Kutub / al-Hayʾah al-Miṣriyyah al-ʿĀmmah, 1927–74.

Jacobi, Renate. "The *Khayāl* Motif in Early Arabic Poetry." *Oriens*, 32 (1990): 50–64.

———. "*Al-Khayalāni*: A Variation of the *Khayāl* Motif." *Journal of Arabic Literature*, 27 (1996): 2–12 .

al-Jāḥiẓ, Abū ʿUthmān ʿAmr ibn Baḥr. *Rasāʾil al-Jāḥiẓ*, edited by ʿAbd al-Salām Muḥammad Hārūn. 4 vols. Cairo: Maktabat al-Khānjī, 1964–79.

———. *Al-Ḥayawān*, edited by ʿAbd al-Salām Muḥammad Hārūn. 8 vols. Cairo: Muṣṭafā al-Bābī al-Ḥalabī, 1965–9.

———. *Al-Bayān wa-l-tabyīn*, edited by ʿAbd al-Salām Muḥammad Hārūn. 4 vols. Cairo: Maktabat al-Khānjī, 1968.

———. *Al-Burṣān wa-l-ʿurjān wa-l-ʿumyān wa-l-ḥūlān*, edited by ʿAbd al-Salām Muḥammad Hārūn. Beirut: Dār al-Jīl, 1990.

al-Jahshiyārī, Abū ʿAbd Allāh Muḥammad ibn ʿAbdūs. *Al-Wuzarāʾ wa-l-kuttāb*, edited by Muṣtafā al-Saqqā et al. Cairo: Maktabat Muṣṭafā l-Bābī al-Ḥalabī, 1980.

[Jamīl Buthayna] – Francesco Gabrieli. "Ǧamīl al-ʿUdrī: Studio critic e raccolta dei frammenti." *Rivista degli Studi Orientali* 17 (1938–9): 41–71, 133–72.

Jones, Alan, ed., trans. and comm. *Early Arabic Poetry, Volume One: Marāthī and Ṣuʿlūk Poems*. Reading: Ithaca Press, 1992

———, ed., trans. and comm. *Early Arabic Poetry, Volume Two: Select Odes*. Reading: Ithaca Press, 1996.

al-Jundī, Muḥammad Salīm. *Al-Jāmiʿ fī akhbār Abī l-ʿAlāʾ al-Maʿarrī wa-āthārih*. With annotations by ʿAbd al-Hādī Hāshim. Damascus: al-Majmaʿ al-ʿIlmī al-ʿArabī, 1962.

al-Jurjānī, al-Qāḍī ʿAlī ibn ʿAbd al-ʿAzīz. *Al-Wasāṭah bayn al-Mutanabbī wa-khuṣūmihi*, edited by Muḥammad Abū l-Faḍl Ibrāhīm and ʿAlī Muḥammad al-Bajāwī. Cairo: Dār Iḥyāʾ al-Kutub al-ʿArabiyyah, n.d.

[al-Kalbī, Hishām ibn Muḥammad], Werner Caskel. *Ǧamharat an-nasab. Das genealogische Werk des Hišām ibn Muhammad al-Kalbī*, I: Tafeln, II: Register. Leiden: Brill, 1966.

al-Kalbī, Hishām ibn Muḥammad. *Nasab Maʿadd wa-l-Yaman al-kabīr*, edited by Nājī Ḥasan. 2 vols. Beirut: ʿĀlam al-Kutub, 1988.

al-Khālidiyyān, Abū Bakr Muḥammad ibn Hāshim and Abū ʿUthmān Saʿīd ibn Hāshim. *Al-Ashbāh wa-l-naẓāʾir min ashʿār al-mutaqaddimīn wa-l-jāhiliyyah wa-l-mukhaḍramīn*, edited by al-Sayyid Muḥammad Yūsuf. 2 vols. Cairo: Lajnat al-Taʾlīf wa-l-Tarjamah wa-l-Nashr, 1958, 1965.

al-Khalīl ibn Aḥmad. *Al-ʿAyn*, edited by Mahdī al-Makhzūmī and Ibrāhīm al-Sāmarrāʾī. 8 vols. Baghdad: Dār al-Rashīd, 1980–85.

al-Khaṭīb al-Baghdādī. *Tārīkh Baghdād*. 14 vols. Cairo: Maktabat al-Khānjī, 1931.

al-Khaṭṭābī, Abū Sulaymān Ḥamd ibn Muḥammad. *Al-ʿUzlah*, edited by Yāsīn Muḥammad al-Sawwās. Beirut: Dār Ibn Kathīr, 1990.

Kister, M.J. "*Labbayka, allāhumma, labbayka*: On a Monotheistic Aspect of a Jāhiliyya Practice." *Jerusalem Studies in Arabic and Islam*, 2 (1980): 33–57.

Kratschkovsky, I. "Zur Entstehung und Komposition von Abū 'l-ʿAlā''s *Risālat al-ghufrān*." *Islamica*, 1 (1925): 344–56.

Kremers, Dieter. "Islamische Einflüsse auf Dantes «Göttliche Komödie»." In Wolfhart Heinrichs, ed. *Orientalisches Mittelalter* (Neues Handbuch der Literaturwissenschaft, Bd. 5), Wiesbaden: Aula-Verlag, 1990: 202–15.

Kuthayyir. *Dīwān*, edited by Qadrī Māyū. Beirut: Dār al-Jīl, 1995.

Labīd. *Dīwān*. Beirut: Dār Ṣādir, 1966.

Lane, Edward William. *An Arabic-English Lexicon*. 8 vols. London: Williams and Norgate, 1863–77.

Laoust, Henri. "La vie et la philosophie d'Abou-l-ʿAlā' al-Maʿarrī." *Bulletin d'Études Orientales*, 10 (1934–44): 119–58.

Lichtenstadter, Ilse. *Introduction to Classical Arabic Literature*. New York: Twayne, 1974.

Lucian. *Chattering Courtesans and Other Sardonic Sketches*, translated with an Introd. and Notes by Keith Sidwell. London: Penguin, 2004.

Lyall, Charles. *The Dīwāns of ʿAbīd ibn al-Abrās of Asad, and ʿĀmir ibn aṭ-Ṭufail, of ʿĀmir ibn Ṣaʿṣaʿah*. Cambridge: E. J. W. Gibb Memorial Trust, 1913.

al-Maʿarrī, Abū l-ʿAlā'. *Al-Fuṣūl wa-l-ghāyāt fī tamjīd Allāh wa-l-mawāʿiẓ*, edited by Maḥmūd Ḥasan Zanātī. Cairo, 1938, repr. Beirut: al-Maktab al-Tijārī, n.d.

———. *Al-Luzūmiyyāt (Luzūm mā lā yalzam)*, edited by Amīn ʿAbd al-ʿAzīz al-Khānjī. 2 vols. Cairo: Maktabat al-Khānjī, 1924.

———. *Risālat al-Ghufrān*, edited by ʿĀ'isha ʿAbd al-Raḥmān "Bint al-Shāṭi'." 9th ed. Cairo: Dār al-Maʿārif, 1993 [the basis of the present translation; 1st edition 1954, based on her doctoral dissertation, University of Cairo, 1950].

———. *Risālat al-Ghufrān*, edited by Ibrāhīm al-Yāzijī. Cairo: al-Maṭbaʿah al-Hindiyyah, 1903.

———. *Risālat al-Ghufrān*, edited by Kāmil Kaylānī (Kīlānī). Cairo, Dār al-Maʿārif, [1943].

———. *Risālat al-Ghufrān*, edited by Mufīd Qumayḥah. Beirut: Dār Maktabat al-Hilāl, 1986.

———. *Risālat al-Ghufrān*, edited by ʿAlī Ḥasan Fāʿūr. Beirut: Dār al-Kutub al-ʿIlmiyyah, 2001 [not consulted].

———. *Risālat al-Ghufrān*, edited by Muḥammad al-Iskandarānī and Inʿām Fawwāl. Beirut: Dār al-Kātib al-ʿArabī, 2011.

———. *Risālat al-Hanā'*, edited by Kāmil Kaylānī. Cairo: Dār al-Kutub, 1944.

———. *Siqṭ (or Saqṭ) al-zand*. Beirut: Dār Ṣādir, 1980.

———. *Risālat al-ṣāhil wa-l-shāḥij*, edited by ʿĀʾishah ʿAbd al-Raḥmān. Cairo: Dār al-Maʿārif, 1984.

[———] — Abou' l'Ala de Maarra. *Le Message du Pardon*, translated by M.-S. Meïssa. Paris: Librairie Orientaliste Paul Geuthner, 1932.

[———] — Abul Ala' Al Maʿarri. *Risalat ul Ghufran: A Divine Comedy*, translated from the Arabic by G. Brackenbury. Cairo: al-Maaref, n.d. [preface dated 1943].

[———] — Abûl-ʿAlâ al-Maʿarrî. *L'Épître du pardon*, trad., introd. et notes par Vincent-Mansour Monteil. Paris: Gallimard, 1984.

———. *Paradies und Hölle. Die Jenseitsreise aus dem «Sendschreiben über die Vergebung»*. Aus dem Arabischen übersetzt und herausgegeben von Gregor Schoeler. München: C. H. Beck, 2002.

———. *L'epistola del perdone. Il viaggio nell'aldilà*, cura e tradizione di Martino Diez, Torino: Nuova Universale Einaudi, 2011.

———. *Risālat al-Malāʾikah*, edited by Muḥammad Salīm al-Jundī. Beirut: Dār Ṣādir, 1992.

———. *Zajr al-nābiḥ: Muqtaṭafāt*, edited by Amjad al-Ṭarābulusī. Damascus: Majmaʿ al-Lughah al-ʿArabiyyah, 1982.

Majnūn Laylā. *Dīwān*, edited by ʿAdnān Zakī Darwīsh. Beirut: Dār Ṣadir, 1994.

al-Mallūḥī, ʿAbd al-Muʿīn. ""Ashʿār al-luṣūṣ wa-akhbāruhum."" *Majallat Majmaʿ al-Lughah al-ʿArabiyyah bi-Dimashq*, 19 (1974): 362–76, 595–608; 50 (1975): 588–612, 814–28; 56 (1981): 273–97, 444; 57 (1982): 383–402; 59 (1984): 65–80; also published in book form, Damascus: Dār Ṭlās, 1988.

Margoliouth, D. S. "Abū 'l-ʿAlāʾ al-Maʿarrī's Correspondence on Vegetarianism." *Journal of the Royal Asian Society*, 1902: 289–332.

al-Marzubānī, Abū ʿUbayd Muḥammad ibn ʿImrān. *Muʿjam al-shuʿarāʾ*, edited by ʿAbd al-Sattār Farrāj. Cairo: Dār Iḥyāʾ al-Kutub al-ʿArabiyyah, 1960.

———. *Nūr al-qabas al-mukhtaṣar min al-Muqtabas fī akhbār al-nuḥāh wa-l-udabāʾ wa-l-shuʿarāʾ wa-l-ʿulamāʿ, ikhtiṣār Yūsuf ibn Aḥmad al-Yaghmūrī / Die Gelehrtenbiographien des Abū ʿUbaidallāh al-Marzubānī in der Rezension des Ḥāfiẓ al-Yaġmūrī*, edited by Rudolf Sellheim. Teil I: Text. Wiesbaden: Franz Steiner, 1964.

———. *Al-Muwashshaḥ*, edited by ʻAlī Muḥammad al-Bajāwī. Cairo: Dār Nahḍat Miṣr, 1965.

al-Marzūqī, Abū ʻAlī Aḥmad ibn Muḥammad. *Sharḥ Dīwān al-Ḥamāsah*, edited by Aḥmad Amīn and ʻAbd al-Salām Hārūn. Repr. Beirut: Dār al-Jīl, 1991.

Massignon, Louis. *Essay on the Origins of the Technical Language of Islamic Mysticism*. Notre Dame, Indiana: University of Notre Dame Press, 1997.

———. *The Passion of al-Hallāj, Mystic and Martyr of Islam*, translated by Herbert Mason. 4 vols. Princeton: Princeton University Press, 1982.

al-Masʻūdī. *Murūj al-dhahab wa-maʻādin al-jawhar*, éd. Barbier de Meynard & Pavet de Courteille, revue et corrigée par Charles Pellat. 7 vols. Beirut: al-Jāmiʻah al-Lubnāniyyah, 1966–79.

al-Maydānī, Abū l-Faḍl Aḥmad ibn Muḥammad. *Majmaʻ al-amthāl*, edited by Naʻīm Ḥusayn Zarzūr. 2 vols. Beirut: Dār al-Kutub al-ʻIlmiyyah, 1988.

Merali, Zeeya. "Dune Tune: The Greatest Hits." *New Scientist*, 17 Sept. 2005: 11.

Montgomery, James E. *The Vagaries of the Qaṣīdah: The Tradition and Practice of Early Arabic Poetry*. [Cambridge:] E. J. W. Gibb Memorial Trust, 1997.

Moreh, Shmuel. *Live Theatre and Dramatic Literature in the Medieval Arabic World*. Edinburgh: Edinburgh University Press, 1992.

al-Mubarrad, Abū l-ʻAbbās Muḥammad ibn Yazīd. *Al-Kāmil fī l-lughah wa-l-adab*, edited by ʻAbd al-Ḥamīd Hindāwī. 4 vols. Beirut: Dār al-Kutub al-ʻIlmiyyah, 1999.

The Mufaḍḍalīyāt: An Anthology of Ancient Arabian Odes compiled by al-Mufaḍḍal, edited by Charles James Lyall. *Vol. II: Translation and Notes*. Oxford: Clarendon Press, 1918.

al-Mufaḍḍaliyyāt, edited by Aḥmad Muḥammad Shākir and ʻAbd al-Salām Muḥammad Hārūn. Cairo: Dār al-Maʻārif, 1964.

al-Murtaḍā, ʻAlī ibn al-Ḥusayn al-Mūsawī al-ʻAlawī al-Sharīf. *Al-Amālī (Ghurar al-fawāʼid wa-durar al-qalāʼid)*, edited by Muḥammad Abū l-Faḍl Ibrāhīm. 2 vols. Cairo: ʻĪsā al-Bābī al-Ḥalabī, 1954.

al-Mutanabbī. *Dīwān*, edited by F. Dieterici. Berlin: Mittler, 1861.

Muth, Franz-Christoph. "Zopyros bei den Arabern. Streiflichter auf ein Motif Herodots in der arabischen Literatur." *Oriens*, 33 (1992): 230–67.

al-Nābighah al-Jaʿdī. *Dīwān*, edited by Wāḍiḥ al-Ṣamad. Beirut: Dār Ṣādir, 1998.

Nagel, Tilman. "The *Risālat al-ghufrān* and the Crisis of the Certainty of Faith." In *Proceedings, 10th Congress [of the] UEAI, Edinburgh, 9–16 Sept. 1980*, edited by Robert Hillenbrand, Edinburgh: Union Européenne des Arabisants et Islamisants, 1982: 55–60.

Naqāʾiḍ Jarīr wa-l-Akhṭal, edited by Anṭūn Ṣāliḥānī (A. Salhani). Beirut: Dār al-Mashriq, 1922.

Naqāʾiḍ Jarīr wa-l-Farazdaq. See Abū ʿUbaydah.

Nicholson, Reynold A. *Literary History of the Arabs*. London: 1907. Reprinted Cambridge: Cambridge University Press, 1966.

———. "The Meditations of Maʿarrī." In Reynold A. Nicholson, *Studies in Islamic Poetry*. Cambridge: Cambridge University Press, 1921, repr. 1979: 43–289.

———. "Persian Manuscripts attributed to Fakhru'ddīn Rāzī with a Note on *Risālatu 'l Ghufrān* by Abū 'l ʿAlā al-Maʿarrī and other MSS in the same collection." *Journal of the Royal Asiatic Society* (1899): 669–74.

———. "The Risālatu 'l-Ghufrān by Abū 'l-ʿAlāʾ al-Maʿarrī." *Journal of the Royal Asiatic Society* (1900): 637–720; (1902): 75–101, 337–62, 813–47.

al-Nushshābī (or Nashshābī), Asʿad ibn Ibrāhīm al-Irbilī. *Al-Mudhākarah fī alqāb al-shuʿarāʾ*, edited by Shākir al-ʿĀshūr. Baghdad: Dār al-Shuʾūn al-Thaqāfiyyah al-ʿāmmah, 1988.

Osman, Hassan. "Dante in Arabic." *Annual Reports of the Dante Society*, 73 (1955): 47–52.

Pavić, Milorad:. *Dictionary of the Khazars: A Lexicon Novel in 100,000 Words*. New York: Knopf, 1988. (Originally published as *Hazarski rečnik: roman leksikon u 100.000 reči*. Belgrad: Prosveta, 1985; a Serbian novel that contains an entry on Abū Hadrash).

Peltz, Christian. *Der Koran des Abū l-ʿAlāʾ al-Maʿarrī*. Teil 1*: Materialien und Überlegungen zum* K. al-Fuṣūl-wa-l-ġāyāt *des al-Maʿarrī*. Teil 2*: Glossar*. Wiesbaden: Harrassowitz, 2013 (Arabische Studien 11).

al-Qālī, Abū ʿAlī Ismāʿīl ibn al-Qāsim. *Al-Amālī*. Cairo: Dār al-Kutub al-Miṣriyyah, 1926.

———. *Dhayl al-Amālī (al-Nawādir)*. Cairo: Dār al-Kutub al-Miṣriyyah, 1926.

Qays ibn al-Khaṭīm. *Dīwān*, edited by Nāṣir al-Dīn al-Asad. Cairo: Dār al-ʿUrūbah, 1962.

al-Qaysī, Abū ʿAlī al-Ḥasan ibn ʿAbd Allāh. *Īḍāḥ shawāhid al-Īḍāḥ*, edited by Muḥammad ibn Ḥammūd al-Daʿjānī. 2 vols. Beirut: Dār al-Gharb al-Islāmī, 1987.

al-Qifṭī, Jamāl al-Dīn Abū l-Ḥasan ʿAlī ibn Yūsuf (Ibn). *Inbāh al-ruwāh ʿalā anbāʾ al-nuḥāh*, edited by Muḥammad Abū l-Faḍl Ibrāhīm. 4 vols. Cairo: Dār al-Fikr al-ʿArabī, 1986.

al-Qurashī, Abū Zayd Muḥammad ibn Abī l-Khaṭṭāb. *Jamharat ashʿār al-ʿarab*. Beirut: Dār Ṣādir, 1963.

al-Rāghib al-Iṣfahānī. *Muḥāḍarāt al-udabāʾ wa-muḥāwarāt al-shuʿarāʾ wa-l-bulaghāʾ*. 2 vols. Būlāq: Jamʿiyyat al-Maʿārif al-Miṣriyyah, 1287.

Reckendorf, H. *Arabische Syntax*. Heidelberg: Carl Winter, [1921], repr. 1977.

Rosenthal, Franz. *Gambling in Islam*. Leiden: Brill, 1975.

Ru'bah ibn al-ʿAjjāj. *Dīwān*, edited by Wilhelm Ahlwardt. Berlin, 1903 (*Sammlungen alter arabischer Dichter: Der Dīwān des Reǧezdichters Rūba ben Elʿaǧǧāǧ*). Reprinted Beirut: Dār al-Āfāq al-Jadīdah, 1973.

al-Ṣafadī, Ṣalāḥ al-Dīn Khalīl ibn Aybak. *Al-Wāfī bi-l-Wafayāt*. 30 vols. Beirut - Wiesbaden - Berlin: Franz Steiner - Klaus Schwarz, 1931–2010.

Saleh, Moustapha. "Abū 'l-ʿAlāʾ al-Maʿarrī (363–449/979–1057): bibliographie critique." *Bulletin d'Études Orientales*, 22 (1969): 133–204; 23 (1970): 197–309.

al-Ṣanawbarī. *Dīwān*, edited by Iḥsān ʿAbbās. Beirut: Dār Ṣādir, 1998.

al-Sarrāj, Abū Muḥammad Jaʿfar ibn Aḥmad. *Maṣāriʿ al-ʿushshāq*. 2 vols. Beirut: Dār Ṣādir, n.d.

Schoeler, Gregor. "Abū l-Alā' al-Ma'arrīs Prolog zum *Sendschreiben über die Vergebung*." In *Islamstudien ohne Ende. Festschrift für Werner Ende zum 65. Geburtstag*, edited by Rainer Brunner et al. Würzburg: Ergon Verlag, 2002 (Abhandlungen für die Kunde des Morgenlandes, Deutsche Morgenländische Gesellschaft, LIV, 1): 417–28.

———. "Die Vision, die auf einer Hypothese gründet: Zur Deutung von Abū 'l-'Alā' al-Ma'arrīs *Risālat al-Ġufrān*." In *Problems in Arabic Literature*, edited by Miklós Maróth. Piliscsaba: The Avicenna Institute of Middle Eastern Studies, 2004: 27–41.

Seidensticker, Tilman. "Sources for the History of Pre-Islamic Religion." In: *The Qur'ān in context: Historical and Literary Investigations into the Qur'ānic Milieu*, edited by Angelika Neuwirth, Nicolai Sinai, and Michael Marx. Leiden - Boston: Brill, 2010, 293–321.

Sells, Michael A. *Desert Tracings: Six Classic Arabian Odes by 'Alqama, Shánfara, Labíd, 'Antara, Al-A'sha, and Dhu al-Rúmma*. Middletown, Connecticut: Wesleyan University Press, 1989.

Sezgin, Fuat. *Geschichte des arabischen Schrifttums. Band II: Poesie bis ca. 430 H.* Leiden: Brill, 1975.

al-Shirbīnī, Yūsuf. *Yūsuf al-Shirbīnī's Brains Confounded by the Ode of Abū Shādūf Expounded*, translated by Humphrey Davies. Leuven: Peeters, 2007.

Sībawayh. *Kitāb Sībawayh*. 2 vols. Cairo: Dār al-Ṭibā'ah, 1318.

Šidfar, Betsi Jakovlevna. *Abu-l'-Alja al'-Maari*. (*Pisateli i učenye Vostoka* [= Writers and Scholars of the East/Orient]). Moscow: Nauka, 1985. (Biography of al-Ma'arrī). (Not seen).

al-Sīrāfī, Abū Muḥammad Yūsuf. *Sharḥ abyāt Sībawayh*, edited by Muḥammad 'Alī Sulṭānī. 2 vols. Damascus: Majma' al-Lughah al-'Arabiyyah, 1976.

Smoor, Pieter. *Kings and Bedouins in the Palace of Aleppo as reflected in Ma'arrī's works*. Manchester, 1985 (*Journal of Semitic Studies*, Monographs, 8).

———. "al-Ma'arrī." In *Encyclopaedia of Islam*, New [=Second] Edition, vol. V, Leiden: Brill, 1986: 927–35.

Stetkevych, Suzanne Pinckney. *The Poetics of Islamic Legitimacy: Myth, Gender, and Ceremony in the Classical Arabic Ode*. Bloomington, Indiana: Indiana University Press, 2002.

———. "The Snake in the Tree in Abū al-ʿAlāʾ al-Maʿarrī's *Epistle of Forgiveness*: Critical Essay and Translation." *Journal of Arabic Literature*, 45 (2014): 1–80.

Strohmaier, Gotthard. "Chaj ben Mekitz – die unbekannte Quelle der Divina Commedia." In Gotthard Strohmaier, *Von Demokrit bis Dante*. Hildesheim, Zürich, New York: Georg Olms, 1996: 449–65.

al-Subkī, Tāj al-Dīn. *Ṭabaqāt al-Shāfiʿiyyah*, edited by Maḥmūd Muḥammad al-Ṭanāḥī and ʿAbd al-Fattāḥ al-Ḥulw. 10 vols. Cairo: ʿĪsā al-Bābī al-Ḥalabī, 1964–76.

Suḥaym ʿAbd Banī l-Ḥasḥās. *Dīwān*, edited by ʿAbd al-ʿAzīz al-Maymanī. Cairo: Dār al-Kutub, 1950.

al-Sukkarī, Abū Saʿīd al-Ḥasan ibn Ḥusayn. *Sharḥ ashʿār al-Hudhaliyyīn*, edited by ʿAbd al-Sattār Aḥmad Farrāj. 3 vols. Cairo: Dār al-ʿUrūbah, 1965.

al-Ṣūlī, Abū Bakr Muḥammad ibn Yaḥyā. *Al-Awrāq (Akhbār al-Rāḍī li-llāh wa-l-Muttaqī li-llāh)*, edited by J. Heyworth Dunne. London: Luzac, 1936.

———. *Al-Awrāq (Ashʿār awlād al-khulafāʾ)*, edited by J. Heyworth Dunne. London: Luzac, 1936.

———. *Akhbār Abī Tammām*, edited by Khalīl Maḥmūd ʿAsākir, Maḥmūd ʿAbduh ʿAzzām, and Naẓīr al-Islām al-Hindī. Cairo: Lajnat al-Taʾlīf, 1937.

al-Suyūṭī, Jalāl al-Dīn ʿAbd al-Raḥmān. *Al-Muzhir fī ʿulūm al-lughah wa-anwāʿihā*, edited by Muḥammad Aḥmad Jād al-Mawlā et al. 2 vols. Cairo: Dār Iḥyāʾ al-Kutub al-ʿArabiyyah, n.d.

———. *Bughyat al-wuʿāh fī ṭabaqāt al-lughawiyyīn wa-l-nuḥāh*, edited by Muḥammad Abū l-Faḍl Ibrāhīm. repr. Beirut: Dār al-Fikr, 1979.

———. *Tārīkh al-khulafāʾ*, edited by Muḥammad Muḥyī l-Dīn ʿAbd al-Ḥamīd. Beirut: Dār al-Jīl, 1988.

al-Ṭabarī, Muḥammad ibn Jarīr. *Tārīkh al-rusul wa-l-mulūk*, edited by M. J. de Goeje et al. 3 vols. Leiden: Brill, 1879–1901.

———. *The History of al-Ṭabarī, vol. IV: The Ancient Kingdoms*, translated by Moshe Perlmann. Albany, NY: State University of New York Press, 1987.

al-Tanūkhī, Abū ʿAlī al-Muḥassin ibn ʿAlī. *Nishwār al-muḥāḍarah*, edited by ʿAbbūd al-Shāljī. 8 vols. Beirut: Dār Ṣādir, 1971–3.

Taʿrīf al-qudamāʾ bi-Abī l-ʿAlāʾ. Cairo: al-Dār al-Qawmiyyah, 1965.

al-Thaʿālibī, Abū Manṣūr ʿAbd al-Malik ibn Muḥammad. *Ghurar akhbār mulūk al-Furs wa-siyarihim / Histoire des rois des Perses*, edited and translated by H. Zotenberg. Paris: Imprimerie Nationale, 1900.

———. *Yatīmat al-dahr*, edited by Muḥammad Muḥyī l-Dīn ʿAbd al-Ḥamīd. 4 vols. Cairo: Maktabat al-Ḥusayn al-Tijāriyyah, 1947.

———. *Al-Tamthīl wa-l-muḥāḍarah*, edited by Muḥammad ʿAbd al-Fattāḥ al-Ḥulw. Beirut: al-Dār al-ʿArabiyyah li-l-Kitāb, 1983.

———. *Tatimmat al-Yatīmah*, edited by Mufīd Muḥammad Qumayḥah. Beirut: Dār al-Kutub al-ʿIlmiyyah, 1983.

———. *Thimār al-qulūb*, edited by Muḥammad Abū l-Faḍl Ibrāhīm. Cairo: Dār al-Maʿārif, 1985.

———. *Aḥsan mā samiʿtu*, edited by Khalīl ʿImrān al-Manṣūr. Beirut: Dār al-Kutub al-ʿIlmiyyah, 2000.

Thaʿlab, Abū l-ʿAbbās Aḥmad ibn Yaḥyā. *Majālis Thaʿlab*, edited by ʿAbd al-Salām Muḥammad Hārūn. 2 vols. Cairo: Dār al-Maʿārif, 1978, 1980.

Tibbets, G. R., and Shawkat M. Toorawa. "Wāḳwāḳ. 2(b). The tree." In *The Encyclopaedia of Islam*, New [=Second] Edition, vol. XI, Leiden: Brill, 2002: 107–08.

al-Tibrīzī, al-Khaṭīb. *Sharḥ al-qaṣāʾid al-ʿashr*, edited by Charles James Lyall. Calcutta, 1894. Reprinted Ridgewood, NJ: Gregg Press, 1965.

———. *Al-Wāfī fī l-ʿarūḍ wa-l-qawāfī*, edited by ʿUmar Yaḥyā and Fakhr al-Dīn Qabāwah. Damascus: Dār al-Fikr, 1979.

Ṭufayl al-Ghanawī. *Dīwān*, edited by Muḥammad ʿAbd al-Qādir Aḥmad. Beirut: Dār al-Kitāb al-ʿArabī, 1968.

Ullmann, Manfred. "Aἴξ τὴν μάχαιραν." In Rotraud Hansberger, M. Afifi al-Akiti and Charles Burnett (eds), *Medieval Arabic Thought: Essays in Honour of Fritz Zimmermann*, 197–208. London - Turin: The Warburg Institute - Nino Aragno Editore, 2012.

———. *Der Neger in der Bildersprache der arabischen Dichter*. Wiesbaden: Harrassowitz, 1998.
ʿUmar ibn Abī Rabīʿah. *Dīwān*. Cairo: al-Hay'ah al-Miṣriyyah al-ʿĀmmah, 1978.
Usāmah ibn Munqidh. *The Book of Contemplation*, translated by Paul M. Cobb. London: Penguin, 2008.
van Ess, Josef. *Theologie und Gesellschaft im 2. und 3. Jahrhundert Hidschra. Eine Geschichte des religiösen Denkens im frühen Islam*. 6 vols. Berlin - New York: de Gruyter, 1991–7.
———. *Der Eine und das Andere. Beobachtungen an islamischen häresiographischen Texten*. 2 vols. Berlin – New York: de Gruyter, 2011.
Wagner, Ewald. "Sprechende Tiere in der arabischen Prosa." *Asiatische Studien*, 45 (1994): 937–57.
al-Walīd ibn Yazīd. *Dīwān*, edited by Ḥusayn ʿAṭwān. Beirut: Dār al-Jīl, 1998.
Walther, Wiebke. "Altarabische Kindertanzreime." In *Studia Orientalia in memoriam Caroli Brockelmann*, edited by Manfred Fleischhammer, 217–33. Halle: Martin Luther-Universität, 1968.
———. Review of Schoeler's translation of *Risālat al-Ghufrān*. *Zeitschrift der Deutschen Morgenländischen Gesellschaft*, 157 (2007): 225–28.
al-Washshā'. *Al-Muwashshā*, edited by Rudolph E. Brünnow. Leiden: Brill, 1886.
al-Wazīr al-Maghribī, al-Ḥusayn ibn ʿAlī. *Al-Īnās bi-ʿilm al-ansāb*, edited by Ibrāhīm al-Ibyārī. Beirut: Dār al-Kutub al-Islāmiyyah, 1980.
Wensinck, A. J. et al., *Concordance et indices de la Tradition Musulmane*. Leiden: Brill, 1992.
WKAS = *Wörterbuch der klassischen arabischen Sprache*. Bearbeitet von Manfred Ullmann. Wiesbaden: Harrassowitz, 1970–2009.
Wright, O. "Music." In A. F. L. Beeston et al. (eds), *Arabic Literature to the End of the Umayyad Period*, Cambridge: Cambridge University Press, 1983 (The Cambridge History of Arabic Literature): 433–59.
Wright, W. *Grammar of the Arabic Language*. 3rd ed. rev. by W. Robertson Smith and M. J. de Goeje. 2 vols. Cambridge: Cambridge University Press, 1896–8.

al-Ya'qūbī, Aḥmad ibn Abī Ya'qūb. *Tārīkh.* 2 vols. Beirut: Dār Bayrūt, n.d.

Yāqūt, Shihāb al-Dīn Abū 'Abd Allāh al-Ḥamawī. *Mu'jam al-udabā'*, edited by Aḥmad Farīd Rifā'ī. 20 vols. Cairo, 1936–8, repr. Beirut: Iḥyā' al-Turāth al-'Arabī, n.d.

———. *Mu'jam al-buldān.* 7 vols. Beirut: Dār Ṣādir, 1995.

Yarshater, E. "Zuhāk." In *Encyclopaedia of Islam*, New [= Second] Edition, vol. XI, Leiden: Brill, 2002: 554–55.

al-Zabīdī, Murtaḍā. *Tāj al-'arūs*, edited by 'Abd al-Sattār Aḥmad Farrāj. 40 vols. Kuweit: Maṭba'at Ḥukūmat al-Kuwayt, 1965–2001.

al-Zamakhsharī. *Asās al-balāghah.* Beirut: Dār Ṣādir, 1979.

———. *Rabī' al-abrār*, edited by Salīm al-Nu'aymī. 4 vols. Baghdad: Maṭba'at al-'Ānī, 1967–82.

———. *Tafsīr al-kashshāf 'an ḥaqā'iq ghawāmiḍ al-tanzīl*, edited by Muḥammad Mursī 'Āmir. 3 vols. Cairo: Dār al-Muṣḥaf, 1977.

Further Reading

Main pre-modern sources for al-Maʿarrī's life

Most of the following and many other shorter passages are also found in two compilations of biographical material on al-Maʿarrī: *Taʿrīf al-qudamāʾ bi-Abī l-ʿAlāʾ*, and Muḥammad Salīm al-Jundī, *al-Jāmiʿ fī akhbār Abī l-ʿAlāʾ*. For bibliographical details see the Bibliography.

al-Thaʿālibī (d. 429/1038), *Tatimmat al-Yatīmah*, p. 16.

al-Khaṭīb al-Baghdādī (d. 463/1071), *Tārīkh Baghdād*, iv, 240.

al-Bākharzī (d. 467/1075), *Dumyat al-qaṣr*, i, 129–37.

Abū l-Barakāt Ibn al-Anbārī (d. 577/1181), *Nuzhat al-alibbāʾ fī ṭabaqāt al-udabāʾ*, pp. 257–59.

Ibn al-Jawzī (d. 597/1201), *al-Muntaẓam*, xvi, 22–27.

Yāqūt (d. 626/1229), *Muʿjam al-udabāʾ*, iii, 107–218.

(Ibn) al-Qifṭī (d. 646/1248), *Inbāh al-ruwāh ʿalā anbāh al-nuḥāh*, i, 81–118.

Ibn al-ʿAdīm (d. 660/1262), *Bughyat al-ṭalab fī tārīkh Ḥalab*, pp. 863–913.

———, *al-Inṣāf wa-l-taḥarrī fī dafʿ al-ẓulm wa-l-tajarrī ʿan Abī l-ʿAlāʾ al-Maʿarrī, in Taʿrīf al-qudamāʾ bi-Abī l-ʿAlāʾ*, pp. 483–578.

Ibn Khallikān (d. 681/1282), *Wafayāt al-aʿyān*, i, 113–16.

al-Dhahabī (d. 748/1348), *Tārīkh al-Islām: Ḥawādith wa-wafayāt 441–50, 451–60*, pp. 198–220.

al-Ṣafadī (d. 764/1363), *al-Wāfī bil-Wafayāt*, vii, 94–111.

ʿAbd al-Raḥīm ibn ʿAbd al-Raḥmān al-ʿAbbāsī (d. 963/1556), *Maʿāhid al-tanṣīṣ*, i, 48–52.

Editions of *Risālat Ibn al-Qāriḥ* and *Risālat al-Ghufrān*

Ibrāhīm al-Yāzijī, ed. Cairo: al-Maṭbaʻah al-Hindiyyah, 1903.

Kāmil Kaylānī (Kīlānī), ed. Cairo: Dār al-Maʻārif, [1943].

Michel Dechico, "La Risāla d'Ibn al-Qāriḥ: traduction et étude lexicographique," Thèse pour le Doctorat de 3e Cycle, Paris: Université de Paris III, Sorbonne Nouvelle, 1980 [also contains an edition of the Arabic text].

Mufīd Qumayḥah, ed. Beirut: Dār Maktabat al-Hilāl, 1986.

ʻĀ'isha ʻAbd al-Raḥmān Bint al-Shāṭi', ed., 9th ed. Cairo: Dār al-Maʻārif, 1993 [the basis of the present translation; 1st edition 1954, based on her doctoral dissertation, University of Cairo, 1950].

Muḥammad al-Iskandarānī and Inʻām Fawwāl, eds. Beirut: Dār al-Kātib al-ʻArabī, 2011.

ʻAlī Ḥasan Fāʻūr, ed. Beirut: Dār al-Kutub al-ʻIlmiyyah [not consulted].

Translations of *Risālat Ibn al-Qāriḥ* and *Risālat al-Ghufrān*

Abou' l'Ala de Maarra. *Le Message du Pardon.* Tr. M.-S. Meïssa. Paris: Librairie Orientaliste Paul Geuthner, 1932.

Abul Ala' Al Maʻarri. *Risalat ul Ghufran: A Divine Comedy.* Tr. from the Arabic by G. Brackenbury. Cairo: al-Maaref, n.d. [preface dated 1943].

Abu-l'-Alja al'-Maarri. *Izbrannoe. Perevod s arabskogo [Selected Works, translated from Arabic].* Sostavlenie, predislovie, primečanie [Edition, preface, notes]: Betsi Jakovlena Šidfar. Moscow: Chudožestvennaja literatura [Publishing House: Belles-Lettres]: 1960, 165–392. (Russian.) (Not seen).

Abu al-Ala al-Maʻarri. *Poslanica o oproštenju* [The Epistle of Forgiveness]. Priredio, prevedio, pristup, napomene, pogovor [Edition, translation, introduction, notes, afterword]: Suleijman Grozdanić. Sarajevo (etc.): Matica srpska, 1979. (Bosnian.) (Not seen.)

Abûl-ʿAlâ al-Maʿarrî. *L'Épître du pardon.* Trad., introd. et notes par Vincent-Mansour Monteil. Paris: Gallimard, 1984 (also contains a translation of *Risālat Ibn al-Qāriḥ*).

Abū l-ʿAlāʾ al-Maʿarrī. *Paradies und Hölle. Die Jenseitsreise aus dem Sendschreiben über die Vergebung.* Aus dem Arabischen übersetzt und herausgegeben von Gregor Schoeler. München: C. H. Beck, 2002 [For a study and translation of the Preamble, *see* Gregor Schoeler, "Abū l-Alāʾ al-Maʿarrīs Prolog zum *Sendschreiben über die Vergebung*," in Rainer Brunner et al., ed., *Islamstudien ohne Ende. Festschrift für Werner Ende zum 65. Geburtstag*, Würzburg: Ergon Verlag, 2002 (Abhandlungen für die Kunde des Morgenlandes, Deutsche Morgenländische Gesellschaft, LIV, 1), pp. 417–28 (translation pp. 422–28)].

Abū l-ʿAlāʾ al-Maʿārrī. *L'epistola del perdone. Il viaggio nell'aldilà.* Cura e tradizione di Martino Diez. Torino: Nuova Universale Einaudi, 2011.

Some modern studies

ʿAbbūd, Mārūn. *Zawbaʿat al-duhūr.* [Beirut:] Dār al-Makshūf, 1945.

al-ʿAbd, ʿAbd al-Ḥakīm ʿAbd al-Salām. *Abū l-ʿAlāʾ al-Maʿarrī wa-naẓrah jadīdah ilayh: Tamḥīṣ naqdī ḥaḍārī wa-fannī.* 2 vols. Alexandria: Dār al-Maṭbūʿāt al-Jadīdah, 1993.

ʿAbd al-Raḥmān ʿĀʾishah "Bint al-Shāṭiʾ". *Abū l-ʿAlāʾ al-Maʿarrī.* Cairo, [1965, date of preface], also published as *Maʿa Abī l-ʿAlāʾ fī riḥlat ḥayātih.* Beirut: Dār al-Kitāb al-ʿArabī, 1972.

———. "Abū l-ʿAlāʾ al-Maʿarrī." In Julia Ashtiany et al. (eds), *ʿAbbasid Belles-Lettres.* Cambridge: Cambridge University Press, 1990 (The Cambridge History of Arabic Literature), 328–38.

al-ʿAlāyilī, ʿAbd Allāh. *Al-Maʿarrī dhālika l-majhūl.* Beirut: Manshūrat al-Adīb, 1944.

ʿAlī, ʿAdnān ʿUbayd. *Al-Maʿarrī fī fikrihī wa-sukhriyyatih.* Amman: Dār Usāmah, 1999.

ʿAlī al-Dawlah, Nādiyā. *Naqd al-shiʿr fī āthār Abī l-ʿAlāʾ al-Maʿarrī.* Damascus [s.n.], 1998.

al-ʿAqqād, ʿAbbās Maḥmūd. *Rajʿat Abī l-ʿAlāʾ.* Cairo: Dār al-Hilāl [1966].

Asín Palacios, M. *La Escatología musulmana en la Divina Comedia.* Madrid: E. Maestre, 1919; translated by H. Sutherland as *Islam and the Divine Comedy.* London: J. Murray, 1926.

ʿAwaḍ, Luwīs. *ʿAlā hāmish al-Ghufrān.* Cairo: Dār al-Hilāl, 1966.

Bāshā, ʿUmar Mūsā. *Naẓarāt jadīdah fī Ghufrān Abī l-ʿAlāʾ.* Beirut: Dār Ṭlās, 1989.

Blachère, Régis. "Ibn al-Qāriḥ et la génèse de *l'Épître du Pardon* d'al-Maʿarrī." *Revue des Études Islamiques,* 1941–6: 5–15, also in his *Analecta,* Damascus: Institut Français, 1975, 431–42.

Brockelmann, Carl. *Geschichte der Arabischen Litteratur.* 2. Aufl. Leiden: Brill, 1937–47, I, 254–55, Suppl. I, 449–54.

Cerulli, Enrico. *Il «Libro della Scala» e la questione delle fonti arabo-spagnole della Divina Commedia.* Vatican City: Bibliotheca Apostolica Vaticana, 1949.

Farrūkh, ʿUmar. *Ḥakīm al-Maʿarrah.* Beirut: Dār Lubnān, 1986.

Grotzfeld, Heinz. "*wa-ʿallama Ādama l-asmāʾ kullahā* „und er lehrte Adam alle Namen" (Sure 2:31). Spekulationen über Adams Sprache im arabisch islamischen Mittelalter." (Farewell Lecture, University of Münster, 25 June 1999). Münster: Universität Münster, 1999.

Ḥabābī, Fāṭimah al-Jāmiʿī. *Lughat Abī l-ʿAlāʾ al-Maʿarrī fī Risālat al-Ghufrān.* Cairo: Dār al-Maʿārif, 1988.

al-Ḥakīm, Suʿād. *Abū l-ʿAlāʾ al-Maʿarrī: Bayna baḥr al-shiʿr wa-yābisat al-nās.* Beirut: Dār al-Fikr al-Lubnānī, 2003.

al-Hāshimī, Muḥammad Yaḥyā. *Lughz Abī l-ʿAlāʾ.* Aleppo [s.n.], 1968.

Ḥimṣī, Muḥammad Ṭāhir. *Abū l-ʿAlāʾ al-Maʿarrī: Malāmiḥ ḥayātihī wa-adabih.* Damascus: Dār Ibn Kathīr, 1999.

———. *Madhāhib Abī l-ʿAlāʾ al-Maʿarrī fī l-lughah wa-ʿulūmihā.* Damascus: Dār al-Fikr, 1986.

Ḥusayn, Ṭāhā. *Dhikrā Abī l-ʿAlāʾ.* Cairo: Maṭbaʿat al-Wāʿiẓ, 1915.

———. *Tajdīd dhikrā Abī l-ʿAlāʾ.* Cairo: Dār al-Maʿārif, 1922.

———. *Maʿa Abī l-ʿAlāʾ fī sijnih.* Cairo: Maṭbaʿat al-Maʿārif, 1944.

Kennedy, Philip F. "Muslim Sources of Dante?". In Dionisius A. Agius and Richard Hitchcock, eds., *The Arab Influence in Medieval Europe.* Reading: Ithaca, 1993, 63–82.

Khuraybānī, Jaʿfar. *Abū l-ʿAlāʾ al-Maʿarrī rahīn al-maḥbisayn*. Beirut: Dār al-Kutub al-ʿIlmiyyah, 1990.

Kratschkovsky, I. "Zur Entstehung und Komposition von Abū 'l-ʿAlā''s *Risālat al-ghufrān*." *Islamica*, 1 (1925): 344–56.

Kremers, Dieter. "Islamische Einflüsse auf Dantes «Göttliche Komödie»." In Wolfhart Heinrichs, ed., *Orientalisches Mittelalter* (Neues Handbuch der Literaturwissenschaft, Bd. 5). Wiesbaden: Aula-Verlag, 1990, 202–15.

Laoust, Henri. "La vie et la philosophie d'Abou-l-ʿAlāʾ al-Maʿarrī." *Bulletin d'Études Orientales*, 10 (1934–44): 119–58.

al-Mallūḥī, ʿAbd al-Muʿīn. *Difāʿ ʿan Abī l-ʿAlāʾ al-Maʿarrī*. Beirut: Dār al-Kunūz al-Adabiyyah, 1994.

Margoliouth, D. S. "Abū 'l-ʿAlāʾ al-Maʿarrī's Correspondence on Vegetarianism." *Journal of the Royal Asian Society*, (1902): 289–312.

al-Maymanī al-Rājakūtī, ʿAbd al-ʿAzīz. *Abū l-ʿAlāʾ wa-mā ilayh*. Cairo: al-Maṭbaʿah al-Salafiyyah, 1925.

Nagel, Tilman. "The *Risālat al-ghufrān* and the Crisis of the Certainty of Faith." In *Proceedings, 10th Congress [of the] UEAI, Edinburgh, 9–16 Sept. 1980*. Edited by R. Hillenbrand. Edinburgh, 1982, 55–60.

Nicholson, Reynold Alleyne. "The Meditations of Maʿarrī," = Chapter II of his *Studies in Islamic Poetry*. Cambridge: CUP, 1979, 43–289 [also contains many verses from *Luzūm mā lā yalzam*, in Arabic and English].

Rizq, Ṣalāḥ. *Nathr Abī l-ʿAlāʾ al-Maʿarrī: Dirāsah fanniyyah*. Cairo: Dār al-Thaqāfah al-ʿArabiyyah, 1985.

Saleh, Moustapha. "Abū 'l-ʿAlāʾ al-Maʿarrī (363–449/979–1057): bibliographie critique." *Bulletin d'Études Orientales*, 22 (1969): 133–204; 23 (1970): 197–309.

al-Sāmarrāʾī, Ibrāhīm. *Dirāsāt fī turāth Abī l-ʿAlāʾ al-Maʿarrī*. Amman: Dār al-Ḍiyāʾ, 1999.

———. *Maʿa l-Maʿarrī al-lughawī*. Beirut: Muʾassasat al-Risālah, 1984.

Schoeler, Gregor. "Die Vision, die auf einer Hypothese gründet: Zur Deutung von Abū 'l-ʿAlāʾ al-Maʿarrīs *Risālat al-Ġufrān*." In *Problems in Arabic Literature*. Edited by Miklós Maróth. Piliscsaba: The Avicenna Institute of Middle Eastern Studies, 2004, 27–41.

Smoor, P. "al-Maʿarrī." *Encyclopaedia of Islam*, New [=Second] Edition, vol. V (Leiden, 1986), 927–35.

———. *Kings and Bedouins in the Palace of Aleppo as reflected in Maʿarrī's works*, Manchester: University of Manchester, 1985 (*Journal of Semitic Studies*, Monographs, 8).

Stetkevych, Suzanne Pinckney. "The Snake in the Tree in Abū al-ʿAlāʾ al-Maʿarrī's *Epistle of Forgiveness*: Critical Essay and Translation." *Journal of Arabic Literature*, 45 (2014): 1–80.

Strohmaier, Gotthard. "Die angeblichen und die wirklichen orientalischen Quellen der ‚Divina Comedia.'" In Gotthard Strohmaier, *Von Demokrit bis Dante*. Hildesheim, Zürich, New York: Georg Olms Verlag, 1996, 471–86.

———. "Chaj ben Mekitz – die unbekannte Quelle der Divina Commedia." In Gotthard Strohmaier, *Von Demokrit bis Dante*. Hildesheim: Wissenschaftliche Buchgesellschaft, 1996, 449–65.

al-Ṭarābulusī, Amjad. *Al-Naqd wa-l-lughah fī Risālat al-Ghufrān*. Damascus: Jāmiʿat Dimashq, 1951.

Taymūr, Aḥmad. *Abū l-ʿAlāʾ al-Maʿarrī*. Cairo: al-Maktabah al-Anjlū al-Miṣriyyah, 1940.

ʿUthmānī, Yūsuf. *Al-Ihtimāmāt al-lughawiyyah fī āthār Abī l-ʿAlāʾ al-Maʿarrī*. Tunis: Kulliyyat al-ʿUlūm al-Insāniyyah wa-l-Ijtimāʿiyyah, 2005.

Zaydān,ʿAbd al-Qādir. *Qaḍāyā l-ʿaṣr fī adab Abī l-ʿAlāʾ al-Maʿarrī*. Cairo: al-Hayʾah al-Miṣriyyah al-ʿĀmmah, 1986.

Index

If no death date is given, this is because it is unknown or because the person is legendary or fictional. Book titles are listed under *Kitāb*.

poems, poetry (cont.)
xxix–xxxiv, xxxvi, xxxviii, xl–xli, xliv–xlvi, *IQ* §§2.7.1–2, §8, *Gh* §1.2, §3.4, §4.1, §7.2, §7.6.1, §8.4, §9.2, §10.5, §§11.3–4, §12.2.1, §12.2.4, §17.3.4, §17.3.6, §17.4.1, §18.1.2, §18.2, §18.5, §20.2, 305n100, 310n180, 311n193, 311n198, 316n246, 316n247, 319n290, 321n319, 323n335, 323n340, 325n367, 326n375, 327n386, 330n432, 331n438, 332n447, 333n466, 335n486, 337n512, 338n518, 339n526, 340n547, 341n554, 341n559, 342n571, 343n574, 344n591, 345n602, 348n637, 350n661, 360n788, 361n795, 361n800, 361n801, 362n812, 365n847, 369n880, 369n884, 370n891, 375n949, 376n965, 379n997, 385n1060, 386n1067, 396n1199, 397n1211, 397n1214, 401n1253, 405n1289, 410n1339, 421n1454; abandoned by some poets in Paradise, *Gh* §8.3.1; definition of, *Gh* §11.2.2, §17.3.1; eulogy dedicated to Muḥammad (al-Aʿshā), *Gh* §5.2, §5.4;improvised, *IQ* §7.5 *Gh* §11.2.1, §11.3, §11.4;of the *jinn*, *Gh* §§15.2.2–5; transmitters of, *Gh* §3.2, §5.2, §§7.4.2–3, §17.3.1, §17.5.2, §17.7.1, §19.1.1, 342n566, 351n674. See also *rajaz*, spurious verses and stanzaic poem
poems, collected. See collected verse
poet, the best, *Gh* §43.3.3
poetic talent, *Gh* §17.10, §29.1.3, §44.1.2, §44.2.1
praise, Ibn al-Qāriḥ's vain, *Gh* §22.1; of Maʿarrat al-Nuʿmān, *IQ* §4.4; of al-Maʿarrī, *IQ* §§2.1–5, §8, *Gh* §22.1, §§22.2.1–3, 357n754
prayers. See ritual prayers
Predestinarians, predestination, *Gh* §30.3, 381n1019, 395n1184
Progeny, Chosen ('Pure Imams') (the Prophets's descendants), *Gh* §11.6.1, §11.7
promiscuity (practiced by al-Ṣanādīqī), *IQ* §3.4
the Prophet. See Muḥammad ibn ʿAbd Allāh
prophetic mission of Muḥammad, *IQ* §3.9, *Gh* §6.2.1, §15.2.7, §17.4.1, beginnings, *IQ* §§5.1–4
prophetic signs, *Gh* §26.5
prosody. See metrical issues
proverbs and common sayings, *Gh* §10.4.1, §18.1.1, §22.1, §§24.3.1–2, §25.1.1, §32.1, §37.2.1, §38.1, §39.2.2, §41.2.1, §43.3.2, 304n79, 306n120, 306n124, 307n139, 308n142, 332n455, 335n478, 339n535, 343n579, 347n620, 349n643, 349n645, 350n662, 350n667,357n762, 357n763, 363n819, 363n824, 363n825, 364n827, 375n952, 383n1042, 383n1047, 399n1228, 401n1253, 402n1265, 403n1274, 403n1276, 406n1304, 407n1305, 409n1324, 412n1357, 419n1431, 421n1459
Qaḍīb (place), *Gh* §31.3.1
Qābīl (Cain), *Gh* §15.2.8.4, §19.1.3, 338n519
Qafūṣ, *Gh* §6.2.2.3
Qanān, *Gh* §44.1.1, 424n1482
Qarmaṭians. See Carmathians
Qārūn, *Gh* §43.3.5
Qasāmah ibn Zuhayr (1st/7th c.), 413n1364

youths, immortal (in Paradise), xxxiii, *Gh* §3.1, §13.1.3, §13.6, §17.1, §20.3, 340n544
Yūnus ibn Ḥabīb al-Ḍabbī (d. 182/798), *Gh* §4.1, §27.2.1
Yūsuf. See Joseph
al-Zabbā', 337n226, 333n464, 403n1276
Zabībah, *Gh* §1.2
al-Zafayān al-Sa'dī (fl. ca. 80/700), 330n417
Zāhid, Abū 'Umar al-. See Ghulām Tha'lab
al-Ẓāhir, *IQ* §3.7.2
Zahrajī, Abū l-Faraj al-, *IQ* §§2.6.1–2, §12, *Gh* §24.1.1, 362n808
Ẓamyā (woman's name), *Gh* §17.7.1, 347n624
Zanj (East African Blacks), *IQ* §3.6.1, *Gh* §28.4.1, §28.5.1, §30.3, 301n49, 301n50, 376n960, 377n968, 381n1017
Zayd (Adī's father), *Gh* §6.5
Zayd ibn 'Alī ibn al-Ḥusayn ibn 'Alī ibn Abī Ṭālib (d. 122/740), *Gh* §11.6.1
Zayd ibn 'Amr ibn Nufayl (d. before ad 610), *Gh* §37.1.4
Zayd ibn Ḥārithah (d. 8/629), *Gh* §37.1.4
Zayd ibn Muhalhil (d. between 9/630 and 23/644), *Gh* §33.2.2, 390n1115
Zayd al-Khayl. See Zayd ibn Muhalhil
Zaynab (woman's name), *Gh* §15.2.8.5, 339n526
Zenobia, 314n226, 333n464, 403n1276
al-Zibriqān ibn Badr (d. mid-1st/7th c.), *Gh* §16.3, §25.2, 340n538
zindīqs (heretics). See apostates, apostasy
Ziyād ibn Rib'ī al-Qutabī, 384n1051
Zoroastrian, Zoroastrians, xxxviii, *IQ* §3.5.1, *Gh* §15.2.8.3, 303n76
al-Zubayr, 339n531
Zoroastrians, *IQ* §3.5.1, *Gh* §15.2.8.3, §30.2, §43.1.1, 373n934
Zubaydah bint al-Manṣūr (d. 216/831–32), *Gh* §29.1.2
Zufar (angel of Paradise), *Gh* §11.3
Zuhayr (pre-Islamic), *Gh* §§5.5.1–2, §6.5, §17.3.2, §22.1, §43.3.1, §44.1.2, 308n144, 316n251, 324n349, 364n829, 420n1446, 421n1448
Zuhayr ibn Janāb al-Kalbī (pre-Islamic), *Gh* §18.1.2
Zuhayr ibn Mas'ūd al-Ḍabbī (pre-Islamic), *Gh* §17.4.2
Zuhayr(ah) (woman's name), *Gh* §17.10, 349n648

About the NYU Abu Dhabi Institute

The Library of Arabic Literature is supported by a grant from the NYU Abu Dhabi Institute, a major hub of intellectual and creative activity and advanced research. The Institute hosts academic conferences, workshops, lectures, film series, performances, and other public programs directed both to audiences within the UAE and to the worldwide academic and research community. It is a center of the scholarly community for Abu Dhabi, bringing together faculty and researchers from institutions of higher learning throughout the region.

NYU Abu Dhabi, through the NYU Abu Dhabi Institute, is a world-class center of cutting-edge research, scholarship, and cultural activity. The Institute creates singular opportunities for leading researchers from across the arts, humanities, social sciences, sciences, engineering, and the professions to carry out creative scholarship and conduct research on issues of major disciplinary, multidisciplinary, and global significance.

About the Translators

Geert Jan van Gelder was Laudian Professor of Arabic at the University of Oxford from 1998 to 2012. He has published widely on classical Arabic literature in Dutch and English, particularly on the history of poetics and criticism and on literary themes as diverse as food, the hammam, and incest. His books include *Beyond the Line: Classical Arabic Literary Critics on the Coherence and Unity of the Poem* and *Of Dishes and Discourse: Classical Arabic Literary Representations of Food.*

Gregor Schoeler was the chair of Islamic Studies at the University of Basel from 1982 to 2009. His books in the fields of Islamic Studies and classical Arabic literature include *The Oral and the Written in Early Islam,* and *Paradies und Hölle,* a partial German translation of *The Epistle of Forgiveness.*

The Library of Arabic Literature

Classical Arabic Literature
Selected and translated by Geert Jan Van Gelder

A Treasury of Virtues, by al-Qāḍī al-Quḍāʿī
Edited and translated by Tahera Qutbuddin

The Epistle on Legal Theory, by al-Shāfiʿī
Edited and translated by Joseph E. Lowry

Leg over Leg, by Aḥmad Fāris al-Shidyāq
Edited and translated by Humphrey Davies

Virtues of the Imām Aḥmad ibn Ḥanbal, by Ibn al-Jawzī
Edited and translated by Michael Cooperson

The Epistle of Forgiveness, by Abū l-ʿAlāʾ al-Maʿarrī
Edited and translated by Geert Jan Van Gelder and Gregor Schoeler

The Principles of Sufism, by ʿĀʾishah al-Bāʿūnīyah
Edited and translated by Th. Emil Homerin

The Expeditions, by Maʿmar ibn Rāshid
Edited and translated by Sean W. Anthony

Two Arabic Travel Books
Accounts of China and India, by Abū Zayd al-Sīrāfī
Edited and translated by Tim Mackintosh-Smith
Mission to the Volga, by Ahmad Ibn Faḍlān
Edited and translated by James Montgomery

Disagreements of the Jurists, by al-Qāḍī al-Nuʿmān
Edited and translated by Devin Stewart

Consorts of the Caliphs, by Ibn al-Sāʿī
Edited by Shawkat M. Toorawa and translated by the Editors of the Library of Arabic Literature

What ʿĪsā ibn Hishām Told Us, by Muḥammad al-Muwayliḥī
Edited and translated by Roger Allen

The Life and Times of Abū Tammām, by Abū Bakr al-Ṣūlī
Edited and translated by Beatrice Gruendler

Printed in the USA
CPSIA information can be obtained
at www.ICGtesting.com
LVHW090408071123
763255LV00003B/268

9 781479 834945